Edexcel A-Level

Statistics & Mechanics

Year 1 & AS-Level

This CGP Student Book is the definitive guide to every Statistics & Mechanics topic from Edexcel AS Mathematics and Year 1 of the A-Level course.

It contains clear study notes, advice, examples, hundreds of practice questions and a realistic practice exam — with fully worked answers at the back.

How to access your free Online Edition

Go to **cgpbooks.co.uk/extras** and enter this code:

2044 7014 5010 8260

This code will only work once. If someone has used this book before you, they may have already claimed the Online Edition.

Contents

Contents

This book has been produced to be a complete resource for your learning and practice. Throughout, we've focused on three core concepts of A-level maths — mathematical methods, problem solving and modelling.

Each chapter starts with a page that includes Learning Objectives and a Prior Knowledge Check.

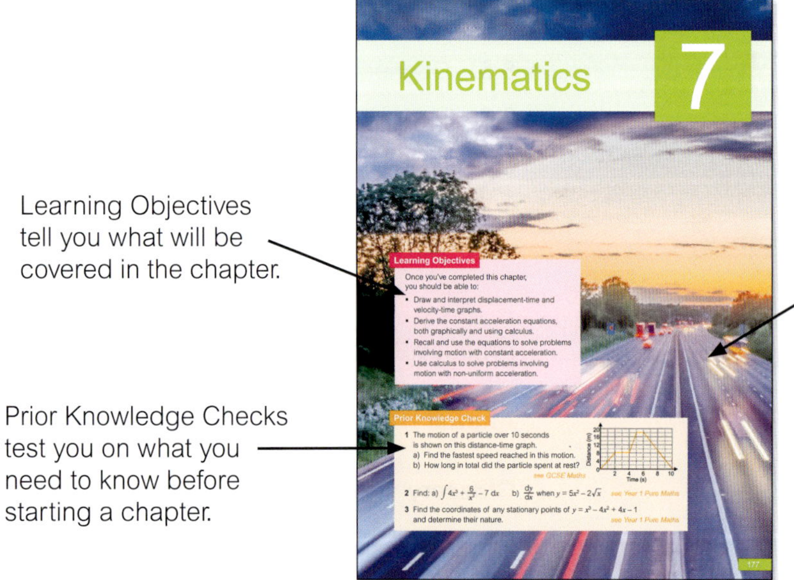

Learning Objectives tell you what will be covered in the chapter.

Prior Knowledge Checks test you on what you need to know before starting a chapter.

Plus — there's an image to illustrate how the maths in the chapter is related to real life.

The main pages have theory, examples and exercises.

Exercises provide lots of practice for every topic, with fully worked answers at the back of the book. Answers to exam-style questions come with a full mark scheme.

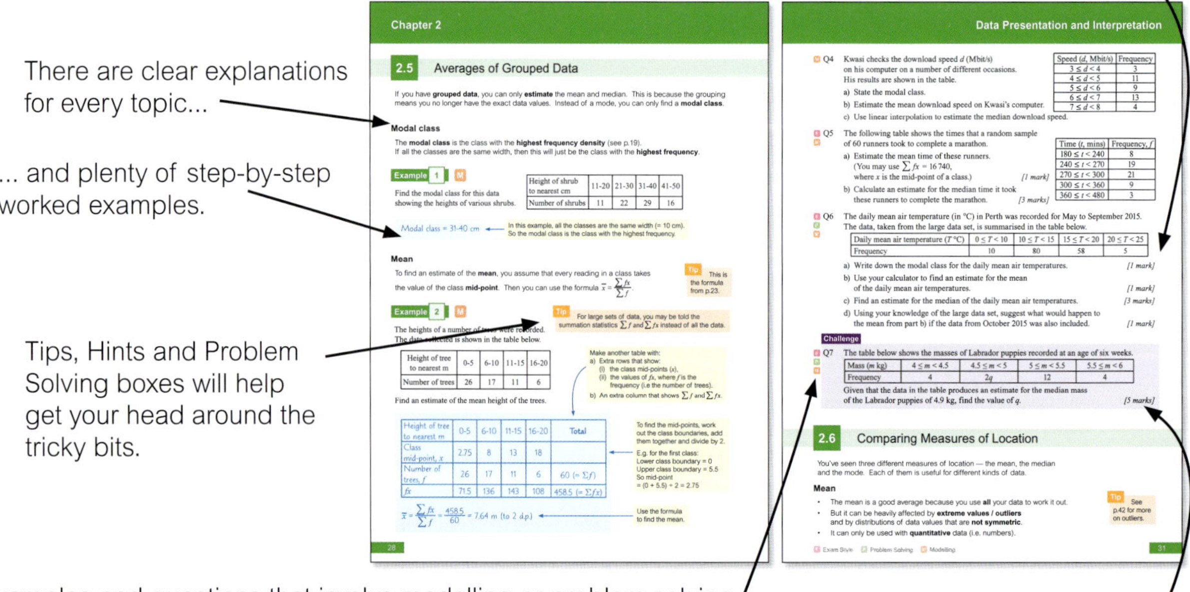

There are clear explanations for every topic...

... and plenty of step-by-step worked examples.

Tips, Hints and Problem Solving boxes will help get your head around the tricky bits.

Examples and questions that involve modelling or problem solving, and questions that are exam style are indicated with stamps:

E Exam Style P Problem Solving M Modelling

The solutions to Problem Solving questions may require knowledge and methods from more than one Chapter of this book.

Challenge Questions at the end of exercises will test your mastery of a topic.

There's a Review Exercise at the end of each chapter and a Practice Paper after the last chapter.

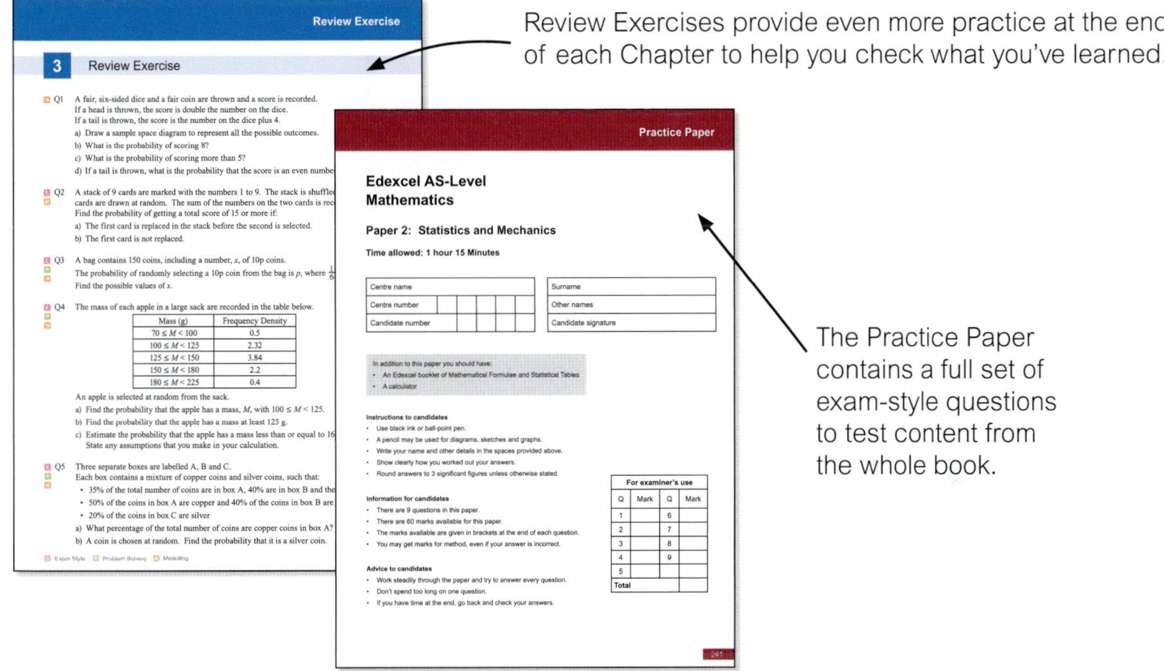

Review Exercises provide even more practice at the end of each Chapter to help you check what you've learned.

The Practice Paper contains a full set of exam-style questions to test content from the whole book.

You can find the Glossary, Statistical Tables and Formula Sheet at the back of the book.

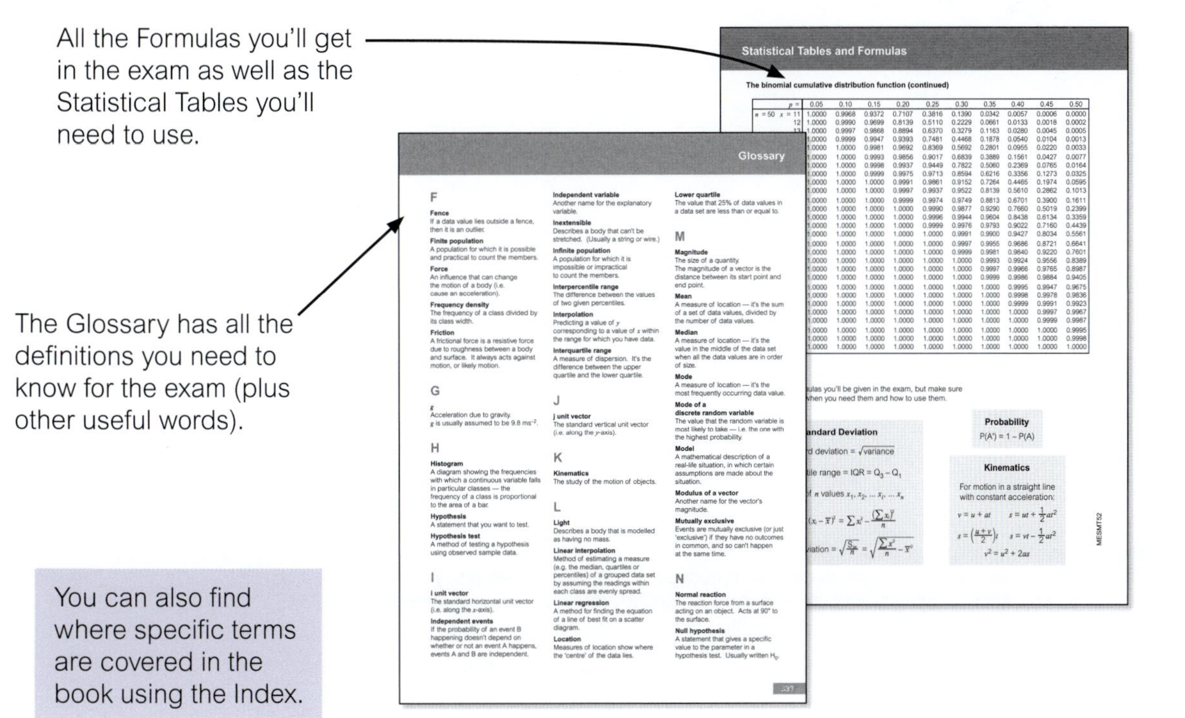

All the Formulas you'll get in the exam as well as the Statistical Tables you'll need to use.

The Glossary has all the definitions you need to know for the exam (plus other useful words).

You can also find where specific terms are covered in the book using the Index.

Published by Coordination Group Publications Ltd
Broughton House, Griffin Street, Broughton-in-Furness, Cumbria, UK, LA20 6HH

www.cgpbooks.co.uk

Text, design, layout and original illustrations
© Coordination Group Publications Ltd (CGP) 2021

Design coordination and Cover design by Beckie Doyle and Kirsty Goodall.

Editors:
Martha Bozic, Michael Bushell, Liam Dyer, Sammy El-Bahrawy, Sarah George, Josie Gilbert, Shaun Harrogate, Rob Hayman, Sharon Keeley-Holden, Simon Little, Samuel Mann, Ali Palin, Rosa Roberts, David Ryan, Ben Train

Contributors:
John Fletcher, Paul Freeman, Charlotte Young

Proofreading:
Mona Allen, Paul Jordin, Lauren McNaughten and Glenn Rogers.

Photo credits:
Cover image © Thamrongpat Theerathammakorn/Moment/Getty Images

Page 1 © Vladimir Zapletin/iStock/Getty Images; Page 13 © vlad61/iStock/Getty Images; Page 72 © kirstypargeter/iStock/Getty Images; Page 101 © kacoates/iStock/Getty Images; Page 141 © sakkmesterke/iStock/Getty Images; Page 168 © adrianam13/iStock/Getty Images; Page 177 © yevtony/iStock/Getty Images; Page 215 © Artur Didyk/iStock/Getty Images.

Clipart from Corel®

Contains public sector information licensed under the Open Government Licence v3.0 (http://www.nationalarchives.gov.uk/doc/open-government-licence/version/3/)
© Crown Copyright, The Met Office 2021.

With thanks to Lottie Edwards for the copyright research.

Printed by Elanders Ltd, Newcastle upon Tyne.

ISBN: 978 1 78908 840 3

Copyright Notice:
All rights reserved. No part of this publication may be reproduced, stored in a retrieval system, or transmitted in any form or by any means, including photocopying, recording, or other electronic or mechanical methods, without the prior written permission of the publisher, except in accordance with the provisions of the Copyright, Designs and Patents Act 1988 or under the terms of a licence issued by the Copyright Licensing Agency Ltd, Barnard's Inn, 86 Fetter Lane, London, EC4A 1EN www.cla.co.uk.

1 Statistical Sampling

Learning Objectives

Once you've completed this chapter, you should be able to:

- Understand what is meant by a population and identify whether a population is infinite or finite.
- Understand what is meant by a census and a sample, and give their advantages and disadvantages.
- Use the following sampling methods: simple random sampling, systematic sampling, stratified sampling, quota sampling and opportunity sampling.
- Comment on the suitability of sampling methods for use in real-world situations.

Prior Knowledge Check

1 A catering company wants to find out what the most popular meals are among secondary school students in the UK. They write a questionnaire for students to fill out.
   a) Give one reason why the company may want to use sampling in this situation.
   b) The company plans to visit a nearby school and give the questionnaire to all of the students there. Explain why this might not give very useful data.
   c) Give one way in which the company could improve the reliability of their sample.

see GCSE Maths

Chapter 1

1.1 Populations and Censuses

Populations

For any statistical investigation, there will be a **group** of something (it could be people, items, animals... or anything else) that you want to **find out about**.

The **whole group**, consisting of **every single** person/item/animal etc. that you want to investigate, is called the **population**. This could be:

- All the students in a maths class
- All the penguins in Antarctica
- All the chocolate puddings produced by a company in a year

A population can be either **finite** or **infinite**. Populations are said to be **finite** if it's possible for someone to **count** how many members there are. Populations are said to be **infinite** if it's **impossible** to know exactly how many members there are — a population might have a **finite number** of members in theory, but if it's impossible to **count** them all in practice, the population is said to be **infinite**.

Finite populations

The number of ... fish in an aquarium.
... trees in a garden.
... members in a pop band.

Infinite populations

The number of ... fish in the Atlantic Ocean.
... leaves in a forest.
... pop fans in the world.

To collect information about your population, you can carry out a **survey**. This means **questioning** the people or **examining** the items.

Censuses

When you collect information from **every member** of a population, it's called a **census** — it's a **survey** of the **whole population**. It helps if the population is fairly **small** and **easily accessible** — so that getting information from every member is a straightforward task.

You need to know the **advantages** and **disadvantages** of carrying out a **census**, so here they are:

Advantage

- It's an **accurate representation** of the population because every member has been surveyed — it's **unbiased**.

Disadvantages

- For **large** populations, it takes a lot of **time** and **effort** to carry out.
- This can make it **expensive** to do.
- It can be difficult to make sure **all** members are surveyed. If some are missed, the survey may be **biased**.
- If the tested items are **used up** or **damaged** in some way by doing a census, a census is **impractical**.

Tip There's only really one main advantage, but it's an important one. See the next page for more on bias.

Tip Watch out for anything that might make doing a census a silly idea.

1.2 Sampling

If doing a census is **impossible** or **impractical**, you can find out about a population by questioning or examining just a **selection** of the people or items. This selected group is called a **sample**.

Before selecting your sample, you need to identify the **sampling units** — these are the **individual members** of the population that **can be sampled**.

A **full list** of all the sampling units is called a **sampling frame**. This list must give a **unique name** or **number** to each sampling unit, and is used to represent the population when selecting a sample (see page 4).

Ideally, a sampling frame would be the **whole population** — but this is often **impractical**, especially with **infinite** populations. For example, the electoral roll of the UK is a **sampling frame** for the adult population of the UK — the **sampling units** are adults who live in the UK. Ideally it would contain every adult living in the country, but in practice it doesn't contain absolutely everyone.

M

For each situation below, explain why taking a sample is more practical than carrying out a census.

a) A company produces 100 chocolate puddings every day, and each pudding is labelled with a unique product number. Every day, a sample of 5 puddings is eaten as a quality control test.

If they did a census of all the puddings, they'd have to eat all of the puddings and there would be none left to sell.

b) Mr Simson runs an online pet store and wants to know if customers are satisfied with the new fish food that he's selling this month. He decides to send fish-food customers an online questionnaire by collecting their email addresses during the checkout process.

If he emailed all customers who bought the new fish food in a month, he'd have a lot of data to process. A sample would be much quicker and easier.

It's usually **more practical** to survey a **sample** rather than carry out a **census**, but your results might not be as **reliable** — make sure you can explain **why**.

Advantages
- Sample surveys are **quicker** and **cheaper** than a census, and it's easier to get hold of all the required information.
- It's the only option when surveyed items are **used up** or **damaged**.

Disadvantages
- There'll be **variability** between samples — each possible sample will give **different** results, so you could just happen to select one which doesn't **accurately reflect** the population.
- Samples can easily be affected by **sampling bias**.

Tip One way to reduce the likelihood of large variability is by using a large sample size. The larger the sample, the more reliable the information should be.

Representative and biased samples

Data collected from a sample is often used to draw **conclusions** about the **whole population**, so the sample must be as similar to the population as possible — it must be a **representative sample**.

If a sample is not representative, it is **biased** and the sample **doesn't fairly represent** the population. A sample could be biased for a **number of reasons** and it can be difficult to get a completely unbiased sample — but there are a few rules you can use to **avoid** introducing bias.

To avoid sampling bias:

1. Select from the correct population and make sure no member of the population is **excluded**.

   E.g. if you want to find out the views of residents from a particular street, your sample should:
   - **include only** residents from that street, and
   - be chosen from a **complete list** of all the residents.

2. Select your sample at **random**.

   Non-random sampling methods include, for example, the sampler:
   - asking friends, who may all give similar answers, or
   - asking for volunteers, who may all have strong views.

3. Make sure all your sample members **respond**.

   E.g. if some of your sampled residents are out when you go to interview them, it's important to go back and get their views another time.

Simple random sampling

Taking a random sample is important for avoiding bias — one way to make sure your sample is completely random is to use **simple random sampling**:

- Every person or item in the population has an **equal chance** of being in the sample.
- Each selection is **independent** of every other selection.

To choose a simple random sample:

- Give a **number** to each population member, from a **full list** of the population.
- Generate a list of **random numbers** using a calculator or a random-number table and **match** them to the numbered members to select your sample.

Here's an example of **simple random sampling** using a **random-number table**.

8330	3992	1840
0330	1290	3237
9165	4815	0766

A zoo has 80 cottontop tamarins. Describe how the random-number table on the right could be used to select a sample of five of them for a study on tail lengths.

Create a list of the 80 cottontop tamarins, giving each cottontop tamarin a 2-digit number between 01 and 80.

First draw up a sampling frame.

Use each 4-digit number in the table as two 2-digit numbers next to each other.
The first few numbers are: 83, 30, 39, 92, 18, 40, 03

Use the random-number table to choose five numbers — start at the beginning and find the first five numbers between 01 and 80.

Ignore numbers bigger than 80,
so the five random numbers are 30, 39, 18, 40 and 03.

Choose the cottontop tamarins with the matching numbers.

Match the random numbers to the sampling frame members.

To decide whether a simple random sample is suitable for investigating a real-world problem, you need to know its advantages and disadvantages. See the next page for these.

Advantage Every member of the population has an **equal chance** of being selected, so it's **completely unbiased**.

Disadvantage It can be **inconvenient** if the population is spread over a **large area** — it might be difficult to track down the selected members (e.g. in a nationwide sample).

Systematic sampling (sampling every n^{th} member)

To make choosing a sample faster, you could use a **systematic sample** — this chooses **every n^{th} member** from the population to be sampled.

To choose a systematic sample:

- Give a **number** to each population **member**, from a **full list** of the population.
- Calculate a **regular interval** to use (e.g. every 10th member of the population) by dividing the population size by the sample size.
- Generate a **random** starting point that is less than or equal to the size of the interval — you could roll a dice or use a random-number generator to choose a suitable starting point. The corresponding member of the population is the **first member** of your sample.
- Keep **adding** the interval to the starting point to select your sample.

Example 3 

50 000 fans attended a football match. Describe how a systematic sample could be used to select a sample of 100 people.

Give each fan a 5-digit number between 00 001 and 50 000 — this could be done e.g. by ticket number. ← Work out how to assign a number to each fan.

50 000 ÷ 100 = 500, so the interval is 500 — i.e. select every 500th fan. ← Calculate the interval to use.

Use a calculator to randomly generate a number between 1 and 500 — e.g. if 239 is randomly generated, the starting point will be 00 239. ← Describe how to find the starting point.

Find the rest of the sample by repeatedly adding 500: ← Use the starting point and the interval to select a sample.

00 239, 00 739, 01 239, ..., 49 239, 49 739

+500 +500 ...

Then select the fans with matching ticket numbers.

You could be asked about the pros and cons of systematic sampling:

Advantages

- It can be used for quality control on a production line — a **machine** can be set up to sample every n^{th} item.
- It should give an **unbiased sample**.

Disadvantage The regular interval could coincide with a **pattern** — e.g. if every 10th item produced by a machine is faulty and you sample every 10th item, your sample will appear to show that **every item** produced is faulty, or that **no items** are faulty. Either way, your sample will be **biased**.

Stratified sampling

If a population is divided into **categories** (e.g. age or gender), you can use a **stratified sample** — this uses the same proportion of each category in the sample as there is in the population.

To choose a stratified sample:

- Divide the population into **categories**.
- Calculate the **total** population.
- Calculate the number needed for each category in the sample, using:

$$\textbf{Size of category in sample} = \frac{\text{size of category in population}}{\text{total size of population}} \times \text{total sample size}$$

- Select the sample for each category at **random**.

Tip You can define your categories using more than one characteristic — e.g. categories could be females under 18, males under 18, females aged 18-25, etc.

Example 4 M

A teacher takes a sample of 20 pupils from her school, stratified by year group. The table shows the number of pupils in each year group.

Year Group	No. of pupils
7	120
8	80
9	95
10	63
11	42

Calculate how many pupils from each year group should be in her sample.

$120 + 80 + 95 + 63 + 42 = 400$ ← Find the total population.

$\text{Year } 7 = \frac{120}{400} \times 20 = 6$ ← Calculate the number needed for each category in the sample.

$\text{Year } 8 = \frac{80}{400} \times 20 = 4$

$\text{Year } 9 = \frac{95}{400} \times 20 = 4.75 \approx 5$

$\text{Year } 10 = \frac{63}{400} \times 20 = 3.15 \approx 3$

$\text{Year } 11 = \frac{42}{400} \times 20 = 2.1 \approx 2$

$6 + 4 + 5 + 3 + 2 = 20$ ✓ ← Check that the total of the categories is the sample size.

Problem Solving You can't have decimal amounts of pupils, so the answers for Years 9, 10 and 11 are rounded to the nearest whole number.

Stratified sampling is useful in certain situations:

Advantages
- If the population has **disjoint categories** (where there is no overlap), this is likely to give you a **representative** sample.
- It's useful when results may **vary** depending on categories.

Disadvantage It can be **expensive** because of the extra detail involved.

Quota sampling

Quota sampling also involves dividing the population into categories — however, it's different from stratified sampling because no effort is made to select members at random.

To choose a quota sample:

- Divide the population into **categories**.
- Give each category a **quota** (number of members to sample).
- Collect data until the quotas are met in **all** categories (**without** using random sampling).

This method is often used in market research. An interviewer will be told the quotas to fulfil, but can choose who to interview within each quota.

Example 5 M

A video-game company wants to gather opinions on a new game. The interviewer is asked to interview 65 people aged under thirty and 35 people aged thirty or above.

Give one advantage and one disadvantage of this quota sample.

Advantage: the company doesn't have a full list of everyone who has played the game, so random sampling isn't possible.

Disadvantage: people with strong views on the game are more likely to respond to the interviewer, which causes sampling bias.

Problem Solving

The company have divided the population into two age groups. A reason for this could be that they know people aged under thirty are more likely to play their video games.

Once again, you need to know the advantages and disadvantages:

Advantages
- It can be done when there **isn't** a full list of the population.
- The interviewer continues to sample until all the quotas are met, so **non-response** is less of a problem.

Disadvantage It can be **easily biased** by the interviewer — within the quotas the interviewer could **exclude** some of the population (e.g. they could choose to interview only sporty-looking people, which might accidentally lead to a biased sample).

Opportunity sampling

The final sampling method you need to know about is **opportunity** (or **convenience**) **sampling**. This is where the sample is chosen from a section of the population that is **convenient** for the sampler.

Example 6 

Mel thinks that most people watch her favourite television programme. She asks 20 friends whether they watch the television programme.

a) Name the sampling method Mel used.

Opportunity (or convenience) sampling — Mel asks her friends because they are easily available to sample.

b) Give a reason why Mel's sample may be biased.

Mel's friends could be of a similar age or the same gender, which is not representative of the whole population.

or...

Because this is Mel's favourite television programme, she might have encouraged her friends to watch it too.

Tip There is no one right answer in part b) — any sensible comment will do.

Here's the final set of advantages and disadvantages you need to know:

Advantage Data can be gathered very **quickly** and **easily**.

Disadvantage It **isn't random** and can be **very biased** — there's no attempt to make the sample representative of the population.

1 Review Exercise

M Q1 For each population described say whether it is finite or infinite.

a) The members of the Ulverston Musical Appreciation Society.

b) The population of Australia.

c) The stars in the Milky Way galaxy.

d) The 2016 Olympic gold medallists.

e) The jalapeño chilli plants on sale at Church Lane Garden Centre.

f) The cells in a human body.

E Q2 a) In the context of a statistical investigation, briefly describe what is meant by:

(i) a population *[1 mark]*

(ii) a sample *[1 mark]*

b) Explain what a sample is used for. *[1 mark]*

M Q3 Members of a local book club have to be consulted about the next book they'll read.

a) What is the population?

b) Explain whether a sample or a census should be used.

M Q4 A teacher is investigating whether a student's ability to memorise a random string of letters is related to their ability to spell. He plans to ask students from his school, which has 1200 pupils, to do a standard spelling test and then to memorise a random string of 20 letters.

a) What is the population?

b) Give two reasons why he should use a sample rather than carry out a census.

M Q5 For each of the following situations, explain whether it would be more sensible to carry out a census or a sample survey:

a) Marcel is in charge of a packaging department of 8 people.
He wants to know the average number of items a person packs per day.

b) A toy manufacturer produces batches of 500 toys. As part of a safety check, they want to test the toys to work out the strength needed to pull them apart.

c) Prisha has a biased dice. She wants to find the proportion of dice rolls that result in a 'three'.

Q6 a) Explain what is meant by a sampling unit.

b) Explain what is meant by a sampling frame.

M Q7 Hattie has a biased coin. To investigate the probability of getting heads, she takes the results of the first 50 times she flips the coin. Is this data likely to be biased? Explain your answer.

E M Q8 A researcher asks for volunteers to participate in an experiment involving moderate physical activity to investigate general levels of fitness amongst the students at a university. The participants are aware of what the experiment involves before volunteering.

a) Identify the population. *[1 mark]*

b) Explain why this method of selection may produce results that are not representative of the population. *[1 mark]*

M Q9 The animals in a zoo are given a unique 3-digit ID number between 001 and 500. Describe how you could use a random-number generator to choose a simple random sample of 20 of the zoo's animals.

E M Q10 There are 346 books in a bookcase. Explain how the random-number table below could be used to select a random sample of six of the books in the bookcase.

936	390	393	380	990
336	597	321	873	983
821	443	595	211	228
080	060	875	558	544
155	603	359	525	590
781	567	396	874	724
718	663	407	003	298

[2 marks]

Q11 a) Describe the characteristics of simple random sampling.

b) Give an advantage and a disadvantage of the method of simple random sampling.

E M Q12 A factory produces five different types of spring. The quality of a spring is tested by stretching it beyond its elastic limit, which means the spring can no longer be used.

a) Explain why using a census to test the quality of the springs produced by the factory is not appropriate. *[1 mark]*

The factory produces approximately 10 000 springs per day. The factory manager suggests taking a sample of 50 springs produced on a certain day to test for quality.

b) Suggest a suitable sampling method and describe how this sample could be obtained. *[2 marks]*

M Q13 All dogs which are admitted to the Graymar Animal Sanctuary are microchipped with a unique identification number. Between 2015 and 2016, 108 dogs were admitted. A sample of 12 dogs which were admitted between 2015 and 2016 is selected for long-term monitoring.

a) What is the population?

b) Explain how to carry out a systematic sample of 12 dogs.

M Q14 The houses on Park Road are numbered from 1 to 173. Forty households are to be chosen to take part in a council survey. Describe a method for choosing an unbiased sample.

M Q15 A sports centre selects a sample of 10 members, stratified by age.
The table shows the total number of members in each age group.

Age (a)	Under 20	20 to 40	41 to 60	Over 60
No. of members	45	33	15	57

Calculate how many people from each age group should be sampled.

E M Q16 The table shows the adult population of a town, split into age categories.

Age range	18 to 29	30 to 39	40 to 49	50 to 64	Over 64
Frequency	1657	3488	2990	1602	1192

A stratified sample of 150 of the adults is to be chosen, in order to carry out the survey. Use the information in the table to determine how many people from each category should be included in the sample. *[2 marks]*

E P M Q17 A builders' merchant sells four different sizes of flagstones, sent from the same supplier.
The manager decides to inspect a sample of the flagstones in the next delivery.
A stratified sample based on the number of each size of flagstone is to be chosen.
The table shows the number of each size of flagstone in the next delivery.

Small	Medium	Large	Extra Large
300	270	210	120

The manager calculates, without needing to round, that 18 medium flagstones will be included in the stratified sample.
Calculate the number of flagstones in the sample. *[2 marks]*

E M Q18 A wildlife association wants to investigate the prevalence, in the UK, of a disease that occurs in foxes. It is decided that a sample of foxes will be studied.

a) Identify the population. *[1 mark]*

b) Explain whether this population is finite or infinite. *[1 mark]*

c) Explain why it isn't possible to take a random sample from this population. *[1 mark]*

The association studies a sample of 20 foxes from a rural area. It is found that the prevalence of the disease in this sample is much lower than originally expected.

d) Explain why these findings may not be applicable to the whole population. *[1 mark]*

M Q19 For a school project, Neville is investigating the types of music people in the UK like to listen to. He collects data by asking friends from his year group. Is this sample likely to be representative of the population? Give one way in which the sample could be improved.

M Q20 A bookshop owner is interested in the reading habits of people in the local area.
She decides to ask some of her customers how many hours they spend reading per week. Explain why this is not a suitable sampling method.

M Q21 For each of the following, name the sampling method used and give one disadvantage of using that sampling method in the given situation:

a) A tea company is investigating tea-drinking habits of its customers. The interviewer is asked to sample exactly 60 women and 40 men using a non-random sampling method.

b) After a concert, a band is looking for feedback from their fans. Using the ticket numbers, they select every 100th fan to complete a survey.

c) A student is researching shopping habits in the UK. He records how many people enter his local shopping centre between 9 am and 5 pm on a Monday.

E P M Q22 A swimming centre has two separate pools. One pool is used for taught swimming lessons that are held every day, and the other pool is for members to use whenever they wish. The centre wants to carry out a survey of a sample of its 550 members. A member of staff suggests splitting the membership into categories of members who attend taught swimming lessons on each day of the week, and taking a stratified sample of size 55.

a) Explain why a stratified sample chosen in this way would be inappropriate. *[1 mark]*

A second member of staff suggests choosing a systematic sample of size 55.

b) Explain how a systematic sample could be taken. *[1 mark]*

Q23 a) Explain the main differences between quota sampling and stratified sampling.

b) Give one advantage and one disadvantage to using stratified sampling.

E M Q24 A supermarket wants to know what customers think of a new cleaning product. Each customer who purchases the product is given a questionnaire and asked to return it to the supermarket once they have had a chance to try the product.

a) What is this type of sampling method called? *[1 mark]*

b) What is a possible problem with asking the customer to return the questionnaire at a later date? *[1 mark]*

E M Q25 A school has approximately 1000 students. A student wants to investigate the internet usage of the other students at the school. She asks six students sitting in a group to fill out a questionnaire.

a) Give two reasons why this sampling method is not suitable. *[2 marks]*

b) Suggest a better sampling method for the student to use and describe how this sample could be obtained. *[2 marks]*

E M Q26 A company is doing some market research and wants to interview members of the public in a town centre. The company divides the target population into separate age categories and wants to ensure that a certain number of people are interviewed within each category.

a) Suggest an appropriate sampling method that the company could use and describe how the sample may be obtained. *[2 marks]*

b) Give one advantage and one disadvantage to using this method of sampling. *[2 marks]*

1 Chapter Summary

1 In statistics, a population is a whole group that you want to investigate. Populations can be either finite or infinite.

2 A census is a survey of the whole population. A census gives an accurate representation of the population (it's unbiased), but can be impractical or impossible to carry out.

3 Sampling is where a selected group is taken from a population and used to draw conclusions for the whole population. Sampling units are the individual members of the population that can be sampled, and a full list of sampling units is called a sampling frame. Sampling is often preferred to a census as it is usually more practical.

4 Samples can be representative of a population, but they can also be biased — which means they don't accurately represent the population. Bias can occur for a number of different reasons. To avoid sampling bias, sample members should be selected at random.

5 Simple random sampling involves selecting members from a population at random, often using a random-number generator.

- As every population member has an equal chance of being selected, it's unbiased.
- However, it can be inconvenient to track down every selected member of the sample.

6 Systematic sampling is a method where every n^{th} member of a population is sampled using a regular interval (n).

- It should result in an unbiased sample and it can be used in quality control, e.g. machines in production can be set up to sample every n^{th} member.
- However, the interval could coincide with a pattern in the population, making the sample biased.

7 Stratified sampling can be used where the population divides into categories. A random sample is taken from each category within the population.

- It is useful when results might vary across categories, and if the categories are disjoint, the sample should be representative.
- However, the extra step to split the population into categories can add time and costs.

8 Quota sampling is another method where the population is split into categories, this time collecting data within each category (without random sampling) until pre-determined quotas are met.

- It can be done without a full list of the population, and non-response shouldn't be a problem.
- However, it can be easily biased by the interviewer.

9 Opportunity sampling involves a sample being chosen from a convenient group within the population.

- Data can be gathered quickly and easily.
- It isn't random and can be very biased.

Data Presentation and Interpretation

2

Learning Objectives

Once you've completed this chapter, you should be able to:

- Interpret frequency tables, grouped frequency tables and histograms.
- Calculate the mean, median and mode for a data set and estimate the mean and median for a grouped data set.
- Calculate the range, interquartile range and interpercentile range and determine whether a data point is an outlier
- Draw and interpret cumulative frequency diagrams and box plots.
- Calculate and interpret variance and standard deviation.
- Decide whether two variables are positively correlated, negatively correlated, or not correlated from a scatter diagram.
- Use a regression line to predict values of the response variable.

Prior Knowledge Check

1 Draw a scatter diagram to display the data in the table.

x	10	20	30	40	50	60
y	22	31	56	46	37	69

see GCSE Maths

2 Look at this set of data: 41 34 34 30 46 44 32 29
Find the: a) mean b) median c) mode

see GCSE Maths

3 Rearrange $3x = \frac{y-4}{3}$ into the forms:
a) $y = mx + c$ b) $ax + by + c = 0$

see Year 1 Pure Maths

4 A straight line goes through points (7, –2) and (4, 16).
Find the equation for this line.

see Year 1 Pure Maths

2.1 Representing Data

A lot of **statistics** involves analysing **data**. The exam board will provide you with a **large data set**.

- You need to be **familiar** with this data, and be able to carry out all the techniques you'll meet in this chapter on your data.
- As there is a lot of data, you'll have to use a **calculator** or **computer** to carry out some of the analysis — but the basic techniques are covered in this chapter.
- Some **examples** in this chapter will use data from the large data set.

Data consists of a number of **observations** (or **measurements**).
Each observation records a value of a particular **variable**. There are different kinds of variables:

- Variables that take **non-numerical** values (i.e. not numbers) — these are **qualitative** variables.
- Variables that take **numerical** values (i.e. numbers) — these are called **quantitative** variables.

There are then two different types of **quantitative** variables:

- A **discrete** variable can take only **certain values** within a particular range (e.g. shoe sizes) — this means there are 'gaps' between possible values (you can't take size 9.664 shoes, for example).
- A **continuous** variable can take **any value** within a particular range (e.g. lengths or masses) — there are no gaps between possible values.

Example 1

An employer collects information about the computers in his office.
He gathers observations of the four variables shown in this table.

1. Manufacturer	Bell	Banana	Deucer	Deucer
2. Processor speed (in GHz)	2.6	2.1	1.8	2.2
3. Year of purchase	2014	2015	2016	2014
4. Colour	Grey	Grey	Grey	Black

a) Which of the four variables are qualitative?

'Manufacturer' and 'Colour' ← Qualitative variables take non-numerical values.

b) Which of the four variables are quantitative?

'Processor speed' and 'Year of purchase' ← Quantitative variables takes numerical values.

Example 2

The following variables are quantitative: (i) length, (ii) weight, (iii) number of brothers, (iv) time, (v) total value of 6 coins from down the back of my sofa

a) Which of these 5 quantitative variables are continuous?

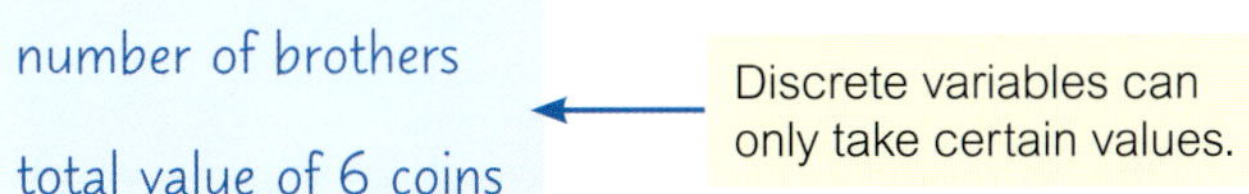

b) Which of these 5 quantitative variables are discrete?

number of brothers

total value of 6 coins

Discrete variables can only take certain values.

Tip 'Number of brothers' can take only whole-number values. 'Total value of 6 coins' can only take certain values — they could be worth 12p or 13p, but not 12.8p.

Data is often shown in the form of a **table**. There are two types you need to be really familiar with:

Frequency tables show the number of observations of various values.
Frequency just means 'the number of times something happens'.

For example, this frequency table shows the number of bananas in thirty 1.5 kg bags.

Number of bananas	8	9	10	11	12
Frequency	3	7	10	6	4

Grouped frequency tables show the number of observations whose values fall within certain classes (i.e. **ranges** or **groups of values**). They're often used when there is a large range of possible values.

For example, this grouped frequency table shows the number of potatoes in thirty 25 kg sacks.

Number of potatoes	50-55	56-60	61-65	66-70	71-75
Frequency	1	8	12	7	2

- Notice how grouped frequency tables **don't** tell you the **exact** value of the observations — just the most and the least they **could** be.
- Notice how the different classes **don't overlap** — in fact, there are '**gaps**' between the classes because the data is **discrete**.

Tip Frequency tables and grouped frequency tables can also be drawn 'vertically', like this:

Number of bananas	Frequency
8	3
9	7
10	10
11	6
12	4

Grouped frequency tables are also used for **continuous** data.
Since there are no 'gaps' between possible data values for continuous variables, there can be no gaps between classes in their grouped frequency tables either.

E.g. this grouped frequency table shows the masses of 50 potatoes.

- **Inequalities** have been used to define the **class boundaries** (the upper and lower limits of each class) — there are no 'gaps' and no overlaps between classes.
- The smallest class doesn't have a **lower limit**, so very small potatoes can still be put into one of the classes. Similarly, the largest class doesn't have an **upper limit**.

Mass of potato (m, in g)	Frequency
$m < 100$	7
$100 \le m < 200$	8
$200 \le m < 300$	16
$300 \le m < 400$	14
$m \ge 400$	5

You don't always need to leave the top and bottom classes without a lower and upper limit — e.g. if you know for a fact that very small or very large data values are impossible.

This grouped frequency table shows the lengths (to the nearest cm) of the same 50 potatoes.

Length of potato (l, in cm)	Frequency
4-5	5
6-7	11
8-9	15
10-11	16
12-13	3

- The shortest potato that could go in the 6-7 class would actually have a length of 5.5 cm (since 5.5 cm would be rounded up to 6 cm when measuring to the nearest cm). So the **lower class boundary** of the 6-7 class is 5.5 cm.
- The **upper class boundary** of the 6-7 class is the same as the lower class boundary of the 8-9 class — this is 7.5 cm. This means there are never any **gaps** between classes. (Even though a potato of length 7.5 cm would go in the 8-9 class, this is still the upper class boundary of the 6-7 class.)

For each class, you can find the **class width** using this formula:

class width = upper class boundary – lower class boundary

And you can find the **mid-point** of a class using this formula:

$$\textbf{mid-point} = \frac{\textbf{lower class boundary + upper class boundary}}{\textbf{2}}$$

Tip A class with a lower class boundary of 50 g and upper class boundary of 250 g can be written in different ways — you might see:
'100-200, to the nearest 100 g',
'50 ≤ mass < 250',
'50-', followed by '250-' for the next class, and so on.
They all mean the same thing.

Example 3 M

A researcher measures the length (to the nearest 10 cm) of 40 cars. Her results are shown in the table.

Length (cm)	Frequency
250-350	5
360-410	11
420-450	17
460-500	7

Add four columns to the table to show:
(i) the lower class boundaries (ii) the upper class boundaries
(iii) the class widths (iv) the class mid-points

The shortest car that measures 250 cm (to the nearest 10 cm) is 245 cm long. So the lower class boundary of the 250-350 class is 245 cm. ← Work out the lower class boundaries.

The upper class boundary of the 250-350 class is 355 cm. ← Work out the upper class boundaries.

Problem Solving 355 cm must be the upper class boundary for the 250-350 class, because no number less than this would work. E.g. it can't be 354.9 cm, because then a car of length 354.99 cm wouldn't fit into any of the classes.

Length (cm)	Frequency	Lower class boundary (cm)	Upper class boundary (cm)	Class width (cm)	Mid-point (cm)
250-350	5	245	355	110	300
360-410	11	355	415	60	385
420-450	17	415	455	40	435
460-500	7	455	505	50	480

← Use the formulas above to find the class widths and the mid-points.

You can represent data from a frequency table with a **frequency polygon**.

Example 4 

The table shows the maximum daily temperature (°C) in Hurn between May and October 2015. Draw a frequency polygon to show the data.

> **Tip** This uses a sample of the large data set.

Maximum daily temperature, t (°C)	Frequency	Mid-point
$10 < t \leq 15$	22	12.5
$15 < t \leq 20$	100	17.5
$20 < t \leq 25$	58	22.5
$25 < t \leq 30$	4	27.5

Calculate the mid-points of each class using the formula from page 16. Adding a column for mid-points makes it easier to plot the points.

Plot the mid-points on the horizontal (x) axis and the frequencies on the vertical (y) axis. So plot the points (12.5, 22), (17.5, 100), (22.5, 58) and (27.5, 4).

Join the points with a straight line (not a curve).

There are lots of other ways of representing data that you'll have come across at GCSE. If you're asked to draw a 'suitable' diagram, think about which will be most appropriate to represent the data you're given — for example, certain types of diagram are better for discrete or continuous variables.

Exercise 2.1

Q1 A mechanic collects the following information about cars he services:

Make, Mileage, Colour, Number of doors, Cost of service

Write down all the variables from this list that are:

a) qualitative b) quantitative

Q2 Amy is an athletics coach. She records the following information about each athlete she trains:

Number of medals won last season, Height, Mass, Shoe size

Write down all the variables from this list that are examples of:

a) discrete quantitative variables b) continuous quantitative variables

M **Q3** A botanist is researching an unusual species of plant. They select 10 of these plants to study. The botanist records the number of leaves on each of the 10 plants and the length of 10 randomly selected leaves from each plant, in millimetres.

a) Write down which of the sets of data collected is continuous, giving a reason for your answer.

b) Explain why all the data the botanist collects for this study is quantitative.

c) Give a reason why the botanist might want to group the data for the length of the leaves.

M **Q4** A group of 50 people were given 30 seconds to see how many words they could make out of a set of 10 letters. The bar chart shows the results.

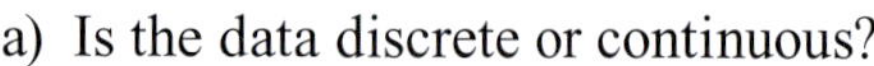

a) Is the data discrete or continuous?

b) How many people found at least 11 words?

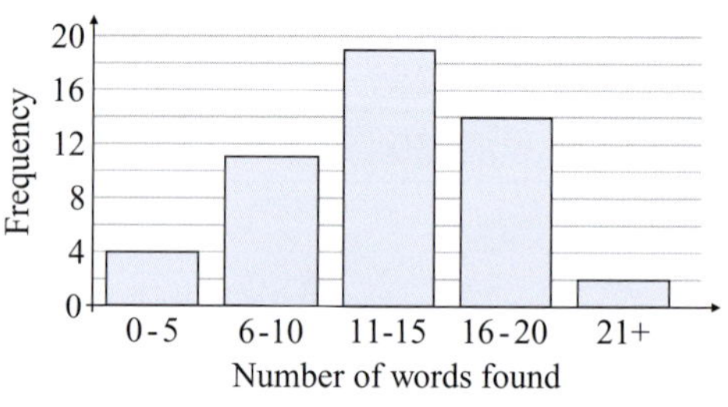

M **Q5** The heights of the members of an art club are shown in the table.

a) Explain why 'height' is a continuous variable.

b) For each class, write down:

(i) the lower class boundary (ii) the upper class boundary

(iii) the class width (iv) the class mid-point

c) Show the information in the table in a frequency polygon.

Height, h (cm)	Number of members
$140 \leq h < 150$	3
$150 \leq h < 160$	9
$160 \leq h < 170$	17
$170 \leq h < 180$	12
$180 \leq h < 190$	5
$190 \leq h < 200$	1

E P M **Q6** The table on the right shows the times taken by 21 members of a running club to complete a half-marathon.

a) Write down the mid-point for the class $1{:}50 \leq t < 1{:}55$ in minutes. *[1 mark]*

b) Draw a frequency polygon for the data, showing the times in minutes. *[3 marks]*

Time, t (h:mm)	Frequency
$1{:}45 \leq t < 1{:}50$	1
$1{:}50 \leq t < 1{:}55$	7
$1{:}55 \leq t < 2{:}00$	7
$2{:}00 \leq t < 2{:}05$	3
$2{:}05 \leq t < 2{:}10$	2
$2{:}10 \leq t < 2{:}15$	1

P M **Q7** The lengths of the bananas in a grocer's shop are shown in the frequency polygon on the right.

a) What type of variable is 'length of banana'?

b) Draw a grouped frequency table using the information in the frequency polygon.

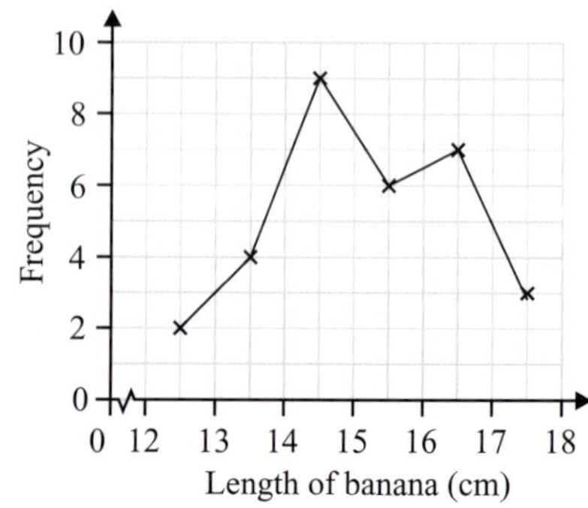

2.2 Histograms

Histograms look like bar charts. However, because they're used to show frequencies of **continuous variables**, there are **no gaps** between the bars. To plot a histogram, you plot the **frequency density** rather than the frequency (as you would in a bar chart). Use this formula to find frequency density:

$$\textbf{Frequency density} = \frac{\textbf{frequency}}{\textbf{class width}}$$

Tip In a histogram, the area of a bar is proportional to the frequency in that class. And if you divide the area of a bar by the total area of all of the bars, you get the probability of a given class.

Here's some data showing the heights of 24 people:

Height (cm)	Lower class boundary (cm)	Upper class boundary (cm)	Class width (cm)	Frequency	Frequency density
$130 \leq h < 150$	130	150	20	3	0.15
$150 \leq h < 160$	150	160	10	4	0.4
$160 \leq h < 165$	160	165	5	5	1
$165 \leq h < 170$	165	170	5	6	1.2
$170 \leq h < 190$	170	190	20	6	0.3

Here's the same data plotted as a histogram.

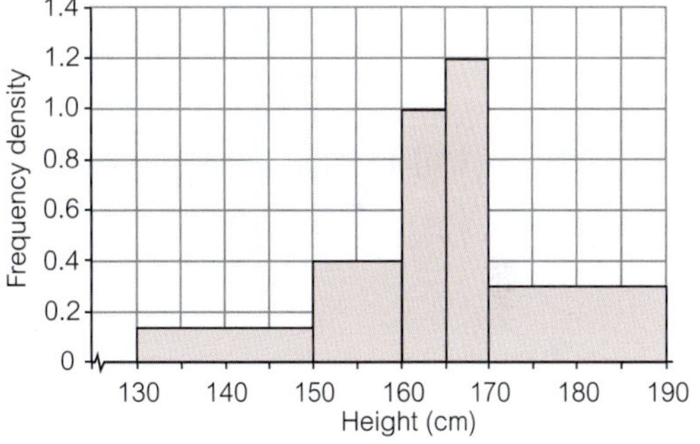

Notice how:

- The vertical axis shows **frequency density**.
- The horizontal axis has a **continuous** scale like an ordinary graph, and there are **no gaps** between the columns.
- A bar's left-hand edge corresponds to the **lower class boundary**, and a bar's right-hand edge corresponds to the **upper class boundary**.

If you plotted the **frequency** (rather than the frequency density), then your graph would look like this.

It looks like there are lots of tall people but this is an illusion created by the width of the final class. If this data was split into classes all the same width, then the graph would look more like the one above.

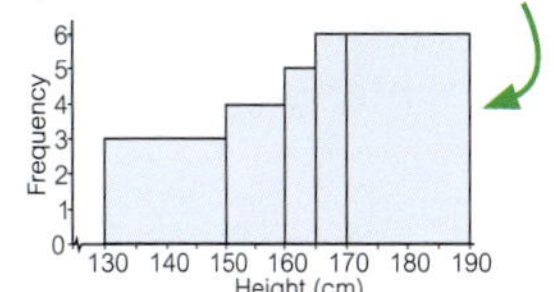

Example 1 

The table shows maximum daily windspeed in knots (kn) in Leuchars, over 30 days in 1987. Draw a histogram to show the data.

Tip This uses a sample of the large data set.

Maximum gust, g (kn)	$5 < g \leq 15$	$15 < g \leq 20$	$20 < g \leq 30$	$30 < g \leq 45$
Frequency	8	9	10	3

Maximum gust, g (kn)	Class width	Frequency	Frequency density
$5 < g \leq 15$	10	8	0.8
$15 < g \leq 20$	5	9	1.8
$20 < g \leq 30$	10	10	1
$30 < g \leq 45$	15	3	0.2

First draw a table showing the class width and the frequency density.

continued on the next page...

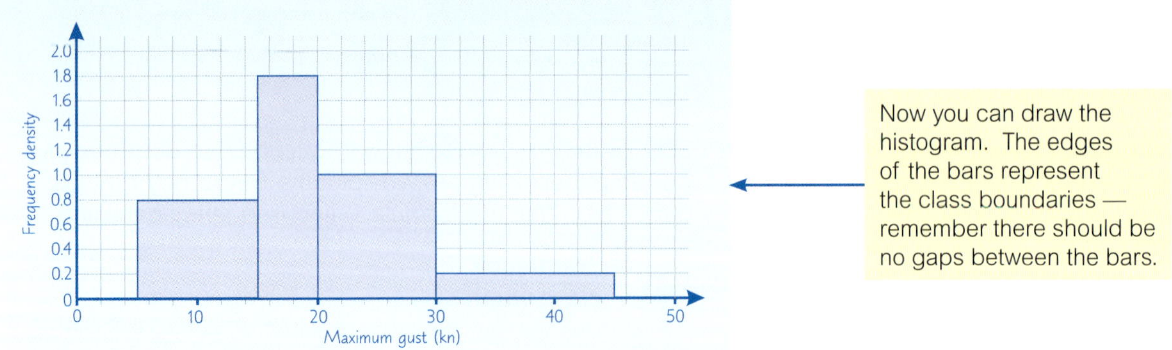

You might be given a histogram with a **missing scale** on the vertical axis. As long as you know the frequency of one of the classes, you can work out what **each interval** on the scale is worth.

Or, you can use the fact that **area is proportional to frequency**, to work out the frequency that **each square** on the grid represents.

Example 2 

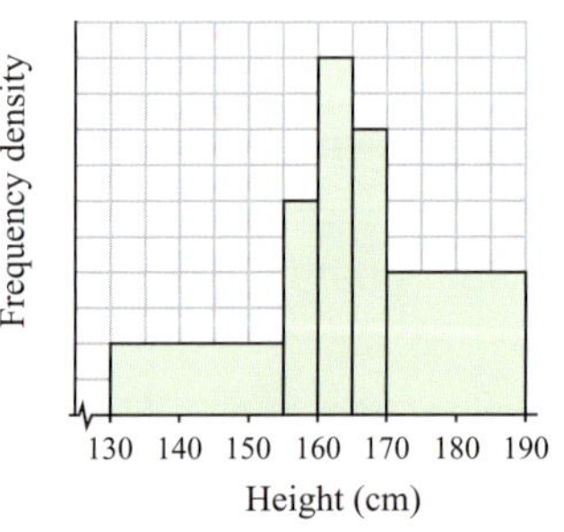

This histogram shows the heights of a group of people.

There were 6 people between 155 cm and 160 cm tall.

a) How many people in the group are between 130 cm and 155 cm tall?

Class width = 160 – 155 = 5

Frequency = 6

So frequency density = 6 ÷ 5 = 1.2

The 155-160 bar is 6 units high, so each interval is worth 1.2 ÷ 6 = 0.2.

Frequency density of 130-155 class = 2 × 0.2 = 0.4, and class width = 25. So frequency = 0.4 × 25 = 10 people.

Before looking at the 130-155 class, you need to use the information you have about the 155-160 class.

Use the frequency density formula to find the frequency density of the 155-160 class.

Use your frequency density to work out what each interval on the scale is worth.

Use the scale to find the frequency density of the 130-155 class, and multiply by the class width to get the frequency.

[**Alternatively**, you could have used the 155-160 bar and the fact that area is proportional to frequency to work out that an area of 6 grid squares represents a frequency of 6, so **1 grid square represents 1 person**. The 130-155 bar has an area of 5 × 2 = 10 squares, which represents a frequency of **10 people.**]

b) How many people in the group are over 165 cm tall?

165-170 cm: Frequency density = 8 × 0.2 = 1.6, so frequency = 1.6 × 5 = 8 people.

170-190 cm: Frequency density = 4 × 0.2 = 0.8, so frequency = 0.8 × 20 = 16 people.

So 8 + 16 = 24 people are over 165 cm tall.

There are two bars representing people over 165 cm tall. You need to find the frequencies represented by both of them.

Add the individual frequencies to find the total frequency.

If a range of data **doesn't** start or end on a **class boundary**, you can only **estimate** the frequency corresponding to that range, as you don't know the individual data values within each class.

Example 3 M

The histogram below shows the speeds of cars along a stretch of road.
Estimate the number of cars travelling at 25 mph or less.

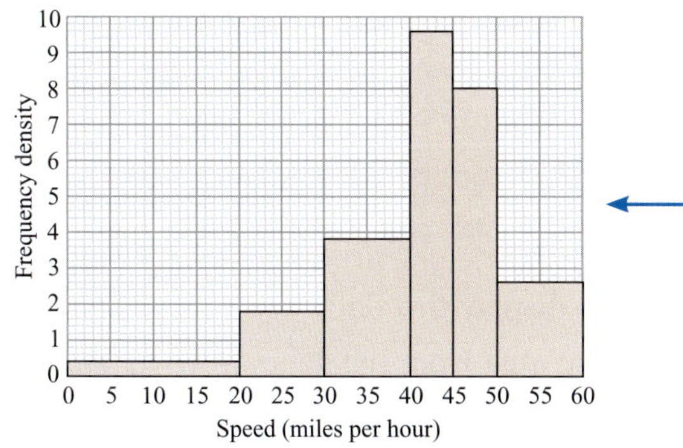

You need to find the frequency represented by the bars to the left of 25 mph on the horizontal axis (the frequency of cars travelling at 25 mph or less).

This is the frequency for the 0-20 bar plus half the frequency for the 20-30 bar (i.e. the frequency between 20 and 25 mph).

Frequency = frequency density × class width
= 0.4 × 20 = 8 cars

Find the frequency for the 0-20 mph bar.

Frequency = frequency density × class width
= 1.8 × 10 = 18

Now find the frequency for the 20-30 mph bar.

18 ÷ 2 = 9 cars

Divide it by 2 — you are making the assumption that half the cars travelling at 20-30 mph were travelling between 20 and 25 mph while the other half were travelling between 25 and 30 mph.

Total travelling at 25 mph or less
= 8 + 9 = 17 cars

Add these figures together to estimate the total number travelling at 25 mph or less.

Exercise 2.2

M **Q1** The table shows maximum daily humidity (%) in Heathrow, over 20 days in 2015.
Draw a histogram to show the data.

Humidity, h (%)	Frequency
$60 < h \leq 80$	2
$80 < h \leq 90$	9
$90 < h \leq 95$	5
$95 < h \leq 100$	4

M **Q2** The histogram on the right shows the audition times (in seconds) for contestants applying for a place on a television talent show.
The auditions for 54 contestants lasted between 30 and 45 seconds.

a) Work out the number of contestants whose auditions lasted less than 30 seconds.

b) Work out the total number of contestants who auditioned.

c) Find the percentage of contestants whose audition lasted more than a minute.

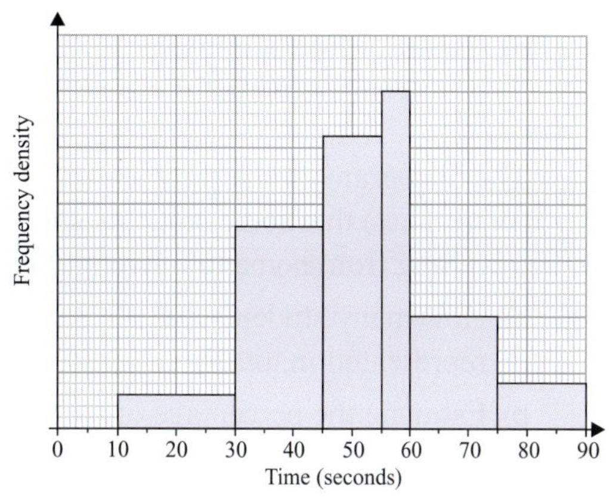

E M **Q3** The daily maximum gust (in knots) in Camborne was recorded from May to October 2015.

The incomplete table and histogram show this data, taken from the large data set.

Max. gust (w kn)	Frequency
$0 \leq w < 10$	1
$10 \leq w < 20$	56
$20 \leq w < 25$	
$25 \leq w < 35$	58
$35 \leq w < 45$	

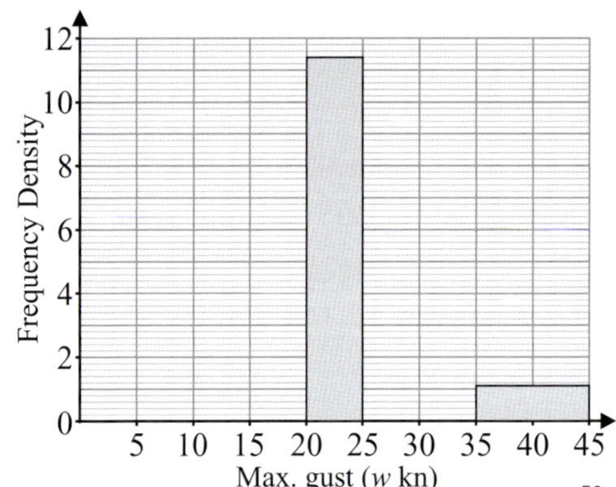

a) Copy and complete the table and the histogram. *[3 marks]*

b) Give two reasons why a histogram is a suitable way to display this data. *[2 marks]*

c) Explain why you can't determine the highest maximum gust from the data. *[1 mark]*

E P M **Q4** A butterfly enthusiast measures the wingspans (w, in mm), to the nearest millimetre, of a sample of tortoiseshell butterflies. She groups her measurements and displays the data in a histogram. The group containing butterflies with a wingspan of 45-47 mm has a frequency of 12. This group is represented on the histogram by a bar of width 1.5 cm and height 9 cm.

a) The bar representing the butterflies with a wingspan of 52-53 mm has an area of 22.5 cm^2. Work out the frequency for this group. *[2 marks]*

b) The frequency for butterflies with a wingspan of 54-58 mm is 14. Find the width and the height of the bar used to represent this group. *[3 marks]*

Q4 Hint The wingspans are measured to the nearest mm, so you need to use upper and lower class boundaries for the class widths (see page 16).

P M **Q5** The histogram below represents the number of people working at a company, grouped by age.

Problem Solving You don't need to know the actual frequencies to work out proportions from histograms — in Q5, just divide the areas of the relevant classes by the total area.

a) Find the percentage of people aged between 26 and 29.

b) Find the fraction of people aged 36 or over.

c) Estimate the percentage of people aged 35 or over.

d) Explain why your answer in part c) is only an estimate.

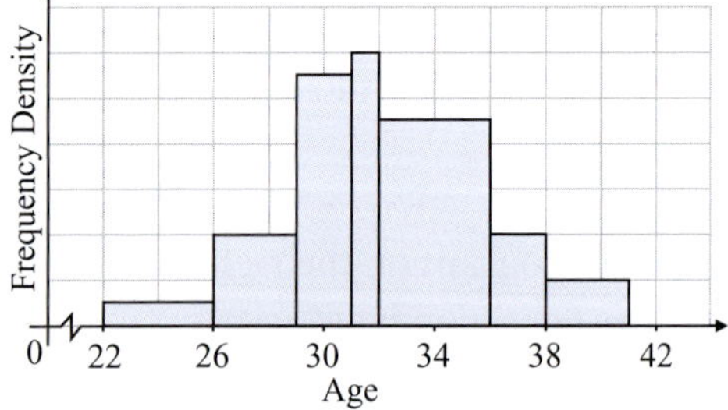

E P M **Q6** The histogram on the right shows the time (in minutes) that some students spend travelling from home to university each day.

a) How many students are represented in total? *[2 marks]*

b) Estimate the percentage of students that spend between 15 and 45 minutes travelling to university. *[4 marks]*

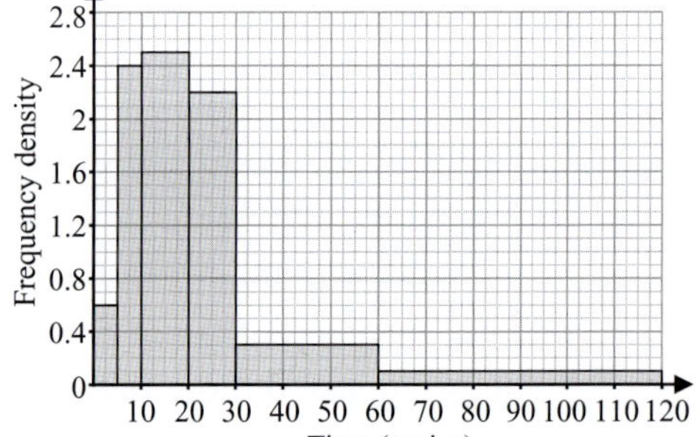

2.3 The Mean

The most common measure of location is called the **mean** (and is often just called 'the average' — but not while you're doing A-level Maths).

The **formula** for the mean ($\bar{x}$, said 'x-bar') is:

$$\text{Mean} = \bar{x} = \frac{\sum x}{n} \text{ or } \frac{\sum fx}{\sum f}$$

where each x is a **data value**, f is the **frequency** of each x (the number of times it occurs), and n is the **total number** of data values.

$\sum$ (sigma) just means you add things together. $\sum x$ means you add up all the values of x, and $\sum f = n$.

If you see $\sum x_i$, imagine there are x-values $x_1, x_2, x_3...$ — $\sum x_i$ means 'add up the values of x_i, for all the different values of i,' which is just another way of telling you to add up all the different values of x.

Example 1

Find the mean of the following list of data: 2, 3, 6, 2, 5, 9, 3, 8, 7, 2

$\sum x = 2 + 3 + 6 + 2 + 5 + 9 + 3 + 8 + 7 + 2 = 47$ ← First, find $\sum x$.

$\bar{x} = \frac{\sum x}{n} = \frac{47}{10} = 4.7$ ← Then divide by $n = 10$ (since there are 10 values).

Example 2 M

A scientist counts the number of eggs in some song thrush nests. His data is shown in this table.

Number of eggs, x	2	3	4	5	6
Number of nests, f	4	9	16	8	3

Calculate the mean number of eggs in these nests.

Number of eggs, x	2	3	4	5	6	Total
Number of nests, f	4	9	16	8	3	40
fx	8	27	64	40	18	157

This time, you have frequencies, so it's a good idea to add to the table:
(i) a row showing the values of fx,
(ii) a column showing the totals $\sum f$ and $\sum fx$.

$\bar{x} = \frac{\sum fx}{\sum f} = \frac{157}{40} = 3.925$ eggs ← Now use the formula for the mean.

Sometimes you have to work backwards from the mean.

Problem Solving

To find the sum of values when you know the mean, rearrange $\overline{x} = \frac{\sum x}{n}$ to give $\sum x = n \times \overline{x}$.

Example 3 

The mean of seven numbers is 9. When an extra number is added the mean becomes 9.5. Find the value of the extra number.

Sum of 7 numbers = $7 \times 9 = 63$ ← Find the sum of the first seven numbers using the formula for the mean.

Sum of 8 numbers = $63 + a$ ← Call the extra number a. Then write an expression for the sum of all eight numbers.

$9.5 = \frac{63 + a}{8} \Rightarrow 76 = 63 + a \Rightarrow 13 = a$ ← The mean of all eight numbers is 9.5, so use this to work out the value of a.

So extra number = 13

If you know a data set of size n_1 has mean $\overline{x_1}$ and another data set of size n_2 has mean $\overline{x_2}$, then the combined mean is $\overline{x}$, where:

$$\overline{x} = \frac{n_1\overline{x_1} + n_2\overline{x_2}}{n_1 + n_2}$$

Example 4 M

A scientist is looking at the amount of rainfall over a week in Hurn in 1987. The mean of the first 5 days is $\overline{x_1} = 5.38$ mm and the mean of the next 2 days is $\overline{x_2} = 22.45$ mm. Find the combined mean ($\overline{x}$) of the rainfall over the week.

Tip This uses a sample of the large data set.

$$\overline{x} = \frac{n_1\overline{x_1} + n_2\overline{x_2}}{n_1 + n_2} = \frac{(5 \times 5.38) + (2 \times 22.45)}{5 + 2}$$

← Use the formula with $n_1 = 5$ and $n_2 = 2$.

$$= \frac{71.8}{7} = 10.25714... = 10.3 \text{ mm (3 s.f.)}$$

Exercise 2.3

M Q1 Katia visits 12 shops and records the price of a loaf of bread. Her results are shown in the table.

£1.08	£1.15	£1.25	£1.19	£1.26	£1.24
£1.15	£1.09	£1.16	£1.20	£1.05	£1.10

Work out the mean price of a loaf of bread in these shops.

M Q2 The number of hours of sunshine per day in Camborne is recorded. The total number of hours of sunshine over 20 days is 99.8 hours. Find the mean number of hours of sunshine per day.

M Q3 In a competition, the 7 members of team A scored a mean of 35 points, and the 6 members of team B scored 252 points altogether. Find the combined mean score.

M Q4 The numbers of goals scored by 20 football teams in their most recent match are shown in the table.

Number of goals, x	0	1	2	3	4
Frequency, f	5	7	4	3	1

Calculate the mean number of goals scored by these teams in their most recent match.

E M Q5 Data was collected regarding the number of days people are absent from work. x is the number of days absent in the last year and n is the number of people in the data set. The summary statistics for the data are $\sum x = 560$, $n = 106$.

a) Find the mean number of days absent per person in the last year. *[1 mark]*

b) Another person is added to the data set. In the last year, they were absent from work on 4 days. Without further calculation, explain the effect this has on the mean. *[2 marks]*

P M Q6 A drama group has 15 members. The mean age of the members is 47.4 years. A 17-year-old joins the drama group. Find the new mean age.

E P M Q7 Students in Classes 12A and 12B took a general knowledge quiz. The mean score for the 18 students in Class 12A was 13. The mean score for students across both classes was 17. Given there are 14 students in Class 12B, find the mean score for the students in Class 12B to 3 s.f. *[3 marks]*

2.4 The Mode and the Median

There are two other important measures of location you need to know about — the **mode** and the **median**.

Mode = most frequently occurring data value.

Tip The mode is often called the modal value.

Example 1

Find the modes of the following data sets.

a) 2, 3, 6, 2, 5, 9, 3, 8, 7, 2

Mode = 2 ← The most frequent data value is 2 — it appears three times.

b) 4, 3, 6, 4, 5, 9, 2, 8, 7, 5

Modes = 4 and 5 ← This time there are two modes — the values 4 and 5 both appear twice.

Tip If a data set has two modes, then it is called bimodal.

c) 4, 3, 6, 11, 5, 9, 2, 8, 7, 12

There is no mode. ← Each value appears just once.

The median is slightly trickier to find than the mode.

Median = value in the middle of the data set when all the data values are placed in order of size.

First put your n data values **in order**, then find the **position** of the median in the ordered list. There are two possibilities:

(i) if $\frac{n}{2}$ is a **whole number** (i.e. n is even), then the median is halfway between the values in this position and the position above.

(ii) if $\frac{n}{2}$ is **not** a **whole number** (i.e. n is odd), **round it up** to find the position of the median.

Example 2

Find the medians of the following data sets.

a) 2, 3, 6, 2, 6, 9, 3, 8, 7

2, 2, 3, 3, 6, 6, 7, 8, 9 ← Put the values in order first.

$\frac{n}{2} = \frac{9}{2} = 4.5$, so the median is the 5th value. ← $\frac{n}{2} = 4.5$ is not a whole number, so round 4.5 up to 5 to find the position of the median.

Median = 6

b) 4, 3, 11, 4, 10, 9, 3, 8, 7, 8

3, 3, 4, 4, 7, 8, 8, 9, 10, 11 ← Put the values in order first.

$\frac{n}{2} = \frac{10}{2} = 5$, so the median is halfway between the 5th and 6th data values. ← $\frac{n}{2} = 5$ is a whole number, so the median is the mean of the 5th and 6th values.

Median = (7 + 8) ÷ 2 = 7.5

If your data is in a **frequency table**, then the mode and the median are still easy to find as long as the data **isn't grouped**.

Example 3 M

The number of letters received one day in a sample of houses is shown in this table.

No. of letters	No. of houses
0	11
1	25
2	27
3	21

a) Find the modal number of letters.

Mode = 2 letters ← The modal number of letters is the number with the highest frequency — that's the one received by the most houses.

b) Find the median number of letters.

No. of letters	No. of houses (frequency)	Cumulative frequency
0	11	11
1	25	36
2	27	63
3	21	84

← It's useful to add a column to show the cumulative frequency (see p.38) — this is just a running total of the frequency column.

$\frac{n}{2} = \frac{84}{2} = 42$, so the median is halfway between the 42nd and 43rd data values. ← The total number of houses is the last cumulative frequency, so $n = 84$. Use this to find the position of the median.

Median = 2 letters ← Using the cumulative frequency, you can see that the data values in positions 37 to 63 all equal 2.

Exercise 2.4

M Q1 The amount of money (in £) raised by seventeen friends is shown below.

250, 19, 500, 123, 185, 101, 45, 67, 194, 77, 108, 110, 187, 216, 84, 98, 140

a) Find the median amount of money raised by these friends.

b) Explain why it is not possible to find the mode for this data.

M Q2 A financial adviser records the interest rates charged by 14 different banks to customers taking out a loan. His findings are below.

6.2%, 6.9%, 6.9%, 8.8%, 6.3%, 7.4%, 6.9%, 6.5%, 6.4%, 9.9%, 6.2%, 6.4%, 6.9%, 6.2%

Find the modal interest rate and the median interest rate charged by these banks.

M Q3 The maximum daily humidity (%) in Leeming recorded over 12 days in 1987 is shown below.

80, 95, 88, 95, 82, 84, 80, 91, 86, 97, 93, 89

a) Write down the mode of this data. b) Find the median humidity recorded.

M Q4 An online seller has received the ratings shown in this table.

a) Write down the modal customer rating.

b) Work out the median customer rating.

Rating	1	2	3	4	5
No. of customers	7	5	25	67	72

E M Q5 27 students in a class are asked how many pets they own. The results are summarised in the table below.

No. of pets	0	1	2	3	4 or more
No. of students	3	5	8	9	2

a) Write down the modal number of pets owned. *[1 mark]*

b) Find the median number of pets owned. *[2 marks]*

c) Three new students join the class, and they each say they own 2 pets. Explain the effect this has on your answers to parts a) and b). *[2 marks]*

E P M Q6 The prices of some calculators from a selection of shops are shown in the table below, where c is an integer such that $2 < c < 10$.

Price	£5	£7	£8	£10	£12	£15	£18
Frequency	2	4	13	11	c	$c - 2$	5

a) Write down the modal price of a calculator. *[1 mark]*

b) Given that the median price of a calculator is £10, show that $3 \leq c \leq 9$. *[3 marks]*

P M Q7 Thomas has an even number of flowers. He counts the number of petals on each flower, and records the results in this frequency table. If the median number of petals is 7, what are the possible values for the number of flowers, p, with 9 petals?

Number of petals	5	6	7	8	9
Number of flowers	4	8	6	2	p

2.5 Averages of Grouped Data

If you have **grouped data**, you can only **estimate** the mean and median. This is because the grouping means you no longer have the exact data values. Instead of a mode, you can only find a **modal class**.

Modal class

The **modal class** is the class with the **highest frequency density** (see p.19).
If all the classes are the same width, then this will just be the class with the **highest frequency**.

Find the modal class for this data showing the heights of various shrubs.

Height of shrub to nearest cm	11-20	21-30	31-40	41-50
Number of shrubs	11	22	29	16

Modal class = 31-40 cm ← In this example, all the classes are the same width (= 10 cm). So the modal class is the class with the highest frequency.

Mean

To find an estimate of the **mean**, you assume that every reading in a class takes the value of the class **mid-point**. Then you can use the formula $\bar{x} = \frac{\sum fx}{\sum f}$.

Tip This is the formula from p.23.

Tip For large sets of data, you may be told the summation statistics $\sum f$ and $\sum fx$ instead of all the data.

The heights of a number of trees were recorded. The data collected is shown in the table below.

Height of tree to nearest m	0-5	6-10	11-15	16-20
Number of trees	26	17	11	6

Find an estimate of the mean height of the trees.

Make another table with:
a) Extra rows that show:
(i) the class mid-points (x),
(ii) the values of fx, where f is the frequency (i.e the number of trees).
b) An extra column that shows $\sum f$ and $\sum fx$.

Height of tree to nearest m	0-5	6-10	11-15	16-20	**Total**
Class mid-point, x	2.75	8	13	18	
Number of trees, f	26	17	11	6	60 (= Σf)
fx	71.5	136	143	108	458.5 (= Σfx)

To find the mid-points, work out the class boundaries, add them together and divide by 2.
E.g. for the first class:
Lower class boundary = 0
Upper class boundary = 5.5
So mid-point
= (0 + 5.5) ÷ 2 = 2.75

$\bar{x} = \frac{\sum fx}{\sum f} = \frac{458.5}{60} = 7.64$ m (to 2 d.p.) ← Use the formula to find the mean.

Median

To find an estimate for the median, use **linear interpolation**.

This table shows the data from Example 2 on the previous page, with an extra row showing the **cumulative frequency**.

Height of tree to nearest m	0-5	6-10	11-15	16-20
Number of trees	26	17	11	6
Cumulative frequency	26	43	54	60

- First, find **which class** the median is in: $\frac{n}{2} = \frac{60}{2} = 30$, so there are 30 values less than or equal to the median — the median must be in the 6-10 class. In this method, you **only** need to find $\frac{n}{2}$ — you **don't** then need to follow the rules described on page 25.
- The idea behind **linear interpolation** is to **assume** that all the readings in this class are evenly spread. So divide the class (whose width is 5) into 17 intervals of equal width (one interval for each of the data values in the class), and assume there's a reading in the middle of each interval.
- The numbers **on the top** of the scale are **heights** (measured in metres). The **upper and lower class boundaries** are shown, and the **median** (m) is also marked (but you don't know its value yet).
- The numbers **underneath** the scale are **cumulative frequencies**. The cumulative frequency at the lower class boundary is 26, while the cumulative frequency at the upper class boundary is 43.
- In fact, you don't need to draw the small intervals and the data points every time — a simplified version like the one on the right is enough to find a median.
- To find the **median**, m, you need to solve: $\frac{a_1}{b_1} = \frac{a_2}{b_2}$

Tip The red crosses in the diagram aren't the actual data values — they're interpolated data values (we've made an assumption about them being at these points).

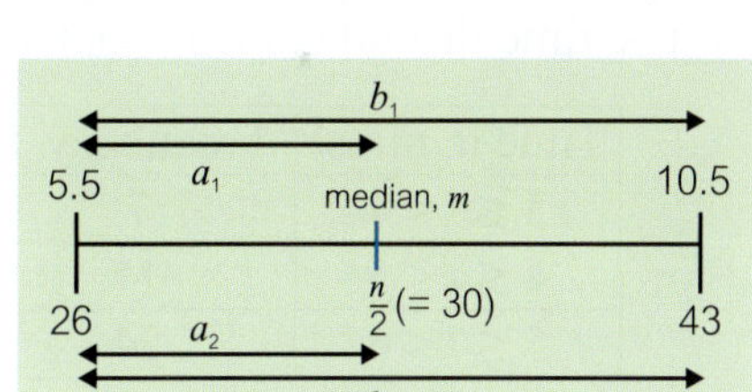

Example 3 M

Estimate the median height for the trees recorded in this table.

Height of tree to nearest m	0-5	6-10	11-15	16-20
Number of trees	26	17	11	6

Tip This is the same data as above — so you know which class contains the median.

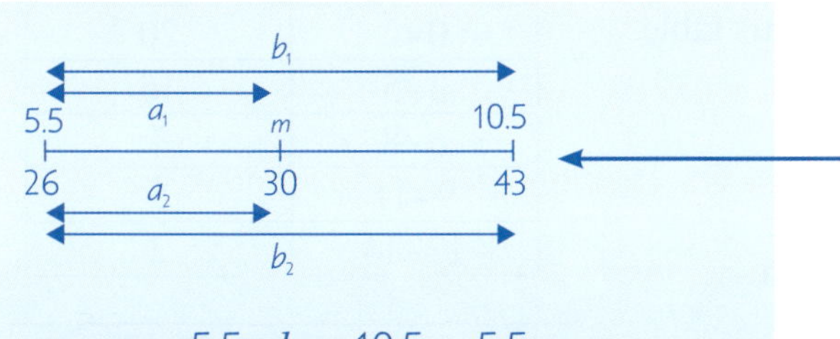

Draw a picture of the class containing the median (m) — just show the important numbers you're going to need.

$a_1 = m - 5.5,\ b_1 = 10.5 - 5.5$
$a_2 = 30 - 26,\ b_2 = 43 - 26$

Work out the values of a_1, b_1, a_2, b_2 from the diagram.

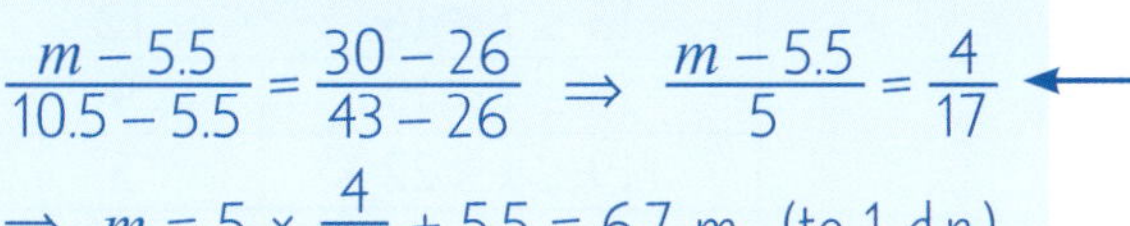

$$\frac{m - 5.5}{10.5 - 5.5} = \frac{30 - 26}{43 - 26} \Rightarrow \frac{m - 5.5}{5} = \frac{4}{17}$$

$$\Rightarrow m = 5 \times \frac{4}{17} + 5.5 = 6.7 \text{ m (to 1 d.p.)}$$

Substitute in the numbers to solve the equation $\frac{a_1}{b_1} = \frac{a_2}{b_2}$ for the value of m.

Example 4 M

Estimate the median length of the newts shown in the table on the right.

Length (to nearest cm)	0 - 2	3 - 5	6 - 8	9 - 11
Number of newts	3	18	12	4

There are $n = 3 + 18 + 12 + 4 = 37$ data values in total.

So $\frac{n}{2} = 18.5$ — the median will be in the 3-5 class.

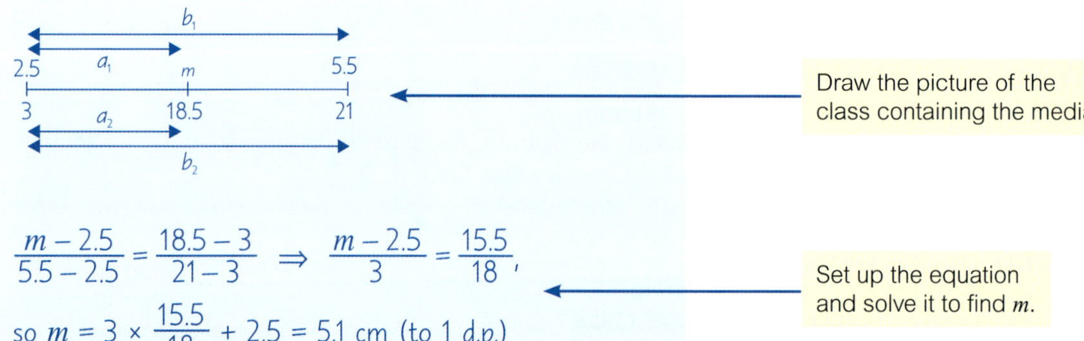

Draw the picture of the class containing the median.

$$\frac{m - 2.5}{5.5 - 2.5} = \frac{18.5 - 3}{21 - 3} \Rightarrow \frac{m - 2.5}{3} = \frac{15.5}{18},$$

so $m = 3 \times \frac{15.5}{18} + 2.5 = 5.1$ cm (to 1 d.p.)

Set up the equation and solve it to find m.

Exercise 2.5

M Q1 The time that 60 students took to change after PE is shown below.

Time (t, mins)	Frequency, f	Mid-point, x	fx
$3 \leq t < 4$	7	3.5	24.5
$4 \leq t < 5$	14	4.5	
$5 \leq t < 6$	24		
$6 \leq t < 8$	10		
$8 \leq t < 10$	5		

Q1 Hint Don't give your answers to too many decimal places when you're estimating something.

a) Copy and complete the table.

b) Use the table to work out an estimate of the mean time it took these students to change.

M Q2 A postman records the number of letters delivered to each of 50 houses one day. The results are shown in this table.

a) State the modal class.

b) Estimate the mean number of letters delivered to these houses.

c) Write down the interval containing the median.

No. of letters	No. of houses
0 - 2	20
3 - 5	16
6 - 8	7
9 - 11	5
12 - 14	2

M Q3 The table shows the maximum daily temperature t (°C) recorded in Leuchars in June 2015.

Use linear interpolation to estimate the median maximum daily temperature in Leuchars.

Temperature (t, °C)	Frequency
$10 \leq t < 13$	1
$13 \leq t < 16$	12
$16 \leq t < 19$	9
$19 \leq t < 22$	5
$22 \leq t < 25$	3

M **Q4** Kwasi checks the download speed d (Mbit/s) on his computer on a number of different occasions. His results are shown in the table.

Speed (d, Mbit/s)	Frequency
$3 \leq d < 4$	3
$4 \leq d < 5$	11
$5 \leq d < 6$	9
$6 \leq d < 7$	13
$7 \leq d < 8$	4

a) State the modal class.

b) Estimate the mean download speed on Kwasi's computer.

c) Use linear interpolation to estimate the median download speed.

E M **Q5** The following table shows the times that a random sample of 60 runners took to complete a marathon.

Time (t, mins)	Frequency, f
$180 \leq t < 240$	8
$240 \leq t < 270$	19
$270 \leq t < 300$	21
$300 \leq t < 360$	9
$360 \leq t < 480$	3

a) Estimate the mean time of these runners. (You may use $\sum fx = 16\,740$, where x is the mid-point of a class.) *[1 mark]*

b) Calculate an estimate for the median time it took these runners to complete the marathon. *[3 marks]*

E P M **Q6** The daily mean air temperature (in °C) in Perth was recorded for May to September 2015. The data, taken from the large data set, is summarised in the table below.

Daily mean air temperature (T °C)	$0 \leq T < 10$	$10 \leq T < 15$	$15 \leq T < 20$	$20 \leq T < 25$
Frequency	10	80	58	5

a) Write down the modal class for the daily mean air temperatures. *[1 mark]*

b) Use your calculator to find an estimate for the mean of the daily mean air temperatures. *[1 mark]*

c) Find an estimate for the median of the daily mean air temperatures. *[3 marks]*

d) Using your knowledge of the large data set, suggest what would happen to the mean from part b) if the data from October 2015 was also included. *[1 mark]*

Challenge

E P M **Q7** The table below shows the masses of Labrador puppies recorded at an age of six weeks.

Mass (m kg)	$4 \leq m < 4.5$	$4.5 \leq m < 5$	$5 \leq m < 5.5$	$5.5 \leq m < 6$
Frequency	4	$2q$	12	4

Given that the data in the table produces an estimate for the median mass of the Labrador puppies of 4.9 kg, find the value of q. *[5 marks]*

2.6 Comparing Measures of Location

You've seen three different measures of location — the mean, the median and the mode. Each of them is useful for different kinds of data.

Mean

- The mean is a good average because you use **all** your data to work it out.
- But it can be heavily affected by **extreme values / outliers** and by distributions of data values that are **not symmetric**.
- It can only be used with **quantitative** data (i.e. numbers).

Tip See p.42 for more on outliers.

Median

- The median is not affected by extreme values, so this is a good average to use when you have **outliers**.
- This makes it a good average to use when the data set is **not symmetric**.

Tip A symmetric data set is one where the distribution of data values above the mean is the mirror image of the distribution of values below the mean.

Mode

- The mode can be used with **qualitative** (non-numerical) data.
- Some data sets can have **more than one** mode — you saw a bimodal data set (with two modes) on page 25. If every value in a data set occurs just **once** then there's **no mode**.

Exercise 2.6

M Q1 Explain whether the mean, median or mode would be most suitable as a summary of each of the following data sets.

a) Salaries of each employee at a company.

b) Length of adult female adder snakes.

c) Make of cars parked in a car park.

d) Weight of all newborn full-term babies born one year at a hospital.

e) Distance a firm's employees travel to work each morning.

Problem Solving In Q1, think about the shape of the histogram you might expect for each data set — e.g. in part a), think about how many people you might expect to earn a low salary compared to a very high salary.

M Q2 Hosi records the number of bedrooms in the houses lived in by a sample of 10 adults. His results are shown in the table.

Number of bedrooms	1	2	3	4	5	6	7	8
Frequency	1	2	4	2	0	0	0	1

Explain why the mean may not be the most suitable measure of location for the data.

E M Q3 The table below shows some information about the number of WiFi devices households have.

No of devices	0	1	2	3	4	5	6	7
Frequency	66	81	49	78	213	214	212	10

a) Briefly explain why the mode would not be a suitable measure of location for the number of devices per household. *[1 mark]*

b) State whether the mean or the median would be the most suitable measure of location for this data and justify your answer. *[1 mark]*

P Q4 The diagram on the right shows the general pattern of a large amount of data.

Describe the order in which you would expect the mean, median and mode to occur, explaining your answer.

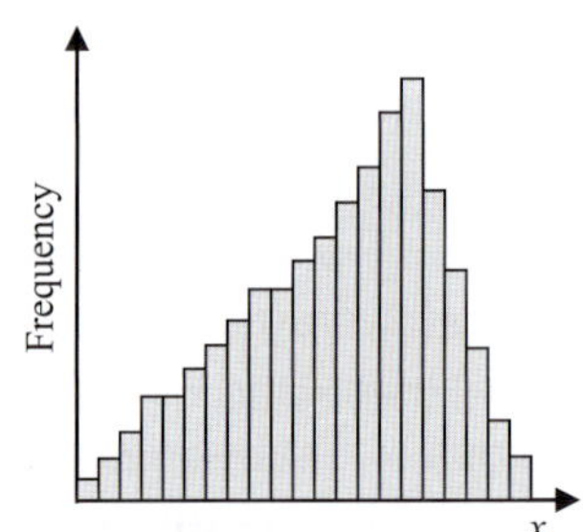

2.7 Range, Interquartile Range and Interpercentile Range

Range

The **range** is about the simplest measure of dispersion you can imagine.

Range = highest value – lowest value

The range is heavily affected by **extreme values**, so it isn't the most useful way to measure dispersion.

Interquartile range

A more useful way to measure dispersion is with the **interquartile range**, but first you have to find the **quartiles**. You've seen how the median divides a data set into two halves. The quartiles are similar — there are three quartiles (usually labelled Q_1, Q_2 and Q_3) and they divide the data into **four parts**.

- Q_1 is the **lower quartile** — 25% of the data is less than or equal to the lower quartile.
- Q_2 is the **median** — 50% of the data is less than or equal to the median.
- Q_3 is the **upper quartile** — 75% of the data is less than or equal to the upper quartile.

For example, the values in the data set on the right have been sorted so that they're in numerical order, starting with the smallest. The three quartiles are shown.

1 2 3 4 4 4 5 | 5 5 6 6 7 7 9

Q_1 Q_2 Q_3

$Q_1 = 4$
$Q_2 = 5$
$Q_3 = 6$

The quartiles are worked out in a similar way to the median — by first finding their **position** in the ordered list of data values. The method below is the same as the one used on p.25 for finding the median, but with $\frac{n}{2}$ replaced by either $\frac{n}{4}$ (Q_1) or $\frac{3n}{4}$ (Q_3).

To find the position of the **lower quartile** (Q_1), first work out $\frac{n}{4}$.

- If $\frac{n}{4}$ is a **whole number**, then the **lower quartile** is halfway between the values in this position and the position above.
- If $\frac{n}{4}$ is not a whole number, **round it up** to find the position of the lower quartile.

To find the position of the **upper quartile** (Q_3), first work out $\frac{3n}{4}$.

- If $\frac{3n}{4}$ is a **whole number**, then the **upper quartile** is halfway between the values in this position and the position above.
- If $\frac{3n}{4}$ is **not** a whole number, **round it up** to find the position of the upper quartile.

Once you've found the upper and lower quartiles, you can find the **interquartile range** (IQR).

Interquartile range (IQR) = upper quartile (Q_3) – lower quartile (Q_1)

Tip You don't need to know the median (Q_2) to calculate the interquartile range.

The interquartile range is a measure of **dispersion**. It actually shows the range of the 'middle 50%' of the data — this means it's not affected by **extreme values**, but it still tells you something about how spread out the data values are.

Example 1

a) Find the median and quartiles of the following data set:

2, 5, 3, 11, 6, 8, 3, 8, 1, 6, 2, 23, 9, 11, 18, 19, 22, 7

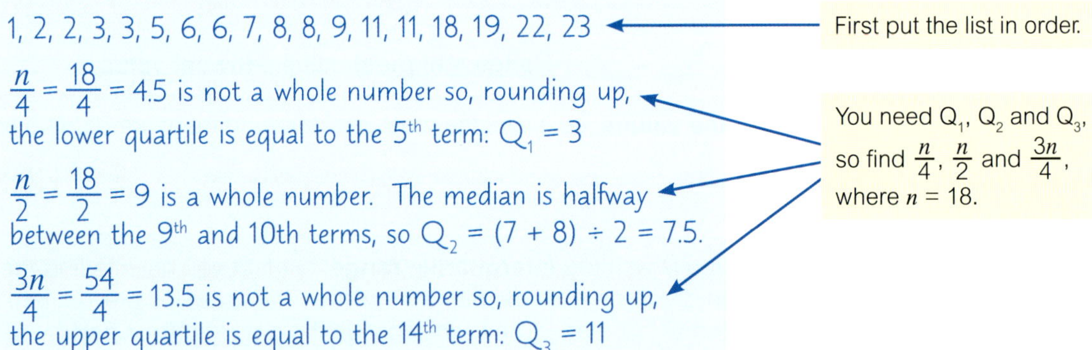

1, 2, 2, 3, 3, 5, 6, 6, 7, 8, 8, 9, 11, 11, 18, 19, 22, 23

First put the list in order.

$\frac{n}{4} = \frac{18}{4} = 4.5$ is not a whole number so, rounding up, the lower quartile is equal to the 5th term: $Q_1 = 3$

$\frac{n}{2} = \frac{18}{2} = 9$ is a whole number. The median is halfway between the 9th and 10th terms, so $Q_2 = (7 + 8) \div 2 = 7.5$.

$\frac{3n}{4} = \frac{54}{4} = 13.5$ is not a whole number so, rounding up, the upper quartile is equal to the 14th term: $Q_3 = 11$

You need Q_1, Q_2 and Q_3, so find $\frac{n}{4}$, $\frac{n}{2}$ and $\frac{3n}{4}$, where $n = 18$.

b) Find the interquartile range for the above data.

Interquartile range $= Q_3 - Q_1 = 11 - 3 = 8$

When your data is **grouped** you don't know the exact values, so you'll need to use **linear interpolation** to find an **estimate** for the lower and upper quartiles.

Example 2 M

a) Estimate the lower and upper quartiles for the tree heights in this table.

Height of tree to nearest m	0-5	6-10	11-15	16-20
Number of trees	26	17	11	6

Height of tree to nearest m	0-5	6-10	11-15	16-20
Number of trees	26	17	11	6
Cumulative frequency	26	43	54	60

First add a row to the table showing cumulative frequency.

$\frac{n}{4} = \frac{60}{4} = 15$, so Q_1 is in the class 0-5.

Now find which class the lower quartile (Q_1) is in. Work out $\frac{n}{4}$ and use the cumulative frequency row.

b_1; 0, a_1, Q_1, 5.5; 0, a_2, 15 $(= \frac{n}{4})$, 26; b_2

Draw a picture of the class containing Q_1 — just show the important numbers you're going to need. Put heights on one side of the line (here, they're on top) and cumulative frequencies on the other side.

$\frac{Q_1 - 0}{5.5 - 0} = \frac{15 - 0}{26 - 0} \Rightarrow \frac{Q_1}{5.5} = \frac{15}{26} \Rightarrow Q_1 = 5.5 \times \frac{15}{26}$

$= 3.2$ m (1 d.p.)

Solve $\frac{a_1}{b_1} = \frac{a_2}{b_2}$ for Q_1.

$\frac{3n}{4} = \frac{3 \times 60}{4} = 45$, so Q_3 is in the class 11-15.

Find the upper quartile (Q_3) in the same way.

b_1; 10.5, a_1, Q_3, 15.5; 43, a_2, 45 $(= \frac{3n}{4})$, 54; b_2

Draw your picture of the class containing Q_3.

continued on the next page...

$$\frac{Q_3 - 10.5}{15.5 - 10.5} = \frac{45 - 43}{54 - 43} \Rightarrow \frac{Q_3 - 10.5}{5} = \frac{2}{11}$$

$$\Rightarrow Q_3 = 10.5 + 5 \times \frac{2}{11} = 11.4 \text{ m (1 d.p.)}$$

Solve $\frac{a_1}{b_1} = \frac{a_2}{b_2}$ for Q_3.

b) Estimate the interquartile range for this data.

Interquartile range (IQR) $= Q_3 - Q_1 = 11.4 - 3.2 = 8.2$ m (1 d.p.)

Interpercentile range

You've seen how the quartiles divide the data into four parts, where each part contains the same number of data values. **Percentiles** are similar, but they divide the data into **100 parts**. The median is the 50th percentile and Q_1 is the 25th percentile, and so on.

The position of the xth percentile (P_x) is $\frac{x}{100}$ × total frequency (n).

For example, to find the 11th percentile in a data set containing 200 values:

- Calculate $\frac{11}{100} \times 200 = 22$.
- Use linear interpolation to estimate the value in this position in the **ordered** list of data values.

You can find **interpercentile ranges** by subtracting two percentiles.

The a% to b% interpercentile range is $P_b - P_a$.

Tip When finding percentiles, the data set is usually large and grouped.

For example, the 20% to 80% interpercentile range is $P_{80} - P_{20}$.

Example 3 M

A reptile specialist records the mass (m, in kilograms) of 150 tortoises. Her results are shown in the table.

a) Estimate the 10th percentile for this data.

Mass (kg)	Frequency	Cumulative frequency
$0.2 \le m < 0.6$	27	27
$0.6 \le m < 1.0$	43	70
$1.0 \le m < 1.4$	35	105
$1.4 \le m < 1.8$	31	136
$1.8 \le m < 2.2$	14	150

Add a column showing cumulative frequency.

Position of P_{10}: $\frac{10}{100} \times 150 = 15$

Now find the position of P_{10}.

Using the cumulative frequency, you can see that this will be in the '$0.2 \le m < 0.6$' class.

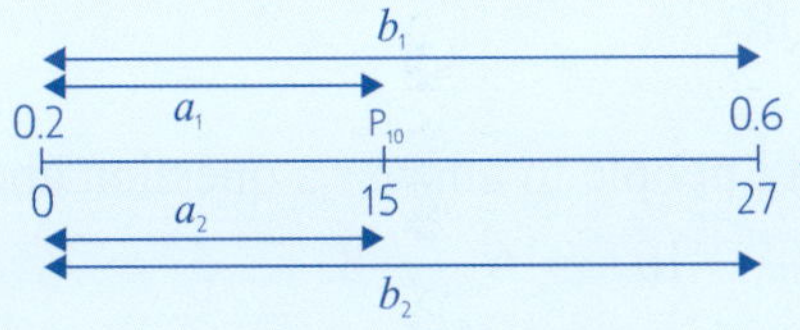

Draw a picture of this class showing the important masses and cumulative frequencies.

$$\frac{P_{10} - 0.2}{0.6 - 0.2} = \frac{15 - 0}{27 - 0} \Rightarrow P_{10} = 0.2 + 0.4 \times \frac{15}{27}$$

$$= 0.42 \text{ kg (2 d.p.)}$$

As always with linear interpolation, solve $\frac{a_1}{b_1} = \frac{a_2}{b_2}$.

b) Estimate the 90th percentile for this data.

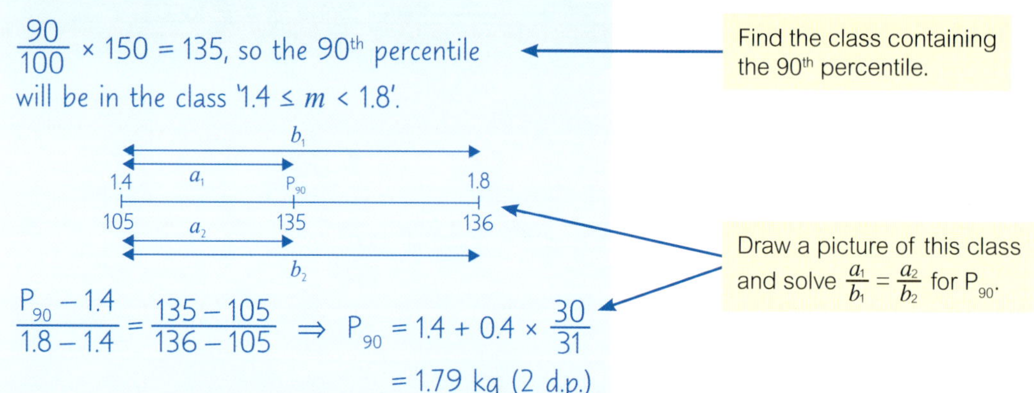

$$\frac{P_{90} - 1.4}{1.8 - 1.4} = \frac{135 - 105}{136 - 105} \Rightarrow P_{90} = 1.4 + 0.4 \times \frac{30}{31}$$
$$= 1.79 \text{ kg (2 d.p.)}$$

c) Estimate the 10% to 90% interpercentile range for this data.

10% to 90% interpercentile range $= P_{90} - P_{10} = 1.79 - 0.42 = 1.37$ kg (2 d.p.)

Exercise 2.7

Q1 Find the range and interquartile range of the following data sets:

a) 41, 49, 26, 20, 31, 9, 32, 39, 4, 21, 9, 12, 48, 23, 26, 10

b) 10.5, 8.6, 9.4, 8.5, 9.0, 12.1, 7.7, 10.3, 13.7, 9.2, 11.3, 8.4

M Q2 The diameters (in miles) of the eight planets in the Solar System are given below:

3032, 7521, 7926, 4222, 88 846, 74 898, 31 763, 30 778

For this data set, calculate:

a) the range
b) the lower quartile (Q_1)
c) the upper quartile (Q_3)
d) the interquartile range (IQR)

M Q3 Each of the three data sets below shows the speeds (in mph) of 18 different cars observed at a certain time and place.

<u>In town at 8:45 am:</u> 14, 16, 15, 18, 15, 17, 16, 16, 18, 16, 15, 13, 15, 14, 16, 17, 18, 15

<u>In town at 10:45 am:</u> 34, 29, 36, 32, 31, 38, 30, 35, 39, 31, 29, 30, 25, 29, 33, 34, 36, 31

<u>On the motorway at 1 pm:</u> 67, 76, 78, 71, 73, 88, 74, 69, 75, 76, 95, 71, 69, 78, 73, 76, 75, 74

For each set of data, calculate:

a) the range
b) the interquartile range (IQR)

E P M Q4 This data shows the times taken, in seconds, by 12 people to answer a question about music.

3 4 2 6 5 4 8 7 16 6 8 5

a) Find the range of the times. *[1 mark]*

b) Find the interquartile range of the times. *[3 marks]*

c) Would the range or the interquartile range be a more appropriate measure of dispersion for this data? Justify your answer. *[2 marks]*

E M **Q5** The frequency table below shows information regarding the number of t-shirts people own.

No of t-shirts	5	6	7	8	9	10	11	12	13
Frequency	20	32	45	55	48	32	24	11	3

a) Find the 30th percentile (P_{30}). *[2 marks]*

b) Find the 30% to 70% interpercentile range. *[3 marks]*

M **Q6** The table shows the maximum temperature (°C) recorded at Heathrow airport each day for 150 days in 1987.
For this data, estimate:

Maximum temperature (t)	Frequency
$10 \le t < 15$	19
$15 \le t < 20$	66
$20 \le t < 25$	49
$25 \le t < 30$	16

a) the lower quartile (Q_1) b) the upper quartile (Q_3)

c) the interquartile range (IQR)

d) the 10th percentile e) the 90th percentile

f) the 10% to 90% interpercentile range

M **Q7** The lengths (l) of a zoo's beetles measured to the nearest mm are shown in this table.
For this data, estimate:

Length (l)	Number of beetles
0 - 5	82
6 - 10	28
11 - 15	44
16 - 30	30
31 - 50	16

a) the 20% to 80% interpercentile range

b) the 5% to 95% interpercentile range

P M **Q8** The daily rainfall (r, mm) in Risebeck was recorded over three months. The results are shown in the table below.

Rainfall (r, mm)	Number of days
$0 \le r < 15$	15
$15 \le r < 35$	21
$35 \le r < 50$	16
$50 \le r < 60$	27
$60 \le r < 75$	13

a) What are the maximum and minimum possible values for the range of the daily rainfall?

Use the table to estimate:

b) the lower (Q_1) and upper quartile (Q_3)

c) the interquartile range (IQR)

d) the 15th and 85th percentile

e) the 15% to 85% interpercentile range

Q9 Hint The data is discrete so the class boundaries come directly from the table.

Challenge

E P M **Q9** The table below shows the 3-dart scores of 300 professional darts players. The lowest 3-dart score was 17 and the highest was 180.

3-dart score	Frequency
0-29	5
30-59	9
60-89	39
90-119	63
120-149	84
150-180	100

a) Find the range of the 3-dart scores. *[1 mark]*

b) Estimate the interquartile range of the 3-dart scores. *[4 marks]*

c) Why might neither the range nor interquartile range be suitable for analysing the 3-dart scores for these players? *[1 mark]*

E Exam Style P Problem Solving M Modelling

2.8 Cumulative Frequency Diagrams

Cumulative frequency means 'running total' — i.e. adding up the frequencies as you go along. A **cumulative frequency diagram** plots this running total so you can estimate the **median** and the **quartiles** easily (see p.29, 33 and 34).

Here's some data showing the weights of 24 sixteen-year-old boys.

Weight (kg)	Frequency	Upper class boundary	Cumulative frequency
$w \le 40$	0	40	0
$40 < w \le 50$	3	50	0 + 3 = 3
$50 < w \le 60$	4	60	3 + 4 = 7
$60 < w \le 70$	8	70	7 + 8 = 15
$70 < w \le 80$	6	80	15 + 6 = 21
$80 < w \le 90$	3	90	21 + 3 = 24

First number = 0 — there are no people who weigh less than 40 kg.

This is the sum of all the frequencies of weights ≤ 70 kg.

Last number = total frequency

- The first number in the cumulative frequency column must be zero — you might need to add a row to the table to show this.
- The last reading should always equal the total number of data values.

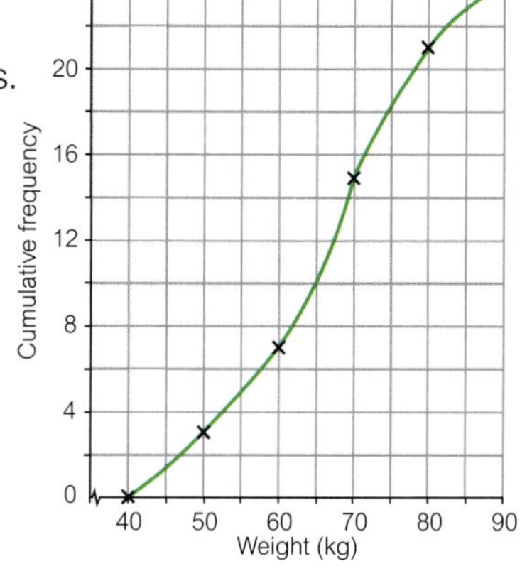

Here's the data plotted as a **cumulative frequency diagram**:

- The vertical axis shows **cumulative frequency**.
- The horizontal axis has a **continuous** scale like an ordinary graph.
- Points are plotted at the **upper class boundary**.
- The line should start at **0** on the vertical axis.

You join the points with a curve or straight lines. If you're asked for a cumulative frequency **polygon**, use straight lines.

a) Draw a cumulative frequency diagram for the data on the right.

Age in completed years	< 11	11-12	13-14	15-16	17-18
Number of students	0	50	65	58	27
Upper class boundary	11	13	15	17	19
Cumulative frequency	0	50	115	173	200

To find the coordinates to plot, extend the table and calculate the upper class boundaries and cumulative frequencies. The upper class boundary of each class = lower class boundary of the next. E.g. for the class 11-12 it's 13 because people are '12' right up until their 13th birthday.

There are 0 students under the age of 11, so the first coordinate is (11, 0).

So you draw the cumulative frequency diagram with coordinates: (11, 0), (13, 50), (15, 115), (17, 173), (19, 200).

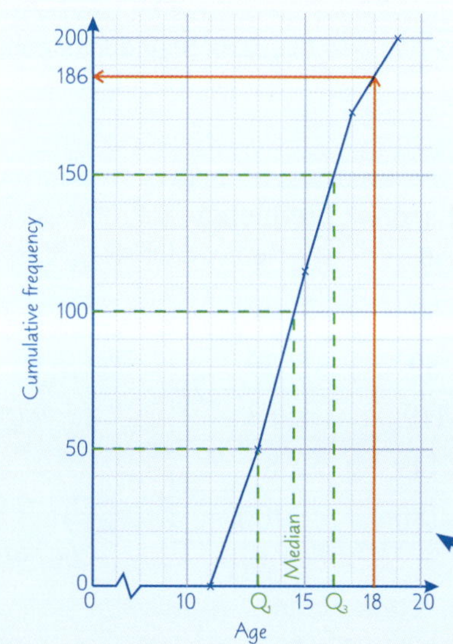

b) Estimate the median and interquartile range from the graph.

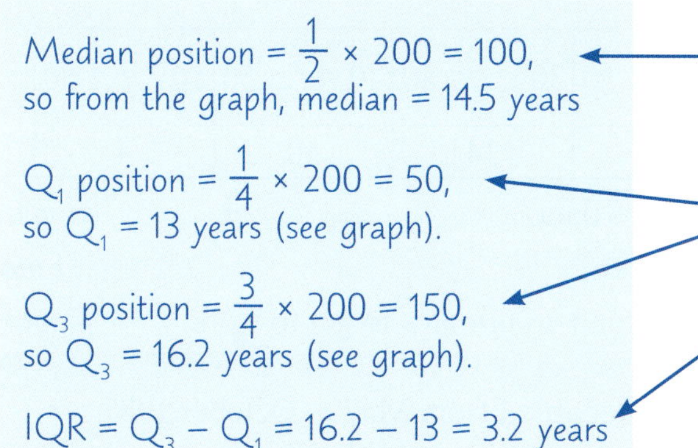

To estimate the median from a graph go to the median position on the vertical scale and read off the value from the horizontal axis.

You can estimate the quartiles in the same way by finding the position first.

Find the interquartile range.

Tip If you drew the graph as a cumulative frequency curve, your estimates might be slightly different.

c) Estimate how many students have already had their 18th birthday.

The number of students aged 18 or over is 200 – 186 = 14

Go up from 18 on the horizontal (age) axis and read off the number of students younger than 18 (= 186 — the orange line on the graph).

Exercise 2.8

M Q1 The amount of water in litres consumed daily by a group of adults is shown in this table.

a) Use the information in the table to draw a cumulative frequency diagram.

b) Use your diagram from part a) to estimate:

(i) the median

(ii) the lower quartile

(iii) the upper quartile

(iv) the interquartile range

Amount of water, w (litres)	Frequency
$w \le 0.8$	0
$0.8 < w \le 1.0$	4
$1.0 < w \le 1.2$	8
$1.2 < w \le 1.4$	12
$1.4 < w \le 1.6$	5
$1.6 < w \le 1.8$	2

Q2 Draw a cumulative frequency diagram for the data given below. Use your diagram to estimate the median and interquartile range.

Distance walked, d (km)	$0 < d \le 2$	$2 < d \le 4$	$4 < d \le 6$	$6 < d \le 8$
Number of walkers	1	10	7	2

M Q3 Using the cumulative frequency diagram for weight on page 38, estimate how many sixteen-year-old boys weigh:

a) Less than 55kg

b) More than 73kg

c) Explain why your answers are estimates.

Q4 Some people were asked how long it takes them to travel to work each day.
The results are shown in the table below.

Time, t (minutes)	$0 < t \leq 10$	$10 < t \leq 20$	$20 < t \leq 30$	$30 < t \leq 40$	$40 < t \leq 50$	$50 < t \leq 60$
Frequency	2	8	22	34	10	4

a) Draw a cumulative frequency diagram for this data. *[3 marks]*

b) Estimate the median time taken to get to work. *[1 mark]*

c) Estimate how many of the people take more than 38 minutes to get to work. *[2 marks]*

Q5 The daily total sunshine (in hours) in Hurn was recorded from May to October 1987.
The data, taken from the large data set, is summarised in the table below.

Daily total sunshine (h hours)	$0 \leq h \leq 3$	$3 < h \leq 5$	$5 < h \leq 8$	$8 < h \leq 12$	$12 < h \leq 16$
Frequency	56	20	43	35	13

a) Draw a cumulative frequency polygon for the data shown in the table. *[3 marks]*

b) Use your diagram to estimate the interquartile range. *[2 marks]*

c) Using your knowledge of the large data set, suggest why the number of days included in the table is smaller than the number of days in this period. *[1 mark]*

Q6 This cumulative frequency diagram shows the monthly earnings of some sixteen-year-olds.

a) How many sixteen-year-olds were sampled?

b) Estimate the median earnings.

c) Estimate how many earned between £46 and £84.

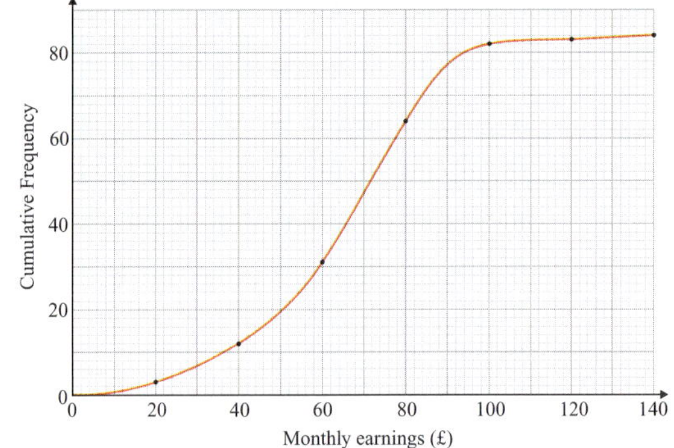

Q7 A company is testing a new video game. In the game, each level lasts for 200 seconds, after which the next level starts immediately. 100 people played the game, and the level they reached before losing is shown in the table:

Level reached	3	4	5	6	7	8	9	10
Frequency, f	6	11	14	28	22	10	7	2

a) Draw a grouped frequency table with 8 classes showing how long the games lasted, in seconds. Include a cumulative frequency column.

b) Draw a cumulative frequency diagram for the data in your new table.

c) Use your cumulative frequency diagram to estimate the number of games that lasted:
(i) less than 500 seconds, (ii) more than 1500 seconds.

d) Use your diagram to estimate the interquartile range of the games' durations.

E M **Q8** The data in the table below shows the speeds, in kilometres per hour, of the deliveries bowled by one player in a cricket match.

Speed (s km/h)	$70 \leq s < 75$	$75 \leq s < 80$	$80 \leq s < 85$	$85 \leq s < 90$	$90 \leq s < 95$	$95 \leq s < 100$
Frequency	7	18	50	83	31	11

a) Draw a cumulative frequency diagram to show the data in the table. *[3 marks]*

b) Use your diagram to estimate the 10% to 90% interpercentile range. *[3 marks]*

c) Estimate the percentage of the deliveries bowled by the player that were faster than 92 km/h. *[3 marks]*

E P M **Q9** The cumulative frequency polygon below shows the lengths of some football pitches from around the UK.

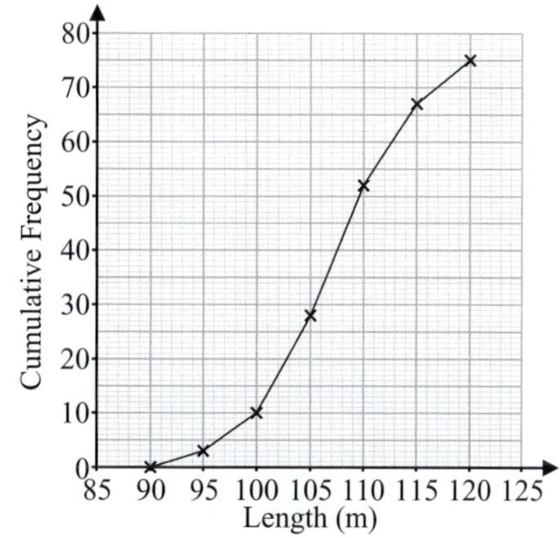

a) Estimate the median length of these football pitches. *[1 mark]*

b) Estimate the interquartile range of the length of these football pitches. *[2 marks]*

c) Estimate the percentage of these football pitches that have a length greater than 110 m. *[3 marks]*

d) Other than the fact that they are estimates, suggest why your answers to parts a)-c) may not give reliable estimates about the lengths of football pitches across the whole of the UK. *[1 mark]*

Challenge

E P M **Q10** The diagram on the right shows a cumulative frequency polygon for the ages of members of a book club.

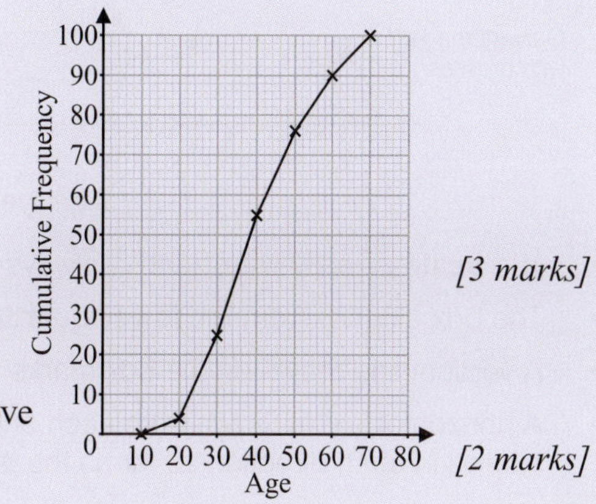

a) Find estimates for two values such that the middle 64% of the ages of the members lie between these values. *[3 marks]*

b) Outliers for this data are defined as values within the lowest 2% or highest 2% of the data. Estimate the value below which and the value above which an age would be considered an outlier. *[2 marks]*

2.9 Outliers and Box Plots

Outliers

An **outlier** is a piece of data that lies a long way from the majority of the readings in a data set.

To decide whether a reading is an outlier, you have to **test** whether it falls **outside** certain limits, called **fences**. A common way to test for outliers is to use the following values for the fences:

- **For the lower fence, use the value $Q_1 - (1.5 \times IQR)$**
- **For the upper fence, use the value $Q_3 + (1.5 \times IQR)$**

So using these fences, x is an **outlier** if either $x < Q_1 - (1.5 \times IQR)$ or $x > Q_3 + (1.5 \times IQR)$. This isn't the only way that fences can be defined — you might be asked to calculate them in a **different** way in the exam, but you'll always be told what **rule** to use.

Example 1

The lower and upper quartiles of a data set are 70 and 100. Use the fences $Q_1 - (1.5 \times IQR)$ and $Q_3 + (1.5 \times IQR)$ to decide whether the data values 30 and 210 are outliers.

$IQR = Q_3 - Q_1 = 100 - 70 = 30$ ← First work out the IQR.

Lower fence: $Q_1 - (1.5 \times IQR) = 70 - (1.5 \times 30) = 25$ ← Then find where your fences are.

Upper fence: $Q_3 + (1.5 \times IQR) = 100 + (1.5 \times 30) = 145$

30 is inside the fences, so it's not an outlier. ← Test the given values.

210 is outside the upper fence, so it is an outlier.

Box plots

A **box plot** is a kind of 'visual summary' of a set of data. Box plots show the **median**, **quartiles** and **outliers** clearly. They look like this:

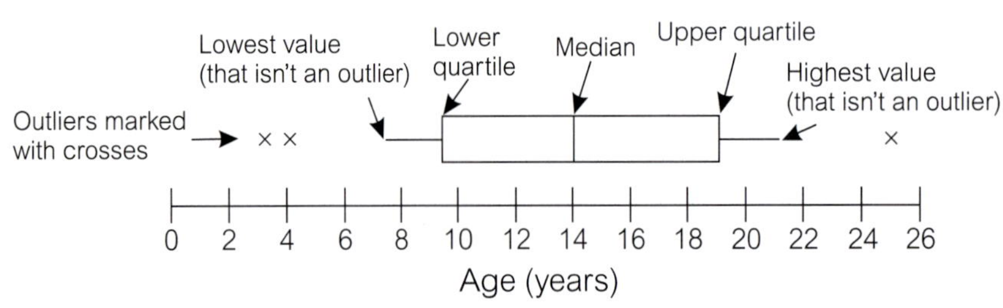

Tip Box plots are sometimes called 'box and whisker diagrams' (where the whiskers are the horizontal lines at either end of the box).

- The **scale** is really important — always include one.
- The box extends from the **lower quartile** to the **upper quartile**.
- A vertical line drawn on the box marks the **median**.
- A horizontal line is drawn from each end of the box. These lines extend in each direction as far as the last data value that **isn't** an outlier.
- **Outliers** are marked with **crosses**.

Tip So the box shows the 'middle 50%' of the data — the interquartile range.

Example 2 

The data below shows the IQs of Year 11 students at Blossom Academy and Cherry High School.

Cherry High School	93, 105, 108, 109, 110, 112, 113, 115, 116, 118, 119, 120, 120, 121, 123, 124, 126, 128, 132, 134, 144
Blossom Academy	98, 101, 103, 105, 106, 106, 107, 108, 109, 111, 112, 114, 116, 118, 122, 124, 127, 131, 136, 140

Problem Solving
Here, the data is already in order, but you should always check.

a) Draw a box plot to represent the data from Cherry High School.
Use $Q_1 - 1.5 \times \text{IQR}$ and $Q_3 + 1.5 \times \text{IQR}$ as your fences for identifying outliers.

The number of data values for Cherry High School (n) is 21.

Since $\frac{n}{2} = 10.5$, the median is the 11th data value. Median (Q_2) = 119

Since $\frac{n}{4} = 5.25$, the lower quartile is the 6th data value. $Q_1 = 112$

Since $\frac{3n}{4} = 15.75$, the upper quartile is the 16th data value. $Q_3 = 124$

$\text{IQR} = Q_3 - Q_1 = 124 - 112 = 12$

Lower fence $= Q_1 - (1.5 \times \text{IQR}) = 112 - (1.5 \times 12) = 94$

Upper fence $= Q_3 + (1.5 \times \text{IQR}) = 124 + (1.5 \times 12) = 142$

93 is below the lower fence (94) and 144 is above the upper fence (142), so both of these values are outliers.

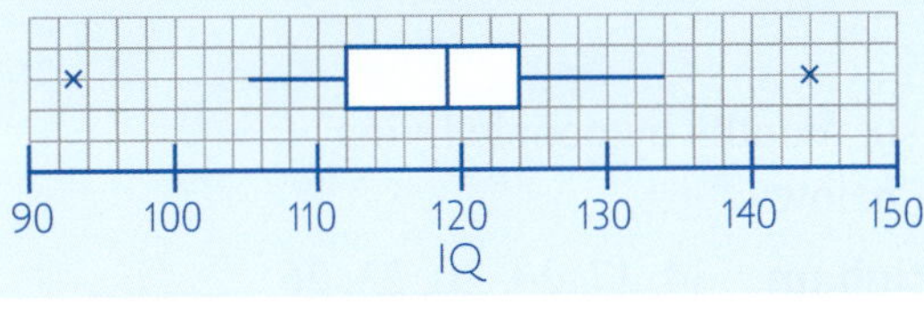

First work out the quartiles (Q_1, Q_2 and Q_3).

Find the interquartile range and the upper and lower fences.

Decide if you have any outliers.

Now you can draw the box plot itself.

Tip
Remember, only extend a line as far as the biggest or smallest data value that isn't an outlier.

b) Draw a box plot to represent the data from Blossom Academy.

The number of data values for Blossom Academy (n) is 20.

$\frac{n}{2} = 10 \Rightarrow$ The median is halfway between the 10th and 11th values: Median = 111.5

$\frac{n}{4} = 5 \Rightarrow$ The lower quartile is halfway between the 5th and 6th values: $Q_1 = 106$

$\frac{3n}{4} = 15 \Rightarrow$ The upper quartile is halfway between the 15th and 16th values: $Q_3 = 123$

$\text{IQR} = Q_3 - Q_1 = 123 - 106 = 17$

Lower fence $= Q_1 - (1.5 \times \text{IQR}) = 106 - (1.5 \times 17) = 80.5$

Upper fence $= Q_3 + (1.5 \times \text{IQR}) = 123 + (1.5 \times 17) = 148.5$

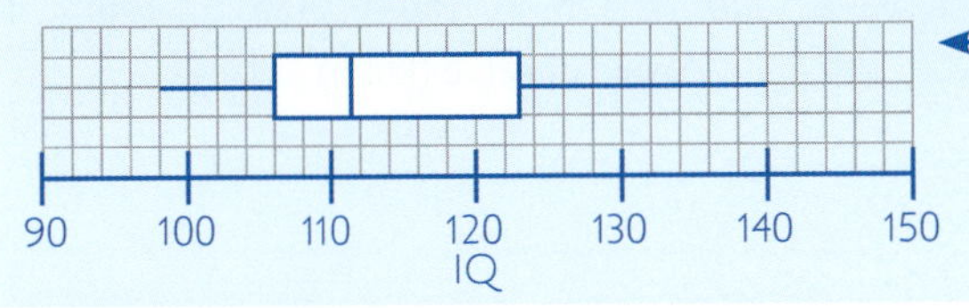

Work out the quartiles (Q_1, Q_2 and Q_3).

Find the interquartile range and the upper and lower fences. All values are between 80.5 and 148.5, so there are **no outliers** at Blossom Academy.

Draw the box plot.

Exercise 2.9

In this exercise, use the fences $Q_1 - (1.5 \times IQR)$ and $Q_3 + (1.5 \times IQR)$ to test for outliers.

Q1 Decide whether the data values 4 and 52 are outliers for data sets where:

a) $Q_1 = 19$ and $Q_3 = 31$ b) $Q_1 = 24$ and $Q_3 = 37$

Q2 A set of data was analysed and the following values were found.

minimum value = 4, maximum value = 49

$Q_1 = 16$, median = 24, $Q_3 = 37$

a) Find the interquartile range.

b) Are there any outliers in this data set?

c) Draw a box plot to illustrate the data set.

M Q3 A meteorologist is analysing the daily maximum humidities (%) from Camborne over 41 days in 2015. The data values are shown below:

95, 100, 100, 99, 99, 90, 91, 99, 98, 99, 99, 95, 97, 99, 99,
100, 92, 100, 82, 90, 97, 100, 100, 100, 100, 100, 99,
96, 92, 99, 99, 98, 99, 97, 99, 99, 90, 88, 85, 86, 74

a) Use the results to calculate the median and interquartile range.

b) Find any data values which are outliers.

c) Draw a box plot to illustrate the data.

M Q4 The numbers of items of junk mail received in six months by people living in the towns of Goossea and Pigham are shown below:

Goossea 0, 2, 6, 13, 15, 17, 19, 24, 27, 28, 28, 31, 32, 35, 41, 44, 50, 75

Pigham 14, 17, 20, 20, 23, 26, 32, 33, 35, 35, 39, 41, 42, 46, 48, 52, 54, 55

a) Are any of the data values from Pigham outliers?

b) Draw a box plot to illustrate the data from Pigham.

c) Draw a box plot to illustrate the data from Goossea.

P M Q5 The speeds of each serve in one tennis match were recorded to the nearest km/h. The data has been summarised in the box plot below. There is one outlier, at the lower end of the data, which is missing from the diagram.

a) What is the lowest recorded speed that is not an outlier?

b) What is the maximum speed, to the nearest km, that the outlier could be?

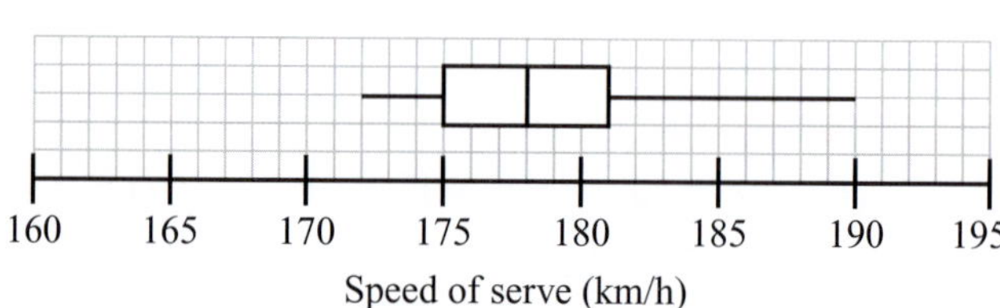

Challenge

E P M Q6 A gardener records the total mass of strawberries (in grams) on plants grown outside and on plants grown in a greenhouse. The results are summarised in the box plots below.

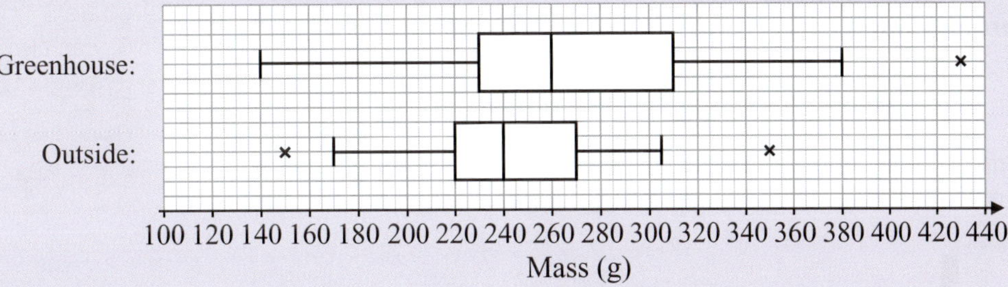

a) Find the difference between the median mass of strawberries for the plants grown in the greenhouse and the plants grown outside. *[1 mark]*

b) Find the interquartile range of the masses for the plants grown outside. *[2 marks]*

c) Explain how you know that the outliers for the plants grown outside would not have been outliers had they been grown in the greenhouse. *[1 mark]*

d) Estimate the percentage of the plants grown in the greenhouse that produced a greater mass of strawberries than the median mass for the plants grown outside. *[3 marks]*

2.10 Variance and Standard Deviation

Variance and standard deviation measure **dispersion** — they show **how spread out** the data values are from the mean. The bigger the variance or standard deviation, the more spread out the values are.

Variance

There are two ways to write the formula for the **variance** — the second one is usually easier to use:

variance = $\frac{\sum(x-\bar{x})^2}{n}$ or **variance =** $\frac{\sum x^2}{n} - \bar{x}^2$

where the x-values are the data, $\bar{x}$ is the mean, and n is the total number of data values.

The second formula above basically says: 'The variance is equal to the mean of the squares $\left(\frac{\sum x^2}{n}\right)$ minus the square of the mean ($\bar{x}^2$).' The first formula makes it easier to understand what the variance actually is — it's 'the average of the squared deviations from the mean'.

The two formulas above are equivalent to each other — you can rearrange one to get the other (although you **won't** be asked to do this in the exam).

$$\frac{\sum(x-\bar{x})^2}{n} = \frac{1}{n}\sum(x^2 - 2x\bar{x} + \bar{x}^2) \quad \text{(multiplying out brackets)}$$

$$= \frac{1}{n}\sum x^2 - 2\cdot\frac{1}{n}\cdot\bar{x}\sum x + \frac{1}{n}\sum\bar{x}^2 \quad \text{(writing as 3 summations)}$$

$$= \frac{1}{n}\sum x^2 - 2\cdot\frac{1}{n}\cdot n\bar{x}^2 + \frac{1}{n}\sum\bar{x}^2 \quad \text{(since } \textstyle\sum x = n\bar{x}\text{)}$$

$$= \frac{1}{n}\sum x^2 - 2\cdot\frac{1}{n}\cdot n\bar{x}^2 + \frac{1}{n}\cdot n\bar{x}^2 \quad \text{(since } \textstyle\sum\bar{x}^2 = n\bar{x}^2\text{)}$$

$$= \frac{1}{n}\sum x^2 - \bar{x}^2 = \frac{\sum x^2}{n} - \bar{x}^2$$

Problem Solving

$\bar{x}$ is just a number, so you can 'take it outside the summation': $\sum x\bar{x} = \bar{x}\sum x$.

Variance is measured in **units²**. For example, if the data values are measured in metres (m), then the variance is measured in metres² (m²).

> **Tip** You might see the variance formula written like this: variance = $\frac{S_{xx}}{n}$, where $S_{xx} = \sum(x - \bar{x})^2$. S_{xx} can also be written as $\sum x^2 - \frac{(\sum x)^2}{n}$. Using this notation, s.d. = $\sqrt{\frac{S_{xx}}{n}}$

Standard deviation

The **standard deviation** (s.d.) is equal to the **square root** of the variance.

standard deviation = $\sqrt{\text{variance}}$

The standard deviation is measured in the **same units** as the data values — this can make it a more useful measure of dispersion than the variance.

Example 1

Find the variance and standard deviation of the following data set: 2, 3, 4, 4, 6, 11, 12

$\sum x = 2 + 3 + 4 + 4 + 6 + 11 + 12 = 42$ ← Find the sum of the numbers first.

$\bar{x} = \frac{\sum x}{n} = \frac{42}{7} = 6$ ← Then finding the mean is easy.

$\sum x^2 = 4 + 9 + 16 + 16 + 36 + 121 + 144 = 346$ ← Next find the sum of the squares.

$\frac{\sum x^2}{n} = \frac{346}{7}$ ← Now finding the 'mean of the squares' is easy.

Variance $= \frac{\sum x^2}{n} - \bar{x}^2 = \frac{346}{7} - 6^2 = 13.428...$ ← The variance is the 'mean of the squares minus the square of the mean'.

$= 13.4$ (3 s.f.)

Standard deviation $= \sqrt{13.428...} = 3.66$ (3 s.f.) ← Take the square root of the variance to find the standard deviation.

Example 2 M

x, the mean daily wind speed in knots, was calculated for 10 days in June 1987 in Leeming. The data is summarised as follows: $\sum x = 38$ and $\sum x^2 = 154$.
Find the variance and standard deviation of the data.

$\bar{x} = \frac{\sum x}{n} = \frac{38}{10} = 3.8$ knots ← Use $\sum x$ to find the mean.

Variance $= \frac{\sum x^2}{n} - \bar{x}^2 = \frac{154}{10} - 3.8^2 = 15.4 - 14.44$ ← Use $\sum x^2$ and $\bar{x}$ to calculate the variance.

$= 0.96$ knots²

Standard deviation $= \sqrt{0.96} = 0.980$ knots (3 s.f.) ← Square root the variance.

If your data is given in a **frequency table**, then the variance formula can be written like this, where f is the frequency of each x.

variance = $\frac{\sum fx^2}{\sum f} - \bar{x}^2$, where $\bar{x} = \frac{\sum fx}{\sum f}$

> **Tip** Remember, $n = \sum f$ and fx^2 means $f \times x^2$ — not $(fx)^2$.

You could also write the formula as variance = $\frac{\sum f(x-\bar{x})^2}{\sum f}$. This is trickier to use though.

Example 3

Find the variance and standard deviation of the data in this table.

x	2	3	4	5	6	7
frequency, f	2	5	5	4	1	1

x	2	3	4	5	6	7
frequency, f	2	5	5	4	1	1
fx	4	15	20	20	6	7

Start by adding an extra row to the table, showing the values of fx.

$\sum f = 2 + 5 + 5 + 4 + 1 + 1 = 18$

$\sum fx = 4 + 15 + 20 + 20 + 6 + 7 = 72$

Find the number of values, $\sum f$, and the sum of the values $\sum fx$.

$\bar{x} = \frac{\sum fx}{\sum f} = \frac{72}{18} = 4$

Then calculate the mean of the values.

x^2	4	9	16	25	36	49
fx^2	8	45	80	100	36	49

Add two more rows to your table showing x^2 and fx^2.

$\sum fx^2 = 8 + 45 + 80 + 100 + 36 + 49 = 318$

Find $\sum fx^2$.

Variance $= \frac{\sum fx^2}{\sum f} - \bar{x}^2 = \frac{318}{18} - 4^2 = 1.666...$

$= 1.67$ (3 s.f.)

Calculate the variance.

Standard deviation $= \sqrt{1.666...} = 1.29$ (3 s.f.)

Then take the square root of the variance to find the standard deviation.

If your data is **grouped**, then you can only **estimate** the variance and standard deviation (because you don't know the actual data values — see page 28). In this case, assume that each data value is equal to the **class mid-point**. Then go through the same steps as in Example 3.

Example 4 

The heights of sunflowers in a garden were measured, and are recorded in the table below.

Height, h (cm)	$150 \le h < 170$	$170 \le h < 190$	$190 \le h < 210$	$210 \le h < 230$
Frequency, f	5	10	12	3

Estimate the variance and the standard deviation of the heights.

Height, h (cm)	$150 \le h < 170$	$170 \le h < 190$	$190 \le h < 210$	$210 \le h < 230$
Frequency, f	5	10	12	3
Class mid-point, x	160	180	200	220
fx	800	1800	2400	660
x^2	25 600	32 400	40 000	48 400
fx^2	128 000	324 000	480 000	145 200

Start by adding extra rows for the class mid-points, x, as well as fx, x^2 and fx^2.

continued on the next page...

$\sum f = 5 + 10 + 12 + 3 = 30$

$\sum fx = 800 + 1800 + 2400 + 660 = 5660$

Find $\sum f$ and $\sum fx$.

$\bar{x} = \frac{\sum fx}{\sum f} = \frac{5660}{30}$

Calculate the mean of the values.

$\sum fx^2 = 128\,000 + 324\,000 + 480\,000 + 145\,200 = 1\,077\,200$

Calculate $\sum fx^2$.

So variance $= \frac{\sum fx^2}{\sum f} - \bar{x}^2 = \frac{1\,077\,200}{30} - \left(\frac{5660}{30}\right)^2 = 311.5555...$

$= 312\text{ cm}^2$ (3 s.f.)

And standard deviation $= \sqrt{311.5555...} = 17.7$ (3 s.f.)

Tip Remember, variance takes 'squared' units.

Outliers (see page 42) are freak pieces of data — you can use the mean and standard deviation to define them. One way to test for outliers is to look for any data values that lie more than 3 standard deviations away from the mean.

So value x is an outlier if:

either: **$x < \bar{x}$ – 3 standard deviations**
or: **$x > \bar{x}$ + 3 standard deviations**

Tip On page 42, outliers were defined using Q_1, Q_3 and the interquartile range.

Outliers can be defined in other ways — you might be asked to calculate the limits (fences) in a **different** way in the exam, but you'll always be told what **rule** to use.

Outliers **affect** the mean, variance and standard deviation so being able to find them is important — this is known as '**cleaning data**'.

Example 5 M

x, the mean daily wind speed in knots (kn), was calculated for 10 days in 2015 in Hurn. The data is summarised as follows: $\sum x = 63$ and $\sum x^2 = 441$.

The highest x-value is 10 knots. Use the fences $\bar{x} - 3$ standard deviations and $\bar{x} + 3$ standard deviations to decide whether this is an outlier.

$\bar{x} = \frac{\sum x}{n} = \frac{63}{10} = 6.3$ kn

Find the mean.

Variance $= \frac{\sum x^2}{n} - \bar{x}^2 = \frac{441}{10} - 6.3^2 = 44.1 - 39.69$

$= 4.41\text{ kn}^2$

Calculate the variance.

Standard deviation $= \sqrt{\text{variance}} = \sqrt{4.41} = 2.1$ kn

Calculate the standard deviation.

$\bar{x}$ – 3 standard deviations $= 6.3 - (3 \times 2.1) = 0$

$\bar{x}$ + 3 standard deviations $= 6.3 + (3 \times 2.1) = 12.6$

Work out the upper and lower fences.

The x-value 10 kn is inside the lower and upper fences, so it is not an outlier.

Just like the different measures of **location** (such as the mean), measures of **dispersion** — the range, interquartile range, variance and standard deviation — can be useful in different ways.

Range

- The range is the **easiest** measure of dispersion to calculate.
- But it's heavily affected by even a single extreme value / outlier. And it depends on only two data values — it **doesn't** tell you anything about how spread out the rest of the values are.

Interquartile range

- It's **not** affected by **extreme values** — so if your data contains **outliers**, then the interquartile range is a good measure of dispersion to use.
- It's fairly **tricky** to work out.

Variance

- The variance depends on **all** the data values — so no values are 'ignored'.
- But it's **tricky** to work out, and is affected by **extreme values / outliers**.
- It's also expressed in **different units** from the actual data values, so it can be difficult to interpret.

Standard deviation

- Like the variance, the standard deviation depends on **all** the data values.
- But it is also **tricky** to work out, and affected by **extreme values / outliers**.
- It has the **same units** as the data values so it is easier to interpret.

In the exam, you might be asked why a particular measure of dispersion (or location) is **suitable** for that data. You'll have to use these pros and cons and **relate** them to the data, as well as saying what they mean **in the context** of the situation.

Exercise 2.10

M Q1 The attendance figures (x) for Wessex Football Club's first six matches of the season were:

756, 755, 764, 778, 754, 759

a) Find the mean ($\bar{x}$) of these attendance figures.

b) Calculate the sum of the squares of the attendance figures, $\sum x^2$.

c) Use your answers to find the variance of the attendance figures.

d) Hence find the standard deviation of the attendance figures.

e) Explain why the standard deviation is a reasonable measure of dispersion to use with this data.

M Q2 The figures for the number of TVs (x) in the households of 20 students are shown in the table on the right.

x	1	2	3	4
frequency, f	7	8	4	1

a) Find the mean number of TVs ($\bar{x}$) in the 20 households.

b) By adding rows showing x^2 and fx^2 to the table, find $\sum fx^2$.

c) Calculate the variance for the data above.

d) Hence find the standard deviation.

Q3 A data set consists of the following values (x):

3.2 2.4 2.8 3.1 2.9 2.5 2.7 2.6

a) Find the mean of the data set.

b) Find $\sum(x-\overline{x})^2$.

c) Hence, find the standard deviation of the data.

E M Q4 x, the daily total rainfall in mm, was measured for 100 days in 1987 in Heathrow. The data is summarised as follows: $\sum x = 290.7$ and $\sum x^2 = 6150.83$

a) Find the standard deviation for this data. *[2 marks]*

b) Using the fences $\overline{x} \pm 3$ standard deviations, decide whether the x-value 35.5 mm is an outlier or not. *[1 mark]*

M Q5 The yields (w, in kg) of potatoes from a number of allotments is shown in the grouped frequency table on the right.

a) Estimate the variance for this data.

b) Estimate the standard deviation.

c) Explain why your answers to a) and b) are estimates.

Yield, w (kg)	Frequency
$50 \leq w < 60$	23
$60 \leq w < 70$	12
$70 \leq w < 80$	15
$80 \leq w < 90$	6
$90 \leq w < 100$	2

E P M Q6 The prices of 80 mobile phones, £x, were collected from an online retailer. The data is summarised as follows: $\sum x = 50\,400$ and $\sum x^2 = 33\,153\,750$.

a) Calculate the mean price of the mobile phones. *[1 mark]*

b) Calculate the standard deviation for the prices of the mobile phones. *[2 marks]*

c) Outliers are defined as values that lie more than 3 standard deviations from the mean. Given that there are no outliers in the data, find the cheapest and most expensive mobile phones that could have been included in the data. *[3 marks]*

Challenge

P Q7 For a small set of data values (x), the mean is 4 and the standard deviation is $\sqrt{2}$. Given that $\sum x^2 - \sum x = 98$, determine the number of values in the data set.

P M Q8 Su and Ellen are collecting data on the durations of the eruptions of the volcano in their garden. Between them, they have recorded the duration of the last 60 eruptions.

- Su has timed 23 eruptions, with an average duration of 3.42 minutes and a standard deviation of 1.07 minutes.
- Ellen has timed 37 eruptions, with an average duration of 3.92 minutes and a standard deviation of 0.97 minutes.

They decide to combine their observations into one large data set.

a) Calculate the mean duration of all the observed eruptions.

b) Find the variance of the set of 60 durations.

c) Find the standard deviation of the set of 60 durations.

Problem Solving

In Q8, find the combined mean using the method on p.24, then use a similar process to find the combined sum of squares (you'll have to substitute the values you know into the variance formula).

2.11 Coding

Coding means doing something to all the readings in your data set to make the numbers easier to work with. That could mean:

- **adding** a number to (or **subtracting** a number from) all your readings
- **multiplying** (or **dividing**) all your readings by a number.
- **both** of the above.

For example, finding the mean of 1831, 1832 and 1836 looks complicated. But if you subtract 1830 from each number, then finding the mean of what's left (1, 2 and 6) is much easier — it's 3. So the mean of the original numbers must be 1833 (once you've 'undone' the coding).

You have to change your original variable, x, to a different one, such as y (so in the example above, if $x = 1831$, then $y = 1$). An **original** data value x will be related to a **coded** data value y by an equation of the form $y = \frac{x - a}{b}$, where a and b are numbers you choose.
The mean and standard deviation of the **original** data values will then be related to the mean and standard deviation of the **coded** data values by the following equations:

- $\bar{y} = \frac{\bar{x} - a}{b}$, where $\bar{x}$ and $\bar{y}$ are the **means** of variables x and y
- **standard deviation of y = $\frac{\text{standard deviation of } x}{b}$**

Because 'a' in the coding formula shifts the entire data set, it doesn't affect the spread — so the formula connecting the coded and uncoded standard deviations depends only on 'b'. If you don't multiply or divide your readings by anything (i.e. if b = 1), then the dispersion isn't changed.

Example 1

Find the mean and standard deviation of: 1 862 020, 1 862 040, 1 862 010 and 1 862 050.

Use the coding $y = \frac{x - 1862\,000}{10}$

So coded (y) values are 2, 4, 1 and 5.

$\bar{y} = \frac{2 + 4 + 1 + 5}{4} = \frac{12}{4} = 3$

Standard deviation $= \sqrt{\frac{2^2 + 4^2 + 1^2 + 5^2}{4} - 3^2}$

$= \sqrt{\frac{46}{4} - 9} = \sqrt{2.5} = 1.58$ (3 s.f.)

$\bar{y} = \frac{\bar{x} - a}{b}$, so $\bar{x} = a + b\bar{y}$.

So $\bar{x} = 1\,862\,000 + 10\bar{y}$
$= 1\,862\,000 + (10 \times 3)$
$= 1\,862\,030$

Standard deviation of $y = \frac{\text{standard deviation of } x}{b}$

Standard deviation of x = b × standard deviation of y
$= 10 \times 1.58 = 15.8$ (3 s.f.)

All the original data values (call them x) start with the same four digits (1862) — so start by subtracting 1 862 000 from every reading. You can then make things even simpler by dividing by 10. These are the coded data values (call them y).

Work out the mean and standard deviation of the (easy-to-use) coded values.

Tip Here, a = 1 862 000 and b = 10.

Then find the mean and standard deviation of the original values using the formulas above.

Carry out the method in exactly the same way with **grouped** data, but assume that all the values equal their **class mid-points** — these are the x-values you use with the coding equation $y = \frac{x - a}{b}$.

Example 2 M

Estimate the mean and standard deviation of this data concerning job interviews, using the coding $y = \frac{x - 15.5}{10}$.

Length of interview, to nearest minute	11-20	21-30	31-40	41-50
Frequency, f	17	21	27	15

Length of interview, to nearest minute	11-20	21-30	31-40	41-50
Frequency, f	17	21	27	15
Class mid-point, x	15.5	25.5	35.5	45.5
Coded value, y	0	1	2	3
fy	0	21	54	45
y^2	0	1	4	9
fy^2	0	21	108	135

Make a new table showing the class mid-points (x) of the original data, and the coded class mid-points (y). Also include rows for fy, y^2 and fy^2.

Number of coded values: $\sum f = 17 + 21 + 27 + 15 = 80$

Sum of the coded values: $\sum fy = 0 + 21 + 54 + 45 = 120$

Mean of the coded values: $\bar{y} = \frac{\sum fy}{\sum f} = \frac{120}{80} = 1.5$

Use your table to find the mean of the coded values ($\bar{y}$).

$\sum fy^2 = 0 + 21 + 108 + 135 = 264$

Variance $= \frac{\sum fy^2}{\sum f} - \bar{y}^2 = \frac{264}{80} - 1.5^2 = 1.05$

So standard deviation of $y = \sqrt{1.05} = 1.02$ (3 s.f.)

Now find the standard deviation.

$\bar{y} = \frac{\bar{x} - a}{b}$, so $\bar{x} = a + b\bar{y} = 15.5 + 10 \times 1.5 = 30.5$ minutes

Standard deviation of $y = \frac{\text{standard deviation of } x}{b}$

So standard deviation of $x = b \times$ standard deviation of y

$= 10 \times 1.02 = 10.2$ minutes (3 s.f.)

Use these figures to find the mean and standard deviation of the original data.

Sometimes, you won't have the data itself — just some **summations**.

Example 3 M

A travel guide employee collects some data on the cost (c, in £) of a night's stay in 10 hotels in a particular town. He codes his data using $d = 10(c - 93.5)$, and calculates the summations below.

$$\sum d = 0 \text{ and } \sum d^2 = 998\,250$$

Calculate the mean and standard deviation of the original costs.

The number of values (n) is 10.

So the mean of the coded values is: $\bar{d} = \frac{\sum d}{n} = \frac{0}{10} = 0$

First find the mean of the coded values.

continued on the next page...

$$\text{Variance} = \frac{\sum d^2}{n} - \overline{d}^2 = \frac{998\,250}{10} - 0^2 = 99\,825$$

So standard deviation $= \sqrt{99\,825} = 316.0$ (4 s.f.)

Find the standard deviation of the coded values.

$\overline{d} = 10(\overline{c} - 93.5)$, so $\overline{c} = 93.5 + \frac{\overline{d}}{10} = 93.5$, i.e. $\overline{c} = £93.50$

Standard deviation of $d = 10 \times$ standard deviation of c,

so standard deviation of $c = \frac{316.0}{10} = 31.6$

$= £31.60$ (to the nearest penny)

Find the mean and standard deviation of the original data.

Exercise 2.11

Q1 A set of data values (x) are coded using $y = \frac{x - 20\,000}{15}$. The mean of the coded data ($\overline{y}$) is 12.4, and the standard deviation of the coded data is 1.34. Find the mean and standard deviation of the original data set.

M Q2 The widths (in cm) of 10 sunflower seeds in a packet are given below.

0.61, 0.67, 0.63, 0.63, 0.66, 0.65, 0.64, 0.68, 0.64, 0.62

a) Code the data values above (x) to form a new data set consisting of integer values (y) between 1 and 10.

b) Find the mean and standard deviation of the original values (x).

M Q3 A pilot regularly flies between the same two destinations. The distances she flies to the nearest 10 km during 12 flights are shown below.

4550, 4510, 4480, 4530, 4480, 4470, 4540, 4490, 4550, 4500, 4460, 4520

a) Code the data values (x) to form new data with integer values (y), where $1 \le y \le 10$.

b) Find the mean and standard deviation of the original data set to the nearest 10 km.

M Q4 The table below shows the weight, x, of 12 items on a production line.

Weight (to nearest g)	100-104	105-109	110-114	115-119
Frequency	2	6	3	1

Use the coding $y = x - 102$ to estimate the mean and standard deviation of the items' weights.

E Q5 Some coded data has been summarised as: $\sum fy = 262.5$, $\sum fy^2 = 4023.4375$ and $\sum f = 20$.

a) Find estimates for the coded mean and coded variance. *[2 marks]*

b) Given that the data was coded using the formula $y = \frac{x - 2500}{4}$, find estimates for the mean and variance of the original data. *[3 marks]*

P Q6 Twenty pieces of data (x) have been summarised as follows:

$$\sum(x + 2) = 7 \text{ and } \sum(x + 2)^2 = 80.$$

Calculate the mean and standard deviation of the data.

Problem Solving In Q6, code the data using $y = x + 2$.

P Q7 A student codes some data values (x) to form a new data set (y). For y, the mean = 7 and the standard deviation = 4.3. For x, the mean = 195 and the standard deviation = 21.5. Find the equation used by the student to code their data.

Challenge

E P M Q8 The widths, x mm, of some cells in the human body are measured, and the mean width of a cell from the data was found to be 0.00011195 mm.

The data was then coded using the formula $y = 10^6x - 100$. The coded results (y) are shown in the table below. One of the frequencies is missing.

y	$0 < y \leq 5$	$5 < y \leq 10$	$10 < y \leq 15$	$15 < y \leq 20$	$20 < y \leq 25$
Frequency, f	22	19	23	p	16

a) Find the missing frequency, p. *[4 marks]*

b) Estimate the standard deviation of the widths of the cells, giving your answer in standard index form correct to 3 significant figures. *[4 marks]*

2.12 Comparing Distributions

In the exam you might be asked to **compare** two distributions. To do this, there are different kinds of things you can say, depending on what information you have about the distributions. You can:

1. Compare measures of **location**: mean, median or mode
   - You need to say which distribution has the higher mean/median/mode, and by how much.
   - Then say what this means **in the context of the question** — this means you need to use the same 'setting' in your answer as the question uses. So if the question is about the weights of tigers in a zoo, you need to talk about the weights of tigers in a zoo in your answer.
2. Compare measures of **dispersion**: standard deviation, range, interquartile/interpercentile range
   - You need to say which distribution's data values are more 'tightly packed', or which distribution's values are more spread out.
   - Then say what this means **in the context of the question**.

Example 1 

This table summarises the marks obtained by a group of students in Maths 'Calculator' and 'Non-calculator' papers. Comment on the location and dispersion of the distributions.

Calculator paper		Non-calculator paper
58	Median, Q_2	42
30	Interquartile range	21
55	Mean	46
21.2	Standard deviation	17.8

The mean and the median are both higher for the Calculator paper (the mean is 9 marks higher, while the median is 16 marks higher). So scores were generally higher on the Calculator paper.

Compare the measures of location (the mean and median values).

continued on the next page...

The interquartile range and the standard deviation are higher for the Calculator paper.
So scores on the Calculator paper are more spread out than those for the Non-calculator paper.

Compare the measures of dispersion (the IQR and standard deviation values).

Example 2 M

The box plots on the right show how the masses (in g) of the tomatoes in two harvests were distributed.
Compare the distributions of the two harvests.

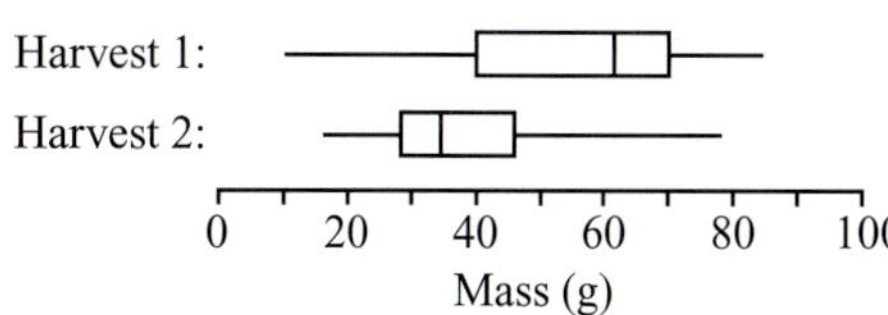

The median is more than 25 g higher for Harvest 1.
So the tomatoes in Harvest 1 were generally heavier.

Compare the measures of location (the median values).

The interquartile range (IQR) and the range for Harvest 1 are higher than those for Harvest 2.
So the masses of the tomatoes in Harvest 1 were more varied than the masses of the tomatoes in Harvest 2.

Compare the measures of dispersion (the IQR values).

Tip This question is about tomato harvests, so make sure you give your answer in this context.

Exercise 2.12

M Q1 The box plots below show the prices of shoes (in £) from two different shops.

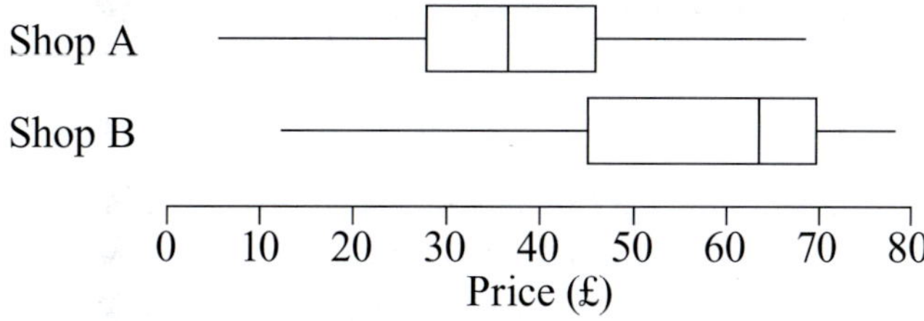

Use the box plots to compare the location and dispersion of the two shops' prices.

M Q2 10 men and 10 women were asked how many hours of sleep they got on a typical night.
The results are shown below.

Men: 6, 7, 9, 8, 8, 6, 7, 7, 10, 5

Women: 9, 9, 7, 8, 5, 11, 10, 8, 10, 8

a) Compare the locations of the two data sets.

b) Compare the dispersion of the two data sets.

Problem Solving In Q2, you need to decide what measures of location and dispersion to find.

E M Q3 The two box plots below summarise the distances that some students in Class A and Class B threw a javelin at a school sports day.

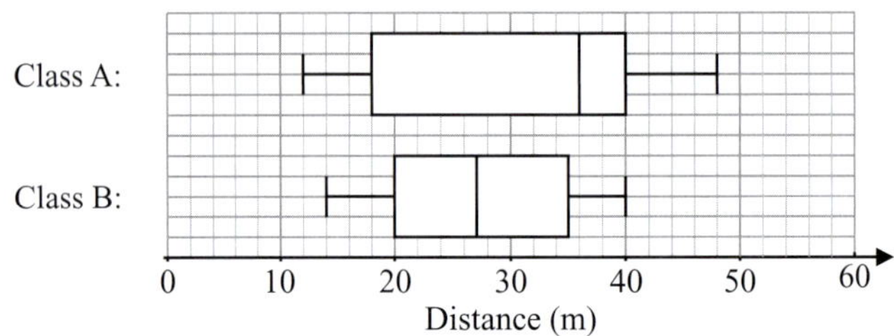

Compare the distances thrown by students in Class A and Class B. *[2 marks]*

E P Q4 The table below shows some percentiles for two data sets, x and y.

Percentile	20th	30th	50th	70th	80th
Data set, x	16.6	19.4	23.8	27.6	30.2
Data set, y	15.9	18.5	23.6	29.5	30.5

Compare the location and dispersion of the two data sets. *[3 marks]*

M Q5 The lengths of brown trout in two samples from different rivers, A and B, were measured (in cm). The data collected was used to produce the values below.

River A: $\sum f = 141$, $\sum fx = 3598$, $\sum fx^2 = 96\ 376$

River B: $\sum f = 120$, $\sum fx = 4344$, $\sum fx^2 = 184\ 366$

a) Compare the location of the lengths in the samples by calculating an appropriate statistic.

b) Compare the dispersion of the lengths in the samples by calculating an appropriate statistic.

E P M Q6 A travel agent is collecting data on two islands, A and B. She records the maximum daily temperature on 100 days. The cumulative frequency curves for her results are shown on the graph below. Compare the location and dispersion of the data for the two islands.

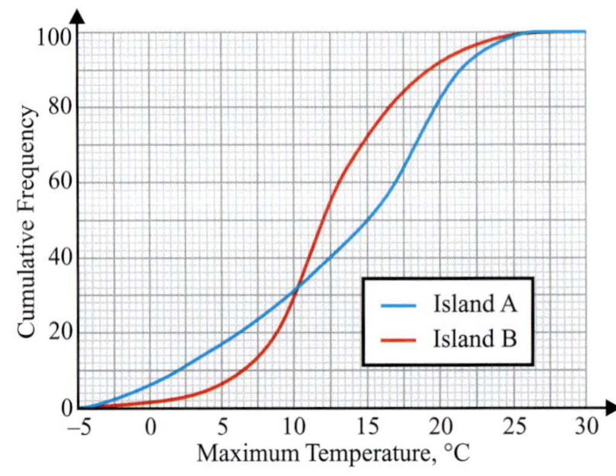

[3 marks]

2.13 Scatter Diagrams and Correlation

Sometimes variables are measured in **pairs** — perhaps because you want to know if they're linked. These pairs of variables might be things like:

- 'my age' and 'length of my feet',
- 'temperature' and 'number of accidents on a stretch of road'.

Data made up of pairs of values (x, y) is called **bivariate data**. You can plot bivariate data on a **scatter diagram** — where each variable is plotted along one of the axes. The pattern of points on a scatter diagram can tell you something about the data.

For example, on this scatter diagram, the variables 'my age' and 'length of my feet' seem linked — you can tell because nearly all of the points lie **close** to a **straight line**. As I got older, my feet got bigger and bigger.

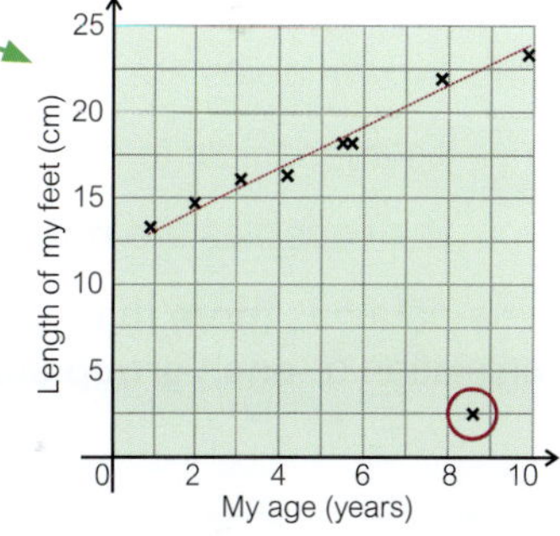

The **line of best fit** on this scatter diagram lies **close** to **most** of the points.

The circled point doesn't fit the pattern of the rest of the data at all, so the line of best fit doesn't need to pass close to it. A point like this could be a measurement error or a 'freak' observation (an **outlier**).

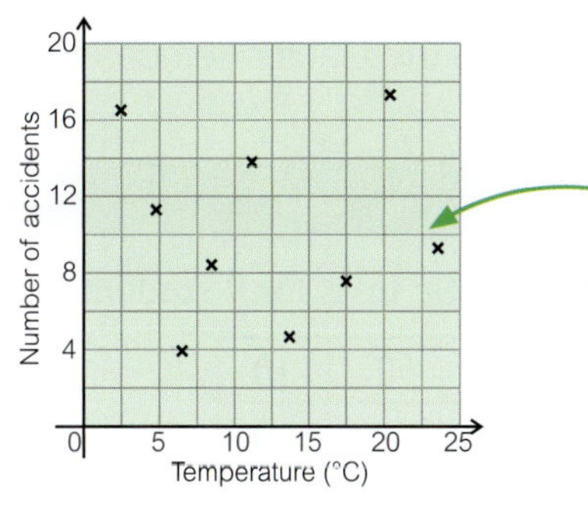

- It's a lot harder to see any connection between the variables 'temperature' and 'number of accidents' on this scatter diagram — the data seems scattered everywhere.
- You can't draw a line of best fit for this data — there isn't a line that lies close to **most** of the points. (It would be hard to draw a line lying close to more than about half the points.)

- You may also see scatter diagrams where it's clear that there is **more than one distinct section** within the population — the data will be in **separate clusters**.
- You may be able to tell from the **context** what the different clusters represent — for example, in this diagram, the longer tracks might all be in a particular style (e.g. classical).

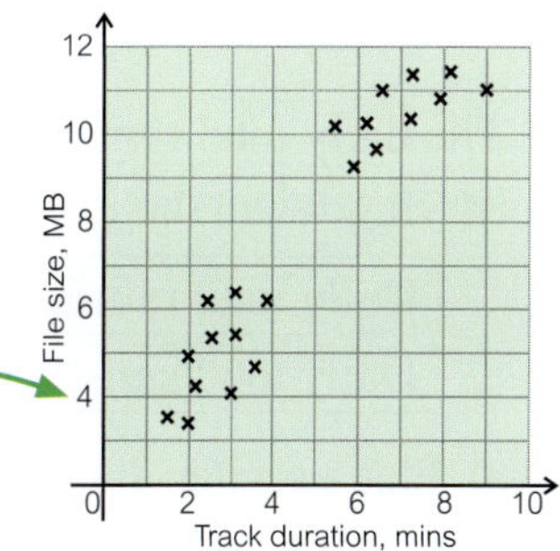

Correlation is all about whether the points on a scatter diagram lie close to a **straight line**.

Sometimes, as one variable gets bigger, the other one also gets bigger — in this case, the scatter diagram might look like this.

- Here, a line of best fit would have a **positive gradient**.
- The two variables are **positively correlated**.

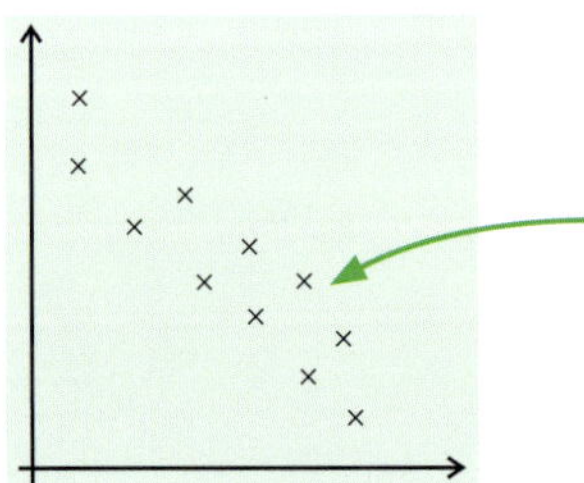

If one variable gets smaller as the other one gets bigger, then the scatter diagram would look like this.

- In this case, a line of best fit would have a **negative gradient**.
- The two variables are **negatively correlated**.

If the points lie **very close** to a straight line, there is **strong** correlation. If they **don't line up** as nicely but you can still draw a line of best fit, there is **weak** correlation.

If the two variables are **not** linked, you'd expect a **random scattering** of points.

- It's impossible to draw a line of best fit close to most of the points.
- The variables are **not correlated** (or there's **zero** correlation).

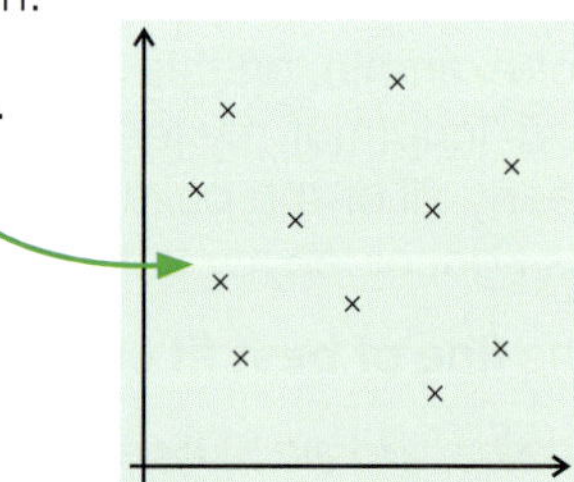

If the data has **more than one** cluster, you should consider the correlation of **each group separately**, as well as the overall correlation.

Be **careful** when writing about two variables that are **correlated** — changes in one variable might **not cause** changes in the other. They could be linked by a third factor, or it could just be coincidence.

For example, sales of barbecues and ice cream might be positively correlated, but higher sales of barbecues don't cause ice cream sales to increase. They're both affected by a third factor (temperature).

Exercise 2.13

M Q1 The data in the table below shows the scores on spelling and arithmetic tests for 9 students.

Spelling score	6	9	11	12	5	6	4	2	10
Arithmetic score	8	10	12	10	7	4	5	1	10

a) Plot a scatter diagram to show this data.

b) Describe the type of correlation shown.

M Q2 The daily total rainfall (mm) and daily total sunshine (hours) on seven random days in Camborne in 1987 are shown in the table below.

Daily total rainfall (mm)	9.3	9.4	2.5	3.5	0.6	7	4.2
Daily total sunshine (hours)	0	11.4	9.1	2.5	5.1	5.9	8.8

a) Plot a scatter diagram to show this data.

b) Describe the type of correlation shown.

M Q3 The table below shows the number of books read and the number of films watched by some students in one year.

No. of books read	3	18	22	12	25	14	37	6	22	33
No. of films watched	16	14	6	23	36	29	12	9	26	19

a) Plot a scatter diagram to show this data.

b) One of the students thinks that the people who had read more books in the year would have watched fewer films. Does the data support this view?

M Q4 This table shows the average length and the average circumference of eggs for several species of bird, measured in cm.

Length	5.9	2.1	3.4	5.1	8.9	6.6	7.2	4.5	6.8
Circumference	19.6	6.3	7.1	9.9	3.5	21	18.7	8.3	18.4

a) Plot a scatter diagram to show this data.

b) Describe any trends in the data.

c) One of the measurements was recorded incorrectly. Use your scatter diagram to determine which one.

M Q5 A town mayor recorded the number of woolly jumpers sold and the number of injuries from ice skating reported over 10 days in her town. Her results are shown in the table.

No. of jumpers sold	25	10	20	5	5	4	18	3	13	15
No. of ice skating injuries	12	5	8	3	2	4	7	1	6	9

a) Plot a scatter diagram to show this data.

b) Describe the type of correlation shown.

c) Why should the mayor be careful when interpreting her data?

E M Q6 Data is collected from different cities regarding the number of cars that pass a point in the city centre in one hour, and the number of cafes per square kilometre in the city centre. The results are shown in the scatter diagram on the right.

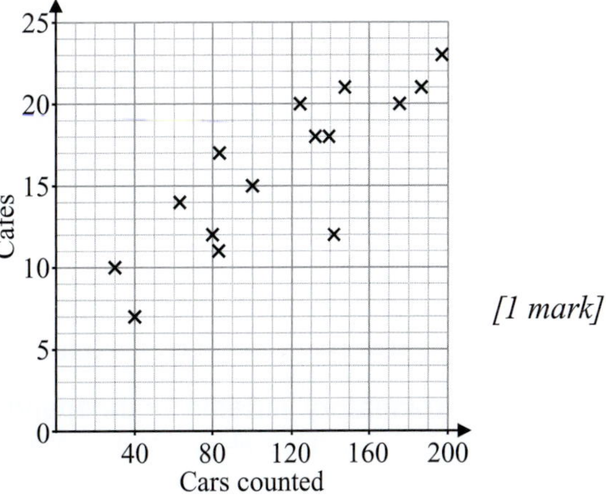

a) Describe any correlation shown by the scatter diagram. *[1 mark]*

A student draws the conclusion from the diagram that more traffic in a city centre leads to it having more cafes.

b) Explain why this statement is incorrect, and suggest an alternative reason for the correlation. *[2 marks]*

E M **Q7** The data below shows the number of police officers employed and the number of reported crimes per year in a country.

Year	2008	2009	2010	2011	2012	2013	2014	2015	2016
Police officers (thousands)	172	163	155	147	140	131	118	112	107
Reported crimes (millions)	1.65	2.10	1.65	1.80	1.85	2.00	1.90	2.20	2.20

a) Draw a scatter diagram to show this data. *[2 marks]*

b) Describe any correlation shown by your scatter diagram. *[1 mark]*

c) Identify any outliers from your scatter diagram. Justify your choice(s). *[1 mark]*

E P M **Q8** The scatter diagram on the right shows the cost of different models of (new) cars plotted against the number of road accidents that model of car has been involved in over the last year.

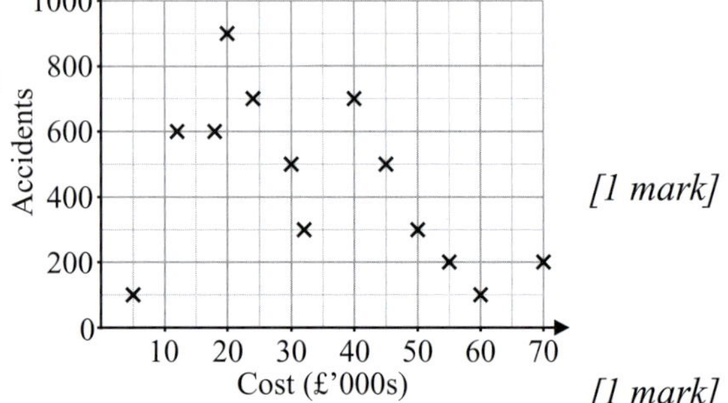

a) Describe the correlation shown. *[1 mark]*

b) A journalist wants to use this data to write an article arguing that the more expensive a car is, the safer it is. Explain why this may not be the case. *[1 mark]*

c) There is an outlier in the data, but all of the values have been plotted correctly. Suggest a reason why this outlier exists. *[1 mark]*

2.14 Explanatory and Response Variables

When you draw a scatter diagram, you always have **two** variables. For example, this scatter diagram shows the load on a lorry, x (in tonnes), and the fuel efficiency, y (in km per litre).

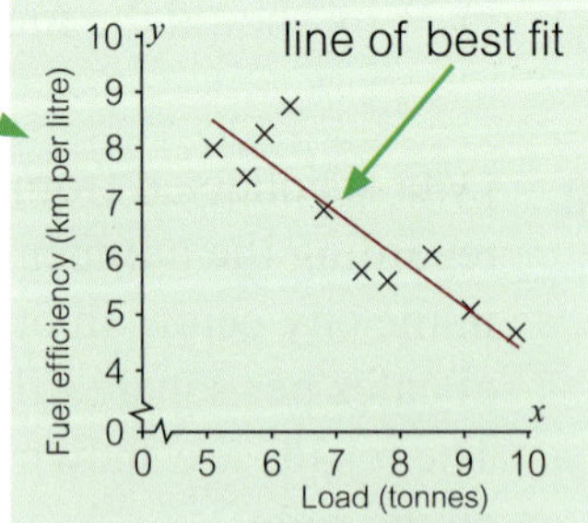

- The two variables are negatively correlated.
- In fact, all the points lie reasonably close to a straight line — the **line of best fit**.
- If you could find the equation of this line, then you could use it as a **model** to describe the relationship between x and y.

Linear regression is a method for finding the equation of a line of best fit on a scatter diagram — you can think of it as a method for **modelling** the relationship between two variables. First, you have to decide which variable is the **explanatory variable** and which is the **response variable**.

- The **explanatory variable** (or **independent variable**) is the variable you can directly control, or the one that you think is **affecting** the other. In the above example, 'load' is the explanatory variable. The explanatory variable is always drawn along the **horizontal axis**.
- The **response variable** (or **dependent variable**) is the variable you think is **being affected**. In the above example, 'fuel efficiency' is the response variable. The response variable is always drawn up the **vertical axis**.

Example 1 M

For each situation below, explain which quantity would be the explanatory variable, and which would be the response variable.

a) A scientist is investigating the relationship between the amount of fertiliser applied to a tomato plant and the eventual yield.

The scientist can directly control the amount of fertiliser they give each plant — so 'amount of fertiliser' is the explanatory variable.

They then measure the effect this has on the plant's yield — so 'yield' is the response variable.

b) A researcher is examining how a town's latitude and the number of days when the temperature rose above 10 °C are linked.

Although the researcher can't control the latitude of towns, it would be the difference in latitude that **leads to** a difference in temperature, and not the other way around.

So the explanatory variable is 'town's latitude', and the response variable is 'number of days when the temperature rose above 10 °C'.

Exercise 2.14

M Q1 For each situation below, explain which quantity would be the explanatory variable, and which would be the response variable.

a) • the time spent practising the piano each week
• the number of mistakes made in a test at the end of the week

b) • the age of a second-hand car
• the value of a second-hand car

c) • the number of phone calls made in a town in a week
• the population of a town

d) • the growth rate of a plant in an experiment
• the amount of sunlight falling on a plant in an experiment

M Q2 a) Suggest a possible explanatory variable for each of the following response variables:

(i) Number of cold drinks sold by a café.

(ii) Amount of a drug in a person's bloodstream.

b) Suggest a possible response variable for each of the following explanatory variables:

(i) Annual income.

(ii) Age of a tree.

M Q3 Look at the sketches of three scatter diagrams below. Suggest how the following variables could be allocated to the axes on the diagrams:

Production efficiency IQ Cost Advertising budget Height Volume of sales

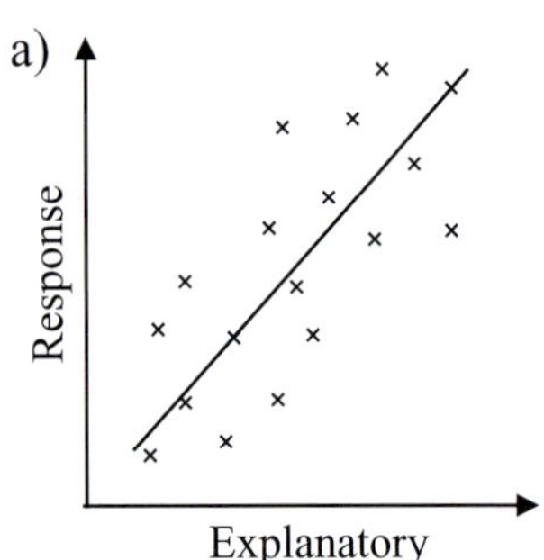

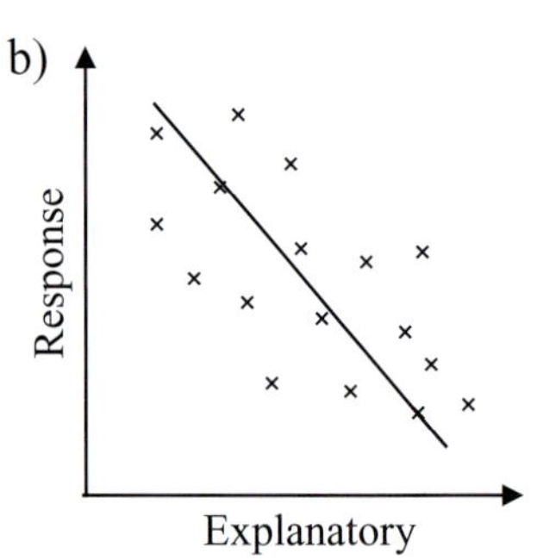

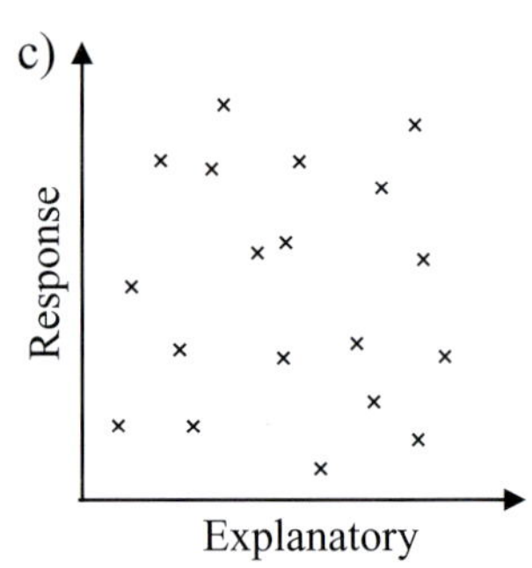

E P M Q4 Ten identical new cars are each fitted with four identical new tyres. After a period of six months, data is collected on the number of miles the cars have been driven, and the average tread depth of the four tyres on each car. None of the tyres were replaced during the six-month period.

a) Sketch a scatter diagram of what you would expect the data to look like, with the explanatory and response variables clearly labelled. *[3 marks]*

b) Justify your selection of explanatory and response variables in part a). *[1 mark]*

2.15 Regression Lines

The **regression line** is essentially what we're going to call the 'line of best fit' from now on. The **regression line of y on x** is a straight line of the form:

Tip 'b' is the **gradient** and 'a' is the **y-intercept**.

$y = \mathbf{a} + \mathbf{b}x$ where a and b are constants

The '**...of y on x**' part means that x is the explanatory variable, and y is the response variable.

You don't need to know how to calculate a and b, but you should be able to **interpret** their values in context — make sure you give your explanations in the context of the question.

Example 1 

A company is collecting data on the fuel efficiency of a type of lorry. They compare the load on a lorry, x (in tonnes), with the fuel efficiency, y (in km per litre), and calculate the regression line of y on x to be: $y = 12.5 - 0.8x$

Interpret the values of a and b in this context.

The value of **a** tells you that a load of 0 tonnes corresponds to a fuel efficiency of 12.5 km per litre — this is the fixed fuel efficiency of the lorry before you have loaded anything on it.

The value of **b** tells you that for every extra tonne carried, you'd expect the lorry's fuel efficiency to fall by 0.8 km per litre (since when x increases by 1, y falls by 0.8).

Interpolation and extrapolation

You can use a regression line to predict values of your **response variable**. There are two forms of this — **interpolation** and **extrapolation**.

Tip You can only use a regression line to predict a value of the response variable — **not** the explanatory variable.

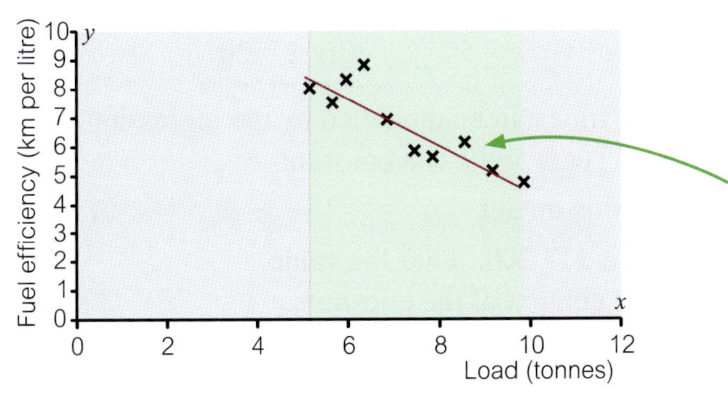

This scatter diagram shows the data from the example on the previous page that was used to calculate the regression line, with the fuel efficiency of a lorry plotted against different loads.

In the data, the values of x are between 5.1 and 9.8.

- When you use values of x within this range (i.e. values of x in the yellow part of the graph) to predict corresponding values of y, this is called **interpolation**. It's okay to do this — the predicted value should be reliable.
- When you use values of x **outside** the range of your original data (i.e. values of x in the grey part of the graph) to predict corresponding values of y, this is called **extrapolation**. These predictions can be **unreliable** — so you need to be very cautious about it. In the example, you'd need to be very careful about using a value of x less than 5.1 or greater than 9.8.
- This is because you don't have any evidence that the relationship described by your regression line is true for values of x less than 5.1 or greater than 9.8 — if the relationship turns out **not to be valid** for these values of x, then your prediction could be wrong.

Example 2 

The length of a spring (y, in cm) when loaded with different masses (m, in g) has the regression line of y on m: $y = 7.8 + 0.01043m$

a) Estimate the length of the spring when loaded with a mass of: (i) 370 g (ii) 670 g

(i) $m = 370$, so $y = 7.8 + 0.01043 \times 370 = 11.7$ cm (1 d.p.)

(ii) $m = 670$, so $y = 7.8 + 0.01043 \times 670 = 14.8$ cm (1 d.p.)

b) The smallest value of m is 200 and the largest value of m is 500. Comment on the reliability of the estimates in part a).

(i) $m = 370$ falls within the range of the original data for m, so this is an interpolation. This means the result should be fairly reliable.

(ii) $m = 670$ falls outside the range of the original data for m, so this is an extrapolation. This means the regression line may not be valid, and you need to treat this result with caution.

Problem Solving Questions can use variables other than x and y — it doesn't change the working out but you may have to identify which is the explanatory variable and which is the response.

Exercise 2.15

Q1 The equation of the regression line of y on x is $y = 1.67 + 0.107x$.

a) Which variable is the response variable?

b) Find the predicted value of y corresponding to: (i) $x = 5$ (ii) $x = 20$

E M Q2 The value (£V) of a particular model of car over time can be modelled by the regression line $V = 30\,000 - ka$, where a is the age of the car in years and k is a constant.

a) Write down the value of a new car based on this model. *[1 mark]*

b) The value of a car that is exactly 8 years old is £17 200. Find the value of k and explain what this value means in the context of the question. *[3 marks]*

c) The newest car in the data set used to generate the model for the value of a car was 2 years old, and the oldest car in the data set was 12 years old. Comment on the reliability of the model for predicting the value of:
(i) a 5-year-old car, (ii) an 18-year-old car. *[2 marks]*

P M Q3 A volunteer counted the number of spots (s) on an area of skin after d days of acne treatment, where d had values 2, 6, 10, 14, 18 and 22. The equation of the regression line of s on d is $s = 58.8 - 2.47d$.

a) Estimate the number of spots the volunteer had on day 7. Comment on the reliability of your answer.

b) She forgot to count how many spots she had before starting to use the product. Estimate this number. Comment on your answer.

c) The volunteer claims that the regression equation must be wrong, because it predicts that after 30 days she should have a negative number of spots. Comment on this claim.

E P M Q4 The average length of the fish in a stocked pond was recorded at the start of every decade since the 1970s. The regression line with equation $l = 67.6 - 2.7d$ models the average length, l cm, of the fish in the pond, in decade d since the 1970s, with the 1970s being decade $d = 1$. The model is based on 5 data values.

a) Use the model to estimate the average length of a fish from the pond in the:
(i) 1990s, (ii) 2010s. *[2 marks]*

b) A local byelaw states that fish less than 18 cm must be released after capture. Find the first decade in which the average length of a fish from the pond is expected to be less than 18 cm. State an assumption you have made and explain why this prediction is unreliable. *[4 marks]*

Challenge

E P Q5 The regression line of y on x is $y = A + Bx$ where A and B are positive constants.

a) Describe the correlation between x and y, justifying your answer. *[1 mark]*

b) The data points (4.5, 9.5) and (10.2, 17.48) lie on the regression line. Find the values of A and B. *[3 marks]*

c) Briefly explain why the strength of the correlation between x and y can't be interpreted from the regression line equation. *[1 mark]*

2 Review Exercise

M Q1 Twenty phone calls were made by a householder one evening.
The lengths of the calls (in minutes to the nearest minute) are recorded in the table below.

Length of calls	0 - 2	3 - 5	6 - 8	9 - 15
Number of calls	10	6	3	1

Show this data on: a) a frequency polygon, b) a histogram.

E P M Q2 Total lung capacity (TLC, x) is the maximum volume a person's lungs can hold, measured in litres. The histogram on the right shows the TLCs recorded for 30 adults. The frequency for the class interval $6 \leq x < 7$ is 5.

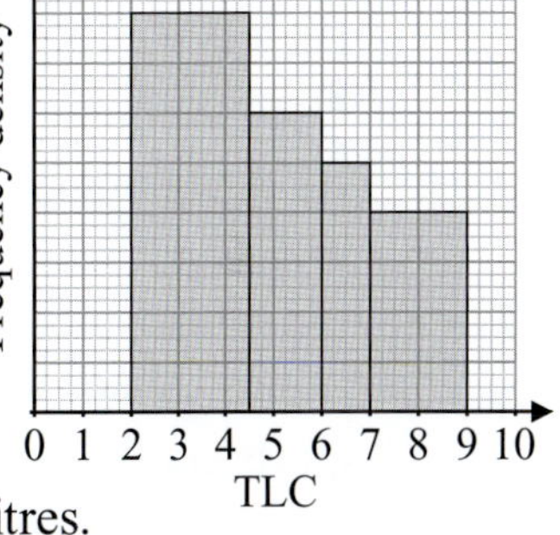

a) Find the number of adults with a TLC between 2 and 6 litres. *[2 marks]*

b) Estimate the number of adults that had a TLC of less than 5 litres. *[1 marks]*

c) Typically, 70% of the population have a TLC between 4 and 8 litres. Are these 30 adults typical of the population? Justify your answer. *[3 marks]*

M Q3 The table below shows how many concerts a group of people attended in 2019.

No. of live concerts	0	1	2	3	4	5	6
Frequency	2	5	16	15	10	9	8

a) Find the mean number of concerts attended.

b) Find the median and the modal number of concerts attended.

Q4 Calculate the mean, median and mode of the data in the table.

x	0	1	2	3	4
f	5	4	4	2	1

M Q5 The speeds of 60 cars travelling in a 40 mph speed limit area were measured to the nearest mph. The data is summarised in the table. Estimate the mean and median, and state the modal class.

Speed (mph)	30 - 34	35 - 39	40 - 44	45 - 50
Frequency	12	37	9	2

P Q6 A set of five values have the following properties:

- The median and the mode are equal.
- The mode occurs three times.
- One value is less than the mode.
- The mean of the values is 6.4.
- There is an outlier with a value twice that of the median.

a) Show that the lowest of the five values is the difference between 32 and five times the mode.

b) Given that the mean of the lowest and highest values is 7, find the five values.

Q7 Two data sets, A and B, are given below:

A: 16, 41, 28, 23, 7, 11, 37, 16, 9, 21, 26, 18, 14, 31, 8

B: 33, 38, 25, 15, 42, 12, 6, 24, 30, 15, 19, 15, 40, 36, 24

Calculate: a) the range of B b) the interquartile range of A

c) the 20% to 80% interpercentile range of B

Q8 a) Draw a cumulative frequency diagram for the following data:

r	$0 \le r < 2$	$2 \le r < 4$	$4 \le r < 6$	$6 \le r < 8$	$8 \le r < 10$
Frequency	2	6	7	4	1

b) Use your cumulative frequency diagram to estimate the number of r-values that are:

(i) less than 3 (ii) more than 5 (iii) between 3.5 and 7

c) Use your cumulative frequency diagram to estimate:

(i) the interquartile range (ii) the 10% to 90% interpercentile range

E P M Q9 The cumulative frequency graph on the right shows the times it takes 160 amateur athletes to run 400 m.

A sports coach uses this graph to determine the qualifying times for Novice, Intermediate and Advanced competitions for 400 m runners. The middle 80% of athletes are entered into the Intermediate competition, with faster runners entered in the Advanced competition, and slower runners in the Novice competition.

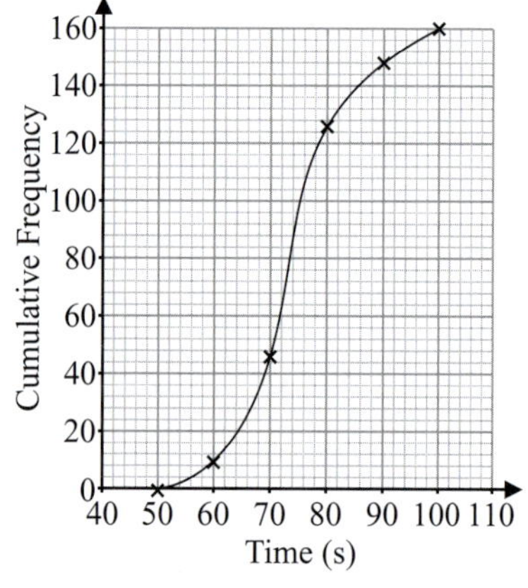

a) Work out the qualifying times the coach should choose for the Intermediate and Advanced competitions. *[4 marks]*

b) The coach decides that if any of the slowest times are outliers, those athletes will not be entered for any of the competitions. Using $Q_3 + 1.5 \times \text{IQR}$ as the upper fence, estimate the percentage of athletes who may not get entered for any competition. *[4 marks]*

M Q10 Two workers iron 10 items of clothing each and record the time, to the nearest minute, that each takes:

Worker A: 3 5 2 7 10 4 5 5 4 12

Worker B: 4 4 8 6 7 8 9 10 11 9

a) For worker A's times, find:

(i) the median,

(ii) the lower and upper quartiles,

(iii) whether there are any outliers, using the fences $Q_1 - 1.5 \times \text{IQR}$ and $Q_3 + 1.5 \times \text{IQR}$.

b) Draw two box plots, using the same scale, to represent the times of each worker.

c) Make one statement comparing the two sets of data.

d) Which worker would be better to employ? Give a reason for your answer.

E P M Q11 This box plot shows the time, in seconds, it took 20 people to complete a 1 km bike ride.

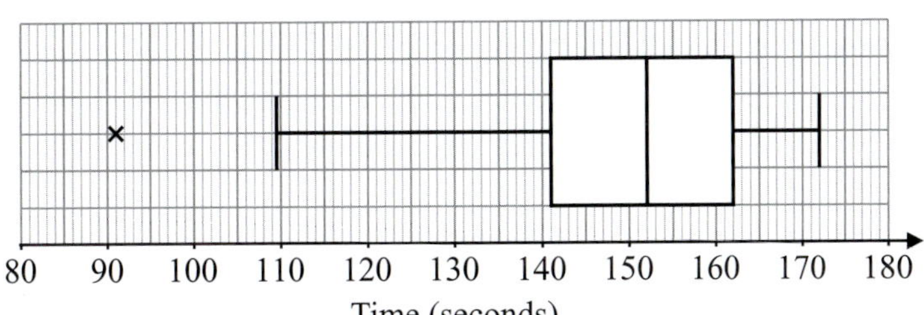

a) Write down the time(s) of any outliers. *[1 mark]*

b) Write down the time of the second quickest bike ride. *[1 mark]*

c) Find the interquartile range. *[2 marks]*

d) Estimate the time by which 90% of participants finish the bike ride. *[3 marks]*

Q12 Find the mean and standard deviation of the following numbers: 11, 12, 14, 17, 21, 23, 27

M Q13 The scores in an IQ test for 50 people are recorded in the table below.

Score	100 - 106	107 - 113	114 - 120	121 - 127	128 - 134
Frequency	6	11	22	9	2

Estimate the mean and variance of the distribution.

E P M Q14 The table below shows the daily total sunshine (s, hours) for Hurn for 15 days in May 1987.

Day	1	2	3	4	5	6	7	8	9	10	11	12	13	14	15
Sunshine (s, hours)	n/a	1.8	13	7	7.1	5.9	6.1	7.4	11.8	7.2	7.1	7.6	4.2	5.7	12.2

a) Use your knowledge of the large data set to explain what is meant by n/a in the table. *[1 mark]*

The data for days 2 to 15 can be summarised as follows:

$$n = 14 \qquad \sum s = 104.1 \qquad \sum s^2 = 896.65$$

b) Calculate the mean and standard deviation for daily total sunshine for days 2 to 15. *[3 marks]*

c) When calculating the standard deviation, a student used the incorrect value of 11.2 hours for day 15. Explain whether their value for the standard deviation will be lower or higher than the real value. *[2 marks]*

An outlier is an observation that lies more than 3 standard deviations from the mean.

d) Show that there are no outliers. *[2 marks]*

P Q15 For a set of data, $n = 100$, $\sum(x - 20) = 125$, and $\sum(x - 20)^2 = 221$.

a) Find the mean and standard deviation of x.

b) Use the fences ($\bar{x} \pm 2$ standard deviations) to test whether the value $x = 19.6$ is an outlier.

M Q16 The time taken (to the nearest minute) for a commuter to travel to work on 20 consecutive work days is recorded in the table. Use the coding $y = x - 35.5$ to estimate the mean and standard deviation of the times, where x is the class mid-point.

Time	Frequency, f
30 - 33	3
34 - 37	6
38 - 41	7
42 - 45	4

E M Q17 The table below represents the daily mean air pressure in Camborne from 1st May to 31st October 1987. The data has been coded using the formula $y = \frac{x - 1000}{4}$, where x is the daily mean air pressure in hPa.

y	$-5 \le y < -3$	$-3 \le y < 0$	$0 \le y < 2$	$2 \le y < 5$	$5 \le y < 7$	$7 \le y < 9$
Frequency	1	7	23	90	55	8

a) Find an estimate of the mean of the original data. *[3 marks]*

b) Find an estimate of the standard deviation of the original data. *[3 marks]*

c) Outliers are defined as values that lie more than 3 standard deviations from the mean. Determine whether there are any outliers in this data. *[3 marks]*

E M Q18 The masses of 40 killer whales were coded using $x = \frac{m - 3000}{1000}$, where m is the mass in kg. The following summary statistics were obtained from the coded data:

$$\sum x = 52.4 \qquad S_{xx} = 9.8$$

Work out the mean and standard deviation of the masses of the killer whales. *[4 marks]*

E M Q19 The table below summarises the distances, to the nearest mile, that 120 people travelled to a sci-fi convention in 2018.

Distance (miles)	Frequency
0 - 10	14
11 - 25	29
26 - 40	31
41 - 60	27
61 - 80	13
81 - 120	6

a) Estimate the mean and standard deviation for this data using your calculator. Give your answer to 3 significant figures. *[3 marks]*

b) Use interpolation to estimate the interquartile range for this data. *[4 marks]*

In 2019, the convention is held again. The mean and standard deviation of the distances travelled were 59.3 miles and 12.1 miles, respectively, for a different group of 120 people.

c) Compare the distances travelled by the two groups. *[2 marks]*

M Q20 The table below shows the results of some measurements concerning alcoholic cocktails. Here, x = total volume in ml, and y = percentage alcohol concentration by volume.

x	90	100	100	150	160	200	240	250	290	300
y	40	35	25	30	25	25	20	25	15	7

a) Draw a scatter diagram representing this information.

b) Does the data suggest any correlation?

E M Q21 The scatter diagram below shows a golfer's score plotted against the number of hours they spent practising each week.

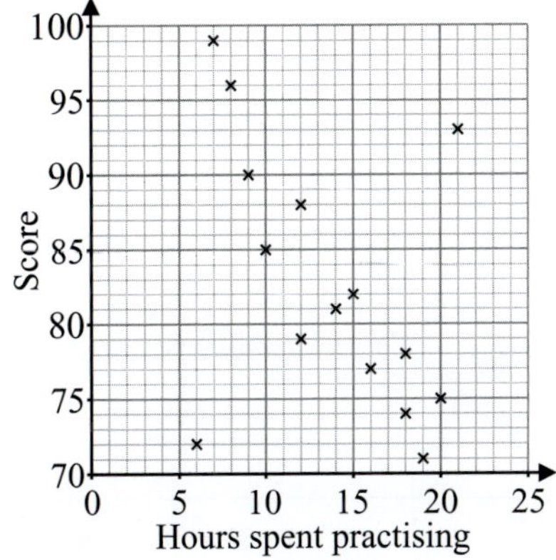

a) Describe the correlation shown on this scatter diagram. *[1 mark]*

b) Identify any possible outliers from the scatter diagram. *[1 mark]*

c) Suggest a possible reason for outliers in this data. *[1 mark]*

M Q22 For each pair of variables below, state which would be the explanatory variable and which would be the response variable.

a) 'number of volleyball-related injuries in a year' and 'number of sunny days that year'

b) 'number of rainy days in a year' and 'number of board game-related injuries that year'

c) 'a person's disposable income' and 'amount they spend on luxuries'

d) 'number of trips to the loo in a day' and 'number of cups of tea drunk that day'

M Q23 The radius in mm, r, and the mass in grams, m, of 10 randomly selected blueberry pancakes are given in the table below.

r	48.0	51.0	52.0	54.5	55.1	53.6	50.0	52.6	49.4	51.2
m	100	105	108	120	125	118	100	115	98	110

The regression line of m on r has equation $m = 3.94r - 94$.

a) Use the regression line to estimate the mass of a blueberry pancake of radius 60 mm.

b) Comment on the reliability of your estimate, giving a reason for your answer.

Challenge

E P M Q24 The histogram below shows the time taken, in hours, by 80 runners to complete the London Marathon. There are 8 runners in the '2-3 hours' class.

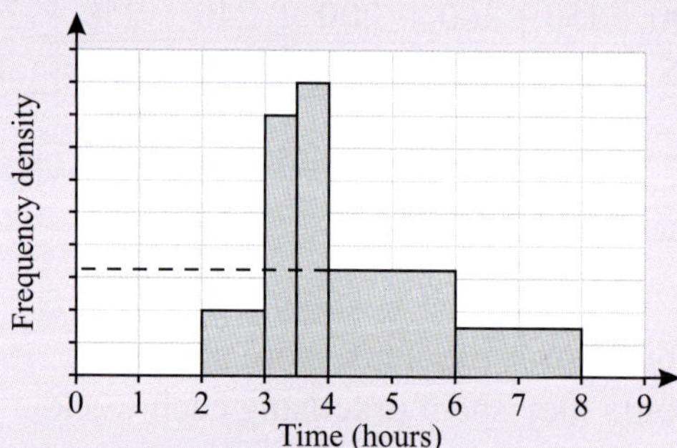

a) Find an estimate for the mean time taken by these runners to complete the marathon. *[6 marks]*

In order to qualify for the Boston Marathon, runners need to complete the London marathon in less than 3 hours 20 minutes.

b) Estimate how many of the 80 runners qualify for the Boston Marathon. *[2 marks]*

P M Q25 The table below shows the heights of sunflowers recorded on the same day.

Height (h cm)	$140 \leq h < 150$	$150 \leq h < 160$	$160 \leq h < 170$	$170 \leq h < 180$
Frequency	24	36	p	18

Given that the data in the table produces an estimate for the mean height of a sunflower of 159 cm, find the value of p.

E P M Q26 The data in the table on the right is taken from the large data set. It concerns the daily mean visibility, measured in decametres (Dm), from 1st May to 31st October at Heathrow, 1987.

Find estimates for two values a and b such that the middle 70% of the data lies in the interval $a \leq v \leq b$. *[5 marks]*

Daily mean visibility, v (Dm)	Frequency
$500 \leq v < 1000$	6
$1000 \leq v < 2000$	25
$2000 \leq v < 2500$	42
$2500 \leq v < 3000$	49
$3000 \leq v < 4000$	57
$4000 \leq v < 4500$	5

P Q27 A data set is such that $Q_3 - Q_2 = 2(Q_2 - Q_1)$. The median is 154 and the interquartile range is 33. The fences to determine outliers are defined as $Q_1 - (1.5 \times \text{IQR})$ and $Q_3 + (1.5 \times \text{IQR})$. Determine whether the data values 88 and 220 are outliers.

E M Q28 The ages, a years, and blood cortisol levels, c in micrograms per decilitre (μg/dl), of 250 adult hospital patients are recorded. The equation of the regression line of c on a is $c = 9.4 + 0.16a$.

a) Describe the correlation between age and blood cortisol level. *[1 mark]*

b) Give an interpretation of 0.16 in the equation of the regression line. *[1 mark]*

c) A researcher claims that the blood cortisol level of a 10-year-old child should be 11 μg/dl. Comment on the validity of this claim, giving a reason for your answer. *[1 mark]*

2 Chapter Summary

1 Data consists of a set of observations, each recording a value of a particular variable.
- Qualitative variables take non-numerical values, e.g. favourite colour.
- Discrete quantitative variables take only specific numerical values, e.g. shoe size.
- Continuous quantitative variables can take any numerical value in a particular range, e.g. height.

2 Histograms represent continuous data from grouped frequency tables.

The vertical axis shows frequency density $\left(= \frac{\text{frequency}}{\text{class width}}\right)$.

The area of each bar is proportional to the frequency in that class.

3 The mean, median and mode are measures of location — they show where the 'centre' of the data lies.
- The mean is calculated using the formula: $\overline{x} = \frac{\sum x}{n}$ or $\frac{\sum fx}{\sum f}$.
- To find the mean of grouped data, use the class mid-point for each reading of x.
- To estimate the median of grouped data use linear interpolation.

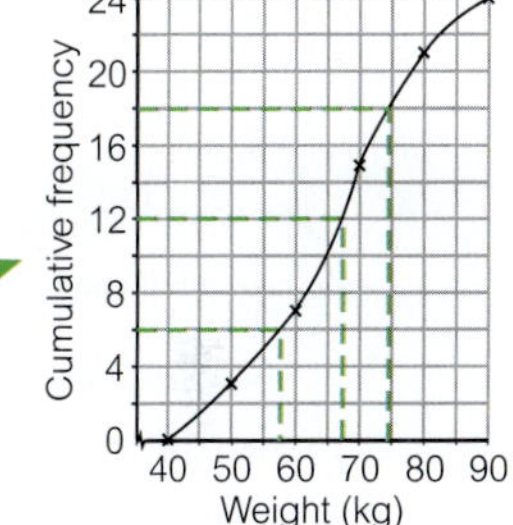

4 The range, the interquartile range, and interpercentile ranges are all measures of dispersion — they measure how spread out data values are. The interquartile range measures the range of the middle 50% of the data.

5 A cumulative frequency diagram plots the running total of frequencies in a data set. You can use it to estimate the median and quartiles.

6 A box plot gives a visual summary of a data set. It shows the position of the median, quartiles and outliers.

7 Variance and standard deviation are measures of dispersion from the mean.
- Variance $= \frac{\sum (x - \overline{x})^2}{n}$ or $\frac{\sum x^2}{n} - \overline{x}^2$ and standard deviation $= \sqrt{\text{variance}}$.
- If the data is given in a frequency table, then variance $= \frac{\sum fx^2}{\sum f} - \overline{x}^2$.

8 You can code data values to make them easier to work with. If the data is coded as $y = \frac{x - \mathrm{a}}{\mathrm{b}}$, then the mean $\overline{y} = \frac{\overline{x} - \mathrm{a}}{\mathrm{b}}$ and standard deviation of $y = \frac{\text{standard deviation of } x}{\mathrm{b}}$.

9 Correlation describes the relationship between a pair of variables — it can be strong or weak, positive or negative. You can see this relationship on a scatter diagram. If the variables are correlated, you can fit a regression line of the form $y = \mathrm{a} + \mathrm{b}x$ to the data.

10 You can use a regression line to predict values of y by interpolating or extrapolating — taking values of x from inside or outside of the known range of data. Extrapolating is often unreliable, as you can't tell if the trend continues outside the observed range.

Probability

3

Learning Objectives

Once you've completed this chapter, you should be able to:

- Find probabilities of events when outcomes are equally likely.
- Identify sample spaces.
- Construct Venn diagrams and two-way tables and use them to find probabilities.
- Use the addition law to find probabilities.
- Recognise mutually exclusive and independent events.
- Use the product law for independent events.
- Understand and use tree diagrams.

Prior Knowledge Check

1 Peter rolls a standard six-sided dice 60 times. It lands on 4 a total of 10 times. Can you conclude whether his dice is biased or not? Give a reason for your answer. *see GCSE Maths*

2 The Venn diagram shows the number of pupils in a class who play tennis (A) and football (B).
Find the probability that a randomly chosen person plays football.

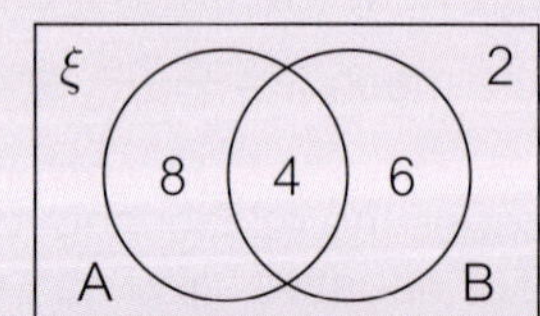

see GCSE Maths

3 A bag contains three white balls and five black balls.
Simran picks two balls at random without replacing either.
a) Draw a tree diagram to show the possible outcomes.
b) Calculate the probability that she picks two white balls. *see GCSE Maths*

3.1 The Basics of Probability

In a **trial** (or experiment), the things that can happen are called **outcomes**.
For example, if you roll a standard six-sided dice, the numbers 1-6 are the outcomes.

Events are 'groups' of one or more outcomes. So a possible event for the dice roll is that 'you roll an odd number' (corresponding to the outcomes 1, 3 and 5). If any outcome corresponding to an event happens, then you can say that the event has also happened.

When all the possible outcomes are **equally likely**, you can work out the **probability** of an event using this formula:

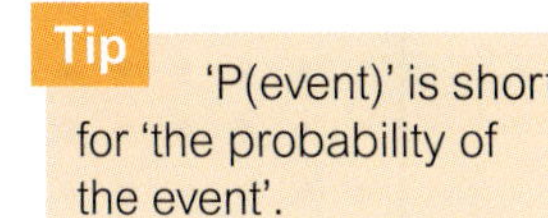

Tip 'P(event)' is short for 'the probability of the event'.

$$P(\text{event}) = \frac{\text{Number of outcomes where event happens}}{\text{Total number of possible outcomes}}$$

This gives a probability **between 0** (the event is impossible) **and 1** (it's certain to happen) — it can be written as a **fraction** or **decimal**. You can also multiply by 100 to give a probability as a **percentage**.

Example 1  M

Tip It's usually best to simplify your answer as much as possible.

A bag contains 15 balls — 5 are red, 6 are blue and 4 are green.
If one ball is selected from the bag at random, find the probability that:

a) the ball is red

The event is 'a red ball is selected'.

$P(\text{red ball}) = \frac{5}{15} = \frac{1}{3}$

There are 5 red balls, so there are 5 outcomes where this event happens out of 15 possible outcomes.

b) the ball is blue

The event is 'a blue ball is selected'.

$P(\text{blue ball}) = \frac{6}{15} = \frac{2}{5}$

There are 6 blue balls, so there are 6 outcomes where this event happens out of 15 possible outcomes.

c) the ball is red or green

The event is 'a red ball or a green ball is selected'.

$P(\text{red or green ball}) = \frac{9}{15} = \frac{3}{5}$

There are 5 red and 4 green balls, so there are 9 outcomes where this event happens out of 15 possible outcomes.

3.2 The Sample Space

The **sample space** (called S) is the set of **all possible outcomes** of a trial. Drawing a **diagram** of the sample space can help you to count the outcomes you're interested in. Then it's an easy task to find probabilities using the formula above.

If a trial consists of **two separate activities**, then a good way to draw your sample space is as a **grid**. If every outcome of one activity is possible with every outcome of the other, then the **total number of outcomes** equals the number of outcomes for one activity multiplied by the number of outcomes for the other activity.

Example 1 M

A fair six-sided dice is rolled twice.

a) Draw a sample space diagram to show all the possible outcomes.

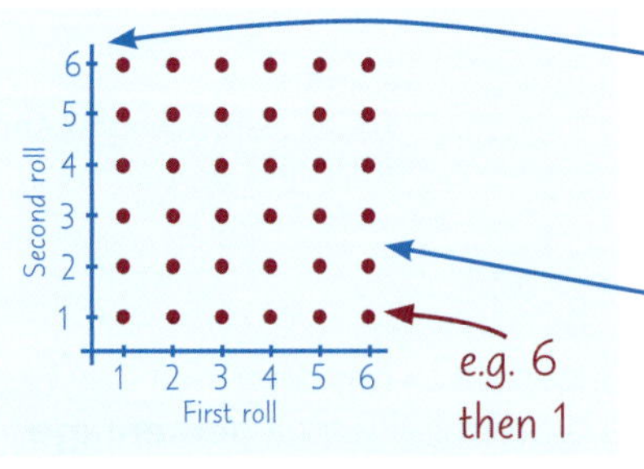

Draw a pair of axes, with the outcomes for the first roll on one axis and the outcomes for the second roll on the other axis.

Mark the intersection of each pair of numbers to show every possible outcome for the two rolls combined.

b) Find the probability of rolling an odd number, followed by a 1.

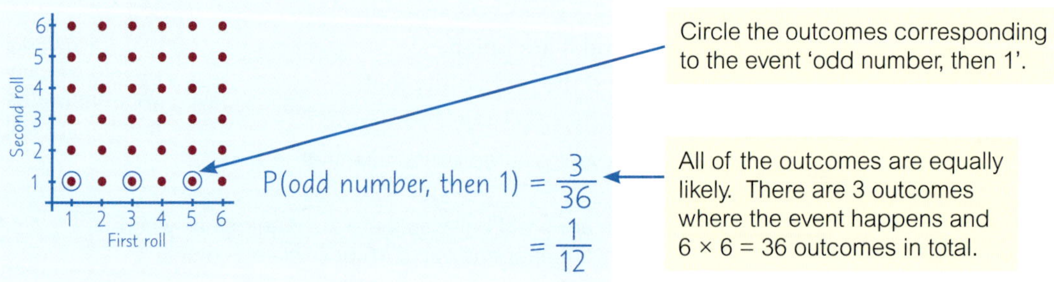

Sometimes, the outcomes you want aren't the numbers themselves, but are calculated from them...

Example 2 

Two bags each contain five cards. Bag A contains cards numbered 1, 3, 3, 4 and 5, and bag B contains cards numbered 1, 2, 4, 4 and 5. A card is selected at random from each bag and the numbers on the two cards are added together to give a total score.

Use a sample space diagram to find the probability that the total score is no more than 6.

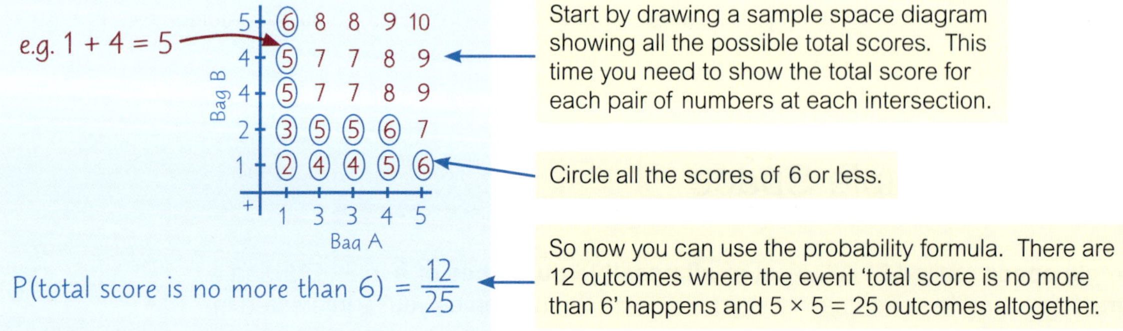

Exercise 3.1-3.2

M Q1 A packet of flower seeds contains 21 marigold, 10 poppy, 19 cornflower and 15 daisy seeds. One seed is taken from the packet at random. Find the probability that the seed is:

a) a poppy seed b) a marigold or cornflower seed c) not a daisy seed

M Q2 A standard pack of 52 playing cards contains four suits: hearts, diamonds, spades and clubs. One card is selected at random from the pack. Find the probability of selecting:

a) the 7 of diamonds b) the queen of spades

c) a 9 of any suit d) a heart or a diamond

M Q3 The sample space diagram on the right represents a dice game where two fair dice are rolled and the product of the two scores is calculated.

a) Find the probability that the product is a prime number.

b) Find the probability that the product is less than 7.

c) Find the probability that the product is a multiple of 10.

×	1	2	3	4	5	6
1	1	2	3	4	5	6
2	2	4	6	8	10	12
3	3	6	9	12	15	18
4	4	8	12	16	20	24
5	5	10	15	20	25	30
6	6	12	18	24	30	36

P M Q4 Ross has a fair dice with an unusual number of sides, and a set of cards with a different number on each card. He picks a card at random and rolls the dice, then adds the two numbers to get a total score. The sample space diagram shows all the possible total scores.

a) How many sides does Ross's dice have?

b) What number is on the third card?

c) What is the probability that the total score is less than 7?

		Dice						
	+	1	2	3	4	5	6	7
Card	2	3	4	5	6	7	8	9
	4	5	6	7	8	9	10	11
	?	6	7	8	9	10	11	12
	7	8	9	10	11	12	13	14
	9	10	11	12	13	14	15	16

M Q5 A game involves picking a card at random from 10 cards, numbered 1 to 10, and tossing a fair coin.

a) Draw a sample space diagram to show all the possible outcomes.

b) Find the probability that the card selected shows an even number and the coin shows 'tails'.

M Q6 Martha rolls two fair six-sided dice numbered 1-6 and calculates a score by subtracting the smaller result from the larger.

a) Draw a sample space diagram to show all the possible outcomes.

b) Find P(the score is zero).

c) Find P(the score is greater than 5).

d) What is the most likely score? And what is its probability?

P Q7 A computer generates a random four-digit number from 0000 to 9999 inclusive. Find the probability that the number generated:

a) has digits which are all consecutive and increasing.

b) ends in a 0.

M Q8 Spinner 1 has five equal sections, labelled 2, 3, 5, 7 and 11, and spinner 2 has five equal sections, labelled 2, 4, 6, 8 and 10. If each spinner is spun once, find the probability that the number on spinner 2 is greater than the number on spinner 1.

E P M Q9 A game involves rolling a six-sided dice, then spinning a five-sided spinner numbered 0-4. The scores from the dice and the spinner are added together to give a final score.

a) Draw a sample space diagram for this game. *[2 marks]*

b) Assuming that the dice and spinner are both fair, find the probability that the final score is at least 7. *[1 mark]*

It is found that the dice is not fair. The probability of it landing on 1 is 0.25 and the probability of it landing on each of the other numbers is 0.15.

c) Given the probabilities above, explain whether the probability that the final score is at least 7 is greater than, equal to, or less than the probability you found in b). You do not need to calculate the probability. *[1 mark]*

E P M Q10 At the start of the day, the ratio of female to male fish in a pet shop tank is 13 : 14. When a customer wants to buy a fish, one is randomly selected from the tank.

a) Find the probability that the next fish selected for a customer will be female. *[1 mark]*

At the start of the day, there were a total of 143 female fish in the tank. Since then, six females and seven males have been sold to customers.

b) Taking account of any fish already sold, find the probability that the next fish selected to be sold to a customer is female. *[2 marks]*

P M Q11 The integers from 1 to $2k + 1$, where $k \geq 100$, are written on separate cards and placed in a bag. One of the cards is selected at random and the number noted. Find expressions in terms of k for the probability that the card has written on it:

a) an odd number less than 20,

b) a square number less than or equal to 100, or an odd number less than 100,

c) an even number.

Challenge

E P M Q12 A circular archery target has three separate regions, A, B and C, as shown in the diagram. The regions are formed by concentric circles of radii 5 cm, 25 cm and 50 cm respectively.

C
B
A

Jon is new to archery. When he hits the target, the probability that the arrow hits a particular region is proportional to the region's area.

a) Show that when he hits the target the probability that Jon's arrow hits region A is 0.01. *[2 marks]*

b) Find the probability that when he hits the target his arrow hits region:

(i) B *[1 mark]*

(ii) C *[1 mark]*

c) Jon's archery coach shoots an arrow and hits the target. Explain why the probabilities calculated in a) and b) may not apply to their shot. *[1 mark]*

3.3 Using Venn Diagrams

A **Venn diagram** shows how a collection of **objects** is split up into different **groups**, where everything in a group has something in common.

Here, for example, the objects are **outcomes** and the groups are **events**.
So the collection of objects, represented by the **rectangle**, is the **sample space** (**S**).
Inside the rectangle are two **circles** representing **two events**, **A** and **B**.

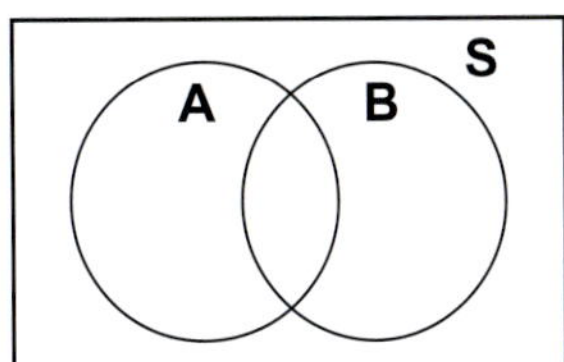

The **circle A** represents all the outcomes corresponding to event A, and the **circle B** represents all the outcomes corresponding to event B.

The diagram is usually labelled with the **number of outcomes** (or the **probabilities**) represented by each area.

As **S** is the set of **all possible outcomes**, the **total probability** in S equals **1**.

The area where the circles overlap represents all the outcomes corresponding to **both event A and event B** happening.

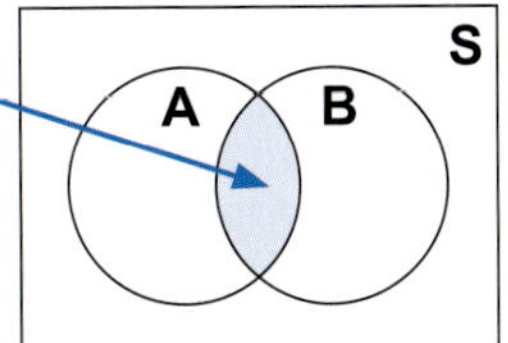

Tip If events don't have any outcomes in common, then the circles won't overlap. These events are called **mutually exclusive**.

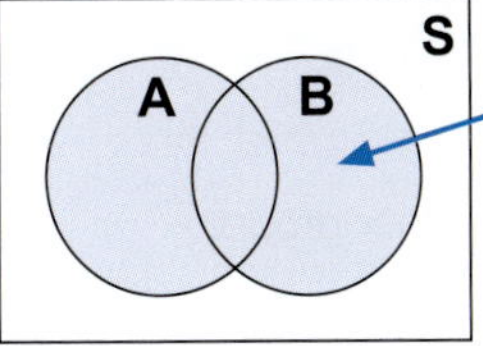

The shaded area represents all the outcomes corresponding to **either event A or event B or both** happening.

In probability questions, "**either event A or event B or both**" is often shortened to just "**A or B**".

The shaded area represents all the outcomes corresponding to **event A not** happening.

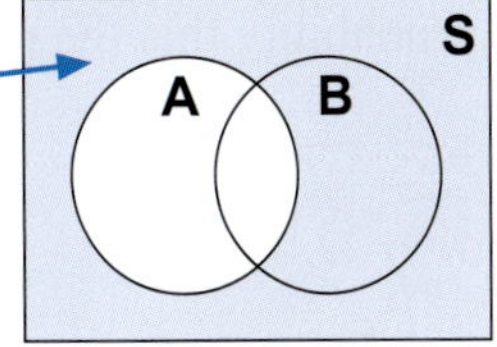

Since an event A must either happen or not happen, and since P(S) = 1:

$$\mathbf{P(A) + P(not\ A) = 1 \Rightarrow P(not\ A) = 1 - P(A)}$$

This can also be written as:

$$\mathbf{P(A) + P(A') = 1 \Rightarrow P(A') = 1 - P(A)}$$

Tip The event "not A" is often written as A', and is called the complement of A.

The shaded area represents all the outcomes corresponding to **event B** happening **and event A not** happening.

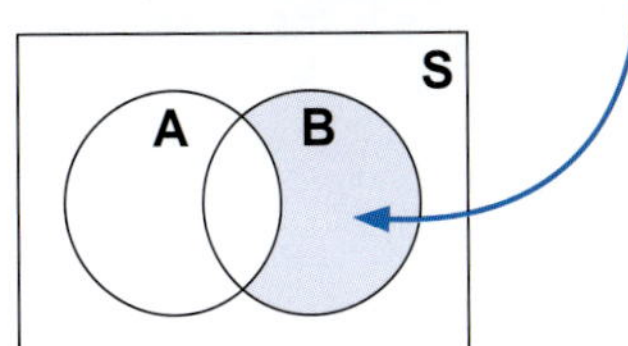

The shaded area represents all the outcomes corresponding to **event A not** happening **and event B not** happening.

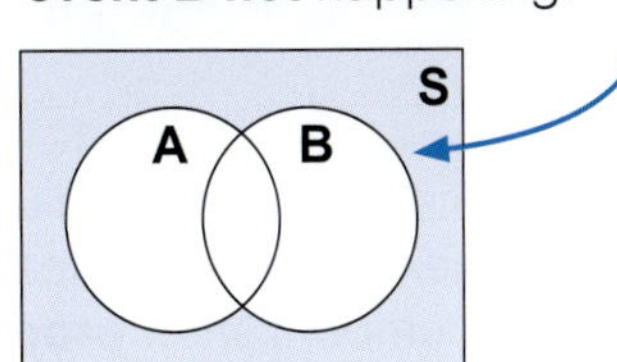

Here's an example where the **objects** are **people**, and they're divided into groups based on whether they have **certain characteristics** in common.

Example 1 

There are 30 boys and girls in a class. 14 of the pupils are girls and 11 of the pupils have brown hair. Of the pupils with brown hair, 6 are boys.

a) Show this information on a Venn diagram.

Let G be the group of girls and BH be the group of pupils with brown hair.

> Firstly, identify the groups. Each group should be defined by a characteristic that a pupil either has or doesn't have.

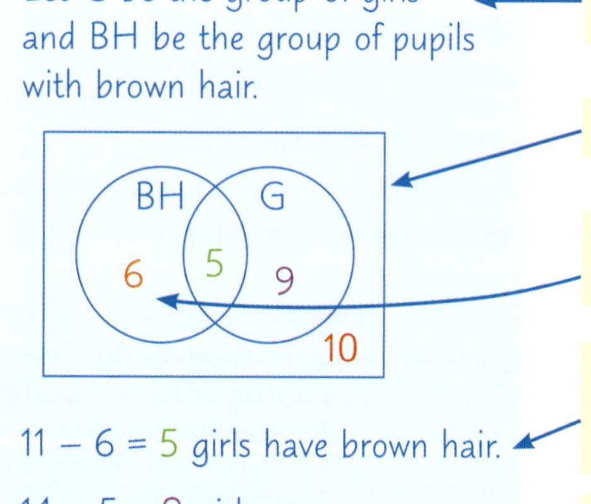

> Draw a Venn diagram with circles representing the groups.

> There are 6 boys with brown hair, so the Venn diagram shows 6 pupils who have brown hair and aren't girls.

$11 - 6 = 5$ girls have brown hair.

> To find the number of pupils that are girls and have brown hair, subtract the number of boys with brown hair from the number of pupils in total with brown hair.

$14 - 5 = 9$ girls don't have brown hair.

> To find the number of pupils who are girls but don't have brown hair, subtract the number of girls with brown hair from the total number of girls.

$30 - (9 + 5 + 6) = 10$ boys don't have brown hair.

> Finally, don't forget the pupils that aren't in either group.

b) A pupil is selected at random from the class.
Find the probability that the pupil is a girl who doesn't have brown hair.

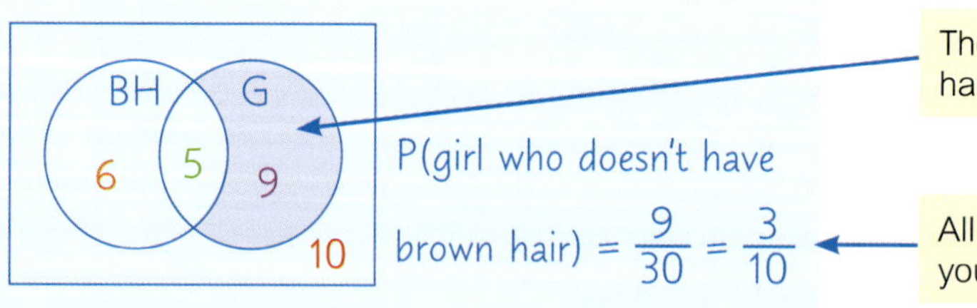

P(girl who doesn't have brown hair) $= \frac{9}{30} = \frac{3}{10}$

> There are 9 girls who don't have brown hair out of the 30 pupils in the class.

> All the outcomes are equally likely so you can use the probability formula.

c) A girl is selected at random from the class. Find the probability that she has brown hair.

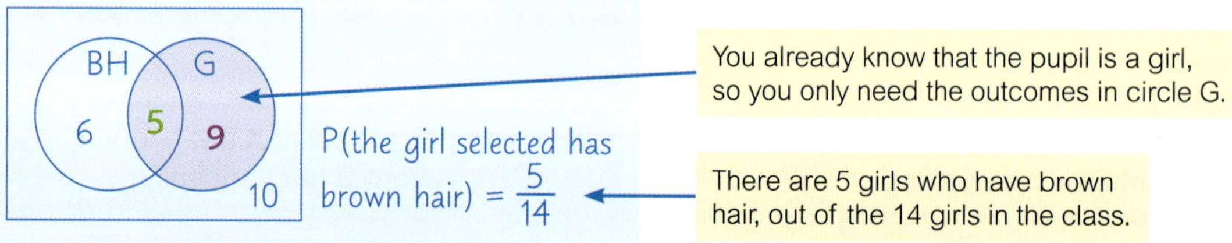

P(the girl selected has brown hair) $= \frac{5}{14}$

> You already know that the pupil is a girl, so you only need the outcomes in circle G.

> There are 5 girls who have brown hair, out of the 14 girls in the class.

You also need to be able to draw and use Venn diagrams for **three groups** (or events). In the next example, instead of showing the 'number of objects' (or outcomes), the numbers show **proportions**, but the ideas are exactly the same.

Example 2 M

A survey was carried out to find out what pets people like.

The proportion who like dogs is 0.6, the proportion who like cats is 0.5, and the proportion who like gerbils is 0.4. The proportion who like dogs and cats is 0.4, the proportion who like cats and gerbils is 0.1, and the proportion who like gerbils and dogs is 0.2. Finally, the proportion who like all three kinds of animal is 0.1.

a) Draw a Venn diagram to represent this information.

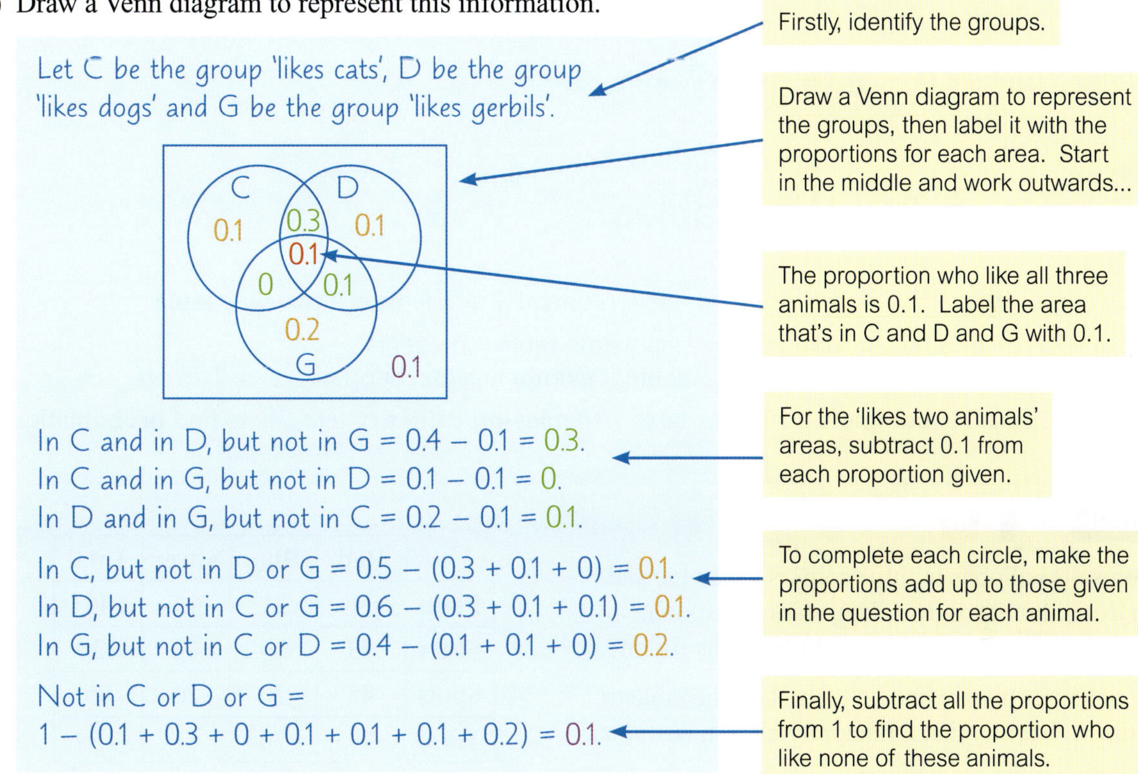

One person who completed the survey is chosen at random.

b) Find the probability that this person likes dogs or cats (or both).

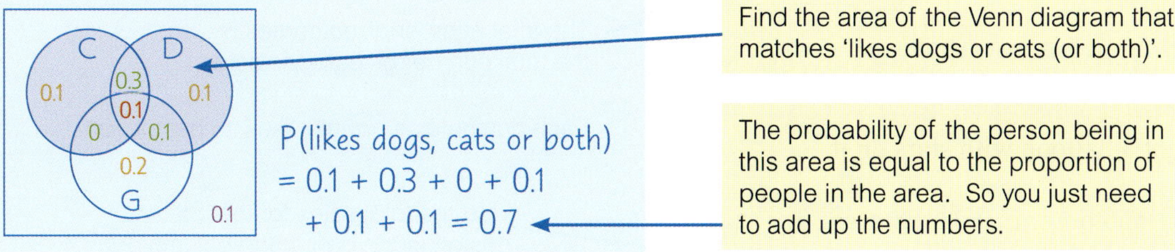

c) Find the probability that this person likes gerbils, but not dogs.

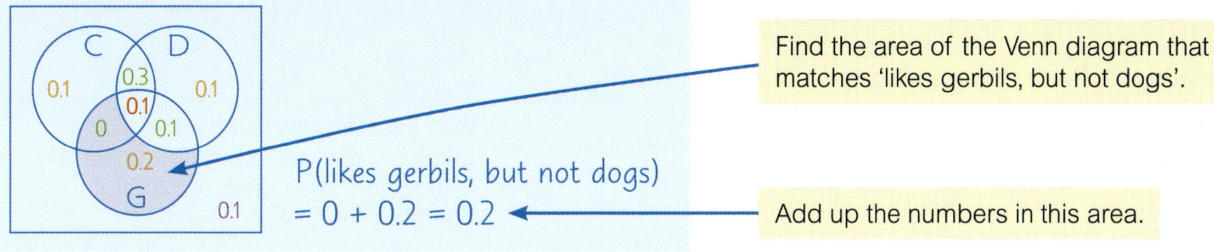

d) One person who said in the survey that they liked dogs is chosen at random. What is the probability this person also said that they like cats?

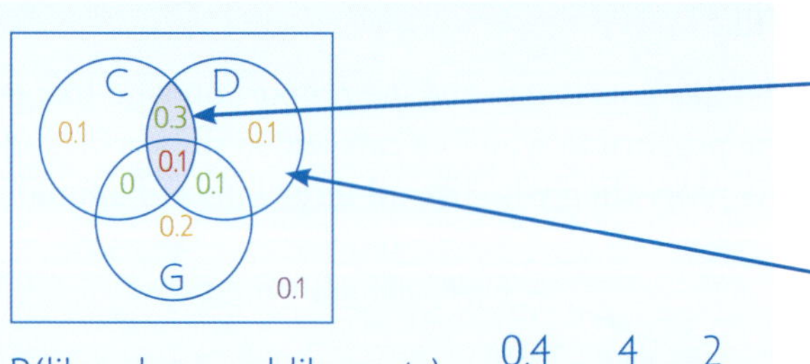

P(likes dogs and likes cats) = $\frac{0.4}{0.6} = \frac{4}{6} = \frac{2}{3}$

This shaded area represents the people who like dogs and also like cats, which is a proportion of 0.3 + 0.1 = 0.4 of the whole group of people.

But you're only interested in the 'likes dogs' circle, not the whole group, so that means you need to divide by 0.3 + 0.1 + 0.1 + 0.1 = 0.6.

3.4 Using Two-Way Tables

Another sort of diagram you can use to represent probability problems is a **two-way table**.

The idea is very similar to Venn diagrams — the **whole table** represents the **sample space** and the **cells** represent different **events** that can happen.

You might be asked to **complete** a two-way table with **missing values** or use one to **find probabilities** of events.

Example 1 

A shop sells balloons in three colours (red, blue and silver), and three designs (plain, stars and spots). The table shows the shop's sales of balloons for one day.

	Red	Blue	Silver	Total
Plain	11	21	13	45
Stars	43	29	48	120
Spots	45	20	20	85
Total	99	70	81	250

Each customer bought one balloon. Use the table to find the probability that a randomly-chosen customer:

a) bought a plain red balloon

11 outcomes match this event, with 250 possible outcomes.

P(bought plain red balloon) = $\frac{11}{250}$

Find the number of customers who bought a plain red balloon. This is the number in the 'Plain' row and the 'Red' column.

The total number of outcomes is the total number of balloons sold.

Each customer is equally likely to be chosen.

b) bought a balloon with stars on it

120 outcomes match the event 'the customer bought a balloon with stars on it'.

P(bought a balloon with stars) = $\frac{120}{250} = \frac{12}{25}$

Find the total sales for the 'Stars' design in the right-hand column.

The total number of possible outcomes is still the total number of balloons sold.

c) bought a balloon that was blue or had spots

70 + 45 + 20 = 135 outcomes

P(bought a blue or spotty balloon) = $\frac{135}{250} = \frac{27}{50}$

Add the numbers of blue balloons to the number of red and silver balloons with spots. Then divide by the total number of possible outcomes.

In the next example, the two-way table shows **proportions** instead of the number of objects (you saw something similar with Venn diagrams on p.79).

Example 2 M

In any week, Carmelita goes to a maximum of two evening classes.
She goes to a dance class, to a knitting class, to both classes, or to neither class.

The probability, P(D), that she attends the dance class is 0.6, the probability, P(K), that she attends the knitting class is 0.3, and the probability that she attends both classes is 0.15.

a) Draw a two-way table showing the probabilities of all possible outcomes.

	D	D'	Total
K	0.15		0.30
K'			
Total	0.60		1.00

Make columns for events D and D' and rows for K and K'. (You could do it the other way round — it doesn't matter which event goes along the top and which goes down the side.)

Now fill in the probabilities you know.
P(D) = 0.6 — that's the total for column D.
P(K) = 0.3 — that's the total for row K.
P(attends both classes) = 0.15 — that goes in the D and K cell.
The total probability is 1, so that goes in the bottom-right cell.

	D	D'	Total
K	0.15	0.15	0.30
K'	0.45	0.25	0.70
Total	0.60	0.40	1.00

Now you can use the totals to fill in the gaps.
For example, for the D' and K cell, 0.3 – 0.15 = 0.15.

b) Find the probability that in a given week:

i) Carmelita attends at least one evening class.

$$P(D \text{ or } K) = 0.15 + 0.45 + 0.15 = 0.75$$

You want the probability that Carmelita attends either the dance class or the knitting class, or both — in other words, P(D or K).

Add up all the probabilities in column D or row K, or both.

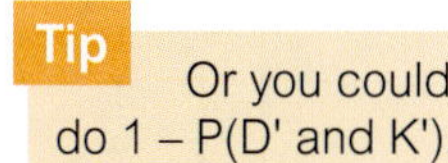

Tip Or you could do 1 – P(D' and K').

ii) She attends exactly one evening class.

$$P(D \text{ and } K') = 0.45$$
$$P(K \text{ and } D') = 0.15$$
$$\text{So } P[(D \text{ and } K') \text{ or } (K \text{ and } D')] = 0.45 + 0.15 = 0.6$$

This time you want the probability that Carmelita attends the dance class but not the knitting class, or the knitting class but not the dance class — P[(D and K') or (K and D')].

Exercise 3.3-3.4

M Q1 The table shows information on the ladybirds being studied by a scientist. Find the probability that a randomly selected ladybird:

a) is red or orange

b) is yellow or has fewer than 10 spots

	Colour of ladybird		
Number of spots	Red	Yellow	Orange
fewer than 10	20	9	1
10 or more	15	3	2

Q2 For events A and B, P(A) = 0.4, P(B) = 0.5 and P(A and B) = 0.15.

a) Draw a Venn diagram to represent events A and B.

b) Find P(A and not B) c) Find P(B and not A)

d) Find P(A or B) e) Find P(neither A nor B)

Q2 Hint You're given probabilities, rather than numbers of outcomes, so label your diagram with probabilities.

M Q3 Rich only ever buys two brands of tea, 'BC Tops' and 'Cumbria Tea', and two brands of coffee, 'Nenco' and 'Yescafé'. On his weekly shopping trip, Rich buys either one brand of tea or no tea, and either one brand of coffee, or no coffee.

a) Copy and complete the two-way table below, which shows the probabilities for each combination of tea and coffee Rich might buy in any one week.

b) Find the probability that, on any given shopping trip:

(i) Rich buys Cumbria Tea and Yescafé,

(ii) Rich buys coffee,

(iii) Rich buys tea but no coffee.

	BC Tops	Cumbria	No tea	Total
Nenco	0.16	0.07		
Yescafé	0.11			0.18
No coffee		0.12	0.14	
Total	0.51		0.27	1

E M Q4 A footwear manufacturer produces three styles of shoe, Sporty, Smart and Casual, in three different colours, white, brown or black. The table on the right shows the number of pairs of each style and colour produced on a particular day.

	Sporty	Smart	Casual
White	140	0	290
Brown	0	320	320
Black	210	450	380

One pair is chosen at random to test for quality.

a) Find the probability that the pair is:

(i) Sporty (ii) Casual and brown, or Sporty and black *[2 marks]*

b) Given that the chosen pair is Smart, find the probability that it is black. *[1 mark]*

E Q5

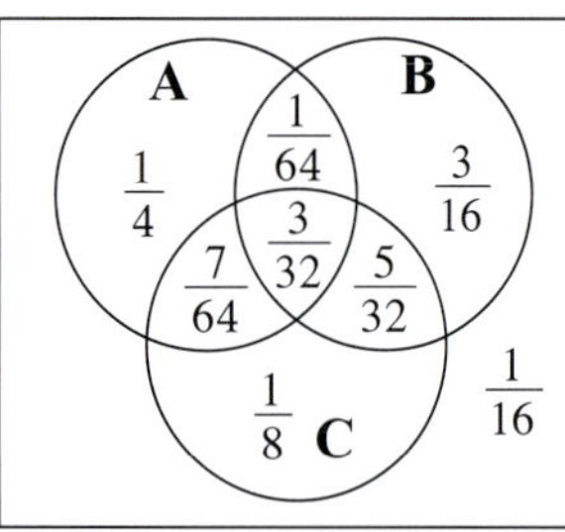

Use the information in the Venn diagram on the left to find the following probabilities:

a) P(A and B and C) *[1 mark]*

b) P(A or B' or C) *[1 mark]*

c) P(A and B' and C') *[1 mark]*

d) P(A' or B' or C) *[1 mark]*

P M Q6 A sixth form college has 144 students.
46 of the students study maths, 38 study physics and 19 study both.

a) Represent the information given above using a two-way table.

b) Find the probability that a randomly selected student from the college studies at least one of either maths or physics.

c) What is the probability that a randomly chosen maths student also studies physics?

Q7 Use the Venn diagram to find the following probabilities:

a) P(L and M) b) P(L and N)

c) P(N and not L) d) P(neither L nor M nor N)

e) P(L or M) f) P(not M)

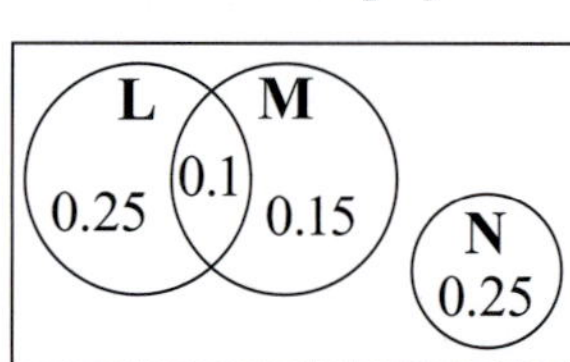

M Q8 Two hundred people were asked which of Spain, France and Germany they have visited. The results are shown in the diagram. Find the probability that a randomly selected person has been to:

a) none of the three countries

b) Germany, given that they have been to France

c) Spain, but not France

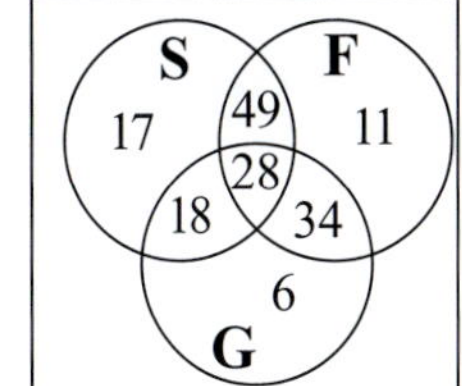

E P M Q9 A researcher is investigating what proportion of the inhabitants of a village are left-handed. They survey the whole village and record the data shown in the table. No-one in the village is both left- and right-handed. If one person surveyed is chosen at random, let L be the event that the person is left-handed and U be the event that the person is under 65.

	Left-handed	Right-handed
Under 65	24	135
65 or over	36	176

a) Write the following events in terms of L and U.

(i) The selected person is right-handed.

(ii) The selected person is 65 or over and left-handed.

(iii) The selected person is under 65 and right-handed. *[3 marks]*

b) Use the table to draw a Venn diagram.
Label each area with the probability of the event. *[2 marks]*

Challenge

P M Q10 1000 football supporters were asked if they go to home league matches, away league matches, or cup matches. 560 go to home matches, 420 go to away matches, and 120 go to cup matches. 240 go to home and away matches, 80 go to home and cup matches, and 60 go to away and cup matches. 40 go to all 3 types of match. Find the probability that a randomly selected supporter goes to:

a) exactly two types of match b) at least one type of match

E P Q11 P(A) = 0.6, P(A' and B) = 0.15 and P(A' or B) = 0.48.

a) Draw a Venn diagram to represent events A and B. *[3 marks]*

b) Using your Venn diagram from part a), state the value of:

(i) P(B)

(ii) P((A' or B')') *[2 marks]*

E P Q12 The Venn diagram below shows probabilities expressed in terms of n.

a) Use the information in the diagram to find the value of n. *[3 marks]*

b) Hence, find the probabilities of the following events:

(i) A

(ii) A and B

(iii) A' or B *[3 marks]*

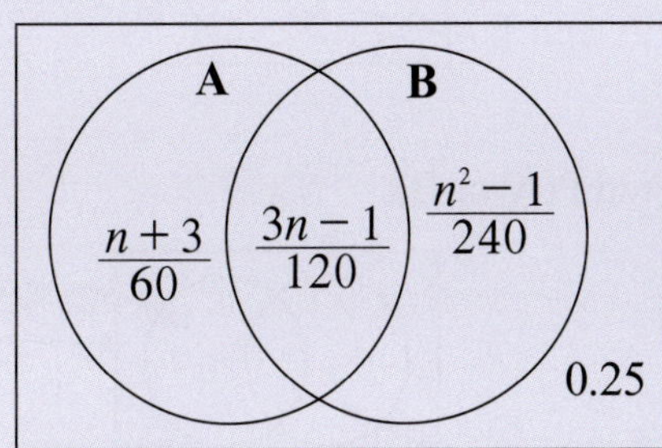

3.5 The Addition Law

For **two events**, A and B: **P(A or B) = P(A) + P(B) – P(A and B)**

You can see why this is true using Venn diagrams.

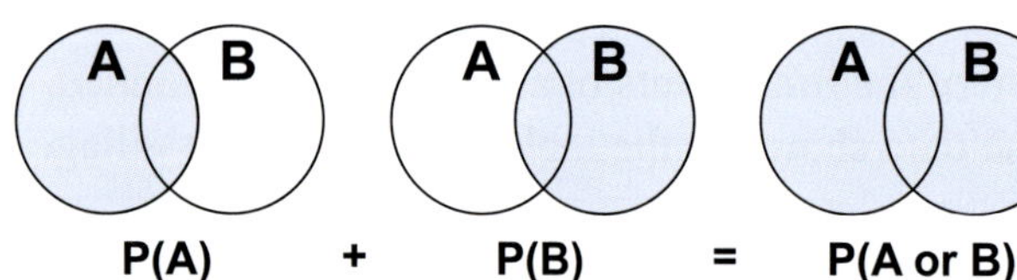

> **Tip**
> If you didn't subtract P(A and B) from P(A) + P(B), you'd be counting it twice — once in A and once in B.

To get P(A or B) on its own, you need to subtract P(A and B) from P(A) + P(B).

The addition law is **really useful** for finding missing probabilities — as long as you know three of the values in the formula, you can **rearrange** the formula to find the remaining probability.

Example 1

For two events A and B, P(A or B) = 0.75, P(A) = 0.45 and P(B') = 0.4.

a) Find P(A and B).

P(B) = 1 – P(B') = 1 – 0.4 = 0.6 ← To use the formula, you need to know P(A), P(B) and P(A or B). You're missing P(B), so start by finding that.

P(A or B) = P(A) + P(B) – P(A and B)
⇒ P(A and B) = P(A) + P(B) – P(A or B) ← Rearrange the addition law formula to make P(A and B) the subject.

P(A and B) = 0.45 + 0.6 – 0.75 = 0.3 ← Substitute in the probabilities to find P(A and B).

b) Find P(A' and B').

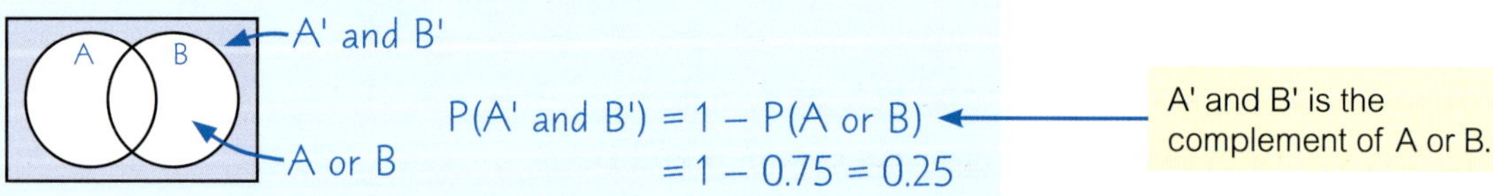

P(A' and B') = 1 – P(A or B)
= 1 – 0.75 = 0.25 ← A' and B' is the complement of A or B.

c) Find P(A and B').

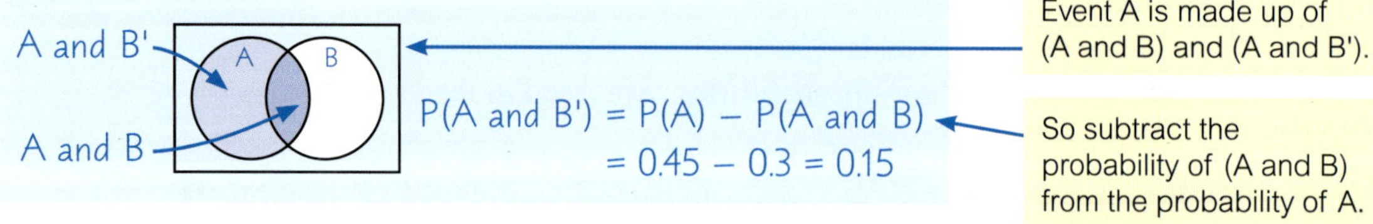

Event A is made up of (A and B) and (A and B').

P(A and B') = P(A) – P(A and B)
= 0.45 – 0.3 = 0.15 ← So subtract the probability of (A and B) from the probability of A.

d) Find P(A' or B).

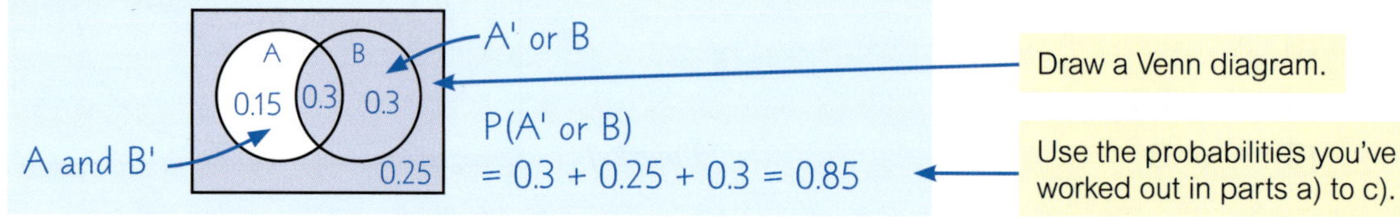

Draw a Venn diagram.

P(A' or B)
= 0.3 + 0.25 + 0.3 = 0.85 ← Use the probabilities you've worked out in parts a) to c).

Example 2 

On any given day, the probability that Jason eats an apple is 0.6, the probability that he eats a banana is 0.3, and the probability that he eats both an apple and a banana is 0.2.

a) Find the probability that he eats an apple or a banana (or both).

A is the event 'eats an apple' and B is the event 'eats a banana' ← Define the events.

$P(A \text{ or } B) = P(A) + P(B) - P(A \text{ and } B) = 0.6 + 0.3 - 0.2 = 0.7$ ← You want to find P(A or B), so use the addition law.

b) Find the probability that he either doesn't eat an apple, or doesn't eat a banana.

$$\begin{aligned} P(A' \text{ or } B') &= P(A') + P(B') - P(A' \text{ and } B') \\ &= [1 - P(A)] + [1 - P(B)] \\ &\quad - [1 - P(A \text{ or } B)] \\ &= (1 - 0.6) + (1 - 0.3) - (1 - 0.7) \\ &= 0.4 + 0.7 - 0.3 = 0.8 \end{aligned}$$

You want to find P(A' or B'). You could use the addition law by replacing A with A' and B with B'.

Problem Solving Alternatively, (A' or B') means everything not in both A and B, i.e. 1 – P(A and B), so P(A' or B') = 1 – 0.2 = 0.8

Exercise 3.5

Q1 If P(A) = 0.3, P(B) = 0.5 and P(A and B) = 0.15, find:

a) P(A') b) P(A or B) c) P(A' and B')

Q2 If P(A') = 0.36, P(B) = 0.44 and P(A and B) = 0.27, find:

a) P(B') b) P(A or B) c) P(A and B') d) P(A or B')

M Q3 A car is selected at random from a car park. The probability of the car being blue is 0.25 and the probability of it being an estate is 0.15. The probability of the car being a blue estate is 0.08.

a) What is the probability of the car not being blue?

b) What is the probability of the car being blue or being an estate?

c) What is the probability of the car being neither blue nor an estate?

Q4 If P(X or Y) = 0.77, P(X) = 0.43 and P(Y) = 0.56, find:

a) P(Y') b) P(X and Y) c) P(X' and Y') d) P(X' or Y')

Q5 If P(C' or D) = 0.65, P(C) = 0.53 and P(D) = 0.44, find:

a) P(C' and D) b) P(C' and D') c) P(C' or D') d) P(C and D)

P M Q6 The probability that a student has read 'To Kill a Mockingbird' is 0.62. The probability that a student hasn't read 'Animal Farm' is 0.66. The probability that a student has read at least one of these two books is 0.79. Find:

a) The probability that a student has read both the books.

b) The probability that a student has read 'Animal Farm' but not 'To Kill a Mockingbird'.

c) The probability that a student has read neither of the books.

E Q7 P(A) = 0.24, P(A and B) = 0.12, and P(A or B) = 0.56.

a) Find P(B'). *[2 marks]*

b) Draw a Venn diagram to represent the events A and B. *[1 mark]*

E M Q8 A large company employs 124 computer programmers.
They use two main programming languages, Adder (A) and Baliscript (B).
Of the 124 programmers, 53 know A and 72 know B.

a) Explain why there must be at least one programmer who knows both programming languages. *[1 mark]*

There are 24 programmers who know both A and B.
A programmer working for the company is chosen at random.

b) Find the probability that the programmer knows at least one of A or B. *[2 marks]*

c) Find the probability that the programmer knows exactly one of A or B. *[2 marks]*

d) Find the probability that the programmer knows neither of the languages. *[1 mark]*

Challenge

P Q9 A and B are two events.

a) Given that P(A) = 0.49 and P(B) = 0.78, find the minimum value of p and the maximum value of q for which $p \leq$ P(A or B) $\leq q$.

b) When P(A or B) takes its maximum value q:

(i) find the value of P(A and B),

(ii) draw a Venn diagram to represent the events A and B.

3.6 Mutually Exclusive Events

Events can happen at the same time when they have one or more outcomes in common. For example, the events 'I roll a 3' and 'I roll an odd number' both happen if the outcome of my dice roll is a '3'. Events which have **no outcomes** in common **can't happen** at the same time. These events are called **mutually exclusive** (or just 'exclusive').

If A and B are mutually exclusive events, then **P(A and B) = 0**.

The addition law was defined on p.84 as: P(A or B) = P(A) + P(B) – P(A and B). When A and B are mutually exclusive, P(A and B) = 0 can be substituted to give a simpler version.

For two events, A and B, where A and B are **mutually exclusive**:

P(A or B) = P(A) + P(B)

And you can write a general form of this for n mutually exclusive events. For mutually exclusive events $A_1, A_2, ..., A_n$:

$$\mathbf{P(A_1 \text{ or } A_2 \text{ or } ... \text{ or } A_n) = P(A_1) + P(A_2) + ... + P(A_n)}$$

Tip In a Venn diagram, mutually exclusive events A and B are shown as non-overlapping circles.

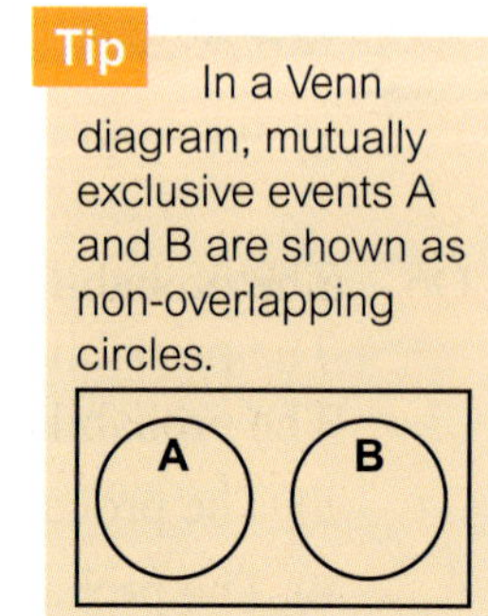

Example 1 

A card is selected at random from a standard pack of 52 cards. Find the probability that the card is either a picture card (a Jack, Queen or King), or the 7, 8 or 9 of clubs.

Let A be the event 'select a picture card' and B be the event 'select the 7, 8 or 9 of clubs'. ← Start by defining the two events.

P(A or B) = P(A) + P(B) ← You want to find the probability of A or B. The card can't be both a picture card and the 7, 8, or 9 of clubs, so A and B are mutually exclusive.

$P(A) = \frac{12}{52}$ and $P(B) = \frac{3}{52}$ ← There are a total of 52 equally likely outcomes. There are 12 outcomes where A happens. There are 3 outcomes where B happens.

$P(A \text{ or } B) = P(A) + P(B) = \frac{12}{52} + \frac{3}{52} = \frac{15}{52}$ ← Substitute in your probabilities to find P(A or B).

To show whether or not events A and B are **mutually exclusive**, you just need to show whether P(A and B) is **zero** or non-zero. To show that A and B are **not** mutually exclusive, you could also show that P(A or B) ≠ P(A) + P(B) — that's the **same** as showing that P(A and B) ≠ 0.

Example 2

a) For two events, A and B, P(A) = 0.38, P(B) = 0.24 and P(A or B) = 0.6. Show whether or not events A and B are mutually exclusive.

P(A or B) = P(A) + P(B) – P(A and B)
⇒ P(A and B) = P(A) + P(B) – P(A or B)
= 0.38 + 0.24 – 0.6 = 0.02 ← Use the addition law to find P(A and B).

P(A and B) ≠ 0, which means A and B are not mutually exclusive. ← Give your reasoning.

b) For two events, A and B, P(A) = 0.75 and P(A and B') = 0.75. Show whether or not events A and B are mutually exclusive.

P(A) = P(A and B) + P(A and B')
⇒ P(A and B) = P(A) – P(A and B') = 0.75 – 0.75 = 0 ← Think about the areas that make up event A. Then rearrange to make P(A and B) the subject.

P(A and B) = 0, which means that A and B are mutually exclusive. ← Give your reasoning.

Exercise 3.6

Q1 If X and Y are mutually exclusive events, with P(X) = 0.48 and P(Y) = 0.37, find:

a) P(X and Y) b) P(X or Y) c) P(X' and Y')

Q2 P(L) = 0.28, P(M) = 0.42 and P(N) = 0.33. If the pairs of events (L and M) and (L and N) are mutually exclusive, and P(M and N) = 0.16, find:

a) P(L or M) b) P(L or N) c) P(M or N) d) P(L and M and N)

e) Draw and label a Venn diagram to show events L, M and N.

M Q3 Kwame is planning his evening. The probabilities that he will go bowling, to the cinema or out for dinner are 0.17, 0.43 and 0.22 respectively. Given that he only has time to do one activity:

a) Find the probability that he either goes bowling or to the cinema.

b) Find the probability that he doesn't do any of the 3 activities.

P Q4 For events A, B and C, P(A) = 0.28, P(B) = 0.66, P(C) = 0.49, P(A or B) = 0.86, P(A or C) = 0.77 and P(B or C) = 0.92. Find each of the probabilities below and say whether or not each pair of events is mutually exclusive.

a) P(A and B) b) P(A and C) c) P(B and C)

P Q5 For events C and D, P(C') = 0.6, P(D) = 0.25 and P(C and D') = 0.4.

a) Show that C and D are mutually exclusive.

b) Find P(C or D)

E Q6 Given that, for events A and B, P(A' and B') = 0.61, P(A) = 0.32 and P(B) = 0.07, show that A and B are mutually exclusive. *[2 marks]*

P M Q7 A box contains 50 biscuits. Of the biscuits, 20 are chocolate-coated and the rest are plain. Half of all the biscuits are in wrappers. One biscuit is selected at random from the box.

If P is the event 'the biscuit is plain', and W is the event 'the biscuit is in a wrapper', show that events P and W are not mutually exclusive.

E Q8 a) Using a Venn diagram, explain why the events (A and B) and (A and B') are mutually exclusive. *[1 mark]*

b) Use the result from part a) to write an expression for P(A) in terms of P(A and B) and P(A' and B). *[1 mark]*

c) Write an expression for P(B) in terms of P(A and B) and P(A' and B). *[1 mark]*

E P Q9 Let A, B and C be three events, where P(B) = P(A and B).

a) Show that P(A) = P(A or B). *[2 marks]*

Events A and C are mutually exclusive.

b) Use a Venn Diagram to explain why B and C must also be mutually exclusive. *[2 marks]*

Challenge

E P Q10 Let A, B and C be three events.

a) On separate Venn diagrams, show the regions corresponding to the events:

(i) A or B

(ii) C' *[2 marks]*

b) Hence, show on a Venn diagram the region corresponding to the event ((A or B) and C'). *[1 mark]*

The probabilities P(A), P(B) and P(C) are all non-zero.
P(A' and C) = 0.36, and P((A or B) and C') = 0.64.

c) Using a Venn diagram and the result from b), or otherwise, show that A and C are mutually exclusive events. *[3 marks]*

3.7 Independent Events

If the probability of an event B happening **doesn't depend** on whether an event A has happened or not, events A and B are **independent**.

For example, if a dice is rolled **twice**, the events A = 'first roll is a 4' and B = 'second roll is a 4', are **independent**, because the number rolled on the second roll **doesn't** depend on the number rolled on the first roll.

Or, suppose a card is selected at **random** from a pack of cards, then replaced, then a second card is selected at random. The events A = 'first card is a 7' and B = 'second card is a 7', are **independent** because P(B) is **unaffected** by what was selected on the first pick.

Tip If the first card isn't replaced, then A and B aren't independent.
If A happens, P(B) = $\frac{3}{51}$.
Otherwise, P(B) = $\frac{4}{51}$.

For two events, A and B, the **product law** for **independent events** is: **P(A and B) = P(A)P(B)**

Example 1

V and W are independent events, where P(V) = 0.2 and P(W) = 0.6.

a) Find P(V and W).

P(V and W) = P(V)P(W) = 0.2 × 0.6 = 0.12 ← Use the product law for independent events.

b) Find P(V or W).

P(V or W) = P(V) + P(W) − P(V and W)
= 0.2 + 0.6 − 0.12 = 0.68 ← You know all the probabilities that you need to use the addition law.

To show that events A and B are independent, you just need to show that P(A) × P(B) = P(A and B).

Example 2 M

A scientist is investigating the likelihood that a person will catch two diseases, after being exposed to one and then the other. The probability of catching the first disease is 0.25, the probability of catching the second disease is 0.5, and the probability of catching both diseases is 0.2.

Show that the events 'catch first disease' and 'catch second disease' are not independent.

A = 'catch first disease' and B = 'catch second disease' ← Define the events.

P(A) × P(B) = 0.25 × 0.5 = 0.125, P(A and B) = 0.2
0.125 ≠ 0.2, so the events are not independent. ← Find P(A) × P(B) and compare with P(A and B).

Example 3 P

For events A and B, P(A) = 0.4, P(A and B) = 0.1 and P(A' and B) = 0.2.
Say whether or not A and B are independent.

P(B) = P(A and B) + P(A' and B) = 0.1 + 0.2 = 0.3 ← Find P(B) using the information given.

P(A) × P(B) = 0.4 × 0.3 = 0.12, P(A and B) = 0.1
0.12 ≠ 0.1, so the events are not independent. ← Find P(A) × P(B) and compare with P(A and B).

Exercise 3.7

Q1 If X and Y are independent events, with P(X) = 0.62 and P(Y) = 0.32, calculate P(X and Y).

Q2 P(A and B) = 0.45 and P(B') = 0.25. If A and B are independent events, what is P(A)?

P Q3 X, Y and Z are independent events, with P(X) = 0.84, P(Y) = 0.68 and P(Z) = 0.48. Find the following probabilities:

a) P(X and Y) b) P(Y' and Z')

c) P(X and Z') d) P(Y' and Z)

Problem Solving

In Q3, if A and B are independent, then A' and B' are also independent.

Q4 Events M and N are independent, with P(M) = 0.4 and P(N) = 0.7. Calculate the following probabilities:

a) P(M and N) b) P(M or N) c) P(M and N')

M Q5 A card is picked at random from a standard pack of 52 cards. The card is replaced and the pack is shuffled, before a second card is picked at random.

a) What is the probability that both cards picked are hearts?

b) Find the probability that the ace of hearts is chosen both times.

Q6 Given that A and B are independent events, P(A) = 0.58 and P(A and B') = 0.36, find the following probabilities:

a) P(B) b) P(A or B) c) P(A' and B')

P M Q7 Rupa has some socks of different colours, which are all mixed up in a drawer. Rupa picks one sock from the drawer at random, then puts it back in and mixes up the socks. She then picks a sock at random from the drawer again.
The probability of picking a black sock from the drawer is $\frac{2}{5}$.
The probability of picking a black sock and then a pink sock is $\frac{1}{25}$.
What is the probability of picking a pink sock from the drawer?

P M Q8 Harrison has a fair n-sided dice, which has sides numbered 1 to n.
When Harrison rolls the dice twice, the probability that he rolls a 2 and then a 5 is $\frac{1}{64}$.
What is the value of n?

Q9 For events A, B and C:
$P(A) = \frac{3}{11}$, $P(B) = \frac{1}{3}$, $P(C) = \frac{15}{28}$, $P(A \text{ and } B) = \frac{1}{11}$, $P(A \text{ and } C) = \frac{2}{15}$ and $P(B \text{ and } C) = \frac{5}{28}$.
Show whether or not each of the pairs of events (A and B), (A and C) and (B and C) are independent.

P M Q10 Jess, Keisha and Lucy go shopping independently. The probabilities that they will buy a book are 0.66, 0.5 and 0.3 respectively.

a) What is the probability that all three of them buy a book?

b) What is the probability that at least two of them buy a book?

Q10 Hint The product law for independent events applies for any number of events.

P M Q11 The probability that Stephen walks to work on any given workday is 0.75, and the probability that he drives to work is 0.25.
For any two consecutive workdays, the probability that he walks on the first and drives on the second is 0.3125. Are the events 'walks to work' and 'drives to work' independent?

E P M Q12 A car dealership classifies the cars it sells into three categories — Budget, Mid-Range and Luxury. The car dealership also records the ages, a, of its customers and puts them into three distinct age-ranges. The dealership records all car sales over a month and presents the data in a two-way table.

	Budget	Mid-range	Luxury
$a < 35$	24	7	6
$35 \leq a < 60$	29	10	26
$a \geq 60$	4	3	21

Let B, M and L be the events that a customer bought a budget, mid-range or luxury car respectively. Let X, Y and Z be the events that a customer was in the age-range $a < 35$, $35 \leq a < 60$ or $a \geq 60$ respectively. A randomly-chosen customer is to be contacted as part of a customer satisfaction survey.

a) Find the probability that the randomly-chosen customer:
 (i) bought a mid-range car
 (ii) was in the age range $35 \leq a < 60$ *[2 marks]*

b) Use your answer to part a) to show that the events M and Y are independent. *[2 marks]*

c) Show that the events L and Z are not independent. *[3 marks]*

3.8 Tree Diagrams

Tree diagrams show probabilities for **sequences** of two or more events.

Here's a tree diagram representing two **independent** trials. There are two possible results for the first trial — events A and not A, and there are two possible results for the second trial — events B and not B.

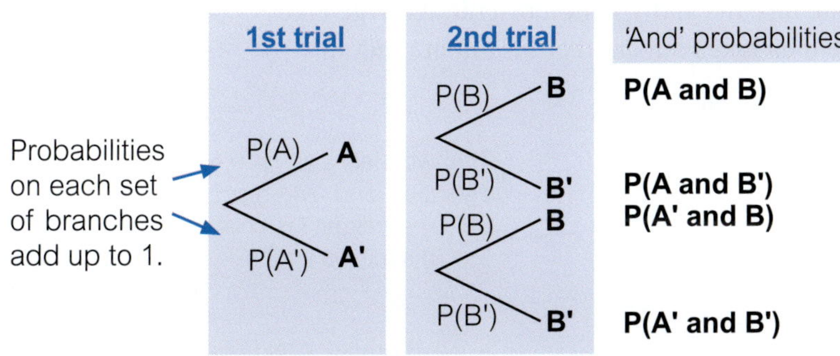

Tip This tree diagram is for independent events A and B, where P(B) is the same whether A happens or not.

Each '**column**' of the diagram represents one **trial**.

Each **branch** of a 'column' is a **possible result** of the trial.

To find the **probability** of a sequence of events, you **multiply along the branches** representing those events.

The **total** of the '**and**' probabilities is always **1**.

Problem Solving The 'and' probabilities are the probabilities of the different sequences of events, and are found by multiplying the various probabilities together. Answers to questions are then often found by adding two or more of these probabilities together.

Example 1 

A bag contains 10 balls, 6 of which are red and 4 of which are purple. One ball is selected from the bag at random, then replaced. A second ball is then selected at random.

Tip 'Then replaced' here means that the two events are independent.

a) By drawing a tree diagram, find the probability that both balls are red.

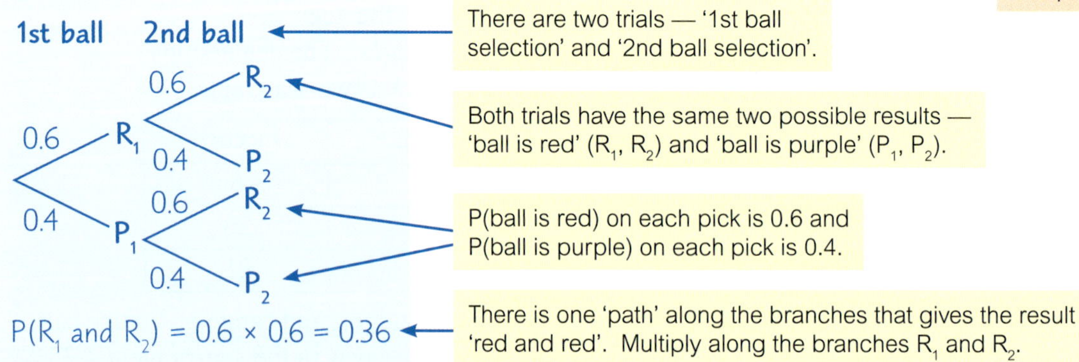

b) Find the probability that one ball is red and the other is purple.

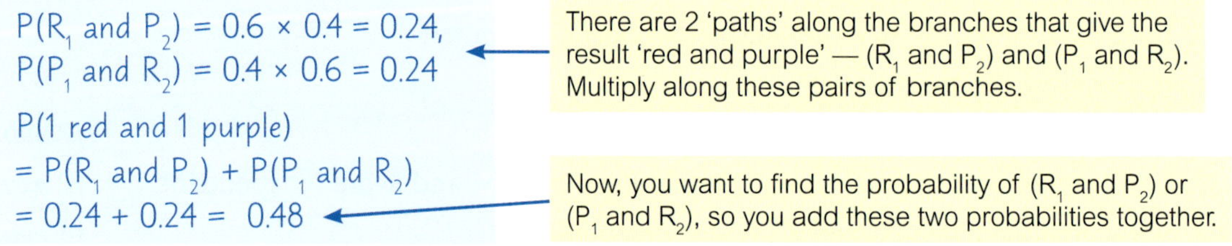

Tree diagrams for dependent events

Events are **dependent** if the probability of one event happening is **affected** by whether or not the other happens. For dependent events, the probabilities on the second set of branches **depend** on the result of the first set.

Example 2 

A box of 6 biscuits contains 5 chocolate biscuits and 1 lemon biscuit. George takes out a biscuit at random and eats it. He then takes out another biscuit at random.

Tip 'And eats it' here means that the two events are dependent.

a) Draw a tree diagram to show this information.

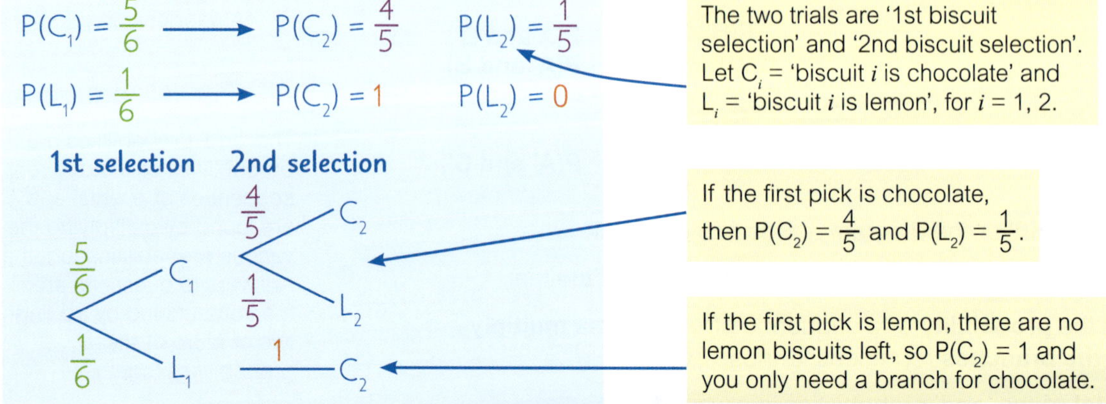

b) Find the probability that George takes out two chocolate biscuits.

$P(C_1 \text{ and } C_2) = \frac{5}{6} \times \frac{4}{5} = \frac{20}{30} = \frac{2}{3}$ ← There is 1 'path' along the branches that gives this result. Multiply along the branches C_1 and C_2.

c) Find the probability that the second biscuit he takes is chocolate.

Possible results are (C_1 and C_2) and (L_1 and C_2). ← There are 2 'paths' that give the result 'second biscuit is chocolate'.

$P(L_1 \text{ and } C_2) = \frac{1}{6} \times 1 = \frac{1}{6}$ ← You already found $P(C_1 \text{ and } C_2)$, so find $P(L_1 \text{ and } C_2)$ in the same way.

P(2nd biscuit is chocolate)
$= P(C_1 \text{ and } C_2) + P(L_1 \text{ and } C_2) = \frac{2}{3} + \frac{1}{6} = \frac{5}{6}$ ← Now add the probabilities for the two 'paths' together.

Exercise 3.8

M Q1 The probability that Jake will win two consecutive darts matches is shown on the tree diagram.

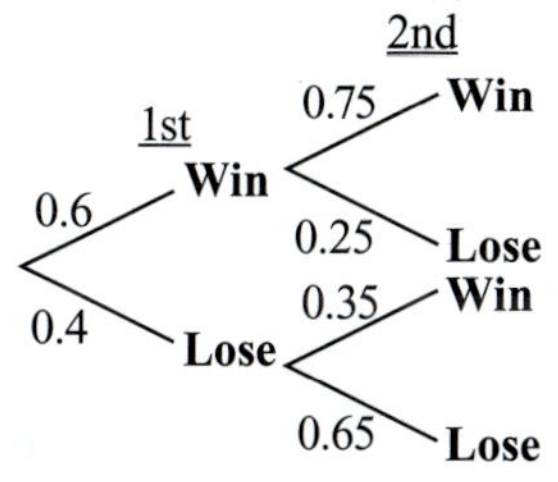

a) Explain whether the events 'wins 1st match' and 'wins 2nd match' are independent.

b) Find the probability that Jake will win:

(i) both matches (ii) at least one match

M Q2 A game involves rolling a fair, six-sided dice and tossing a fair coin. A player wins if they roll a '6' and the coin shows 'tails'.

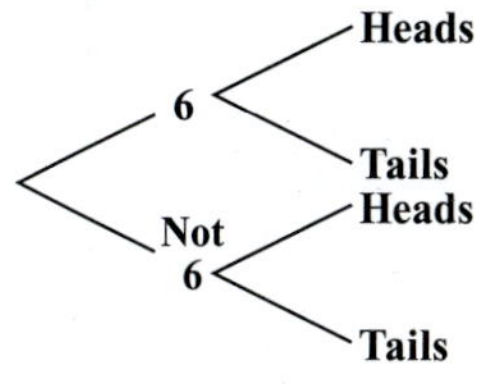

a) Complete the tree diagram by showing the probability on each branch.

b) Find the probability that a person wins the game.

M Q3 The probability that a randomly selected Year 13 student has passed their driving test is 0.3. The probability that they intend to go to university is 0.75.

a) Assuming that 'passed driving test' and 'intends to go to university' are independent, draw a tree diagram to show this information.

b) Find the probability that a randomly selected student hasn't passed their driving test and does not intend to go to university.

E M Q4 A box of eggs contains 4 brown eggs and 2 white eggs.
3 eggs are chosen at random, one at a time, to be used in an omelette.

a) Draw a tree diagram to represent the possible ways in which the eggs could be chosen. *[3 marks]*

By considering the relevant branches of the tree diagram:

b) Find the probability that all the eggs used are brown. *[1 mark]*

c) Find the probability that at least one egg of each colour is used. *[2 marks]*

d) Find the probability that exactly one white egg is used. *[2 marks]*

M Q5 A restaurant has found that if a diner orders a roast dinner, the probability that they order apple pie for pudding is 0.72. If they order a different main course, they order apple pie with probability 0.33. The probability that a diner orders a roast dinner is 0.56.

By drawing a tree diagram, find the probability that a randomly selected diner will order apple pie for pudding.

E P M Q6 A game involves picking two balls at random from a bag containing 12 balls — 5 red, 4 yellow and 3 green — where the first ball isn't replaced. A player wins if they pick two balls of the same colour.

a) Draw a tree diagram to show the possible results of each pick. *[2 marks]*

b) Find the probability that a player wins the game. *[2 marks]*

c) The game changes so that the first ball is replaced before the second one is picked. Is a player more or less likely to win now? Explain your answer. *[1 mark]*

P M Q7 Juan and Callum write movie reviews for every movie they watch. For any given movie, Juan and Callum give it a positive review with independent probabilities 0.4 and 0.3 respectively. Using tree diagrams or otherwise, find the probability that exactly one positive review is written, if:

a) Juan and Callum watch a movie together.

b) Callum watches two movies on his own.

c) Juan watches three movies on his own.

d) Juan and Callum watch a movie together, then Callum watches another movie on his own.

e) Juan watches two movies on his own, then Callum watches a movie on his own.

Challenge

P M Q8 The partly completed tree diagram shows the probability that an athlete knocks over two consecutive hurdles. 'Yes' means the hurdle is knocked over, and 'No' means it isn't.

The probability that the athlete knocks over both hurdles is 0.08 and the probability that they knock over neither hurdle is 0.72.

Use this information to fill in the missing probabilities a, b, c and d on the diagram.

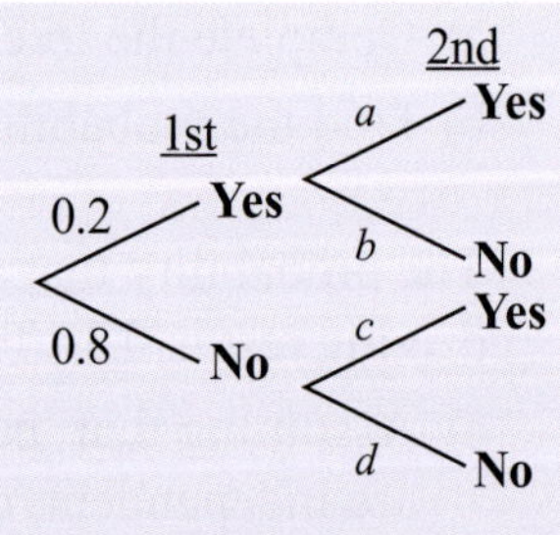

E P M Q9 Josie plays a game with a coin and a spinner. The coin is biased and the probability of it landing on heads is $\frac{2}{5}$. The spinner is fair and is split into three equal-size sectors — red, blue and yellow. To play the game, Josie flips the coin then spins the spinner. If the spinner lands on red or yellow, she flips the coin again and the game ends. If the spinner lands on blue, the game ends without another coin flip.

a) Draw a tree diagram to represent the possible results of this game. *[3 marks]*

b) What is the probability of Josie flipping one head and one tail and getting red on the spinner, in any order? *[2 marks]*

c) What is the probability that she flips two heads? *[2 marks]*

3 Review Exercise

M Q1 A fair, six-sided dice and a fair coin are thrown and a score is recorded.
If a head is thrown, the score is double the number on the dice.
If a tail is thrown, the score is the number on the dice plus 4.

a) Draw a sample space diagram to represent all the possible outcomes.

b) What is the probability of scoring 8?

c) What is the probability of scoring more than 5?

d) If a tail is thrown, what is the probability that the score is an even number?

E M Q2 A stack of 9 cards are marked with the numbers 1 to 9. The stack is shuffled and two cards are drawn at random. The sum of the numbers on the two cards is recorded.
Find the probability of getting a total score of 15 or more if:

a) The first card is replaced in the stack before the second is selected. *[3 marks]*

b) The first card is not replaced. *[2 marks]*

E P M Q3 A bag contains 150 coins, including a number, x, of 10p coins.
The probability of randomly selecting a 10p coin from the bag is p, where $\frac{1}{6} < p < \frac{1}{5}$.
Find the possible values of x. *[3 marks]*

E P M Q4 The mass of each apple in a large sack are recorded in the table below.

Mass (g)	Frequency Density
$70 \le M < 100$	0.5
$100 \le M < 125$	2.32
$125 \le M < 150$	3.84
$150 \le M < 180$	2.2
$180 \le M < 225$	0.4

An apple is selected at random from the sack.

a) Find the probability that the apple has a mass, M, with $100 \le M < 125$. *[2 marks]*

b) Find the probability that the apple has a mass at least 125 g. *[1 mark]*

c) Estimate the probability that the apple has a mass less than or equal to 165 g.
State any assumptions that you make in your calculation. *[4 marks]*

E P M Q5 Three separate boxes are labelled A, B and C.
Each box contains a mixture of copper coins and silver coins, such that:

- 35% of the total number of coins are in box A, 40% are in box B and the rest are in box C
- 50% of the coins in box A are copper and 40% of the coins in box B are copper
- 20% of the coins in box C are silver

a) What percentage of the total number of coins are copper coins in box A? *[1 mark]*

b) A coin is chosen at random. Find the probability that it is a silver coin. *[2 marks]*

M Q6 Half the students in a sixth-form college eat sausages for dinner and 20% eat chips. 2% eat sausages and chips together.

a) Draw a Venn diagram to show this information.

b) Find the percentage of students who eat chips but not sausages.

c) Find the percentage of students who eat either chips or sausages but not both.

d) Find the probability that a randomly selected student eats sausages but not chips.

e) Find the probability that a randomly selected student eats neither sausages nor chips.

f) Find the probability that a randomly selected student who eats chips also eats sausages.

P M Q7 100 people were asked if they enjoy activity holidays, beach holidays and/or skiing holidays. Each person asked enjoys at least one of these types of holiday.

10 people enjoy all three types of holiday. 25 people enjoy both activity and beach holidays, 22 people enjoy both activity and skiing holidays, and 21 people enjoy both beach and skiing holidays. 41 people enjoy activity holidays, 59 people enjoy beach holidays, and 58 people enjoy skiing holidays.

One person is selected at random. Find the probability that they like beach holidays but don't like skiing holidays.

E P M Q8 A choir is going to perform a concert. Of the 75 members of the choir, 60 are able to sing in the concert. 20 members have been in the choir for 10 or more years, and 18 of those will be in the concert.

Using a Venn diagram, work out the probability that a randomly selected member has been in the choir for less than 10 years and is not singing in the concert. *[3 marks]*

M Q9 The hot-beverage choices of a company's 30 workers are shown in the table below.

If one worker is selected at random, find the probability that he or she:

a) drinks coffee

b) drinks milky tea without sugar

c) either drinks tea or takes only sugar

Drink	Milk or sugar			
	Only milk	Only sugar	Both	Neither
Tea	7	4	6	1
Coffee	5	3	2	2

E P Q10 Given that P(A) = 0.46, use the information in the Venn diagram on the right to find the values of x and y.

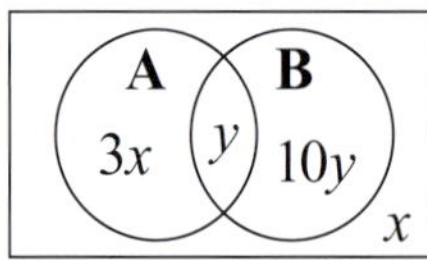

[4 marks]

M Q11 On any shopping trip, the probability that Aiden buys clothes is 0.7, the probability that he buys music is 0.4 and the probability that he buys both clothes and music is 0.2. Find the probability that:

a) He buys clothes or music or both.

b) He buys neither clothes nor music.

M Q12 For a certain biased dice, P(roll a 1) = 0.3 and P(roll a 3) = 0.2. This dice is rolled once.

a) Find the probability that a 1 or a 3 is rolled.

b) Find the probability that neither a 1 nor a 3 is rolled.

c) The dice is rolled twice. Find the probability of rolling:

(i) two 1s, (ii) a 1, then a 3, (iii) a 3, then neither a 1 nor a 3.

Q13 R and S are independent events with P(R) = 0.9 and P(S) = 0.8. Find:

a) P(R and S) b) P(R or S) c) P(R' and S') d) P(R' or S')

P M Q14 As part of a game-show, four contestants, A, B, C and D, are presented with ten boxes numbered from 1 to 10. Each box contains some prize money. In the order A, B, C, D, each contestant chooses a box at random without knowing the choice of any other contestant.

a) What is the probability that contestant A chooses the box numbered 4?

b) Show that the probability that contestants A and B choose different boxes is $\frac{9}{10}$.

c) What is the probability that all four contestants choose different boxes?

d) What is the probability that at least two contestants choose the same box?

E M Q15 A sample of 60 students was chosen from all the students at a school. 24 study Maths, 20 study Art and 8 study both Maths and Art. If one of the 60 students is selected at random, are the events 'student studies Maths' and 'student studies Art' independent? Explain your answer. *[3 marks]*

P M Q16 Hafsa rolls two fair, six-sided dice numbered 1-6 and calculates her score by adding the two results together.

a) What is the probability that her score is a prime number?

b) What is the probability that her score is a square number?

Let P be the event 'Hafsa's score is a prime number' and S be the event 'Hafsa's score is a square number'.

c) Explain whether or not the events P and S are mutually exclusive.

d) Find P(P or S).

Hafsa carries out the experiment twice. Let S_1 be the event 'score from first pair of rolls is a square number' and S_2 be the event 'score from second pair of rolls is a square number'.

e) Explain whether or not the events S_1 and S_2 are independent.

f) Find P(S_1 and S_2).

Q17 a) Explain, using probability notation, what it means for two events, A and B, to be statistically independent.

b) Use the information in the Venn diagram on the right to show that:

(i) A and B are independent events

(ii) A and C are independent events

(iii) B and C are independent events

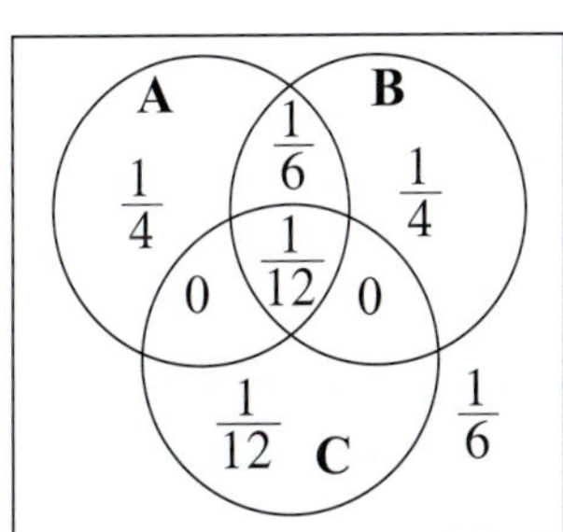

Q18 An A-Level maths student makes the following claim:

"Since P(A and B) is equal to P(A)P(B), then the addition law of probability can be re-written as simply P(A or B) = P(A) + P(B) – P(A)P(B)."

a) Explain why this statement is incorrect. *[1 mark]*

The student makes another claim:

"If A and B are independent and B and C are independent, then it must follow that A and C are independent."

A B
0.075 0.125 0.175
0
0.05 0.2
0.15
C 0.225

b) Use the information in the Venn diagram to show that the second statement is also incorrect. *[3 marks]*

Q19 Given that P(A and B') = $\frac{1}{4}$, P(A' and B) = $\frac{1}{6}$ and P(A and B) = k, where $k > 0$, determine the possible values of k for which the events A and B are statistically independent. *[4 marks]*

Q20 Evelyn has these five coins in her pocket: 5p, 10p, 10p, 20p, 50p.
She selects two coins at random, without replacement, and defines three events as follows:

A: a 10p is selected B: the total value is more than 60p C: the second coin is round

a) Find P(B). *[2 marks]*

b) Event A and one of the other events are mutually exclusive.
Explain which of B and C is the other event. *[2 marks]*

c) Find P(A and C). *[3 marks]*

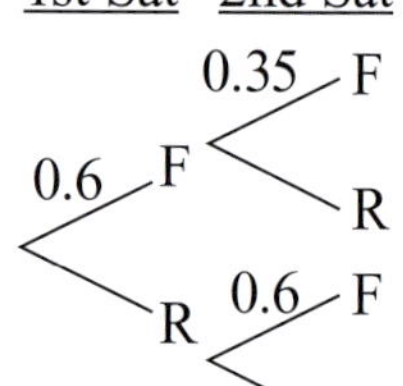

Q21 Kai plays either football or rugby every Saturday.
The tree diagram on the right shows the probabilities that he plays football (F) or rugby (R) on each of the next two Saturdays.

a) Fill in the three missing probabilities to complete the tree diagram.

b) Find the probability that Kai plays football on at least one of the next two Saturdays.

c) Find the probability that Kai plays the same sport on both of the next two Saturdays.

Q22 A fridge contains twelve cans of pop. Eight cans are cola and four are lemonade.
Three cans are chosen at random from the fridge.

a) Draw a tree diagram to represent this situation. *[3 marks]*

b) Find the probability that the first can is cola and the third can is lemonade. *[3 marks]*

c) Find the probability that exactly two of the cans are the same. *[4 marks]*

Q23 A bakery sells plain doughnuts and jam doughnuts. Two customers each buy one doughnut at random. Initially, there are 5 jam doughnuts and k plain doughnuts, where k is a positive integer. The probability that the two customers bought one of each type of doughnut between them is $\frac{11}{24}$.

a) Draw a tree diagram to represent this situation, expressing relevant probabilities in terms of k. *[2 marks]*

b) Use the tree diagram from a) to find the original number of plain doughnuts. *[4 marks]*

E M Q24 A child is skimming stones across the surface of a lake. Each time a stone hits the surface of the water, it can either bounce or sink. It is assumed that the probability of a stone bouncing when it first hits the water is 0.72, and that the probability of it bouncing decreases by 0.24 each time it hits the water.

a) Draw a tree diagram to represent this situation. *[2 marks]*

b) What is the greatest number of times that a stone will bounce in this model? *[1 mark]*

c) What is the probability that the stone bounces exactly once then sinks? *[1 mark]*

d) What is the probability that the stone bounces the maximum number of times? *[1 mark]*

Challenge

E P M Q25 An ice cream vendor sells ice creams in three sizes — small, medium and large. The ice creams can be served plain or topped with one of sprinkles or sauce. The ice cream vendor records the number of sales on a certain day, as shown in the incomplete table on the right.

	Small	Medium	Large	Total
Plain	5		6	18
Sprinkles				
Sauce	15	9		
Total	25	y	23	x

Given that P(Medium and Sprinkles) = 0.2 and P(Large and Sauce) = 0.05:

a) Find an expression in terms of x for the number of medium ice creams with sprinkles sold. *[1 mark]*

b) Find the values of x and y. *[4 marks]*

c) Copy and complete the table. *[1 mark]*

d) Use the information in the table to find the probability that a randomly selected ice cream sold was:

(i) large

(ii) small and plain

(iii) medium or topped with sprinkles *[3 marks]*

E P M Q26 A child plays a game with a fair dice. The dice is repeatedly rolled until a 1 is rolled for the first time. When this happens, the game ends.

a) Write an expression for the probability of rolling the 1 on the nth roll. *[2 marks]*

b) Hence, calculate the probability that the 1 occurs on the fourth roll. *[1 mark]*

c) What is the probability of rolling the 1 on either the second or eighth roll? *[2 marks]*

d) Find the probability that the number of rolls is at least four. *[3 marks]*

E P M Q27 Sue rehearses with an orchestra four times per week. She chooses to either walk or cycle to rehearsals. The probability that she chooses to walk is 0.34. Her choice to walk or cycle on any given day is random.

a) List all the possible sets of outcomes of Sue's choice to walk or cycle for a week where she walks at least three times *[1 mark]*

b) Using your answer to part a) and a tree diagram, find the probability that Sue walks at least three times in a given week. *[3 marks]*

3 Chapter Summary

1 When all possible outcomes of a trial or experiment are equally likely, the probability of an event happening is $\text{P(event)} = \dfrac{\text{Number of outcomes where event happens}}{\text{Total number of possible outcomes}}$.

2 A sample space diagram shows all possible outcomes of a trial or experiment.
If there are two separate activities happening in the trial, you can draw the diagram as a grid.

3 A Venn diagram can be used to show the probabilities of two or more events happening.
In a Venn diagram showing events A and B, the complement of A (A') is everything that is not inside the circle A and represents every outcome corresponding to event A not happening. Venn diagrams can show the number of outcomes or the proportion for each outcome.

4 A two-way table shows combinations of two events, where each cell of the table represents a different combined event. Like Venn diagrams, they can be filled with values or proportions.

5 The addition law for two events, A and B, is: P(A or B) = P(A) + P(B) – P(A and B).

6 Mutually exclusive events are events that cannot happen at the same time.
For two mutually exclusive events, A and B: P(A and B) = 0 and P(A or B) = P(A) + P(B).
Or for more than two events: $P(A_1 \text{ or } A_2 \text{ or } ... \text{ or } A_n) = P(A_1) + P(A_2) + ... + P(A_n)$.

7 Independent events are events whose probabilities don't depend on the other happening.
The product law for two independent events, A and B, is: P(A and B) = P(A)P(B).
To show that two events are independent, show that P(A) × P(B) = P(A and B).

8 A tree diagram shows probabilities for two or more events.
Tree diagrams can be used for independent or dependent events. For dependent events, the probabilities of the second trial will be affected by the outcome of the first.

Statistical Distributions

4

Learning Objectives

Once you've completed this chapter, you should be able to:

- Understand what is meant by a discrete random variable.
- Find and use probability distributions, probability functions and cumulative distribution functions.
- Calculate and use binomial coefficients.
- Recognise where to use a binomial distribution.
- Find probabilities using the binomial probability function.
- Use binomial tables to find probabilities.
- Model real-life situations using the binomial distribution.

Prior Knowledge Check

1 One card is drawn at random from a standard pack of 52 playing cards. Find the probability that the card is:

a) the 6 of clubs b) a spade c) an ace d) an even-numbered diamond

see pages 73-74

2 Without using a calculator, work out the values of the following:

a) 6! b) $\frac{20!}{18!}$ c) ${}^{7}C_{6}$

see Year 1 Pure Maths

Chapter 4

4.1 Discrete Random Variables

First things first, you'll need to know what a discrete random variable is:

- A **variable** is just something that can take a variety of values — its value isn't fixed.
- A **random variable** is a variable that takes different values with different probabilities.
- A **discrete random variable** is a random variable which can take only a certain number of values.

A **discrete random variable** is usually represented by an **upper case** letter such as X.
The **particular values** that X can take are represented by the **lower case** letter x.

These examples should help you to get used to the difference between x and X.

Rolling a fair dice and recording the score:

X is the name of the random variable. It's '**score on dice**'.

x is a particular value that X can take.
Here x could be **1**, **2**, **3**, **4**, **5** or **6**.

Tossing a fair coin twice and counting the number of heads:

X is '**number of heads**'.

x could be **0**, **1** or **2**.

In these two examples, the discrete random variable can take only a few different values.
The possible values are all whole numbers — but they don't have to be.

4.2 Probability Distributions and Functions

A **probability distribution** is a **table** showing all the possible values a discrete random variable can take, plus the **probability** that it'll take each value.

Example 1

Draw the probability distribution table for X, where X is the score on a fair, six-sided dice.

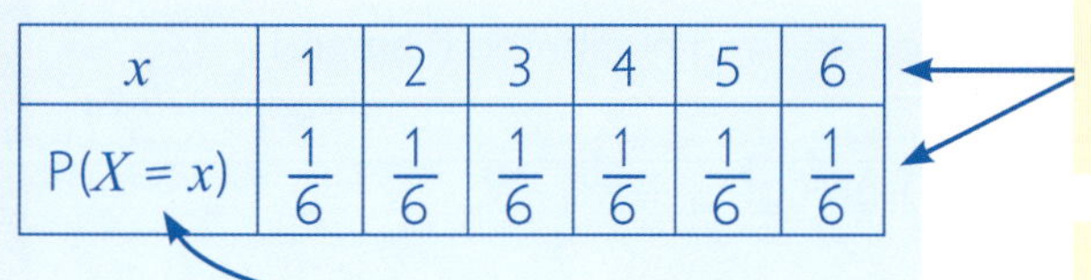

x	1	2	3	4	5	6
$P(X = x)$	$\frac{1}{6}$	$\frac{1}{6}$	$\frac{1}{6}$	$\frac{1}{6}$	$\frac{1}{6}$	$\frac{1}{6}$

X can take the values 1, 2, 3, 4, 5 and 6, each with probability $\frac{1}{6}$.

This notation means the probability that X takes the value x.

A **probability function** is a formula that generates the probability of X taking the value x, for every possible x. It is written **P($X = x$)** or sometimes just **p(x)**. A probability function is really just another way of representing the information in the probability distribution table.

Example 2

a) A fair coin is tossed once and the number of tails, X, is counted. Write down the probability function of X.

$X = 0$ when coin lands on heads
$X = 1$ when coin lands on tails
The probability of each outcome is $\frac{1}{2}$.

The coin can land on either heads or tails. Write down the value of X and the probability for each outcome.

$P(X = x) = \frac{1}{2} \quad x = 0, 1$

Now write down the probability function, listing the possible values of x after the 'formula'.

b) A biased coin, for which the probability of heads is $\frac{3}{4}$ and tails is $\frac{1}{4}$, is tossed once and the number of tails, X, is counted. Write down the probability function of X.

$X = 0$ when coin lands on heads
$X = 1$ when coin lands on tails

The possible outcomes are the same as above.

$P(X = 0)$ is $\frac{3}{4}$ $\quad P(X = 1)$ is $\frac{1}{4}$

However, the probabilities are different for different values of x.

$$P(X = x) = \begin{cases} \frac{3}{4} & x = 0 \\ \frac{1}{4} & x = 1 \end{cases}$$

It's best to use two 'formulas', one for each x-value. Write the probability function as a bracket, and put each value of x next to the 'formula' which gives its probability.

There's an important rule about probabilities that you'll use in solving lots of discrete random variable problems:

The **probabilities** of **all** the possible values that a discrete random variable can take **add up to 1**.

Using summation notation this can be written as:

$$\sum_{\text{all } x} P(X = x) = 1$$

Tip
The $\sum$ (sigma) symbol means 'sum of' and the writing underneath tells you what to put into the expression.
In this case, 'all x' means you add the probabilities for all the different values of x.

We can check this works for the **fair coin** in **Example a)** above:

$$\sum_{\text{all } x} P(X = x) = \sum_{x=0,1} P(X = x) = P(X = 0) + P(X = 1) = \frac{1}{2} + \frac{1}{2} = 1 \checkmark$$

The only values of x are 0 and 1.

The probability of each outcome is $\frac{1}{2}$.

You can use the fact that all the probabilities add up to 1 to solve problems where **probabilities** are **unknown** or contain unknown factors.

Example 3

The random variable X has probability function $P(X = x) = kx$, $x = 1, 2, 3$. Find the value of k.

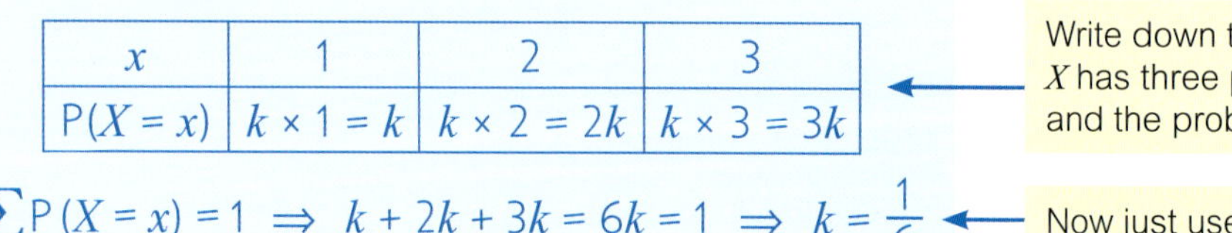

x	1	2	3
$P(X = x)$	$k \times 1 = k$	$k \times 2 = 2k$	$k \times 3 = 3k$

Write down the probability distribution. X has three possible values (x = 1, 2, 3), and the probability of each is kx.

$$\sum_{\text{all } x} P(X = x) = 1 \Rightarrow k + 2k + 3k = 6k = 1 \Rightarrow k = \frac{1}{6}$$

Now just use the rule for the sum of the probabilities to find k.

You may be asked to find the probability that X is **greater** or **less** than a value, or **lies between** two values. You just need to identify all the values that X can now take and then it's a simple case of **adding up** all their **probabilities**.

Example 4 M

The number of hot beverages drunk by GP Pits Tea staff each day is modelled by the discrete random variable X, which has this probability distribution:

x	$P(X = x)$
0	0.1
1	0.2
2	0.3
3	0.2
4 or more	a

a) Find the value of a.

$0.1 + 0.2 + 0.3 + 0.2 + a = 1 \Rightarrow 0.8 + a = 1 \Rightarrow a = 0.2$

Use $\sum_{\text{all } x} P(X = x) = 1$.

b) Find $P(2 \le X < 4)$.

$$P(2 \le X < 4) = P(X = 2 \text{ or } 3)$$
$$= P(X = 2) + P(X = 3)$$
$$= 0.3 + 0.2 = 0.5$$

This is asking for the probability that 'X is greater than or equal to 2, but less than 4', which means $X = 2$ or $X = 3$. These events are mutually exclusive (see page 86) so you can add the probabilities.

c) Find the mode.

The highest probability in the table is 0.3 when $X = 2$, so the mode = 2.

The mode is the most likely value — so it's the value with the highest probability.

When it's not clear what the probability distribution or function should be, it can be helpful to draw a **sample space diagram** of all the **possible outcomes** and work it out from that. For more on sample space diagrams, see pages 73-74.

Example 5

An unbiased six-sided dice has faces marked 1, 1, 1, 2, 2, 3. The dice is rolled twice. Let X be the random variable 'sum of the two scores on the dice'.

a) Find the probability distribution of X.

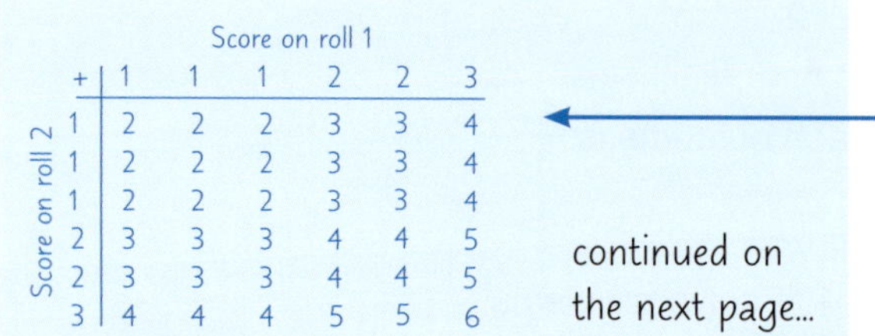

Score on roll 1 (columns), Score on roll 2 (rows)

+	1	1	1	2	2	3
1	2	2	2	3	3	4
1	2	2	2	3	3	4
1	2	2	2	3	3	4
2	3	3	3	4	4	5
2	3	3	3	4	4	5
3	4	4	4	5	5	6

You need to identify all the possible values, x, that X could take and the probability of each. Draw a sample space diagram showing the 36 possible outcomes of the dice rolls.

continued on the next page...

$x = 2, 3, 4, 5, 6$

From the diagram you can see that there are only five values X can take.

9 out of the 36 outcomes give a score of 2.

So $P(X = 2) = \frac{9}{36} = \frac{1}{4}$

Since all 36 outcomes are equally likely, you can find the probability of each value by counting how many times it occurs in the diagram and dividing by 36.

12 out of the 36 outcomes give a score of 3.

So $P(X = 3) = \frac{12}{36} = \frac{1}{3}$

Similarly, $P(X = 4) = \frac{10}{36} = \frac{5}{18}$,

$P(X = 5) = \frac{4}{36} = \frac{1}{9}$, $P(X = 6) = \frac{1}{36}$

Simplify fractions where possible.

x	2	3	4	5	6
$P(X = x)$	$\frac{1}{4}$	$\frac{1}{3}$	$\frac{5}{18}$	$\frac{1}{9}$	$\frac{1}{36}$

Write the probability distribution in a table. Always check that the probabilities add up to 1.

b) Find $P(X < 5)$.

$P(X < 5) = P(X = 2) + P(X = 3) + P(X = 4)$

$= \frac{1}{4} + \frac{1}{3} + \frac{5}{18} = \frac{31}{36}$

This is asking for the probability that X is strictly less than 5, in other words X takes values 2, 3 or 4. Just add the probabilities together.

Example 6 **M**

A game involves rolling two fair dice. If the sum of the scores is greater than 10 then the player wins 50p. If the sum is between 8 and 10 (inclusive) then they win 20p. Otherwise they get nothing.

a) If X is the random variable 'amount player wins', find the probability distribution of X.

$x = 0, 20, 50$

There are three possible values that X can take.

$P(X = 0) = P(\text{Sum of scores} < 8)$
$P(X = 20) = P(8 \leq \text{Sum of scores} \leq 10)$
$P(X = 50) = P(\text{Sum of scores} > 10)$

For each x value, you need to find the probability of getting a sum of scores which results in that value of x.

21 out of 36 outcomes give a sum of scores strictly less than 8, so

$P(X = 0) = P(\text{Sum of scores} < 8) = \frac{21}{36} = \frac{7}{12}$

12 out of 36 outcomes give a sum of scores between 8 and 10 inclusive, so

$P(X = 20) = P(8 \leq \text{Sum of scores} \leq 10) = \frac{12}{36} = \frac{1}{3}$

3 out of 36 outcomes give a sum of scores strictly greater than 10, so

$P(X = 50) = P(\text{Sum of scores} > 10) = \frac{3}{36} = \frac{1}{12}$

To find these probabilities, draw a sample space diagram showing the 36 possible outcomes of the dice rolls. Mark on your diagram all the outcomes that give each value of x.

Score on dice 1 (columns), Score on dice 2 (rows):

+	1	2	3	4	5	6
1	2	3	4	5	6	7
2	3	4	5	6	7	8
3	4	5	6	7	8	9
4	5	6	7	8	9	10
5	6	7	8	9	10	11
6	7	8	9	10	11	12

continued on the next page...

x	0	20	50
$P(X = x)$	$\frac{7}{12}$	$\frac{1}{3}$	$\frac{1}{12}$

Using this information, draw the probability distribution table.

b) The game costs 15p to play. Find the probability of making a profit.

$$P(X > 15) = P(X = 20) + P(X = 50)$$
$$= \frac{1}{3} + \frac{1}{12} = \frac{5}{12}$$

A player will make a profit if they win more than 15p, so they must win 20p or 50p.

Add the corresponding probabilities to find the answer.

The discrete uniform distribution

Sometimes you'll have a random variable where every value of X is **equally likely** — this is called a **uniform** distribution. E.g. rolling a normal, unbiased dice gives you a **discrete uniform distribution**.

Example 7 M

A lottery involves a ball being picked at random from a box of 30 balls numbered from 11 to 40. The random variable X represents the number on the first ball to be picked. Write down the probability function of X, and find $P(X < 20)$.

$$P(X = x) = \frac{1}{30}, \quad x = 11, 12, ..., 40$$

Each ball has a probability of $\frac{1}{30}$ of being picked first, so the distribution is uniform.

$$P(X < 20) = P(X = 11) + P(X = 12) + ... + P(X = 19)$$
$$= \frac{1}{30} + \frac{1}{30} + ... + \frac{1}{30}$$
$$= \frac{9}{30} = \frac{3}{10}$$

To find $P(X < 20)$, add together the probabilities of the first ball to be picked being 11, 12, ..., 19.

Exercise 4.1-4.2

Q1 For each of the following random experiments, identify:

(i) The discrete random variable, X.

(ii) All possible values, x, that X can take.

a) Tossing a fair coin 4 times and recording the number of tails.

b) Rolling a fair four-sided dice (with sides numbered 1, 2, 3 and 4) twice, and recording the sum of the scores.

Q2 A fair six-sided dice is rolled.
Write down the probability distribution for the following random variables:

a) A = 'score rolled on the dice'.

b) B = '1 if the score is even, 0 otherwise'.

c) C = '5 times the score rolled on the dice'.

Q3 Draw a table showing the probability distribution for the following probability functions:

a) $P(X = x) = \frac{x}{10}$, $x = 1, 2, 3, 4$

b) $p(x) = 0.55 - 0.1x$, $x = 0, 3, 4, 5$

c) $p(x) = 0.2$, $x = 10, 20, 30, 40, 50$

d) $P(X = x) = 0.01x^2$, $x = 1, 3, 4, 5, 7$

Q4 A biased coin, for which the probability of heads is $\frac{2}{3}$ and tails is $\frac{1}{3}$, is tossed once and the number of heads, X, is counted. Write down the probability function of X.

M Q5 a) The number of items bought, X, in the 'less than five items' queue at a shop is modelled as a random variable with probability distribution:

x	1	2	3	4
$P(X = x)$	0.2	0.4	0.1	a

(i) Find a

(ii) Find $P(X \geq 2)$

b) Tommy sells pieces of square turf. The size of turf (in m²), X, requested by each of his customers is modelled as a random variable with probability distribution:

x	1	4	9	16	25	36
$P(X = x)$	k	k	k	k	k	k

(i) Find k

(ii) Find $P(X \geq 5)$

(iii) Find $P(X \geq 10)$

(iv) Find $P(3 \leq X \leq 15)$

(v) Find P(X is divisible by three)

Q6 For each of the probability functions in a) to c) below:
(i) find k and (ii) write down the probability distribution of X.

a) $P(X = x) = kx^2 \quad x = 1, 2, 3$

b) $P(X = x) = \frac{k}{x} \quad x = 1, 2, 3$

c) $P(X = x) = \begin{cases} kx & x = 1, 2, 3, 4 \\ k(8-x) & x = 5, 6, 7 \end{cases}$

Problem Solving In Q6c, remember that when a probability function is written in brackets, different values of x have probabilities given by different formulas.

M Q7 An unbiased four-sided dice with possible scores 1, 2, 3 and 4 is rolled twice. X is the random variable 'product of the two scores on the dice'. Find $P(3 < X \leq 10)$.

Q8 A random variable, X, has a discrete uniform distribution and can take all integer values between 12 and 15 inclusive. Draw a table showing the distribution of X, and find $P(X \leq 14)$.

P M Q9 In a game, the score is recorded from rolling a fair 20-sided dice that has sides numbered 0, 2, 5 or 10. The probability of scoring 2 is three times the probability of scoring 5. The probability of scoring anything else is $\frac{1}{10}$. The random variable X represents the score on the dice for one roll. Write down the probability distribution of X and find $P(X > 0)$.

P M Q10 In a raffle, the winning ticket is randomly picked from a box of 150 tickets, numbered from 1 to 150. The random variable Y represents the number on the winning ticket. Write down the probability function of Y and find $P(60 < Y \leq 75)$.

E P **Q11** The four sides of an unbiased tetrahedral dice are numbered with the first four prime numbers. The discrete random variable X is the 'sum of the sides showing' when the dice is rolled.

a) Draw a table to show the probability distribution of X. *[2 marks]*

b) Explain why X has a discrete uniform distribution. *[1 mark]*

c) Find the probability that X is an even number. *[1 mark]*

d) The prime number 2 is replaced with another prime number. What is the probability that X is an even number now? Explain your answer. *[2 marks]*

P M **Q12** Liam is designing a game where the possible outcomes are "wins two prizes", "wins one prize" and "wins no prizes". He sets it up so that the probability of winning two prizes is half of the probability of winning one prize, which is half of the probability of winning no prizes. Draw a table showing the probability distribution of the number of prizes won, X, and find the probability of winning at least one prize.

E P **Q13** A random variable X has the probability function $p(x) = k(x^3 - 6x^2 + 11x)$ for $x = 1, 2, 3$. Show that X has a discrete uniform distribution and find the value of k. *[3 marks]*

E P **Q14** The discrete random variable X has the probability function defined as:

$$P(X = x) = \begin{cases} \frac{1}{kx} & x = 10, 20 \\ \frac{k}{x} & x = 30, 40, 50 \\ 0 & \text{otherwise} \end{cases} \quad \text{where } k > 1 \text{ and is a constant.}$$

a) Show that $47k^2 - 600k + 90 = 0$. *[2 marks]*

b) Hence show that $k = 12.6$ to 3 significant figures. *[2 marks]*

c) Using $k = 12.6$, find $P(X \leq 20)$. *[2 marks]*

Challenge

E P **Q15** The table below shows the probability distribution for the discrete random variable X where a and b are non-zero constants.

x	a	$2a$	b	$2b$
$P(X = x)$	$\frac{1}{2b}$	$\frac{a}{2b}$	$\frac{3a}{2b}$	$\frac{1}{2a}$

Given $P(2a \leq X \leq b) = \frac{2}{3}$, find the values of a and b. *[5 marks]*

4.3 The Cumulative Distribution Function

The **cumulative distribution function**, written **F(*x*)**, gives the probability that X will be **less than or equal to** a particular value, x. It's like a **running total** of probabilities.

To find $F(x_0)$ for a given value x_0, you **add up** all of the probabilities of the values X can take which are less than or equal to x_0.

$$F(x_0) = P(X \leq x_0) = \sum_{x \leq x_0} P(X = x)$$

Tip This is written in summation notation and is the sum of all the probabilities for which $x \leq x_0$. You'll sometimes see this written as $F(x_0) = \sum_{x \leq x_0} p(x)$.

Remember that $p(x)$ is just the same as writing $P(X = x)$.

Example 1

The table shows the probability distribution of the discrete random variable H.

Draw a table to show the cumulative distribution function $F(h)$.

h	0.1	0.2	0.3	0.4
$P(H = h)$	$\frac{1}{4}$	$\frac{1}{4}$	$\frac{1}{3}$	$\frac{1}{6}$

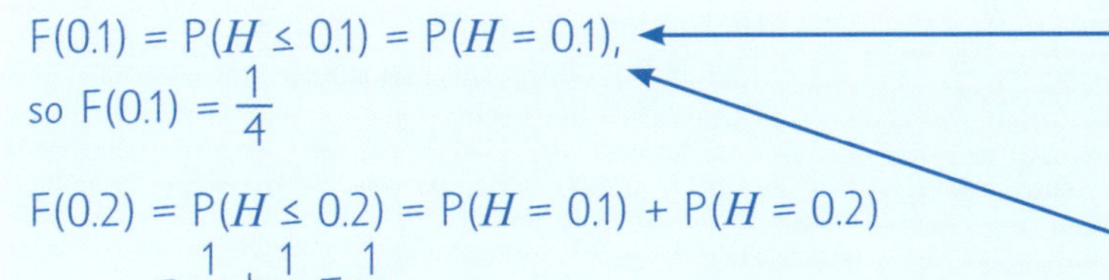

$F(0.1) = P(H \leq 0.1) = P(H = 0.1)$,

so $F(0.1) = \frac{1}{4}$

There are 4 values of h, so you have to find the probability that H is less than or equal to each of them in turn. Start with the smallest value of h.

H can't be less than 0.1.

$F(0.2) = P(H \leq 0.2) = P(H = 0.1) + P(H = 0.2)$

$= \frac{1}{4} + \frac{1}{4} = \frac{1}{2}$

$F(0.3) = P(H \leq 0.3) = P(H = 0.1) + P(H = 0.2) + P(H = 0.3)$

$= \frac{1}{4} + \frac{1}{4} + \frac{1}{3} = \frac{5}{6}$

$F(0.4) = P(H \leq 0.4)$

$= P(H = 0.1) + P(H = 0.2) + P(H = 0.3) + P(H = 0.4)$

$= \frac{1}{4} + \frac{1}{4} + \frac{1}{3} + \frac{1}{6} = 1$

The probability of H being less than or equal to the largest value of h is always 1, as it's the sum of all the possible probabilities.

h	0.1	0.2	0.3	0.4
$F(h) = P(H \leq h)$	$\frac{1}{4}$	$\frac{1}{2}$	$\frac{5}{6}$	1

Write all the values you've found in a table.

Sometimes you'll be asked to work backwards — you can work out the **probability function**, given the cumulative distribution function.

- The probability that X is **equal** to a certain x value is the same as the probability that X is less than or equal to that x value, but not less than or equal to the next lowest x value.
- To describe these x values, it can be useful to use the notation x_i. For example, if X can take the values $x = 2, 4, 6, 9$, then you can label these as $x_1 = 2$, $x_2 = 4$, $x_3 = 6$ and $x_4 = 9$.
- Using this notation, the probability that '$X = x_i$' is the same as the probability that 'X is **less than or equal** to x_i, but **NOT** less than or equal to x_{i-1}'.
- This clever trick can be written: $\mathbf{P(X = x_i) = P(X \leq x_i) - P(X \leq x_{i-1}) = F(x_i) - F(x_{i-1})}$

Example 2

The cumulative distribution function $F(x)$ for a discrete random variable X is: $F(x) = kx$, for $x = 1, 2, 3$ and 4.

Find k, and the probability function for X.

Problem Solving As before, questions with an unknown quantity usually want you to use the fact that all probabilities add up to 1.

$F(4) = P(X \leq 4) = 1$

You know that X has to be 4 or less and that all the probabilities add up to 1.

$F(4) = 1 \Rightarrow 4k = 1$ so $k = \frac{1}{4}$

Substitute 4 in for 'x' in 'kx'.

continued on the next page...

$F(1) = P(X \le 1) = 1 \times k = \frac{1}{4}$,
$F(2) = P(X \le 2) = 2 \times k = \frac{1}{2}$,
$F(3) = P(X \le 3) = 3 \times k = \frac{3}{4}$

Work out the probabilities of X being less than or equal to 1, 2 and 3 by substituting $k = \frac{1}{4}$ into $F(x) = kx$ for each x value.

$P(X = 4) = P(X \le 4) - P(X \le 3) = 1 - \frac{3}{4} = \frac{1}{4}$
$P(X = 3) = P(X \le 3) - P(X \le 2) = \frac{3}{4} - \frac{1}{2} = \frac{1}{4}$
$P(X = 2) = P(X \le 2) - P(X \le 1) = \frac{1}{2} - \frac{1}{4} = \frac{1}{4}$
$P(X = 1) = P(X \le 1) = \frac{1}{4}$

You need to find the probabilities of X being equal to 1, 2, 3 and 4. This is the clever bit, just use: $P(X = x_i) = F(x_i) - F(x_{i-1})$

$P(X = x) = \frac{1}{4}$ for $x = 1, 2, 3, 4$

Now you can write out the probability function.

Exercise 4.3

Q1 Each of a)-d) shows the probability distribution for a discrete random variable, X. Draw up a table to show the cumulative distribution function F(x) for each one.

a)

x	1	2	3	4	5
p(x)	0.1	0.2	0.3	0.2	0.2

b)

x	−2	−1	0	1	2
p(x)	$\frac{1}{5}$	$\frac{1}{5}$	$\frac{1}{5}$	$\frac{1}{5}$	$\frac{1}{5}$

c)

x	1	2	3	4
p(x)	0.3	0.2	0.3	0.2

d)

x	2	4	8	16	32	64
p(x)	$\frac{1}{2}$	$\frac{1}{4}$	$\frac{1}{8}$	$\frac{1}{16}$	$\frac{1}{32}$	$\frac{1}{32}$

Q2 Each of a)-b) shows the probability distribution for a discrete random variable, X. For each part, draw up a table showing the cumulative distribution function, F(x), and use it to find the required probabilities.

a)

x	1	2	3	4
p(x)	0.3	0.1	0.45	0.15

Find: (i) $P(X \le 3)$ and (ii) $P(1 < X \le 3)$

b)

x	−2	−1	0	1	2
p(x)	$\frac{1}{10}$	$\frac{2}{5}$	$\frac{1}{10}$	$\frac{1}{5}$	$\frac{1}{5}$

Find: (i) $P(X \le 0)$ and (ii) $P(X > 0)$

E Q3 The discrete random variable X has probability function:
$P(X = x) = \frac{1}{8}, x = 1, 2, 3, 4, 5, 6, 7, 8$

a) Draw up a table showing the cumulative distribution function, F(x). *[2 marks]*

b) Find: (i) $P(X \le 3)$ and (ii) $P(3 < X \le 7)$ *[3 marks]*

Q4 Each table shows the cumulative distribution function of a discrete random variable, X. Write down the probability distribution for X.

a)

x	1	2	3	4	5
F(x)	0.2	0.3	0.6	0.9	1

b)

x	−2	−1	0	1
F(x)	0.1	0.2	0.7	1

c)

x	2	4	8	16	32	64
F(x)	$\frac{1}{32}$	$\frac{1}{8}$	$\frac{1}{4}$	$\frac{1}{2}$	$\frac{3}{4}$	1

E Q5 The discrete random variable X has the following probability distribution:

x	1	4	9	16	25
P($X = x$)	$\frac{k}{30}$	$\frac{3k-2}{60}$	$\frac{k}{20}$	$\frac{2k-1}{30}$	$\frac{k}{15}$

a) Find the value of the constant k. *[2 marks]*

b) Draw up a table showing the cumulative distribution function, F(x). *[2 marks]*

c) Find P($X \geq 16$). *[1 mark]*

d) Find P($4 < X \leq 16$). *[2 marks]*

P Q6 The discrete random variable X has the cumulative distribution function:

x	1	2	3	4
F(x)	0.3	a	0.8	1

Given that P($X = 2$) = P($X = 3$), draw a table showing the probability distribution of X.

P Q7 For each cumulative distribution function, find the value of k, and give the probability distribution for the discrete random variable, X.

a) $F(x) = \frac{(x+k)^2}{25}, x = 1, 2, 3$

b) $F(x) = \frac{(x+k)^3}{64}, x = 1, 2, 3$

c) $F(x) = 2^{(x-k)}, x = 1, 2, 3$

Challenge

E P Q8 The discrete random variable X has cumulative distribution function:

$$F(x) = \frac{(x-1)^2}{64} \quad x = x_1, x_2, 7, x_3$$

where $x_1, x_2, 7, x_3$ are positive integers in ascending order.

a) Find the values of x_3 and P($X = x_3$). *[2 marks]*

In this cumulative distribution function, $F(x_2) = \frac{1}{4}$.

b) Find the values of x_2 and P($X = 7$). *[2 marks]*

c) Given that P($X = x_2$) = 3P($X = x_1$), find the value of x_1. *[2 marks]*

P Q9 The discrete random variable X = 'the larger score showing when a pair of fair six-sided dice are rolled (or either score if they are the same)'.

a) Show that the cumulative distribution function, F(x), is given by:

$F(x) = \frac{x^2}{36}, \quad x = 1, 2, 3, 4, 5, 6$

b) Hence, find the probability distribution for X.

4.4 Binomial Coefficients

It's really important in probability to be able to **count** the possible **arrangements** of various objects. This is because **different** arrangements of outcomes can sometimes correspond to the **same** event — there's more detail about this on the next few pages.

It's slightly easier to get your head round some of these ideas if you think about things that are less 'abstract' than outcomes. So first of all, think about arranging n **different** objects on a shelf.

> n **different** objects can be arranged in $n!$ ('n factorial') different orders, where $n! = n \times (n-1) \times (n-2) \times \ldots \times 3 \times 2 \times 1$.

Example 1

a) In how many orders can 4 different ornaments be arranged on a shelf?

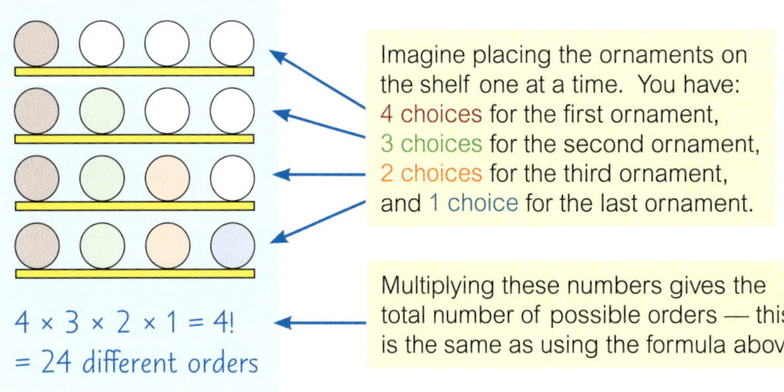

Tip The picture shows one possible order — 1st, 2nd, 3rd, 4th. The white areas are alternate choices for where the ornaments could be placed.

b) In how many orders can 8 different objects be arranged?

$8 \times 7 \times 6 \times 5 \times 4 \times 3 \times 2 \times 1$
$= 8! = 40\,320$ different orders

This time there are 8 choices for the first ornament, 7 for the second, and so on.

Keep thinking about arranging n objects on a shelf — but imagine that x of those objects are the **same**.

> n objects, of which x are **identical**, can be arranged in $\frac{n!}{x!}$ orders.

Example 2

a) In how many different orders can 5 objects be arranged if 2 of those objects are identical?

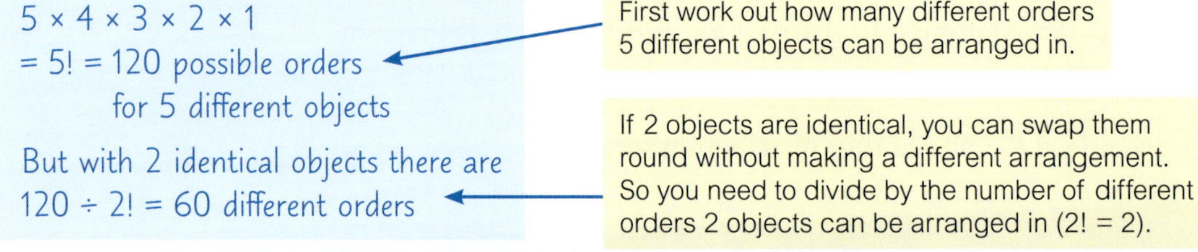

b) In how many different orders can 7 objects be arranged if 4 of those objects are identical and two of the remaining objects are also identical to each other?

$7! = 5040$ possible orders for 7 different objects ← Work out how many different orders 7 different objects can be arranged in.

$4! = 24$ and $2! = 2$

$\frac{7!}{4! \times 2!} = \frac{5040}{24 \times 2} = 105$ possible orders ← Divide by the number of ways the 4 identical objects can be arranged and the number of ways the 2 identical objects can be arranged.

Now imagine you have n objects, but x of these are identical to each other, and the other $n - x$ are also identical to each other (so there are really only two different types of object — x of one type, and $n - x$ of the other).

x objects of **one type** and $(n - x)$ objects of **another type** can be arranged in $\frac{n!}{x!(n-x)!}$ different orders.

Tip Your calculator may have an nCr button or function to calculate binomial coefficients.

You'll have seen $\frac{n!}{x!(n-x)!}$ before in the Pure part of this course — it's a **binomial coefficient**. Remember, binomial coefficients can also be written as $\binom{n}{x}$ and ${}^nC_x$.

Example 3

In how many different orders can 8 identical blue books and 5 identical green books be arranged on a shelf?

$n = 8 + 5 = 13$ and $x = 8$ (or 5),

so there are $\binom{13}{8} = \frac{13!}{8!5!} = 1287$ orders ← You can use the binomial coefficient. It doesn't matter whether x represents the number of green or the number of blue books, since $8!5! = 5!8!$.

Counting 'numbers of arrangements' crops up in all sorts of places.

Example 4 M

a) How many ways are there to select 11 players from a squad of 16?

$\binom{16}{11} = \frac{16!}{11!5!} = 4368$ ← Imagine the 16 players are lined up — then you could 'pick' or 'not pick' players by giving each of them a tick or a cross symbol. So just find the number of ways to order 11 ticks and 5 crosses.

b) How many ways are there to pick 6 lottery numbers from 59?

$\binom{59}{6} = \frac{59!}{6!53!} = 45\,057\,474$ ← Again, numbers are either 'picked' or 'unpicked'. Notice how binomial coefficients get large very quickly as n gets larger.

Chapter 4

Back to the subject of **probability**...

When there are only **two** possible outcomes, these outcomes are often **labelled** 'success' and 'failure'. For example, when you toss a coin, there are two possible outcomes — heads and tails. So 'success' could be heads, while 'failure' could be tails.

In this section, you're going to be working out the **probability** of getting x successes (in **any** order) when you try something n times in total (i.e. in n 'trials'). For example, if you toss a coin 3 times, then you're going to find the probability of getting, say, 2 heads (so here, $n = 3$ and $x = 2$).

But the probability of getting x successes in n trials depends **in part** on how many ways there are to **arrange** those x successes and $(n - x)$ failures. So to find the probability of getting 2 heads in 3 coin tosses, you'd need to find out how many ways there are to get 2 heads and 1 tail in any order.

Tip The 'in part' is explained on page 116.

You could get: (i) heads on 1st and 2nd tosses, tails on the 3rd
(ii) heads on 1st and 3rd tosses, tails on the 2nd
(iii) heads on 2nd and 3rd tosses, tails on the 1st

Tip The 3 possible arrangements of heads and tails are given by: $\binom{3}{2} = \frac{3!}{2!1!} = 3$.

These **different** arrangements of successes and failures are important when you're finding the total probability of '2 heads and 1 tail'.

Example 5

15 coins are tossed. How many ways are there to get:

a) 9 heads and 6 tails?

This is $\binom{15}{9} = \frac{15!}{9!(15-9)!} = \frac{15!}{9! \times 6!} = 5005$

b) 6 heads and 9 tails?

This is $\binom{15}{6} = \frac{15!}{6!(15-6)!} = \frac{15!}{6! \times 9!} = 5005$

Problem Solving It doesn't matter whether you consider heads a 'success' or 'failure'. There are just as many ways to arrange '9 successes and 6 failures' as there are ways to arrange '6 successes and 9 failures'. In fact $\binom{n}{x} = \binom{n}{n-x}$ for any n and x.

Exercise 4.4

Q1 For each word below, find the number of different orders in which the letters can be arranged.

a) RANDOM b) STARLING c) TART
d) START e) STARLINGS f) SASSIEST
g) STARTER h) STRESSLESS i) STARTERS

M Q2 A school football squad consists of 20 players.
How many different ways are there for the coach to choose 11 players out of 20?

Q3 Ten 'success or failure' trials are carried out.
In how many different ways can the following be arranged:

a) 3 successes and 7 failures? b) 5 successes and 5 failures?
c) 1 success and 9 failures? d) 8 successes and 2 failures?

Q4 Twenty 'success or failure' trials are carried out.
In how many different ways can the following be arranged:

a) 10 successes and 10 failures? b) 14 successes and 6 failures?

c) 2 successes and 18 failures? d) 5 successes and 15 failures?

M Q5 A fair coin is tossed 11 times. How many ways are there to get:

a) 4 heads? b) 6 heads? c) 8 heads?

d) 11 heads? e) 5 tails? f) 9 tails?

E P M Q6 Habibah wants to arrange a total of 15 milk bottles in a line.
There are 7 identical bottles of one type, and 4 identical bottles of a different type. The remaining milk bottles are all unique.

a) Find the number of different ways in which Habibah could arrange the 15 milk bottles. *[1 mark]*

The 7 identical bottles each have one of two codes printed on the bottom.
4 of the bottles have one code and 3 have the other.

b) If the two sets of bottles with different codes are treated as separate types, how many different ways can Habibah arrange the 15 milk bottles? *[1 mark]*

P M Q7 In a quiz, a contestant loses if they answer 3 out of 8 questions incorrectly.
Once a contestant has lost, or once it is no longer possible for them to lose, the quiz ends and they don't have to answer the rest of the questions.
In how many ways could a contestant win the quiz without answering all 8 questions?

P M Q8 In a board game, a player selects four coloured pegs from a large number of pegs that are available in six different colours.

a) The pegs are placed in a line in the order that they are selected. How many different arrangements are there if there are no restrictions on the colour chosen?

b) If the order in which the pegs are chosen is irrelevant, in how many ways can a player choose four pegs if each peg has to be a different colour?

Challenge

E P M Q9 Amy is moving x of the 12 plant pots she has in her back garden to her front garden.
There are 792 combinations of plant pots she could choose to move.
Given that Amy is moving fewer than half of the plant pots, find the value of x. *[3 marks]*

E P M Q10 There are twice as many ways of choosing 3 items from n items as there are of choosing 2 items from $(n - 1)$ items.
Find the value of n. *[4 marks]*

4.5 The Binomial Distribution

On page 114, it said that the probability of getting x successes in n trials depended **in part** on the number of ways those x successes could be arranged.

But there's another factor as well — the **probability of success** in any of those trials. This example involves finding the probability of 3 successes in 4 trials.

Example 1

a) I roll a fair dice 4 times. Find the probability of getting a five or a six on 3 of those rolls.

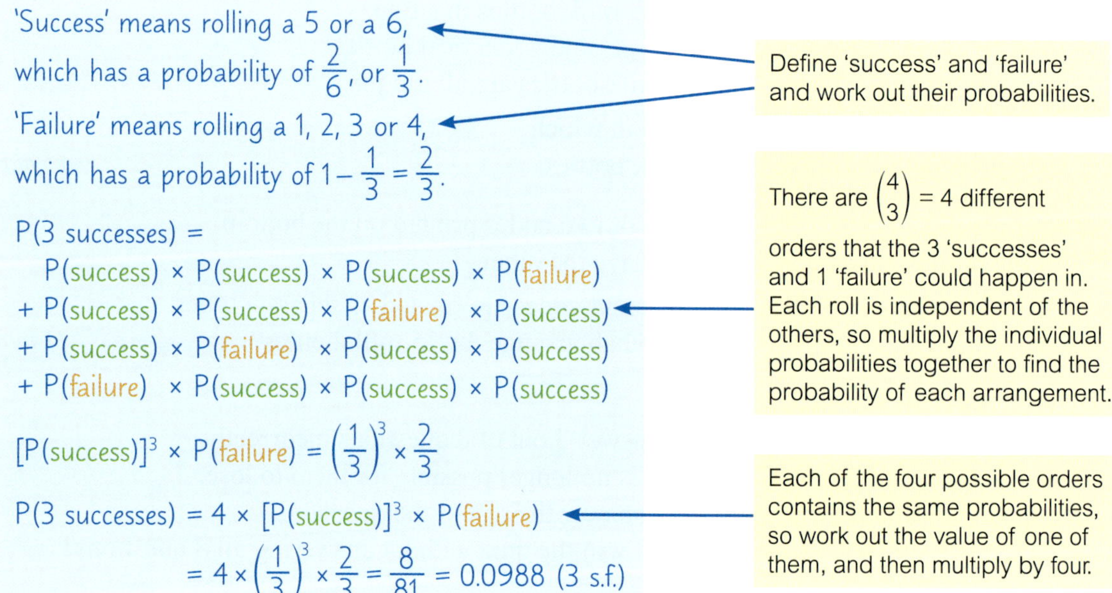

'Success' means rolling a 5 or a 6, which has a probability of $\frac{2}{6}$, or $\frac{1}{3}$.

'Failure' means rolling a 1, 2, 3 or 4, which has a probability of $1 - \frac{1}{3} = \frac{2}{3}$.

Define 'success' and 'failure' and work out their probabilities.

P(3 successes) =
P(success) × P(success) × P(success) × P(failure)
+ P(success) × P(success) × P(failure) × P(success)
+ P(success) × P(failure) × P(success) × P(success)
+ P(failure) × P(success) × P(success) × P(success)

There are $\binom{4}{3} = 4$ different orders that the 3 'successes' and 1 'failure' could happen in. Each roll is independent of the others, so multiply the individual probabilities together to find the probability of each arrangement.

$[\text{P(success)}]^3 \times \text{P(failure)} = \left(\frac{1}{3}\right)^3 \times \frac{2}{3}$

$\text{P(3 successes)} = 4 \times [\text{P(success)}]^3 \times \text{P(failure)}$

$= 4 \times \left(\frac{1}{3}\right)^3 \times \frac{2}{3} = \frac{8}{81} = 0.0988 \text{ (3 s.f.)}$

Each of the four possible orders contains the same probabilities, so work out the value of one of them, and then multiply by four.

b) I roll a fair dice 4 times. Find the probability of getting a six on 3 of those rolls.

'Success' means rolling a 6, which has probability $\frac{1}{6}$.

'Failure' means rolling a 1, 2, 3, 4 or 5, which has probability $1 - \frac{1}{6} = \frac{5}{6}$.

Define 'success' and 'failure' and work out their probabilities.

$\text{P(3 successes)} = 4 \times [\text{P(success)}]^3 \times \text{P(failure)}$

$= 4 \times \left(\frac{1}{6}\right)^3 \times \frac{5}{6} = \frac{4 \times 5}{6^4} = \frac{20}{1296}$

$= 0.0154 \text{ (3 s.f.)}$

You're still looking for 3 successes in 4 rolls, as in part a), so there are still 4 ways to arrange the 3 successes and 1 failure. The only difference is the probabilities.

You could use exactly the same logic to work out the formula for the probability of x successes in n trials, for any values of x and n:

$$\text{P}(x \text{ successes in } n \text{ trials}) = \binom{n}{x} \times [\text{P(success)}]^x \times [\text{P(failure)}]^{n-x}$$

This is the **probability function** for the **binomial distribution**. It tells you the probability that in a total of n separate trials, there will be x successes, for any value of x from 0 to n.

There are **5 conditions** that lead to a binomial distribution. If just one of these conditions is **not met**, then the logic you've just seen to get the formula won't hold, and you **won't** have a binomial distribution.

A random variable X follows a **binomial distribution** as long as these 5 conditions are satisfied:

1. There is a **fixed** number (n) of trials.
2. Each trial involves either '**success**' or '**failure**'.
3. All the trials are **independent**.
4. The probability of 'success' (p) is the **same** in each trial.
5. The variable is the **total** number of **successes** in the n trials.

In this case, $\mathbf{P}(X = x) = \binom{n}{x} \times p^x \times (1 - p)^{n-x}$

for $x = 0, 1, 2, ..., n$, and you can write $X \sim \mathrm{B}(n, p)$.

> **Tip** Binomial random variables are discrete, since they only take values 0, 1, 2, ... , n.

> **Tip** n and p are the two parameters of the binomial distribution. (Or n is sometimes called the 'index'.)

Example 2 

Which of the random variables described below would follow a binomial distribution? For those that do, state the distribution's parameters.

a) The number of red cards (R) drawn from a standard, shuffled 52-card pack in 10 picks, not replacing the cards each time.

Not binomial, since the probability of 'success' changes each time (as the cards are not replaced).

b) The number of red cards (R) drawn from a standard, shuffled 52-card pack in 10 picks, replacing the card each time.

Binomial — there's a fixed number (10) of independent trials with two possible results ('red' or 'black/not red'), a constant probability of success (as the cards are replaced), and R is the number of red cards drawn. So $R \sim \mathrm{B}(10, 0.5)$.

c) The number of times (T) I have to toss a coin before I get heads.

Not binomial, since the number of trials isn't fixed.

d) The number of left-handed people (L) in a sample of 500 randomly chosen people if the proportion of left-handed people in the population of the United Kingdom is 0.13.

Binomial — there's a fixed number (500) of independent trials with two possible results ('left-handed' or 'not left-handed'), a constant probability of success (0.13), and L is the number of left-handers. So $L \sim \mathrm{B}(500, 0.13)$.

> The population of the UK is huge compared to the sample size. This means the probability of choosing a left-handed person isn't affected by the number of left-handed people already selected.

Sometimes you might need to make an **assumption** in order to justify using a binomial distribution. Any assumptions you need to make will be in order to satisfy the 5 conditions for a binomial distribution on the previous page.

Example 3 M

State any assumptions that would need to be made in order for N to be modelled by a binomial distribution, where N is the total number of defective widgets produced by a machine in a day, if it produces 5000 widgets every day.

There's a fixed number (5000) of trials, and each trial has two possible results ('defective' or 'not defective'). N is the number of 'successes' over the 5000 trials. So there are two more conditions to satisfy.

You'd need to assume that the trials are independent (e.g. that one defective widget doesn't lead to another), and that the probability of a defective widget being produced is always the same (if the machine needed to 'warm up' every morning before it started working properly, then this might not be true).

Exercise 4.5

M **Q1** In each of the following situations, explain whether or not the random variable follows a binomial distribution. For those that follow a binomial distribution, state the parameters n and p.

a) The number of spins (X) of a five-sided spinner (numbered 1-5) until a 3 is obtained.

b) The number of defective light bulbs (X) in a batch of 2000 new bulbs, where 0.5% of light bulbs are randomly defective.

c) The number of boys (Y) out of the next 10 children born in a town, assuming births are equally likely to produce a girl or a boy.

M **Q2** Kaitlin believes that it is sunny in Philadelphia on 30% of the days in a year. She claims that the number of sunny days in any given week, X, can be modelled by the binomial distribution $X \sim B(7, 0.3)$. Explain why this model may not be accurate.

M **Q3** A circus performer successfully completes his act on 95% of occasions. He will perform his act on 15 occasions and X is the number of occasions on which he successfully completes the act.

State the assumptions that would need to be made in order for X to be modelled by a binomial distribution.

M **Q4** Ahmed picks 10 cards from a standard, shuffled pack of 52 cards. If X is the number of picture cards (i.e. jacks, queens or kings), state the conditions under which X would follow a binomial distribution, giving the parameters of this distribution.

M **Q5** A sewing machine operator sews buttons onto jackets. The probability that a button sewed by this operator falls off a jacket before it leaves the factory is 0.001. On one particular day, the sewing machine operator sews 650 buttons, and X is the number of these buttons that fall off a jacket before it leaves the factory.

Can X be modelled by a binomial distribution?
State any assumptions you make and state the value of any parameters.

E M Q6 A broadband provider randomly chooses 150 customers to call as part of a marketing campaign. Previous campaigns show that the probability of a customer answering their call is 45%. The number of customers that answer their call is modelled as a discrete random variable following a binomial probability distribution.

a) State an assumption that is needed to satisfy the binomial distribution condition that all trials are independent. *[1 mark]*

b) Explain how the information given satisfies any two of the other requirements needed for a binomial distribution. *[2 marks]*

c) Write down the parameters for the required binomial distribution. *[1 mark]*

E M Q7 Kamali selects 8 different songs randomly from a large library of music online. Kamali assumes each song has an 80% chance of having a running time longer than 3 minutes. Kamali decides to model the number of songs in her selection that are not longer than 3 minutes as a discrete random variable X, following a binomial distribution.

a) Give two reasons why a binomial distribution is suitable for this scenario. *[2 marks]*

b) Write down the parameters for the required binomial distribution. *[1 mark]*

4.6 Using the Binomial Probability Function

You've seen the conditions that give rise to a binomial probability distribution. And you've seen where the binomial probability function (see below) comes from.

For a random variable X, where $X \sim B(n, p)$:

$$P(X = x) = \binom{n}{x} \times p^x \times (1-p)^{n-x} \quad \text{for } x = 0, 1, 2, ..., n$$

Tip This formula is in the formula booklet — but you'll have to look in the A-level section to find it.

Now you need to make sure you know how to use it.

You can also find the value of $P(X = x)$ really easily using your calculator. Be careful as some calculators have a probability function (PD or PDF) and a cumulative distribution function (CD or CDF, see p.108) — you should be using the probability function for this type of question.

Example 1

If $X \sim B(12, 0.16)$, find:

a) $P(X = 0)$

$$P(X=0) = \binom{12}{0} \times 0.16^0 \times (1-0.16)^{12-0} = \frac{12!}{0!12!} \times 0.16^0 \times 0.84^{12}$$
$$= 0.123 \text{ (3 s.f.)}$$

Use the formula with $n = 12$, $p = 0.16$ and $x = 0$.

b) $P(X = 2)$

$$P(X=2) = \binom{12}{2} \times 0.16^2 \times (1-0.16)^{12-2} = \frac{12!}{2!10!} \times 0.16^2 \times 0.84^{10}$$
$$= 0.296 \text{ (3 s.f.)}$$

Use the formula with $n = 12$, $p = 0.16$ and $x = 2$.

Don't be put off if the question is asked in some kind of context.

Example 2 

I spin the fair spinner on the right 7 times.
Find the probability that I spin:

a) 2 fives

Let X = number of fives spun, then $X \sim B(7, \frac{1}{5})$

Call 'spin a five' a success and 'spin anything else' a failure.

$$P(X = 2) = \binom{7}{2} \times \left(\frac{1}{5}\right)^2 \times \left(\frac{4}{5}\right)^5$$
$$= \frac{7!}{2!5!} \times \frac{1}{25} \times \frac{1024}{3125} = 0.275 \text{ (3 s.f.)}$$

You want to find the probability of 2 successes in 7 spins, so use the binomial probability function with $n = 7$ and p = P(spin a five) = $\frac{1}{5}$.

b) 4 numbers less than three

Let X = number of spins less than three, then $X \sim B(7, \frac{2}{5})$

Call 'spin a number less than three' a success and 'spin anything else' a failure.

$$P(X = 4) = \binom{7}{4} \times \left(\frac{2}{5}\right)^4 \times \left(\frac{3}{5}\right)^3$$
$$= \frac{7!}{4!3!} \times \frac{16}{625} \times \frac{27}{125}$$
$$= 0.194 \text{ (3 s.f.)}$$

You want to find the probability of 4 successes in 7 spins, so use the binomial probability function with $n = 7$ and p = P(spin less than a three) = $\frac{2}{5}$.

Sometimes you might need to find several individual probabilities, and then add the results together.

Example 3

If $X \sim B(6, 0.32)$, find:

Tip If $X \sim B(n, p)$, then X can take only integer values from 0 to n.

a) $P(X \leq 2)$

If $X \leq 2$, then X can be 0, 1 or 2.

Work out which probabilities you need.

$$P(X = 0) = \binom{6}{0} \times 0.32^0 \times (1 - 0.32)^{6-0}$$
$$= \frac{6!}{0!6!} \times 0.32^0 \times 0.68^6 = 0.0988...$$

$$P(X = 1) = \binom{6}{1} \times 0.32^1 \times (1 - 0.32)^{6-1}$$
$$= \frac{6!}{1!5!} \times 0.32^1 \times 0.68^5 = 0.2791...$$

$$P(X = 2) = \binom{6}{2} \times 0.32^2 \times (1 - 0.32)^{6-2}$$
$$= \frac{6!}{2!4!} \times 0.32^2 \times 0.68^4 = 0.3284...$$

Use the formula to find $P(X = 0)$, $P(X = 1)$ and $P(X = 2)$. Here $n = 6$ and $p = 0.32$.

$$P(X \leq 2) = P(X = 0) + P(X = 1) + P(X = 2)$$
$$= 0.0988... + 0.2791... + 0.3284... = 0.706 \text{ (3 s.f.)}$$

Add the results together to find $P(X \leq 2)$. You can add these probabilities as they are mutually exclusive (see page 86).

b) $P(2 \leq X < 4)$

If $2 \leq X < 4$, then X can be 2 or 3.

$P(X = 3) = \binom{6}{3} \times 0.32^3 \times (1 - 0.32)^{6-3}$

$= \frac{6!}{3!3!} \times 0.32^3 \times 0.68^3 = 0.2060...$

$P(2 \leq X < 4) = P(X = 2) + P(X = 3)$

$= 0.3284... + 0.2060... = 0.534$ (3 s.f.)

Work out which probabilities you need.

You've already found $P(X = 2)$, so you just need to find $P(X = 3)$ now.

Now add the probabilities together.

Sometimes you're better off using a bit of cunning and coming at things from a different direction.

Example 4 **M**

A drug with a success rate of 83% is tested on 8 people.
X, the number of people the drug is successful on, can be modelled by the binomial distribution $X \sim B(8, 0.83)$. Find $P(X \leq 6)$.

$P(X \leq 6) = 1 - P(X > 6) = 1 - P(X = 7) - P(X = 8)$

$P(X = 7) = \binom{8}{7} \times 0.83^7 \times (1 - 0.83)^{8-7}$

$= \frac{8!}{7!1!} \times 0.83^7 \times 0.17^1 = 0.3690...$

$P(X = 8) = \binom{8}{8} \times 0.83^8 \times (1 - 0.83)^{8-8}$

$= \frac{8!}{8!0!} \times 0.83^8 \times 0.17^0 = 0.2252...$

$P(X \leq 6) = 1 - P(X = 7) - P(X = 8)$

$= 1 - 0.3690... - 0.2252... = 0.406$ (3 s.f.)

You could use the method above — i.e. $P(X \leq 6) = P(X = 0) + P(X = 1) + ... + P(X = 6)$. But it's quicker here to work out the probabilities you **don't** want, and then subtract them from 1.

Use the formula to find $P(X = 7)$, where $n = 8$ and $p = 0.83$.

Now find $P(X = 8)$.

Finally subtract them both from 1.

Example 5 **M**

When I toss a grape in the air and try to catch it in my mouth, my probability of success is always 0.8. The number of grapes I catch in 10 throws is described by the discrete random variable X.

a) Explain why X can be modelled by a binomial distribution and give the values of any parameters.

There's a fixed number (10) of independent trials with two possible results ('catch' and 'not catch'), a constant probability of success (0.8), and X is the total number of catches. Therefore X follows a binomial distribution, $X \sim B(10, 0.8)$.

b) Find the probability of me catching at least 9 grapes in 10 throws.

$P(X \geq 9) = P(X = 9) + P(X = 10)$

$= \left\{\binom{10}{9} \times 0.8^9 \times 0.2^1\right\} + \left\{\binom{10}{10} \times 0.8^{10} \times 0.2^0\right\}$

$= 0.2684... + 0.1073... = 0.376$ (3 s.f.)

To find P(at least 9 catches), add P(9 catches) and P(10 catches) together.

Exercise 4.6

Q1 Find the probabilities below. Give your answers to 3 significant figures.

a) For $X \sim B(10, 0.14)$:

(i) $P(X = 2)$ (ii) $P(X = 4)$ (iii) $P(X = 5)$

b) For $X \sim B(8, 0.27)$:

(i) $P(X = 3)$ (ii) $P(X = 5)$ (iii) $P(X = 7)$

c) For $X \sim B(22, 0.55)$:

(i) $P(X = 10)$ (ii) $P(X = 15)$ (iii) $P(X = 20)$

Q2 Find the probabilities below. Give your answers to 3 significant figures.

a) For $X \sim B(12, 0.7)$:

(i) $P(X \geq 11)$ (ii) $P(8 \leq X \leq 10)$ (iii) $P(X > 9)$

b) For $X \sim B(20, 0.16)$:

(i) $P(X < 2)$ (ii) $P(X \leq 3)$ (iii) $P(1 < X \leq 4)$

c) For $X \sim B(30, 0.88)$:

(i) $P(X > 28)$ (ii) $P(25 < X < 28)$ (iii) $P(X \geq 27)$

d) For $X \sim B(14, 0.62)$:

(i) $P(X = 6)$ (ii) $P(X \geq 12)$ (iii) $P(X \leq 11)$

Q3 Find the probabilities below. Give your answers to 3 significant figures.

a) For $X \sim B(5, \frac{1}{2})$:

(i) $P(X \leq 4)$ (ii) $P(X > 1)$ (iii) $P(1 \leq X \leq 4)$

b) For $X \sim B(8, \frac{2}{3})$:

(i) $P(X < 7)$ (ii) $P(X \geq 2)$ (iii) $P(0 \leq X \leq 8)$

c) For $X \sim B(6, \frac{4}{5})$:

(i) $P(X > 0)$ (ii) $P(X \geq 3)$ (iii) $P(1 \leq X < 6)$

M Q4 A biased coin, for which the probability of heads is $\frac{2}{5}$, is tossed 9 times. Find the probability of getting:

a) 2 heads b) 5 heads c) 9 tails

E M Q5 There are 8 lights above a stage. The colour displayed by each light is chosen at random by a computer from a choice of 10 colours, including red. The discrete random variable X is the number of lights displaying red and follows a binomial probability distribution.

a) State a distribution that can be used to model X. *[1 mark]*

b) Find the probability that there are exactly 4 lights displaying red. *[1 mark]*

c) Find the probability that no lights display red. *[1 mark]*

P M Q6 A fair, six-sided dice is rolled 5 times. Find the probability of rolling:

a) exactly 2 sixes
b) at least 1 five
c) more than 3 threes
d) 3 scores of more than two
e) no multiples of 3
f) 4 or fewer square numbers

M Q7 A multiple-choice test has three possible answers to each question, only one of which is correct. A student guesses the answer to each of the twelve questions at random. The random variable X is the number of correct answers.

a) State the distribution of X and explain why this model is suitable.

b) Find the probability that the student gets fewer than three questions correct.

M Q8 22.5% of the avocados in a crate are ripe. Seb picks out 3 avocados at random. After selecting each avocado, he replaces it and mixes them all up before selecting again. What is the probability that all the avocados he picks are ripe?

M Q9 5% of the items made using a particular production process are defective. A quality control manager samples 15 items at random. What is the probability that there are between 1 and 3 defective items (inclusive)?

P M Q10 For each dart thrown by a darts player, the probability that it scores 'treble-20' is 0.75.

a) The player throws 3 darts. Find the probability that she gets a 'treble-20' with at least 2 darts.

b) She throws another 30 darts for a charity challenge. If she gets a 'treble-20' with at least 26 of the darts, she wins the charity a prize. What is the probability that she wins the prize?

E P M Q11 A random sample of 50 people from across the country are asked whether they intend to switch their energy supplier. From previous surveys, the probability that someone intends to switch their energy supplier is assumed to be 0.35.

a) State the distribution to model the number of people in the sample who intend to switch their energy supplier. *[1 mark]*

b) Find the probability that either exactly 20 people or exactly 30 people in the sample intend to switch their energy supplier. *[2 marks]*

c) Find the probability that fewer than 3 people in the sample do not intend to switch their energy supplier.
Give your answer in standard form to 4 significant figures. *[3 marks]*

Challenge

E P Q12 The discrete random variable X has the binomial probability distribution $X \sim B(15, p)$.

a) Find $P(X \geq 14)$ in terms of p, giving your answer in its simplest form. *[3 marks]*

b) Given that $P(X = 4) = P(X = 11)$, show that $p = 0.5$. *[3 marks]*

4.7 Using Binomial Tables to Find Probabilities

Binomial tables show the sum of all the binomial probabilities less than or equal to a given number, for certain values of n and p. Here's an example of a problem solved **without** binomial tables.

Example 1 M

I have an unfair coin. When I toss this coin, the probability of getting heads is 0.35. Find the probability that it will land on heads fewer than 3 times when I toss it 12 times in total.

Let X represent the number of heads in 12 tosses, then $X \sim B(12, 0.35)$.

$$P(X \leq 2) = P(X = 0) + P(X = 1) + P(X = 2)$$

$$= \left\{\binom{12}{0} \times 0.35^0 \times 0.65^{12}\right\} + \left\{\binom{12}{1} \times 0.35^1 \times 0.65^{11}\right\} + \left\{\binom{12}{2} \times 0.35^2 \times 0.65^{10}\right\}$$

$$= 0.005688... + 0.036753... + 0.108846...$$

$$= 0.1513 \text{ (4 s.f.)}$$

Define the random variable X and state its distribution.

You need to find $P(X < 3)$, which is the same as $P(X \leq 2)$.

But it's much quicker to use tables of the binomial **cumulative distribution function** (c.d.f.). These tables show $P(X \leq x)$, for $X \sim B(n, p)$.
So have another look at the problem in the previous example.
Here, $X \sim B(12, 0.35)$, and you need to find $P(X \leq 2)$.

- First find the table for the correct value of n. The table below is for $n = 12$.
- Then find the right value of p across the top of the table — here, $p = 0.35$.

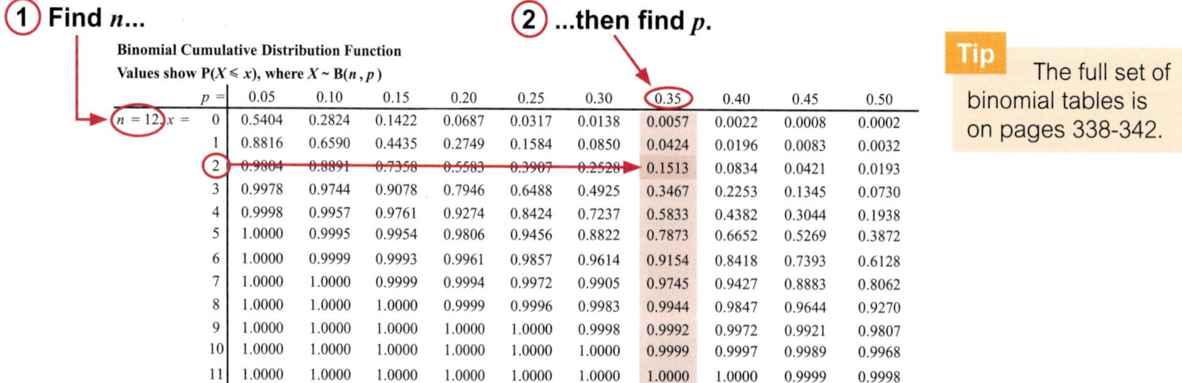

Binomial Cumulative Distribution Function
Values show $P(X \leq x)$, where $X \sim B(n, p)$

p =	0.05	0.10	0.15	0.20	0.25	0.30	0.35	0.40	0.45	0.50
$n = 12$, x = 0	0.5404	0.2824	0.1422	0.0687	0.0317	0.0138	0.0057	0.0022	0.0008	0.0002
1	0.8816	0.6590	0.4435	0.2749	0.1584	0.0850	0.0424	0.0196	0.0083	0.0032
2	0.9804	0.8891	0.7358	0.5583	0.3907	0.2528	0.1513	0.0834	0.0421	0.0193
3	0.9978	0.9744	0.9078	0.7946	0.6488	0.4925	0.3467	0.2253	0.1345	0.0730
4	0.9998	0.9957	0.9761	0.9274	0.8424	0.7237	0.5833	0.4382	0.3044	0.1938
5	1.0000	0.9995	0.9954	0.9806	0.9456	0.8822	0.7873	0.6652	0.5269	0.3872
6	1.0000	0.9999	0.9993	0.9961	0.9857	0.9614	0.9154	0.8418	0.7393	0.6128
7	1.0000	1.0000	0.9999	0.9994	0.9972	0.9905	0.9745	0.9427	0.8883	0.8062
8	1.0000	1.0000	1.0000	0.9999	0.9996	0.9983	0.9944	0.9847	0.9644	0.9270
9	1.0000	1.0000	1.0000	1.0000	1.0000	0.9998	0.9992	0.9972	0.9921	0.9807
10	1.0000	1.0000	1.0000	1.0000	1.0000	1.0000	0.9999	0.9997	0.9989	0.9968
11	1.0000	1.0000	1.0000	1.0000	1.0000	1.0000	1.0000	1.0000	0.9999	0.9998

Tip The full set of binomial tables is on pages 338-342.

The numbers underneath your value of p tell you $P(X \leq x)$ for all the different values of x down the left-hand side of the table. Here, you need $P(X \leq 2)$. So reading across, the table tells you $P(X \leq 2) = \mathbf{0.1513}$.

You might find it easier to use your calculator rather than the tables to find these values in your exam. For these questions, you should use the binomial cumulative distribution function (CD or CDF) instead of the binomial probability function (see page 119). You could even use both tables and calculator to check that you get the same answer from both, if you have time.

Example 2 

I have an unfair coin. When I toss this coin, the probability of getting heads is 0.35.
Find the probability that it will land on heads fewer than 6 times when I toss it 12 times in total.

Let X be the number of heads, then $X \sim B(12, 0.35)$.

Using the table for $n = 12$ and $p = 0.35$, $P(X \leq 5) = 0.7873$.

> Since $n = 12$ again, you can use the table at the bottom of the previous page. And since $p = 0.35$, the probability you need will also be in the highlighted column. But this time, you need to find $P(X \leq 5)$, so find $x = 5$ down the left-hand side of the table, and then read across.

For these next examples, the value of n is also 12, so you can still use the table on the previous page. The value of p is different, though — so you'll need to use a different column.

But be warned... in these examples, looking up the value in the table is just the start of the solution.

Example 3 

I have a different unfair coin. When I toss this coin, the probability of getting heads is 0.4.
Find the probability that it will land on heads more than 4 times when I toss it 12 times in total.

Let X be the number of heads, then $X \sim B(12, 0.4)$

Using the table for $n = 12$ and $p = 0.4$, $P(X \leq 4) = 0.4382$.

$$P(X > 4) = 1 - P(X \leq 4) = 1 - 0.4382 = 0.5618$$

> This time, $p = 0.4$ — so find $p = 0.4$ along the top of the table, and look at that column. The tables only show $P(X \leq x)$, whereas you need to find $P(X > 4)$. But $P(X > 4) = 1 - P(X \leq 4)$ — so you can still use the information in the table to quickly find the answer.

With a bit of cunning, you can get binomial tables to tell you almost anything you want to know...

Example 4 

The probability of getting heads when I toss my unfair coin is 0.4.
When I toss this coin 12 times in total, find the probability that:

a) It will land on heads exactly 6 times.

Let X be the number of heads, then $X \sim B(12, 0.4)$.

$P(X = 6) = P(X \leq 6) - P(X \leq 5)$

> To find $P(X = 6)$, use $P(X \leq 6) = P(X \leq 5) + P(X = 6)$.

Using the table for $n = 12$ and $p = 0.4$: $P(X \leq 6) = 0.8418$
$P(X \leq 5) = 0.6652$

> You can find both $P(X \leq 6)$ and $P(X \leq 5)$ from the tables — use the '$p = 0.4$' column in the '$n = 12$' table.

$$P(X = 6) = P(X \leq 6) - P(X \leq 5) = 0.8418 - 0.6652 = 0.1766$$

> Then plug in those values.

Problem Solving

If A and B are mutually exclusive events, then P(A or B) = P(A) + P(B). If you call A the event '$X \leq 5$', and B the event '$X = 6$', then: P(A or B) = $P(X \leq 5 \text{ or } X = 6)$ = $P(X \leq 6)$.

b) It will land on heads more than 3 times but fewer than 6 times.

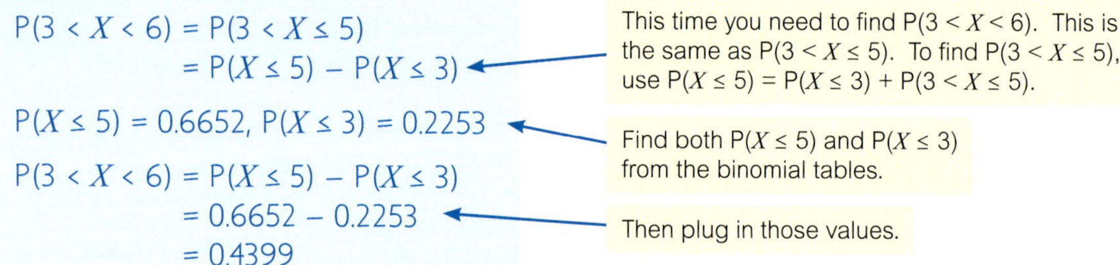

$P(3 < X < 6) = P(3 < X \leq 5)$
$= P(X \leq 5) - P(X \leq 3)$

This time you need to find $P(3 < X < 6)$. This is the same as $P(3 < X \leq 5)$. To find $P(3 < X \leq 5)$, use $P(X \leq 5) = P(X \leq 3) + P(3 < X \leq 5)$.

$P(X \leq 5) = 0.6652$, $P(X \leq 3) = 0.2253$

Find both $P(X \leq 5)$ and $P(X \leq 3)$ from the binomial tables.

$P(3 < X < 6) = P(X \leq 5) - P(X \leq 3)$
$= 0.6652 - 0.2253$
$= 0.4399$

Then plug in those values.

There's an easy way to remember which probability you need to subtract. For example, suppose you need to find $P(a < X \leq b)$.

- Use the table to find **$P(X \leq b)$** — the probability that X is less than or equal to the largest value satisfying the inequality '$a < X \leq b$'...
- **...and subtract $P(X \leq a)$** to 'remove' the probability that X takes one of the smaller values not satisfying the inequality '$a < X \leq b$'.

Problem Solving

You could work out all the individual probabilities and add them together, but it would take a lot longer.

Example 5

If $X \sim B(12, 0.45)$, find:

a) $P(5 < X \leq 8)$

Using the table for $n = 12$ and $p = 0.45$, $P(X \leq 8) = 0.9644$.

The largest value satisfying the inequality $5 < X \leq 8$ is $X = 8$. So you need to find $P(X \leq 8)$.

From the table, $P(X \leq 5) = 0.5269$.
So $P(5 < X \leq 8) = P(X \leq 8) - P(X \leq 5)$
$= 0.9644 - 0.5269$
$= 0.4375$

You need to subtract the probability $P(X \leq 5)$, since $X = 5$ doesn't satisfy the inequality $5 < X \leq 8$, and neither does any value smaller than 5.

b) $P(4 \leq X < 10)$

Using the table for $n = 12$ and $p = 0.45$, $P(X \leq 9) = 0.9921$.

The largest value satisfying the inequality $4 \leq X < 10$ is $X = 9$. So you need to find $P(X \leq 9)$.

From the table, $P(X \leq 3) = 0.1345$.
So $P(4 \leq X < 10) = P(X \leq 9) - P(X \leq 3)$
$= 0.9921 - 0.1345$
$= 0.8576$

Now subtract the probability $P(X \leq 3)$, since $X = 3$ doesn't satisfy the inequality $4 \leq X < 10$, and neither does any value smaller than 3.

Using the tables is relatively straightforward as long as you can find the value of p you need. But the values of p only go as high as $p = 0.5$ — so if $p > 0.5$, you need to think about things slightly differently.

- Suppose $X \sim B(12, 0.65)$, and you need to find $P(X \leq 5)$. This means you need to find the probability of 5 or fewer 'successes', when the probability of 'success' is $p = 0.65$.
- But you can switch things round and say you need to find the probability of 7 or more 'failures', where the probability of 'failure' is $1 - p = 0.35$.
- It's easiest if you rewrite the problem using a new variable, Y, say. Y will represent the number of 'failures' in 12 trials, so $Y \sim B(12, 0.35)$.

- You can use tables to find $P(Y \geq 7) = 1 - P(Y < 7) = 1 - P(Y \leq 6) = 1 - 0.9154 = \mathbf{0.0846}$
- So the probability of 7 or more 'failures' is 0.0846 if the probability of each 'failure' is 0.35. This must equal the probability of 5 or fewer 'successes' if the probability of 'success' is 0.65.
- So if $X \sim B(12, 0.65)$, then $P(X \leq 5) = \mathbf{0.0846}$.

> Where $X \sim B(n, p)$, but $p > 0.5$...
>
> First define $Y = n - X$, where $Y \sim B(n, 1 - p)$.
> Then, for constants k and h:
>
> - $P(X \leq k) = P(Y \geq n - k)$ and $P(X < k) = P(Y > n - k)$
> - $P(X \geq k) = P(Y \leq n - k)$ and $P(X > k) = P(Y < n - k)$
> - $P(h < X \leq k) = P(n - k \leq Y < n - h)$

Example 6 M

The probability of this spinner landing on blue is 0.7.
The spinner is spun 12 times, and the random variable X represents the number of times the spinner lands on blue.

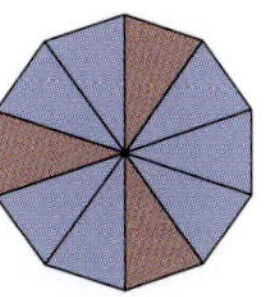

a) Find $P(X > 8)$.

$X \sim B(12, 0.7)$

Let Y = number of reds = $12 - X$,
$P(\text{red}) = 1 - P(\text{blue}) = 1 - 0.7 = 0.3$.
This means $Y \sim B(12, 0.3)$

$P(X > 8) = P(Y < 4) = P(Y \leq 3) = 0.4925$

Write down the distribution that X follows. X represents the number of 'blues' in 12 spins and P(land on blue) = 0.7.

Since $p > 0.5$, you can't use the tables for X. So define a new random variable Y, where Y represents the number of 'reds' in 12 spins.

Use the tables for Y to work out $P(X > 8)$.

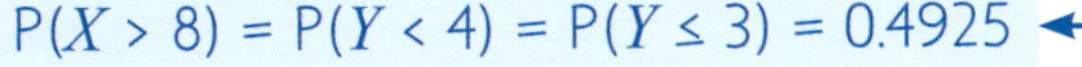

b) Find $P(X \leq 4)$.

$P(X \leq 4) = P(Y \geq 8) = 1 - P(Y < 8) = 1 - P(Y \leq 7)$
$= 1 - 0.9905 = 0.0095$

Write the probability in terms of Y, then use the tables.

c) Find $P(5 \leq X < 8)$.

$P(5 \leq X < 8) = P(4 < Y \leq 7) = P(Y \leq 7) - P(Y \leq 4)$
$= 0.9905 - 0.7237 = 0.2668$

This time you'll need to find two values from the tables.

Exercise 4.7

Q1 The random variable $X \sim B(10, 0.25)$. Use the binomial table for $n = 10$ to find:

a) $P(X \leq 2)$ b) $P(X \leq 7)$ c) $P(X \leq 9)$ d) $P(X < 10)$
e) $P(X < 5)$ f) $P(X < 4)$ g) $P(X < 6)$ h) $P(X < 2)$

Q2 The random variable $X \sim B(15, 0.4)$. Use the appropriate binomial table to find:

a) $P(X > 3)$ b) $P(X > 6)$ c) $P(X > 10)$ d) $P(X \geq 5)$
e) $P(X \geq 3)$ f) $P(X \geq 13)$ g) $P(X > 11)$ h) $P(X \geq 1)$

Q3 The random variable $X \sim B(20, 0.35)$. Use the appropriate binomial table to find:

a) $P(X = 7)$ b) $P(X = 12)$ c) $P(2 < X \leq 4)$

d) $P(10 < X \leq 15)$ e) $P(7 \leq X \leq 10)$ f) $P(3 \leq X < 11)$

Q4 The random variable $X \sim B(25, 0.8)$. Use the appropriate binomial table to find:

a) $P(X \geq 17)$ b) $P(X \geq 20)$ c) $P(X > 14)$

d) $P(X = 21)$ e) $P(3 \leq X < 14)$ f) $P(12 \leq X < 18)$

M Q5 The probability of having green eyes is known to be 0.18. In a class of thirty children, find the probability that fewer than ten children have green eyes.

Q5 Hint You'll need to use the c.d.f on your calculator to find the probability in this question.

M Q6 In a production process it is known that approximately 5% of items are faulty. In a random sample of 25 objects, estimate the probability that fewer than 6 are faulty.

M Q7 I have an unfair coin. When tossed, the probability of getting heads is 0.85. If I toss it 15 times, find the probability that it will land on heads at least 11 times but fewer than 14 times.

E M Q8 A second-hand car salesperson claims that the probability of each car they have for sale having a mileage of 50 000 miles or less is 90%. A random sample of 40 cars is chosen to test this claim. The number of cars in the sample with a mileage of more than 50 000 miles is modelled by the random variable X, following a binomial distribution.

a) State the parameters for the distribution of X. *[1 mark]*

b) Find the probability that no more than 6 cars in the sample have a mileage of more than 50 000 miles. *[1 mark]*

c) 3 of the cars in the sample had a mileage of more than 50 000 miles. Find the probability of this result, assuming the salesperson's claim is true. *[2 marks]*

M Q9 A shop delivers newspapers to a customer 7 days a week. The probability that any random newspaper is undelivered is known to be 0.05. If the customer has more than one paper undelivered in a week they get free newspapers for that week. The number of newspapers undelivered in a week, X, can be modelled by a binomial distribution. Find the probability that the customer gets free newspapers for the week, in any random week.

Challenge

E P M Q10 Abbie receives 25 emails one day. The probability of an email she receives being spam is 0.65.

a) State a distribution that can be used to model the number of spam emails she receives on this day. *[1 mark]*

b) Find the probability that Abbie receives exactly 10 spam emails on this day. *[2 marks]*

c) Using your answer to part b) and stating any necessary assumptions, find the probability that Abbie receives exactly 10 spam emails per day on at least 2 days out of a period of 5 days. *[4 marks]*

d) Comment on the assumption made in your answer to part c). *[1 marks]*

4.8 Using Binomial Tables 'Backwards'

Sometimes, you'll need to use the tables 'the other way round'. So far you've been given a value for x, and you've had to find a probability such as $P(X \le x)$, $P(X > x)$, $P(X = x)$,... and so on. But you could be given a probability (c, say) and asked to find a value of x. These kinds of questions can get quite complicated.

If your calculator has an Inverse Binomial function, you can use that to answer these questions really easily. If not, you can instead use the binomial cumulative distribution function on your calculator 'backwards'. Your calculator might allow you to produce a table of values for your n and p — otherwise you'll have to use trial and error to find the probability for different x-values.

Example 1

If $X \sim B(25, 0.2)$, find:

a) c if $P(X \le c) = 0.7800$

Using the table for $n = 25$ and $p = 0.2$:
$P(X \le 6) = 0.7800$, so $c = 6$

Use the binomial table for $n = 25$, and the column for $p = 0.2$. Go down the column until you reach 0.7800.

b) d if $P(X \ge d) = 0.7660$

If $P(X \ge d) = 0.7660$, then
$P(X < d) = P(X \le d - 1) = 1 - 0.7660 = 0.2340$

Rewrite the information you're given as a probability of the form $P(X \le x)$.

$P(X \le 3) = 0.2340$, so $d - 1 = 3 \Rightarrow d = 4$

Go down the 0.2 column until you reach 0.2340. The value of x gives you $d - 1$, so add 1 to find d.

Example 2

If $X \sim B(30, 0.4)$, find:

a) the maximum value a such that $P(X \le a) < 0.05$.

Using the table for $n = 30$ and $p = 0.4$:
$P(X \le 7) = 0.0435$
$P(X \le 8) = 0.0940$

Use the binomial table for $n = 30$, and go down the column for $p = 0.4$ until you find two probabilities either side of 0.05.

So $a = 7$

a is the largest value of x where $P(X \le x)$ is less than 0.05.

b) the minimum value b such that $P(X > b) < 0.05$.

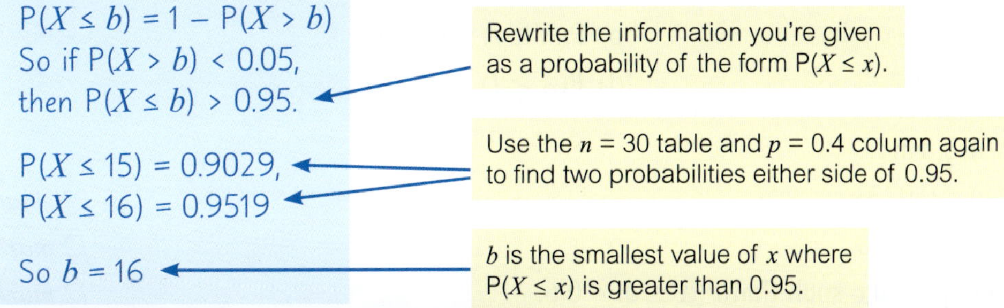

$P(X \le b) = 1 - P(X > b)$
So if $P(X > b) < 0.05$,
then $P(X \le b) > 0.95$.

Rewrite the information you're given as a probability of the form $P(X \le x)$.

$P(X \le 15) = 0.9029$,
$P(X \le 16) = 0.9519$

Use the $n = 30$ table and $p = 0.4$ column again to find two probabilities either side of 0.95.

So $b = 16$

b is the smallest value of x where $P(X \le x)$ is greater than 0.95.

This kind of question occurs in real-life situations.

Example  P M

A teacher is writing a multiple-choice test, with 5 options for each of the 20 questions. She wants the probability of someone passing the test by guessing the answer to each question to be 10% or less. How high should the pass mark be to give a student guessing the answer to every question less than a 10% probability of passing the test?

Each question has 5 possible answers, so P(correct guess) = $1 \div 5 = 0.2$.

Work out the probability of correctly guessing each individual answer.

Let X be the overall score of a student who always guesses. There are 20 questions altogether, so $X \sim B(20, 0.2)$.

Define the random variable and its probability distribution.

Let m be the pass mark. We need to find the minimum value m such that $P(X \geq m) < 0.1$. So $P(X < m) > 0.9$ or $P(X \leq m - 1) > 0.9$.

Write down the condition that the pass mark needs to satisfy so that the probability of the student passing the test is less than 10%.

$P(X \leq 5) = 0.8042$, but $P(X \leq 6) = 0.9133$

$P(X \leq 6) > 0.9$, so $m - 1 = 6 \Rightarrow m = 7$, so the pass mark should be 7.

Use the table for $n = 20$, with $p = 0.2$. Look for the lowest value of x where $P(X \leq x)$ is greater than 0.9. This gives you $m - 1$, so add 1 to get the answer.

Check:

$P(X \geq 6) = 1 - P(X \leq 5)$
$= 1 - 0.8042 = 0.1958 > 0.1$

$P(X \geq 7) = 1 - P(X \leq 6)$
$= 1 - 0.9133 = 0.0867 < 0.1$ ✓

You can check this value of m satisfies the teacher's requirements by checking that it's the lowest value of x for which $P(X \geq x) < 0.1$.

Exercise 4.8

Q1 The random variable $X \sim B(8, 0.35)$. Find the values of a, b, c and d such that:

a) $P(X \leq a) = 0.4278$
b) $P(X < b) = 0.9747$
c) $P(X > c) = 0.8309$
d) $P(X \geq d) = 0.1061$

Q2 The random variable $X \sim B(12, 0.4)$. Find the values of e, f, g and h such that:

a) $P(X < e) = 0.2253$
b) $P(X \leq f) = 0.8418$
c) $P(X \geq g) = 0.0003$
d) $P(X > h) = 0.0573$

Q3 The random variable $X \sim B(30, 0.15)$. Find the values of i, j, k and l such that:

a) $P(X < i) = 0.9903$
b) $P(X \geq j) = 0.2894$
c) $P(X > k) = 0.9520$
d) $P(X \geq l) = 0.1526$

E P Q4 If $X \sim B(40, 0.45)$, find:

a) a if $P(X < a) = 0.9233$ *[1 mark]*
b) b if $P(X > b) = 0.3156$ *[2 marks]*
c) the maximum value c such that $P(X \leq c) < 0.6$. *[2 marks]*

E P **Q5** If $X \sim B(25, 0.25)$, find:

a) a if $P(X \leq a) = 0.0962$ *[1 mark]*

b) b if $P(X \geq b) = 0.4389$ *[2 marks]*

c) the minimum value c such that $P(X > c) < 0.1$. *[2 marks]*

E P M **Q6** A factory produces 40 dining chairs per hour. The probability that a chair fails its quality control inspection is p. The discrete random variable, X, is the number of chairs produced in a randomly-chosen hour that fail their quality control inspection.

a) State the probability distribution for X in terms of p. *[1 mark]*

b) Given that $P(X = 3) = 0.0816$, find the value of p. *[3 marks]*

E P M **Q7** A sample of used cricket balls is taken and each ball is tested to see if it is damaged. The number of damaged cricket balls in the sample is modelled by the discrete random variable X, which follows a binomial probability distribution with $X \sim B(30, a)$.

The probability that more than 7 but no more than 10 cricket balls in the sample are damaged is 0.3840. Find the value of a. *[3 marks]*

E P M **Q8** A rifle shooter places ten tin cans in a line and has one attempt at shooting each can in turn. The probability that they hit a can with their one shot is k. The number of cans they hit is modelled as a binomial probability distribution, and the probability they hit at least 8 of the cans is 0.9298. Find the value of k. *[4 marks]*

P M **Q9** A teacher is writing a multiple-choice test, with 4 options for each of the 30 questions. He wants the probability of someone passing the test by guessing the answer to each question to be 10% or less.

a) What is the lowest score that should be set as the pass mark?

b) Another teacher says the probability of passing by guessing should be less than 1%. What should the minimum pass score be now?

P M **Q10** In a fairground competition, a fair coin is tossed 20 times by a contestant. If the contestant scores x heads or more, they win a prize. If the random variable X represents the number of heads obtained, find the minimum number of heads that are needed to win if the probability of winning is to be kept below 0.05.

P M **Q11** In the final round of a TV gameshow, contestants get to spin a giant spinning wheel 5 times. The wheel is split into four equal-sized 'zones'. To win the grand prize, the wheel must land in the golden zone at least b times. The probability of winning the grand prize is 0.1035.

a) How many successful spins does a contestant need to win the grand prize?

b) The show's producers want to increase the total number of spins a contestant is allowed to 10, without increasing their probability of winning the grand prize. What should they set the minimum number of successful spins, g, to in order to achieve this?

Challenge

P **Q12** The discrete random variable X has probability distribution $X \sim B(6, p)$. It is given that $P(a < X \leq a + 3) = 0.4673$, $p > 0.5$ and a is non-zero. Use statistical tables to deduce the values of a and p.

4.9 Modelling Real Problems with B(n, p)

M

The first step with a real-world problem is to **model** it using a sensible probability distribution. If the situation satisfies all the conditions on p.117, then you'll need to use a **binomial distribution**.

When you've decided how to model the situation, you can do the calculation. Don't forget to include units in your answer where necessary. You may then need to **interpret** your solution — saying what your answer means in the **context** of the question.

Tip Make sure you write down any assumptions you're making in order to use the binomial distribution (unless you've been told them in the question).

Example 1

A double-glazing salesman is handing out leaflets in a busy shopping centre. He knows that the probability of a passing person taking a leaflet is always 0.3. During a randomly chosen one-minute interval, 30 people passed him.

a) Suggest a suitable model to describe the number of people (X) who take a leaflet.

During this one-minute interval:
(i) there's a fixed number (30) of trials,
(ii) all the trials are independent,
(iii) there are two possible results ('take a leaflet', 'do not take a leaflet'),
(iv) there's a constant probability of success (0.3),
(v) X is the total number of people taking leaflets.

All the conditions for a binomial distribution are satisfied. So $X \sim B(30, 0.3)$

Tip You don't always need to write down the 5 conditions for a binomial distribution — but make sure they're satisfied. You should always specify the values of n and p though.

b) What is the probability that more than 10 people take a leaflet?

$P(X > 10) = 1 - P(X \leq 10)$
$= 1 - 0.7304 = 0.2696$

You can get this probability from the binomial tables, or your calculator.

Example 2

I am tossing a coin that I know is three times as likely to land on heads as it is on tails.

a) What is the probability that it lands on tails for the first time on the third toss?

P(heads) = 3 × P(tails), but P(heads) + P(tails) = 1.
This means that P(heads) = 0.75 and P(tails) = 0.25.

First you need to know the probabilities for heads and tails.

If it lands on tails for the first time on the third toss, then the first two tosses must have been heads.

Interpret the information given in the question.

continued on the next page...

P(lands on tails for the first time on the third toss)
$= 0.75 \times 0.75 \times 0.25 = 0.141$ (3 s.f.)

Since all the tosses are independent:
P(heads then heads then tails)
= P(heads) × P(heads) × P(tails)

b) What is the probability that in 10 tosses, it lands on heads at least 7 times?

If X represents the number of heads in 10 tosses, then $X \sim B(10, 0.75)$.

First define your random variable, and state how it is distributed.

The number of tails in 10 tosses can be described by the random variable $Y = 10 - X$, where $Y \sim B(10, 0.25)$.

$p = 0.75$ isn't in your tables, so define a new binomial random variable Y with probability of success $p = 0.25$.

$P(X \geq 7) = P(Y \leq 3) = 0.7759$

You need the probability of 'at least 7 heads' — this is the same as '3 or fewer tails'.

Exercise 4.9

E M Q1 A hairdresser hands out leaflets. She knows there is always a probability of 0.25 that a passer-by will take a leaflet. During a five-minute period, 50 people pass the hairdresser.

a) Suggest a suitable model for X, the number of passers-by who take a leaflet in the five-minute period. Explain why this is a suitable model. *[1 mark]*

b) What is the probability that more than 4 people take a leaflet? *[2 marks]*

c) What is the probability that exactly 10 people take a leaflet? *[2 marks]*

M Q2 As part of a magic trick, 50 people must pick a card at random from a standard deck of 52 cards and say whether it is a heart. The magician uses a binomial distribution to model the number of people who pick a heart.

a) Explain why, for the model to be suitable, the magician must replace each selected card and shuffle the pack before the next person picks their card.

b) What is the probability that exactly 15 people pick a heart?

c) What is the probability that more than 20 people pick a heart?

E P M Q3 Clinical trials have shown a new drug to be 88% effective.
20 people are given the drug and the number of people who show a positive response, X, is modelled using a binomial distribution.

a) Write down the parameters for the required binomial distribution. *[1 mark]*

b) Find the probability that the number of people who show a positive response is:

(i) less than or equal to 17, *[1 mark]*

(ii) exactly 17. *[1 mark]*

c) The drug is considered suitable if $P(X > r) < 0.35$, where r is the actual number of positive responses in the sample. Find the minimum value of r for the drug to be considered suitable. *[3 marks]*

M Q4 Jasmine plants 15 randomly selected seeds in each of her plant trays. She knows that 35% of this type of plant grow with yellow flowers, and the rest grow with white flowers. All her seeds grow successfully, and she counts how many plants in each tray grow with yellow flowers.

a) Find the probability that a randomly selected tray has exactly 5 plants with yellow flowers.

b) Find the probability that a randomly selected tray contains more plants with yellow flowers than plants with white flowers.

Challenge

P M Q5 Simon tries to solve the crossword puzzle in his newspaper every day for 18 days. He either succeeds or fails to solve the puzzle.

a) Simon believes that the number of successes, X, can be modelled by a random variable following a binomial distribution. State two conditions needed for this to be true.

b) He believes that the situation has distribution $X \sim \mathrm{B}(18, p)$, where p is the probability Simon successfully completes the crossword. If $\mathrm{P}(X = 4) = \mathrm{P}(X = 5)$, find p.

E P M Q6 In a game using a fair, six-sided dice, a player wins a prize if they roll a number less than 3. If they roll any other number, they get another go, up to a maximum of three attempts. The game is played 10 times. The discrete random variable X is the number of prizes won.

a) (i) Find the probability that a player wins a prize within the three attempts. *[2 marks]*

(ii) Hence, write down a suitable distribution for X, and justify why this distribution is an appropriate model. *[1 mark]*

b) Find the probability that a player wins a prize on at least half the games they play. *[2 marks]*

c) The probability that a player wins x or fewer prizes is less than 10%. Find the largest possible value of x. *[2 marks]*

E P M Q7 A quality controller is testing a sample of 40 toys made at a factory. The probability that a toy made at this factory is faulty is 0.15. The number of faulty toys in the sample can be modelled as a discrete random variable X, following a binomial distribution.

a) Find the probability that exactly 3 of the 40 toys are faulty. *[1 mark]*

b) Find the probability that fewer than 6 toys are faulty. *[1 mark]*

c) Find the probability that between 5 and 10 toys (inclusive) are faulty. *[2 marks]*

d) The number of faulty toys in the sample, t, is recorded. If $\mathrm{P}(X \geq t) < 0.01$, production is stopped. Find the minimum value of t that would stop production. *[3 marks]*

E P M Q8 An online shop typically receives 12 orders every ten minutes. The probability that an order will be cancelled later on is 36%. The discrete random variable X is the number of orders from a ten-minute period that are cancelled.

a) Estimate the probability that no orders from a ten-minute period are cancelled. *[1 mark]*

b) Estimate the probability that more orders from a ten-minute period are cancelled than are not cancelled. *[2 marks]*

c) (i) Estimate the probability that fewer than 3 orders from a ten-minute period are cancelled. *[1 mark]*

(ii) Estimate the probability that fewer than 3 orders are cancelled for exactly 4 ten-minute periods in a single hour. *[3 marks]*

4 Review Exercise

E Q1 The probability distribution of Y is:

y	0	1	2	3
$P(Y = y)$	0.5	k	k	$3k$

a) Find the value of k. *[1 mark]*

b) Find $P(Y < 2)$. *[1 mark]*

M Q2 A game is played by rolling a fair, six-sided dice twice. If the sum of the two results is a multiple of 3, then the player scores 3 points. If the sum is a multiple of 5, they score 5 points, and if the sum is a multiple of 7, they score 7 points. Otherwise, they score 2 points. X is the random variable 'number of points scored'. Draw a table showing the probability distribution of X and find $P(X \leq 5)$.

E M Q3 A fair six-sided dice has numbers 1, 2 and 3 on it. One side has a 1, two sides have a 2 and three sides have a 3.

a) If Y is the random variable 'number rolled', draw a table to show the probability distribution of Y. *[2 marks]*

b) Find $P(Y < 3)$. *[1 mark]*

c) The dice is rolled twice. Find the probability that the product of the two numbers rolled is even. *[2 marks]*

E M Q4 The score spun on a spinner X has probability function $P(X = x) = kx^2$ for $x = 2, 4, 6, 8$.

a) Find the value of k. *[2 marks]*

b) A fair coin is tossed and the spinner is spun. Find the probability that the coin lands on tails and the spinner lands on a prime number. *[2 marks]*

E Q5 The discrete random variable X has the probability function defined as:

$$P(X = x) = \begin{cases} kx & x = 1, 2, 3 \\ kx^2 & x = 4, 5 \\ 0 & \text{otherwise} \end{cases} \quad \text{where } k \text{ is a constant.}$$

a) Find the value of k. *[2 marks]*

b) Find $P(X = 2)$. *[1 mark]*

c) Find $P(X \leq 3.5)$. *[1 mark]*

d) Find $P(2.1 \leq X \leq 4.2)$. *[2 marks]*

E P Q6 The table below shows the probability distribution for the discrete random variable M.

m	2	8	24	36
$P(M = m)$	$\frac{k}{4}$	$\frac{k^2}{16}$	$\frac{k^2}{32}$	$\frac{k}{16}$

a) Show that $3k^2 + 10k - 32 = 0$. *[2 marks]*

b) Hence show that $k = 2$, explaining why there is only one possible value of k. *[2 marks]*

c) Find $P(4 \leq M \leq 28)$. *[2 marks]*

Q7 The probability distribution for the random variable W is given in the table.

w	0.2	0.3	0.4	0.5
$P(W = w)$	0.2	0.2	0.3	0.3

Draw up a table to show the cumulative distribution function.

Q8 Each probability function below describes a discrete random variable, X. In each case, draw a table showing the cumulative distribution function, and use it to find the required probabilities.

a) $P(X = x) = \frac{(x+2)}{25}$ $\quad x = 1, 2, 3, 4, 5$

Find (i) $P(X \leq 3)$ (ii) $P(1 < X \leq 3)$

b) $P(X = x) = \frac{1}{6}$ $\quad x = 1, 2, 3, 4, 5, 6$

Find (i) $P(X \leq 3)$ (ii) $P(3 < X < 6)$

E Q9 The cumulative distribution function for the discrete random variable Y is:

$$F(y) = \begin{cases} \frac{y}{2} & y = 0.1, 0.2, 0.3 \\ 2y & y = 0.4, 0.5 \end{cases}$$

a) Find $P(Y \leq 0.3)$. *[1 mark]*

b) Find $P(Y = 0.4)$. *[2 marks]*

c) Find $P(0.2 \leq Y \leq 0.4)$. *[2 marks]*

E P Q10 The sides of a biased five-sided spinner are labelled 1, 2, 3, p and q, where p and q are integers such that $3 < p < q$.
The discrete random variable X is the outcome when the spinner is spun once.

a) Given that $F(p) = 0.5$ and $P(q) = \frac{q}{20}$, find the value of q. *[2 marks]*

b) Given that the sum of the numbers on the spinner is a triangular number, find the value of p. *[2 marks]*

Q11 In how many different orders can the following be arranged?

a) 15 identical red balls, plus 6 other balls, all of different colours.

b) 4 red counters, 4 blue counters, 4 yellow counters and 4 green counters.

c) 7 green counters and 5 blue counters.

d) 3 'heads' and 4 'tails' in seven coin tosses.

E M Q12 A bakery makes ten different flavours of doughnut.
Joan buys six doughnuts, each of which is a different flavour.

a) In how many ways could Joan buy six different flavours of doughnut? *[2 marks]*

b) The following week, Joan buys four doughnuts from the same bakery.
Explain why the number of ways in which Joan could buy different flavoured doughnuts doesn't change from part a). *[1 mark]*

M Q13 Which of the following would follow a binomial distribution? Explain your answers.

a) The number of prime numbers you throw in 30 throws of a standard dice.

b) The number of aces in a 7-card hand dealt from a standard pack of 52 cards.

c) The number of shots I have to take before I score from the free-throw line in basketball.

M Q14 Use the binomial probability function to find the probability of the following.

a) Getting exactly 8 heads when you spin a fair coin 10 times.

b) Getting at least 8 heads when you spin a fair coin 10 times.

Q15 If $X \sim B(14, 0.27)$, find:

a) $P(X = 4)$ b) $P(X < 2)$ c) $P(5 < X \leq 8)$ d) $P(X \geq 11)$

E M Q16 The probability that a paraglider canopy made by a particular company has an imperfection is 1%. 30 of their canopies are tested, and any with imperfections are rejected before sale.

a) State the assumption needed to model this situation as a binomial distribution. *[1 mark]*

b) Write down a suitable distribution to model the number of canopies that have an imperfection. *[1 mark]*

c) Find the probability that exactly 2 of the canopies tested have imperfections. *[1 mark]*

E M Q17 For each arrow fired by an archer towards a target, the probability of it hitting the bullseye is 0.45. On a particular occasion, the archer fires 40 arrows towards the target. The number of arrows that hit the bullseye is modelled by the random variable X.

a) State a distribution that can be used to model X. *[1 mark]*

b) Find the probability that the archer hits the bullseye exactly 12 times. *[1 mark]*

c) Find the probability that the archer hits the bullseye fewer than two times, giving your answer in standard form to 3 significant figures. *[2 marks]*

E M **Q18** Darshan has a faulty alarm clock. It means the probability of him being late to college on any given day is 0.2, independently of all other days.

a) Suggest and justify a model for the number of days Darshan is late in a five-day week. *[1 mark]*

b) During a five-day week, calculate the probability that:

(i) He is late only once. *[1 mark]*

(ii) He is late more than twice. *[2 marks]*

Q19 If $X \sim B(25, 0.15)$ and $Y \sim B(15, 0.65)$ find:

a) $P(X \leq 3)$
b) $P(X \leq 7)$
c) $P(X \leq 15)$
d) $P(2 < X < 8)$
e) $P(Y \leq 3)$
f) $P(Y \leq 7)$
g) $P(Y \leq 15)$
h) $P(Y \geq 9)$
i) $P(8 \leq Y < 13)$

Q20 Find the required probability for each of the following binomial distributions.

a) $P(X \leq 15)$ if $X \sim B(20, 0.4)$
b) $P(X < 4)$ if $X \sim B(40, 0.15)$
c) $P(X > 7)$ if $X \sim B(25, 0.45)$
d) $P(X \geq 40)$ if $X \sim B(50, 0.8)$
e) $P(X = 20)$ if $X \sim B(30, 0.7)$
f) $P(X = 7)$ if $X \sim B(10, 0.75)$

E P **Q21** If $X \sim B(30, 0.35)$, find:

a) a if $P(X \leq a) = 0.8737$ *[1 mark]*

b) b if $P(X \geq b) = 0.8762$ *[2 marks]*

c) the maximum value c such that $P(X \leq c) < 0.05$. *[2 marks]*

E M **Q22** A person has a 5% chance of receiving at least one call on their home phone each day. They wish to model the number of days over a 30-day period on which they receive at least one call on their home phone using a binomial probability distribution.

a) State the required probability distribution, justifying why a binomial distribution is an appropriate model for this scenario. *[1 mark]*

b) Find the probability that at least one call is received on fewer than 5 days. *[1 mark]*

E M **Q23** A takeaway shop sends vouchers to people. There is a probability of 0.15 that a person uses the voucher they receive. During a two-hour period, 40 people are each sent one voucher.

a) Suggest and justify a suitable model for X, the number of people who use the voucher they received in this two-hour period. *[1 mark]*

b) Find the probability that at least 10 people use the voucher. *[2 marks]*

c) Find the probability that exactly 6 people use the voucher. *[2 marks]*

M Q24 A chocolate shop sells selection boxes of 12 chocolates, where each chocolate is randomly selected from all the varieties of chocolates they sell. Forrest likes 70% of the varieties they sell and dislikes the rest. He buys one of the selection boxes at random.

a) Find the probability that Forrest's selection box contains exactly 10 chocolates that he likes.

b) Find the probability that his selection box contains more chocolates that he likes than chocolates that he dislikes.

E P M Q25 A café sells 20 different drinks, 8 of which contain caffeine. A group of 10 customers each order a drink chosen at random from the 20 drinks available.

a) Write down the binomial distribution for X, the discrete random variable "number of drinks ordered by the group that contain caffeine". *[1 mark]*

b) Find the probability that fewer than half of the drinks ordered contain caffeine. *[1 mark]*

c) Find the probability that more than 75% of the drinks ordered contain caffeine. *[2 marks]*

d) Show that there is approximately a 45% chance that the group order contains either 4 or 5 drinks containing caffeine. *[2 marks]*

Challenge

P M Q26 A bowls club holds a draw to decide which members will play each other in a tournament. There are 120 ways of selecting the first two members from the draw. How many members are in the draw?

P M Q27 During a football match, Messy tries to dribble past a certain player 11 times. He either succeeds or fails to dribble past the player.

a) Messy believes that the number of successes, X, can be modelled by a random variable following a binomial distribution. State two conditions needed for this to be true.

b) He believes that the situation has distribution $X \sim B(11, p)$, where p is the probability that Messy successfully dribbles past the player. If $P(X = 3) = P(X = 4)$, find p.

E P M Q28 A snooker player practises a particular shot 24 times per day. The probability of them successfully completing the shot is 0.12.

a) Using a binomial distribution, find the probability that the snooker player successfully completes the shot:

(i) exactly 3 times per day (ii) at least twice per day. *[3 marks]*

b) The player practises the shot every day for 7 days. Find the probability that they successfully complete the shot at least twice per day on at least 4 days. *[3 marks]*

c) Explain why a binomial distribution may not be a valid model. *[2 marks]*

E P M Q29 Eggs from a certain farm come in boxes of twelve. 8% of all the eggs from this farm are cracked. Boxes that contain more than two cracked eggs are considered defective.

a) Use a binomial distribution to find the probability that a box is defective. *[2 marks]*

Eight boxes are stacked into a crate. If a crate has more than one defective box, it is to be sent back to the farm.

b) Use a binomial distribution to find the probability that a crate is sent back. *[3 marks]*

c) Explain why a binomial distribution may not be the perfect model in these cases. *[2 marks]*

4 Chapter Summary

1 Discrete random variables can take only a certain number of values with different probabilities. You use upper case letters, such as X, for random variables, and lower case letters, such as x, for their values.

2 A probability distribution is a table showing all the possible values of a discrete random variable and the probability that it'll take each value.

3 A probability function is a formula that generates the probability of a random variable X taking the value x, for every possible x. It is written $\text{P}(X = x)$ or sometimes just $\text{p}(x)$.

4 The probabilities of all possible values that a discrete random variable can take add up to 1. This fact is written as $\sum_{\text{all } x} \text{P}(X = x) = 1$.

5 A discrete uniform distribution is where every value of a discrete random variable is equally likely.

6 A cumulative distribution function, $\text{F}(x)$, gives the probability that a random variable X will be less than or equal to x.

7 For a discrete random variable X: $\text{F}(x_0) = \text{P}(X \leq x_0) = \sum_{x \leq x_0} \text{P}(X = x)$.

8 You can calculate the probability function from the cumulative distribution function. If x_{i-1} and x_i are two consecutive values that X can take, then $\text{P}(X = x_i) = \text{F}(x_i) - \text{F}(x_{i-1})$.

9 n different objects can be arranged in $n! = n \times (n-1) \times .... \times 1$ different orders.
n objects, where x of them are identical, can be arranged in $\frac{n!}{x!}$ different orders.
x objects of one type and $n - x$ objects of another type can be arranged in $\frac{n!}{x!(n-x)!}$ different orders — this is just the binomial coefficient $\binom{n}{x}$.

10 A random variable X follows a binomial distribution if these 5 conditions are satisfied:

- There is a fixed number (n) of trials.
- Each trial involves either 'success' or 'failure'.
- All the trials are independent.
- The probability of 'success' (p) is the same in each trial.
- The variable is the total number of successes in the n trials.

11 If a random variable X follows a binomial distribution, $X \sim \text{B}(n, p)$, then its probability function is: $\text{P}(X = x) = \binom{n}{x} \times p^x \times (1-p)^{n-x}$ for $x = 0, 1, 2, ..., n$. Find the value of $\text{P}(X = x)$ on your calculator using the probability function.

12 Binomial tables show the cumulative distribution function for a binomial distribution, i.e. $\text{P}(X \leq x)$ for $X \sim \text{B}(n, p)$, for certain values of n and p. Find the value of $\text{P}(X \leq x)$ on your calculator using the cumulative distribution function.

Statistical Hypothesis Testing

5

Learning Objectives

Once you've completed this chapter, you should be able to:

- Formulate null and alternative hypotheses.
- Decide when to use a one- or two-tailed test.
- Understand what is meant by significance levels.
- Understand what is meant by a test statistic and find a test statistic's sampling distribution.
- Test an observed value of a test statistic for significance by calculating the p-value.
- Find a critical region and identify the actual significance level of a test.
- Conduct hypothesis tests about probabilities or proportions using a test statistic with a binomial distribution.

Prior Knowledge Check

1 A random variable $X \sim B(40, 0.25)$. Use the binomial table for $n = 40$ to find:
a) $P(X \leq 12)$ b) $P(X < 5)$ c) $P(X > 8)$

see page 124

2 The probability of a biased dice landing on 4 is 0.3. The dice is rolled 50 times.
a) Suggest a model for X, the number of times the dice lands on 4.
b) What is the probability of the dice landing on 4 less than 15 times?

see page 132

5.1 Null and Alternative Hypotheses

Parameters are quantities that **describe** the characteristics of a **population** — e.g. the **mean** (μ), **variance** (σ^2), or a **proportion** (p). **Greek letters** such as μ and σ are often used for parameters.

A **hypothesis** (plural: **hypotheses**) is a claim or a statement that **might** be true, but which might **not** be.

A **hypothesis test** is a method of testing a hypothesis about a population using **observed data** from a **sample**. You'll need **two** hypotheses for every hypothesis test — a **null** hypothesis and an **alternative** hypothesis.

> **Tip** Hypothesis testing is sometimes called significance testing.

Null hypothesis

The **null hypothesis** is a statement about the **value** of a population parameter. The null hypothesis is always referred to as $\mathbf{H_0}$.

H_0 needs to give a **specific value** to the parameter, since all the calculations in your hypothesis test will be based on this value.

The example below (which I'll keep coming back to throughout the section) shows how you could use a hypothesis test to check whether a coin is 'fair' (i.e. whether it's equally likely to land on heads or tails).

> Aisha wants to test whether a coin is fair. She tosses it 100 times and then carries out a hypothesis test.
>
> Testing whether a coin is fair is a test about the probability (p) that it lands on heads.
>
> If the coin is **fair**, then the value of p will be 0.5.
> If the coin is **biased**, then the value of p could be **anything except 0.5**.
>
> Aisha's null hypothesis needs to assume a **specific** value for p.
> So Aisha's null hypothesis is H_0: $p = 0.5$

> **Tip** So if X is the number of heads, $X \sim B(100, 0.5)$.

> **Tip** Aisha's using p as the probability that the coin lands on heads, but you could equally use it as the probability the coin lands on tails.

The fact that Aisha is carrying out this test at all probably means that she has some doubts about whether the coin really is fair.

But that's okay, you **don't** have to **believe** your null hypothesis — it's just an assumption you make for the purposes of carrying out the test. In fact, as you'll soon see, it's pretty common to choose a null hypothesis that you think is **false**.

Depending on your data, there are **two** possible results of a hypothesis test:

a) "**Fail to reject H_0**" — this means that your data provides **no evidence** to think that your null hypothesis is **untrue**.

b) "**Reject H_0**" — this means that your data provides evidence to think that your null hypothesis is **unlikely to be true**.

If you need to reject H_0, you need an alternative hypothesis 'standing by'.

Two kinds of alternative hypothesis

Your **alternative hypothesis** is what you're going to conclude if you end up rejecting H_0 — i.e. what you're rejecting H_0 in favour of. The alternative hypothesis is always referred to as $\mathbf{H_1}$.

There are **two kinds** of alternative hypothesis:

A **one-tailed** alternative hypothesis specifies whether the parameter you're investigating is **greater than** or **less than** the value you used in H_0. Using a one-tailed alternative hypothesis means you're carrying out a **one-tailed hypothesis test**.

A **two-tailed** alternative hypothesis **doesn't specify** whether the parameter you're investigating is greater than or less than the value you used in H_0 — all it says is that it's **not equal** to the value in H_0. Using a two-tailed alternative hypothesis means you're carrying out a **two-tailed hypothesis test**.

Aisha has a choice of alternative hypotheses, and she'll need to choose which to use **before** she starts collecting data.

She could use a **one-tailed** alternative hypothesis — there are two possibilities:

$H_1: p > 0.5$ — this would mean the coin is biased towards **heads**

or $H_1: p < 0.5$ — this would mean the coin is biased towards **tails**

She could use a **two-tailed** alternative hypothesis:

$H_1: p \neq 0.5$ — this would mean the coin is biased, but it doesn't say whether it's biased in favour of heads or tails.

Tip Notice that H_1 does not give a specific value to the population parameter — it gives a range of values.

To decide which alternative hypothesis to use, you have to consider:

- **What you want to find out** about the parameter:
  For example, if you were investigating the proportion (q) of items produced in a factory that were faulty, then you might only want to test whether q has **increased** (testing whether it's decreased might not be as important).

- Any **suspicions** you might already have about the parameter's value:
  For example, if Aisha in the example above thought that the coin was actually biased towards heads, then she'd use $H_1: p > 0.5$.

Possible conclusions after a hypothesis test

I'm going to assume now that you've written your null and alternative hypotheses, and **collected some data**. You need to know the two **possible conclusions** that you can come to after performing a hypothesis test.

> **Tip** 'Under the null hypothesis' or 'under H_0' just means 'assuming that the null hypothesis is true'.

Your **observed data** is **really unlikely** under the null hypothesis, H_0.

- If your observed data is **really unlikely** when you assume that H_0 is true, then you might start to think 'Well, maybe H_0 isn't true after all.'
- It could be that your observed data is actually much more **likely** to happen under your **alternative hypothesis**. Then you'd perhaps think H_1 is more likely to be true than H_0.
- In this case, you would **reject H_0** in favour of H_1.
- This **doesn't** mean that H_0 is **definitely false**. After all, as long as your observed data isn't impossible under H_0, then H_0 could still be true. All it means is that 'on the balance of probabilities', H_1 seems to be **more likely** to be true than H_0.

> **Tip** How unlikely your results need to be before you reject H_0 is called the significance level (see page 147).

The **observed data isn't** especially unlikely under the null hypothesis, H_0.

- If your observed data could easily have come about under H_0, then you **can't reject H_0**.
- In this case, you would '**fail to reject H_0**'.
- However, this is **not** the same as saying that you have evidence that H_0 is **true** — all it means is that H_0 appears to be **believable**, and that you have **no evidence** that it's false.
- But it's not really any better than having collected **no data** at all — you had **no evidence** to disbelieve the null hypothesis before you did your experiment... and you **still** don't. That's all this conclusion means. Notice that you 'fail to reject H_0' — you never 'accept H_0'.

Because the conclusion of 'not rejecting H_0' is so **weak**, it's actually more meaningful when you can 'reject H_0' **in favour** of H_1.

This is why the alternative hypothesis H_1 is usually **more interesting** than the null hypothesis H_0.

For example, with Aisha and her coin (pages 142-143), it was the **alternative** hypothesis that contained the claim that the coin was **biased**.

It's also why H_0 often says something that you think is **false**. Your aim is to gather evidence to reject H_0 in favour of H_1 (and this is why H_1 might be what you actually **believe**).

> If Aisha **rejects H_0**:
>
> She has **evidence** that H_0 is false (i.e. the coin is biased).
>
> She **can't** be certain, but H_1 appears **more likely** to be true.
>
> If Aisha **fails to reject H_0**:
>
> She has **no** evidence that H_0 is false (i.e. that the coin is biased).
>
> H_0 **could** be true, but she has no evidence to say so.
>
> H_0 **could** also be false, but she has no evidence for that either.

> **Tip** A hypothesis test can provide evidence that H_1 is likely to be true, but it can't provide evidence that H_0 is likely to be true.

Example 1

A 4-sided spinner has sides labelled A–D. Adam thinks that the spinner is biased towards side A. He wants to do a hypothesis test to test this theory.

a) Write down a suitable null hypothesis to test Adam's theory.

p = the probability of the spinner landing on side A

Identify the population parameter.

Adam thinks the spinner is biased. So his null hypothesis should be that the spinner is unbiased, and that each side has a probability of 0.25 of being spun. So:

H_0: $p = 0.25$

The null hypothesis must give a specific value to p, and it's the statement that Adam is trying to get evidence to reject.

b) Write down a suitable alternative hypothesis.

If the spinner is biased towards side A, then the probability, p, of spinning A will be greater than 0.25. So:

This is the hypothesis that Adam actually believes.

H_1: $p > 0.25$

Write out the hypothesis using the correct notation.

c) State whether this test is one- or two-tailed.

The alternative hypothesis specifies that p is greater than 0.25, so the test is one-tailed.

Problem Solving

The question will usually give you a hint about what H_1 should be. Here it says Adam suspects the spinner is biased towards side A, which means he thinks p is greater than 0.25.

Example 2

In a particular post office, the average probability over the course of a day that a customer entering the post office has to queue for more than 2 minutes is 0.6. The manager of the post office wants to test whether the probability of having to queue for more than 2 minutes is different between the hours of 1 pm and 2 pm.

a) Write down a suitable null hypothesis.

p = the probability of having to queue for more than 2 minutes between 1 pm and 2 pm.

Identify the population parameter.

The null hypothesis is that the probability of having to queue for more than 2 minutes is the same as at other times.

H_0: $p = 0.6$

The null hypothesis must give a specific value to p.

b) Write down a suitable alternative hypothesis.

H_1: $p \neq 0.6$

The manager wants to test for any difference (rather than just an increase or just a decrease).

c) State whether this test is one- or two-tailed.

The alternative hypothesis only specifies that p is not equal to 0.6, so the test is two-tailed.

Exercise 5.1

M Q1 Over the last few years Jules has had a 90% success rate in germinating her geranium plants. This year she has bought an improved variety of seeds and hopes for even better results.

a) Which quantity is Jules investigating?

b) What value has this quantity taken over the last few years?

c) Write down a suitable null hypothesis.

d) Write down a suitable alternative hypothesis.

e) State whether this test is one- or two-tailed.

M Q2 Each week, the probability that a cat catches a mouse is 0.7. The cat's owner has put a bell on its collar and wants to test if it now catches fewer mice.

a) State the quantity that the owner is investigating.

b) What value did this quantity take before?

c) Write down a suitable null hypothesis using parts a) and b).

d) Write down a suitable alternative hypothesis.

e) State whether this test is one- or two-tailed.

M Q3 The school health team checks teenagers for the presence of an antibody before vaccinating them. Usually 35% of teenagers have the antibody present. The team visits a remote Scottish island where they think that the proportion of teenagers with the antibody may be different.

a) Write down the quantity that is being investigated.

b) Formulate the null and alternative hypotheses, H_0 and H_1.

c) State whether this test is one- or two-tailed.

M Q4 The local council found that only 16% of residents were aware that grants were available to help pay to insulate their houses. The council ran a campaign to publicise the grants, and now want to test whether there is an increased awareness in the area. Write down suitable null and alternative hypotheses involving the proportion of residents aware of the grants.

M Q5 In a village shop, 3% of customers buy a jar of chilli chutney. The owner has changed the packaging of the chutney and wants to know if the proportion of customers buying a jar of chilli chutney has changed. Write down suitable null and alternative hypotheses.

M Q6 It is claimed that the proportion of members of a particular gym who watch Australian soaps is 40%. Boyd wants to test his theory that the proportion is higher. Write down suitable null and alternative hypotheses.

M Q7 The probability that one brand of watch battery lasts for more than 18 months is 0.64. Elena thinks that a new brand of watch battery is more likely to last for more than 18 months. Write down suitable null and alternative hypotheses and state whether her test is one-tailed or two-tailed.

M Q8 In a primary school, the proportion of students not reaching the expected standard in the Year 6 SATs over a 4-year period is 20%.
The headteacher introduces some different teaching methods to see if that has an impact on the proportion of students not reaching the expected standard.

a) State the null and alternative hypotheses that could be used to carry out a test.

b) State whether this is a one- or two-tailed test.

P M Q9 The milk yield from the cows on a farm is such that the probability of collecting over 2000 litres in a day during winter is 0.95. Following a change of winter feed, 24 out of 30 randomly-selected days give a yield of more than 2000 litres.

a) Suggest a theory that could be tested using this data.

b) Write down suitable null and alternative hypotheses that could be used to test the theory you suggested in part a).

c) State whether your test is one- or two- tailed.

5.2 Significance Levels and Test Statistics M

You've seen that you would reject H_0 if the data you collect is 'really unlikely' under H_0. But you need to decide exactly **how unlikely** your results will need to be before you decide to reject H_0.

The **significance level** of a test shows how far you're prepared to believe that unlikely results are just down to **chance**, rather than because the assumption in H_0 is wrong.

> The **significance level** of a test (α) determines **how unlikely** your data needs to be under the null hypothesis (H_0) before you reject H_0.

Tip Significance levels can be written as percentages or decimals.

If your results under H_0 have a probability of α **or below**, then you can say that your results are **significant**.

For example, your significance level could be $\alpha = 0.05$ (or 5%). This would mean that you would **only** reject H_0 if your observed data fell into the **most extreme** 5% of possible outcomes.

You'll usually be told what significance level to use, but the most common values are $\alpha = 0.1$ (or 10%), $\alpha = 0.05$ (or 5%) and $\alpha = 0.01$ (or 1%).

The value of α also determines the strength of the evidence that the test has provided if you reject H_0 — the **lower** the value of α, the **stronger the evidence** you have that H_0 is false.

- For example, if you use $\alpha = 0.05$ and your data lets you reject H_0, then you have evidence that H_0 is false.
- But if you use $\alpha = 0.01$ and your data lets you reject H_0, then you have **stronger** evidence that H_0 is false.

Also, the **lower** the value of α, the **lower** the probability of **incorrectly rejecting H_0** when it is in fact **true** — i.e. of getting extreme data due to chance rather than because H_0 was false.

But although a **low** value of α sounds like a good thing, there's an important **disadvantage** to using a low significance level — you're **less likely to be able to reject H_0**. This means your experiment is more likely to end up 'failing to reject H_0' and concluding nothing.

Test statistics

To see if your results are **significant**, you need to find their probability under H_0. The way you do this is to '**summarise**' your data in something called a **test statistic**.

A **test statistic** for a hypothesis test is a statistic calculated from **sample data**, which is used to **decide** whether or not to reject H_0.

The **probability distribution** of a statistic is called the **sampling distribution**. It gives all the possible values of the statistic, along with the corresponding probabilities (assuming H_0 is true). In this course, the sampling distribution of the test statistics you'll use will be a **binomial distribution** $B(n, p)$.

Once you've found your test statistic (X), you then need to work out the p-value — this is the probability of a value **at least as extreme** as X using the parameter in your null hypothesis.

If your p-value is less than or equal to the significance level α, you can reject H_0.

Tip A statistic is a quantity that is calculated from known observations — i.e. from a sample.

Tip Don't mix up the p-value with the binomial probability p.

Deciding whether or not to reject H_0

1. Comparing the probability of the test statistic with α

Right... back to Aisha and her coin. Let's assume first that Aisha is carrying out a **one-tailed test** to check if the coin is biased **towards heads**.

For this one-tailed test, Aisha's null and alternative hypotheses will be:

$$\mathbf{H_0: p = 0.5} \quad \text{and} \quad \mathbf{H_1: p > 0.5}$$

Aisha's going to use a significance level of α **= 0.05**.

Aisha then throws the coin 30 times and records the number of heads.

Her test statistic X is the **number of heads** she throws — so X follows a binomial distribution $B(n, p)$. In fact, under H_0, $X \sim \mathbf{B(30, 0.5)}$.

First suppose Aisha records **19 heads** — i.e. $X = 19$.

- The probability of a result **at least as extreme** as $X = 19$ is $\mathbf{P(X \geq 19)}$.
- Under H_0, this is $1 - P(X < 19) = 1 - P(X \leq 18) = 1 - 0.8998 = \mathbf{0.1002}$
- This p-value of 0.1002 is **greater than** the significance level α, so she **cannot reject H_0**.
- Aisha has **no evidence** at the 5% level of significance that the coin is biased in favour of heads.

Suppose instead that Aisha records **20 heads** — i.e. $X = 20$.

- The probability of a result **at least as extreme** as $X = 20$ is $\mathbf{P(X \geq 20)}$.
- Under H_0, this is $1 - P(X < 20) = 1 - P(X \leq 19) = 1 - 0.9506 = \mathbf{0.0494}$
- This p-value of 0.0494 is **less than** the significance level α, so she **can reject H_0**.
- Aisha has **evidence** at the 5% level of significance that the coin is biased in favour of heads.

Tip Remember... n is the number of trials — 30, and p is the probability of success in each of those trials — 0.5 (because we're assuming that H_0 is true).

Tip A result 'at least as extreme as 19' means '19 or more'.

Tip In fact, any value for X of 20 or more would lead Aisha to reject H_0.

Levels of significance can be shown on a graph of the **probability function** for your test statistic. Under H_0, $X \sim B(30, 0.5)$, so each probability is worked out using $P(X = x) = \binom{30}{x} 0.5^x 0.5^{30-x}$.

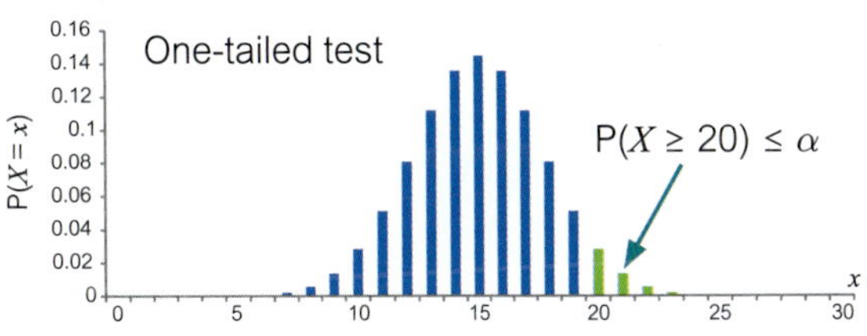

The green bars form the 'one tail' of the test statistic's distribution where values of the test statistic would lead you to reject H_0 in favour of H_1. They're at the 'high' end of the distribution — because H_1 was of the form H_1: $p > 0.5$ (so high values of X are more likely under H_1 than under H_0).

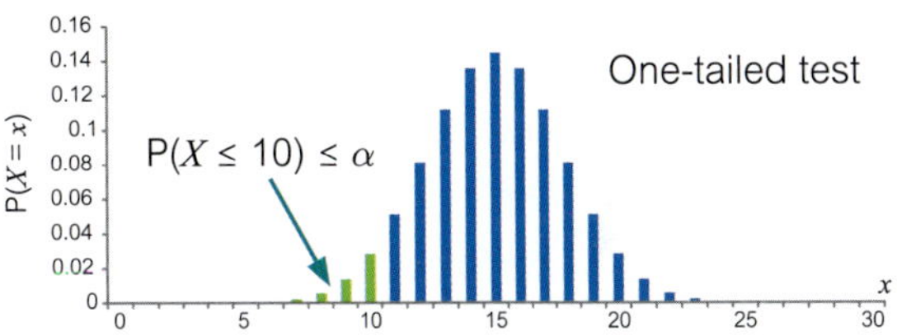

If Aisha had chosen her alternative hypothesis to be: H_1: $p < 0.5$, then the values that would lead her to reject H_0 would be at the 'low' end. She would reject H_0 for $X = 10$ or lower, since $P(X \leq 10) = 0.0494 < \alpha$, but $P(X \leq 11) = 0.1002 > \alpha$.

Now assume that Aisha is carrying out a **two-tailed test** to check if the coin is biased towards **either heads or tails**.

There's one important difference from the one-tailed test.

For this two-tailed test, Aisha's null and alternative hypotheses will be:

$$\mathbf{H_0: p = 0.5} \quad \text{and} \quad \mathbf{H_1: p \neq 0.5}$$

Again, Aisha's going to use a significance level of α **= 0.05**.

Aisha then throws the coin 30 times and records the number of heads.

Her test statistic X is the **number of heads** she throws — so X follows a binomial distribution $B(n, p)$. In fact, under H_0, $\mathbf{X \sim B(30, 0.5)}$.

Problem Solving

You need to write down all these pieces of information for every hypothesis test you do.

So up to this point, things are pretty much identical to the one-tailed test.

But now think about which 'extreme' outcomes for the test statistic would favour H_1 over H_0.

This time, extreme outcomes at **either** the 'high' end **or** the 'low' end of the distribution would favour your alternative hypothesis, H_1: $p \neq 0.5$.

But the significance level is the **total** probability of the results that'd lead to you rejecting H_0. So for a two-tailed test, you have to **divide α by 2** and use **half** of the significance level ($\frac{\alpha}{2} = 0.025$) at each end of the distribution.

So suppose Aisha records **20 heads** — i.e. $\mathbf{X = 20}$.

- The probability of a result **at least as extreme** as $X = 20$ is $\mathbf{P(X \geq 20)}$.
- Under H_0, this is $1 - P(X < 20) = 1 - P(X \leq 19) = 1 - 0.9506 = \mathbf{0.0494}$.
- This p-value of 0.0494 is **greater than** 0.025, so she **cannot reject H_0**.
- Aisha has **no evidence** at the 5% level of significance that the coin is biased (in either direction).

Suppose instead that Aisha records **21 heads** — i.e. $X = 21$.

- The probability of a result **at least as extreme** as $X = 21$ is $P(X \geq 21)$.
- Under H_0, this is $1 - P(X < 21) = 1 - P(X \leq 20) = 1 - 0.9786 = \mathbf{0.0214}$
- This p-value of 0.0214 is **less than** 0.025, so she **can reject H_0**.
- Aisha has **evidence** at the 5% level of significance that the coin is biased (towards either heads or tails).

Notice how in this two-tailed test, Aisha needs 21 heads to reject H_0, whereas in the one-tailed test, she only needed 20 heads.

This is why you need to be careful when you choose your alternative hypothesis. Choosing the wrong H_1 can make it harder to reject H_0.

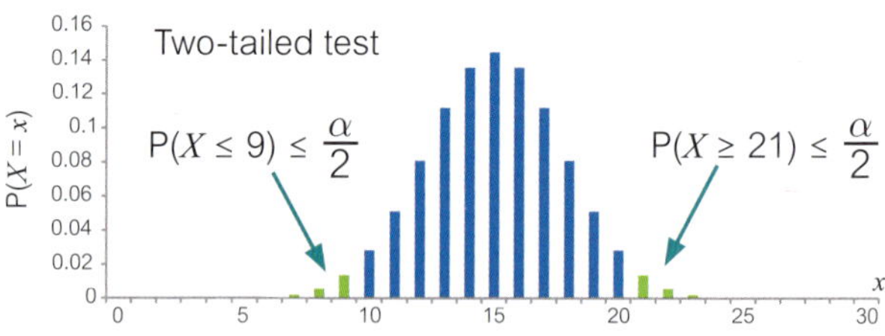

At the low end, she would reject H_0 for $X = 9$ or lower, since $P(X \leq 9) = 0.0214 < \frac{\alpha}{2}$, but $P(X \leq 10) = 0.0494 > \frac{\alpha}{2}$.

2. Finding the critical region

When Aisha was deciding whether to reject H_0 or not reject H_0:

1) she worked out her test statistic using her data,
2) then she calculated the probability (under H_0) of getting a value for the test statistic at least as extreme as the value she had found (the p-value).

Finding the **critical region** is another way of doing a hypothesis test. You work out all the values of the test statistic that would lead you to reject H_0.

Tip The critical region is just a set of values that X can take which fall far enough away from what's expected under the null hypothesis to allow you to reject it.

The **critical region** (CR) is the **set** of all values of the **test statistic** that would cause you to **reject H_0**.

Using a critical region is like doing things the other way round, because:

1) you work out all the values that would make you reject H_0,
2) then you work out the value of your test statistic using your data, and check if it is in the critical region (and if it is, then reject H_0).

So if you find the **critical region** first, you can quickly say whether any observed value of the test statistic, X, is **significant**.

As you've seen, **one-tailed tests** have a **single critical region**, containing either the highest or lowest values. Here are the graphs from before again — the values of x which are green would all cause you to reject H_0, so they are the values that make up the critical region.

One-tailed test:

$H_0: p = 0.5$
$H_1: p > 0.5$
$\alpha = 0.05$

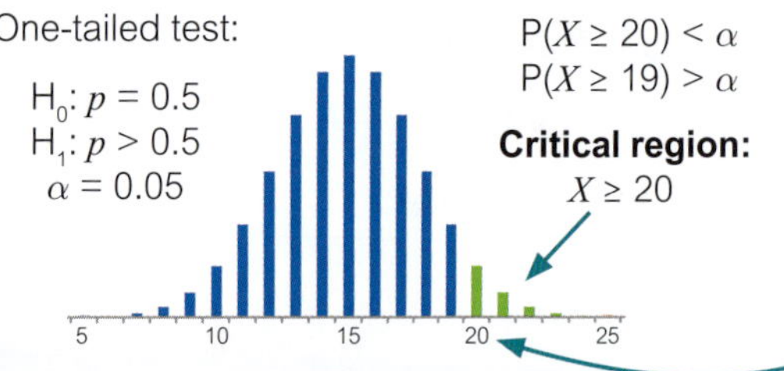

$P(X \geq 20) < \alpha$
$P(X \geq 19) > \alpha$

Critical region: $X \geq 20$

- When $X = 19$, Aisha couldn't reject H_0, so $X = 19$ is **not** in the critical region.
- But $X = 20$ **is** in the critical region, since in this case Aisha **could** reject H_0.
- $\mathbf{X = 20}$ is called the **critical value** — it's the value on the 'edge' of the critical region.

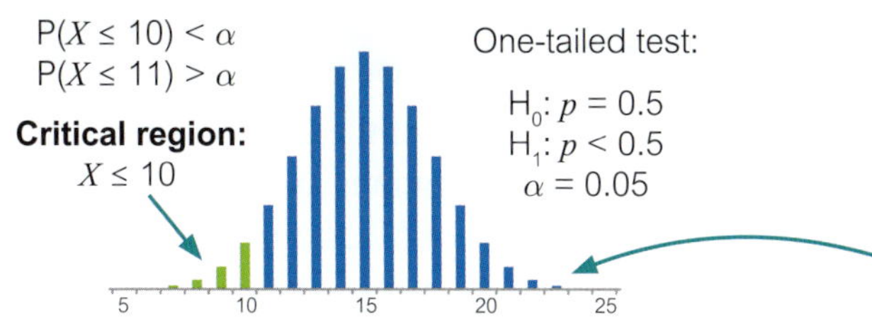

- For this test with H_1: $p < 0.5$, $X = 10$ is the **critical value**.
- The **acceptance region** is the set of all values of the test statistic for which you have **no evidence to reject H_0** — i.e. the blue bars on the diagrams.

A **two-tailed test** has a **critical region** that's split into two 'tails' — one tail at each end of the distribution. Again, the green values of x make up the two parts of the critical region.

The **critical values** for this two-tailed test are: $X = 9$ and $X = 21$.

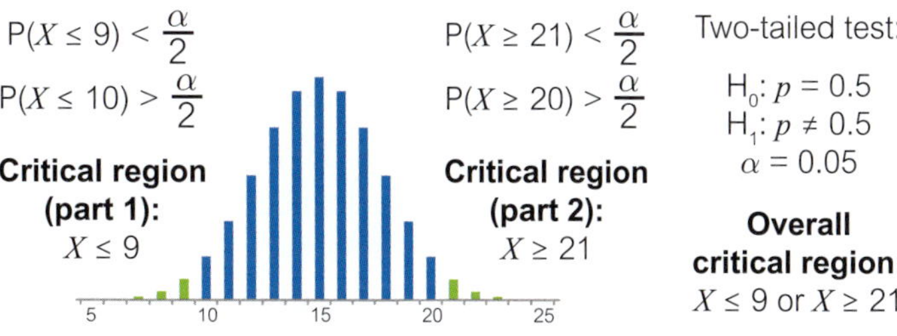

Once you've calculated the critical region, you can easily find what's called the **actual significance level**. The **actual significance level** of the test is usually **slightly different** from the significance level you use to find the critical region in the first place.

The **actual significance level** of a test is the **probability** of **rejecting H_0** when it is true. So the actual significance level is the probability of **incorrectly rejecting H_0**. You find the actual significance level by calculating the **probability** of X taking a value in the **critical region** (assuming H_0 is true).

Back to Aisha and her coin for the final time...

> Aisha's one-tailed test has a critical region of $\boldsymbol{X \geq 20}$.
> She found this using a significance level $\alpha = 0.05$.
>
> But the **actual significance level** of this test is $P(X \geq 20) = \mathbf{0.0494}$
>
> So the probability of Aisha rejecting H_0 when it is true is 0.0494.
>
> In other words, this means that there is a probability of 0.0494 of Aisha **incorrectly** rejecting H_0 when $H_{0\text{ is}}$ true — i.e. of the test producing this kind of **wrong result**.

The actual significance level of a **one-tailed test** will always be **less than or equal to α**.

> Similarly, Aisha's two-tailed test has a critical region of $X \geq 21$ or $X \leq 9$.
> She found this using a significance level $\alpha = 0.05$.
>
> But the **actual significance level** of this test is
> $P(X \geq 21) + P(X \leq 9) = 0.0214 + 0.0214 = \mathbf{0.0428}$
>
> So the probability of Aisha rejecting H_0 when it's true this time is 0.0428.
>
> In other words, there is a 0.0428 probability of Aisha incorrectly rejecting H_0 when H_0 is true — i.e. of the test producing this kind of wrong result.

Problem Solving

Remember you need to find the probability of each end of the critical region and add them up here.

There are **two** different ways that you might be asked to find a critical region for a **two-tailed test**:

1. So that the probability in each tail is **no greater** than $\frac{\alpha}{2}$.
2. So that the probability in each tail is **as close as possible** to $\frac{\alpha}{2}$. In this case, the **total** probability in the two tails **might** be slightly **greater** than α.

So that's what hypothesis tests are — see the next topic for lots more binomial hypothesis tests.

Exercise 5.2

M Q1 After trialling a new flavour of ice cream, a shopkeeper wants to see if the proportion of her customers buying her homemade ice cream has changed from its previous average of 15%. She carries out a hypothesis test using data from a random sample of 50 customers.

a) Suggest suitable hypotheses for this test. Is this a one- or two-tailed test?

b) Identify the test statistic, X.

c) The critical region for this test is $X \leq 3$ or $X \geq 13$. Nine of the customers in the sample buy her ice cream. Comment on whether there is sufficient evidence to reject H_0.

d) The probability of $X \leq 3$ is 0.0460, and the probability of $X \geq 13$ is 0.0301. Calculate the actual significance level of this test.

P M Q2 A company which makes light bulbs claims that 60% of its light bulbs last 800 hours or more. Quality Control Officers test a random sample of 30 light bulbs, and find that 13 of them last 800 hours or more.

a) The Quality Control Officers are interested in the proportion of light bulbs lasting less than 800 hours. Write suitable hypotheses to test whether this proportion is higher than the company says.

b) Define the test statistic, X.

c) The critical region for this test using a 5% level of significance is $X \geq 17$. State, with a reason, whether there is sufficient evidence to reject H_0.

P M Q3 A chocolatier offers a gift wrap service as an option with each purchase of a luxury box. Over one year, they observe that for every 60 luxury boxes they sell, 24 get gift wrapped. Then one day, the greetings card shop next door closes down, which the chocolatier thinks might affect the amount of gift wrapping they provide. Over the following month, they sell 50 luxury boxes, 14 of which get gift wrapped.

a) Suggest a suitable test statistic, X, to test whether the probability of a luxury box getting gift wrapped has changed, and give null and alternative hypotheses for this test.

b) The critical region for this test at the 10% level is $X \leq 13$ or $X \geq 27$. State, with a reason, whether there is sufficient evidence for rejecting the null hypothesis.

P M Q4 A company claims that 95% of the bags of jelly sweets it produces and sells as 200 g bags have a mass exceeding 205 g. Bertie buys 20 bags and finds that 15 have a mass exceeding 205 g. She carries out a hypothesis test to determine whether the company is exaggerating to make itself look better.

a) Give suitable null and alternative hypotheses for Bertie's test.

b) Explain why this situation calls for a one-tailed rather than a two-tailed test.

c) The p-value for Bertie's result is 0.0026. State, with a reason, whether there is enough evidence at the 5% significance level for Bertie to reject her null hypothesis.

5.3 Hypothesis Tests for a Binomial Distribution

Setting up the test

In the last topic, you saw that there were **two** different methods you could be asked to use in a hypothesis-test question — **testing for significance** and **finding a critical region**.

In both cases, you'll always **set up** the hypothesis to test in the same way. Follow this method:

1) Define the **population parameter** in **context** — for a binomial distribution it's always p, a **probability** of success, or **proportion** of a population.
2) Write down the **null** hypothesis (H_0) — H_0: $p = a$ for some constant a.
3) Write down the **alternative** hypothesis (H_1) — H_1 will either be 'H_1: $p < a$' or 'H_1: $p > a$' (one-tailed test) or H_1: '$p \neq a$' (two-tailed test).
4) State the **test statistic**, X — always just the number of '**successes**' in the sample.
5) Write down the **sampling distribution** of the test statistic under H_0 — $X \sim B(n, p)$ where n is the sample size.
6) State the **significance level,** α — you'll usually be given this.

Example 1

Cleo wants to test whether a coin is more likely to land on heads than tails. She plans to flip it 15 times and record the results. Write down suitable null and alternative hypotheses. Define the test statistic, X, and give its sampling distribution under the null hypothesis.

p = probability of the coin landing on heads ← Define the population parameter.

Null hypothesis: the coin is unbiased, so H_0: $p = 0.5$ ← Write out the null hypothesis.

Cleo thinks that the coin is more likely to land on heads, so H_1: $p > 0.5$ ← Write out the alternative hypothesis.

X = the number of heads in the sample of 15 throws. Under H_0, $n = 15$ and $p = 0.5$, so X follows a binomial distribution with $X \sim B(15, 0.5)$. ← Define the test statistic and state its sampling distribution under H_0.

Testing for significance

If you're asked to test an observed value for significance, you need to work out the p-value using either the **binomial tables** or the **binomial cumulative distribution function** on your calculator (see p.124), and then compare it to α for a one-tailed test, or $\frac{\alpha}{2}$ if it's a two-tailed test.

The binomial **tables** (see p.338-342) show the cumulative distribution function **P($X \le x$)** — this lets you quickly find the probability of results '**at least as extreme**' as the observed value.

You can also use the binomial **cumulative distribution function** on your calculator to find **P($X \le x$)** — in fact, you'll **need** to when the tables don't include the probability or value of n that you need.

The next three examples will guide you through one-tailed hypothesis tests — from forming the hypotheses to the final conclusion.

Example 2

A student believes that a five-sided spinner is biased towards landing on 5. He spins the spinner 20 times and it lands on 5 ten times. Using a 5% level of significance, test the hypothesis that the spinner is biased towards landing on 5.

p = the probability of the spinner landing on 5 ← Identify the population parameter.

Null hypothesis: the spinner is not biased, so H_0: $p = 0.2$

Alternative hypothesis: the spinner is more likely to land on 5, so H_1: $p > 0.2$

← Formulate the null and alternative hypotheses for p.

Let X = number of times the spinner lands on a 5 in the sample. Under H_0, $X \sim B(20, 0.2)$. ← State the test statistic X and its sampling distribution under H_0.

The significance level is $\alpha = 0.05$. ← State the test's significance level.

Using the binomial tables: $P(X \geq 10)$
$= 1 - P(X < 10)$
$= 1 - P(X \leq 9)$
$= 1 - 0.9974$
$= 0.0026$

← Test for significance — your p-value is the probability of X being at least as extreme as the value you've observed, i.e. the probability of X being 10 or more, under the null hypothesis.

Under the null hypothesis $p = 0.2$.

Binomial Cumulative Distribution Function
Values show P(X ≤ x), where X~B(n, p)

p =	0.05	0.10	0.15	0.20
n = 20, x = 0	0.3585	0.1216	0.0388	0.0115
...	...	...	...	...
8	1.0000	0.9999	0.9987	0.9900
9	1.0000	1.0000	0.9998	0.9974
10	1.0000	1.0000	1.0000	0.9994

Since $0.0026 < 0.05$, the result is significant.

There is evidence at the 5% level of significance to reject H_0 and to support the student's claim that the spinner is biased towards landing on 5. ← Write your conclusion — you will either reject the null hypothesis H_0 or have insufficient evidence to do so.

Example 3

Pen-Gu Inc. sells stationery to 60% of the schools in the country. The manager of Pen-Gu Inc. claims that there has recently been a decrease in the number of schools buying their stationery. She rings 30 schools at random and finds that 16 buy Pen-Gu Inc. stationery. Test her claim using a 1% significance level.

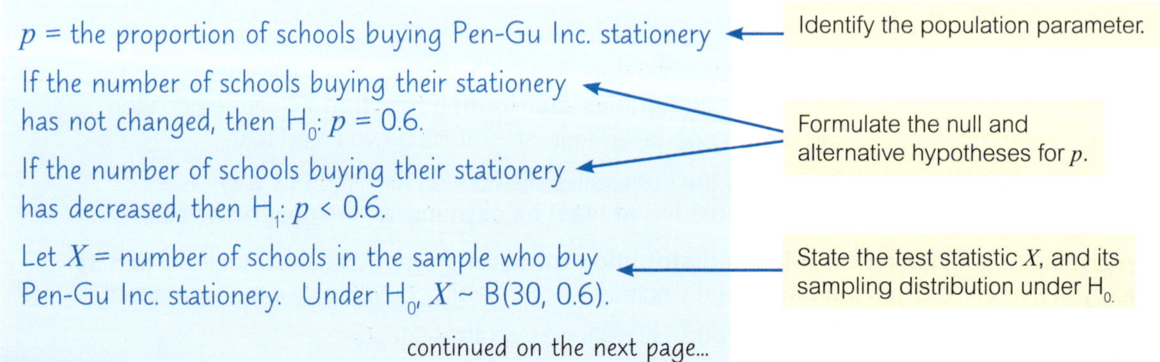

p = the proportion of schools buying Pen-Gu Inc. stationery ← Identify the population parameter.

If the number of schools buying their stationery has not changed, then H_0: $p = 0.6$.

If the number of schools buying their stationery has decreased, then H_1: $p < 0.6$.

← Formulate the null and alternative hypotheses for p.

Let X = number of schools in the sample who buy Pen-Gu Inc. stationery. Under H_0, $X \sim B(30, 0.6)$. ← State the test statistic X, and its sampling distribution under H_0.

continued on the next page...

The significance level is $\alpha = 0.01$.

State the significance level of the test.

Let Y = number of schools in the sample who do not buy Pen-Gu Inc. stationery. Then $Y \sim B(30, 0.4)$.

The value of p under H_0 is greater than 0.5, so you need to do a bit of fiddling to be able to use the binomial tables (or you could use your calculator instead).

Using the binomial tables: $P(X \leq 16) = P(Y \geq 14)$
$= 1 - P(Y < 14)$
$= 1 - P(Y \leq 13)$
$= 1 - 0.7145$
$= 0.2855$

Binomial Cumulative Distribution Function
Values show P(X ≤ x), where X~B(n, p)

p =	...	0.35	0.40
n = 30, x = ...	...	...	...
12	...	0.7802	0.5785
13	...	0.8737	0.7145
14	...	0.9348	0.8246

Test for significance — your p-value is the probability of X being at least as extreme as the value you've observed, i.e. the probability of X being 16 or less, under the null hypothesis.

Since $0.2855 > 0.01$, the result is not significant.

There is insufficient evidence at the 1% level of significance to reject H_0 in favour of the manager's claim.

Write your conclusion.

Tip Always say: 'there is sufficient evidence to reject H_0' or 'there is insufficient evidence to reject H_0' — never talk about 'accepting H_0' or 'rejecting H_1'.

If the value of p or n isn't in the tables, you can use the **binomial probability function** to work things out — or just go straight to the answer by using your **calculator**.

Tip You will need to be able to use your calculator for certain questions, so make sure you've had plenty of practice answering questions with both methods.

Example 4

The proportion of pupils at a school who support a particular football team is found to be 1 in 3. Nigel claims that there is less support for this team at his school. In a random sample of 20 pupils from Nigel's school, 3 support the team. Use a 10% level of significance to test Nigel's claim.

p = proportion of pupils who support the team at Nigel's school

Identify the population parameter.

$H_0: p = \frac{1}{3}$ $\quad H_1: p < \frac{1}{3}$

Formulate the hypotheses.

Let X = number of sampled pupils supporting the team. Under H_0, $X \sim B(20, \frac{1}{3})$.

State the test statistic and its sampling distribution under H_0.

The significance level is $\alpha = 0.1$.

State the significance level of the test.

$$P(X \leq 3) = P(X = 0) + P(X = 1) + P(X = 2) + P(X = 3)$$
$$= \left(\frac{2}{3}\right)^{20} + 20\left(\frac{1}{3}\right)\left(\frac{2}{3}\right)^{19} + 190\left(\frac{1}{3}\right)^2\left(\frac{2}{3}\right)^{18}$$
$$+ 1140\left(\frac{1}{3}\right)^3\left(\frac{2}{3}\right)^{17} = 0.0604$$

You want the probability under H_0 of getting a value less than or equal to 3. The tables don't have values for $p = \frac{1}{3}$, so either work out the probabilities individually using the binomial probability function and add them up, or use the binomial cumulative distribution function on your calculator to go straight to the answer.

$0.0604 < 0.1$, so the result is significant.

There is sufficient evidence at the 10% level of significance to reject H_0 and to support Nigel's claim that there is less support for the team at his school.

Write your conclusion.

With two-tailed tests, the only difference is the value that you compare the probability to in the test for significance.

Example 5

A wildlife photographer is taking photographs of a rare glass frog.

He's established over a long period of time that the probability that he'll sight a glass frog during any day of searching is 0.05.

He moves to another part of the rainforest believing that the probability will be different. During his first 6 days searching he spots the frog on 3 of the days.

Use a 1% level of significance to test his claim.

Problem Solving

The photographer believes he'll see a glass frog on 5% (= 0.05) of days when he looks.
So in 6 days, he'd expect to see a glass frog on 0.05 × 6 = 0.3 days.
For a binomial distribution in general: expected value = np.

p = probability that the wildlife photographer will spot a glass frog in a day of searching — Identify the population parameter.

H_0: $p = 0.05$ H_1: $p \neq 0.05$ — Formulate the hypotheses.

Let X = number of sampled days that he spots a glass frog. Under H_0, $X \sim B(6, 0.05)$. — State the test statistic and its sampling distribution under H_0.

The significance level is $\alpha = 0.01$. So $\frac{\alpha}{2} = 0.005$. — State the significance level of the test.

Using the binomial tables: $P(X \geq 3)$
$= 1 - P(X < 3)$
$= 1 - P(X \leq 2)$
$= 1 - 0.9978$
$= 0.0022$

Test for significance — you're interested in the probability of X being at least as extreme as the value you've observed.

Under H_0, the expected number of days on which a frog is seen is 0.3. 3 is greater than this expected value, so the p-value will be the probability of X being 3 or more, under the null hypothesis.

Binomial Cumulative Distribution Function
Values show $P(X \leq x)$, where $X \sim B(n, p)$

	$p =$ 0.05	0.10
$n = 6$, $x = 0$	0.7351	0.5314
1	0.9672	0.8857
2	0.9978	0.9842

Since $0.0022 < 0.005$, the result is significant.

There is sufficient evidence at the 1% level of significance to reject H_0 in favour of the wildlife photographer's claim that the probability of sighting a glass frog is different in the other part of the rainforest. — Write your conclusion.

Tip

Since the test is two-tailed, you need to work out which 'tail' you are working in — i.e. do you need to find the probability that X is less than, or more than, the observed value?

Problem Solving

If the observed value was less than the expected value under H_0, the p-value would be the probability that X was less than or equal to that value.

Exercise 5.3

M Q1 For each hypothesis test below, write down suitable null and alternative hypotheses, define the test statistic, X, and give its probability distribution under the null hypothesis.

a) Callie believes a 10-sided spinner is biased towards landing on 7. She plans to test this by spinning the spinner 50 times and recording the results.

b) The probability of being stopped at a particular set of traffic lights is thought to be 0.25. Eli thinks he is less likely to be stopped. He passes the lights once a day for 2 weeks and records whether or not he has to stop.

c) A taxi company's drivers get lost on average on 1 in every 40 journeys. The company employs some new drivers and wants to test whether this proportion has changed, using a random sample of 100 journeys.

d) Lucy believes that only 50% of students in her school will have seen a particular film. Rahim thinks that a higher proportion of students will have seen the film, so asks a random sample of 30 students.

Problem Solving

In Q2, Charlotte thinks she can do better than just randomly guessing.

P M Q2 Charlotte claims she can read Milly's mind. To test this claim Milly chooses a number from 1 to 5 and concentrates on it while Charlotte attempts to read her mind. Charlotte is right on 4 out of 10 occasions.

a) Write down the population parameter and suitable null and alternative hypotheses.

b) Define the test statistic and write down its sampling distribution under the null hypothesis.

c) Are these results significant at a 5% level of significance?

E M Q3 Last year 45% of students said that the chicken dinosaurs in the school canteen were good value. After this year's price increase Ellen says fewer students think they are good value. She asked 50 randomly selected students and found only 16 said that the chicken dinosaurs were good value. Test Ellen's claim at the 10% level. *[5 marks]*

E M Q4 Last year, 25% of shoppers at a supermarket used at least one voucher at the checkout. Recent records suggest that the proportion using at least one voucher may be changing. A random sample of 30 shoppers is taken and it is found that 13 of them used at least one voucher.

a) Write down hypotheses that can be used to test whether there has been a change in the proportion using at least one voucher. *[1 mark]*

b) Carry out this test at the 5% significance level and conclude whether or not there is sufficient evidence that the proportion has changed. *[4 marks]*

E P M Q5 Alice claims that a pack of 52 cards is not a standard pack as she thinks the probability of drawing a Heart is different to the probability of drawing the other suits. She tests her claim by drawing 15 cards at random from the pack, replacing each card and shuffling before each pick. 8 of the cards she draws are Hearts. Is there evidence to support her claim at the 5% level? *[5 marks]*

E M Q6 In the past, 25% of John's violin pupils have gained distinctions in their exams. He's using a different examination board and wants to know if the percentage of distinctions will be significantly different. His first 12 exam candidates gained 6 distinctions. Test whether the percentage of distinctions is significantly different at the 1% level. *[5 marks]*

E M Q7 Jin is a keen birdwatcher. Over time he has found that 15% of the birds he sees are classified as 'rare'. He has bought a new type of birdseed and is not sure whether it will attract more or fewer rare birds. On the first day only 2 out of 40 of the birds were rare. Test whether the percentage of rare birds is significantly different at the 10% level. *[5 marks]*

E M Q8 10% of customers at a village newsagent's buy Pigeon Spotter Magazine. The owner has just opened a new shop in a different village and wants to know whether this proportion will be different in the new shop. One day 8 out of a random sample of 50 customers bought Pigeon Spotter Magazine. Is this significant at the 5% level? *[5 marks]*

E M Q9 On average, 32% of the customers buying a single cookie at a bakery choose white choc chip. The baker changes the recipe and wants to know if this will change the proportion of white choc chip cookies he sells. One month after the recipe change, he takes a random sample of 50 customers who buy a single cookie and finds that 11 chose white choc chip. Test whether the proportion of white choc chip cookies sold is significantly different, at the 10% level. *[5 marks]*

E P M Q10 Pete's Driving School advertises that 70% of its clients pass the driving test at their first attempt. Hati and three other random clients failed. Four random other clients did pass first time. She complained that the advertisement was misleading and that the percentage was actually lower. Test whether there is evidence to support Hati's complaint at the 1% level. *[5 marks]*

E M Q11 For her previous team, a footballer scored in 55% of the games she played. She has joined a new team and claims that the proportion of games she scores in has changed. For her new team, she has scored in 22 out of 30 games played. Test whether there is evidence to support the footballer's claim at the 5% level. *[5 marks]*

Challenge

E P M Q12 During her previous years at secondary school, the probability of Yawen getting at least one detention on any day is 0.17. At the start of the new school year she aims to get detentions on fewer days. For the first N days of the new year she doesn't get any detentions, and concludes at the 5% significance level that the probability of her getting a detention has decreased. Show that N must be at least 17. *[5 marks]*

5.4 Critical Regions for Binomial Hypothesis Tests

Remember that the critical region is just the **set of all values** which are **significant** under H_0. You use the binomial tables (or the binomial probability function) to find it.

If the test is **one-tailed**, the critical region will be at only **one end** of the distribution. If the test is **two-tailed**, the critical region will be **split in two** with a bit at each end.

For a two-tailed test, you could either be asked to make the probability of rejection in the tails **less than** $\frac{\alpha}{2}$, or **as close** to $\frac{\alpha}{2}$ as possible.

The **actual significance level** is the probability (under H_0) that H_0 is rejected, which is found by calculating the **probability** that the observed value of the test statistic will fall in the critical region.

Example 1

A company manufactures kettles. Its records over the years show that 20% of its kettles will be faulty. Simon claims that the proportion of faulty kettles must be lower than this. He takes a sample of 30 kettles to test his claim.

a) Find the critical region for a test of Simon's claim at the 5% level.

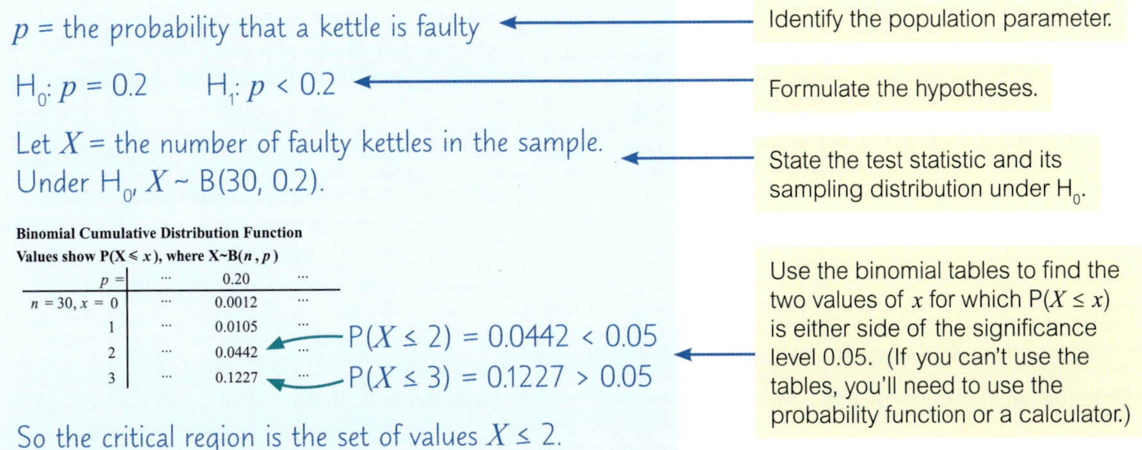

$p =$	...	0.20	...
$n = 30, x = 0$	...	0.0012	...
1	...	0.0105	...
2	...	0.0442	...
3	...	0.1227	...

b) State the actual significance level.

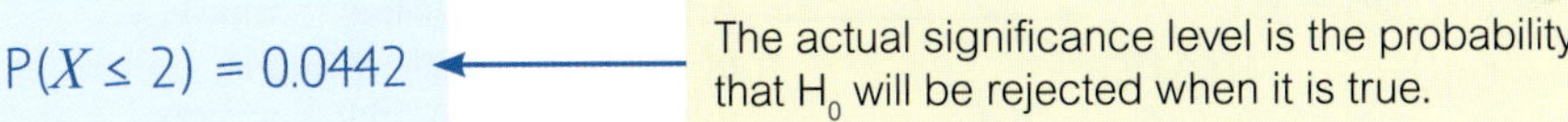

Tip
The number $X = 2$ in this example is the critical value.

c) Simon found that 1 kettle in his sample was faulty.
Say whether this is significant evidence to reject H_0.

1 lies in the critical region, so it is significant evidence to reject H_0 in favour of H_1.

Example 2

Records show that the proportion of trees in a wood that suffer from a particular leaf disease is 15%. Hasina thinks that recent weather conditions might have affected this proportion. She examines a random sample of 20 of the trees.

a) Using a 10% level of significance, find the critical region for a two-tailed test of Hasina's theory. The probability of rejection in each tail should be as close to 0.05 as possible.

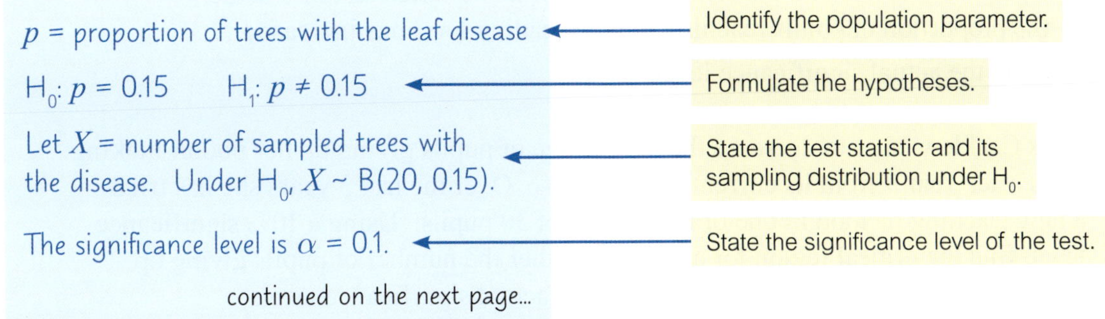

Lower tail:
$P(X \leq 0) = 0.0388 < 0.05$
$P(X \leq 1) = 0.1756 > 0.05$

0.0388 is closer to 0.05, so the lower tail is $X \leq 0$.

Upper tail:
$P(X \geq 6) = 1 - P(X \leq 5) = 1 - 0.9327$
$= 0.0673 > 0.05$

$P(X \geq 7) = 1 - P(X \leq 6) = 1 - 0.9781$
$= 0.0219 < 0.05$

0.0673 is closer to 0.05, so the upper tail is $X \geq 6$.

The lower tail is $X \leq 0$ and the upper tail is $X \geq 6$ so the critical region is $X = 0$ or $X \geq 6$.

Problem Solving This is a two-tailed test, so look at both ends of the sampling distribution — the lower tail is the set of 'low' values of X with a total probability as close to 0.05 as possible, and the upper tail is the set of 'high' values of X with a total probability as close to 0.05 as possible.

For the lower tail, use the binomial tables to find the two values of x such that $P(X \leq x)$ is either side of 0.05, and choose the closest.

For the upper tail, you need to find two values of x such that $P(X \geq x)$ is either side of 0.05, and choose the closest.
In the tables, this means looking for two values of x such that $P(X \leq x)$ is either side of 0.95.

Write the critical region using both tails.

b) Find the actual significance level of a test based on your critical region from part a).

$P(X = 0) + P(X \geq 6) = 0.0388 + 0.0673$
$= 0.1061$ or 10.61%

Add the probabilities (under H_0) of the test statistic falling in each part of the critical region.

c) Hasina finds that 8 of the sampled trees have the leaf disease. Comment on this finding.

The observed value of 8 is in the critical region. So there is evidence at the 10% level of significance to reject H_0 and to support Hasina's theory that there has been a change in the proportion of affected trees.

Exercise 5.4

M Q1 A primary school hopes to increase the percentage of pupils reaching the top level in reading from its current value of 25% by limiting the time pupils spend playing games online. Twenty parents will be limiting their child's use of online games.

a) Using a 5% level, find the critical region for a one-tailed test of whether the proportion of pupils reaching the top reading level has increased.

b) State the actual significance level.

M Q2 Miss Cackle wishes to decrease the percentage of pupils giving up her potion-making class after Year 9 from its current level of 20%. Over the last 3 years she has tried a new teaching method in one of her classes of 30 pupils. Using a 10% significance level, find the critical region for a test of whether the number of pupils giving up potions after Year 9 has decreased. State the actual significance level.

E M Q3 A travel agent thinks that fewer people are booking their holidays early this year. In the past, 35% have booked their summer holiday by February 1st. She intends to ask 15 people on 2nd February whether they have booked their summer holiday.

a) Find the critical region for a test at the 5% level of whether fewer people are booking their holidays early this year. *[4 marks]*

b) State the actual significance level. *[1 mark]*

c) The travel agent finds that 3 of the people she asked had already booked their summer holiday. Is this result significant at the 5% level? *[1 mark]*

E M Q4 The manager of a sports centre wants to increase the proportion of its members playing squash from its current level of 15%. She runs a campaign to promote the squash facilities, and after three months, she asks a sample of 40 randomly selected members if they play squash at the sports centre.

a) Using a 5% significance level, find the critical region for a test of whether the proportion of members playing squash at the sports centre has increased. *[4 marks]*

b) State the actual significance level of the test. *[1 mark]*

c) The manager finds that 12 of the 40 people play squash at the sports centre. Is this a significant result at the 5% level? *[1 mark]*

E M Q5 When Isla eats a certain brand of cheese, the probability that she gets a headache is 0.3. She wants to try a different brand of cheese, to see if it affects how frequently she gets headaches. She plans to eat the new brand of cheese every day for 40 days, keeping other conditions the same, and record whether she gets a headache on each day.

a) Using a binomial model and clearly stating your hypotheses, find the critical region for a hypothesis test at the 10% significance level of whether the probability that Isla gets a headache has changed. The probability of each tail should be less than 5%. *[5 marks]*

Out of the 40 days, Isla gets a headache on 9 days and no headache on 31 days.

b) State, with a reason, whether Isla rejects or fails to reject the null hypothesis. *[1 mark]*

c) Criticise the suitability of using a binomial model in this context. *[1 mark]*

M Q6 Politicians are testing for a difference in local councils' rubbish collection service between the North and the South. They've found that 40% of the northern councils provide a weekly service. They have randomly chosen 25 councils in the south of the country to investigate. Find the critical region for a test of whether the number of councils providing weekly collections is significantly different in the south at the 5% level. The probability of each tail should be as close to 2.5% as possible. Calculate the actual significance level.

M Q7 A takeaway business wants to see if the proportion of their customers spending over £25 will change if they offer free delivery. Before offering free delivery, 30% of their customers spent over £25. They select a random sample of 50 customers in the month after starting to offer free delivery. Using a significance level of 10%, find the critical region for a test of whether free delivery has changed the proportion of customers spending over £25. The probability of each tail should be less than 5%. Calculate the actual significance level of the test.

M Q8 A new drug is to be tested on 50 people to see if they report an improvement in their symptoms. In the past it has been found that with a placebo treatment, 15% of people report an improvement, so the new drug has to be significantly better than this. Find the critical region for a test at the 1% level of significance of whether the new drug is significantly better than a placebo. The probability of the tail should be less than 1%. State the actual significance level.

M Q9 Tests conducted on five-year-old girls have found that 5% of them believe that they have magical powers. A group of 50 five-year-old boys are to be tested to see if the same proportion of boys believe that they have magical powers. Find the critical region for a test at the 10% level of whether the proportion of boys who believe they have magical powers is different from that of girls. The probability of each tail should be as close to 5% as possible. Calculate the actual significance level.

E M Q10 Trains run by a certain operating company arrive late 25% of the time. A new rail operator has recently taken over, who claims it has significantly improved the service. Local train enthusiasts choose 20 trains at random from the schedule over a period of one week and monitor whether or not they arrive on time.

a) Using a significance level of 10%, find the critical region for a test of whether a significantly smaller proportion of trains arrive late under the new operator. *[4 marks]*

b) Two trains in the sample arrive late. Comment on the operator's claim. *[1 mark]*

P M Q11 The British Furniture Company's top salesman has persuaded 60% of customers to take out a loyalty card. He has been on a motivational course and aims to improve even further. On his first day's work after the course he serves 12 customers.

a) Find the critical region for a test of whether the salesman has improved at the 5% level.

b) State the actual significance level.

c) He persuades 10 customers to get a loyalty card. Is this result significant at the 5% level?

P M Q12 A bookseller decides to change the books in the window of her shop. She wants to see if this changes the proportion of customers who buy children's books. Over the last year, 65% of customers bought children's books. In the month after changing the window display, she chooses a random sample of 15 customers and records whether each customer buys any children's books. Find the critical region for a test at the 5% level of significance of whether the proportion of customers buying children's books has changed. The probability of each tail should be as close to 2.5% as possible. Calculate the actual significance level of the test.

Challenge

P M Q13 A company claims that 8 out of 10 parrots prefer their birdseed, Polly-No-Meal, to the next best-selling brand. Ava believes the company is exaggerating the popularity of the birdseed, so she carries out a test with 10 parrots to see how many of them prefer Polly-No-Meal. Ava's result is the smallest value that is not in the critical region at a 5% significance level.

a) Find the number of parrots who preferred Polly-No-Meal in Ava's test.

b) Ava then carries out the same experiment with another 10 parrots and obtains the same result, which she says is still not significant evidence at the 5% level to conclude that the company's claim is exaggerated. Is she correct? Fully justify your answer.

5 Review Exercise

M Q1 Michael's journey to work involves going through one set of traffic lights. During 2020, he was able to go straight through without being stopped by the lights on 15% of journeys. He suspects that the timing of the lights has since been changed, improving his chance of getting through without stopping. He decides to conduct a hypothesis test and presents the following working: "Let p = the probability of going through without stopping. Then H_0: $p = 0.15$ and H_1: $p = 0.25$. The test is two-tailed."
Find and explain the errors in his working.

M Q2 Sweets are put into packets of 12 on a factory production line. It is found that the probability that a packet contains fewer than 12 sweets is 9%. A new packaging system is introduced and the factory owner is interested in whether this is a better system for ensuring packets contain at least 12 sweets.

a) State the null and alternative hypotheses for the factory owner's test.

b) Is this a one- or two-tailed test?

M Q3 The probability that each item a machine produces is faulty is thought to be 0.05. The manager takes a sample of 50 items to check this claim. Write down suitable null and alternative hypotheses for his test, define the test statistic and give its probability distribution under the null hypothesis.

M Q4 Tommy likes 55% of the songs which play on his favourite radio station. He decides to try listening to Tunes FM instead. Over a week, he listens to 50 songs on Tunes FM and likes 36 of them. He decides to carry out a test using the following hypotheses:

H_0: the probability of me not liking a song on Tunes FM is 0.45.
H_1: the probability of me not liking a song on Tunes FM is not 0.45.

a) What is the test statistic, X?

b) Given that his test gives a critical region of $X \leq 15$ or $X \geq 30$ at the 5% level, determine whether he rejects H_0, explaining your answer.

M Q5 Milo correctly answers 84% of questions in a quiz. Tina claims that she is better at quizzes than Milo. In a sample of 10 questions, she answers 9 questions correctly.

a) Write down the population parameter and appropriate hypotheses to test Tina's claim.

b) What is the test statistic? What is its probability distribution under the null hypothesis?

c) Test Tina's claim at the 5% significance level.

Q6 Carry out the following tests of the binomial parameter p.
Let X represent the number of successes in a random sample of size 20:

a) Test H_0: $p = 0.2$ against H_1: $p < 0.2$, at the 5% significance level, using $x = 2$.

b) Test H_0: $p = 0.4$ against H_1: $p > 0.4$, at the 1% significance level, using $x = 15$.

E M Q7 Maisie and her brother flip a coin to decide who gets to borrow their mum's car. Maisie suspects that the coin her brother uses is biased towards heads. To test her claim, she flips the coin 20 times, and it lands on heads 13 times. Test, at a 5% significance level, if there is evidence to support her claim. *[5 marks]*

E P M Q8 Hiral suspects that a five-sided dice numbered 1 to 5 might be biased and that the probability of rolling a 5 is higher than it would be on a fair five-sided dice. To test this suspicion, she rolls the dice 20 times and records her results as follows:

Score	1	2	3	4	5
Frequency	4	2	4	1	9

a) Give null and alternative hypotheses for testing whether the dice is biased toward rolling a 5. *[1 mark]*

b) Showing your working, write down the range of significance levels which would cause her to reject the null hypothesis. *[3 marks]*

E M Q9 A writer finds that, on average, 1 out of every 20 pages in his previous book contains an error. For his new book, he has used a different proofreader. The writer checks 50 pages and finds that 2 of them contain errors. Test whether the error rate for his new book is significantly different at the 5% level. *[5 marks]*

E M Q10 25% of the students taught by a statistics teacher have gained an A grade in their final exam. The teacher changes exam boards and is worried that the proportion of her students gaining an A grade might change. In the first year of the new exam, 9 out of her 40 students get A grades. Test, at the 5% significance level, whether the proportion of students gaining A grades has changed under the new exam board. *[5 marks]*

E P M Q11 A botanist attempts to grow a rare variety of orchid. These orchid seeds germinate approximately 15% of the time. He plants 20 seeds and uses a new fertiliser to improve the chances of germination. Of the 20 seeds planted, 7 germinate.

a) Test, at the 5% level, if the proportion of seeds germinating is significantly higher using the new fertiliser. Outline any necessary assumptions to be able to carry out this test. *[6 marks]*

b) Explain why an assumption made in part a) may, in fact, not be true. *[1 mark]*

Q12 Find the critical region for the following test where $X \sim B(10, p)$:
Test H_0: $p = 0.3$ against H_1: $p < 0.3$, at the 5% significance level.

M Q13 The owner of a restaurant wants to improve its reviews on a website. Currently, the restaurant has 45% positive reviews. After changing the menu and carrying out staff training, the owner wants to know if the proportion of positive reviews has increased. He checks a random sample of 20 new reviews on the website.

a) Find the critical region for a hypothesis test at the 1% significance level.

b) Find the actual significance level.

c) Find the acceptance region.

P M Q14 A company makes chocolate eggs that sometimes contain a toy. They claim that 10% of their eggs contain a toy. Hector buys 50 eggs and counts the number which contain a toy.

His hypotheses are: H_0: 10% of the eggs contain toys.
H_1: Fewer than 10% of the eggs contain toys.

a) Is his test one- or two-tailed? Give a reason for your answer.

b) Given that he rejects H_0 at the 5% significance level, find all possible values of X, the number of eggs he bought which contain a toy.

E P M Q15 Cherlan sets himself the challenge of going for a jog every day for a (non-leap) year. He goes for a jog on 146 days of the year. At the start of the following year, he goes for a jog on only 1 day out of the first 7 days. He is worried that he is less motivated to go for a jog this year.

a) Find the critical region for a hypothesis test at the 10% significance level to determine whether the proportion of days Cherlan goes for a jog is lower in the new year. *[4 marks]*

b) Comment on Cherlan's suspicion that he is less motivated. *[1 mark]*

c) State one thing that may affect the validity of his test. *[1 mark]*

E M Q16 85% of students are happy with the service their bus company provides. 100 randomly selected students from another school are asked if they are happy with their bus company.

a) Find the critical region for a hypothesis test at the 10% significance level of whether the proportion of 'happy' students is different at the second school. The probability in each tail should be as close to 5% as possible. *[5 marks]*

b) Find the actual significance level. *[1 mark]*

c) 75 students from the second school are happy with the bus company. Is this result significant at the 10% level? *[1 mark]*

E M Q17 The manufacturer of a particular cleaning product claims that 70% of households use their product. A market research company is employed to investigate this claim. They conduct an online survey to get information from 50 households.

a) Write down the hypotheses that could be used to test the manufacturer's claim. *[1 mark]*

b) Using a 5% significance level, find the critical region for this test, and calculate the actual significance level. *[5 marks]*

c) 26 of the 50 households surveyed said they use the product. Comment on the manufacturer's claim, given this information. *[2 marks]*

E P M **Q18** A student reads in a report that in a group of children, 40% chose to play with building blocks over a remote control car. She is interested in whether age affects this choice. She offers a group of children from a younger age group the chance to play with either building blocks or a remote control car. Her results are shown in the table below.

Building blocks	Remote control car	Total
20	20	40

a) Give the critical region for a test at the 10% level to determine whether the proportion of children who choose to play with building blocks is different for the younger group of children. The probability in each tail should be less than 5%. *[5 marks]*

b) Interpret the outcome of this hypothesis test in context. *[2 marks]*

c) Give one consideration the student should have made to make sure the test was fair. *[1 mark]*

Challenge

E P M **Q19** The Venn diagram shows the numbers of diners who visit a restaurant over a two-month period sorted by whether they ordered starters, mains and puddings.

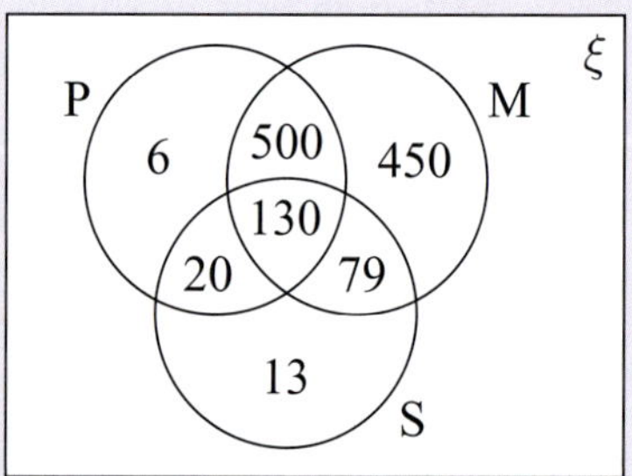

The management introduces a discount when you order exactly two courses and they want to know whether this is encouraging people to order two courses. During the first two days of the discount, they take a random sample of 40 diners and 26 of them order exactly two courses.

a) Use hypothesis testing at the 5% level to determine whether there is evidence to suggest that the incentive is working. *[5 marks]*

b) Give the critical region for a test of the hypothesis from part a) at the 10% level. *[2 marks]*

P M **Q20** Ayo selects a card from a pack of 52 cards twenty times, replacing the card and shuffling the pack between each selection. He picks out 12 red and 8 black cards. He thinks that the pack might not contain an even number of red and black cards and writes out the following:

X = number of red cards selected,
p = probability of selecting a red card
$H_0: p = 0.5$, $H_1: p \neq 0.5$

a) Give the minimum significance level needed to reject the null hypothesis.

b) What would you advise Ayo about whether his pack of cards contains equal numbers of red and black cards?

E P M **Q21** The canteen at a sixth form college has previously received a 68% approval rating from students. A new catering company has taken over the canteen and want to see if this rating has changed. They survey groups of students leaving the canteen and find that 34 out of 42 students approve of the service provided.

a) Test, at the 1% level, if the approval rating for the canteen has changed since the new company took over. *[5 marks]*

b) Give one reason why a binomial distribution model may not be valid for the above test. *[1 mark]*

5 Chapter Summary

1 A hypothesis test is a method of testing a claim or statement about a population, that might or might not be true, using observed data from a sample.

2 A hypothesis test requires two hypotheses:
- The null hypothesis (H_0) is a statement about the value of a population parameter p.
- The alternative hypothesis (H_1) is what you'll conclude if you decide to reject H_0.

3 There are two kinds of alternative hypothesis:
- A one-tailed H_1 specifies whether p is greater than or less than the value used in H_0.
- A two-tailed H_1 only states that p is not equal to the value in H_0.

4 A hypothesis test can have two possible conclusions: reject H_0 in favour of H_1 — if the observed data provides strong evidence that H_0 is unlikely to be true — or fail to reject H_0.

5 The significance level, α, of a test determines how unlikely the data needs to be under the null hypothesis before you reject H_0 — if the results under H_0 have a probability of α or below then you can say they are 'significant'.

6 The most common significance levels are $\alpha = 0.1$ (10%), $\alpha = 0.05$ (5%) and $\alpha = 0.01$ (1%).

7 Using a lower value of α will give stronger evidence that H_0 is false if it is rejected, but it also makes it less likely that you'll be able to reject H_0 in the first place.

8 A test statistic, X, for a hypothesis test is a quantity calculated from sample data, which is used to decide whether or not to reject H_0.

9 The sampling distribution gives all possible values of a statistic, X, with its corresponding probabilities. In this course, you'll use the binomial distribution $B(n, p)$.

10 The p-value is the probability of a value at least as extreme as x, i.e. $P(X \leq x)$ or $P(X \geq x)$, using the parameter in H_0. If the p-value is less than or equal to α, you can reject H_0.

11 Use binomial tables or the binomial cumulative distribution function to find p-values.

12 In a two-tailed test, use $\frac{\alpha}{2}$ as the significance level at each end of the distribution.

13 The critical region is the set of all values of the test statistic that would lead you to reject H_0.

14 The actual significance level is the probability of rejecting H_0 when it is true. You can find it by calculating the probability of X taking a value in the critical region (assuming H_0 is true).

15 In a two-tailed test, you could be asked to find the critical region so that the probability in each tail is either no greater than $\frac{\alpha}{2}$ or as close as possible to $\frac{\alpha}{2}$.

Quantities and Units in Mechanics

6

Learning Objectives

Once you've completed this chapter, you should be able to:

- Understand and use base units in the S.I. system for length, time and mass.
- Use derived units for quantities such as force and velocity.
- Understand and use terminology used in mechanics.
- Explain and evaluate assumptions made in modelling situations.

Prior Knowledge Check

1 Convert each of these measurements into the units given:
   a) 3200 m into km
   b) 825 mm into cm
   c) 0.07 km into m see GCSE Maths

2 Find the combined total of 2500 g, 45 kg and 0.5 tonnes. Give your answer in kg. see GCSE Maths

6.1 S.I. Units

The International System of Units (S.I.) was developed to make measurements consistent around the world. S.I. units, which include the **metre**, **kilogram** and **second**, are set by certain scientific constants.

These units are referred to as **base units**, which means that they can be used to derive all other units of measurement. They're also mutually independent — you can't derive one base unit from another.

Derived units

Other units, such as **newtons**, are called **derived** S.I. units because they are combinations of the base units. All quantities can be measured in units derived from the base S.I. units. There are also non-S.I. derived units, such as miles per hour — the mile isn't part of the S.I. system as it's an imperial unit.

Example 1

a) Derive the S.I. units of velocity and acceleration.

Velocity is defined as the change in displacement divided by the time taken. Displacement is measured in metres, and time in seconds, so velocity is measured in $m \div s = ms^{-1}$ (or m/s).

Similarly, acceleration is the change in velocity over time, so is measured in $ms^{-1} \div s = ms^{-2}$.

b) Express the newton in terms of S.I. base units.

1 newton is the force that will cause a mass of 1 kg to accelerate at a rate of 1 ms^{-2}.
The formula for the force exerted on an object is the mass of the object multiplied by its acceleration (see page 221).
So in terms of base units, this is $kg \times ms^{-2} = kgms^{-2}$.

Exercise 6.1

Q1 The following should have been given in SI base units, but these were missed off. Add the correct SI units for each part.

a) velocity = 7
b) displacement = 0.2
c) time = 5
d) acceleration = 2.6
e) speed = 9
f) area = 1020

Q2 Give the derived units of the following measurements using the S.I. base units kg, m and s:

a) Volume = length × width × height
b) Density = mass ÷ volume
c) Momentum = mass × velocity
d) Jerk = acceleration ÷ time
e) Energy = force × distance
f) Pressure = force ÷ area

6.2 Modelling in Mechanics

M

Modelling is a **cycle** — you can improve your model by making more (or fewer) assumptions.

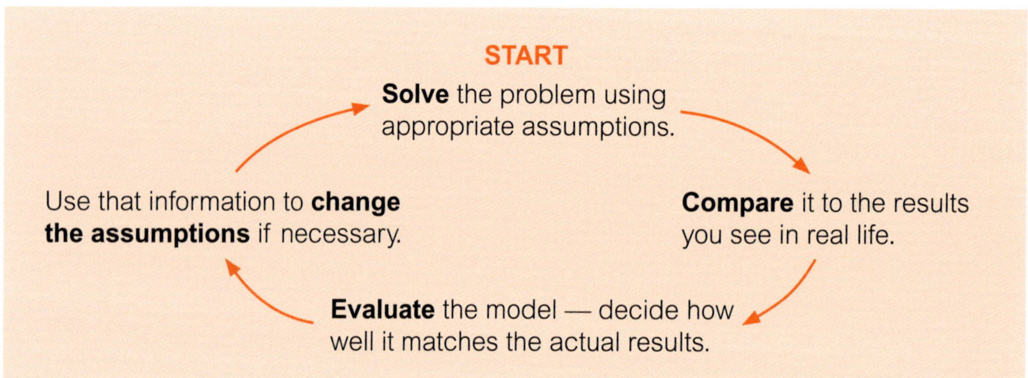

Keep going until you're satisfied with the model.

Mathematical models use lots of words that you already know, but which are used to mean something very precise.

Light — the body has negligible mass.

Static — the body is not moving.

Rough — a body in contact with the surface will experience a frictional force which will act to oppose motion.

Smooth — a body in contact with the surface will not experience a frictional force.

Rigid — the body does not bend.

Thin — the body has negligible thickness.

Inextensible — the body can't be stretched.

Equilibrium — there is no resultant force acting on the body.

> **Tip** These definitions refer to a '**body**' — this is just another way of saying 'an object'. You won't be tested on these terms, but you need to be familiar with what they mean as they come up all the time.

Particle — a body whose mass acts at a point, so its dimensions don't matter.

Plane — a flat surface.

Beam or **Rod** — a thin, straight, rigid body.

Wire — a thin, inextensible, rigid, light body.

String — a thin body, usually modelled as being light and inextensible.

Peg — a fixed support which a body can hang from or rest on.

Pulley — a wheel, usually modelled as fixed and smooth, over which a string passes.

Labelling forces

You have to know what **forces** are acting on a body when you're creating a mathematical model, so you need to understand what each **type** of force is.

Weight (W)

Due to the particle's mass, m, and the acceleration due to gravity, g: $W = mg$
Weight always acts **downwards**. The effect of gravity can be assumed to be constant: $g = 9.8$ ms^{-2} (unless you're given a different value).

The Normal Reaction (R or N)

The reaction from a surface — always at **90° to the surface**.
(The 'normal' to an object is the line or direction that is perpendicular to it, which is why this is called the normal reaction force.)

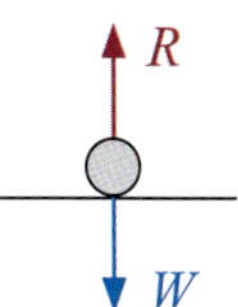

Tension (T)

Force in a **taut** rope, wire or string.

Tip Taut means that the string is tight and straight.

Friction (F)

A **resistance** force due to **roughness** between a body and surface.
Always acts **against motion**, or likely motion.

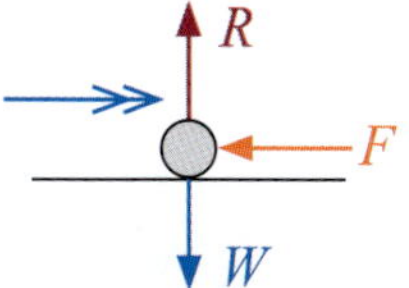

Thrust or Compression

Force in a rod (e.g. the pole of an open umbrella).

Example 1

Draw a diagram to model each of the following situations.
In each case, state the assumptions you have made.

a) A brick is resting flat on a horizontal table.

Assumptions:

- The brick is a particle.
- There's no wind or other external forces involved.

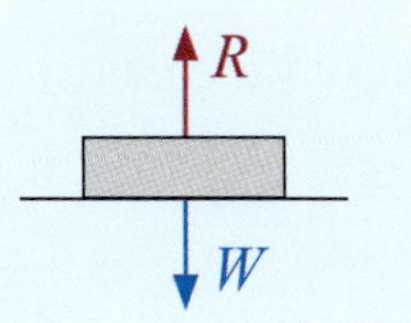

Tip 'Resting' or 'at rest' means that the object isn't moving.

b) An ice hockey player is accelerating across an ice rink.

Assumptions:

- The skater is a particle.
- There is no friction between the skates and the ice.
- There is no air resistance.
- The skater generates a constant forward force, S.

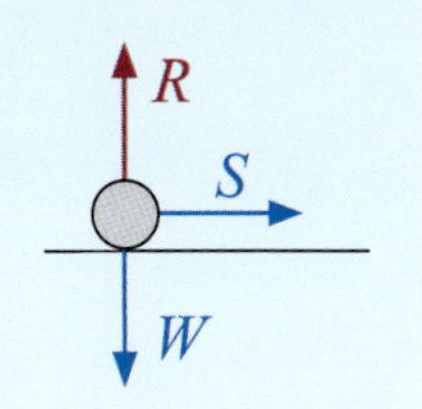

Tip It's quicker and easier to use just a letter for each force in your diagram, e.g. S for the forward force.

c) A golf ball is dropped from a tall building.

Assumptions:

- The ball is a particle.
- Air resistance can be ignored.
- There's no wind or other external forces involved.
- The effect of gravity (g) is constant.

d) A book is put flat on a table. One end of the table is slowly lifted and the angle to the horizontal is measured when the book starts to slide.

Assumptions:

- The book is a particle.
- The book is rigid, so it doesn't bend or open.
- The surface of the table is rough, so there will be a frictional force acting between it and the book.
- There are no other external forces acting.

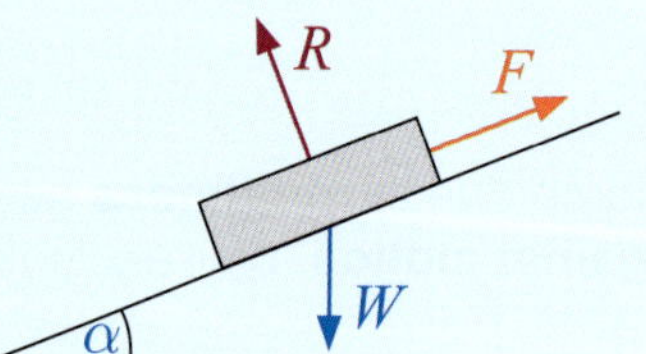

e) A sledge is steadily pulled along horizontal ground by a small child with a rope.

Assumptions:

- The sledge is a particle.
- Friction is too big to be ignored (i.e. it's not ice).
- The rope is a light, inextensible string.
- The rope is horizontal (it's a small child).

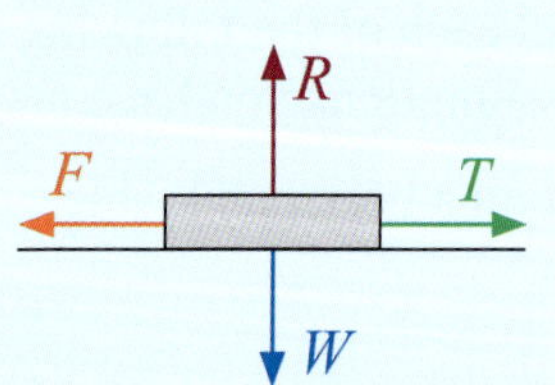

Tip The weight of a rigid object can be assumed to act at a single point — the centre of mass of the object.

f) A ball is held by two strings, A and B, at angles α and β to the vertical.

Assumptions:

- The ball is a particle.
- The strings are light.
- The strings are inextensible.

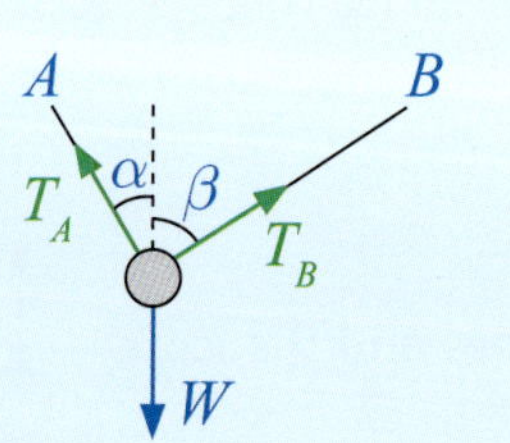

Exercise 6.2

For questions 1-9, draw a diagram to model the situation and state any assumptions you make.

M Q1 An apple falls from a tree.

M Q2 A shoe lace is threaded through a conker. The conker hangs vertically in equilibrium from the shoe lace.

M Q3 A sledge is steadily pulled up an icy hill by a rope.

M Q4 a) A wooden box is pushed across a polished marble floor.

b) A crate is pulled across a carpeted floor by a horizontal rope.

M Q5 A person pushes a small package along the road with a stick. The stick makes an angle of 20° with the horizontal.

M Q6 a) A car is driven up a hill. b) A car is driven down a hill.

P M Q7 A strongman pulls a lorry along a horizontal road by a rope parallel to the road.

Q6-7 Problem Solving

Both the car's engine and the strongman will generate a driving force D.

M Q8 A toboggan travels down an icy slope, at an angle α to the horizontal.

P M Q9 A pendulum on a string is pushed by a rod, so that it is at an angle α to the vertical.

E P M Q10 A box (modelled as a particle) is positioned halfway up a rough ramp, which is secured against a vertical wall. The ramp makes an angle of 60° with horizontal ground. Draw a diagram showing the forces which act on the box. *[2 marks]*

Q11 In mechanics modelling, what are the differences between each of the following sets of terms?

a) Rough and smooth

b) A rod and a wire

c) A peg and a pulley

M Q12 The diagram shows a ball which has been thrown from ground level at an angle of 70° to the horizontal and is moving through the air (which offers no resistance). Copy the diagram and mark the force(s) acting on the ball.

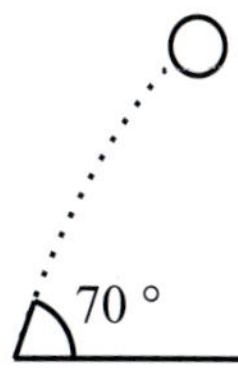

Challenge

E M Q13 A car tows a trailer up a steep road, using a tow rope. Make a copy of the diagram and show the forces acting on the car and on the trailer.

State two assumptions that you make. *[5 marks]*

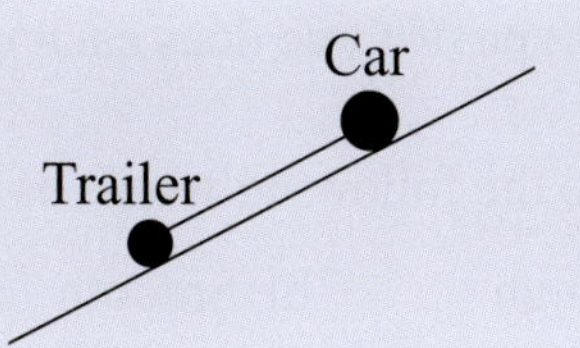

6 Review Exercise

E P Q1 Power is defined as work done per second. Its units are Nms^{-1}.
Show that energy and work done are measured in the same units.
A formula for energy is energy = force × distance. *[2 marks]*

E Q2 A formula for final velocity, v (ms^{-1}), is $v = u + at$, where u (ms^{-1}) is the initial velocity, a (ms^{-2}) is the constant acceleration and t (seconds) is the total time taken.
Verify that each term within the formula has the same units. *[1 mark]*

E Q3 A formula for displacement, s (m), is $s = ut + \frac{1}{2}at^2$, where u (ms^{-1}) is the initial velocity, a (ms^{-2}) is the constant acceleration and t (seconds) is the total time taken.
Verify that each term within the formula has the same units. *[1 mark]*

P Q4 What must a density, measured in gcm^{-3}, be multiplied by to give the density measured in SI base units?

E P Q5 E, the elastic potential energy of a spring, is given by the formula $E = \lambda x^2$, where λ is the spring constant and x is the extension of the spring, given in m.
What are the SI units of λ? A formula for energy is energy = force × distance. *[2 marks]*

E P M Q6 A cyclist travels 6 km at a speed of 30 000 cm/min.
She then cycles for a further 0.0125 days at a speed of 12 km/hour.
How long did she cycle in total? Give your answer in SI base units. *[3 marks]*

Q7 In the following, m represents mass (kg), a represents acceleration (ms^{-2}), s represents displacement (m), v represents velocity (ms^{-1}), t represents time (seconds) and F represents force ($kgms^{-2}$).

a) Which pairs of expressions have equivalent units?

ma $\frac{mv}{t^2}$ $\frac{v^2}{a} \times \frac{m}{t^2}$ $\frac{ma}{t}$

b) Which of the following expressions have equivalent units to acceleration?

$v \times s$ $\frac{Fvt}{ms}$ $vs \div t$

Q8 The letters W, F, R, N and T are commonly used in diagrams to represent forces.
What type of force does each usually stand for?

Q9 Define the following words as they apply in mechanics models:

a) Rough b) Smooth c) Plane d) Body

Q10 What are the missing words in the following paragraph?

> In mechanics, we will often __(1)__ a real-life situation, making approximations so that what we are working on is more __(2)__ than the reality.
>
> When a model is too simple, results which we calculate will tend to be ____(3)____ . A model which is too complex may give accurate results but be __(4)__ than necessary to work with. Modelling assumptions show our simplifications.
>
> When we say that something is __(5)__, we mean that it has negligible mass. A body which is not moving is described as __(6)__ . When no resultant force is acting on a body, the body is said to be in ____(7)____ . A body which does not bend is referred to as __(8)__. A body which cannot be stretched is known as _____(9)_____ .

E P Q11 Describe the orientation of the surface in each case if:

a) the normal reaction acting upwards from the surface on a particle is vertical. *[1 mark]*

b) the normal reaction acting upwards from the surface on a particle is at an angle of 20° to the vertical. *[1 mark]*

Challenge

M Q12 The diagram below shows an object at rest on a sloping shelf with a fixed bookend attached to the shelf.

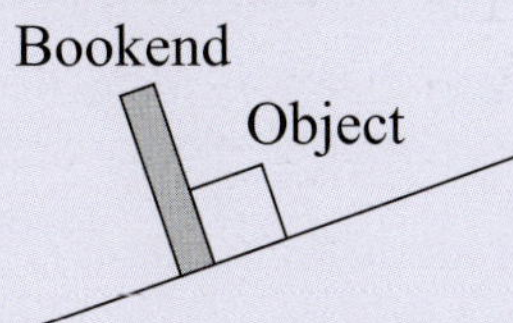

Show the forces acting on the object. State two assumptions that you make.

E P Q13 A graph shows time in seconds on the x-axis and displacement in m on the y-axis for a particle acted upon by a varying force. It has equation $y = 0.5x^2 + 3$ for $0 \leq x < 3$. What are the units of the constants 0.5 and 3 in the equation? *[2 marks]*

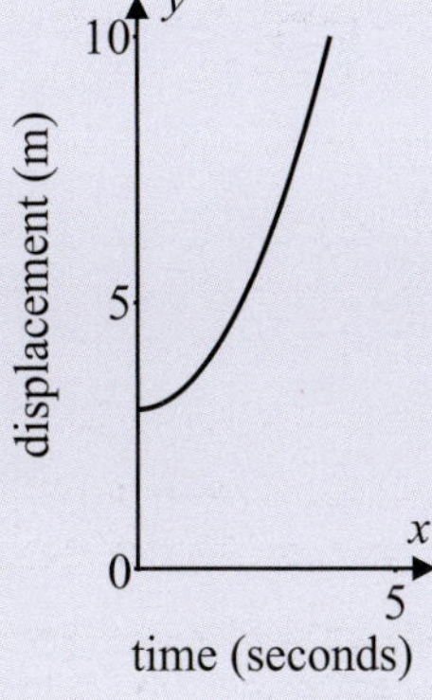

6 Chapter Summary

1 The metre (for distance), kilogram (for mass) and second (for time) are S.I. base units.

2 S.I. base units can be combined to create derived S.I. units.

3 In mechanics, real world situations can be simplified by modelling the situation as more basic than it actually is. But any model will involve making assumptions.

4 Lots of the terms used in mechanical modelling have very precise meanings — e.g. particle, light, rough. These properties will dictate which forces act on the body in a model.

5 A body will always have forces acting on it. Different forces act in different directions. Common types of forces include:

- Weight (= mass × gravity)
- The normal reaction (always perpendicular to a surface)
- Tension
- Friction
- Thrust or compression

Kinematics

7

Learning Objectives

Once you've completed this chapter, you should be able to:

- Draw and interpret displacement-time and velocity-time graphs.
- Derive the constant acceleration equations, both graphically and using calculus.
- Recall and use the equations to solve problems involving motion with constant acceleration.
- Use calculus to solve problems involving motion with non-uniform acceleration.

Prior Knowledge Check

1 The motion of a particle over 10 seconds is shown on this distance-time graph.

a) Find the fastest speed reached in this motion.

b) How long in total did the particle spent at rest?

see GCSE Maths

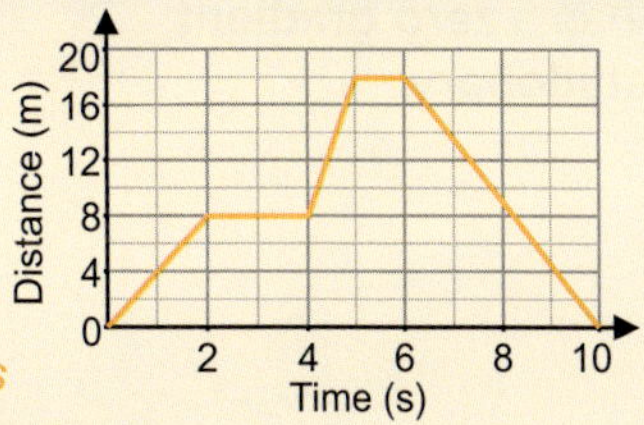

2 Find: a) $\int 4x^3 + \frac{6}{x^2} - 7\,dx$ b) $\frac{dy}{dx}$ when $y = 5x^2 - 2\sqrt{x}$ see Year 1 Pure Maths

3 Find the coordinates of any stationary points of $y = x^3 - 4x^2 + 4x - 1$ and determine their nature. see Year 1 Pure Maths

7.1 Displacement, Velocity and Acceleration

Displacement is an object's **distance from a particular point** (often its starting point), measured in a straight line. It's not necessarily the same as the total distance travelled.

Velocity is the **rate of change of displacement** with respect to **time**. It can be thought of as a measure of how **fast** an object is moving. It's different from **speed** because it takes into account the direction of movement. If distance is measured in metres (m) and time is measured in seconds (s), then velocity is measured in metres per second (ms^{-1}).

Acceleration is the **rate of change** of an object's **velocity** with respect to **time** — i.e. how much an object is **speeding up** or **slowing down**. If velocity is measured in ms^{-1} and time is measured in s, then acceleration is measured in ms^{-2}.

Tip
Displacement, velocity and acceleration are all vector quantities — they have a magnitude and a direction.

7.2 Displacement-Time Graphs

A **displacement-time (x-t) graph** shows how an object's **displacement** from a particular point changes over time. Displacement is plotted on the vertical axis, and time is plotted on the horizontal axis.

- The **height** of the graph gives the object's **displacement** at that time.
- The **gradient** of the graph at a particular point gives the object's **velocity** at that time — the **steeper** the line, the **greater** the velocity.
- A **negative gradient** shows that the object is moving in the **opposite direction** to when the gradient is positive.
- A horizontal line has a **zero gradient**, so the object is **stationary**.

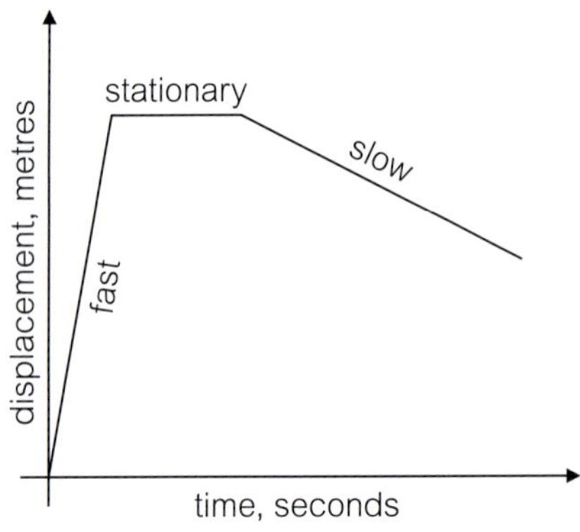

Tip
A displacement-time graph is not the same as a distance-time graph. The height of a distance-time graph gives the **total distance** that a body has travelled up to that point. The gradient of a distance-time graph gives an object's **speed**, rather than its velocity (i.e. it says nothing about the direction in which the object is moving).

Example 1 M

A girl goes for a run along a straight path. Her journey is detailed below:

She runs 1.5 km in 5 minutes, then rests for 2 minutes.
She then jogs 0.5 km in 4 minutes, in the same direction as before.
Finally, she runs 2.5 km back in the direction she came, passing her starting point on the way. She finishes 20 minutes after she first set off.

Show her journey on a displacement-time graph.

Tip The 'straight path' bit tells you that all motion is in a straight line — so, given the distance travelled, you can work out the girl's displacement after each stage of the journey, measured from her starting point, $x = 0$.

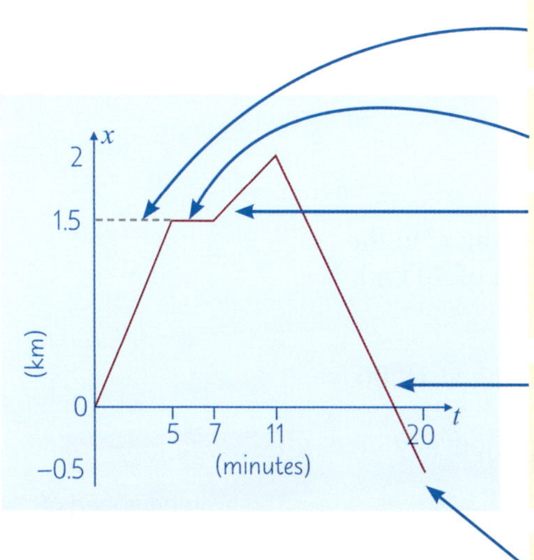

The graph should start at (0, 0) ($t = 0$ minutes, $x = 0$ km), then increase to a height of 1.5 km over 5 minutes.

In the next stage, the girl rests for 2 minutes, so this part of the graph will be a horizontal line.

The girl then jogs 0.5 km, from a displacement of 1.5 km to 2 km, over 4 minutes. She is travelling in the same direction as before, so the graph still has a positive gradient, but she is not travelling as fast, so the line is not as steep.

In the final stage, she travels in the opposite direction for 2.5 km, finishing at (20, –0.5) ($t = 20$ mins, $x = -0.5$ km). The graph has a negative gradient because she is moving in the opposite direction to before.

The girl's final displacement is –0.5 km, i.e. she goes back through her starting point and finishes 0.5 km away in the opposite direction to her initial motion.

Example 2 M

A cyclist's journey is shown on this displacement-time graph. Given that the cyclist starts from rest and cycles in a straight line, describe the motion.

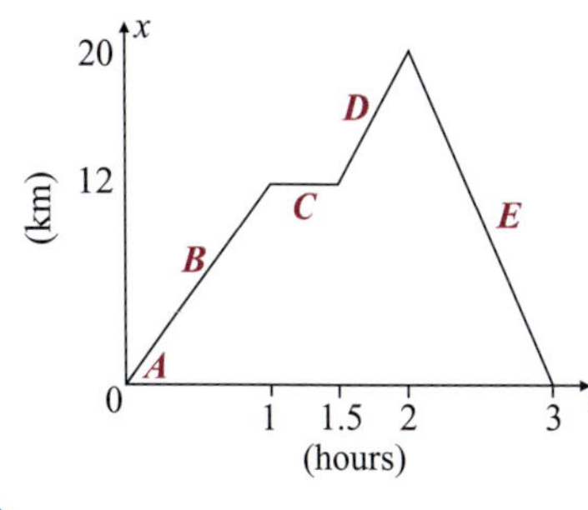

The cyclist starts from rest at point A (when $t = 0$, $x = 0$).

At B, the gradient $= m = \frac{y_2 - y_1}{x_2 - x_1}$ so their velocity $= \frac{(12 - 0)\text{ km}}{(1 - 0)\text{ hours}}$ $= 12$ kmh^{-1} — the cyclist cycles 12 km in 1 hour.

Calculate the gradient of the graph to find the velocity.

At C, the line is horizontal, so there is no movement — the cyclist rests for half an hour ($v = 0$).

At D, they cycle 8 km (from 12 km to 20 km) in half an hour, so their velocity $= \frac{(20 - 12)\text{ km}}{(2 - 1.5)\text{ hours}} = 16$ kmh^{-1}.

At E, the cyclist returns to their starting position, cycling 20 km in 1 hour, so their velocity $= \frac{(0 - 20)\text{ km}}{(3 - 2)\text{ hours}} = -20$ kmh^{-1}.

Problem Solving The gradient is negative at E because the cyclist is travelling in the opposite direction to stages B and D.

Exercise 7.1-7.2

M Q1 The displacement-time graph shows the journey of a car travelling in a straight line. Calculate the velocity of the car during each stage of the journey.

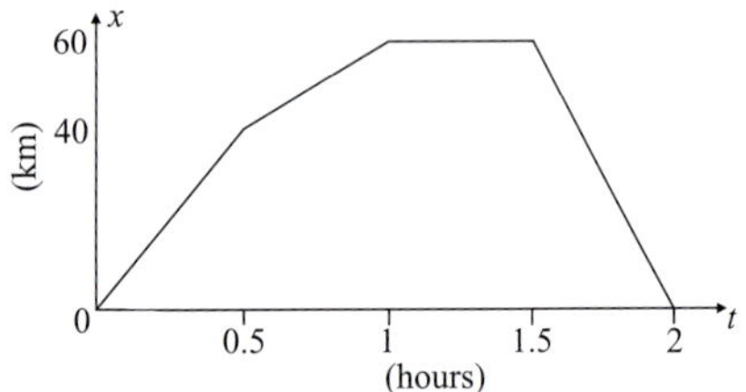

Q1 Hint Make sure you get your signs right — remember that a negative gradient means a negative velocity.

M Q2 A coach travels in a straight line between three stops, A, B and C. Its journey is as follows:

- Leaves A at midday.
- Travels 30 km at a constant speed to B in one hour.
- Stops for 30 minutes.
- Leaves B and travels 60 km at a constant speed to point C in the same direction as before, moving at a constant speed of 40 kmh^{-1}.
- Stops for 30 minutes.
- Leaves C and returns to A at a constant speed, arriving at 18:00.

a) Draw a displacement-time graph to show the coach's journey. Plot the time of day on the horizontal axis, and the coach's displacement from A on the vertical axis.

b) Find the velocity of the coach during the final stage of the journey.

c) Find the average speed of the coach over the whole journey.

Problem Solving The average speed of an object is given by: $\dfrac{\text{total distance travelled}}{\text{total time taken}}$

M Q3 The displacement-time graph on the right shows a girl's motion during a running game. The game is played on a straight track, and she starts and ends at rest.

a) Calculate her velocity at each stage of the game.

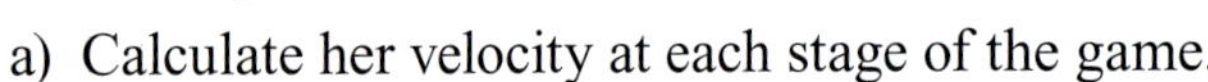

b) Find: (i) her total distance travelled,
(ii) her total displacement.

c) Find her average speed during the game.

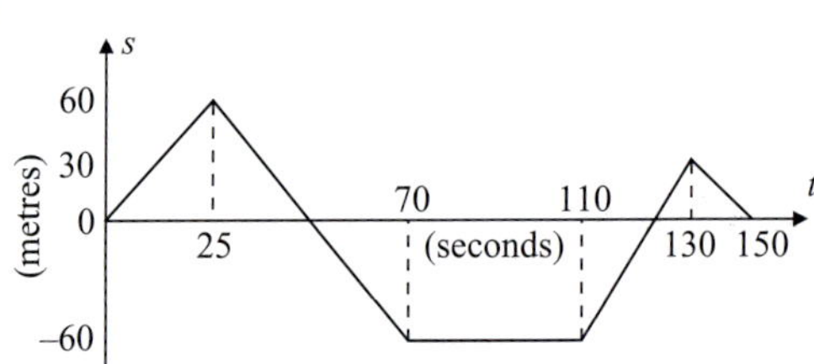

E M Q4 The graph represents the displacement of a horse from its stable as it travels along a straight horizontal road.

a) The horse stopped to eat grass twice. How far from the stable was this, and how long did it stop for in total? *[2 marks]*

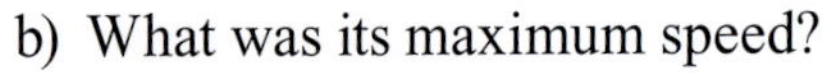

b) What was its maximum speed? *[2 marks]*

c) How far did the horse travel in total? *[1 mark]*

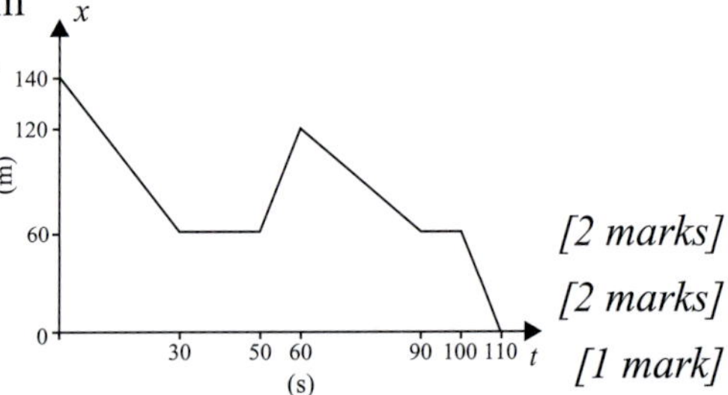

d) What was the average speed of the horse (including its rest time) to 1 d.p.? *[1 mark]*

e) What was the average velocity of the horse (including its rest time) to 1 d.p.? *[1 mark]*

M Q5 A man leaves his house at 13:00. He walks in a straight line at a speed of 5 mph for one hour, then at a speed of 3 mph in the same direction for the next hour. He then rests for an hour. The man's wife leaves their house at 14:30 and travels at a constant speed to meet him at 15:30. Draw a displacement-time graph to show the two journeys.

P M Q6 A train travels 1000 m along a straight track for 50 seconds at a constant speed. It is then held at a signal for 90 seconds before continuing to travel in the same direction at a speed of U ms^{-1} for a further 60 seconds. The total displacement of the train is 2.4 km.

a) Draw a displacement-time graph to show the movement of the train.

b) What was the speed in ms^{-1} of the train in the first 50 seconds?

c) Find the value of U to 3 s.f.

d) What was the average speed of the train during this motion (including time spent at rest)?

P M Q7 Which of the following situations could this graph not describe? Explain your answer(s).

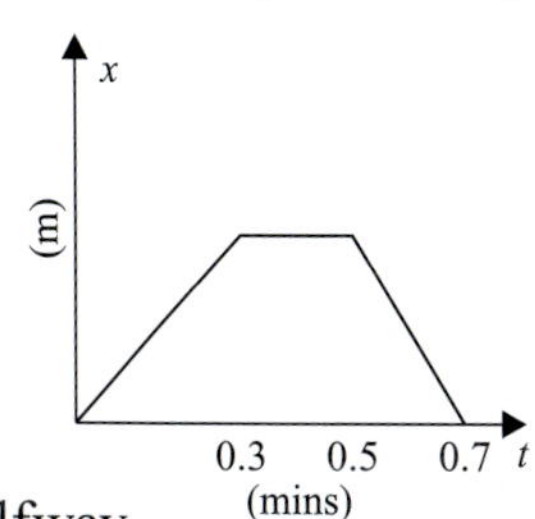

A: The displacement (x), from a hive, of a bee which flies from the hive slowly but steadily in a straight line, circles the hive and then returns to the hive faster along a different straight line.

B: The displacement (x) of a cyclist who sets off from home, rides halfway along a straight road, stops to check his phone, then rides along the rest of the road.

C: The distance travelled (x) of a walker, who climbs a hill, stops at the top to catch her breath then walks down more quickly.

P M Q8 The carriage on a theme park ride moves vertically up and down in a straight line. The ride lasts 30 seconds and the carriage goes above and below the ground. The displacement-time graph on the right shows the motion of the ride.

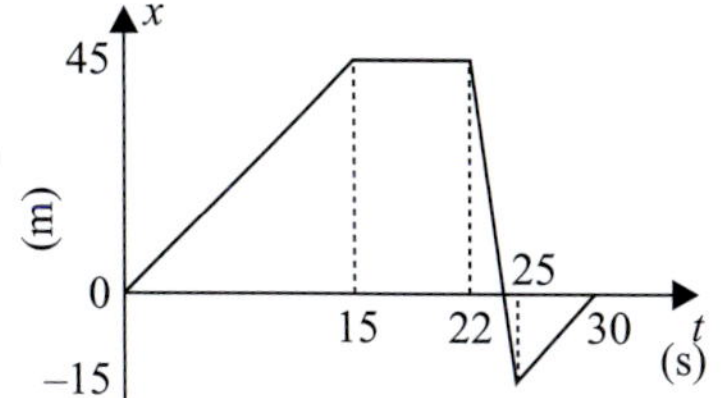

a) Sketch a distance-time graph of the motion.

b) Find the distance travelled by the carriage.

P M Q9 A man walks with velocity u ms^{-1} for 500 m, then with velocity $-2u$ ms^{-1} for 700 m. He then walks 600 m with velocity $1.5u$ ms^{-1}.

a) Find the man's final displacement.

b) Show his journey on a displacement-time graph.

c) Find his total journey time. Give your answer in terms of u.

d) Find his average speed in terms of u.

Challenge

P M Q10 A car travels in a straight line with speed u ms^{-1} for t seconds, stops for 100 seconds, then returns back the way it came with speed $2u$ ms^{-1}.

a) Draw a displacement-time graph to show the movement of the car.

b) Find an expression in terms of u and t for the total distance travelled by the car.

c) Find the car's average speed (including its rest time). Give your answer in terms of u and t.

7.3 Velocity-Time Graphs

A **velocity-time (v-t) graph** shows how an object's **velocity** changes over time.

- The **height** of a velocity-time graph gives the object's **velocity** at that time, and its **gradient** gives its **acceleration**.
- A **negative gradient** can mean that the object is **decelerating** in the **positive direction**, or that it is **accelerating** in the **negative direction**.
- A **horizontal** line means the object is moving at a **constant velocity**.
- The **area** under the graph gives the object's **displacement**.

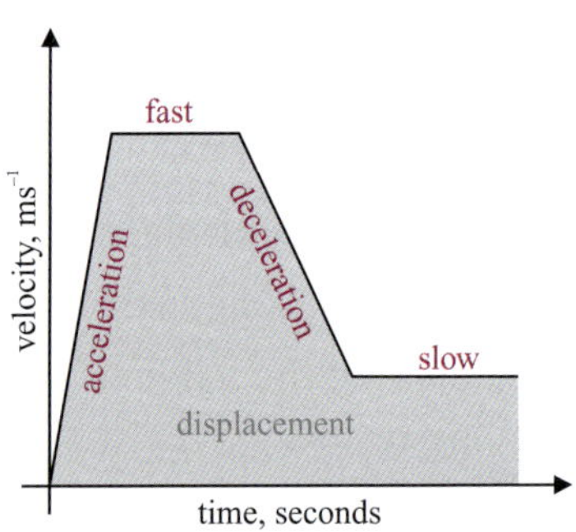

Remember that velocity is different from speed in that the **direction** of motion is important. So for velocity-time graph questions, you need to decide which direction is positive.

Example 1

A car starts from rest and reverses in a straight line with constant acceleration to a velocity of -5 ms^{-1} in 12 seconds.

Still reversing, it then decelerates to rest in 3 seconds and remains stationary for another 3 seconds.

The car then moves forward along the same straight line as before (but in the opposite direction), accelerating uniformly to a velocity of 8 ms^{-1} in 6 seconds. It maintains this speed for 6 seconds.

a) Show the car's movement on a velocity-time graph.

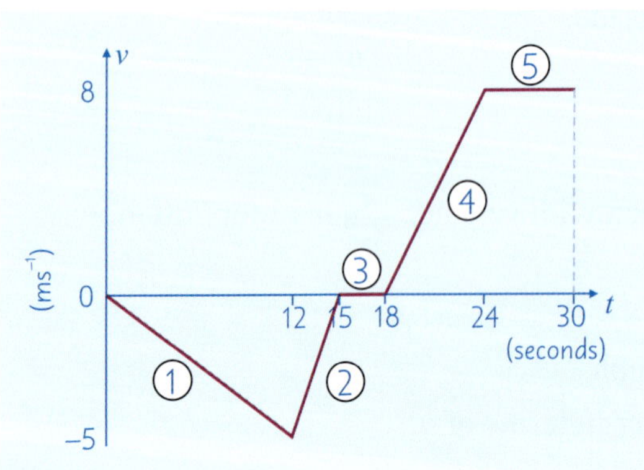

1. If an object is moving with negative velocity, then the graph will go below the t axis. The graph should start at (t = 0 s, v = 0 ms^{-1}), then decrease to -5 ms^{-1} over 12 seconds.
2. In the next stage, the graph should return to (v = 0 ms^{-1}) in 3 seconds.
3. The car is then stationary, so the graph should remain at (v = 0 ms^{-1}) for 3 seconds.
4. In the next stage, the graph should increase to (v = 8 ms^{-1}) in 6 seconds.
5. Finally, the car travels at a constant velocity for 6 seconds — shown by a horizontal line.

b) Use your graph to find the car's final displacement from its starting point.

Area below axis = $\frac{1}{2} \times 15 \times -5 = -37.5$ m ← First find the area below the horizontal axis.

continued on the next page...

Area above axis $= \frac{1}{2}(6 + 12) \times 8 = 72$ m ← Then find the area above the horizontal axis. Use the formula for the area of a trapezium.

Displacement $= -37.5 + 72 = 34.5$ m ← Now add the areas together to find the final displacement.

Problem Solving For the **total distance** travelled, add the **magnitudes** of the areas together: $37.5 + 72 = 109.5$ m

Exercise 7.3

M Q1 The velocity-time graph on the right shows a bus journey. Describe the motion of the bus, given that it travels in a straight line.

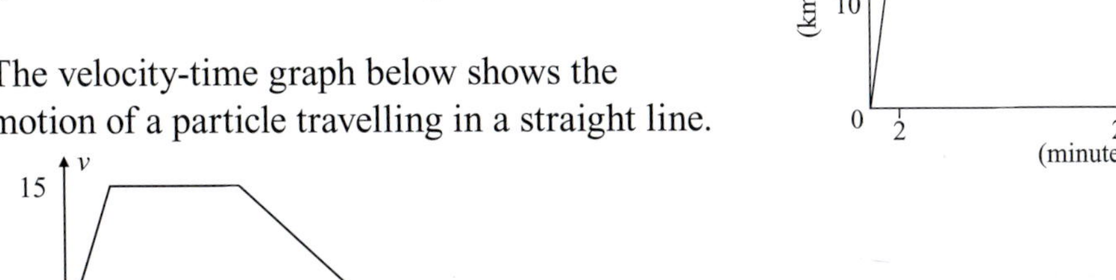

Q2 The velocity-time graph below shows the motion of a particle travelling in a straight line.

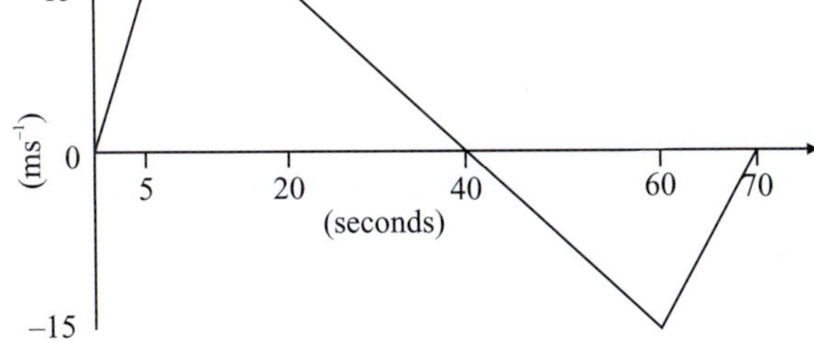

Find the particle's acceleration:

a) during the first 5 seconds of motion. b) between 40 and 60 seconds.

c) during the final 10 seconds of motion.

P M Q3 A train starts from rest at station A and travels with constant acceleration for 30 s. It then travels with constant speed V ms^{-1} for 3 minutes. It then decelerates with constant deceleration for 1 minute before coming to rest at station B. The total distance between stations A and B is 6.3 km.

a) Sketch a speed-time graph for the motion of the train between stations A and B.

b) Hence or otherwise find the value of V.

c) Calculate the distance travelled by the train while decelerating.

E M Q4 A cat moves in a straight line and always in the same direction, from rest. For 5 seconds, it accelerates at a constant rate, to reach a velocity of 10 ms^{-1}. It then maintains this constant velocity for 5 seconds, before decelerating at a constant rate over 2 seconds to come to rest.

a) Draw a velocity-time graph to represent the cat's movement over this period. *[2 marks]*

b) How far did the cat move in total? *[2 marks]*

c) What was the cat's acceleration during the first 5 seconds? *[1 mark]*

d) What was the average velocity of the cat to 1 decimal place? *[1 mark]*

E Exam Style P Problem Solving M Modelling

P Q5 A particle is travelling in a straight line. It passes point A with velocity 10 ms^{-1}. Immediately after passing A, it accelerates at 4 ms^{-2} for x metres up to a velocity of 50 ms^{-1}, then decelerates at 10 ms^{-2} for y metres to point B. It passes B with velocity 10 ms^{-1}. The particle takes T seconds to travel between A and B.

a) Show the particle's motion on a velocity-time graph.

b) Find the area under the graph in terms of T.

c) Calculate the values of x, y and T.

M Q6 A train is travelling at a steady speed of 30 ms^{-1} along a straight track. As it passes a signal box, it begins to decelerate steadily, coming to rest at a station in 20 seconds. The train remains stationary for 20 seconds, then sets off back in the direction it came with an acceleration of 0.375 ms^{-2}. It reaches a speed of 15 ms^{-1} as it passes the signal box.

a) Draw a velocity-time graph to show the motion of the train. How long after leaving the station does the train reach the signal box?

b) Find the train's deceleration as it comes into the station.

c) Find the distance between the signal box and the station.

Q6 Hint Decide which direction is positive — then velocities in the opposite direction will be negative. At these times, the graph will go below the horizontal axis.

P M Q7 A stone is held out over the edge of a cliff and thrown vertically upwards with a speed of 9.8 ms^{-1}. It decelerates until it becomes stationary at its highest point, 1 second after being thrown, then begins to fall back down. It lands in the sea below the cliff edge with speed 29.4 ms^{-1}, 4 seconds after it was thrown.

a) Draw a velocity-time graph to show the motion of the stone.

b) Use your graph to find:

(i) the distance the stone travels before it reaches its highest point,

(ii) the distance the stone travels from its highest point to the sea,

(iii) the height of the cliff above the sea.

Q7 Hint Displacement is not the same as distance travelled.

Challenge

E P M Q8 The velocity-time graph below shows two sprinters in a 100 m race on a straight track.

a) What was the highest velocity reached by either sprinter during the race? *[1 mark]*

b) What was the highest positive acceleration reached by either sprinter during the race? Show your working. *[2 marks]*

c) Who was quicker to run 100 m? Show your working. *[4 marks]*

d) Was the winner always in the lead? Give a reason for your answer. *[1 mark]*

e) State a limitation of this model. *[1 mark]*

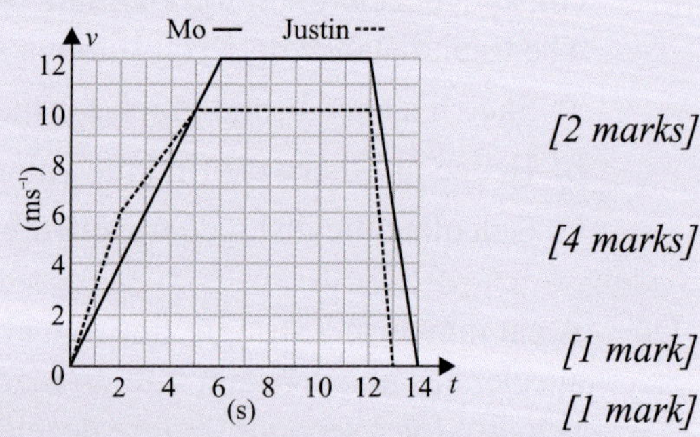

7.4 Constant Acceleration Equations

The constant acceleration equations are:

$$v = u + at$$
$$s = ut + \frac{1}{2}at^2$$
$$s = \left(\frac{u+v}{2}\right)t$$
$$v^2 = u^2 + 2as$$
$$s = vt - \frac{1}{2}at^2$$

s = displacement in m

u = initial speed (or velocity) in ms^{-1}

v = final speed (or velocity) in ms^{-1}

a = acceleration in ms^{-2}

t = time that passes in s (seconds)

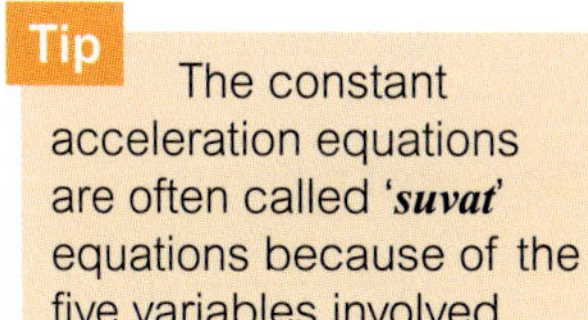

Tip The constant acceleration equations are often called '*suvat*' equations because of the five variables involved.

Remember — these equations only work if the acceleration is **constant**.

You'll usually be given three variables — your job is to **choose the equation** that will help you find the missing fourth variable. In this book, all the motion you'll deal with will be in a **straight line**. You should choose which direction is **positive**, then any velocity, acceleration or displacement in the **opposite direction** will be **negative**.

You can derive the *suvat* equations using motion graphs and a bit of algebra:

Deriving the SUVAT equations

Consider a particle moving with constant acceleration a.
The particle will accelerate from an initial velocity u to a final velocity v.
As it accelerates, it will cover a distance s over time t.

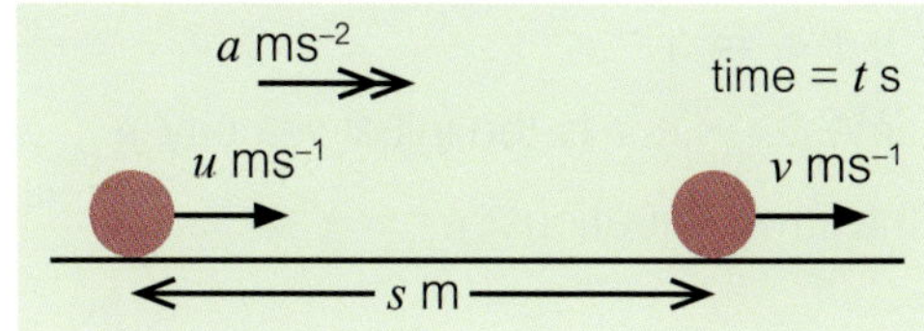

The velocity-time graph on the right shows the movement of the particle.

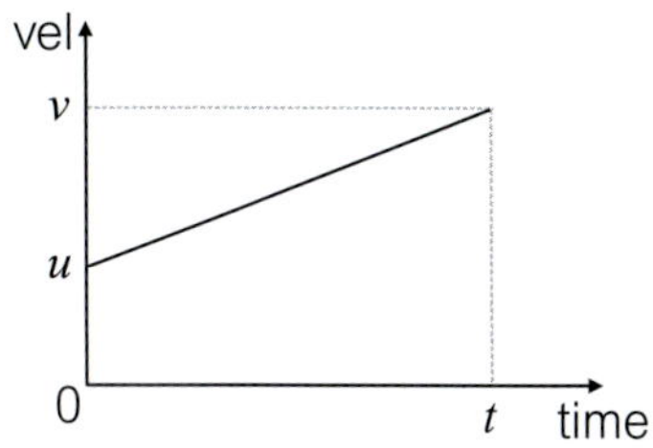

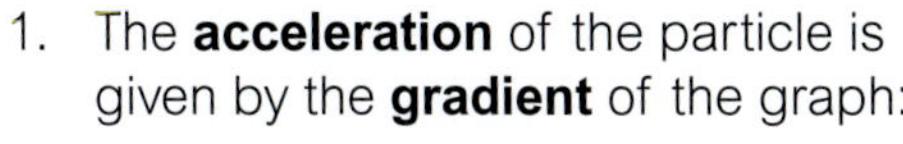

1. The **acceleration** of the particle is given by the **gradient** of the graph:

   $a = \frac{v-u}{t}$, or $v = u + at$

2. The **distance travelled** is given by the **area** under the graph:

   Area of A = ut

   Area of B = $\frac{1}{2}(v-u)t$

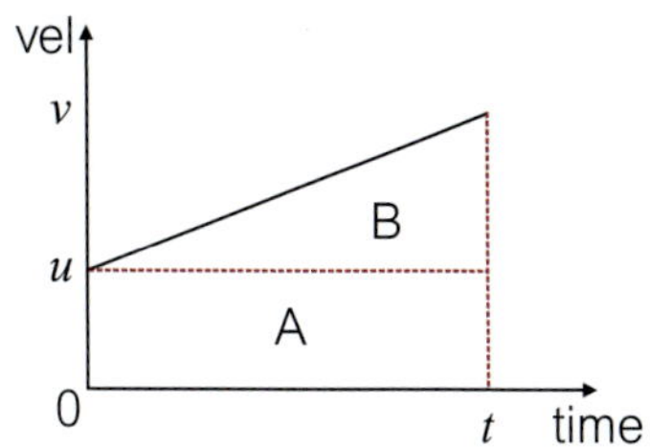

So $s = ut + \frac{1}{2}(v - u)t = ut + \frac{1}{2}vt - \frac{1}{2}ut = \frac{1}{2}ut + \frac{1}{2}vt$

This gives $\mathbf{s = \left(\frac{u+v}{2}\right)t}$

Problem Solving You could also find this area using the formula for the area of a trapezium: $s = \frac{1}{2}(u + v) \times t$

Now you can rearrange these two equations and make some substitutions to derive the remaining formulas.

3. Substituting $v = u + at$ into $s = \left(\frac{u+v}{2}\right)t$ gives:
   $s = \left(\frac{u+u+at}{2}\right)t = \left(u + \frac{1}{2}at\right)t \Rightarrow \mathbf{s = ut + \frac{1}{2}at^2}$

4. Substituting $t = \left(\frac{v-u}{a}\right)$ into $s = \left(\frac{u+v}{2}\right)t$ gives:
   $s = \left(\frac{u+v}{2}\right)\left(\frac{v-u}{a}\right) \Rightarrow 2as = (u + v)(v - u) = v^2 - u^2 \Rightarrow \mathbf{v^2 = u^2 + 2as}$

5. Substituting $u = v - at$ into $s = \left(\frac{u+v}{2}\right)t$ gives:
   $s = \left(\frac{v-at+v}{2}\right)t = \left(v - \frac{1}{2}at\right)t \Rightarrow \mathbf{s = vt - \frac{1}{2}at^2}$

You can also derive these equations using calculus — you need to understand both methods.

- Acceleration is the **rate of change of velocity (v) with respect to time (t)**. This can be written as $a = \frac{dv}{dt}$.
- From the Fundamental Theorem of Calculus, this means that $v = \int a\,dt$.
- Since a is constant, you can calculate this integral: $v = \int a\,dt = at + c$
- When $t = 0$, you get $v = a(0) + c \Rightarrow v = c$
- So c is just the velocity at time 0 — i.e. c is the initial velocity, u.
- This gives you the first of the *suvat* equations: $v = u + at$

- Similarly, velocity is the **rate of change of displacement with respect to time**, i.e. $v = \frac{ds}{dt} \Rightarrow s = \int v\,dt$.
- From before, you know that $v = u + at \Rightarrow s = \int u + at\,dt = ut + \frac{1}{2}at^2 + C$
- The place where the object begins at time $t = 0$ is the starting point where $s = 0$ as well. At $t = 0$, $s = 0 \Rightarrow u(0) + \frac{1}{2}a(0) + C = 0 \Rightarrow C = 0$
- This gives you the second *suvat* equation: $s = ut + \frac{1}{2}at^2$

Rearranging and substituting one equation into the other will give you the other *suvat* equations, as above. You can now use these results to solve all sorts of Mechanics problems.

Example 1 M

A jet ski travels in a straight line along a river. It passes under two bridges 200 m apart and is observed to be travelling at 5 ms^{-1} under the first bridge and at 9 ms^{-1} under the second bridge. Calculate its acceleration.

$s = 200 \quad u = 5 \quad v = 9 \quad a = a$ — List the variables. (You're not told or asked for t, so don't bother writing it down.)

$v^2 = u^2 + 2as$ — Choose the equation with s, u, v and a in it.

$9^2 = 5^2 + (2 \times a \times 200)$ — Substitute the values you're given and solve for a.

$81 = 25 + 400a$

$400a = 81 - 25 = 56$

$a = 56 \div 400 = 0.14 \text{ ms}^{-2}$

Example 2

A particle accelerates from rest for 8 seconds at a rate of 12 ms^{-2}.
The particle's motion is restricted to a straight path.

a) Find the velocity of the particle at the end of the 8 seconds.

$s = s \quad u = 0 \quad v = v \quad a = 12 \quad t = 8$ — List the variables. If a particle 'starts from rest', then $u = 0$. You'll need to find s in part b)

$v = u + at$ — Choose the equation with u, a, t and v in it.

$v = 0 + (12 \times 8) = 96 \text{ ms}^{-1}$ — Substitute the values you're given.

b) Find the distance travelled by the particle during this time.

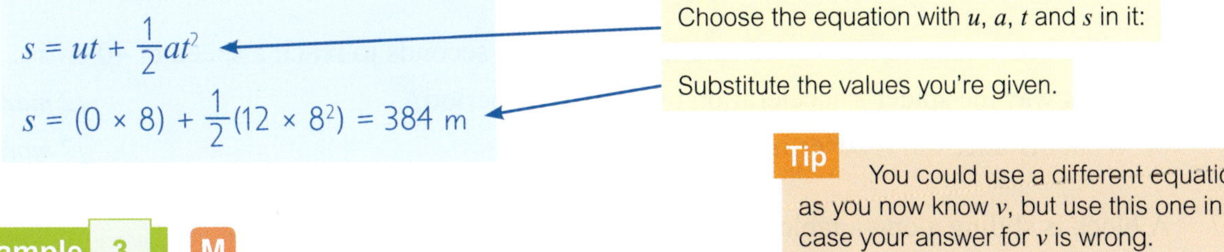

Tip You could use a different equation as you now know v, but use this one in case your answer for v is wrong.

Example 3 M

A car decelerates at a rate of 16 kmh^{-2} for 6 minutes.
It travels 1.28 km along a straight road during this time.
Find the velocity of the car at the end of the 6 minutes.

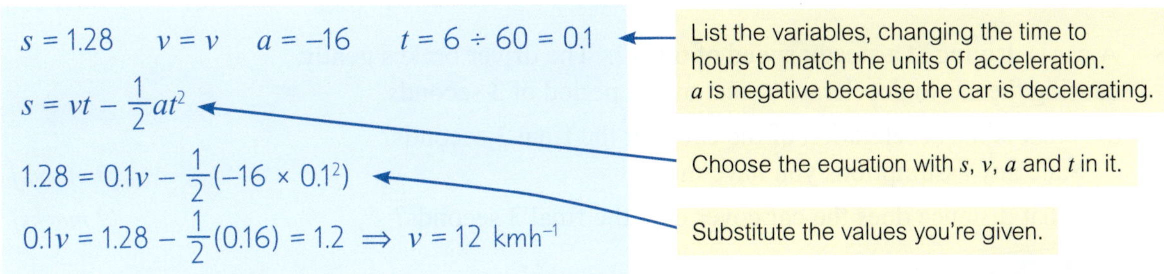

Exercise 7.4

> **Hint**
> Remember — always write out the *suvat* variables.

M Q1 A car travels along a straight horizontal road. It accelerates uniformly from rest to a velocity of 12 ms^{-1} in 5 seconds.

a) Find the car's acceleration.

b) Find the total distance travelled by the car.

M Q2 A cyclist is travelling at 18 kmh^{-1}. He brakes steadily, coming to rest in 50 m.

a) Calculate the cyclist's initial speed in ms^{-1} .

b) Find the time it takes him to come to rest.

c) Find his deceleration.

> **Problem Solving**
> To convert from kmh^{-1} to ms^{-1}, multiply by 1000, then divide by 60^2.

M Q3 A skier accelerates from 5 ms^{-1} to 25 ms^{-1} over a distance of 60 m.

a) Find the skier's acceleration.

b) What modelling assumptions have you made?

P M Q4 A car travels with uniform acceleration between three lamp posts, equally spaced at 18 m apart. It passes the second post 2 seconds after passing the first post, and passes the third post 1 second later.

a) Find the car's acceleration.

b) Calculate the car's velocity when it passes the first post.

M Q5 A sprinter accelerates at a constant rate from rest to 6 ms^{-1} over a distance of 30 m.

a) Find the acceleration over the first 30 m.

b) How long does it take the sprinter to run this distance?

E M Q6 A spider accelerates at a constant rate from rest for 2 seconds to reach a speed of 40 cms^{-1}.

a) What was the spider's acceleration over the time period? *[2 marks]*

b) What distance did it cover in this time? *[2 marks]*

P M Q7 A block is sliding along a table. It starts at one end of the table with an initial velocity of 1.2 ms^{-1} and decelerates at a constant rate of 0.4 ms^{-2}.

a) Calculate how long the block has been sliding for when its velocity is 0.7 ms^{-1}.

b) Determine the minimum length of the table necessary such that the block comes to a stop before it slides off.

E M Q8 A car is driving at a steady speed of 6 ms^{-1}. The driver brakes gently, causing the car to decelerate to rest over a period of 3 seconds.

a) What is the acceleration of the car over the final 3 seconds? State any assumptions you have made. *[3 marks]*

b) What distance does the car cover over the final 3 seconds? *[2 marks]*

E P M **Q9** A gate in a racing game opens every 2 minutes and remains open for 40 seconds. A player's car is 800 m away from the gate and is travelling at 10 ms^{-1} at the instant when the gate opens.

a) What acceleration is required to reach the gate before it closes? *[2 marks]*

b) The speed limit in the game is 60 mph. Determine whether accelerating at a constant rate to reach the gate in time would cause the player to break the speed limit. (Use the approximation 1609 m ≈ 1 mile) *[4 marks]*

E **Q10** A particle moves from rest with constant acceleration of 6 ms^{-2}.

a) Find the time it takes for the particle to travel 300 m. *[2 marks]*

b) After travelling 300 m, the particle decelerates uniformly to come to rest in 150 m. How long will it take to come to rest? *[3 marks]*

E M **Q11** A speedboat accelerates at a constant rate from 6 ms^{-1} at 1 ms^{-2} for 5 seconds. It then accelerates steadily at 2 ms^{-2}, to reach a speed of 14 ms^{-1}. Finally, it travels a further 60 m at constant velocity of 14 ms^{-1}.

a) How far does the speedboat travel during the first interval of acceleration? *[2 marks]*

b) What is the velocity of the speedboat after its first interval of acceleration? *[2 marks]*

c) How far does the speedboat travel during the second interval of acceleration? *[2 marks]*

d) How long does the second period of acceleration take? *[2 marks]*

e) What is the average velocity of the speedboat over the time period (to 1 d.p.)? *[3 marks]*

E P M **Q12** A driver travelling at 30 ms^{-1} sees an obstacle in the road ahead. She starts braking at a distance of 150 m from the obstacle. Find the range of values of acceleration for which she is able to stop in time. *[4 marks]*

Challenge

P M **Q13** A bus is approaching a tunnel. At time $t = 0$ seconds, the driver begins slowing down steadily from a speed of U ms^{-1} until, at $t = 15$ s, he enters the tunnel, travelling at 20 ms^{-1}. The driver maintains this speed while he drives through the tunnel. After emerging from the tunnel at $t = 40$ s, he accelerates steadily, reaching a speed of U ms^{-1} at $t = 70$ s.

a) Calculate the length of the tunnel.

b) Given that the total distance travelled by the coach is 1580 m, find the value of U.

Problem Solving

In Q13, the motion you're interested in is between 15 and 40 seconds, so you can use $t = 40 - 15 = 25$ in your calculations.

7.5 Gravity

An object moving through the air will experience an **acceleration** towards the centre of the earth due to **gravity**.

This acceleration is denoted by the letter g, where g **= 9.8 ms⁻²**.

Acceleration due to gravity always acts **vertically downwards**.

For an object moving freely under gravity, you can use the *suvat* equations to find information such as the **speed of projection**, **time of flight**, **greatest height** and **landing speed**.

Tip

You might be given a different value of g in a particular question (e.g. $g = 10$ ms^{-2}). Use the one you're given, otherwise your answer might not match the examiner's.

Example 1 M

A pebble is dropped into an empty well 18 m deep and moves freely under gravity until it hits the bottom. Calculate the time it takes to reach the bottom.

Taking downwards as positive:
$s = 18 \quad u = 0 \quad a = 9.8 \quad t = t$ ← Decide which direction should be taken as positive and list the variables.

$s = ut + \frac{1}{2}at^2$ ← You need the equation with s, u, a and t in it.

$18 = (0 \times t) + \left(\frac{1}{2} \times 9.8 \times t^2\right) = 4.9t^2$ ← Substitute values.

$t^2 = \frac{18}{4.9} = 3.67...$

$t = \sqrt{3.67...} = 1.92$ s (3 s.f.)

Tip Watch out for tricky questions like this — at first it looks like they've only given you one variable. You have to spot that the pebble was dropped (so u = 0) and that it's moving freely under gravity (so $a = g = 9.8$ ms^{-2}).

Example 2 M

A ball is projected vertically upwards at 3 ms^{-1} from a point 1.5 m above the ground.

a) How long does it take to reach its maximum height?

Taking upwards as positive:
$u = 3 \quad v = 0 \quad a = -9.8 \quad t = t$ ← Decide which direction should be taken as positive and list the variables.

When projected objects reach the top of their motion, they stop momentarily, so $v = 0$. Because g always acts downwards and up was taken as positive, a is negative.

$v = u + at$ ← Use the equation with u, v, a and t in it.

$0 = 3 + (-9.8 \times t) = 3 - 9.8t$ ← Substitute values.

$t = \frac{3}{9.8} = 0.306$ s (3 s.f.)

b) What is the ball's speed when it hits the ground?

The ball lands on the ground, 1.5 m below the point of projection. ← Think about the complete path of the ball.

So $s = -1.5$.

$v = v \quad u = 3 \quad a = -9.8 \quad s = -1.5$ ← List the variables.

$v^2 = u^2 + 2as$ ← Choose the best equation.

$v^2 = 3^2 + 2(-9.8 \times -1.5) = 38.4$ ← Substitute values.

So speed $= \sqrt{38.4} = 6.20$ ms^{-1} (to 3 s.f.)

Problem Solving Remember that s is **displacement** — the object's final position relative to its starting point, not its total distance travelled. Here, the ball lands below its initial point, and since upwards is positive, s is negative.

Tip The question asks for its **speed**, so you can ignore the negative root.

Example 3

A particle is projected vertically upwards from ground level with a speed of u ms^{-1}. The particle takes 2.6 s to return to ground level.

a) Draw a velocity-time graph to show the particle's motion.

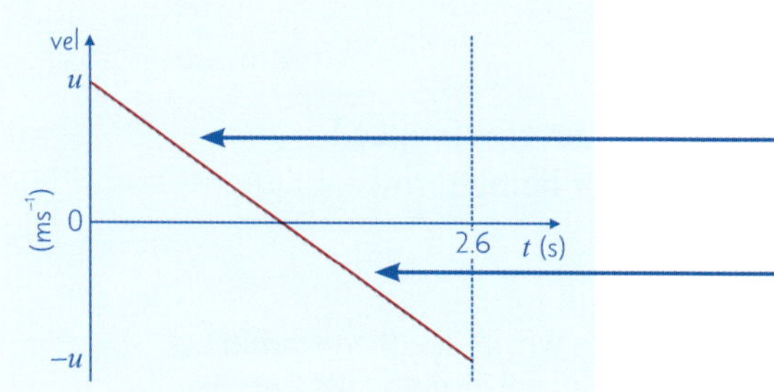

The particle is projected with speed u, then decelerates due to gravity until it is momentarily at rest at its highest point.

It then falls to the ground, accelerating due to gravity and reaching its initial speed u (but in the opposite direction to before) when it lands.

Tip Remember that velocity takes into account the direction of motion, so can be positive or negative. Speed is all about the magnitude, so the direction doesn't matter.

Tip Here we've taken upwards as positive, so the particle's initial velocity is u. If you'd taken downwards as positive you'd get a graph going up from $-u$ to u instead.

b) Find u, the particle's speed of projection.

$u = u \quad v = 0 \quad a = -9.8 \quad t = 2.6 \div 2 = 1.3$

Think about the first half of the particle's motion, from ground level to its highest point. As you're looking at half of the flight, t is half of 2.6. $v = 0$ at the highest point.

$v = u + at$, so

$0 = u - 9.8 \times 1.3$

Substitute values into $v = u + at$

So $u = 9.8 \times 1.3 = 12.74$ ms^{-1}

Example 4

A particle is fired vertically upwards from ground level with speed 49 ms^{-1}.

Assuming that air resistance can be ignored, find the amount of time that the particle is over 78.4 m above the ground.

Problem Solving The particle will pass 78.4 m twice: once on its way up and once on its way back down. So find these two times and work out the difference between them.

Taking upwards as positive:

$s = 78.4 \quad u = 49 \quad a = -9.8 \quad t = t$

Decide which direction should be taken as positive and list the variables.

$s = ut + \frac{1}{2}at^2$

$78.4 = 49t - 4.9t^2$

Substitute values into $s = ut + \frac{1}{2}at^2$ and rearrange to find the two moments in time that the particle is at 78.4 m.

$\Rightarrow t^2 - 10t + 16 = 0$

continued on the next page...

Problem Solving It's assumed here that the particle will actually reach a height of 78.4 m — if it doesn't, then the quadratic will have **no real solutions**.

$\Rightarrow (t-2)(t-8)=0 \Rightarrow t=2, t=8$

So the particle is 78.4 m above the ground 2 seconds after being fired (on the way up), and 8 seconds after being fired (on the way back down).

This means that the particle is above 78.4 m for $8-2=6$ seconds.

Find the difference between the two times.

Example 5 M

A boot is thrown vertically upwards from a point x m above ground level. Its speed of projection is 4 ms^{-1}. The boot lands on the ground 2 seconds after being thrown.

a) Find the value of x.

Taking upwards as positive:
$s=-x \quad u=4 \quad a=-9.8 \quad t=2$

Decide which direction should be taken as positive and list the variables. $s=-x$ because the boot lands x m below its point of projection.

$-x=(4\times 2)+\frac{1}{2}(-9.8\times 2^2)=-11.6$

Substitute values into $s=ut+\frac{1}{2}at^2$

So $x=11.6$ m

b) Find the speed and direction of the boot 0.8 seconds after it is thrown.

Taking upwards as positive:
$u=4 \quad v=v \quad a=-9.8 \quad t=0.8$

$v=4+(-9.8\times 0.8)=-3.84$ ms^{-1}

Using $v=u+at$

v is negative, so the boot is moving downwards at 3.84 ms^{-1}.

Notice that for all of these examples, the **mass** of the object is **not** part of the calculations. This is because the acceleration due to gravity does not depend on an object's mass.

Exercise 7.5

M Q1 A pebble is dropped down a hole to see how deep it is. It reaches the bottom of the hole after 3 seconds. How deep is the hole?

Q1 Hint The pebble is dropped, so $u=0$.

M Q2 An orange is thrown vertically upwards with initial speed 14 ms^{-1}. How long does it take to reach its maximum height?

M Q3 A ball is dropped from a second floor window that is 5 metres from the ground.

a) How long will it take to reach the ground?

b) At what speed will it hit the ground?

E M Q4 A stone is dropped from the top of a cliff and takes 4 seconds to hit the water below.

a) What is the height of the cliff above the water? *[2 marks]*

b) What is the speed of the stone as it hits the water? *[2 marks]*

M Q5 A toy rocket is projected vertically upwards from ground level with a speed of 30 ms^{-1}.

a) Find the maximum height reached by the rocket.

b) Find the time it takes the rocket to reach the ground.

c) Find the toy rocket's speed and direction 2 seconds after launch.

M Q6 A ball is projected vertically upwards with a speed u ms^{-1} from a point d metres above the ground. After 3 seconds the ball hits the ground with a speed of 20 ms^{-1}.

a) Calculate the value of u. b) Calculate the value of d.

P M Q7 An apple is thrown vertically upwards with speed 8 ms^{-1} from a height of 5 m above the ground.

a) Calculate the apple's maximum height above the ground.

b) For how long is the apple 8 m or more above the ground?

Q7 Hint Remember that the apple is not thrown from ground level.

P M Q8 The displacement-time graph on the right shows the motion of an object fired vertically upwards with speed 24.5 ms^{-1} over the edge of a cliff. The object travels in a vertical line and hits the ground below (at $x = 0$).

a) Find the value of p. b) Find the value of q.

c) Find the value of r.

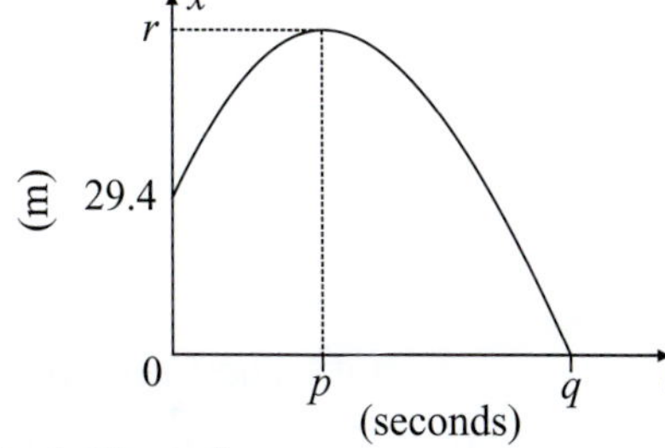

E M Q9 The acceleration due to gravity on the moon is approximately 1.62 ms^{-2}. Object A is dropped from a height of 10 m from the surface of the moon. Object B is dropped from a height of 10 m from the surface of the Earth.

a) Without performing calculations, explain which object would travel more quickly. *[1 mark]*

b) Find the velocity of object A as it hits the moon's surface, to 1 decimal place. *[2 marks]*

c) Object B bounces off the surface of the Earth and reaches a height of 10 m. What velocity did it rebound upwards at? *[2 marks]*

d) State one other difference that could be considered between the two situations on the moon and the Earth in a refined model. *[1 mark]*

E P M Q10 In an attempt to dislodge a flying disc from a tree, a stone is thrown vertically up in the air from a height of 1.7 m with a velocity of 9 ms^{-1}. However, it doesn't reach the height of the disc and travels without encountering any obstacles.

a) How much time passes before the stone hits the ground? *[4 marks]*

b) What is the maximum height that the stone reaches? *[2 marks]*

c) The height of the disc is 2 m above the maximum height reached by the stone. What is the minimum initial velocity which would ensure that the stone would reach the height of the disc? *[2 marks]*

E P M Q11 A boy stands on a desk and projects an eraser downwards. It hits the ground 0.2 seconds later. The desk is between 70 cm and 80 cm tall and he projects it from a height between 1.2 m and 1.4 m above this. What is the minimum velocity which he could have projected the eraser with? *[3 marks]*

P M Q12 A ball is dropped from the edge of the roof of a building. It hits the ground 2 seconds later. The ball is retrieved and this time is thrown vertically upwards from the same point on the edge of the roof, with a velocity of 29.4 ms^{-1}.

a) From what height was the ball dropped the first time?

b) At what speed did the ball hit the ground the first time?

c) With what speed will the ball hit the ground the second time?

d) How long will the ball take to hit the ground the second time?

e) Give one modelling assumption you have made in your solution.

P M Q13 An acorn drops from a tree. 0.1 seconds before it hits the ground, it is travelling at 2 ms^{-1}. From what height above the ground did the acorn drop? Give your answer to 2 d.p.

Challenge

P M Q14 A decorator is painting the frame of a fifth floor window and catapults a brush up to her friend exactly three floors above her. She catapults it vertically with a speed of 12 ms^{-1}, and it is at its maximum height when her friend catches it.

a) Find the distance between the decorator and her friend.

b) For how long is the brush in the air?

c) She later catapults a tub of putty vertically at the same speed but her friend fails to catch it. The floors of the building are equally spaced apart, and the decorator is positioned at the base of the fifth floor. At what speed does it hit the ground?

E P Q15 An object is projected vertically upwards, from ground level, at a speed of 40 ms^{-1}.

a) Give the times at which the object is 77.5 m above the ground. *[4 marks]*

b) Use symmetry to find the other time that the object is at the same height as it is after 3.5 seconds. *[2 marks]*

P M Q16 A projectile is fired from a point 50 m below ground level vertically upwards. It passes a target 100 m above ground level and 3 seconds later passes another target which is 220 m above ground level. Assume that air resistance can be ignored.

a) Find the speed of projection of the projectile.

b) Find the maximum height above the ground reached by the projectile.

c) Find the time taken by the projectile to reach the first target.

Problem Solving

In Q16, work out part a) in two separate stages.

7.6 More Complicated Problems

Now you're familiar with the constant acceleration equations, it's time for some trickier problems.

- Some questions will involve **motion graphs** — you may have to find areas and gradients as well as use the *suvat* equations.
- Some will involve **more than one** moving object. For these questions, t is often the same (or at least connected) because time ticks along for both objects at the same rate. The distance travelled might also be connected.

Example 1  

A jogger and a cyclist are travelling along a straight path. Their movements are as follows:

The jogger runs with constant velocity.
At the moment the jogger passes the cyclist, the cyclist accelerates from rest, reaching a velocity of 5 ms^{-1} after 6 seconds, and then continues at this velocity. The cyclist overtakes the jogger after 15 seconds.

a) Taking the time that the cyclist begins to accelerate as $t = 0$ s, sketch a speed-time graph to show their motion.

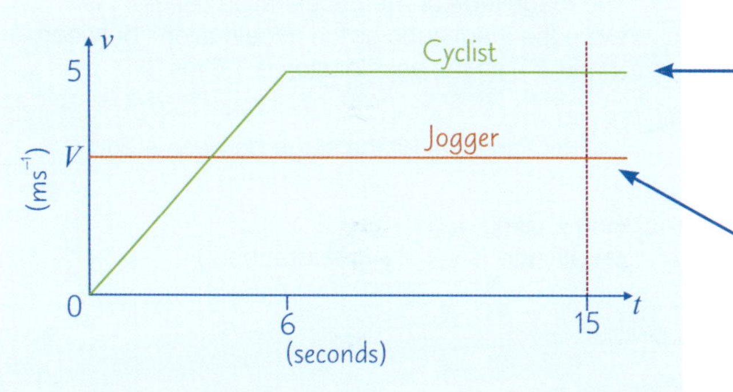

The graph of the cyclist's motion will increase from ($t = 0$ s, $v = 0$ ms^{-1}) to ($t = 6$ s, $v = 5$ ms^{-1}), then will become horizontal.

The graph of the jogger's motion will be a horizontal line, as the speed is constant. Call the jogger's speed V. You know that the cyclist overtakes the jogger, so V must be less than 5 ms^{-1}.

b) Find the speed of the jogger.

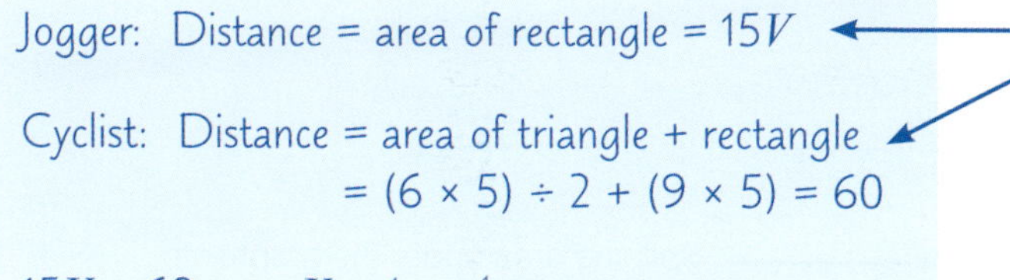

Find the area under the graphs for the cyclist and jogger — this represents the distance they each travelled in 15s.

Tip You could also use the formula for the area of a trapezium here instead.

We know that after 15s, the distances travelled by the jogger and cyclist are the same, so put 15V equal to 60.

Example 2  

A bus is travelling along a straight road at V ms^{-1}. When it reaches point A it accelerates uniformly for 4 s, reaching a speed of 21 ms^{-1} as it passes point B.
At point B, the driver brakes uniformly until the bus comes to a halt 7 s later.
The magnitude of the deceleration is twice the magnitude of the previous acceleration.

a) Sketch a velocity-time graph to show the motion of the bus.

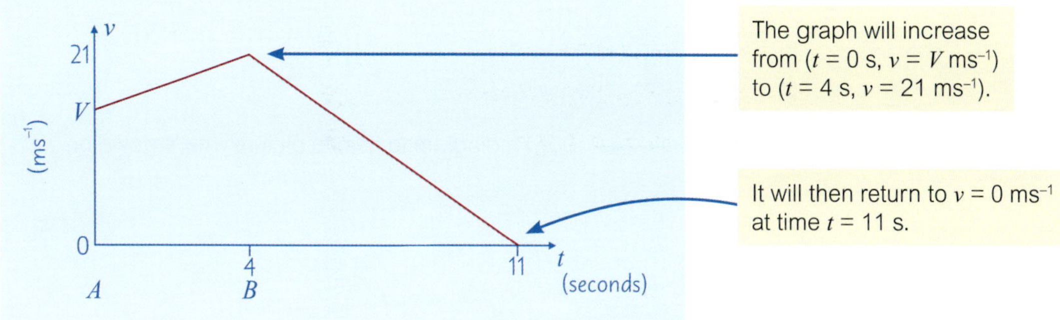

b) Find the value of V.

<u>After B:</u>

$u = 21 \quad v = 0 \quad a = a \quad t = 7$

$$a = \frac{(0 - 21)}{7} = -3 \text{ ms}^{-2}$$

<u>Between A and B:</u>

$a = 3 \div 2 = 1.5 \text{ ms}^{-2}$

$u = V \quad v = 21 \quad a = 1.5 \quad t = 4$

$V = 21 - (1.5 \times 4) = 15 \text{ ms}^{-1}$

List the variables for the stage after B.

To find the deceleration use $a = \dfrac{(v-u)}{t}$
(This is just $v = u + at$ rearranged.)

Problem Solving You can also use the graph to find the deceleration — it's the gradient of the line.

The magnitude of the deceleration ('after B') is twice the magnitude of the acceleration ('between A and B'), so the acceleration is 1.5 ms^{-1}.

List the variables for the stage between A and B.

Find V using $u = v - at$
(Again, this is $v = u + at$ rearranged.)

c) Find the distance travelled by the bus during the measured time.

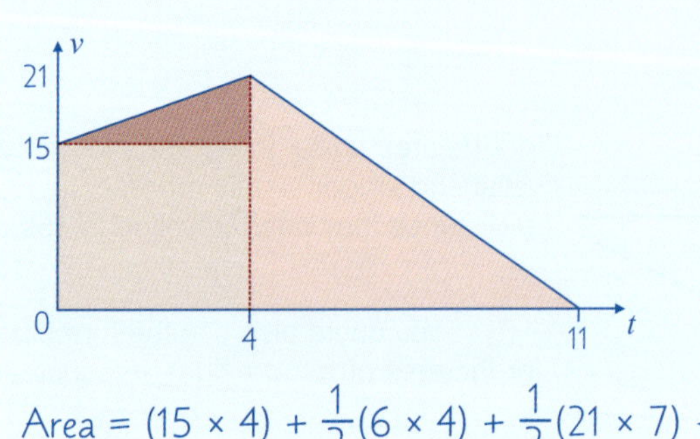

$$\text{Area} = (15 \times 4) + \frac{1}{2}(6 \times 4) + \frac{1}{2}(21 \times 7)$$
$$= 145.5 \text{ m}$$

Split the area under the graph into simple shapes and find the area.

Example 3  

A car, A, travelling along a straight road at a constant 30 ms^{-1}, passes point R at time $t = 0$.

Exactly 2 seconds later, a second car, B, passes point R with velocity 25 ms^{-1}, moving in the same direction as car A.

Car B accelerates at a constant 2 ms^{-2}.

Find the time when the two cars are level.

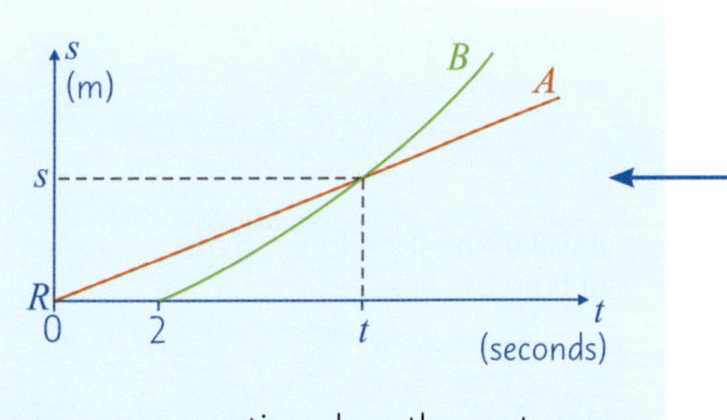

Draw a diagram to help to picture what's going on.

continued on the next page...

Car A:
$s_A = s \quad u_A = 30 \quad v_A = 30 \quad a_A = 0 \quad t_A = t$

Car B:
$s_B = s \quad u_B = 25 \quad v_B = v \quad a_B = 2 \quad t_B = (t-2)$

For each car, there are different *suvat* variables, so write separate lists and separate equations. s is the same for both cars because they're level.

Problem Solving Car A travels at a constant speed, so $a_A = 0$. Car B passes R 2 seconds after A passes point R, so $t_B = t - 2$.

Car A:
$s = 30t + \left(\frac{1}{2} \times 0 \times t^2\right)$
$s = 30t$

Car B:
$s = 25(t-2) + \left(\frac{1}{2} \times 2 \times (t-2)^2\right)$
$s = 25t - 50 + (t-2)(t-2)$
$s = 25t - 50 + (t^2 - 4t + 4)$
$s = t^2 + 21t - 46$

Use $s = ut + \frac{1}{2}at^2$ for each car.

$30t = t^2 + 21t - 46$
$\Rightarrow t^2 - 9t - 46 = 0$

Make the expressions for s equal to each other (because the cars have travelled the same distance).

$t^2 - 9t - 46 = 0$
$t = \frac{-b \pm \sqrt{b^2 - 4ac}}{2a} = \frac{9 \pm \sqrt{9^2 - (4 \times 1 \times (-46))}}{2 \times 1}$
$\Rightarrow t = 12.639...$ or $t = -3.639...$

Use the quadratic formula to solve for t.

So the cars are level 12.6 seconds after car A passes R (correct to 3 s.f.).

Tip You can ignore the negative value of t, as time is always positive.

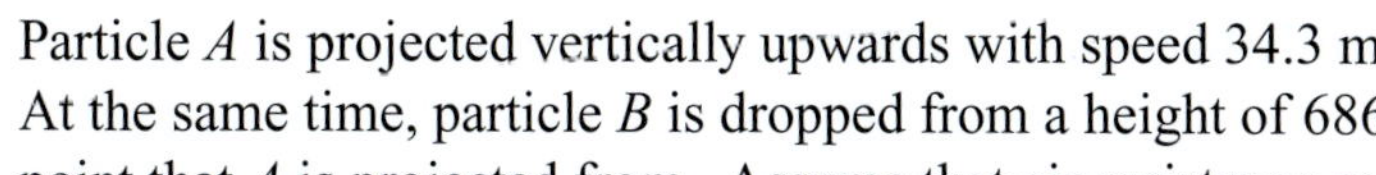

Particle A is projected vertically upwards with speed 34.3 ms^{-1} from ground level. At the same time, particle B is dropped from a height of 686 m directly above the point that A is projected from. Assume that air resistance can be ignored.

Find the time that the two particles collide.

Taking upwards as positive for Particle A:
$s_A = s_A \quad u_A = 34.3 \quad v_A = v_A \quad a_A = -9.8 \quad t_A = t$

Taking upwards as positive for Particle B:
$s_B = s_B \quad u_B = 0 \quad v_B = v_B \quad a_B = -9.8 \quad t_B = t$

continued on the next page...

Decide which direction should be taken as positive and write the *suvat* variables for each particle.
s_A = displacement above ground
s_B = displacement from where B is dropped.

Tip t is the same for both particles, as they set off at the same time.

Particle A:

$s_A = 34.3t + \left(\frac{1}{2} \times (-9.8) \times t^2\right) \Rightarrow s_A = 34.3t - 4.9t^2$

Particle B:

$s_B = 0 + \left(\frac{1}{2} \times (-9.8) \times t^2\right) \Rightarrow s_B = -4.9t^2$

To find the time that the particles collide, you need to know how far they have moved. Use $s = ut + \frac{1}{2}at^2$.

$34.3t - 4.9t^2 = 686 - 4.9t^2$

$34.3t = 686$

$t = 686 \div 34.3 = 20$

So, after t seconds, A is $(34.3t - 4.9t^2)$ m above the ground and B has moved $4.9t^2$ m downwards from a height of 686 m — i.e. B is $(686 - 4.9t^2)$ m above the ground. Equate these two heights and solve for t.

So the particles collide 20 seconds after being released.

Exercise 7.6

P Q1 A particle moves with constant acceleration a. The particle will accelerate from an initial velocity u to a final velocity v. As it accelerates, it will cover a distance s over time t.

a) Derive $s = \left(\frac{u+v}{2}\right)t$ using a velocity-time graph.

b) Use $s = \left(\frac{u+v}{2}\right)t$ and $v = u + at$ to derive $v^2 = u^2 + 2as$.

E P M Q2 A scooter is ridden along a straight horizontal road. It accelerates uniformly from rest to a velocity of 5 ms^{-1} over a period of 8 seconds. It then maintains this velocity for a further 20 seconds before decelerating at 2.5 ms^{-2} to rest. A velocity-time graph describes its motion.

a) Would the graph be steeper during the acceleration period or the deceleration period? Explain your answer. *[2 marks]*

b) Find the time taken for the deceleration stage. *[2 marks]*

c) How far did the scooter travel in total? *[2 marks]*

P Q3 At time $t = 0$, an object passes point W with speed 2 ms^{-1}. It travels at this constant speed for 8 seconds, until it reaches point X. Immediately after passing X, the object accelerates uniformly to point Y, 28 m away. The object's speed at Y is 6 ms^{-1}. Immediately after passing Y, the object decelerates uniformly to V ms^{-1} (where $V > 2$) in 5 seconds. The object travels a total distance of 67 m.

a) Find the time taken for the object to travel between X and Y.

b) Draw a velocity-time graph to show the motion of the object.

c) Find the value of V.

P M Q4 A van is travelling at a constant speed of 14 ms^{-1} along a straight road. At time $t = 0$, the van passes a motorbike, which then sets off from rest and travels along the same road in the same direction as the van. The motorbike accelerates uniformly to a speed of 18 ms^{-1} in 20 seconds, then maintains this speed.

a) Draw a velocity-time graph to show the motion of the two vehicles.

b) How long after setting off does the motorbike overtake the van?

P M Q5 Two remote-controlled cars, X and Y, lie on a straight line 30 m apart. At time $t = 0$, they are moving towards each other. X has initial speed 15 ms^{-1} and accelerates at a rate of 1 ms^{-2}. Y has initial speed 20 ms^{-1} and accelerates at a rate of 2 ms^{-2}.

a) Calculate the time taken for the cars to collide.

b) Calculate the speed of each car when they collide.

c) How far from the initial position of X do the two cars collide?

P M Q6 Ava and Budi are both cyclists. At time $t = 0$, Ava, travelling at a constant velocity of U ms^{-1}, passes Budi at rest on a straight path. Budi immediately accelerates at a constant rate for 6 seconds until he reaches a velocity of V ms^{-1}, where $V > U$, and continues at this constant velocity. At time $t = 7$ seconds, Ava accelerates at a constant rate for 4 seconds until she is cycling alongside Budi at the same constant speed.

a) Sketch a velocity-time graph of this motion.

b) Express V in terms of U.

c) Each cyclist travels 36 m from their position at $t = 0$ to their position at $t = 11$ s. Calculate the values of U and V.

P Q7 A particle travels between three points, P, Q and R. At time $t = 0$, the particle passes P with speed 15 ms^{-1}. Immediately after passing P, the particle accelerates uniformly at 3 ms^{-2} for 4 seconds, until it reaches Q with speed U ms^{-1}. It then travels at this constant speed in a straight line for 6 seconds to point R. Immediately after passing R, the particle decelerates uniformly for T seconds until it comes to rest.

a) Draw a velocity-time graph to show the particle's motion.

b) Find the value of U.

c) Given that the particle travels a total distance of 405 m, find how long after passing P the particle comes to rest.

d) Find the deceleration of the particle in coming to rest.

E P M Q8 Two golf carts are at the same point on a straight, horizontal road. Golf cart A is travelling at 27 kmh^{-1} and golf cart B at 6 ms^{-1}. They maintain these speeds for the next 2 minutes.

a) Draw the following graphs, showing the progress of the golf carts over the 2 minutes:

(i) a velocity-time graph *[2 marks]*

(ii) a displacement-time graph *[2 marks]*

b) At the end of the 2 minute period, golf cart A comes to a stop after a further 50 m and golf cart B decelerates at 0.06 ms^{-2} until they have travelled the same distance as golf cart A. How many seconds has golf cart B travelled for at this point? *[4 marks]*

P M Q9 A car accelerates uniformly from rest for 10 seconds until it reaches a velocity of $3U$ ms^{-1}. The driver then immediately brakes and decelerates for 5 seconds, then drives at a constant velocity of U ms^{-1} for 13 seconds.

a) Sketch a velocity-time graph to show the motion of the car.

b) Find the deceleration of the car between $t = 10$ and $t = 15$ in terms of U.

c) The total distance covered by the car in this motion is 304 m. Find the value of U.

P M Q10 A ball A is dropped from a height of 8 m at time $t = 0$. At the same moment, a second ball B is projected vertically upwards with speed 6 ms^{-1} from a point 4 m above the ground directly below ball A. Assume that air resistance can be ignored.

a) Find the time taken for the two balls to collide.

b) Find the height above the ground of the two balls when the collision occurs.

P M Q11 At time $t = 0$, a ball is rolled across a mat with speed 5 ms^{-1}. It decelerates at a rate of 0.5 ms^{-2} until it comes to rest. 3 seconds later, a second ball is rolled along a smooth floor, in a direction parallel to the first. This ball travels with a constant velocity of 4 ms^{-1}. The starting points of the two balls are side-by-side.

Problem Solving

In Q11, the second ball is rolled 3 seconds after the first ball, so if $t_1 = t$, then $t_2 = t - 3$.

a) How long after the first ball is rolled does the second ball pass the first ball?

b) Find the distance travelled by each ball before the second ball passes the first ball.

c) How far ahead of the first ball is the second ball 15 seconds after the first ball is rolled?

Q12 Car X travels at a constant speed of 16 ms^{-1} along a straight horizontal road. Car Y has initial speed 28 ms^{-1} and starts to decelerate with a constant rate of 3 ms^{-2} at time $t = 0$. X and Y are alongside each other at $t = 0$ and travel in the same direction.

a) How long after $t = 0$ are the two cars level again?

b) Calculate the distance travelled by the cars at the point when they're level.

P Q13 An object is projected vertically upwards from a position 3 m above the ground. The object reaches a maximum height of 4 m above its initial position before falling to the ground.

a) Sketch a displacement-time graph for this motion, where $s = 0$ is the initial position of the object.

b) Calculate the time taken for the object to reach its maximum height.

c) Calculate the velocity of the object when it hits the ground.

Challenge

E P M Q14 Two drones hover above a straight, horizontal path. Drone A begins to move with constant acceleration from 0 ms^{-1} to 7 ms^{-1} over a period of 3 seconds, then continues at a constant velocity. Drone B begins its journey 50 m in front of Drone A and sets off 12 seconds later in the same direction. Drone B accelerates at 3 ms^{-2} for 3 seconds, then maintains a constant velocity. After reaching constant velocity, Drone B overtakes Drone A.

a) Draw a velocity-time graph to show this information. *[3 marks]*

b) How much time elapsed between when Drone A set off and when Drone B overtook it? *[4 marks]*

P M Q15 At time $t = 0$, a ball A is dropped from a bridge 40 m above the ground. One second later, a second ball B is thrown vertically upwards with speed 5 ms^{-1} from a point 10 m above the ground.

a) Find the distance travelled by ball A when ball B is at the highest point in its motion.

b) How long after the ball A is dropped do the two balls become level?

c) How far from the ground are they at this time?

7.7 Displacement with Non-Uniform Acceleration

When acceleration is constant, displacement, s, can be written as $s = ut + \frac{1}{2}at^2$ — i.e. it can be written as a quadratic in terms of t. However, when acceleration **isn't** constant, displacement can be given by **any** function, not just a quadratic.

If you're given an equation for s in terms of t, then you can use differentiation to find the velocity and acceleration. Remember that:

$$v = \frac{ds}{dt} \quad \text{and} \quad a = \frac{dv}{dt} = \frac{d^2s}{dt^2}$$

Displacement might also be given by another letter such as r, d or x — so you would have $v = \frac{dr}{dt}$, etc.

Example 1

An object's displacement s (in metres) at time t (in seconds) is given by the equation:
$s = t^3 - 3t^2 + 2t$, where $t \geq 0$

a) Find its displacement at time $t = 4$.

$s = 4^3 - 3(4)^2 + 2(4) = 64 - 48 + 8 = 24$ m ← Substitute $t = 4$ into the equation.

b) Calculate the object's velocity at time $t = 1$.

$v = \frac{ds}{dt} = 3t^2 - 6t + 2$ ← For this, you need to find the velocity function using $v = \frac{ds}{dt}$.

$v = 3(1)^2 - 6(1) + 2 = 3 - 6 + 2 = -1$ ms^{-1} ← Now you can substitute $t = 1$.
(i.e. 1 ms^{-1} in the negative direction)

Example 2

An object has displacement s (in miles) at time t (in hours) given by $s = \frac{1}{9}t^4 - t^3 + 12t$, where $t \geq 0$.

a) Calculate the object's initial velocity.

$v = \frac{ds}{dt} = \frac{4}{9}t^3 - 3t^2 + 12$ ← First, differentiate to find the equation for velocity.

$v = \frac{4}{9}(0)^3 - 3(0)^2 + 12 = 0 - 0 + 12$ ← The question asks for the initial velocity — i.e. when $t = 0$.
$= 12$ miles per hour

b) Find its acceleration at time $t = 3$.

$v = \frac{4}{9}t^3 - 3t^2 + 12 \Rightarrow a = \frac{4}{3}t^2 - 6t$ ← Now you need the object's acceleration. $a = \frac{dv}{dt}$ tells you that you need to differentiate the velocity equation.

$a = \frac{4}{3}(3)^2 - 6(3) = 12 - 18 = -6$ miles/hour^2 ← Substitute $t = 3$.

Exercise 7.7

Q1 An object's displacement in metres at t seconds is given by the function: $s = 2t^3 - 4t^2 + 3$

a) Calculate the object's displacement at time $t = 3$.

b) Find the object's velocity equation.

c) What is its velocity at time $t = 3$?

Q2 An object's displacement in metres at t seconds is given by the function: $s = \frac{1}{3}t^4 - 2t^3 + 3t^2$.

a) Find the object's displacement at time $t = 4$.

b) Find the object's acceleration at time $t = 3$.

E Q3 A particle's displacement, s, in m is given by $s = t^4 + t^3 + 2t^2$, where t represents time, is measured in seconds and is greater than or equal to 0.

a) Show that the initial velocity and initial displacement of the particle are both 0. *[4 marks]*

b) Give the acceleration of the particle after 5 seconds. *[3 marks]*

M Q4 At time $t = 0$, a dog breaks its lead and runs along a straight path, until it is caught again at $t = 4$. Its displacement in metres at time t seconds while it is running free is modelled by the equation: $s = \frac{1}{5}t^5 - 2t^4 + 7t^3 - 10t^2 + 5t$

a) Calculate the dog's initial velocity.

b) What is the dog's acceleration at time $t = 2$?

E P M Q5 A rabbit's journey is modelled by the formula $s = t^2(t - 3)(t - 4)$ for $0 \leq t \leq 4$, where t is time measured in seconds and s is the displacement from the entrance of its burrow, in m. The rabbit always travels along a straight line.

a) Sketch the displacement-time graph for the rabbit. *[4 marks]*

b) What is the rabbit's displacement when $t = 2$? *[1 mark]*

c) What is the acceleration of the rabbit when $t = 3.5$? *[4 marks]*

Q5 Hint Make sure that you know how to sketch quartics.

Challenge

E P Q6 A particle's displacement, $s(t)$ is a cubic function, where s is measured in m and t is measured in seconds. The particle has 0 m displacement at 3 seconds, 5 seconds and 10 seconds. At 1 second, the displacement is 14.4 m. The function is valid for $t \geq 0$.

a) Find $s(t)$. *[4 marks]*

b) Find the displacement when $t = 4$. *[1 mark]*

c) Find the velocity when $t = 4$. *[4 marks]*

d) Determine whether there is a time when the numerical value of the velocity (in ms^{-1}) is equal to the numerical value of the acceleration (in ms^{-2}). *[4 marks]*

E P Q7 Particles A and B move in a straight line. Particle A's displacement is given by $s = 0.2t^3 - 3t^2$, with s measured in metres and time, t, measured in seconds, for $t \geq 0$. Particle B moves in the same way and with the same starting position, but with a delay of 5 seconds.

a) Find an expression, in terms of t, for the displacement of particle B. *[1 mark]*

b) What is the distance between the two particles after 10 seconds? *[2 marks]*

c) What is the difference in the speeds of the two particles after 10 seconds? *[4 marks]*

7.8 Velocity and Acceleration Equations

Instead of being given the displacement function, sometimes you'll be told the object's acceleration or velocity. From this, you can then find an equation for its displacement.

Remember that: $s = \int v \, dt$ and $v = \int a \, dt$

Initial conditions

You will always get a constant of integration, C, when finding the equation for displacement (or when finding velocity from acceleration). This is because different displacement equations can give you the same velocity equation:

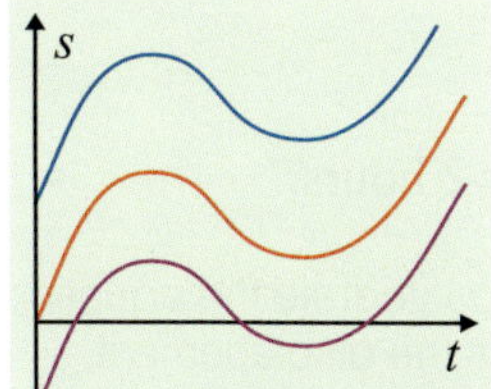

$s = \frac{1}{3}t^3 - \frac{3}{2}t^2 + 2t + 3$

$s = \frac{1}{3}t^3 - \frac{3}{2}t^2 + 2t$ → $v = t^2 - 3t + 2$

$s = \frac{1}{3}t^3 - \frac{3}{2}t^2 + 2t - \frac{3}{4}$

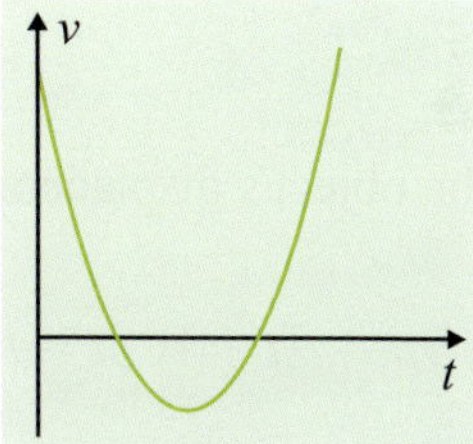

Because of this, you'll often be given a **condition** so you can find C. Usually this will be the displacement (or velocity) at time $t = 0$, i.e. the initial displacement. However, some questions may make things harder by giving you conditions at a different time — always check that you're substituting the right value for t.

Example 1

An object's velocity is given by $v = t^2 - 3t + 2$. Find its displacement as a function of t, given that:

a) the object is at $s = 0$ when $t = 0$.

$s = \int (t^2 - 3t + 2)\, dt = \frac{1}{3}t^3 - \frac{3}{2}t^2 + 2t + C$ ← Using $s = \int v \, dt$, integrate the velocity to find the displacement.

$0 = \frac{1}{3}(0)^3 - \frac{3}{2}(0)^2 + 2(0) + C \Rightarrow 0 = C$ ← You are told that when $t = 0$, $s = 0$, so substitute these values to find C.

$s = \frac{1}{3}t^3 - \frac{3}{2}t^2 + 2t$ ← Put C back in the equation.

b) the object is at $s = 2.5$ when $t = 3$.

$2.5 = \frac{1}{3}(3)^3 - \frac{3}{2}(3)^2 + 2(3) + C$ ← You already know that the displacement is given by $s = \frac{1}{3}t^3 - \frac{3}{2}t^2 + 2t + C$. Now Substitute in the conditions $t = 3$, $s = 2.5$.

$2.5 = 9 - 13.5 + 6 + C$

$C = 2.5 - 1.5 = 1$

$s = \frac{1}{3}t^3 - \frac{3}{2}t^2 + 2t + 1$ ← Put C back in the equation.

Example 2

The equation $a = 20t^3 + 18t - 2$ gives the acceleration of an object in kmh^{-2} at time t hours.

a) Given that its initial velocity is $1\ \text{kmh}^{-1}$, find the equation for its velocity in terms of t.

$$v = \int (20t^3 + 18t - 2)\ dt$$

Begin by integrating the acceleration.

$$= 20\left(\frac{t^4}{4}\right) + 18\left(\frac{t^2}{2}\right) - 2t + C$$

$$= 5t^4 + 9t^2 - 2t + C$$

$$1 = 0 + C \Rightarrow C = 1$$

You know that $v = 1$ when $t = 0$, so substitute in these values to calculate C.

$$v = 5t^4 + 9t^2 - 2t + 1$$

b) After 1 hour, the object's displacement was 4 km. Find its displacement after 2 hours.

$$s = \int (5t^4 + 9t^2 - 2t + 1)\ dt = t^5 + 3t^3 - t^2 + t + C$$

You need to integrate the equation again to get the displacement.

$$4 = 1^5 + 3(1)^3 - 1^2 + 1 + C \Rightarrow C = 0$$

The condition $s = 4$ when $t = 1$ will give you the value of C.

$$s = t^5 + 3t^3 - t^2 + t$$

$$s = 2^5 + 3(2)^3 - 2^2 + 2 = 32 + 24 - 4 + 2 = 54\ \text{km}$$

Substitute $t = 2$ into the equation.

Exercise 7.8

Q1 The velocity (in cms^{-1}) of a particle, t seconds after a chemical reaction, is found to be:

$$v = 1 + 6t + 6t^2 - 4t^3$$

a) Given that the particle starts at $s = 0$, give an equation for its displacement.

b) Find the displacement and velocity of the particle at $t = 2$.

Q2 The velocity (in ms^{-1}) of a particle, after t seconds, is given by the equation $v = 12t^3 - 18t^2 + 2t$.

a) Given that the particle starts at $s = 2$, give an equation for its displacement.

b) Find the displacement and velocity of the particle at $t = 2$.

Q3 The acceleration of an object can be modelled by the equation $a = 3t^3 - 9t^2 + 4t + 6$. Given that the velocity of the object is $6\ \text{ms}^{-1}$ after 2 seconds, and the initial displacement is 0 m, find an equation for the displacement of the object.

P M Q4 A shuttlecock is hit horizontally from a height of 3 m. The shuttlecock's vertical velocity is $0\ \text{ms}^{-1}$ at time $t = 0$ seconds. The wind affects its motion such that its vertical acceleration is given by the function $a = -6t^2 + 6t - 6$ (where upwards is the positive direction). Find the vertical velocity of the shuttlecock at time $t = 1$.

E Q5 The velocity, in ms^{-1}, of a particle is given as $v = 3t^2 - 4t$, where $t \geq 0$ and is measured in seconds.

a) Find the velocity when $t = 2$ seconds. *[1 mark]*

b) Write an expression in terms of t for the acceleration of the particle. *[1 mark]*

c) The displacement of the particle is given by the function $s(t)$. Find $s(t)$, given that $s(2) = 0$. *[2 marks]*

E Q6 The velocity, in ms^{-1}, of a particle is given as $v = t^3 + 4t^2$, where $t \geq 0$ and is measured in seconds. The initial displacement of the particle is 4 m.

a) Find the velocity of the particle when $t = 2$. *[1 mark]*

b) Find an expression, in terms of t, for the displacement of the particle. *[2 marks]*

c) Find the displacement when $t = 3$. *[1 mark]*

Q7 The acceleration, in ms^{-2}, of a particle is given as $a = t + 4$, where $t \geq 0$ and is measured in seconds. After 5 seconds, the velocity of the particle is 6 ms^{-1}. Find the velocity of the particle when the acceleration is 6 ms^{-2}.

E P Q8 A particle moves along the x-axis, such that its velocity, $\frac{dx}{dt} = 1 + t^2$, where x is given in m and t is given in seconds.

a) The displacement when $t = 2$ is double the displacement when $t = 4$. Find an expression for the displacement of the particle. *[4 marks]*

b) What is the acceleration of the particle after 8 seconds? *[2 marks]*

P M Q9 A paper aeroplane is thrown from a height of 2 m. The plane's vertical velocity is 0 ms^{-1} at time $t = 1$ second. It experiences air resistance such that its vertical acceleration is given by the function: $a = -3t^2 + 6t - 4$. Find the formula for the plane's vertical displacement, measured in metres above the ground (upwards is the positive direction).

Challenge

E P Q10 The acceleration of a body is given as a quadratic in t, for time $t \geq 0$. Its velocity is 0 at 2, 4 and 6 seconds. Its initial velocity is 24 ms^{-1}.

a) Find an expression, in terms of t, for the velocity of the body. *[3 marks]*

b) The expression for the displacement of the body is in the form $s(t) = wt^4 + xt^3 + yt^2 + zt + 10$. What is the displacement of the body after 5 seconds? *[4 marks]*

7.9 Maximum and Minimum Points

You can also find maximum and minimum points of these functions — you'll have seen how to do this in the Pure part of the course. In this context, this means finding the maximum (or minimum) displacement or velocity that an object reaches.

For example, you can find where an object's velocity has a local maximum where $\frac{dv}{dt}$ (i.e. its acceleration) is zero.

Tip The second derivative is negative at maximum points (because the gradient is decreasing) and positive at minimum points (because the gradient is increasing).

Example 1 M

A ball is rolled up a slope. Its displacement from the bottom, s m, at time t seconds after being released, is modelled by the function: $s = 8 + 2t - t^2$, $0 \le t < 4$

a) Explain the limits on t.

The limits on t are that $t \ge 0$ and $t < 4$.

When $t < 0$, the ball has yet to be released so its motion is not given by the same function.

When $t = 4$, $s = 8 + 2(4) - 4^2 = 8 + 8 - 16 = 0$ — that is, at time $t = 4$, the ball reaches the bottom of the slope, at which point you would expect its motion to change.

Problem Solving

The best way to approach a question like this is to investigate what happens at the limits. A sketch of the graph might also help.

b) Find the maximum displacement reached by the ball.

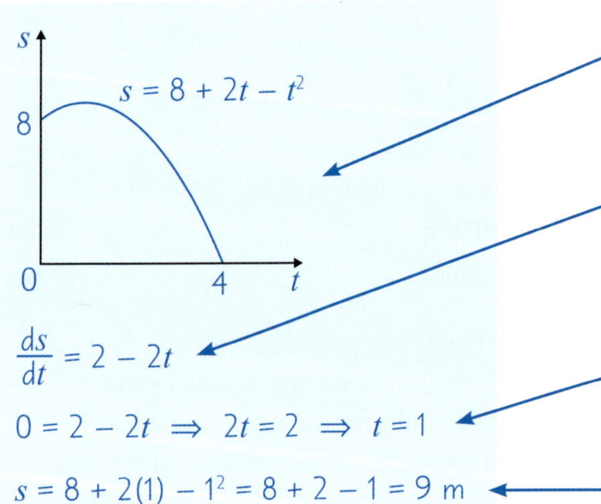

To help visualise the problem, sketch the graph of the function.

$\frac{ds}{dt} = 2 - 2t$

You want the maximum displacement — i.e. the peak of the curve, where the gradient is zero. So you need to differentiate the displacement function (which will give you the velocity).

$0 = 2 - 2t \Rightarrow 2t = 2 \Rightarrow t = 1$

Setting the velocity equal to zero will tell you the time at which it reaches its maximum displacement — once the velocity becomes negative, the object starts moving back towards $s = 0$.

$s = 8 + 2(1) - 1^2 = 8 + 2 - 1 = 9$ m

Now you just need to substitute this back into the original equation.

Example 2

At time t (s), an object's displacement (cm) follows the function: $s = 10 - 8t + t^3 - \frac{1}{6}t^4$, $t \ge 0$.

Find the time at which the object reaches its maximum velocity.

$v = \frac{ds}{dt} = -8 + 3t^2 - \frac{2}{3}t^3$

First, find an equation for the object's velocity.

$\frac{dv}{dt} = 6t - 2t^2 = 0 \Rightarrow 2t(3 - t) = 0$
$\Rightarrow t = 0$ or $t = 3$

You know that when the object reaches a local maximum velocity, $\frac{dv}{dt} = 0$. So find $\frac{dv}{dt}$ by differentiating and set it equal to 0.

$t = 0 \Rightarrow \frac{d^2v}{dt^2} = 6 - 4t$
$= 6 - 4(0) = 6$

$6 > 0 \Rightarrow$ minimum at $t = 0$

So there are two roots for t to check. Calculate $\frac{d^2v}{dt^2}$ and look for $\frac{d^2v}{dt^2} < 0$ to find the maximum point.

continued on the next page...

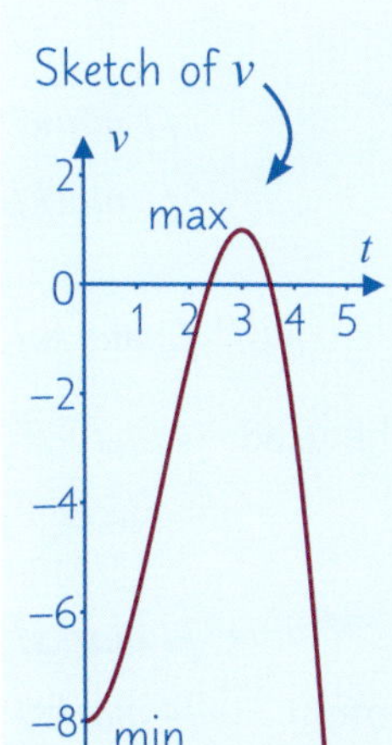

$t = 3 \Rightarrow \frac{d^2v}{dt^2} = 6 - 4t$
$= 6 - 4(3)$
$= 6 - 12 = -6$

$-6 < 0 \Rightarrow$ maximum at $t = 3$

So the object reaches its maximum velocity at $t = 3$ seconds.

You're asked for the time at its maximum velocity, not for the velocity itself. So make sure you give the right value as your answer.

Problem Solving $t = 3$ is a local maximum value for v. To make sure it's the **overall** maximum value, sketch the graph of v using the information you know about the turning points. Then check the graph doesn't go above the local maximum anywhere.

Exercise 7.9

M Q1 The displacement of a yo-yo is measured as it extends out as far as the string allows and then retracts. The motion is modelled by the function: $s = 2t^4 - 8t^3 + 8t^2$, $0 \leq t \leq 2$ where t is measured in seconds and s is measured in feet from the starting point.

a) What happens at the limits $t = 0$ and $t = 2$?

b) Find the length of the string (i.e. the maximum displacement of the yo-yo).

M Q2 The velocity of a cat (in ms^{-1}) at time t (seconds) over a period of three seconds is approximated by the function: $v = t^3 - 6t^2 + 9t$

a) Find the time at which the cat is travelling at the greatest velocity.

b) The cat's displacement at $t = 0$ is 5 metres.
What is its displacement at $t = 2$ (assuming that its motion is in a straight line)?

Q3 Find the maximum displacement of the objects whose displacement functions are given below (where displacement, s, is measured in metres, and time, t ($t \geq 0$) is measured in seconds):

a) $s = 2 + 3t - 2t^2$

b) $s = t^2 + t^3 - 1.25t^4$

c) $s = -3t^4 + 8t^3 - 6t^2 + 16$

Problem Solving In Q3, these all start from $t = 0$, so any stationary points where t is negative can be ignored.

Q4 Given that s is measured in metres and t in seconds, find the maximum (positive) velocity of an object whose displacement is given by:

a) $s = 15t + 6t^2 - t^3$

b) $s = \frac{-t^5}{20} + \frac{t^4}{4} - \frac{t^3}{3} + 11t$

Q3-4 Hint If a point has a second derivative of zero, it could be a maximum, minimum or a point of inflection, which means you'll have to test it anyway.

Q5 A particle moves with velocity v ms^{-1} defined by: $v = -\frac{1}{4}t^4 + 2t^3 + 4t - 3$, $t \geq 0$
Find the maximum acceleration of the particle.

E Q6 An object's displacement, s, in m, is given by the equation $s = 3t^2 + 2t + 5$, where t is the time, measured in seconds, and $t \geq 0$.

a) Give the initial displacement of the object. *[1 mark]*

b) Give an expression for the velocity of the object, in terms of t. *[1 mark]*

c) What is the minimum displacement of the object? Justify why it is the minimum. *[2 marks]*

E Q7 To find the displacement in metres of a particle, the following formula can be used: $s = t^3 - 14t^2 + 56t - 64$, which is valid for $t \geq 0$, with t measured in seconds.

a) Find all times when the particle is changing direction. Explain whether each represents a local maximum or a local minimum. *[4 marks]*

b) Find the minimum velocity of the particle and explain why it is the minimum. *[4 marks]*

E Q8 $s = -t^3 + 6t^2 - 11t + 6$ is used to find the displacement in metres of a particle. The function is valid for $t \geq 0$, where t measured in seconds.

a) Find the maximum displacement of the particle in the interval $1 \leq t \leq 3$, justifying that this is the maximum. *[5 marks]*

b) Find the maximum velocity of the particle and explain why it is the maximum. *[4 marks]*

E P M Q9 A remote-control car moves on a straight track. Displacement from a marked point on the track is given as positive when it is to the right of the starting point and negative when it is to the left. The displacement, s, in metres, of the car is given by the equation $s = t^2 - 8t + 12$, where t is time given in seconds and $t \geq 0$.

a) What is the velocity of the car after 10 seconds? *[2 marks]*

b) Find the minimum displacement of the car. *[2 marks]*

c) How long is the car to the left of the marked point? *[2 marks]*

P M Q10 A computer is used to track the motion of a lizard, running back and forth along a track. The computer logs its position over a 7 second interval and computes that its displacement can be approximated by the following quartic function:

$$s = \frac{1}{6}t^4 - 2t^3 + 5t^2 + 2t \quad \text{for } 0 \leq t \leq 7,$$

where s is measured in metres and t in seconds.

Calculate the lizard's greatest speed (i.e. the velocity of greatest magnitude) over these 7 seconds.

Problem Solving

In Q10, you're asked for the greatest speed, rather than velocity, so you need to check all the stationary points here and the limits.

Challenge

P Q11 The acceleration in ms^{-2} of an object is given by $a = 2t - 6t^2$.

a) Given that the initial velocity of the object is 1 ms^{-1}, find its maximum velocity.

b) Find the maximum displacement of the object from its starting position.

P Q12 Find the maximum displacement, in metres, of an object with acceleration given by $a = (6t - 4)$ ms^{-1}, where $0 \leq t \leq 1$ and such that $s = 0$ at both $t = 0$ and $t = 1$.

7 Review Exercise

Q1 An object starts with zero displacement and has a negative value for the average velocity over its total journey. Which two of the following statements must be true?

A: The moving object is reversing.

B: The moving object moves in the negative direction at some point.

C: The moving object's final displacement is a lower value than its initial displacement.

D: The moving object is decelerating.

M Q2 The displacement-time graph below shows a motorcycle journey.
Find the velocity of the motorcycle during each stage of the journey.

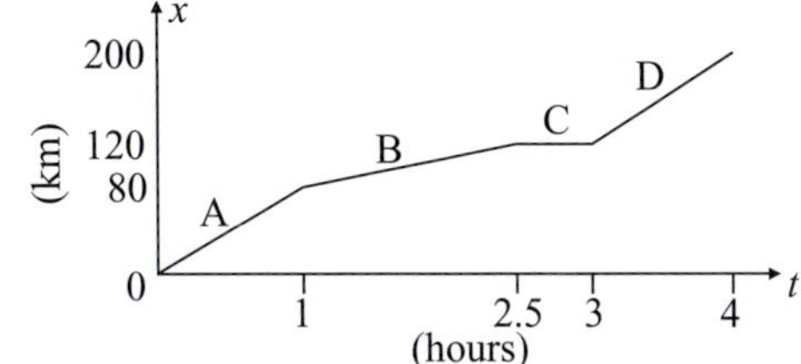

E M Q3 A straight train track passes through Appleton, Broughby and Carlford, in that order. A train on this track leaves Appleton at 14:25 and travels at an average speed of 160 km/h, passing through but not stopping at Broughby after 15 minutes. 20 minutes later, it arrives in Carlford, 45 km from Broughby.

a) Represent this information on a distance-time graph. *[2 marks]*

b) Would the graph have a different shape if it showed displacement against time instead of distance against time? Explain your answer. *[1 mark]*

M Q4 A runner starts from rest and accelerates at 0.5 ms^{-2} for 5 seconds. She then maintains a constant velocity for 20 seconds before decelerating to a stop at 0.25 ms^{-2}. Draw a velocity-time graph to show the motion and find the distance the runner travels.

Q5 A journey is shown on the speed-time graph on the right.

a) Find the acceleration during the first 3 seconds of motion.

b) Find the deceleration during the final 1 second of motion.

c) Find the distance travelled between $t = 3$ and $t = 6$.

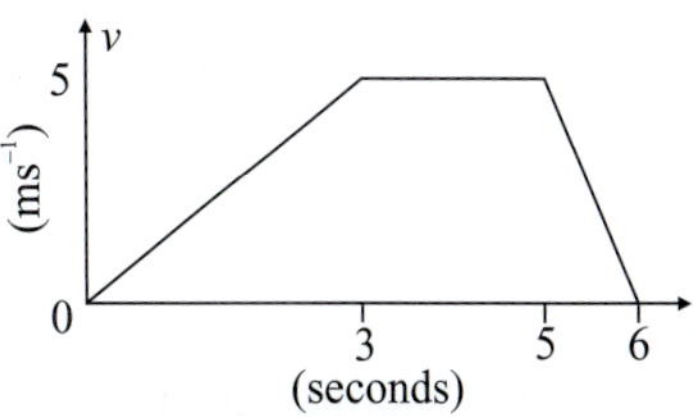

E M Q6 The velocity-time graph shows a car's progress along a straight horizontal road.

a) For how long is the car decelerating? *[1 mark]*

b) Find the total distance travelled by the car in the 18-second period. *[3 marks]*

c) Calculate the first time at which the car is travelling at 12 ms^{-1}. *[2 marks]*

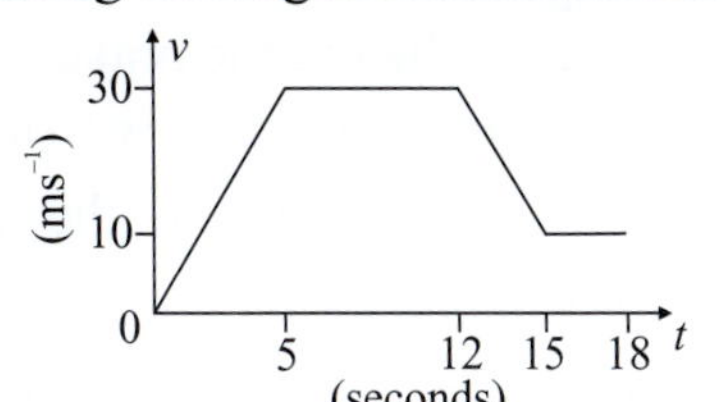

E M Q7 The velocity-time graph below shows the motion of a diver as he jumps up from a static diving board, dives into the pool below and then swims to the surface.

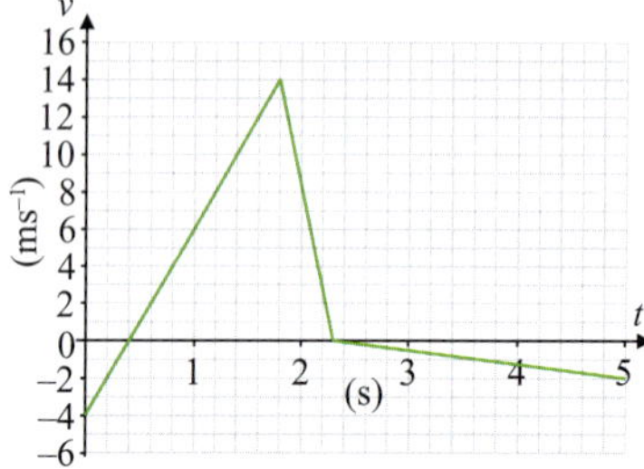

a) At what time is the diver at his greatest height? *[1 mark]*

b) Find the acceleration at time $t = 5$ seconds. *[2 marks]*

c) What is the height of the diving board above the pool? *[4 marks]*

M Q8 A runner accelerates at a rate of 0.2 ms^{-2} along a straight road. At the start of the road, her velocity is 6 ms^{-1}. It takes her 20 seconds to run the length of the road.

a) How long is the road?

b) What is her velocity as she reaches the end of the road?

E P M Q9 A child holds an umbrella and runs in a straight line at a constant velocity of 3 ms^{-1}. The wind increases and causes the child to decelerate at a constant rate of 0.85 ms^{-2}. How long does it take for the child to return to the position they were in when the wind changed? *[3 marks]*

P M Q10 A horse runs directly towards the edge of a cliff with velocity 11 ms^{-1}. The horse begins to decelerate at a rate of 3.8 ms^{-2} when it is a distance of 25 m from the cliff edge. Will the horse stop before it reaches the cliff edge?

E P M Q11 A dog runs in a straight line on an obstacle course. He accelerates uniformly from rest at a constant 1.5 ms^{-2} until he reaches a checkpoint, then decelerates at a constant 1 ms^{-2} until he stops at an obstacle. The total distance travelled is 32 m. Find the total time taken. *[6 marks]*

Q12 A particle is projected vertically upwards from the ground with velocity 35 ms^{-1}.

a) Find the maximum height reached by the particle.

b) Find the time the particle is in the air before it lands again.

M Q13 On a theme park ride, the carriage is fired vertically downwards from a height of 20 m above ground level. The carriage is modelled as a particle and moves freely under gravity before the brakes are applied, 10 m below ground level. When the brakes are applied, the carriage is travelling at 25 ms^{-1}.

a) Find the speed of projection of the carriage.

b) Find the time taken for the carriage to reach ground level.

c) Suggest one reason why this may not be a suitable model.

E M Q14 A ball is thrown vertically upwards from the edge of a cliff with velocity 20 ms^{-1}.

a) Find the time taken for the ball to reach its greatest height. *[3 marks]*

b) Given that it takes 5.24 seconds for the ball to hit the ground at the base of the cliff, find the height of the cliff to 3 significant figures. *[3 marks]*

E M Q15 Anish and Bethany are taking part in a 60 m sprint race. Anish starts at rest, accelerates uniformly at a rate of 1.5 ms^{-2} for 3 seconds, then runs at a constant velocity for the rest of the race. Bethany starts at rest, accelerates uniformly at 1.8 ms^{-2} for 5 seconds, then decelerates uniformly at a rate of –2 ms^{-2} for 3 seconds and maintains that velocity for the rest of the race.

a) On the same diagram, sketch velocity-time graphs to illustrate the motion of the runners in the race, labelling the points where the velocity changes. *[3 marks]*

b) Using the graph, or otherwise, identify who won the race. *[6 marks]*

P M Q16 A swimmer and a fish set off from the same place at the same time. The swimmer swims in a straight line with constant velocity 1 ms^{-1}. The fish accelerates uniformly from rest to U ms^{-1} in 2 seconds, then maintains this speed. It moves in a straight line throughout its motion, and overtakes the swimmer 5 seconds after they set off.

a) Draw a velocity-time graph to show the motion of the swimmer and the fish.

b) Use your graph to find the value of U.

E P M Q17 Athlete A starts jogging from a point on a straight horizontal track, from rest. He accelerates to a velocity of 5 ms^{-1} over a period of 3 seconds then maintains this speed for 10 seconds before coming to an instantaneous rest.

5 seconds after athlete A starts jogging, athlete B starts from the same point, from rest. He accelerates for 2 seconds at 3 ms^{-2} then runs at a constant velocity for a further T seconds before coming to an instantaneous rest.

a) Sketch a velocity-time graph, showing the motion of both athletes. *[5 marks]*

b) After how many seconds are both athletes moving at the same velocity? *[3 marks]*

c) They both cover the same distance prior to coming to rest. How much quicker does athlete B cover the distance than athlete A? *[4 marks]*

Q18 An object's displacement in metres at t seconds is given by the function: $s = \frac{1}{4}t^4 - t^3 - t^2$.

a) Find the object's velocity at time $t = 5$.

b) Find the object's acceleration at time $t = 2$.

Q19 A particle's acceleration after t seconds is a ms^{-2}, where a is given by the function $12 - 3t^2$.

a) Given that the initial velocity of the particle is 4 ms^{-1}, find an equation for the velocity, v.

b) Find the velocity and acceleration of the particle after 3 seconds.

E Q20 A particle starts from rest and moves in a straight line. At t seconds after the beginning of the motion, the acceleration of the particle is given by $a = 4t^2 - 9t + 32$, where $t \geq 0$. Find the displacement of the particle after 2 seconds. *[6 marks]*

Q21 Match each particle to its displacement-time graph and velocity-time graph below.

Particle X's displacement, s, in metres, at t seconds, is given by the equation $s = 4$.
Particle Y's displacement is given by the equation $s = 4t - 1$.
Particle Z's displacement is given by the equation $s = t^2 + 1$.

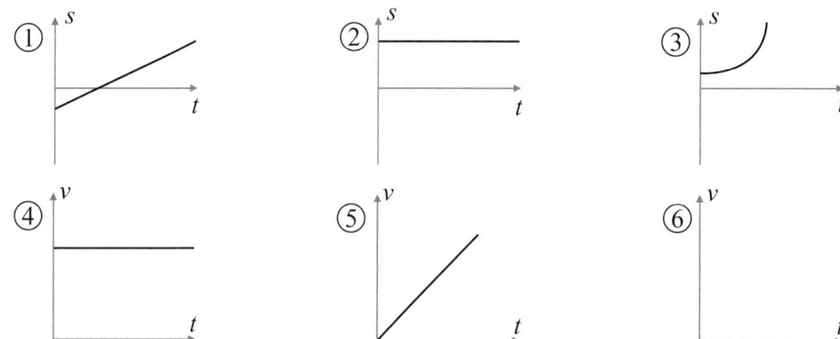

Q22 The displacement of an object is modelled by the equation $s = 8t^2 - \frac{1}{2}t^4$.

a) What happens at the limits $t = 0$ and $t = 4$?

b) Find the greatest displacement the object reaches from its initial position.

E Q23 A particle moves with velocity v, measured in ms^{-1}, where:

$v = 3t - t^2, \quad 0 \le t \le 3 \qquad\qquad v = 21 - 7t, \quad t \ge 3$

t is measured in seconds, and when $t = 0$, the particle's displacement is 0.

a) Find the velocity of the particle when $t = 5$. *[1 mark]*

b) Find the displacement of the particle when $t = 5$. *[6 marks]*

E P Q24 The displacement s, in metres, and time t, in seconds, of a particle is given as follows:

$$s = t^3 \text{ when } 0 \le t \le 1$$
$$s = t^4 \text{ when } 1 < t \le 2$$
$$s = -t^3 + 24 \text{ when } 2 < t \le 3,$$

a) Find the displacement of the particle when $t = 1.5$ seconds. *[1 mark]*

b) Find the maximum displacement of the particle. Justify your answer. *[3 marks]*

c) Find the velocity of the particle when $t = 2.5$ seconds. *[3 marks]*

E P M Q25 The acceleration of a runner is $a = 0.25t^2$, where a is in ms^{-2} and t is in seconds, $0 \le t \le 3$. The runner's initial displacement is 0 m and her initial velocity is 0 ms^{-1}.

a) Find her maximum acceleration, explaining how you know that it represents the maximum. *[2 marks]*

b) Find an expression for her velocity, in terms of t. *[3 marks]*

c) Find an expression for her displacement, in terms of t. *[3 marks]*

d) What was her change in displacement during the third second? *[3 marks]*

e) Without performing further calculations, would you expect her change in displacement between 1 and 2 seconds to be more or less than the answer to part d)? *[1 mark]*

Challenge

P M Q26 The graph shows the displacement of two people from a bank along a straight horizontal high street, over a 10-minute period.

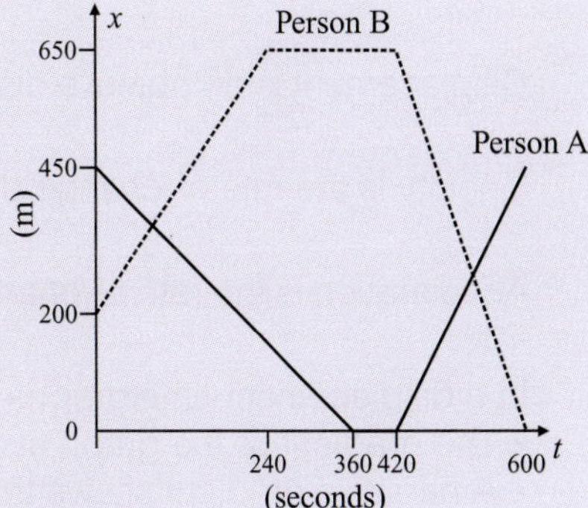

a) How long did person A spend at the bank?

b) Who walked the greater distance and by how much?

c) Whose displacement from the bank was greater at the end of the 10-minute period and by how much?

d) What was the greatest speed achieved?

e) After how many seconds were the two people the same distance from the bank for the second time?

P Q27 A projectile is fired from a point 10 m below ground level vertically upwards. It passes a target 20 m above ground level and 2 seconds later passes another target which is 50 m above ground level. Assume that air resistance can be ignored.

a) Find the speed of projection of the projectile.

b) Find the maximum height above the ground reached by the projectile.

c) Find the amount of time that the projectile spends over 30 m above the ground.

P Q28 At time $t = 0$, particle A is dropped from a crane 35 m above the ground. Two seconds later, particle B is projected vertically upwards with speed 3 ms^{-1} from a point 5 m above the ground.

a) Find the distance travelled by A when B is at the highest point in its motion.

b) How long after A is dropped do the two particles become level?

c) How far from the ground are they at this time?

M Q29 An athlete's displacement during a training exercise can be modelled by the quartic function:

$$s = -\frac{1}{40}t^4 - \frac{1}{15}t^3 + 2t^2 \quad \text{for} \quad 0 \le t \le 6$$

where s is measured in metres and t in seconds.

Calculate the athlete's greatest speed over the 6 second interval.

7 Chapter Summary

1 Displacement is an object's distance from a particular point.

2 Velocity is the rate of change of displacement with respect to time.

3 Acceleration is the rate of change of an object's velocity with respect to time.

4 In a displacement-time graph:
- The gradient of the graph at a particular point gives the object's velocity.
- A negative gradient shows that the object is moving in the opposite direction.

5 In a velocity-time graph:
- The gradient of the graph at a particular point gives the object's acceleration.
- The area under the graph gives the object's displacement.

6 There are five constant acceleration equations:

$$v = u + at$$
$$s = ut + \frac{1}{2}at^2$$
$$s = \left(\frac{u+v}{2}\right)t$$
$$v^2 = u^2 + 2as$$
$$s = vt - \frac{1}{2}at^2$$

where

s = displacement in m

u = initial speed (or velocity) in ms^{-1}

v = final speed (or velocity) in ms^{-1}

a = acceleration in ms^{-2}

t = time that passes in s (seconds)

7 Acceleration due to gravity is denoted by the letter g, where $g = 9.8$ ms^{-2}.

8 Given any function for displacement, s, in terms of time, t, you can differentiate to find functions for velocity and acceleration, e.g. $v = \frac{ds}{dt}$ and $a = \frac{dv}{dt} = \frac{d^2s}{dt^2}$.

9 Integrating a function for the acceleration, a, of an object will give you velocity, v. Integrating velocity will give you displacement, e.g. $v = \int a\,dt$ and $s = \int v\,dt$.

10 You can find the maximum or minimum displacement or velocity of an object by calculating the turning points of the function (e.g. by checking where $\frac{ds}{dt}$ or $\frac{dv}{dt}$ is equal to zero).

11 You need to calculate the second derivative $\left(\frac{d^2s}{dt^2} \text{ or } \frac{d^2v}{dt^2}\right)$ of the function to determine the nature of any turning points. If the second derivative is negative, then the point is a local maximum, and if it's positive, the point is a local minimum.

Forces and Newton's Laws

8

Learning Objectives

Once you've completed this chapter, you should be able to:

- Understand and use the fact that forces are vectors.
- Find magnitudes and directions of forces.
- Know and understand Newton's three laws of motion, and apply them to constant acceleration problems.
- Solve problems involving resistance forces when a particle is moving.
- Solve problems involving two connected particles, including connected particles moving over a smooth peg or pulley.

Prior Knowledge Check

1 Find the magnitude and direction of the following vectors to 1 decimal place:

a) $\begin{pmatrix} 12 \\ 9 \end{pmatrix}$ b) $(3\mathbf{i} - 5\mathbf{j})$ c) $\begin{pmatrix} -2 \\ 2 \end{pmatrix}$ d) $(-4\mathbf{i} - 8\mathbf{j})$

see Year 1 Pure Maths

2 A crate is being pulled up a smooth slope by a light inextensible string.

a) Explain what is meant by the term: (i) smooth (ii) light

b) Draw a diagram showing the forces acting on the crate.

see page 170

3 A particle starts from rest and accelerates in a straight line at a rate of 5 ms^{-2} for 6 seconds. Find:

a) the final velocity of the particle,

b) the displacement of the particle over these 6 seconds.

see page 185

8.1 Treating Forces as Vectors

Forces are **vectors** — they have a **magnitude** (size) and a **direction** that they act in.

- The magnitude of a force is measured in **newtons** (**N**). For a force $\boldsymbol{F}$, you would write its magnitude as $|\boldsymbol{F}|$.
- A force's direction is an **angle** that is measured **anticlockwise** from the **horizontal** (unless a question says otherwise).
- A **component of a force** is the part of the force that acts in a **particular direction**.

Tip Use **bolding** or underlining to show that something is a vector (e.g. $\boldsymbol{F}$ or $\underline{F}$). It's tricky to make your handwriting bold, so underlining works better.

A force acting on an object can cause that object's **velocity** to change (see p.221).

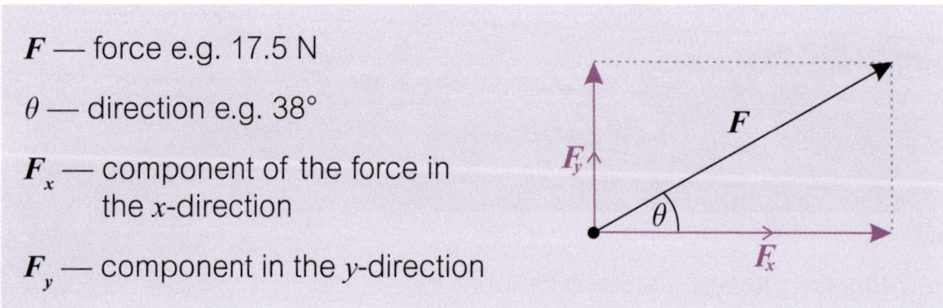

You can describe forces using the **unit vectors i** and **j**. Unit vectors are a pair of **perpendicular** vectors, each of **magnitude one unit**. The number in front of the **i** is the horizontal force component, and the number in front of the **j** is the vertical force component.

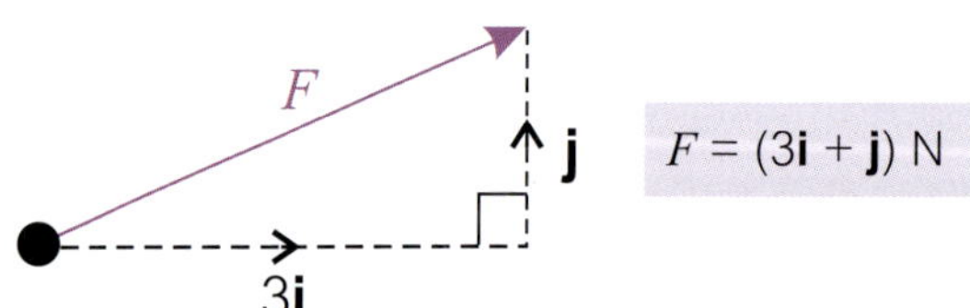

You can also represent a force with a column vector. The top number is the horizontal (**i**) component and the bottom number is the vertical (**j**) component.

For example, $3\mathbf{i} + \mathbf{j}$ can be given as the vector $\begin{pmatrix}3\\1\end{pmatrix}$.

For a force $\boldsymbol{F} = x\mathbf{i} + y\mathbf{j}$, its magnitude is $|\boldsymbol{F}| = \sqrt{x^2 + y^2}$

and the direction θ can be found by first finding the angle with the horizontal, which is given by $\tan^{-1}\left(\frac{y}{x}\right)$.

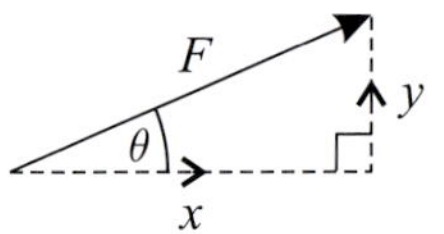

Tip $\tan^{-1}\left(\frac{y}{x}\right)$ will be the direction θ when $0 < \theta < 90°$. When θ is between 90° and 360°, you may need to add or subtract this angle to/from 180° or 360° — drawing a diagram will be very helpful.

Example 1

A force $F = (3\mathbf{i} - 2\mathbf{j})$ N acts on a particle P. Find the magnitude and direction of the force.

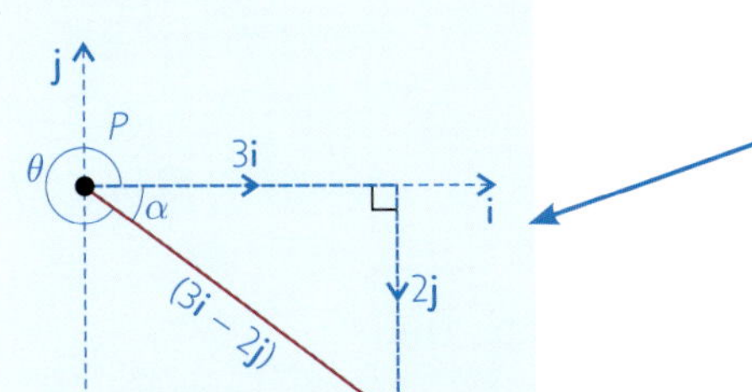

Draw a diagram of the force acting on the particle to get a clear idea of what's going on.

Tip As a column vector, this force would be given by $\begin{pmatrix} 3 \\ -2 \end{pmatrix}$.

Magnitude of $\boldsymbol{F} = \sqrt{3^2 + 2^2} = \sqrt{13} = 3.61$ N (to 3 s.f.)

The force and its **i** and **j** components form a right-angled triangle, so you can use Pythagoras' theorem to find the magnitude of the force.

$\tan\alpha = \frac{2}{3} \Rightarrow \alpha = \tan^{-1}\left(\frac{2}{3}\right) = 33.690...$

$\theta = 360 - \alpha$, so $\theta = 326.4°$ (1 d.p.)

Use trigonometry to find the acute angle α. You can see from the diagram that the direction is between 270° and 360°, so subtract α from 360° to get the answer in the correct range.

Exercise 8.1

Give your answers to an appropriate degree of accuracy unless otherwise stated.

Q1 Find the magnitude and direction of the following forces.

a) $7\mathbf{i}$ N b) $(2\mathbf{i} + 2\mathbf{j})$ N c) $(3\mathbf{i} + 4\mathbf{j})$ N

d) $(-3\mathbf{i} + 4\mathbf{j})$ N e) $(12\mathbf{i} - 5\mathbf{j})$ kN f) $(-\mathbf{i} - 4\mathbf{j})$ N

Problem Solving Estimate the direction before doing the calculation — drawing a diagram might help.

Q2 Find the magnitude and direction of each force.

a) $\begin{pmatrix} 3 \\ 1 \end{pmatrix}$ N b) $\begin{pmatrix} -4 \\ -2 \end{pmatrix}$ N c) $\begin{pmatrix} 12 \\ -3 \end{pmatrix}$ N d) $\begin{pmatrix} -0.5 \\ 0.5 \end{pmatrix}$ kN

e) $\begin{pmatrix} 0 \\ -11 \end{pmatrix}$ N f) $\begin{pmatrix} 15 \\ 25 \end{pmatrix}$ kN g) $\begin{pmatrix} -5 \\ -7 \end{pmatrix}$ N h) $\begin{pmatrix} -8 \\ 9 \end{pmatrix}$ N

Q3 Find the direction of the force $(\mathbf{i} + \sqrt{3}\,\mathbf{j})$ N.

Q4 Find the magnitude of the force $\begin{pmatrix} 15 \\ -8 \end{pmatrix}$ kN, and give its direction.

P Q5 The force $\begin{pmatrix} 56a \\ -42a \end{pmatrix}$ N (where a is a constant) has a magnitude of 35 N. Find the value of a.

P Q6 The forces $\begin{pmatrix} 3 \\ 4 \end{pmatrix}$ N and $\begin{pmatrix} 4 \\ 3 \end{pmatrix}$ N act at the same point. Find the angle between these forces.

P Q7 A force $\boldsymbol{F}$ has a magnitude of 6 N, a horizontal component of $5\mathbf{i}$ N and a direction at an angle θ below the positive $\mathbf{i}$ direction such that $\tan\theta = \frac{a}{5}$, where $a > 0$. Find the value of a.

E P **Q8** A force, $\boldsymbol{F}_1 = \begin{pmatrix} 3 \\ 2 \end{pmatrix}$ N, acts in the same direction as a force, $\boldsymbol{F}_2$.
Given that $|\boldsymbol{F}_2| = 8$ N, find $\boldsymbol{F}_2$. *[4 marks]*

E **Q9** Two forces, $\begin{pmatrix} 3 \\ 5 \end{pmatrix}$ N and $\begin{pmatrix} -1 \\ a \end{pmatrix}$ N, have equal magnitude.
Find the possible values of a. *[3 marks]*

E P **Q10** A force, $\boldsymbol{F} = \begin{pmatrix} 2 \\ -1 \end{pmatrix}$ N, acts on a particle. Giving your answers to 2 d.p., find:

a) the force, $\boldsymbol{F}_1$, which acts directly downwards with a magnitude 5 N greater than the magnitude of $\boldsymbol{F}$. *[2 marks]*

b) the force which is parallel to $\boldsymbol{F}$ and has magnitude 1 N. *[2 marks]*

Challenge

E P **Q11** The diagram shows how two forces, $\boldsymbol{F}$ and $\boldsymbol{G}$, act on a particle. In the diagram, 1 square represents 1 newton.

a) Find the magnitudes of $\boldsymbol{F}$ and $\boldsymbol{G}$. *[3 marks]*

b) Find the obtuse angle between the two forces. *[2 marks]*

c) The x-component of $\boldsymbol{G}$ is changed, resulting in a force that has twice the magnitude of $\boldsymbol{F}$. Find the two column vectors which could represent the revised force $\boldsymbol{G}$. *[3 marks]*

8.2 Resultant Forces and Equilibrium

The **resultant force** on an object is the **single** force that has the **same effect** as all the forces acting on the object combined.

To calculate the resultant force on an object, you need to **add the components** of the forces acting on the object in each direction (i.e. add all of the **i**-components and all of the **j**-components). The total force in each direction will be the component of the resultant force in that direction.

1

An object is being pulled along a rough surface by a force of 12 N (acting parallel to the surface). It experiences a resistance force of 5 N directly opposing the motion.
Draw a diagram showing the forces on the object, and calculate the resultant force on the object.

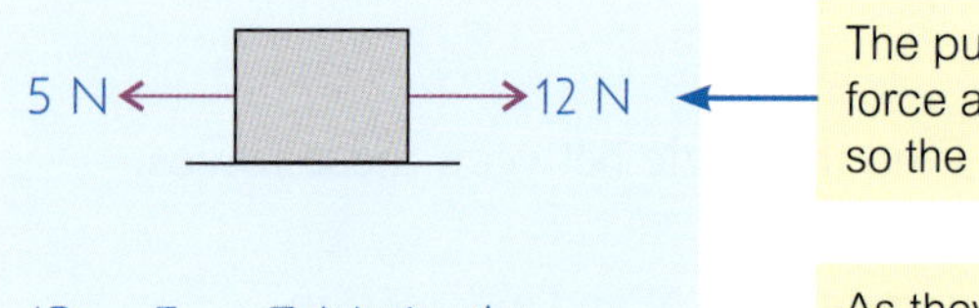

The pull force and the resistance force are acting in opposite directions, so the diagram looks like this.

$12 - 5 = 7$ N in the direction of the 12 N force.

As they're acting in opposite directions, subtract the smallest force from the largest. This is the resultant force on the object.

Problem Solving

Resistance forces always act in the opposite direction to the movement of an object (see p.171).

It's often useful to determine, and work with, two perpendicular components of a force — this is called **resolving** the force. Usually it's in terms of the **i** and **j** unit vectors.

Example 2

Two forces, given by the vectors $(3\mathbf{i} - \mathbf{j})$ N and $(-2\mathbf{i} + 4\mathbf{j})$ N, act on an object. Calculate the resultant force on the object in both the **i**- and **j**-directions.

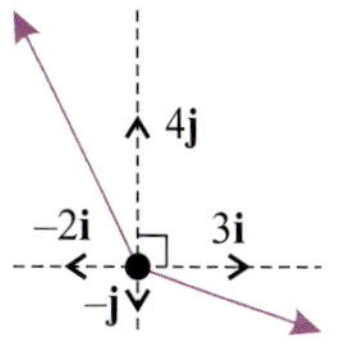

i: $3\mathbf{i} + (-2\mathbf{i}) = \mathbf{i}$ N

j: $(-\mathbf{j}) + 4\mathbf{j} = 3\mathbf{j}$ N

Add the forces in each direction.

When the resultant force on an object is **zero** (usually when all the forces on the object **cancel** each other out), the object is in **equilibrium**.

Example 3 

Four children are having a tug-of-war contest. The diagram below shows the forces acting on the rope.

35 N, 40 N ← → 32 N, D N

Given that the rope is being held in equilibrium, find the force D.

$-35 - 40 + 32 + D = 0$

$\Rightarrow D = 35 + 40 - 32$

$\Rightarrow D = 43$ N

The rope is in equilibrium, so the resultant force is zero.

Solve the equation to find D.

Tip When you're resolving or adding components, draw an arrow to show which direction you're taking as positive.

Example 4

A particle is suspended in equilibrium by three light, inextensible strings. The diagram shows all of the forces acting on the particle (in N).

Find the missing force $\begin{pmatrix} x \\ y \end{pmatrix}$.

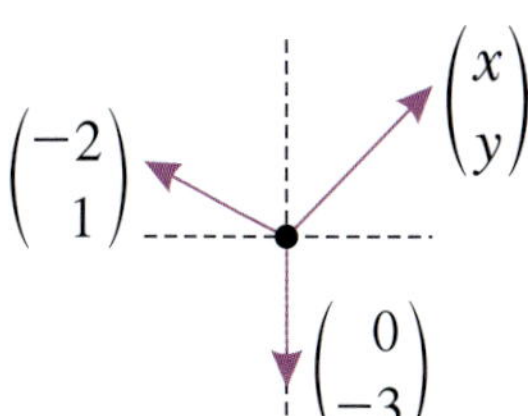

$-2 + 0 + x = 0$

$1 - 3 + y = 0$

Resolve the forces horizontally (→) and vertically (↑). The particle is in equilibrium, so the resultant force in both directions must be zero.

$-2 + 0 + x = 0 \Rightarrow x = 2$

$1 - 3 + y = 0 \Rightarrow y = 2$

So the missing force is given by $\begin{pmatrix} 2 \\ 2 \end{pmatrix}$.

Solve the equations to find the components of the missing force.

Tip Check the definitions on page 170 if you're not sure what "light" or "inextensible" mean in this modelling context.

Exercise 8.2

Give your answers to an appropriate degree of accuracy unless otherwise stated.

Q1 An object hangs in equilibrium on a string, as shown in the diagram. Find the tension in the string, T.

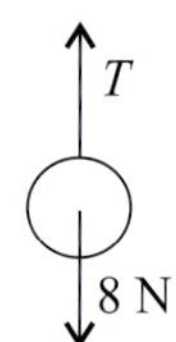

Q2 Find the resultant of the two forces $(8\mathbf{i} + 5\mathbf{j})$ N and $(3\mathbf{i} - 2\mathbf{j})$ N.

Q3 A particle is acted on by the forces $(-7\mathbf{i} - 9\mathbf{j})$ N and $(3\mathbf{i} - 2\mathbf{j})$ N.

a) Find the resultant of the two forces.

b) After a third force $\boldsymbol{F}$ is applied, the particle is now in equilibrium. Write down force $\boldsymbol{F}$.

M Q4 A diver uses a diving jet to move around underwater. The forces on the diver and his jet are shown in the diagram. Find the resultant force, giving your answer in terms of $\mathbf{i}$ and $\mathbf{j}$.

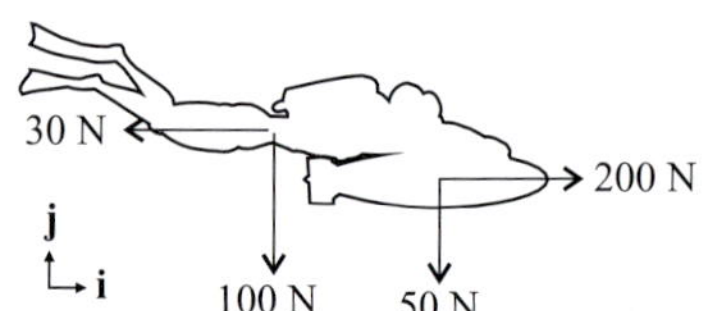

Q5 An object is held in equilibrium by three forces: $(3\mathbf{i} + 2\mathbf{j})$ N, $(x\mathbf{i} - 4\mathbf{j})$ N and $(-5\mathbf{i} + 2\mathbf{j})$ N. Find the value of the constant x.

E Q6 A particle is in equilibrium on a horizontal table. It has weight 14 N and is acted upon by a force, $\boldsymbol{G} = 7$ N, in a horizontal direction. The other forces acting on it are friction and the normal reaction exerted by the table.
Show this information on a diagram, including the values of the friction and normal reaction forces. *[2 marks]*

P Q7 Three forces $\begin{pmatrix} 3 \\ a \end{pmatrix}$ N, $\begin{pmatrix} -2 \\ 1 \end{pmatrix}$ N and $\begin{pmatrix} b \\ 7 \end{pmatrix}$ N act on an object, where a and b are constants.
Find the values of a and b, given that the object is held in equilibrium.

P M Q8 As part of an experiment on magnetism, a magnetic stone is held in place on a table, while some students hold two magnets on the table. The forces exerted on the stone by the magnets are given by $\mathbf{i}$ N and $(-5\mathbf{i} - 2\mathbf{j})$ N respectively.

a) Draw a diagram showing the stone and the magnetic forces acting on it.

b) Find the resultant force acting on the stone.

c) Another two magnets are added, resulting in two new forces on the stone given by $(4\mathbf{i} + \mathbf{j})$ N and $\boldsymbol{F}$ N respectively. Given that the stone is now in equilibrium, find the force $\boldsymbol{F}$.

E P Q9 A stone, in equilibrium, is acted upon by 3 forces, $\boldsymbol{F}_1$, $\boldsymbol{F}_2$ and $\boldsymbol{F}_3$. $\boldsymbol{F}_1$ has direction of 315° and $\boldsymbol{F}_2$ has direction of 225°, where direction is measured anticlockwise from the positive x-axis.
The magnitude of $\boldsymbol{F}_1$ is double the magnitude of $\boldsymbol{F}_2$. $\boldsymbol{F}_3 = \begin{pmatrix} -3 \\ c \end{pmatrix}$, where c is a constant.
Find c, $\boldsymbol{F}_1$ and $\boldsymbol{F}_2$ *[6 marks]*

Challenge

E P Q10 The resultant force acting on a particle is $\begin{pmatrix} 6 \\ -2 \end{pmatrix}$. One of the two forces which combine to give this result is $\begin{pmatrix} 4 \\ a \end{pmatrix}$ and the other has a horizontal component which is double its vertical component. Find the angle between the two forces acting on the particle. *[6 marks]*

8.3 Newton's Laws of Motion

Newton's first law:

A body will stay at **rest** or maintain a **constant velocity** unless a **resultant force** acts on the body.

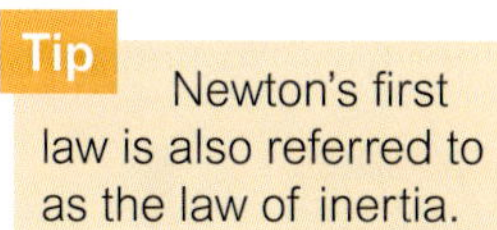

So if the forces acting on something are perfectly **balanced**, then it **won't accelerate**. If it's stationary, it'll **stay stationary** and if it's moving in a straight line with constant speed, it'll carry on moving in the **same straight line** with the same **constant speed**.

Newton's second law:

The **overall resultant force** (F_{net}) acting on a body is equal to the **mass** of the body multiplied by the body's **acceleration**.

So if the forces acting on a body **aren't** perfectly **balanced**, then the body will **accelerate** in the **direction** of the resultant force. The magnitude of the acceleration will be proportional to the magnitude of F_{net}.

A body's mass, its acceleration and the resultant force acting on it are related by the following formula, sometimes called the **equation of motion**: $\boldsymbol{F_{net} = ma}$
This is often written as $F = ma$, but the F always means resultant force.

A common use of this formula is calculating the **weight** of an object. An object's weight is a **force** caused by **gravity**. Gravity causes a constant acceleration of approximately 9.8 ms^{-2}, denoted $\boldsymbol{g}$.

Putting this into $F = ma$ gives the equation for weight (W): $W = mg$

Remember that weight is a force and is measured in **newtons**, while mass is measured in **kg**. 1 newton is defined as the force needed to make a 1 kg mass accelerate at a rate of 1 ms^{-2}.

Newton's third law:

For **two bodies**, A and B, the force exerted by A on B is **equal in magnitude** but **opposite in direction** to the force exerted by B on A.

So for a particle sat on a horizontal surface, the particle exerts a **downward force** upon the surface and the surface exerts a force vertically **upwards** upon the particle with the **same magnitude**. This is called a **reaction force**, and is normally labelled R.

Newton's third law also applies to forces like tension, where an object and a connected rope pull on each other with equal force.

8.4 Using Newton's Laws

Newton's laws are a lot easier to understand once you start **using them**.
If you're doing calculations, you'll probably use the second law ($F_{net} = ma$) more than the other two. You might also need to use the **constant acceleration equations** from Chapter 7.

Example 1

A particle of mass 12 kg is attached to the end of a light, vertical string. The particle is accelerating vertically downwards at a rate of 7 ms^{-2}.

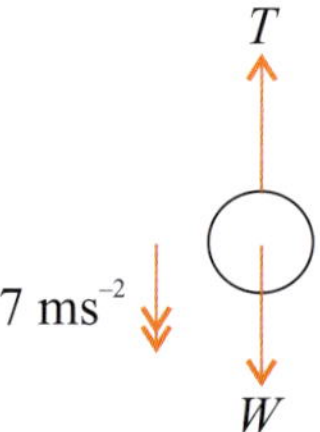

a) Find W, the weight of the particle.

$W = mg$ ← Use the formula for weight.
$= 12 \times 9.8$
$= 117.6$ N

Tip Unless a question tells you otherwise, take $g = 9.8$ ms^{-2}.

b) Find T, the tension in the string.

$F_{net} = ma$ ← Use the equation of motion.
$117.6 - T = 12 \times 7$ ← Resolve vertically (↑).
$T = 117.6 - 84 = 33.6$ N

Tip You don't have to work out the resultant force separately before using $F = ma$. You can do the whole thing in one 'resolving' step.

c) Find the resultant force acting horizontally on the particle.

The particle is not accelerating horizontally, so from Newton's first law, there is no resultant force acting horizontally on the particle.

The next example uses the **normal reaction force** — see page 171 for a reminder of this.

Example 2

A 4 kg mass, initially at rest on a smooth horizontal plane, is acted on by a horizontal force of 5 N. Find the magnitude of the acceleration of the mass and the normal reaction from the plane, R.

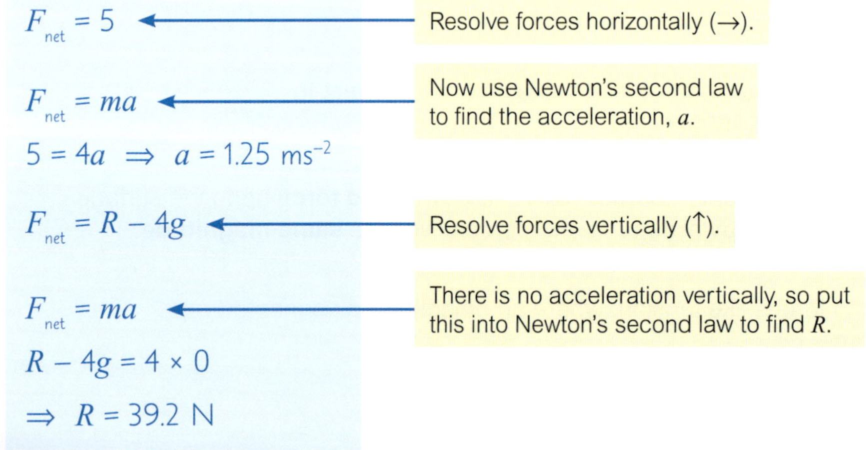
$F_{net} = 5$ ← Resolve forces horizontally (→).

$F_{net} = ma$ ← Now use Newton's second law to find the acceleration, a.
$5 = 4a \Rightarrow a = 1.25$ ms^{-2}

$F_{net} = R - 4g$ ← Resolve forces vertically (↑).

$F_{net} = ma$ ← There is no acceleration vertically, so put this into Newton's second law to find R.
$R - 4g = 4 \times 0$
$\Rightarrow R = 39.2$ N

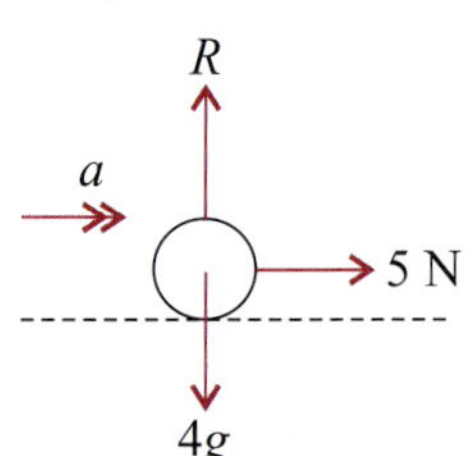

Tip It's pretty common for the normal reaction force to have the same magnitude as the weight of the object.

Example 3

A particle of weight 30 N is being accelerated across a rough horizontal plane by a force of 6 N acting parallel to the horizontal, as shown. The particle experiences a constant resistance force of 2.5 N. Given that the particle starts from rest, find its speed after 4 s.

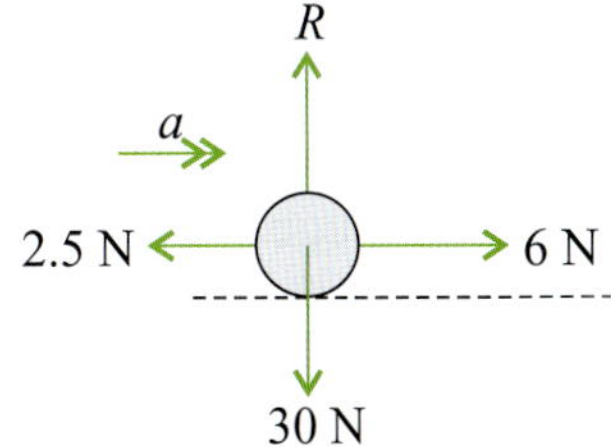

$W = mg \Rightarrow m = \frac{W}{g}$ ← You're given the weight, so you need to calculate the mass of the particle.

$\Rightarrow m = \frac{30}{9.8} = 3.061... \text{ kg}$

$F_{net} = ma$ ← Now resolve forces horizontally (→), using Newton's second law to find the acceleration, a.

$6 - 2.5 = 3.061... \times a$

$\Rightarrow a = 3.5 \div 3.061... = 1.143... \text{ ms}^{-2}$

$u = 0, \quad v = v, \quad a = 1.143..., \quad t = 4$

$v = u + at$ ← Use one of the constant acceleration equations to find the speed.

$= 0 + 1.143... \times 4$

$= 4.57 \text{ ms}^{-1}$ (to 3 s.f.)

Tip It always helps to draw a diagram showing the forces acting on a body and the direction of acceleration.

Tip Look back at page 185 if you need a reminder of any of the constant acceleration equations.

Newton's second law still works when the force and acceleration are in vector form. Make sure it's clear in your working when you're using vectors by underlining the letters.

Example 4

A particle of mass m kg is acted upon by a force F of $(-8\mathbf{i} + 6\mathbf{j})$ N, resulting in an acceleration of magnitude 8 ms^{-2}.

a) Find the value of m.

$F_{net} = \sqrt{(-8)^2 + 6^2} = \sqrt{100} = 10 \text{ N}$ ← Find F_{net} — it's the magnitude of $\boldsymbol{F}$.

$F_{net} = ma$ ← Now use Newton's second law to find m.

$10 = 8m$

$m = 1.25 \text{ kg}$

b) The force on the particle changes to a force of $(4\mathbf{i} + 7\mathbf{j})$ N. Find the new acceleration of the particle in vector form.

$\boldsymbol{F}_{net} = m\boldsymbol{a}$ ← You can use Newton's second law with vectors to get the acceleration.

$(4\mathbf{i} + 7\mathbf{j}) = 1.25\boldsymbol{a}$

$\boldsymbol{a} = (4 \div 1.25)\mathbf{i} + (7 \div 1.25)\mathbf{j}$

$\boldsymbol{a} = (3.2\mathbf{i} + 5.6\mathbf{j}) \text{ N}$

Exercise 8.3-8.4

Give your answers to an appropriate degree of accuracy unless otherwise stated.

Q1 A particle with mass 15 kg is accelerating at 4 ms^{-2}.
Find the magnitude of the resultant force acting on the particle.

Q2 A block of mass 5 kg is acted on by a resultant force of 10 N. Find:

a) the acceleration of the block,

b) the speed of the block after 8 s (given that it starts from rest).

E Q3 The resultant force acting on a particle of mass 5 kg is 8 N, in a horizontal direction. Find the acceleration of the particle, indicating the direction. *[2 marks]*

E Q4 A particle of mass 2 kg has initial velocity –5 ms^{-1}. It is acted on by a 3 N force in the positive direction. Find its velocity after 2 seconds. *[2 marks]*

Q5 A particle of mass 18 kg is attached to the end of a light, vertical string. Given that the particle is accelerating vertically upwards at 0.4 ms^{-2}, find T, the tension in the string.

M Q6 A model car, initially at rest on a horizontal plane, is acted on by a resultant horizontal force of magnitude 18 N, causing it to accelerate at 5 ms^{-2}. Find:

a) the mass of the model car, b) the car's speed after 4 seconds,

c) the magnitude of the normal reaction from the plane.

M Q7 A sack of flour of mass 55 kg is attached to the end of a light vertical rope. The sack starts from rest and accelerates vertically upwards at a constant rate so that after 4 seconds it is moving with speed 2.5 ms^{-1}.

a) Find the magnitude of the acceleration of the sack of flour.

b) Assuming that the sack experiences a non-gravitational constant resistance to motion of magnitude 120 N, find the tension in the rope.

E Q8 A particle of mass 2 kg has initial velocity 5 ms^{-1}. 10 seconds later, it has velocity 3 ms^{-1}. Given that its acceleration was constant over this period, find the resultant force which acted on the particle over that time. *[2 marks]*

P M Q9 A stone of mass 300 grams is dropped from the surface of a lake and descends vertically down to the lake floor. It hits the bottom 12 seconds after being released from rest. Assuming that the stone experiences a constant resistance of 1.5 N, find the depth of the lake.

Q9 Hint Use Newton's second law to find the acceleration of the stone first.

E M Q10 A pebble is pushed along a horizontal table, with a force of 10 N acting on it horizontally. There is a frictional force of 5 N between the table and the pebble. The pebble moves from rest to a velocity of 8 ms^{-1} in a period of 4 seconds. Find the normal reaction of the table on the pebble. *[4 marks]*

Q11 A particle of mass 10 kg is acted on by a force of $(8\mathbf{i} - 2\mathbf{j})$ N.

a) Find the acceleration of the particle in vector form.

b) Find the magnitude of the acceleration.

c) Assuming that the particle is initially at rest, find the speed of the particle after 6 seconds.

Problem Solving Just like Newton's second law, you can use the equation $\mathbf{v} = \mathbf{u} + \mathbf{a}t$ with vectors. Notice that t is a scalar.

P Q12 A particle of mass m kg is acted on by a force of $(8\mathbf{i} + 6\mathbf{j})$ N. Given that the particle is initially at rest and accelerates to a velocity of $(32\mathbf{i} + 24\mathbf{j})$ ms^{-1} in 2 seconds, find the value of m.

P Q13 Two constant forces are acting on a body of mass 2 kg. 10 seconds after starting to accelerate from rest, the velocity of the body is given by $(30\mathbf{i} + 20\mathbf{j})$ ms^{-1}.

a) Calculate the resultant force acting on the body. Give your answer in vector form.

b) If one of the forces is given by $(10\mathbf{i} - 3\mathbf{j})$ N, what is the magnitude of the other force?

P Q14 Two constant forces act on a body of mass x kg. 3 seconds after starting to accelerate from rest, the velocity of the body is given by $(6\mathbf{i} - 9\mathbf{j})$ ms^{-1}.

a) Given that the resultant force is $(10\mathbf{i} - 15\mathbf{j})$ N, find x.

b) One of the forces is given by $(\mathbf{i} + 7\mathbf{j})$ N. Calculate the magnitude of the other force.

Challenge

E P M Q15 Two remote-control cars each have a mass of 2 kg. Car 1 is placed on a track and is acted on by a resultant force of $\begin{pmatrix} 2 \\ 3 \end{pmatrix}$ N. Car 2 is placed 2 seconds later, at the same point, and is acted on by a resultant force of $\begin{pmatrix} 4 \\ 6 \end{pmatrix}$ N.

a) Verify that the motion for the cars is along the same path. *[1 mark]*

b) How long after Car 1 sets off will the cars collide? *[7 marks]*

8.5 Connected Particles

In situations where you have two (or more) particles **joined together**, you can still consider the motion of each **individually** and resolve the forces acting on each particle separately.

However, if the connection between the particles is **light**, **inextensible** and remains **taut**, and the particles are moving in the **same straight line**, they can also be considered to be moving as **one particle** with the **same acceleration**.

Example 1 

A person of mass 70 kg is standing in a lift of mass 500 kg. The lift is attached to a vertical light, inextensible cable, as shown. By modelling the person as a particle, and given that the lift is accelerating vertically upwards at a rate of 0.6 ms^{-2}, find:

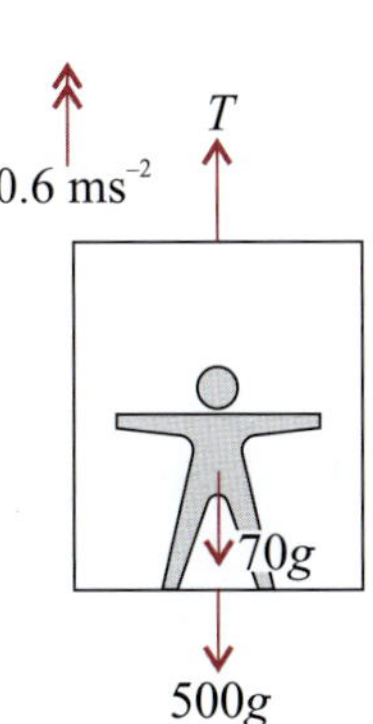

a) T, the tension in the cable,

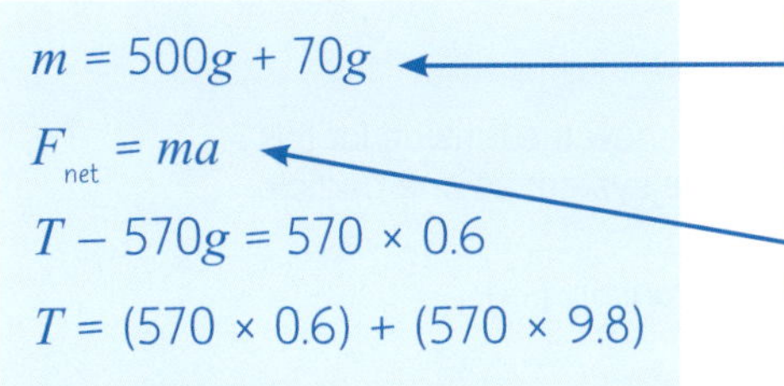

$m = 500g + 70g$

$F_{net} = ma$

$T - 570g = 570 \times 0.6$

$T = (570 \times 0.6) + (570 \times 9.8)$

$T = 5928$ N

The whole system is accelerating together, so you can treat the whole system as one particle.

Resolve vertically (↑) for the whole system.

b) the magnitude of the force exerted by the person on the floor of the lift.

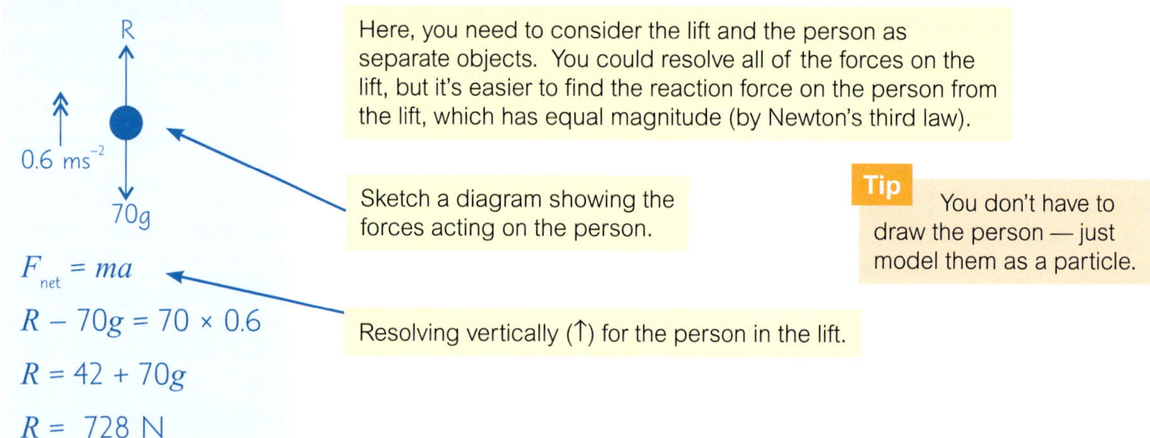

Tension and thrust

When two objects are **connected** by a **light**, **taut** and **inextensible string**, the string exerts an equal **tension** force at both ends, usually (but not always) in **opposite directions**. For example, if the string passes over a **pulley**, then the tension forces will both act **towards the pulley** (see p.229).

Thrust (or **compression**) is the opposite effect, where a **rigid rod** pushes on two connected objects with equal force. For example, the legs of a **table** could be modelled as rigid rods, exerting a thrust force on both the **tabletop** and the **floor**.

A 30-tonne locomotive engine is pulling a single 10-tonne carriage, as shown.
They are accelerating at 0.3 ms^{-2} due to the force P generated by the engine.
The coupling between the engine and the carriage can be modelled as light and inextensible.
It is assumed that there are no forces resisting the motion.

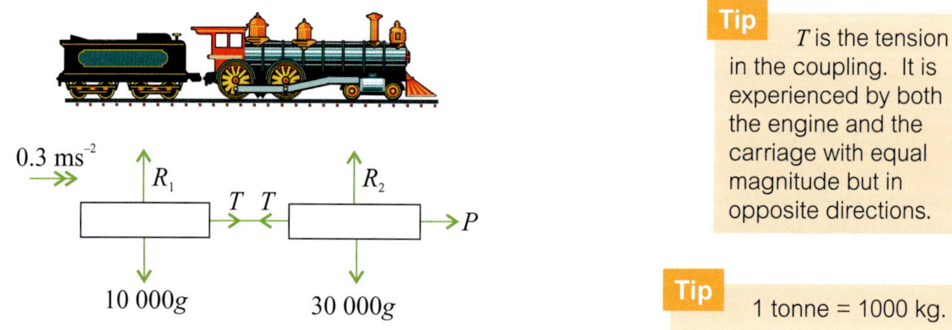

a) Find the magnitude of the driving force P.

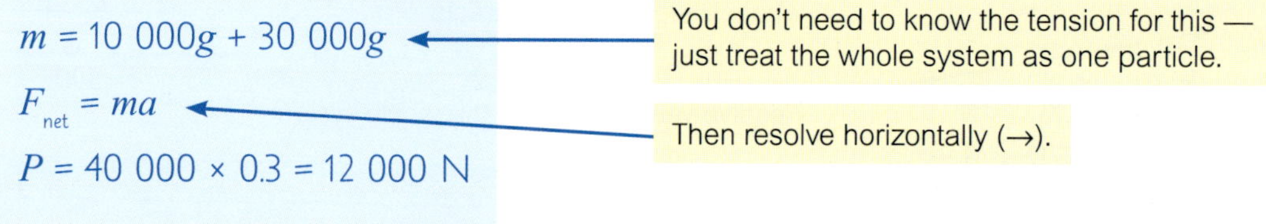

b) Find the magnitude of the tension in the coupling.

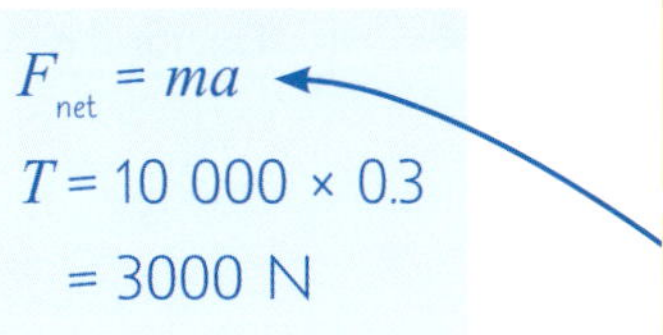

The coupling is modelled as being light and inextensible, so the tension will be constant throughout the coupling.

Resolve horizontally (→), considering only the forces acting on the carriage.

Tip You could consider only the forces acting on the engine instead, but there are fewer acting on the carriage, so the calculation is easier.

c) When the engine and carriage are travelling at 15 ms^{-1}, the coupling breaks. Given that the driving force remains the same, find the distance travelled by the engine in the first 5 seconds after the coupling breaks.

$F_{net} = ma$

$P = 30\ 000 \times a$

$a = 12\ 000 \div 30\ 000 = 0.4$ ms^{-2}

Resolve horizontally (→), considering only the forces acting on the engine to find its new acceleration.

$s = s \quad u = 15 \quad a = 0.4 \quad t = 5$

$s = ut + \frac{1}{2}at^2$

$s = (15 \times 5) + \left(\frac{1}{2} \times 0.4 \times 5^2\right) = 80$ m

Now use a constant acceleration equation to find the distance travelled.

Exercise 8.5

Give your answers to an appropriate degree of accuracy unless otherwise stated.

M Q1 A lift of mass 2000 kg is carrying a load of weight 4000 N.

a) Calculate the tension in the lift cable, given that the lift is accelerating vertically upwards at 0.2 ms^{-2} and that the cable is light, inextensible and vertical.

b) Find the reaction force between the floor of the lift and the load.

M Q2 A lift is being tested for safety. The lift has a mass of 1000 kg and contains a load of mass 1400 kg. The lift is attached to a vertical light, inextensible cable.

a) Calculate the tension in the cable given that the lift is accelerating vertically downwards at a rate of 1.5 ms^{-2}.

b) Find the reaction force between the floor of the lift and the load.

c) The lift is raised to a height of 30 m above the ground. The cable is cut and the lift falls freely from rest to the ground. Find the speed of the lift as it hits the ground.

E M Q3 A cement mixer of mass 80 kg is on a platform of mass 1000 kg. The platform is attached to a vertical light, inextensible cable, attached to a crane. The tension in the cable is 11 124 N.

a) Find the acceleration of the system. *[2 marks]*

b) Find the force exerted by the cement mixer on the platform. *[2 marks]*

M Q4 A tractor of mass 2 tonnes is pulling a trailer of mass 1.5 tonnes by means of a light, rigid coupling, as shown on the right. The tractor applies its brakes and both tractor and trailer decelerate at a rate of 0.3 ms^{-2}.

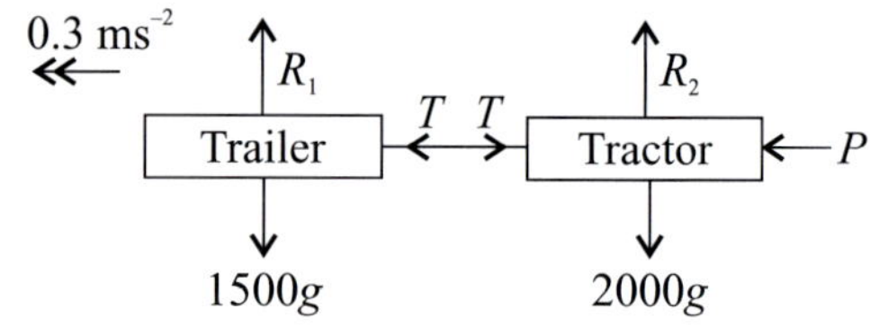

a) Calculate the braking force, P, generated by the tractor.

b) Find the magnitude of T, the thrust in the coupling between the tractor and the trailer.

c) State an assumption that has been made in this model of the motion of the tractor and trailer.

Q4 Hint Remember — thrust is the force in a rigid rod. In this question, thrust acts just like tension would, but in the opposite directions.

P M Q5 A car is towing a caravan along a level road. The car has mass 1200 kg and the caravan has mass 800 kg. Resistance forces of magnitude 600 N and 500 N act on the car and the caravan respectively. The acceleration of the car and caravan is 0.2 ms^{-2}.

a) Calculate the driving force of the car.

b) Find the tension in the tow bar.

c) The car and caravan are travelling at a speed of 20 ms^{-1} when the tow bar breaks. Given that the resistance forces remain constant, how long does the caravan take to come to rest?

Q5a) Hint Add together the individual resistance forces to find the total resistance of the whole system.

P M Q6 A locomotive with mass 4000 kg is connected to a carriage with mass 2500 kg by a light, rigid coupling. Resistance forces of 1200 N and 950 N act on the locomotive and carriage respectively. The driving force created by the locomotive's engine is 4500 N.

a) Find the acceleration of the locomotive and carriage to 2 decimal places.

b) The locomotive and carriage are travelling at 30 ms^{-1} when the coupling breaks. Calculate the distance travelled by the carriage in the five seconds after the coupling breaks.

Challenge

E P M Q7 A car is towing an empty trailer along a level road, using a tow rope. The car has mass 900 kg and the trailer has mass 400 kg. The resistance forces on the car and the trailer are 400 N and 200 N, respectively. The driving force of the car is 1900 N.

a) Calculate the acceleration of the car. *[2 marks]*

b) Find the magnitude of the tension in the tow rope. *[2 marks]*

c) A load of mass 500 kg is added to the trailer, which causes an increase to the resistance force on the trailer to 300 N. There is no change to the resistance force on the car or the driving force. How much longer would it take the car's speed to increase by 10 ms^{-1} now than before the load was added? *[4 marks]*

E P M Q8 A lift is moving upwards. It decelerates from a velocity of 20 ms^{-1} to rest over a 10 second interval. A person is standing in the lift. The mass of the lift only is 900 kg and the lift is attached to a light, inextensible cable. The tension in the cable is 7605 N.

a) Find the mass of the person. *[3 marks]*

b) Find the force exerted by the person on the floor of the lift. *[2 marks]*

c) If the maximum acceleration of the lift is 1.2 ms^{-2} upwards, find the minimum height of the lift shaft. *[3 marks]*

8.6 Pegs and Pulleys

Particles connected by a string which passes over a **peg** or **pulley** will move with the **same magnitude of acceleration** as each other (as long as the string is inextensible and remains taut). However, the two connected particles **cannot** be treated as one because they will be moving in different directions.

You may see pegs and pulleys described as '**fixed**' — this just means that the peg or pulley is held in place so that it won't move when the string passes over it.

If the peg or pulley is **smooth**, then the **magnitude** of the **tension** in the string connecting the particles will be the **same** either side of the peg or pulley. Pulleys aren't usually completely smooth, but **modelling** them this way makes the calculations much easier.

Example 1

Masses of 3 kg and 5 kg are connected by a light, inextensible string and hang vertically either side of a smooth, fixed pulley. They are released from rest.

a) Find the magnitude of the acceleration of each mass.

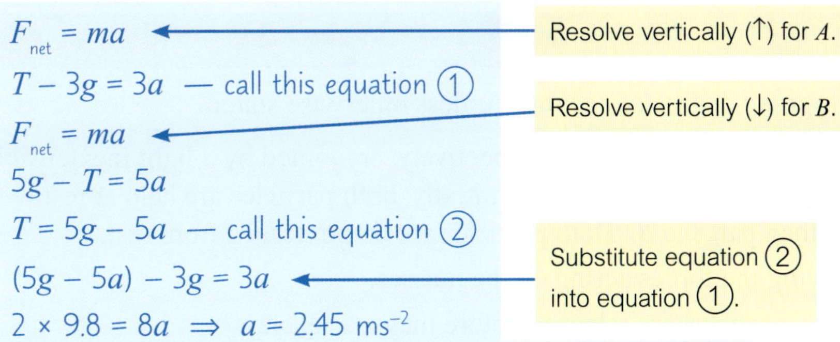

$F_{net} = ma$ ← Resolve vertically (↑) for A.

$T - 3g = 3a$ — call this equation ①

$F_{net} = ma$ ← Resolve vertically (↓) for B.

$5g - T = 5a$

$T = 5g - 5a$ — call this equation ②

$(5g - 5a) - 3g = 3a$ ← Substitute equation ② into equation ①.

$2 \times 9.8 = 8a \Rightarrow a = 2.45 \text{ ms}^{-2}$

The string is inextensible, so the acceleration of each particle will have the same magnitude, but opposite direction.

Tip: When the particles are released from rest, the heavier particle will move downwards, and the lighter particle will move upwards.

b) Find the time it takes for each mass to move 40 cm.

$s = 0.4, u = 0, a = 2.45, t = t$

$s = ut + \frac{1}{2}at^2$ ← Use one of the constant acceleration equations.

$0.4 = (0 \times t) + \left(\frac{1}{2} \times 2.45 \times t^2\right) \Rightarrow 0.4 = 1.225t^2$

So $t = \sqrt{\frac{0.4}{1.225}} = 0.571$ s (3 s.f.)

c) State any assumptions made in your model.

- A does not hit the pulley and B does not hit the ground.
- There's no air resistance.
- The string is 'light' so the tension is the same for both A and B, and the string doesn't break.
- The string is inextensible so the acceleration is the same for both masses.
- The pulley is fixed and smooth.
- Acceleration due to gravity is constant ($g = 9.8 \text{ ms}^{-2}$).

Example 2

A particle of mass 3 kg is placed on a smooth, horizontal table. A light, inextensible string connects it over a smooth, fixed peg to a particle of mass 5 kg which hangs vertically, as shown. Find the tension in the string if the system is released from rest.

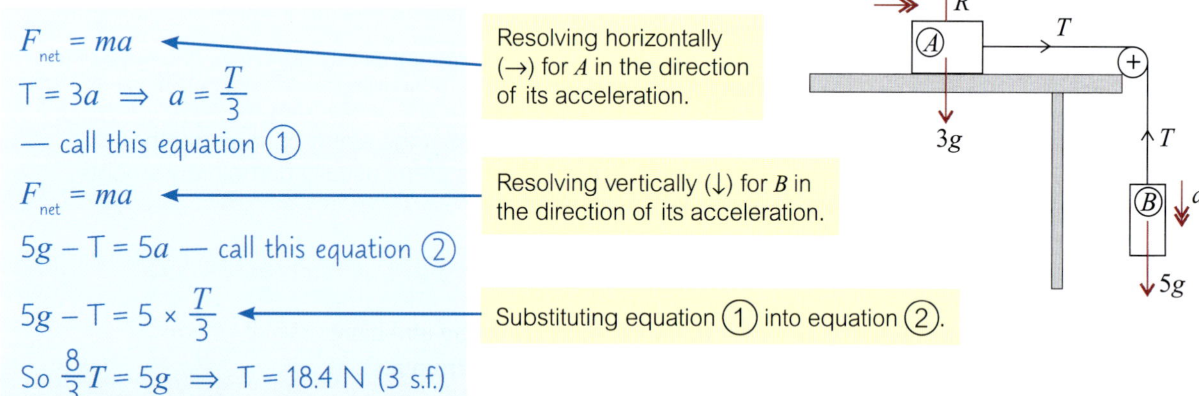

$F_{net} = ma$ — Resolving horizontally (→) for A in the direction of its acceleration.

$T = 3a \Rightarrow a = \frac{T}{3}$

— call this equation ①

$F_{net} = ma$ — Resolving vertically (↓) for B in the direction of its acceleration.

$5g - T = 5a$ — call this equation ②

$5g - T = 5 \times \frac{T}{3}$ — Substituting equation ① into equation ②.

So $\frac{8}{3}T = 5g \Rightarrow T = 18.4$ N (3 s.f.)

Exercise 8.6

Give your answers to an appropriate degree of accuracy unless otherwise stated.

Q1 Two particles, A and B, of mass 3 kg and 2 kg respectively, are joined by a light inextensible string which passes over a fixed, smooth pulley. Initially, both particles are held at rest with particle A 60 cm higher than particle B. Both particles are then released from rest.

a) Draw a diagram showing the forces acting on the masses.

b) How long is it after the particles are released before they are level?

E Q2 Particle A, mass 2 kg, and particle B, mass 6 kg, are connected by a light, inextensible string and hang vertically either side of a smooth, fixed pulley. They are released from rest.

a) Find the magnitude of the acceleration of each mass. *[3 marks]*

b) Find the tension, T, in the string. *[1 mark]*

Q3 Particle A, mass 35 kg, and particle B, mass M kg ($M < 35$), are connected by a light, inextensible rope which passes over a fixed, smooth peg, as shown. Initially both particles are level and they are released from rest.

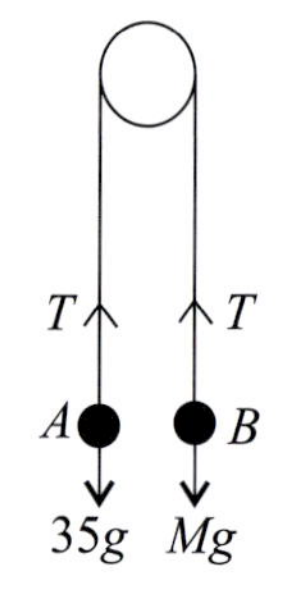

a) Calculate T, the tension in the rope, given that the particles move 5 m vertically in the first 2 seconds after they are released.

b) Find M.

Q4 Particles A and B, of mass 5 kg and 7 kg respectively, are connected by a light, inextensible string which passes over a fixed, smooth pulley. Particle A is resting on a smooth horizontal surface and particle B is hanging vertically, as shown. The system is released from rest.

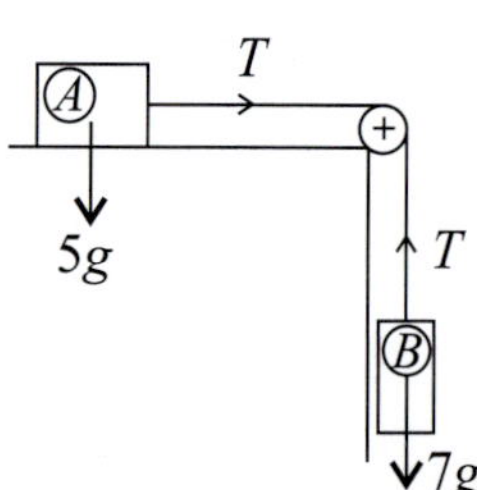

a) Find the magnitude of the acceleration of the particles.

b) Find the tension in the string.

c) What assumptions have you made in your model?

Q5 A particle of mass 2 kg is placed on a smooth, horizontal table. A light, inextensible horizontal string connects it over a smooth peg, fixed to the edge of the table, to a particle of mass M kg which hangs vertically. Given that the tension in the string is 16 N when the system is released from rest, calculate M to two decimal places.

M Q6 A bucket of stones with mass 50 kg is attached to one end of a light inextensible rope, the other end of which is attached to a counterweight of mass 10 kg. The rope passes over a smooth fixed pulley. The bucket is raised from rest on the ground to a height of 12 m in a time of 20 s by the addition of a constant force F acting vertically downwards on the counterweight.

a) Draw a diagram to show the forces acting on this system.

b) Calculate the tension in the rope.

c) Find the magnitude of F.

d) When the bucket is 12 m above the ground, the stones are removed and the force F stops acting on the counterweight. Given that the bucket weighs 11 kg and the system is released from rest, find the speed of the bucket as it hits the ground.

Q7 Two particles, P and Q, of mass 2.5 kg and 1.5 kg respectively are attached to either end of a light, inextensible string which passes over a fixed, smooth pulley. The particles are released from rest at a height of 2 m above the ground.

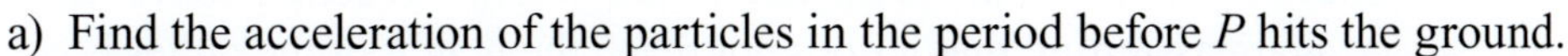

a) Find the acceleration of the particles in the period before P hits the ground.

b) Calculate the height Q reaches above the ground after 0.8 seconds.

c) Find the speed of P at the exact instant it hits the ground.

P Q8 Two particles, A and B, of mass 15 kg and 12 kg respectively, are attached to the ends of a light, inextensible string which passes over a fixed, smooth pulley. The particles are held at rest so that the string is taut and they are both 6 m above the horizontal ground, as shown.

a) Find the acceleration of the particles immediately after they are released.

b) Find the magnitude of the force which the string exerts on the pulley.

c) Particle A strikes the ground without rebounding. Particle B then moves freely under gravity without striking the pulley. Find the time between particle A hitting the ground and particle B coming to rest for the first time.

Q8b) Hint Consider the parts of the string either side of the pulley separately and remember that the tension is constant throughout the string.

Q8c) Hint The string is inextensible, so at the instant that A hits the ground, both A and B will be travelling with the same speed.

E P Q9 Masses of $4m$ kg and $3m$ kg are connected by a light, inextensible string and hang vertically, either side of a smooth, fixed pulley. They are released from rest.

a) Show, algebraically, that the magnitude of the acceleration of the particles does not depend on the value of m. *[4 marks]*

b) Show, algebraically, that the tension in the string is proportional to m. *[1 mark]*

P Q10 Two particles, P and Q, of mass 8 kg and 10 kg respectively, are attached to the ends of a light, inextensible string which passes over a fixed, smooth pulley. P is held at rest on a smooth horizontal surface, 4 m from the pulley, and Q hangs vertically, 9 m above the horizontal ground, as shown. The system is released from rest and P begins to accelerate towards the pulley. At the instant P hits the pulley, the string breaks and Q then moves freely under gravity until it hits the ground. Find the time between the instant the particles are released from rest and the instant when Q hits the ground.

4 m
T
P(8 kg)
T
Q(10 kg)
9 m

Challenge

E P Q11 Two particles, A and B, with masses of 1 kg and 6 kg respectively, are connected by a light, inextensible string and hang vertically, either side of a smooth, fixed pulley. They are released from rest, both at a height of 3 m above the ground. It is assumed that the pulley is high enough above the starting position that the lighter particle does not reach it.

a) Find the magnitude of the acceleration of each mass. *[4 marks]*

b) Find the tension in the string. *[1 mark]*

c) How many seconds after release does the heavier particle hit the ground? *[1 mark]*

d) When the heavier particle hits the ground, the lighter particle continues to move under the influence of gravity. What is the maximum height it reaches, above its starting position, again assuming that it does not reach the height of the pulley? *[3 marks]*

8.7 Harder Problems involving Pegs and Pulleys

These questions are just like those on the previous few pages, but they also include **resistance forces**. The method for answering them is exactly the same as for the problems on the previous pages: resolve the forces acting on **each particle** separately in the **direction of acceleration**.

Remember that as long as the string connecting the particles is **light** and **inextensible**, and the peg or pulley is **smooth**, the **tension** in the string will be **constant** and the two particles will have the same **magnitude** of **acceleration**.

Example 1

A block, A, of mass 6 kg, is placed on a rough horizontal table. A light, inextensible string connects A to a second block, B, of mass 12 kg. The string passes over a fixed, smooth peg and B hangs vertically, as shown. The system is released from rest.

Given that A experiences a fixed resistance force F of 30 N, find the tension in the string.

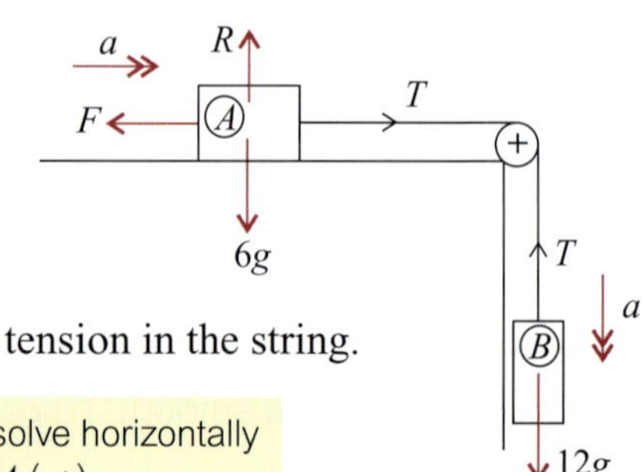

$F_{net} = ma \Rightarrow T - F = 6a$ ← Resolve horizontally for A (→).

$\Rightarrow a = \frac{1}{6}(T - 30)$ — call this equation ①

$F_{net} = ma \Rightarrow 12g - T = 12a$ — call this equation ② ← Resolve vertically for B (↓).

continued on the next page...

Tip
A well-drawn force diagram is really important for these trickier problems.

$12g - T = 12 \times \frac{1}{6}(T - 30) \Rightarrow 12g - T = 2T - 60$ ← Substitute equation 1 into equation 2.

$\Rightarrow 3T = 117.6 + 60 = 177.6 \Rightarrow T = 59$ N (to 2 s.f.)

Exercise 8.7

Give your answers to an appropriate degree of accuracy unless otherwise stated.

P **Q1** Two particles A and B, of mass 6 kg and M kg respectively, are joined by a light, inextensible string which passes over a fixed, smooth pulley. The particles are held at rest with A on a rough, horizontal surface and B hanging vertically, as shown on the right. Given that A experiences a constant resistance force, F, of 10 N and that the tension in the string has magnitude 12 N, find:

a) the acceleration of A immediately after the particles are released,

b) the value of M.

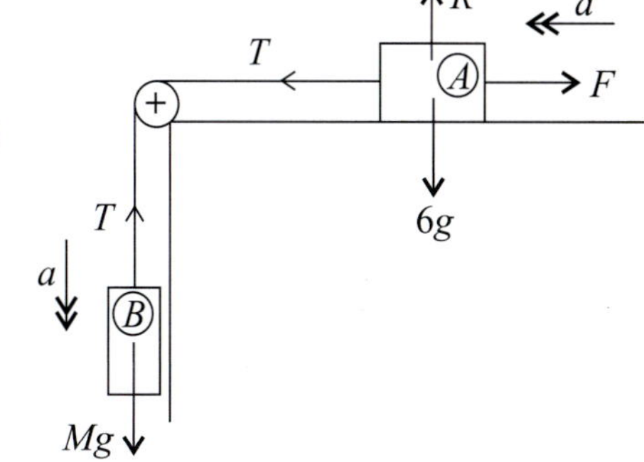

P **Q2** Two particles, A and B, have mass 3 kg and M kg respectively. Particle A lies on a rough table and is attached to one end of a light, inextensible string that passes over a smooth pulley P, as shown. Particle B is attached to the other end of the string and hangs freely, vertically below P and 1.5 m above the ground. A constant resistance force of 15 N acts on Particle A. Particle B hits the ground 3 seconds after the system is released from rest and before A reaches the pulley.

Find the value of M.

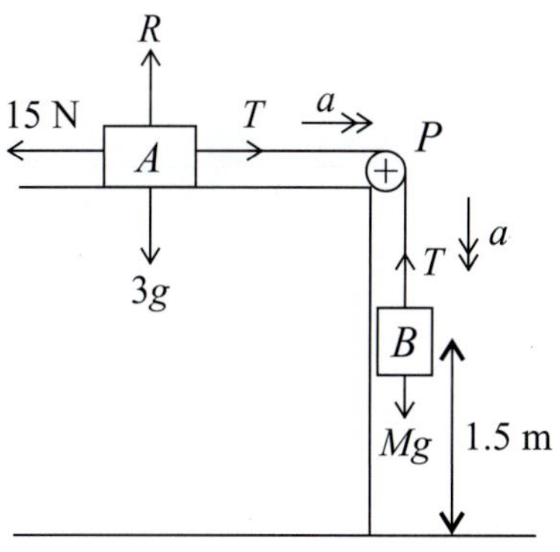

E P **Q3** Two particles, A and B, of mass 2 kg and 4 kg respectively, are joined by a light, inextensible string. The string passes over a fixed, smooth pulley at the edge of a rough horizontal surface. Particle A is resting on the surface and B hangs vertically. The frictional force acting on A is constant at 5 N.

a) Find the acceleration of the particles, following their release. *[4 marks]*

b) Find the tension in the string, on release. *[1 mark]*

c) What value would the frictional force need to be in order for the system not to move when released? *[2 marks]*

P M **Q4**

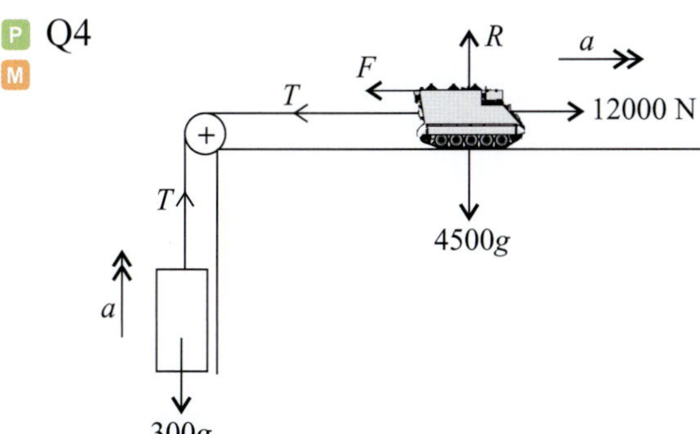

A 4500 kg buggy is lifting a 300 kg stone slab using a light, inextensible rope which passes over a fixed, smooth pulley, as shown. Initially, the slab is at rest on the ground below the pulley and the rope is taut. The buggy produces a driving force of 12 000 N and is slowed by a constant resistance force of F N.

The slab reaches 2 ms^{-1} after 6 seconds. Find the magnitude of the resistance force F N.

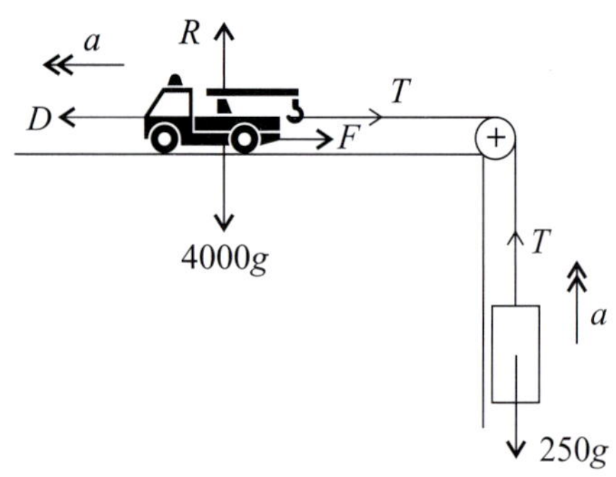

P M **Q5** A 4000 kg truck is lifting a 250 kg crate of building materials, using a light inextensible rope which passes over a fixed smooth pulley, as shown. Initially, the crate is at rest on the ground below the pulley and the rope is taut. The truck produces a driving force of D newtons and is slowed by a constant resistance force F of 500 N.

a) The crate reaches 3 ms^{-1} after 5 seconds. Find the magnitude of the driving force, D.

b) When the crate reaches 3 ms^{-1}, the rope snaps. Given that the driving force remains the same, what is the truck's new acceleration?

Q5b) Hint When the rope snaps, the tension force T will disappear.

c) After the rope snaps, the crate travels freely, experiencing no resistance forces. How much time elapses between the moment when the rope snaps, and when the crate hits the ground?

d) Give a possible improvement that could be made to this model.

E P **Q6** Two particles, A and B, of mass 3 kg and M kg respectively, are joined by a light, inextensible string, which passes over a fixed, smooth pulley. Particle A is held at rest on a rough horizontal surface and B hangs vertically, as shown. The frictional force acting on A is constant at 3 N.

a) Steve says that, in order for the system to move on release, the mass of B must exceed the mass of A. Explain why he is wrong and find the minimum value of M required for movement. *[4 marks]*

b) Given that the acceleration of the system is 2 ms^{-2} on release, find the mass of particle B and the tension in the string. *[4 marks]*

Challenge

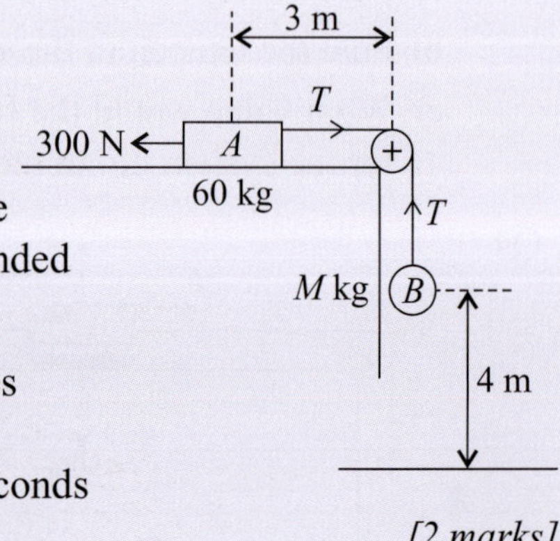

E P M **Q7** A paving slab, A, is positioned 3 m from the edge of a flat, horizontal roof. It is attached to a light, inextensible rope, which passes over a smooth, fixed pulley at the edge of the roof and is attached to a rock, B, with mass M kg, as shown in the diagram. The paving slab has a mass of 60 kg and the frictional force between it and the roof is 300 N. B is suspended 4 m above horizontal ground. The system is held at rest.

a) The system is released from rest. Find the range of values for acceleration, a, that would result in the paving stone reaching the edge of the roof in an interval less than 3 seconds and more than 1 second from release. *[2 marks]*

b) Hence find the range of possible values of M for this interval. *[7 marks]*

8 Review Exercise

Give your answers to an appropriate degree of accuracy unless otherwise stated.

Q1 Find the magnitude and direction of the following forces, giving your answers to 3 s.f.

a) (5**i** + 12**j**) kN b) (2**i** – 5**j**) N c) (–3**i** + 8**j**) kN d) (–4**i** – 11**j**) N

Q2 A force (x**i** + y**j**) N, with direction parallel to the vector (2**i** + 7**j**) N, acts on a particle, P. Find the angle between the vector **j** and the force.

P Q3 An object is acted upon by two forces of $\begin{pmatrix} 11 \\ -6 \end{pmatrix}$ N and $\begin{pmatrix} -8 \\ 4 \end{pmatrix}$ N.

a) Find the resultant force acting on the object as a column vector.

b) A third force is applied such that the object is now in equilibrium. Find the magnitude and direction of this additional force to 1 d.p.

E Q4 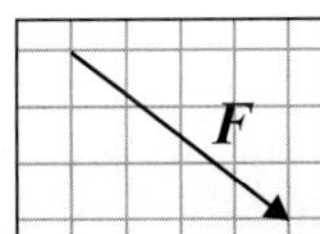

The diagram shows how a force, $\boldsymbol{F}$, acts on a particle. In the diagram, the side length of 1 square represents 1 newton.

a) Write $\boldsymbol{F}$ as a column vector. *[1 mark]*

b) The force $\boldsymbol{G}$ is perpendicular to $\boldsymbol{F}$, has positive coefficients of **i** and **j** and has equal magnitude to $\boldsymbol{F}$. Write $\boldsymbol{G}$ as a vector in terms of the components **i** and **j**. *[1 mark]*

E P Q5 Three forces $\boldsymbol{F}_1$ = (2**i** + a**j**) N, $\boldsymbol{F}_2$ = (3a**i** – 2b**j**) N and $\boldsymbol{F}_3$ = (b**i** + 2**j**) N act on a particle P.

a) Find the resultant force, $\boldsymbol{R}$, in terms of a and b. *[2 marks]*

b) Given that the force $\boldsymbol{F}_1$ acts at an angle of 45° to **i** and that $a > 0$, find the value of a. *[1 mark]*

c) The magnitude of the resultant force $\boldsymbol{R}$ is $3\sqrt{10}$ N. Find all of the possible values for b. *[3 marks]*

E Q6 In this question, **i** represents the unit vector in the easterly direction and **j** represents the unit vector in the northerly direction. A force, $\boldsymbol{F}$, acts in an exact north-easterly direction. Its magnitude is 5 N.

a) Write the force as a column vector. *[2 marks]*

b) Write, as column vectors, the two forces which are perpendicular to $\boldsymbol{F}$ and which have magnitude equal to $\boldsymbol{F}$. *[2 marks]*

E Q7 Two forces, $\begin{pmatrix} -4 \\ 6 \end{pmatrix}$ N and $\begin{pmatrix} 1 \\ -7 \end{pmatrix}$ N, act on a particle.

a) Find the resultant force. *[1 mark]*

b) Find the magnitude of the resultant force. *[2 marks]*

c) Find the direction of the resultant force. *[2 marks]*

d) A third force is now added to the system. The resultant force is now $\begin{pmatrix} 3 \\ 4 \end{pmatrix}$ N. Find the third force. *[1 mark]*

E P Q8 Two forces, $\boldsymbol{F} = \begin{pmatrix} -4 \\ a \end{pmatrix}$ N and $\boldsymbol{G} = \begin{pmatrix} 2 \\ a \end{pmatrix}$ N, where a is a positive constant, act on an object.
Show that the angle, θ, between the two forces satisfies the equation $\cos\theta = \frac{a^2 - 8}{\sqrt{(a^2 + 16)(a^2 + 4)}}$. *[3 marks]*

Q9 A horizontal force of 2 N acts on a 1.5 kg particle which is initially at rest on a smooth horizontal plane. Find the speed of the particle 3 seconds after it is released from rest.

Q10 A horizontal force of F N acts on a 7 kg particle which is initially at rest on a smooth horizontal plane. After 6 seconds the particle is travelling at 3 ms^{-1}. Find the force F.

Q11 A particle with mass 300 g is accelerating at 5 ms^{-2}.
Find the magnitude of the resultant force acting on the particle.

E Q12 A particle is released from a height of 5 m above the ground. It hits the ground 1.2 seconds later. During the period of its fall, there is a constant resistive force, R, acting vertically upwards. Given that the particle's mass is 8 kg, find the size of R. *[3 marks]*

E Q13 A particle, mass 4 kg, has initial velocity 10 ms^{-1}. Two forces act on it in the horizontal direction — a tension force of 3 N in the direction of travel, and a frictional force of 1.2 N. How far will the particle have travelled after 4 seconds? *[3 marks]*

M Q14 A 3 kg parcel is attached to a light, inextensible rope. It starts at rest on the ground with the rope taut, and then is pulled vertically upwards by a constant force for 3 seconds, reaching a height of 2.7 m.

a) Find the acceleration of the parcel.

b) Find the tension in the rope.

Q15 A particle of mass 2 kg is attached to the end of a taut, vertical string. Given that the particle is accelerating vertically downwards at 2 ms^{-2}, find T, the tension in the string.

E Q16 A constant force of $(15\mathbf{i} + 9\mathbf{j})$ N begins acting on a particle which is initially at rest. The particle has mass 6 kg. What is the velocity of the particle after 4 seconds? *[2 marks]*

Q17 A particle of mass 4 kg is acted on by a force $\boldsymbol{F} = (4\mathbf{i} - 2\mathbf{j})$ N.

a) Find the acceleration of the particle as a vector in the form $(x\mathbf{i} + y\mathbf{j})$ ms^{-2}.

b) The particle starts and continues to move across a rough surface, experiencing a resistive force of $(-\mathbf{i} + 2\mathbf{j})$ N. Find the magnitude of the acceleration of the particle across the rough surface.

P Q18 Two forces act on a particle of mass 8 kg which is initially at rest on a smooth horizontal plane. The two forces are $(24\mathbf{i} + 18\mathbf{j})$ N and $(6\mathbf{i} + 22\mathbf{j})$ N (with $\mathbf{i}$ and $\mathbf{j}$ being perpendicular unit vectors in the plane). Find:

a) the magnitude and direction of the resulting acceleration of the particle,

b) the particle's distance from its starting point after 3 seconds.

E P Q19 A particle of mass 5 kg moves along a straight, narrow track with initial velocity $(12\mathbf{i} + 5\mathbf{j})$ ms^{-1}. It encounters a resultant force of $(-1.2\mathbf{i} - 0.5\mathbf{j})$ N.

a) What angle does the track make with the x-axis? *[2 marks]*

b) How far will the particle travel before it comes to rest? *[3 marks]*

M Q20 A lift of mass 320 kg is carrying a crate with mass 40 kg. The crate and lift are accelerating vertically downwards at a rate of 0.4 ms^{-2}. The lift is suspended from a light, inextensible cable.

a) Find the tension, T, in the cable.

b) Find the reaction force between the crate and the bottom of the lift.

M Q21 A tractor of mass 2 tonnes experiences a resistance force of 1000 N while driving along a straight horizontal road. The tractor engine provides a forward force of 1500 N and it pulls a trailer of mass 1 tonne. Given that the tractor is accelerating at 0.05 ms^{-2}, find:

a) the resistance force, F, acting on the trailer,

b) the tension in the coupling between the tractor and trailer.

Q22 Particles A and B, of mass 3 kg and 4 kg respectively, are connected by a light, inextensible string which passes over a fixed, smooth pulley at the edge of a smooth horizontal surface. Particle A is resting on the surface and particle B is hanging vertically. The system is released from rest.

a) Find the magnitude of the acceleration of the particles.

b) Find the tension in the string.

c) What assumptions have you made in your model?

P Q23 Two particles are connected by a light, inextensible string and hang in a vertical plane either side of a fixed, smooth pulley. When released from rest the particles accelerate at 1.2 ms^{-2}. Given that the heavier particle has mass 4 kg, find the mass of the other particle.

E Q24 Particle A, of mass 2 kg, is at rest on a smooth, horizontal surface. It is connected by a light, inextensible string which passes over a smooth pulley to particle B, of mass m kg, which hangs vertically, as shown.

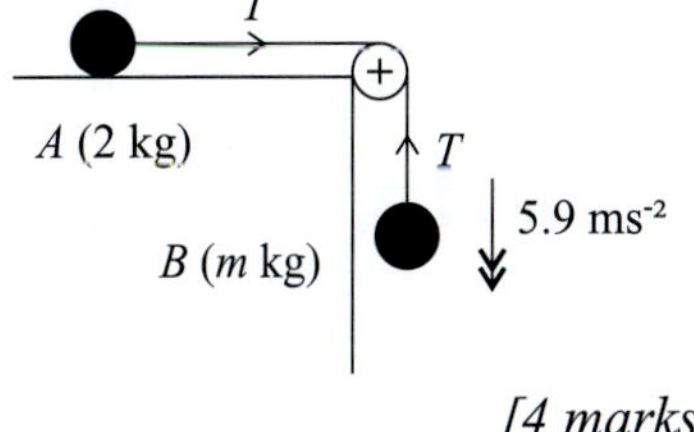

The system is released from rest and moves with acceleration 5.9 ms^{-2}. Find the tension, T, in the string and the value of m. *[4 marks]*

E P Q25 Particles A and B of mass m kg and $(m + 5)$ kg respectively are attached to the ends of a light, inextensible string. The string passes over a smooth, fixed pulley and the particles hang with the string taut and both particles 1 m above the floor. The system is released from rest.

a) Show that the acceleration in the string before B hits the floor is $\frac{49}{2m+5}$. *[4 marks]*

b) Given that the tension in the string before B reaches the floor is 36.75 N, find m. *[4 marks]*

c) B reaches the floor before A reaches the pulley, and A moves vertically and freely under gravity in the subsequent motion. Find the greatest height above the floor reached by A. *[4 marks]*

Q26 A light, inextensible string passing over a smooth pulley connects boxes A and B, of mass 10 kg and 8 kg respectively, as shown in the diagram.

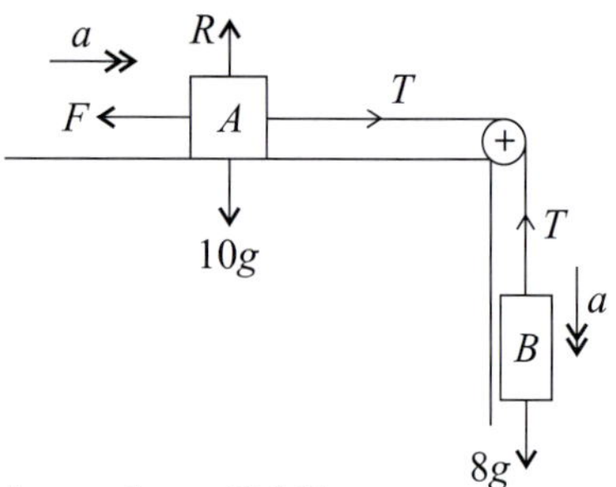

The system is released from rest and the boxes begin to accelerate at a rate of 0.5 ms^{-2}. Box A experiences a constant frictional force F. Find the magnitude of F.

E P M Q27 On a building site, a light, inextensible rope passes over a horizontal scaffolding pole (modelled as a smooth peg) 10 m above the ground. A box of sandwiches of mass 3 kg is attached to the end of the rope 1.5 m above the ground.

a) The sandwiches are raised from rest to a height 0.5 m below the peg in 4 seconds. What is the value of the constant force that was applied to the other end of the rope in order to raise the sandwiches? *[3 marks]*

The sandwiches are removed and the rope is lowered. A bucket of mortar (modelled as a particle) weighing 35 kg is now attached to the end of the rope, again 1.5 m above the ground.

b) If a force of 382.4 N is applied to the other end of the rope, how long will it take the bucket to reach the same height as the sandwiches? *[3 marks]*

E P M Q28 A snowmobile with mass 300 kg pulls two sleds, each of mass 120 kg, over horizontal ground. The snowmobile experiences a constant resistive force of $5R$ N, and each sled experiences a constant resistive force of R N. The driving force of the snowmobile is 1900 N and the couplings between both the snowmobile and the first sled, and between the two sleds, are modelled as horizontal, light and rigid.

a) Given that the snowmobile achieves an acceleration of 0.2 ms^{-2}, find R. *[3 marks]*

b) Find the tension in the coupling between the two sleds. *[2 marks]*

c) Find the tension in the coupling between the snowmobile and the first sled. *[2 marks]*

d) More identical sleds are added to the snowmobile. Given that the maximum driving force for the snowmobile is 2500 N, find the maximum number of sleds that the snowmobile can pull, and the acceleration that it can achieve with this number of sleds. Assume the resistive forces for the snowmobile and each sled remain the same. *[5 marks]*

Challenge

E P Q29 $\boldsymbol{F}_1 = (\mathbf{i} + 8\mathbf{j})$ N and $\boldsymbol{F}_2 = (-4\mathbf{i} + k\mathbf{j})$ N. The magnitude of $\boldsymbol{F}_2$ is the same as the magnitude of $\boldsymbol{F}_1$. Find the possible values of θ, the angle between the forces. *[5 marks]*

E P Q30 Two forces, $(-3\mathbf{i} + 2\mathbf{j})$ N and $(4\mathbf{i} - \mathbf{j})$ N, act on a particle.

a) Find the resultant force and its magnitude and direction. *[3 marks]*

b) A third force is now added to the system. The resultant force has a magnitude of 7 N at an angle of +30° to the horizontal. Find the third force. *[7 marks]*

E P **Q31** Three forces, $\begin{pmatrix} a \\ b \end{pmatrix}$, $\begin{pmatrix} 2b \\ -a \end{pmatrix}$, and $\begin{pmatrix} -11 \\ 2 \end{pmatrix}$, act on a particle, where **i** is the unit vector in the positive horizontal (right) direction and **j** is the unit vector in the positive vertical (upwards) direction.

a) If the resultant force on the particle acts in a horizontal direction, find an expression for a in terms of b. *[2 marks]*

b) If the particle is in equilibrium, find a and b. *[2 marks]*

c) If the resultant force acts at an angle of 45° upwards from the positive horizontal direction, find:

(i) an expression for b in terms of a. *[2 marks]*

(ii) the range of possible values of a and b. *[3 marks]*

E P M **Q32** Two marbles are modelled as particles and each has mass 8 g.
Marble A accelerates from rest with a constant acceleration of $\begin{pmatrix} 20 \\ 50 \end{pmatrix}$ cms^{-2} from a point on a straight, horizontal track. Marble B, beginning from rest at the same point, starts to move 4 seconds later, under the influence of a force of $\begin{pmatrix} 0.004 \\ 0.01 \end{pmatrix}$ N.

a) Find the force acting on Marble A. *[2 marks]*

b) How many seconds after Marble A begins its journey will one of the marbles have travelled twice as far as the other? Assume the marbles do not collide. *[7 marks]*

E P M **Q33** An engine of mass 1200 kg is towing a carriage using a light, inextensible rope. The mass of the empty carriage is 200 kg and it has a load of 600 kg. During a period of 10 seconds, the engine accelerates from stationary at a constant rate to reach a velocity of 10 ms^{-1}. The resistive forces on the engine and the carriage are 5% of their weight (in the case of the carriage, this includes the weight of the load).

a) Assuming the driving force of the engine remains the same, what would the load in the carriage have to be reduced to for the engine and carriage to reach 15 ms^{-1} over the same period? *[6 marks]*

b) What would be the difference between the tension, T_1, in the rope in the given scenario and the tension, T_2, in the rope in the scenario in part a)? *[4 marks]*

P **Q34** Two particles, A and B, of mass 500 g and 750 g respectively, are attached to the ends of a light, inextensible string which passes over a fixed, smooth pulley. A is held at rest on a smooth horizontal surface, 2 m from the pulley, and B hangs vertically, 3 m above the horizontal ground, as shown.

The system is released from rest and B begins to accelerate towards the ground. At the instant A hits the pulley, the string breaks and B then moves freely under gravity until it hits the ground.

Find the time between the instant the particles are released from rest and the instant when B hits the ground.

8 Chapter Summary

1 Forces have magnitude (size) and direction, so they can be treated as vectors, $\begin{pmatrix} x \\ y \end{pmatrix}$.

2 The magnitude of a force is measured in newtons (N), the direction of a force is the angle measured anticlockwise from the horizontal. The angle with the horizontal is given by $\tan^{-1}\left(\frac{y}{x}\right)$.

3 A force can be described using the unit vectors **i** (for the horizontal) and **j** (for the vertical), so that a column vector $\begin{pmatrix} x \\ y \end{pmatrix}$ can be written as $x\mathbf{i} + y\mathbf{j}$.

4 The resultant force is the combined effect of all the forces acting on an object. To find this, resolve the forces and add up all the horizontal (**i**-) components and all the vertical (**j**-) components separately.

5 An object is in equilibrium when all the forces acting on the object cancel out and the resultant force is zero.

6 Newton's laws of motion:

- Newton's first law: A body will stay at rest or maintain a constant velocity unless a resultant force acts on the body.
- Newton's second law: The overall resultant force (F_{net}) acting on a body is equal to the mass of the body multiplied by the body's acceleration: $F_{net} = ma$.
- Newton's third law: For two bodies, A and B, the force exerted by A on B is equal in magnitude but opposite in direction to the force exerted by B on A.

7 When two particles are connected by something light, inextensible and taut, and are moving in the same straight line, they can be treated as one particle moving with the same acceleration.

8 When two particles are connected by a light, inextensible and taut string, tension occurs. The string exerts an equal tension force at both ends and usually in opposite directions. The opposite to tension is thrust — this occurs when a rigid rod connects two particles and pushes on them with equal force.

9 If two particles are connected by an inextensible string which passes over a peg or pulley, they will have the same acceleration but in different directions. These types of problem can sometimes involve resistance forces.

Edexcel AS-Level Mathematics

Paper 2: Statistics and Mechanics

Time allowed: 1 hour 15 Minutes

Centre name					
Centre number					
Candidate number					

Surname
Other names
Candidate signature

In addition to this paper you should have:
- An Edexcel booklet of Mathematical Formulae and Statistical Tables
- A calculator

Instructions to candidates
- Use black ink or ball-point pen.
- A pencil may be used for diagrams, sketches and graphs.
- Write your name and other details in the spaces provided above.
- Show clearly how you worked out your answers.
- Round answers to 3 significant figures unless otherwise stated.

Information for candidates
- There are 9 questions in this paper.
- There are 60 marks available for this paper.
- The marks available are given in brackets at the end of each question.
- You may get marks for method, even if your answer is incorrect.

Advice to candidates
- Work steadily through the paper and try to answer every question.
- Don't spend too long on one question.
- If you have time at the end, go back and check your answers.

For examiner's use			
Q	Mark	Q	Mark
1		6	
2		7	
3		8	
4		9	
5			
Total			

SECTION A: STATISTICS

Answer ALL the questions.

Q1 The scatter diagram below shows data from the large data set for Jacksonville for a random sample of days during May-October 1987. A regression line has been drawn for the data.

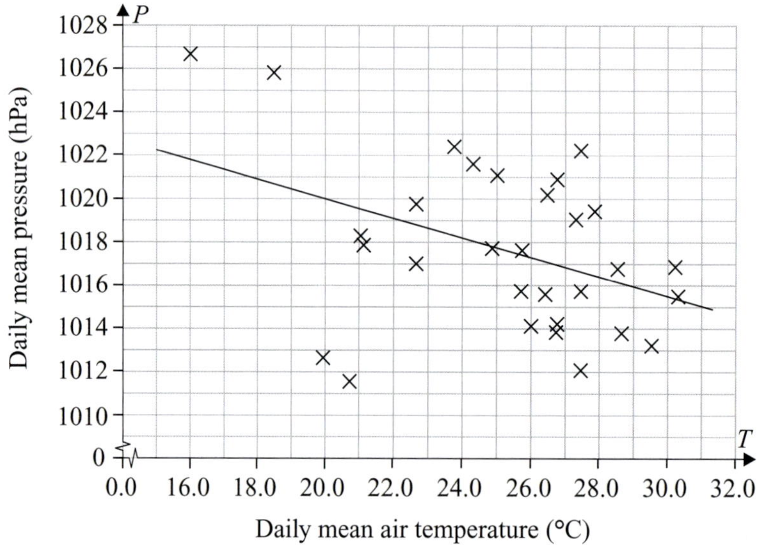

a) State: (i) the explanatory variable,
(ii) the response variable.

(1)

b) Describe the correlation between daily mean air temperature and daily mean pressure shown on the diagram.

(1)

The equation of the regression line of P on T is $P = -0.45T + 1029$.

c) Interpret the gradient of the regression line.

(1)

d) (i) Use the equation of the regression line to predict the daily mean pressure for a daily mean temperature of 10 °C.

(1)

(ii) Comment on the reliability of this prediction, giving a reason for your answer.

(1)

Q2 Philippa is using the large data set to investigate daily total rainfall in Leuchars. She selects a random sample of size 6 from the May, June and July data for 2015. Readings are available for all dates from these months. Philippa wishes to calculate the standard deviation of her sample data.

a) Using your knowledge of the large data set, suggest a difficulty that Philippa might face when calculating the standard deviation.

(1)

Philippa codes her sample data using the coding $y = 10x - 2$, where y is the coded value and x is the original value for daily total rainfall (x mm). The coded values are:

4 0 224 6 152 20

b) Calculate:

(i) $\sum y$ (ii) $\sum y^2$

(2)

c) Using your answers to b), calculate the mean and standard deviation of the coded data.

(2)

d) Find the standard deviation of Philippa's original data.

(1)

Q3 A company employs interpreters who speak a range of languages.

R represents the event that an employee speaks Russian.
S represents the event that an employee speaks Spanish.
M represents the event that an employee speaks Mandarin.

The company wants to select an employee at random to complete a questionnaire. The Venn diagram on the right shows the probabilities of choosing an employee who speaks each language or combination of languages.

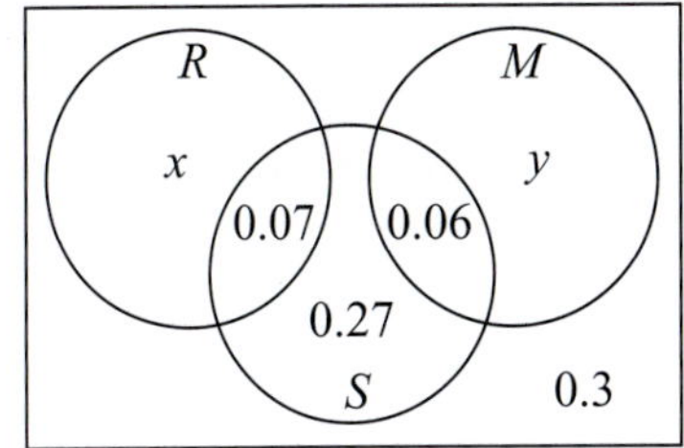

The events *S* and *M* are statistically independent.

a) Find the values of x and y.

(3)

b) Find the probability that a randomly selected employee speaks Mandarin or Spanish, but not both.

(1)

The company decides to send the questionnaire to several employees instead. The employees are listed alphabetically and one of the first 10 is selected at random. That employee and every tenth employee after them is selected to receive the questionnaire.

c) Give the name of the sampling method the company is using.

(1)

Q4 A factory that produces springs selects a random sample of 80 springs. They use this sample to test the amount of force that can be applied to each spring before it breaks. The table on the right summarises the data obtained from the sample.

Maximum force applied before breaking (x newtons)	Frequency
$0 \leq x < 5$	3
$5 \leq x < 10$	20
$10 \leq x < 15$	45
$15 \leq x < 20$	8
$20 \leq x < 25$	3
$25 \leq x < 30$	1

a) Find the class interval containing the median.

(2)

b) Use linear interpolation to find an estimate for the median.

(3)

c) Using the raw data it is found that $Q_1 = 9.4$ N and $Q_3 = 14.2$ N, and that the single value in the class interval $25 \leq x < 30$ is 28.8 N. Using $Q_3 + (1.5 \times \text{IQR})$ as the upper fence, show that the value 28.8 N is an outlier.

(1)

Q5 A biologist inspects potato plants in a large field. The probability, p, that a given potato plant is infected with a certain fungus is thought to be 0.3. The biologist uses a binomial distribution and this probability to model the number of plants infected with the fungus.

a) If the biologist inspects 30 randomly-selected plants, find the probability that at least 12 of these are infected with the fungus.

(2)

The biologist suggests that the value of p has been underestimated. They select a random sample of 25 potato plants from the field and find that 10 of them are infected with the fungus.

b) Using a 5% significance level and clearly stating your hypotheses, find the critical region for a one-tailed hypothesis test to determine whether the value of p has been underestimated.

(3)

c) Explain whether the biologist should reject the null hypothesis. Interpret the outcome of this hypothesis test in context.

(2)

The fungus is known to be easily passed from one plant to another.

d) Given the above information, explain whether a binomial distribution would be appropriate for modelling the infection of the potato plants.

(1)

SECTION B: MECHANICS

Answer ALL the questions.

Unless told otherwise, take $g = 9.8\ \text{ms}^{-2}$ wherever a numerical value is required.

Q6 A particle P of mass m kg is acted upon by two forces, $\boldsymbol{F}_1 = \begin{pmatrix} 2.5 \\ -2 \end{pmatrix}$ N and $\boldsymbol{F}_2 = \begin{pmatrix} 9.5 \\ 5.5 \end{pmatrix}$ N.

a) Find the magnitude of the resultant force acting on P.

(3)

b) Given that P accelerates at $2\ \text{ms}^{-2}$, find the value of m.

(2)

Q7 A particle Q travels along a straight line such that the velocity, $v\ \text{ms}^{-1}$, of the particle at time t seconds is given by the equation $v = 1.4 - 0.9t + 0.1t^2$ for $t \geq 0$. Q is at the origin when $t = 0$.

a) Find the magnitude of the initial acceleration of Q.

(2)

b) Find the times at which Q is instantaneously at rest.

(2)

c) Find the total distance travelled by Q during the first 7 seconds.

(4)

Q8 A stone, S, is projected vertically upwards from a level surface with initial speed $25\ \text{ms}^{-1}$. One second later another stone, T, is projected vertically upwards from the same point with initial speed $32\ \text{ms}^{-1}$. The two stones collide while in mid-air.

After projection, S and T move freely under gravity and are modelled as particles.

a) Find the height above the point of projection at which the stones collide and determine whether the stones are travelling in the same direction or opposite directions when they collide.

(7)

b) Explain how the assumption that the stones move freely under gravity has been used in your calculations.

(1)

Q9 A cage of mass 50 kg has a heavy load of mass 600 kg placed inside it. The cage and its load are initially at rest on a level surface before being raised vertically upwards by means of a light inextensible rope attached to the top of the cage. The cage accelerates upwards at 0.05 ms^{-2}.

a) Find the tension T in the rope.

(2)

b) (i) Find the normal reaction force R exerted by the load on the floor of the cage.

(ii) With reference to Newton's laws, explain how the size of the normal reaction force of the floor of the cage on the load compares to the value of R, found in part (i), as the cage accelerates upwards.

(3)

A velocity-time graph for the motion of the cage is shown below. After accelerating for 6 seconds the cage moves at a constant speed for $3k$ seconds before decelerating and coming to rest in a further k seconds.

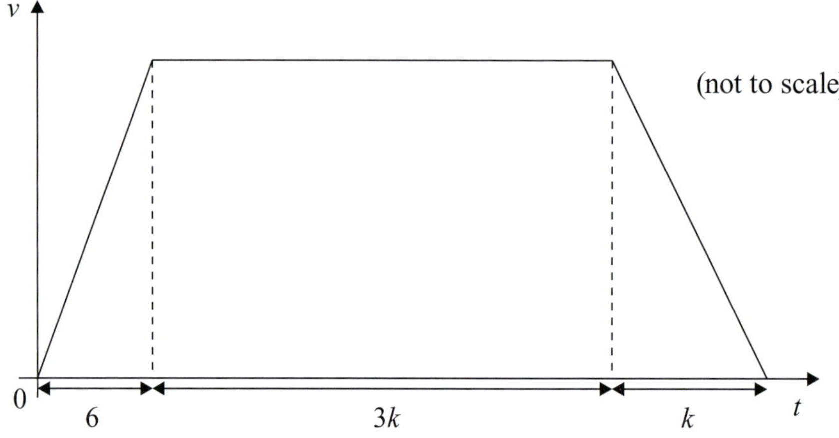

c) The cage is raised a total of 9.3 m. With the aid of the graph, determine the deceleration of the cage as it comes to rest.

(4)

Chapter 1: Statistical Sampling

Prior Knowledge Check

Q1 **a)** E.g. The population, secondary school students in the UK, is too large for them to collect data about every member, so sampling will be much more practical.

b) E.g. If they only obtain data from a single school, their results may be biased and not representative of secondary school pupils across the UK.

c) E.g. By increasing their sample size.

Chapter 1 Review Exercise

Q1 **a)** Finite **b)** Infinite

Although there are technically a finite number of people in Australia, counting them precisely would be impossible.

c) Infinite **d)** Finite

e) Finite **f)** Infinite

Q2 **a)** **(i)** A population is the whole group that you want to investigate. *[1 mark]*

(ii) A sample is a subset of a population. *[1 mark]*

b) A sample is used to draw conclusions about a population when it is impossible or impractical to carry out a census of the whole population. *[1 mark]*

Q3 **a)** The population is all of the members of the book club.

b) A census should be used because all members of the book club should be consulted about the new book. Since it is a local book club, there should be few enough members to ask everyone.

Q4 **a)** The population is the 1200 students at the school.

b) One reason for using a sample is that it would be time-consuming and difficult to test every student in the school. Another reason is that it would be difficult to process the large amount of data.

Q5 **a)** A census would be more sensible. The results will be more accurate and there are only 8 people in the population, so it wouldn't take long to find out the required information for each person.

b) A sample survey should be done — testing all 500 toys would take too long and it would destroy all the toys.

c) A sample survey is the only option. The population is all the possible dice rolls — there are an infinite number of dice rolls, so you can only examine a sample of them.

Q6 **a)** A sampling unit is an individual member of a population that can be sampled.

b) A sampling frame is a full list of all the sampling units.

Q7 E.g. assuming that flipping the coin does not change or damage it in any way, the probability of getting heads would be the same in any flip, so the data won't be biased.

Q8 **a)** All of the students at the university. *[1 mark]*

b) The experiment might attract students who are enthusiastic about participating in physical activity, meaning those who don't enjoy physical activity may be underrepresented. *[1 mark for a suitable comment]*

Q9 Use a random-number generator to generate a list of 20 3-digit numbers, ignoring numbers outside of the range 001-500 and any repeated numbers. Then select the animals with the corresponding ID numbers.

Q10 Assign each book in the bookcase a number from 001 to 346. Use the table to choose six numbers. E.g. start at the top-left corner and go down the first column, looking for numbers that are less than or equal to 346. Then, move to the top of the second column and repeat the process, until you've found six numbers. Using this selection process gives the numbers 336, 080, 155, 060, 321, 211. Then choose the books with the matching numbers.
[2 marks available — 1 mark for a correct description of the use of the table, 1 mark for linking this to the selection of the books]
There are many different ways that a random-number table may be used — this is just one example.

Q11 **a)** Each individual in the population has an equal chance of being selected, and each selection made is independent of any other selection.

b) Advantage: a simple random sample is unbiased, so it should be representative of the population as a whole.
Disadvantage: a simple random sample may be inconvenient if the population is spread over a large area, or impossible if the population isn't completely known.

Q12 **a)** A census would not be appropriate because the springs are destroyed in the testing process, so a census would destroy all of the springs produced. *[1 mark]*

b) E.g. Stratified sampling is a suitable sampling method. There are five different types of springs, so a random sample could be taken from each type such that the proportion of each type in the sample of 50 is the same as the proportion in the total springs produced.
[2 marks available — 1 mark for a suitable sampling method, 1 mark for an explanation of how the sample could be taken]

Q13 **a)** The 108 dogs admitted to the sanctuary between 2015 and 2016.

b) Give each dog a 3-digit number between 001 and 108.
Calculate the regular interval: $108 \div 12 = 9$
Use a random-number generator to choose a starting point from 1 to 9. Keep adding 9 to the starting point and add all these dogs to the sample. e.g. if the starting point is 8, then the sample will be 008, 017, 026, 035, 044, 053, 062, 071, 080, 089, 098, 107

Q14 Give each house a 3-digit number between 001 and 173 corresponding to its house number. Using a random-number table, choose a starting point on the table and move along it 3 digits at a time. For each 3 digits, see if it is a 3-digit number between 001 and 173. If it is, include the house with that number. Choose the first 40 distinct numbers between 001 and 173 that you come across in the table. Survey the 40 houses which match the numbers you have chosen.

Q15 Total population $= 45 + 33 + 15 + 57 = 150$

Under 20: $\frac{45}{150} \times 10 = 3$

20 to 40: $\frac{33}{150} \times 10 = 2.2 \approx 2$

41 to 60: $\frac{15}{150} \times 10 = 1$

Over 60: $\frac{57}{150} \times 10 = 3.8 \approx 4$

Answers have been rounded to the nearest whole number because you can't have decimal amounts of people.

Q16 Total population = 1657 + 3488 + 2990 + 1602 + 1192 = 10 929

18 to 29: $\frac{1657}{10929} \times 150 = 22.742... = 23$

30 to 39: $\frac{3488}{10929} \times 150 = 47.872... = 48$

40 to 49: $\frac{2990}{10929} \times 150 = 41.037... = 41$

50 to 64: $\frac{1602}{10929} \times 150 = 21.987... = 22$

Over 64: $\frac{1192}{10929} \times 150 = 16.360... = 16$

[2 marks available — 2 marks for all values correct, otherwise 1 mark for at least two correct]

Q17 Total flagstones in delivery = 300 + 270 + 210 + 120 = 900.
Medium flagstones are $\frac{270}{900}$ = 30% of the total flagstones, so 18 medium flagstones is 30% of the total number of flagstones in the sample. So the sample size is 60.
[2 marks available — 1 mark for a correct method, 1 mark for the correct sample size]

Q18 a) The population is all of the foxes in the UK. *[1 mark]*

b) Infinite, as the population is impossible to count. *[1 mark]*

c) Knowledge of the whole population is impossible. *[1 mark]*

d) The foxes tested were all from a rural area, so might only be representative of that area/rural areas — the prevalence of the disease may be different in urban environments. *[1 mark]*

Q19 E.g. if the population is 'people in the UK', then his sample is likely to be unrepresentative, since the members are all in the same age range, and since they're friends they might like the same music. The sample could be improved by collecting data from other parts of the UK, other age ranges, etc.

Q20 Customers of the bookshop are likely to spend more time reading per week than people who aren't bookshop customers, so the sample taken is likely to be biased and not representative of the people in the local area.

Q21 a) Quota sample. The sample is non-random, so it could be biased. E.g. the interviewer is not told which ages to sample, so they might ask younger people, whose tea-drinking habits might be different from those of older people.

b) Systematic sample. There could be a pattern making the sample biased. For example: every 100th ticket number could correspond to a seat with a bad view — every 100th seat could be at the end of a row, which could have a worse view than seats in the middle.

c) Opportunity (or convenience) sample. The sample isn't representative of the population. For example: many people work between the hours of 9 am and 5 pm on a Monday — these people are excluded from the sample.

Q22 a) The suggested sample would be inappropriate because e.g. some members might attend lessons on more than one day each week, and some members may attend no taught lessons at all, so the categories suggested are not well-defined and may exclude part of the population.
[1 mark for a suitable reason]

b) A list of the members could be produced, with each member assigned a number from 1 to 550. A random number from 1 to 10 could be generated to indicate the first person selected from the list, and then every 10th person after that would be chosen for the sample.
[1 mark for a suitable explanation]

Q23 a) Stratified sampling selects the sample members from each category at random, but quota sampling doesn't use random sampling.
A stratified sample preserves the proportions of the different categories that the population has been split into, but a quota sample will not necessarily do this.

b) A stratified sample is likely to give a representative sample, and is useful when the results might vary depending on the categories in the population. However, a stratified sample requires full knowledge of the population, and may be expensive to carry out because of the extra detail involved.

Q24 a) Opportunity (or convenience) sampling *[1 mark]*

b) The customer may forget about the questionnaire/lose the questionnaire/not bother to return the questionnaire.
[1 mark for a sensible answer]

Q25 a) This sampling method is not suitable because students sitting together in a group may all be friends and have similar internet usage habits. Also the sample size is very small, so it could be biased as the results can easily be skewed.
[2 marks available — 1 mark for each correct reason]

b) E.g. she could take a stratified sample. She could take a random sample from each year group so the number of students from each year group in the sample are in the same proportions as the number of students from each year group in the school.
[2 marks available — 1 mark for a suitable sampling method, 1 mark for an explanation of how the sample could be taken]

Q26 a) Quota sampling would be an appropriate method, as there is a certain number of people in each category who must be interviewed.
The interviewer will approach people in the town centre to be interviewed. Once the quota has been reached in a certain category, no more individuals will be interviewed in that category. The interviewer will continue interviewing until the quota has been reached for each category.
[2 marks available — 1 mark for suggesting an appropriate sampling method, 1 mark for an accurate description]

b) Advantage: this type of sampling is possible even when it isn't possible to list the whole population.
Disadvantage: the sample could easily be biased, e.g. if the interviewer approaches people at a certain time of day or in a particular location.
[2 marks available — 1 mark for a correct advantage, 1 mark for a correct disadvantage]

Chapter 2: Data Presentation and Interpretation

Prior Knowledge Check

Q1

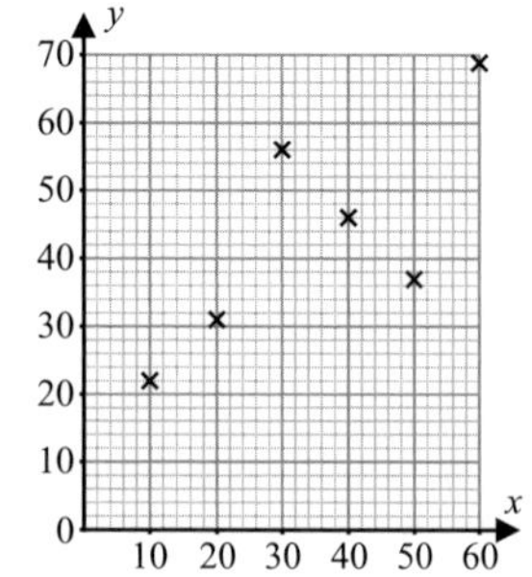

Q2 Put the data in order first: 29, 30, 32, 34, 34, 41, 44, 46

a) Mean = $\frac{29 + 30 + 32 + 34 + 34 + 41 + 44 + 46}{8} = 36.25$

b) $\frac{n}{2} = \frac{8}{2} = 4$, so the median is halfway between the 4th and 5th values.
Median = (34 + 34) ÷ 2 = 34.

c) Mode = 34

Q3 **a)** $3x = \frac{y-4}{3} \Rightarrow 9x = y - 4 \Rightarrow y = 9x + 4$

b) $3x = \frac{y-4}{3} \Rightarrow 9x = y - 4 \Rightarrow 9x - y + 4 = 0$

Q4 Gradient $= \frac{-2-16}{7-4} = \frac{-18}{3} = -6$

$y - (-2) = -6(x - 7) \Rightarrow y + 2 = -6x + 42 \Rightarrow y = -6x + 40$

Exercise 2.1 — Representing Data

Q1 **a)** Make, Colour

b) Mileage, Number of doors, Cost of service

Q2 **a)** Number of medals won last season, Shoe size

b) Height, Mass

Q3 **a)** The length of the leaves is continuous, as it could take any value in a given range — there aren't any gaps between possible lengths.

b) All of the data is numerical.

c) E.g. there are 100 data values in total, which could all be different / the length can only be measured to a certain degree of accuracy.

Q4 **a)** The data can only take integer values, so it is discrete.

b) Add up the frequencies of '11-15', '16-20' and '21+': 19 + 14 + 2 = 35 people.

Q5 **a)** There are no 'gaps' between possible heights.

b)

Height, h (cm)	No. of members	Lower class b'dary (cm)	Upper class b'dary (cm)	Class width (cm)	Class mid-point (cm)
$140 \le h < 150$	3	140	150	10	145
$150 \le h < 160$	9	150	160	10	155
$160 \le h < 170$	17	160	170	10	165
$170 \le h < 180$	12	170	180	10	175
$180 \le h < 190$	5	180	190	10	185
$190 \le h < 200$	1	190	200	10	195

c) Plot the mid-point of the classes on the x-axis and the frequencies on the y-axis.

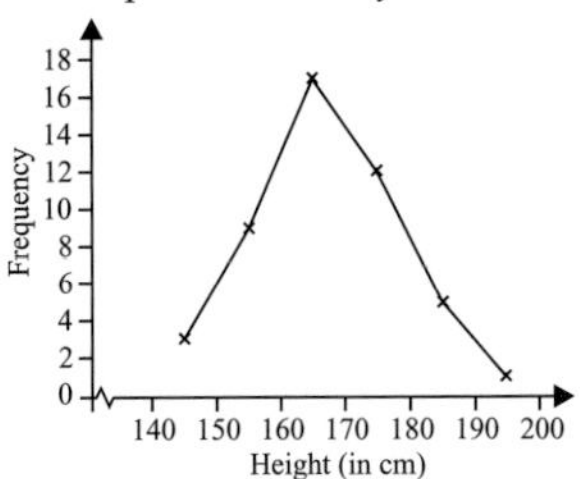

Q6 **a)** 112.5 minutes *[1 mark]*

b)

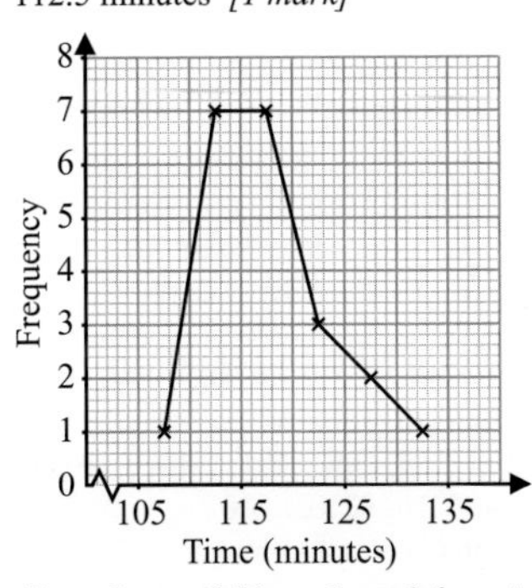

[3 marks available — 1 mark for using the mid-points, 1 mark for plotting the correct mid-point values, 1 mark for joining points to make a frequency polygon]

Q7 **a)** The data is numerical and can take any value, so it is a continuous quantitative variable.

b) The x-values of the points are halfway between whole centimetre intervals — e.g. 12.5 cm is halfway between 12 cm and 13 cm.
These are the mid-points of the classes, so the boundaries of the classes must be at each centimetre interval.

Length, l (cm)	Frequency
$12 \le l < 13$	2
$13 \le l < 14$	4
$14 \le l < 15$	9
$15 \le l < 16$	6
$16 \le l < 17$	7
$17 \le l < 18$	3

You might have written the inequalities slightly differently — you could swap < and ≤ in each inequality, so the classes would be 12 < l ≤ 13, 13 < l ≤ 14, etc. The signs need to be arranged the same way in each class though — you can't mix and match.

Exercise 2.2 — Histograms

Q1 First add columns to the table to show class boundaries, the class widths and the frequency densities.

Humidity, h (%)	Lower class boundary	Upper class boundary	Class width	Freq.	F.D.
$60 < h \le 80$	60	80	20	2	0.1
$80 < h \le 90$	80	90	10	9	0.9
$90 < h \le 95$	90	95	5	5	1
$95 < h \le 100$	95	100	5	4	0.8

Then you can draw the histogram:

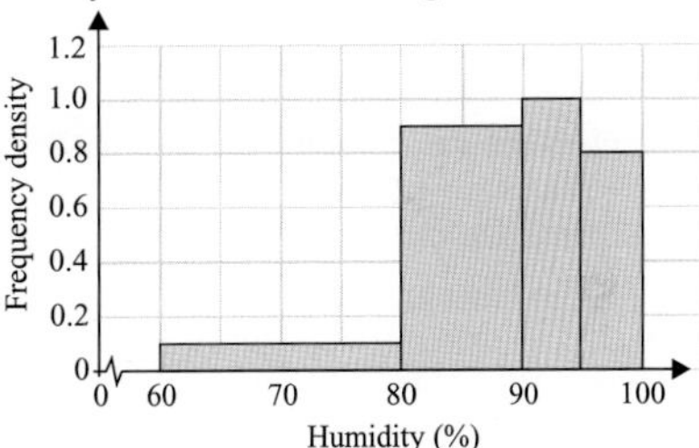

Q2 **a)** First you need to work out the scale on the vertical axis — use the information that the bar for 30-45 seconds represents 54 contestants.

<u>30-45 seconds class</u>:
Class width = 45 – 30 = 15 and frequency = 54
So frequency density = 54 ÷ 15 = 3.6
Height of bar = 18 small rectangles, so each small rectangle is worth 3.6 ÷ 18 = 0.2

<u>Bar for 10-30 seconds</u>:
Class width = 30 – 10 = 20
and frequency density = 3 × 0.2 = 0.6
So frequency = 0.6 × 20 = 12

So 12 auditions lasted less than 30 seconds.

b) Now you need to find the frequencies represented by the other bars as well.
Frequency density for '45-55' bar = 26 × 0.2 = 5.2,
so frequency = 5.2 × 10 = 52 contestants.
Frequency density for '55-60' bar = 30 × 0.2 = 6,
so frequency = 6 × 5 = 30 contestants.
Frequency density for '60-75' bar = 10 × 0.2 = 2,
so frequency = 2 × 15 = 30 contestants.
Frequency density for '75-90' bar = 4 × 0.2 = 0.8,
so frequency = 0.8 × 15 = 12 contestants.

Total number of contestants who auditioned:
12 + 54 + 52 + 30 + 30 + 12 = 190

c) The auditions of 30 + 12 = 42 contestants lasted longer than 60 seconds. So the percentage of contestants whose audition lasted longer than a minute is:
(42 ÷ 190) × 100 = 22.105...% = 22.1% (3 s.f.).

Q3 a) For $0 \le w < 10$ class: frequency density = 1 ÷ 10 = 0.1
$10 \le w < 20$ class: frequency density = 56 ÷ 10 = 5.6
$25 \le w < 35$ class: frequency density = 58 ÷ 10 = 5.8

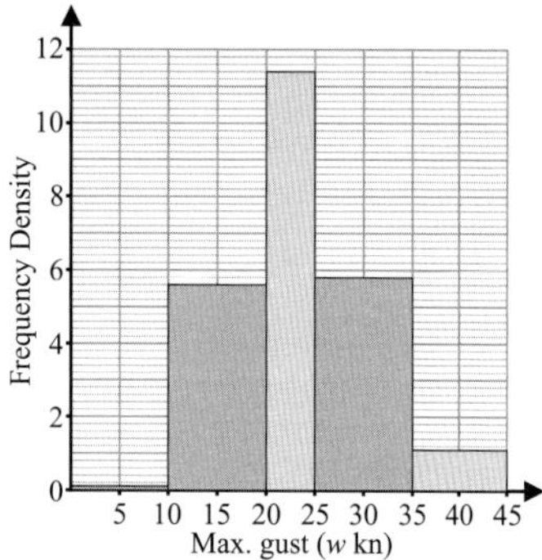

Then, using frequency = frequency density × class width:

Max. gust (w kn)	Frequency
$0 \le w < 10$	1
$10 \le w < 20$	56
$20 \le w < 25$	11.4 × 5 = 57
$25 \le w < 35$	58
$35 \le w < 45$	1.1 × 10 = 11

[3 marks available — 1 mark for all three histogram bars correct, 1 mark for using frequency = frequency density × class width, 1 mark for both entries in table correct]

b) E.g. Intervals have different class widths and the data is continuous.
[2 marks available — 1 mark for each sensible reason]

c) The data is grouped — you know there were 11 days in the highest class interval, but you can't tell what the individual maximum gusts are.
[1 mark for a correct reason]

Q4 a) The area of the 45-47 mm bar is 1.5 × 9 = 13.5 cm^2. This represents 12 butterflies. So each butterfly is represented by an area of 13.5 ÷ 12 = 1.125 cm^2. Then, for the 52-53 mm class, 22.5 ÷ 1.125 = 20, so the frequency is 20.
[2 marks available — 1 mark for finding the area that represents each butterfly, 1 mark for correct frequency]

b) The class 54-58 mm has lower class boundary 53.5 and upper class boundary 58.5. So the class width is 58.5 – 53.5 = 5. The first bar, representing a class of width 3, was 1.5 cm wide. So the bar representing the class 54-58 mm must be 2.5 cm wide.
And because it needs to represent a frequency of 14, its area must be 14 × 1.125 = 15.75 cm^2.
This means it must be 15.75 ÷ 2.5 = 6.3 cm high.
[3 marks available — 1 mark for finding the correct area, 1 mark for the correct width, 1 mark for the correct height]

Q5 a) Find the total area of all the bars:
You don't know the scale on the y-axis, but it doesn't matter as you're working out the percentage not the number of people. So assume each square on the y-axis is 1.

Area of '22-26' bar = 4 × 0.5 = 2
Area of '26-29' bar = 3 × 2 = 6
Area of '29-31' bar = 2 × 5.5 = 11
Area of '31-32' bar = 1 × 6 = 6
Area of '32-36' bar = 4 × 4.5 = 18
Area of '36-38' bar = 2 × 2 = 4
Area of '38-41' bar = 3 × 1 = 3
Total area = 50, so the percentage of people aged 26-29 is 6 ÷ 50 × 100 = 12%.

b) Add the areas of the '36-38' and '38-41' bars: 4 + 3 = 7.
So the fraction of people that are aged 36 or over is $\frac{7}{50}$.

c) Area of '35-36' = Area of '32-36' bar ÷ 4 = 18 ÷ 4 = 4.5
Add this onto area of '36-41' from part b):
7 + 4.5 = 11.5. So the percentage of people aged 35 or over is 11.5 ÷ 50 × 100 = 23%.

d) You have to assume that the data is evenly distributed in the range 32-36, which it may not be.

Q6 a) In total: (0.6 × 5) + (2.4 × 5) + (2.5 × 10) + (2.2 × 10) + (0.3 × 30) + (0.1 × 60) = 77
[2 marks available — 1 mark for a correct method to find the total frequency, 1 mark for the correct answer]

b) Half of the 10-20 frequency is $\frac{1}{2}(2.5 \times 10) = 12.5$
and half of the 30-60 frequency is $\frac{1}{2}(0.3 \times 30) = 4.5$
So approximately 12.5 + 22 + 4.5 = 39 students take between 15 and 45 minutes, which is $\frac{39}{77} \times 100 = 50.64... = 51\%$.
[4 marks available — 1 mark for finding half of the $10 \le t < 20$ class frequency, 1 mark for finding half of the $30 \le t < 60$ class frequency, 1 mark for approximate number of students between 15 and 45 minutes, 1 mark for correct answer]

Exercise 2.3 — The Mean

Q1 The sum of all 12 prices is £13.92.
So the mean price is £13.92 ÷ 12 = £1.16

Q2 99.8 ÷ 20 = 4.99 hours

Q3 The mean score of team B members is 252 ÷ 6 = 42.
Use the formula to find the combined mean score:
$\bar{x} = \frac{n_1\bar{x}_1 + n_2\bar{x}_2}{n_1 + n_2} = \frac{7 \times 35 + 6 \times 42}{7 + 6}$ = 38.2 points (3 s.f.)

Q4

Number of goals, x	0	1	2	3	4	Total
Frequency, f	5	7	4	3	1	20
fx	0	7	8	9	4	28

So the mean is 28 ÷ 20 = 1.4 goals

Q5 a) Mean = $\frac{560}{106}$ = 5.28 (3 s.f.) *[1 mark]*

b) The new value is smaller than the original mean, so the new mean will be smaller.
[2 marks available — 1 mark for stating that the mean gets smaller, 1 mark for sensible justification]

Q6 Old sum of ages = 15 × 47.4 = 711 years
New sum of ages = 711 + 17 = 728 years
So new mean = 728 ÷ 16 = 45.5 years
Or you could have used the combined mean formula with $n_1 = 15$, $\bar{x}_1 = 47.4$, $n_2 = 1$ and $\bar{x}_2 = 17$ to get the same answer.

Q7 Let $\bar{x}$ be the mean score for Class 12B.
Using the combined mean formula:
$17 = \frac{(18 \times 13) + (14 \times \bar{x})}{18 + 14} \Rightarrow 544 = 234 + 14\bar{x}$
$\Rightarrow 310 = 14\bar{x} \Rightarrow \bar{x} = 22.14... = 22.1$ (3 s.f.)
[3 marks available — 1 mark for using the combined mean formula, 1 mark for substituting values into the formula correctly, 1 mark for the correct answer]

Exercise 2.4 — The Mode and the Median

Q1 a) First put the amounts in order:
£19, £45, £67, £77, £84, £98, £101, £108, £110, £123, £140, £185, £187, £194, £216, £250, £500
There are 17 amounts in total. Since 17 ÷ 2 = 8.5 is not a whole number, round this up to 9 to find the position of the median. So the median = £110.

b) All the values occur just once.

Q2 Modal interest rate = 6.9%
The values in order are: 6.2%, 6.2%, 6.2%, 6.3%, 6.4%, 6.4%, 6.5%, 6.9%, 6.9%, 6.9%, 6.9%, 7.4%, 8.8%, 9.9%
There are 14 values in total. Since 14 ÷ 2 = 7 is a whole number, the median is halfway between the 7th and 8th values in the ordered list. So the median = (6.5% + 6.9%) ÷ 2 = 6.7%.

Q3 **a)** 80% and 95%

b) First put the values in order: 80%, 80%, 82%, 84%, 86%, 88%, 89%, 91%, 93%, 95%, 95%, 97%
There are 12 values in total. Since $12 \div 2 = 6$ is a whole number, the median is halfway between the 6th and 7th values in the ordered list.
So the median = (88% + 89%) ÷ 2 = 88.5%.

Q4 **a)** 5

b) There are 176 ratings in total. $176 \div 2 = 88$, so the median is midway between the 88th and 89th values.
Add a row to the table to show cumulative frequencies:

Rating	1	2	3	4	5
No. of customers	7	5	25	67	72
Cumulative frequency	7	12	37	104	176

From the cumulative frequencies, the 88th and 89th values are both 4, so the median = 4.

Q5 **a)** 3 *[1 mark]*

b) $\frac{n}{2} = \frac{27}{2} = 13.5$, so the median is the 14th value, which is 2.
[2 marks available — 1 mark for method, 1 mark for answer]

c) The mode will become 2 pets, since 11 students will have 2 pets, which is the highest frequency.
The median will stay the same. The median is already 2, so these new data values will be added to the middle of the data.
[2 marks available — 1 mark for a correct comment on the mode, 1 mark for a correct comment on the median]

Q6 **a)** £8 *[1 mark]*

b) The total frequency is $2c + 33$. $\frac{n}{2} = \frac{(2c+33)}{2} = c + 16.5$, so the median is the $(c + 17)$th value.
As the median is £10, the position of the median must be between the 20th and 30th values.
$20 \leq c + 17 \leq 30 \Rightarrow 3 \leq c \leq 13$.
However, you are told that $2 < c < 10$ and c is an integer, so $3 \leq c \leq 9$.
[3 marks available — 1 mark for finding the position of the median in terms of c, 1 mark for finding an inequality for c based on the median position, 1 mark for combining with given inequality to get the correct answer]

Q7 Make a table showing the cumulative frequencies:

No. of petals	5	6	7	8	9
No. of flowers	4	8	6	2	p
Cumulative frequency	4	12	18	20	$20 + p$

Let n be the total number of flowers, so that $n = 20 + p$.
n is even so the median = 7 lies halfway between the values in the $\frac{n}{2}$ and $\frac{n}{2} + 1$ positions.
For this to be true, the values in these positions must both be 7. Looking at the cumulative frequencies this means $13 \leq \frac{n}{2} \leq 17$ ($\frac{n}{2}$ can't equal 18 because then the value in the $\frac{n}{2} + 1$ position would be 8). So since n is even, the possible values of n are 26, 28, 30, 32 and 34.
$n = 20 + p$, so the possible values of p are 6, 8, 10, 12, 14.

Exercise 2.5 — Averages of Grouped Data

Q1 **a)**

Time (t, mins)	Frequency, f	Mid-point, x	fx
$3 \leq t < 4$	7	3.5	24.5
$4 \leq t < 5$	14	4.5	63
$5 \leq t < 6$	24	5.5	132
$6 \leq t < 8$	10	7	70
$8 \leq t < 10$	5	9	45

b) $\sum f = 60$, $\sum fx = 334.5$
So estimate of mean = $334.5 \div 60 = 5.6$ mins (1 d.p.).

Q2 **a)** 0-2 letters
All the classes are the same width, so use the frequency to find the modal class (instead of the frequency density).

b) Add some extra columns to the table:

Number of letters	Number of houses, f	Mid-point, x	fx
0-2	20	1	20
3-5	16	4	64
6-8	7	7	49
9-11	5	10	50
12-14	2	13	26

$\sum f = 50$, $\sum fx = 209$
So estimate of mean = $209 \div 50 = 4.18$ letters

c) Since $\sum f \div 2 = 50 \div 2 = 25$, the median is halfway between the values in this position (25) and the next position (26) in the ordered list.
So the median must be in the class 3-5.

Q3 Add a cumulative frequency column to the table:

Temperature (t, °C)	Frequency	Cumulative frequency
$10 \leq t < 13$	1	1
$13 \leq t < 16$	12	13
$16 \leq t < 19$	9	22
$19 \leq t < 22$	5	27
$22 \leq t < 25$	3	30

So $\frac{n}{2} = \frac{30}{2} = 15$, meaning the median must lie in the class '$16 \leq t < 19$'. Now you need to sketch that class.

b_1
16 a_1 m 19
13 a_2 15 22
b_2

Finally, solve $\frac{a_1}{b_1} = \frac{a_2}{b_2}$. This gives: $\frac{m-16}{19-16} = \frac{15-13}{22-13}$

$\Rightarrow \frac{m-16}{3} = \frac{2}{9} \Rightarrow m = 3 \times \frac{2}{9} + 16 = 16.7$ °C (1 d.p.)

Q4 **a)** $6 \leq d < 7$

b) Add some extra columns to the table:

Speed (d, Mbit/s)	Frequency, f	Mid-point, x	fx
$3 \leq d < 4$	3	3.5	10.5
$4 \leq d < 5$	11	4.5	49.5
$5 \leq d < 6$	9	5.5	49.5
$6 \leq d < 7$	13	6.5	84.5
$7 \leq d < 8$	4	7.5	30

$\sum f = 40$, $\sum fx = 224$
So estimate of mean = $224 \div 40 = 5.6$ Mbit/s.

c) Add a cumulative frequency column to the table:

Speed (d, Mbit/s)	Frequency, f	Cumulative frequency
$3 \leq d < 4$	3	3
$4 \leq d < 5$	11	14
$5 \leq d < 6$	9	23
$6 \leq d < 7$	13	36
$7 \leq d < 8$	4	40

So $\frac{n}{2} = 20$, meaning the median must lie in the class '$5 \leq d < 6$'. Now sketch that class.

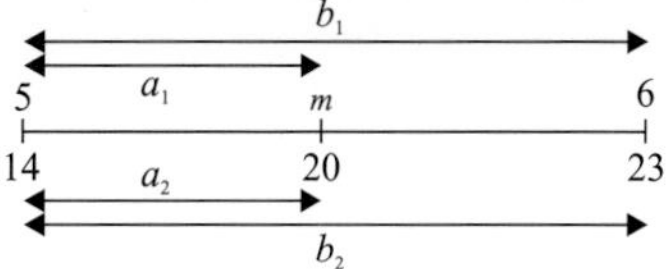

Finally, solve $\frac{a_1}{b_1} = \frac{a_2}{b_2}$. This gives:
$\frac{m-5}{6-5} = \frac{20-14}{23-14} \Rightarrow m - 5 = \frac{6}{9} \Rightarrow m = 5.7$ (1 d.p.)

Q5 **a)** Estimated mean = 16 740 ÷ 60 = 279 minutes *[1 mark]*

b) Add a cumulative frequency column to the table:

Time (t, mins)	Frequency, f	Cumulative frequency
$180 \le t < 240$	8	8
$240 \le t < 270$	19	27
$270 \le t < 300$	21	48
$300 \le t < 360$	9	57
$360 \le t < 480$	3	60

So $\frac{n}{2} = 30$, meaning the median must lie in the class '$270 \le t < 300$'. Now sketch that class.

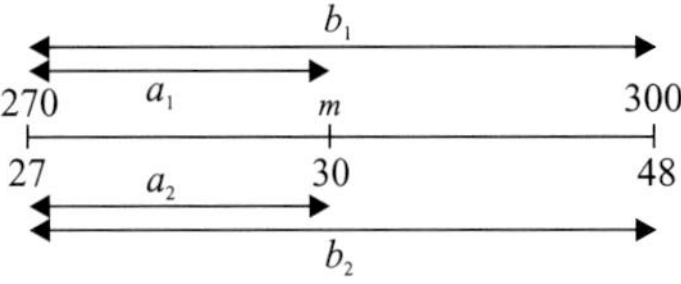

Finally, solve $\frac{a_1}{b_1} = \frac{a_2}{b_2}$. This gives:

$\frac{m-270}{300-270} = \frac{30-27}{48-27} \Rightarrow \frac{m-270}{30} = \frac{3}{21}$

$\Rightarrow m = 30 \times \frac{3}{21} + 270 = 274.2... \approx 274$ minutes (3 s.f.)

[3 marks available — 1 mark for identifying which interval the median lies in, 1 mark for use of linear interpolation, 1 mark for the correct answer]

Q6 **a)** $10 \le T < 15$ *[1 mark]*

b) Work out the mid-points for each class:

(0 + 10) ÷ 2 = 5 (10 + 15) ÷ 2 = 12.5

(15 + 20) ÷ 2 = 17.5 (20 + 25) ÷ 2 = 22.5

$\sum f = 153, \sum fx = 2177.5$

So estimate of mean = 2177.5 ÷ 153 = 14.2 (3 s.f.) *[1 mark]*

c) Add a cumulative frequency row to the table:

Daily mean air temp. (T °C)	$0 \le T < 10$	$10 \le T < 15$	$15 \le T < 20$	$20 \le T < 25$
Frequency, f	10	80	58	5
Cumulative frequency	10	90	148	153

$\frac{n}{2} = \frac{153}{2} = 76.5$, so the median lies in the class $10 \le T < 15$.

Sketch the class:

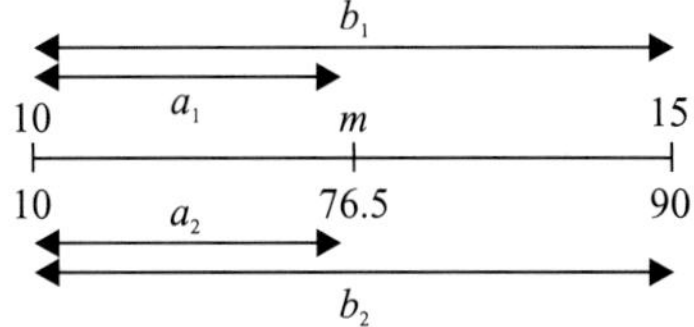

Finally, solve $\frac{a_1}{b_1} = \frac{a_2}{b_2}$. This gives: $\frac{m-10}{15-10} = \frac{76.5-10}{90-10}$

$\Rightarrow \frac{m-10}{5} = \frac{66.5}{80} \Rightarrow m = 5 \times \frac{66.5}{80} + 10 = 14.2$ (1 d.p.)

[3 marks available — 1 mark for identifying which interval the median lies in, 1 mark for use of linear interpolation, 1 mark for the correct answer]

d) Temperatures in Perth tend to be higher in October, so the October values of the daily mean air temperature are likely to be at the high end of the data for the whole period, and so the mean will increase. *[1 mark for a sensible explanation]*

Q7 Total number of puppies = $4 + 2q + 12 + 4 = 2q + 20$

The median is the $(2q + 20) \div 2 = (q + 10)^{\text{th}}$ value, and it is in the $4.5 \le m < 5$ class interval. Sketch the class:

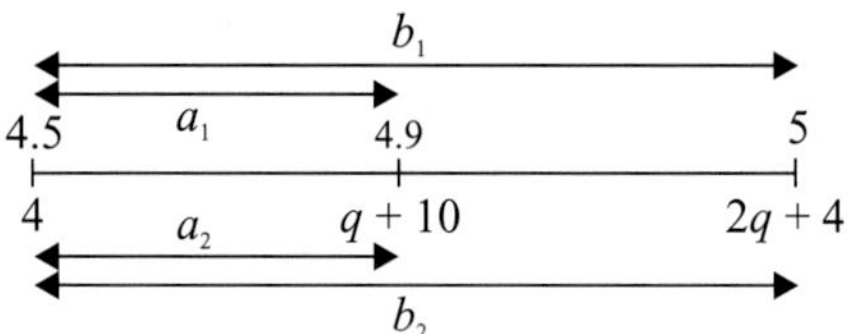

Finally, solve $\frac{a_1}{b_1} = \frac{a_2}{b_2}$. This gives: $\frac{4.9-4.5}{5-4.5} = \frac{(q+10)-4}{(2q+4)-4}$

$\Rightarrow \frac{0.4}{0.5} = \frac{q+6}{2q} \Rightarrow 1.6q = q + 6 \Rightarrow q = 10$

[5 marks available — 1 mark for expressing the total number of puppies in terms of q, 1 mark for finding the position of the median in terms of q, 1 mark for setting up the equation, 1 mark for a correct method to solve the equation, 1 mark for answer for q]

Exercise 2.6 — Comparing Measures of Location

Q1 **a)** Median — most employees will earn relatively low salaries but a few may earn much higher salaries, so the mean could be heavily affected by a few high salaries.

b) Mean — the data should be reasonably symmetrical so the mean would be a good measure of location. The median would be good as well (for a symmetric data set, it should be roughly equal to the mean).

c) Mode — make of car is qualitative data so the mode is the only average that can be found.

d) Mean — the data should be reasonably symmetrical so the mean would be a good measure of location. The median would be good as well (for a symmetric data set, it should be roughly equal to the mean).

e) Median — most employees will perhaps travel fairly short distances to work but a few employees may live further away. The median would not be affected by these few high values.

The mode is unlikely to be suitable in b), d) and e) (and possibly a) as well) because all the values may be different.

Q2 There is a very extreme value of 8 that would affect the mean quite heavily.

Q3 **a)** The mode would be 5 as this number of devices occurs the most. However, the numbers of households with 4 or 6 devices is very similar to the number with 5 devices. Since the frequencies are high, there is little difference between all three values, so stating the mode as 5 could be misleading. *[1 mark for a sensible explanation]*

b) Either: The median is the most suitable measure, because the data is not symmetric/the values for 4-6 devices are much higher than the others, so the mean could give a misleading impression of the location of the data.

Or: The mean is the most suitable measure because it takes all the data into account.

[1 mark for a sensible justification]

Q4 mean < median < mode

There are more lower values of x than higher values of x in the data, so you would expect the mean to be the lowest — it is the measure most affected by extreme values.

The median would be next as it is unaffected by extreme values, and the mode would be the highest measure of location — the tallest bar is further to the right than most of the data, so is one of the higher values of x.

Exercise 2.7 — Range, Interquartile Range and Interpercentile Range

Q1 a) Highest value = 49, lowest value = 4, so range = 49 – 4 = 45
There are 16 values, and the ordered list is
4, 9, 9, 10, 12, 20, 21, 23, 26, 26, 31, 32, 39, 41, 48, 49
Since $\frac{n}{4} = 4$, the lower quartile (Q_1) is halfway between the 4th and 5th values in the ordered list.
So $Q_1 = (10 + 12) \div 2 = 11$.

Since $\frac{3n}{4} = 12$, the upper quartile (Q_3) is halfway between the 12th and 13th values in the ordered list.
So $Q_3 = (32 + 39) \div 2 = 35.5$,
and IQR = $Q_3 - Q_1 = 35.5 - 11 = 24.5$

b) Highest value = 13.7, Lowest value = 7.7
So range = 13.7 – 7.7 = 6
There are 12 values, and the ordered list is: 7.7, 8.4, 8.5, 8.6, 9.0, 9.2, 9.4, 10.3, 10.5, 11.3, 12.1, 13.7
Since $\frac{n}{4} = 3$, the lower quartile (Q_1) is halfway between the 3rd and 4th values in the ordered list.
So $Q_1 = (8.5 + 8.6) \div 2 = 8.55$.

Since $\frac{3n}{4} = 9$, the upper quartile (Q_3) is halfway between the 9th and 10th values in the ordered list.
So $Q_3 = (10.5 + 11.3) \div 2 = 10.9$.
IQR = $Q_3 - Q_1 = 10.9 - 8.55 = 2.35$

Q2 a) Highest value = 88 846 miles, lowest value = 3032 miles
So range = 88 846 – 3032 = 85 814 miles

b) There are 8 values, and the ordered list is: 3032, 4222, 7521, 7926, 30 778, 31 763, 74 898, 88 846
Since $\frac{n}{4} = 2$, the lower quartile (Q_1) is halfway between the 2nd and 3rd values.
So $Q_1 = (4222 + 7521) \div 2 = 5871.5$ miles

c) Since $\frac{3n}{4} = 6$, the upper quartile (Q_3) is halfway between the 6th and 7th values.
So $Q_3 = (31\,763 + 74\,898) \div 2 = 53\,330.5$ miles

d) IQR = $Q_3 - Q_1 = 53\,330.5 - 5871.5 = 47\,459$ miles

Q3 a) and b)
<u>In town at 8:45 am</u>:
The ordered list of 18 values is: 13, 14, 14, 15, 15, 15, 15, 15, 16, 16, 16, 16, 16, 17, 17, 18, 18, 18
So the range = 18 – 13 = 5 mph

Since $\frac{n}{4} = 4.5$, the lower quartile (Q_1) is in position 5 in the ordered list. So Q_1 = 15 mph.

Since $\frac{3n}{4} = 13.5$, the upper quartile (Q_3) is in position 14 in the ordered list. So Q_3 = 17 mph.
This means IQR = $Q_3 - Q_1 = 17 - 15 = 2$ mph.

<u>In town at 10:45 am</u>:
The ordered list of 18 values is: 25, 29, 29, 29, 30, 30, 31, 31, 31, 32, 33, 34, 34, 35, 36, 36, 38, 39
So the range = 39 – 25 = 14 mph
The lower quartile (Q_1) is in position 5 in the ordered list. So Q_1 = 30 mph.
The upper quartile (Q_3) is in position 14 in the ordered list. So Q_3 = 35 mph.
This means IQR = $Q_3 - Q_1 = 35 - 30 = 5$ mph.

<u>On the motorway at 1 pm</u>:
The ordered list of 18 values is: 67, 69, 69, 71, 71, 73, 73, 74, 74, 75, 75, 76, 76, 76, 78, 78, 88, 95
So the range = 95 – 67 = 28 mph
The lower quartile (Q_1) is in position 5 in the ordered list.
So Q_1 = 71 mph.
The upper quartile (Q_3) is in position 14 in the ordered list.
So Q_3 = 76 mph.
This means IQR = $Q_3 - Q_1 = 76 - 71 = 5$ mph.

Q4 Put the data in order first:
2 3 4 4 5 5 6 6 7 8 8 16

a) Range = 16 – 2 = 14 seconds *[1 mark]*

b) There are 12 values, and 12 ÷ 4 = 3, so the lower quartile (Q_1) is halfway between the 3rd and 4th values. So $Q_1 = 4$.
3 × (12 ÷ 4) = 9, so the upper quartile (Q_3) is halfway between the 9th and 10th values. So $Q_3 = 7.5$.
So IQR = 7.5 – 4 = 3.5 seconds
[3 marks available —1 mark for finding Q_1, 1 mark for finding Q_3, 1 mark for finding the IQR]

c) The IQR would be more appropriate for this data as one value (16) is quite large compared with most of the other values so will affect the range.
The IQR will not include this extreme value.
[2 marks available — 1 mark for stating IQR, 1 mark for a sensible justification]

Q5 a) Add a cumulative frequency row to the table:

No of t-shirts	5	6	7	8	9	10	11	12	13
Frequency	20	32	45	55	48	32	24	11	3
Cumulative freq.	20	52	97	152	200	232	256	267	270

$\frac{30}{100} \times 270 = 81$, so P_{30} is the 81st value. So $P_{30} = 7$.
[2 marks available — 1 mark for finding the position, 1 mark for the final answer]

b) $\frac{70}{100} \times 270 = 189$, so P_{70} is the 189th value. So $P_{70} = 9$.
Therefore, $P_{70} - P_{30} = 9 - 7 = 2$
[3 marks available — 1 mark for finding the position of P_{70}, 1 mark for finding the value of P_{70}, 1 mark for the final answer]

Q6 a) Add a cumulative frequency column to the table:

Maximum temperature (t)	Freq.	Cumulative freq.
$10 \le t < 15$	19	19
$15 \le t < 20$	66	85
$20 \le t < 25$	49	134
$25 \le t < 30$	16	150

$\frac{n}{4} = 150 \div 4 = 37.5$, meaning the lower quartile (Q_1) must lie in the class '$15 \le t < 20$'. Now, sketch that class.

b_1
15 a_1 Q_1 20
19 a_2 37.5 85
b_2

Finally, solve $\frac{a_1}{b_1} = \frac{a_2}{b_2}$. This gives:
$\frac{Q_1 - 15}{20 - 15} = \frac{37.5 - 19}{85 - 19} \Rightarrow \frac{Q_1 - 15}{5} = \frac{18.5}{66}$
$\Rightarrow Q_1 = 5 \times \frac{18.5}{66} + 15 = 16.4$ °C (1 d.p.).

b) $\frac{3n}{4} = 150 \div 4 \times 3 = 112.5$, meaning the upper quartile (Q_3) must lie in the class '$20 \le t < 25$'. Now, sketch that class.

b_1
20 a_1 Q_3 25
85 a_2 112.5 134
b_2

Finally, solve $\frac{a_1}{b_1} = \frac{a_2}{b_2}$. This gives:
$\frac{Q_3 - 20}{25 - 20} = \frac{112.5 - 85}{134 - 85} \Rightarrow \frac{Q_3 - 20}{5} = \frac{27.5}{49}$
$\Rightarrow Q_3 = 5 \times \frac{27.5}{49} + 20 = 22.8$ °C (1 d.p.).

c) So IQR = $Q_3 - Q_1 = 22.8 - 16.4 = 6.4$ °C (1 d.p.).

d) $\frac{10}{100} \times n = \frac{10}{100} \times 150 = 15$, meaning the 10th percentile (P_{10}) must lie in the class '$10 \leq t < 15$'.
Now you need to sketch that class.

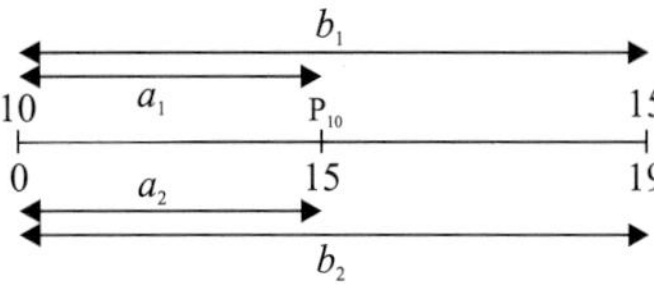

Finally, solve $\frac{a_1}{b_1} = \frac{a_2}{b_2}$. This gives:

$\frac{P_{10} - 10}{15 - 10} = \frac{15 - 0}{19 - 0} \Rightarrow \frac{P_{10} - 10}{5} = \frac{15}{19}$

$\Rightarrow P_{10} = 5 \times \frac{15}{19} + 10 = 13.9$ °C (1 d.p.).

e) $\frac{90}{100} \times n = \frac{90}{100} \times 150 = 135$, meaning the 90th percentile (P_{90}) must lie in the class '$25 \leq t < 30$'.
Now you need to sketch that class.

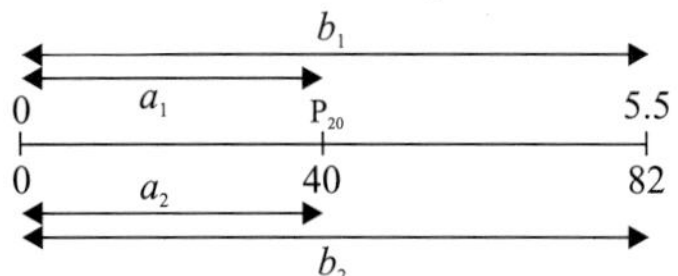

Finally, solve $\frac{a_1}{b_1} = \frac{a_2}{b_2}$. This gives:

$\frac{P_{90} - 25}{30 - 25} = \frac{135 - 134}{150 - 134} \Rightarrow \frac{P_{90} - 25}{5} = \frac{1}{16}$

$\Rightarrow P_{90} = 5 \times \frac{1}{16} + 25 = 25.3$ °C (1 d.p.)

f) So 10% to 90% interpercentile range
$= P_{90} - P_{10} = 25.3 - 13.9 = 11.4$ °C (1 d.p.).

Q7 a) Add a cumulative frequency column to the table:

Length (l)	Number of beetles	Cumulative frequency
0 - 5	82	82
6 - 10	28	110
11 - 15	44	154
16 - 30	30	184
31 - 50	16	200

$\frac{20}{100} \times n = \frac{20}{100} \times 200 = 40$, meaning that P_{20} must lie in the class '0 - 5'. Now you need to sketch that class.

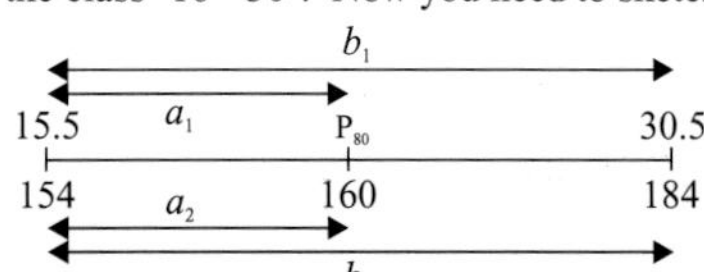

Finally, solve $\frac{a_1}{b_1} = \frac{a_2}{b_2}$.

This gives: $\frac{P_{20} - 0}{5.5 - 0} = \frac{40 - 0}{82 - 0} \Rightarrow \frac{P_{20}}{5.5} = \frac{40}{82}$

$\Rightarrow P_{20} = 5.5 \times \frac{40}{82} = 2.7$ mm (1 d.p.)

$\frac{80}{100} \times n = \frac{80}{100} \times 200 = 160$, meaning that P_{80} must lie in the class '16 - 30'. Now you need to sketch that class.

Finally, solve $\frac{a_1}{b_1} = \frac{a_2}{b_2}$. This gives:

$\frac{P_{80} - 15.5}{30.5 - 15.5} = \frac{160 - 154}{184 - 154} \Rightarrow \frac{P_{80} - 15.5}{15} = \frac{6}{30}$

$\Rightarrow P_{80} = 15 \times \frac{6}{30} + 15.5 = 18.5$ mm

So the 20% to 80% interpercentile range
$= P_{80} - P_{20} = 18.5 - 2.7 = 15.8$ mm (1 d.p.).

b) $\frac{5}{100} \times n = \frac{5}{100} \times 200 = 10$, meaning that P_5 must lie in the class '0 - 5'. Now sketch that class.

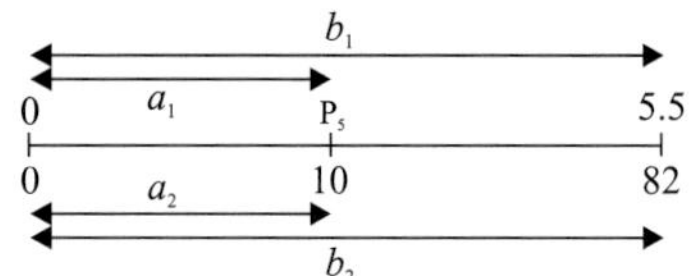

Finally, solve $\frac{a_1}{b_1} = \frac{a_2}{b_2}$.

This gives: $\frac{P_5 - 0}{5.5 - 0} = \frac{10 - 0}{82 - 0} \Rightarrow \frac{P_5}{5.5} = \frac{10}{82}$

$\Rightarrow P_5 = 5.5 \times \frac{10}{82} = 0.7$ mm (1 d.p.)

$\frac{95}{100} \times n = \frac{95}{100} \times 200 = 190$, meaning that P_{95} must lie in the class '31-50'. Now you need to sketch that class.

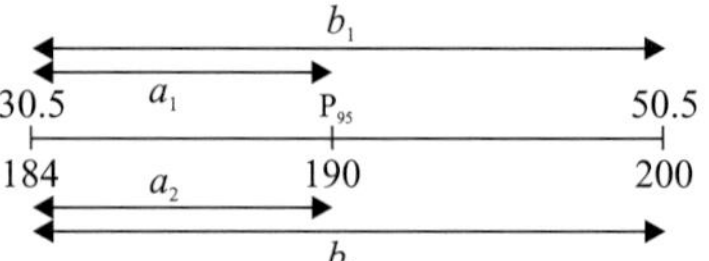

Finally, solve $\frac{a_1}{b_1} = \frac{a_2}{b_2}$. This gives:

$\frac{P_{95} - 30.5}{50.5 - 30.5} = \frac{190 - 184}{200 - 184} \Rightarrow \frac{P_{95} - 30.5}{20} = \frac{6}{16}$

$\Rightarrow P_{95} = 20 \times \frac{6}{16} + 30.5 = 38$ mm

So the 5% to 95% interpercentile range
$= P_{95} - P_5 = 38 - 0.7 = 37.3$ mm (1 d.p.).

You use the lower and upper class boundaries when you sketch the classes because of how the data is grouped.

Q8 a) To find the maximum range, use the minimum and maximum possible rainfall values:
Maximum range = 75 – 0 = 75 mm to the nearest mm.
To find the minimum range, use the highest possible value from the first class and the lowest from the final class:
Minimum range = 60 – 15 = 45 mm to the nearest mm.

You can't know the actual range, because you don't know the exact data values within each class.

b) Add a cumulative frequency column to the table:

Rainfall (r, mm)	Number of days	Cumulative freq.
$0 \leq r < 15$	15	15
$15 \leq r < 35$	21	36
$35 \leq r < 50$	16	52
$50 \leq r < 60$	27	79
$60 \leq r < 75$	13	92

$\frac{n}{4} = 92 \div 4 = 23$, meaning the lower quartile (Q_1) must lie in the class '$15 \leq r < 35$'. Now you need to sketch that class.

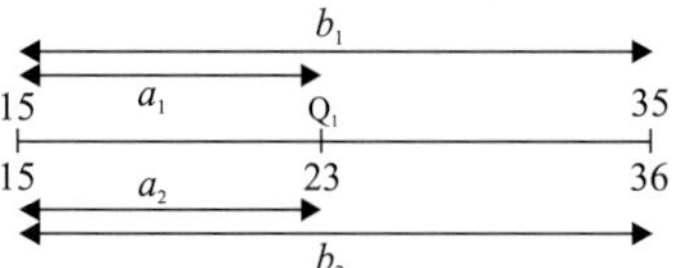

Finally, solve $\frac{a_1}{b_1} = \frac{a_2}{b_2}$. This gives:

$\frac{Q_1 - 15}{35 - 15} = \frac{23 - 15}{36 - 15} \Rightarrow \frac{Q_1 - 15}{20} = \frac{8}{21}$

$\Rightarrow Q_1 = 20 \times \frac{8}{21} + 15 = 22.6$ mm (1 d.p.)

$\frac{3n}{4} = 92 \div 4 \times 3 = 69$, meaning the upper quartile (Q_3) must lie in the class '$50 \leq r < 60$'. Now sketch that class.

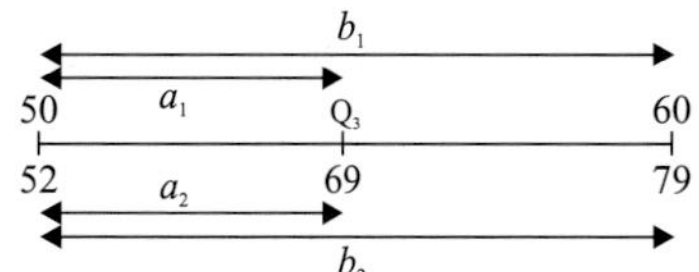

Finally, solve $\frac{a_1}{b_1} = \frac{a_2}{b_2}$. This gives:

$\frac{Q_3 - 50}{60 - 50} = \frac{69 - 52}{79 - 52} \Rightarrow \frac{Q_3 - 50}{10} = \frac{17}{27}$

$\Rightarrow Q_3 = 10 \times \frac{17}{27} + 50 = 56.3$ mm (1 d.p.).

c) IQR = 56.3 – 22.6 = 33.7 mm (1 d.p.)

d) $\frac{15}{100} \times n = \frac{15}{100} \times 92 = 13.8$, meaning that P_{15} must lie in the class '$0 \le r < 15$'. Now sketch that class.

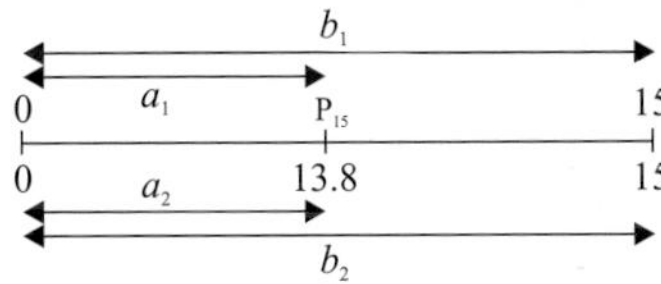

Finally, solve $\frac{a_1}{b_1} = \frac{a_2}{b_2}$.

This gives: $\frac{P_{15} - 0}{15 - 0} = \frac{13.8 - 0}{15 - 0} \Rightarrow \frac{P_{15}}{15} = \frac{13.8}{15}$

$\Rightarrow P_{15} = 15 \times \frac{13.8}{15} = 13.8$ mm (1 d.p.)

$\frac{85}{100} \times n = \frac{85}{100} \times 92 = 78.2$, meaning that P_{85} must lie in the class '$50 \le r < 60$'.
Now you need to sketch that class.

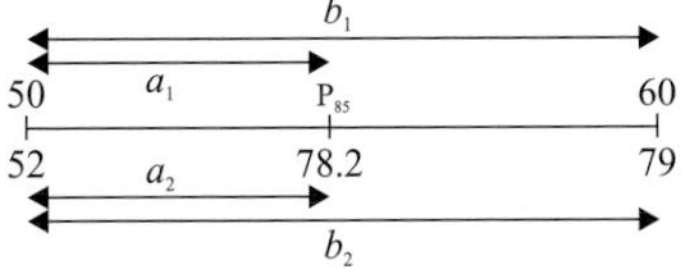

Finally, solve $\frac{a_1}{b_1} = \frac{a_2}{b_2}$. This gives:

$\frac{P_{85} - 50}{60 - 50} = \frac{78.2 - 52}{79 - 52} \Rightarrow \frac{P_{85} - 50}{10} = \frac{26.2}{27}$

$\Rightarrow P_{85} = 10 \times \frac{26.2}{27} + 50 = 59.7$ mm (1 d.p.)

e) So the 15% to 85% interpercentile range $= P_{85} - P_{15} = 59.7 - 13.8 = 45.9$ mm (1 d.p.).

Q9 a) 180 – 17 = 163 *[1 mark]*

b) Add a cumulative frequency row to the table:

3-dart score	0-29	30-59	60-89	90-119	120-149	150-180
Frequency	5	9	39	63	84	100
Cumulative frequency	5	14	53	116	200	300

$\frac{n}{4} = \frac{300}{4} = 75$, meaning the lower quartile (Q_1) must lie in the 90-119 class interval. Now sketch that class:

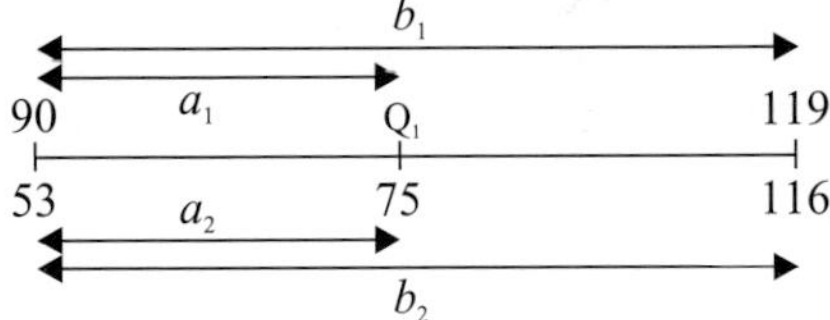

Then, solve $\frac{a_1}{b_1} = \frac{a_2}{b_2}$. This gives:

$\frac{Q_1 - 90}{119 - 90} = \frac{75 - 53}{116 - 53} \Rightarrow \frac{Q_1 - 90}{29} = \frac{22}{63}$

$\Rightarrow Q_1 = 29 \times \frac{22}{63} + 90 = 100.12... = 100.1$ (1 d.p.)

$3 \times \frac{300}{4} = 225$, meaning the upper quartile (Q_3) must lie in the 150-180 class interval. Now sketch that class:

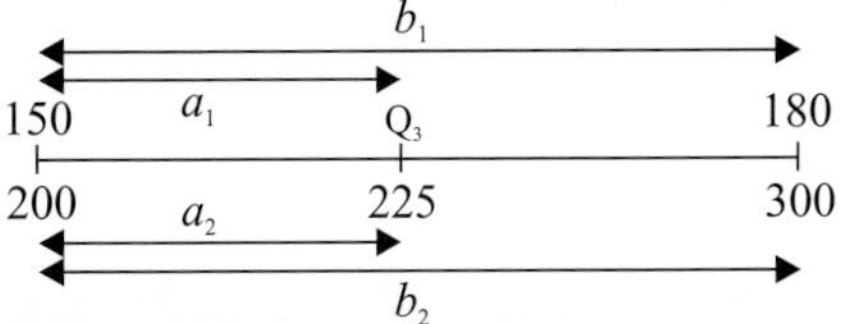

Then, solve $\frac{a_1}{b_1} = \frac{a_2}{b_2}$. This gives:

$\frac{Q_3 - 150}{180 - 150} = \frac{225 - 200}{300 - 200} \Rightarrow \frac{Q_3 - 150}{30} = \frac{25}{100}$

$\Rightarrow Q_3 = 30 \times \frac{25}{100} + 150 = 157.5$

So IQR = 157.5 – 100.1 = 57.4

[4 marks available — 1 mark for use of n to locate Q_1 and Q_3, 1 mark for the correct value of Q_1, 1 mark for the correct value of Q_3, 1 mark for correct IQR]

c) E.g. These 300 players are professionals, so are likely to get top scores regularly — you would expect a lot of data to be in the highest-class interval. The range would pick up any occasional low scores, so it would be too large to accurately represent the dispersion of the data. The IQR would cut off some of the highest scores, even though these are likely to occur regularly. *[1 mark for a sensible reason]*

Exercise 2.8 — Cumulative Frequency Diagrams

Q1 a) Add a cumulative frequency column to the table:

Amount of water, w (litres)	Freq.	Cumulative freq.
$w \le 0.8$	0	0
$0.8 < w \le 1.0$	4	4
$1.0 < w \le 1.2$	8	12
$1.2 < w \le 1.4$	12	24
$1.4 < w \le 1.6$	5	29
$1.6 < w \le 1.8$	2	31

Then you can plot the cumulative frequency diagram.

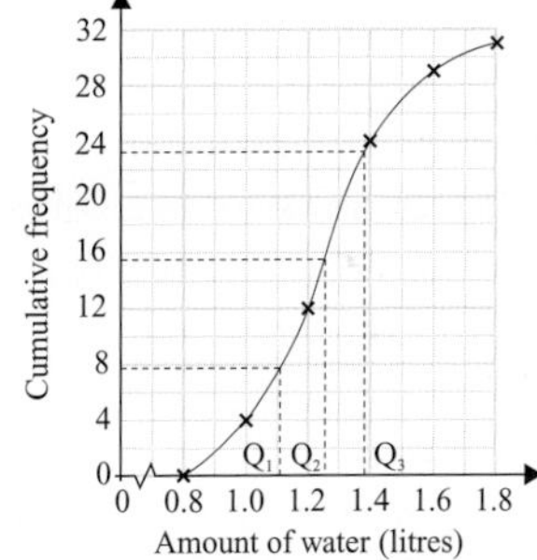

b) Use your diagram from part a) to find Q_1, Q_2 and Q_3.

$n = 31$, so $\frac{n}{4} = 7.75$, $\frac{n}{2} = 15.5$ and $\frac{3n}{4} = 23.25$.

(i) Median ≈ 1.25 litres

(ii) Lower quartile ≈ 1.11 litres

(iii) Upper quartile ≈ 1.38 litres

(iv) IQR ≈ 1.38 – 1.11 = 0.27 litres

Your answers to i)-iv) may be different depending on how you've drawn your diagram, e.g. if you've joined the points with straight lines rather than drawing a curve.

Q2 Add a cumulative frequency column to the table:

Distance walked, d (km)	No. of walkers	Cumulative freq.
$0 < d \leq 2$	1	1
$2 < d \leq 4$	10	11
$4 < d \leq 6$	7	18
$6 < d \leq 8$	2	20

Then you can plot the cumulative frequency diagram.

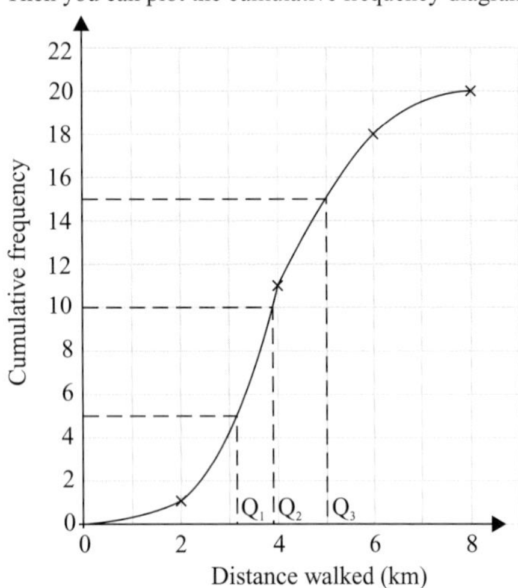

So median = $Q_2 \approx 3.9$ km and
interquartile range = $Q_3 - Q_1 \approx 5 - 3.2 = 1.8$ km.

Q3 **a)** Approximately 5 boys weigh less than 55 kg.

b) Approximately 17 boys weigh less than 73 kg.
So 24 – 17 = 7 boys weigh more than 73 kg.

c) The data is grouped so you don't know the actual values.

Q4 **a)** Add a cumulative frequency column to the table:

Time, t (minutes)	Freq.	Cumulative freq.
$0 < t \leq 10$	2	2
$10 < t \leq 20$	8	10
$20 < t \leq 30$	22	32
$30 < t \leq 40$	34	66
$40 < t \leq 50$	10	76
$50 < t \leq 60$	4	80

Then you can plot the cumulative frequency diagram.

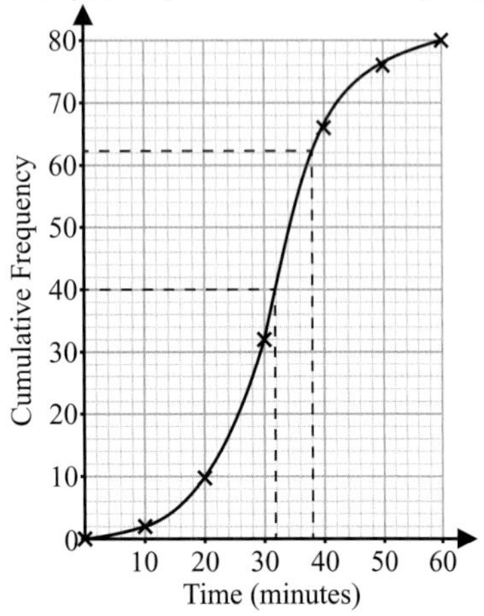

[3 marks available — 1 mark for points plotted at the end of each class interval, 1 mark for joining points with a curve or straight lines, 1 mark for a fully correct diagram]

b) Median position = $\frac{n}{2} = \frac{80}{2} = 40$. Reading from the graph, this is around 32 minutes (see above). *[1 mark]*

c) Reading from the graph, the cumulative frequency at 38 minutes is approximately 62 (see above), so 80 – 62 = 18 people take more than 38 minutes to get to work.
[2 marks available — 1 mark for finding the cumulative frequency at 38 minutes, 1 mark for the correct answer using graph reading at 38 minutes]

Q5 **a)** Add a cumulative frequency column to the table:

Daily total sunshine (h hours)	Freq.	Cumulative Freq.
$0 \leq h \leq 3$	56	56
$3 < h \leq 5$	20	76
$5 < h \leq 8$	43	119
$8 < h \leq 12$	35	154
$12 < h \leq 16$	13	167

Then you can plot the cumulative frequency diagram.

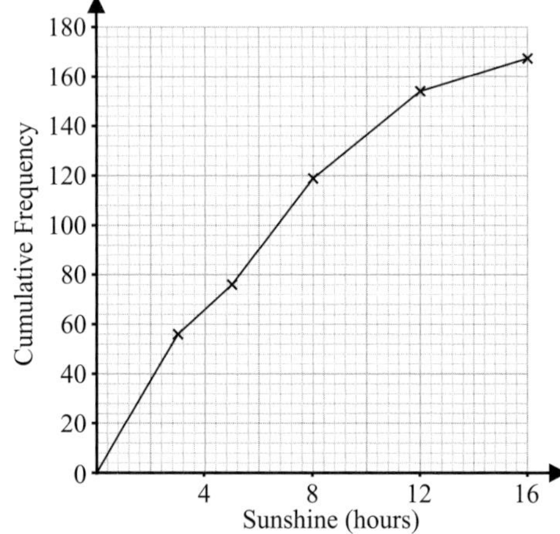

[3 marks available — 1 mark for points plotted at the end of each class interval, 1 mark for joining points with straight lines, 1 mark for a fully correct diagram]

b) Q_1 position = $\frac{n}{4} = \frac{167}{4} = 41.75$.
Reading from the graph, Q_1 is approximately 2.2.

Q_3 position = $3 \times \frac{167}{4} = 125.25$.
Reading from the graph, Q_3 is approximately 8.8.
So estimate of interquartile range is 8.8 – 2.2 = 6.6 hours.
[2 marks available — 1 mark for reading both Q_1 and Q_3 from the graph, 1 mark for finding the IQR]

c) On some days the data was not available, so it is not recorded in the table.
[1 mark for a sensible reason]

Q6 **a)** 84 people

b) Median earnings ≈ £67

c) Approximately 16 people earned less than £46 and approximately 70 people earned less than £84.
70 – 16 = 54, so approximately 54 people earned between £46 and £84.

Q7 **a)** Level 3 starts after 200 × 2 = 400 seconds and lasts until 600 seconds, etc. Use this to work out the classes in the table.

Duration t (seconds)	Freq.	Cumulative freq.
$400 < t \leq 600$	6	6
$600 < t \leq 800$	11	17
$800 < t \leq 1000$	14	31
$1000 < t \leq 1200$	28	59
$1200 < t \leq 1400$	22	81
$1400 < t \leq 1600$	10	91
$1600 < t \leq 1800$	7	98
$1800 < t \leq 2000$	2	100

b)

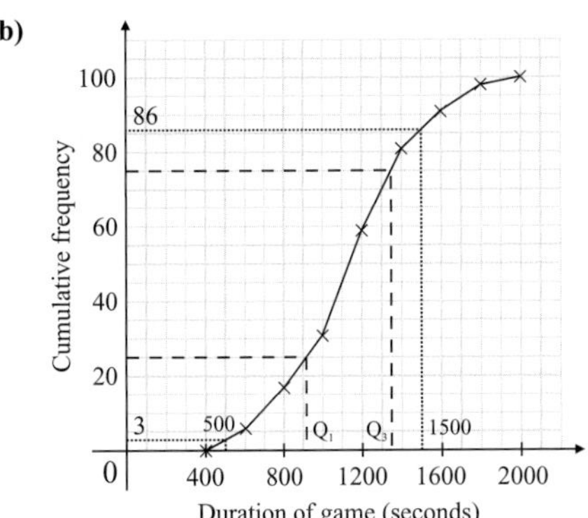

c) From the diagram for part b).
(i) 3 games (ii) 100 – 86 = 14 games

d) From the diagram in part b):
Lower quartile position = $\frac{100}{4}$ = 25, so $Q_1 \approx 920$ seconds
Upper quartile position = $\frac{300}{4}$ = 75, so $Q_3 \approx 1350$ seconds
IQR ≈ 1350 – 920 ≈ 430 seconds

Q8 a) Add a cumulative frequency column to the table:

Speed (s km/h)	Freq.	Cumulative freq.
$70 \le s < 75$	7	7
$75 \le s < 80$	18	25
$80 \le s < 85$	50	75
$85 \le s < 90$	83	158
$90 \le s < 95$	31	189
$95 \le s < 100$	11	200

Then you can plot the cumulative frequency diagram.

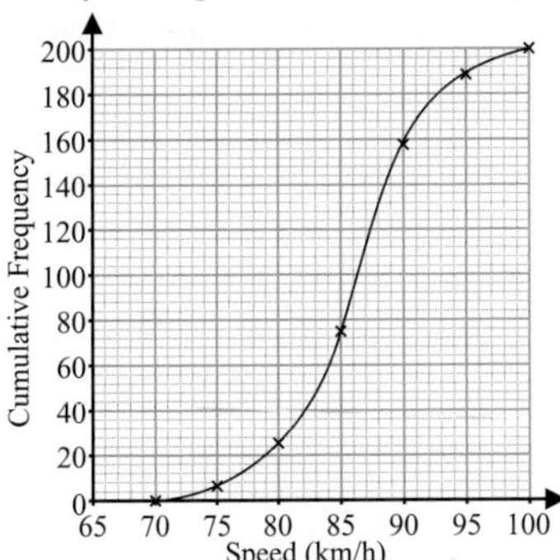

[3 marks available — 1 mark for points plotted at the end of each class interval, 1 mark for joining points with a curve or straight lines, 1 mark for a fully correct diagram]

b) P_{10} position = $\frac{n}{10} = \frac{200}{10}$ = 20.
Reading from the graph, P_{10} is approximately 79 km/h.
P_{90} position = $9 \times \frac{200}{10}$ = 180.
Reading from the graph, P_{90} is approximately 93 km/h.
So the 10% to 90% interpercentile range is $P_{90} - P_{10}$ = 93 – 79 = 14 km/h.
[3 marks available — 1 mark for finding one percentile position, 1 mark for reading both percentiles from the graph, 1 mark for the correct interpercentile range]

c) From the graph, the cumulative frequency at 92 km/h is 176, so approximately 176 deliveries were slower than 92 km/h.
So 200 – 176 = 24 deliveries were faster than 92 km/h.
$\frac{24}{200} \times 100$ = 12%, so approximately 12% of the deliveries were faster than 92 km/h.
[3 marks available — 1 mark for finding the cumulative frequency at 92 km/h, 1 mark for a correct method to find the answer, 1 mark for the final answer]

Q9 a) Median position = $\frac{n}{2} = \frac{75}{2}$ = 37.5. Reading from the graph, the median length is approximately 107 m. *[1 mark]*

b) Q_1 position = $\frac{n}{4} = \frac{75}{4}$ = 18.75.
Reading from the graph, Q_1 is approximately 102.5 m.
Q_3 position = $3 \times \frac{75}{4}$ = 56.25.
Reading from the graph, Q_3 is approximately 111.5 m.
So IQR = $Q_3 - Q_1$ = 111.5 – 102.5 = 9 m
[2 marks available — 1 mark for reading both quartiles from the graph, 1 mark for finding the IQR]

c) From the graph, the cumulative frequency at 110 m is 52.
So, 75 – 52 = 23 pitches have a length greater than 110 m.
So $\frac{23}{75} \times 100$ = 31% (2 s.f.) are longer than 110 m.
[3 marks available — 1 mark for finding the cumulative frequency at 110m, 1 mark for a correct method to find the answer, 1 mark for the final answer]

d) E.g. Data from 75 football pitches has been used for the graph, but there are many more pitches than that in the UK, so the answers are based on a sample that might not be representative of the whole population.
[1 mark for a sensible comment]

Q10 a) The middle 64% of the data will be between the 18th percentile and the 100 – 18 = 82nd percentile.
Reading from the graph, P_{18} is approximately 27, and P_{82} is approximately 54, so the middle 64% of ages are between 27 and 54 years.
[3 marks available — 1 mark for identifying you need the 18th and 82nd percentiles, 1 mark for reading both percentiles from the graph, 1 mark for the final answer]

b) Reading from the graph, P_2 is approximately 15, and P_{98} is approximately 68, so ages below 15 or above 68 would be considered outliers.
[2 marks available —1 mark for reading P_2 and P_{98} from the graph, 1 mark for the final answer]

Exercise 2.9 — Outliers and Box Plots

Q1 a) IQR = $Q_3 - Q_1$ = 31 – 19 = 12
Lower fence = Q_1 – (1.5 × IQR) = 19 – (1.5 × 12) = 1
Upper fence = Q_3 + (1.5 × IQR) = 31 + (1.5 × 12) = 49
The value 4 is inside the fences, so 4 is not an outlier.
The value 52 is outside the upper fence, so 52 is an outlier.

b) IQR = $Q_3 - Q_1$ = 37 – 24 = 13
Lower fence = Q_1 – (1.5 × IQR) = 24 – (1.5 × 13) = 4.5
Upper fence = Q_3 + (1.5 × IQR) = 37 + (1.5 × 13) = 56.5
The value 4 is outside the lower fence, so 4 is an outlier.
The value 52 is inside the fences, so 52 is not an outlier.

Q2 a) IQR = $Q_3 - Q_1$ = 37 – 16 = 21

b) Lower fence = Q_1 – (1.5 × IQR) = 16 – (1.5 × 21) = –15.5
Upper fence = Q_3 + (1.5 × IQR) = 37 + (1.5 × 21) = 68.5
The minimum value and the maximum value both fall inside the fences, so there are no outliers in this data set.

c)

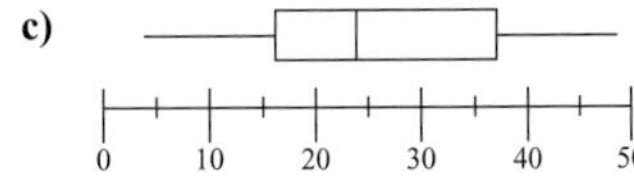

Q3 **a)** Put the values in order: 74, 82, 85, 86, 88, 90, 90, 90, 91, 92, 92, 95, 95, 96, 97, 97, 97, 98, 98, 99, 99, 99, 99, 99, 99, 99, 99, 99, 99, 99, 99, 100, 100, 100, 100, 100, 100, 100, 100, 100

There are 41 data values altogether, i.e. $n = 41$.
Since $41 \div 2 = 20.5$ is not a whole number, round this up to 21 to find the position of the median.
So the median = 99% humidity.

Since $41 \div 4 = 10.25$ is not a whole number, round this up to 11 to find the position of the lower quartile.
So the lower quartile (Q_1) = 92% humidity.

Since $3 \times 41 \div 4 = 30.75$ is not a whole number, round this up to 31 to find the position of the upper quartile.
So the upper quartile (Q_3) = 99% humidity.

IQR = $Q_3 - Q_1 = 99 - 92 = 7$% humidity

b) The lower fence is $Q_1 - (1.5 \times \text{IQR}) = 92 - (1.5 \times 7) = 81.5$%

The upper fence is $Q_3 + (1.5 \times \text{IQR}) = 99 + (1.5 \times 7) = 109.5$%

This is greater than 100% which is impossible, so there are no outliers outside the upper fence. The value 74 is outside the lower fence, so that is the only outlier.

c)

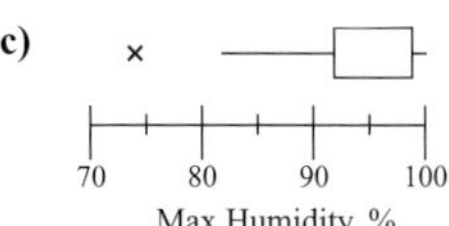

$Q_2 = Q_3 = 99$, so the median and upper quartile are both represented by the right-hand edge of the box.

Q4 **a)** There are 18 data values for Pigham. Since $18 \div 2 = 9$, the median is halfway between the 9th and 10th data values (which are both 35). So the median = 35.

Since $18 \div 4 = 4.5$, the lower quartile (Q_1) is the 5th data value. So $Q_1 = 23$.

Since $3 \times 18 \div 4 = 13.5$, the upper quartile ($Q_3$) is the 14th data value. So $Q_3 = 46$.

Interquartile range = $Q_3 - Q_1 = 46 - 23 = 23$

Lower fence is $Q_1 - (1.5 \times \text{IQR}) = 23 - (1.5 \times 23) = -11.5$
This is less than 0, which is an impossible number of items of junk mail, so there are no outliers outside the lower fence.

The upper fence is $Q_3 + (1.5 \times \text{IQR}) = 46 + (1.5 \times 23) = 80.5$

None of the values fall outside the fences, so there are no outliers.

b)

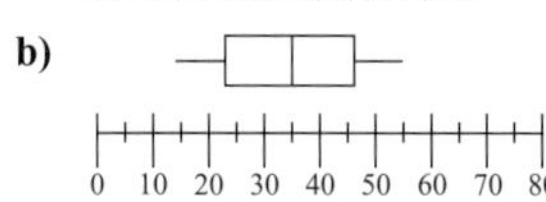

c) There are 18 data values for Goossea, so the median is halfway between the 9th and 10th data values.
So the median = 27.5.

The lower quartile (Q_1) is the 5th data value.
So the lower quartile = 15.

The upper quartile (Q_3) is the 14th data value.
So the upper quartile = 35.

The interquartile range = $Q_3 - Q_1 = 35 - 15 = 20$.

The lower fence is $Q_1 - (1.5 \times \text{IQR}) = 15 - (1.5 \times 20) = -15$
This means there are no 'low outliers'.

The upper fence is $Q_3 + (1.5 \times \text{IQR}) = 35 + (1.5 \times 20) = 65$

This means that the value of 75 is an outlier (but the next highest value, 50, is not an outlier).

So the box plot looks like this:

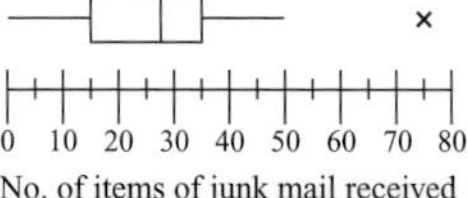

Q5 **a)** The lower end of the horizontal line in the diagram is at 172, so 172 km/h is the lowest speed that is not an outlier.

b) Using the ends of the box to find the quartiles gives $Q_1 = 175$ km/h and $Q_3 = 181$ km/h.
So IQR = $Q_3 - Q_1 = 181 - 175 = 6$ km/h, and
lower fence = $Q_1 - (1.5 \times \text{IQR}) = 175 - (1.5 \times 6) = 166$ km/h
So an outlier at the lower end of the data must be less than 166 km/h. The speeds are measured to the nearest km/h, so the maximum possible value of the outlier is 165 km/h.

Q6 **a)** Median in greenhouse = 260 g. Median outside = 240 g.
So the difference is 260 – 240 = 20 g. *[1 mark]*

b) $Q_1 = 220$ g and $Q_3 = 270$ g, so IQR = 270 – 220 = 50 g
[2 marks available — 1 mark for reading the values for Q_1 and Q_3 from the box plot, 1 mark for the final answer]

c) E.g. The two outliers for the plants grown outside are within the range of non-outlier masses for the plants grown in the greenhouse, so they would not be outliers.
[1 mark for a sensible explanation]

d) Median mass for plants grown outside is 240 g.
For plants grown in the greenhouse, $Q_1 = 230$ g and $Q_2 = 260$ g, so 240 g lies between Q_1 and Q_2.
240 g is $\frac{1}{3}$ of the way between 230 g and 260 g, so using linear interpolation, 240 g is approximately the $25 + \frac{1}{3} \times 25 = 25 + 8.33... = 33.3...$th percentile.
So 100 – 33.3... = 66.6... = 67% (2 s.f.) of the plants in the greenhouse produced a greater mass of strawberries than the median mass for the plants grown outside.
[3 marks available — 1 mark identifying that 240 g lies between Q_1 and Q_2, 1 mark for an attempt to use linear interpolation, 1 mark for the final answer]

Exercise 2.10 — Variance and Standard Deviation

Q1 **a)** $\bar{x} = \frac{756 + 755 + 764 + 778 + 754 + 759}{6} = \frac{4566}{6} = 761$

b) $\sum x^2 = 756^2 + 755^2 + 764^2 + 778^2 + 754^2 + 759^2 = 3\,475\,138$

c) variance $= \frac{\sum x^2}{n} - \bar{x}^2 = \frac{3\,475\,138}{6} - 761^2 = 68.666... = 68.7$ (3 s.f.)

d) standard deviation $= \sqrt{\text{variance}} = \sqrt{68.666...} = 8.29$ (3 s.f.)

e) There are no outliers or extreme values to affect the standard deviation in a way that would make it unrepresentative of the rest of the data set.

Q2 **a)** Start by adding an extra row to the table for fx.

x	1	2	3	4
frequency, f	7	8	4	1
fx	7	16	12	4

Then $\bar{x} = \frac{\sum fx}{\sum f} = \frac{39}{20} = 1.95$

b) Now add two more rows to the table.

x	1	2	3	4
frequency, f	7	8	4	1
fx	7	16	12	4
x^2	1	4	9	16
fx^2	7	32	36	16

So $\sum fx^2 = 7 + 32 + 36 + 16 = 91$

c) variance $= \frac{\sum fx^2}{\sum f} - \bar{x}^2 = \frac{91}{20} - 1.95^2 = 0.7475$

d) standard deviation $= \sqrt{\text{variance}} = \sqrt{0.7475} = 0.865$ (3 s.f.)

Q3 a) Total = 3.2 + 2.4 + 2.8 + 3.1 + 2.9 + 2.5 + 2.7 + 2.6 = 22.2
So mean = 22.2 ÷ 8 = 2.775

b) $(3.2 - 2.775)^2 + (2.4 - 2.775)^2 + (2.8 - 2.775)^2 + (3.1 - 2.775)^2 + (2.9 - 2.775)^2 + (2.5 - 2.775)^2 + (2.7 - 2.775)^2 + (2.6 - 2.775)^2 = 0.555$

c) Variance = 0.555 ÷ 8 = 0.069375
Standard deviation = $\sqrt{\text{variance}} = \sqrt{0.069375}$ = 0.263391... = 0.26 (2 s.f.)

Q4 a) $\bar{x} = \frac{\sum x}{n} = \frac{290.7}{100} = 2.907$ mm

variance = $\frac{\sum x^2}{n} - \bar{x}^2 = \frac{6150.83}{100} - 2.907^2$ = 53.05765... mm²

standard deviation = $\sqrt{\text{variance}} = \sqrt{53.05765...}$ = 7.284068... = 7.28 mm (3 s.f.)

[2 marks available — 1 mark for the correct variance or expression for standard deviation, 1 mark for the correct standard deviation]

b) Outliers are more than 3 standard deviations away from the mean: 2.907 + 3 × 7.284068... = 24.8 (3 s.f.)
The x-value 35.5 > 24.8 so it is an outlier. *[1 mark]*
You only need to consider $\bar{x}$ + 3 standard deviations because the x-value 35.5 is greater than $\bar{x}$.

Q5 a) Add some more columns to the table showing the class mid-points (x), as well as fx, x^2 and fx^2.

Yield, w (kg)	f	Mid-point, x	fx	x^2	fx^2
$50 \le w < 60$	23	55	1265	3025	69575
$60 \le w < 70$	12	65	780	4225	50700
$70 \le w < 80$	15	75	1125	5625	84375
$80 \le w < 90$	6	85	510	7225	43350
$90 \le w < 100$	2	95	190	9025	18050

So $\sum f = 58$, $\sum fx = 3870$, $\sum fx^2 = 266050$.

variance = $\frac{\sum fx^2}{\sum f} - \left(\frac{\sum fx}{\sum f}\right)^2 = \frac{266050}{58} - \left(\frac{3870}{58}\right)^2$
= 134.95838... = 135 kg² (3 s.f.)

b) standard deviation = $\sqrt{134.95838...}$ = 11.6 kg (3 s.f.)

c) Because the data is grouped.

Q6 a) $\bar{x} = \frac{\sum x}{n} = \frac{50\,400}{80}$ = £630 *[1 mark]*

b) Variance = $\frac{\sum x^2}{n} - \bar{x}^2 = \frac{33\,153\,750}{80} - 630^2$
= 17521.875

So standard deviation = $\sqrt{17521.875}$ = 132.370...
= £132.37 (to the nearest penny)

[2 marks available — 1 mark for the correct variance or expression for standard deviation, 1 mark for the correct standard deviation]

c) Upper and lower fences for outliers are 630 ± (3 × 132.37), so lower fence = £232.89 and upper fence = £1027.11.
The cheapest mobile phone that could have been included in the data would cost £232.89, and the most expensive mobile phone that could have been included would cost £1027.11.
[3 marks available — 1 mark for a method to find the fences, 1 mark for both fences correct, 1 mark for sensible interpretation]
You could also have rounded your answers to the nearest pound.

Q7 The mean $\bar{x} = \frac{\sum x}{n} = 4$, so $\sum x = 4n$.
Standard deviation = $\sqrt{2}$, so variance = $\frac{\sum x^2}{n} - \bar{x}^2 = 2$.
So $\sum x^2 = (2 + \bar{x}^2) \times n = (2 + 4^2) \times n = 18n$.
Then $\sum x^2 - \sum x = 18n - 4n = 14n$.
From the question, $\sum x^2 - \sum x = 98$,
so $14n = 98 \Rightarrow n = 7$, so there are 7 values in the data set.

Q8 a) Work out the total duration of all the 23 eruptions that Su has timed. This is $\sum x = n\bar{x} = 23 \times 3.42 = 78.66$ minutes.
Work out the total duration of all the 37 eruptions that Ellen has timed. This is $\sum y = n\bar{y} = 37 \times 3.92 = 145.04$ minutes
So the total duration of the last 60 eruptions is:
$\sum x + \sum y = 78.66 + 145.04 = 223.7$ minutes
So the mean duration of the last 60 eruptions is:
$\frac{223.7}{60} = 3.72833 = 3.73$ minutes (3 s.f.)

b) Work out the sum of squares of the durations of all the 23 eruptions that Su has timed. The s.d. is 1.07, so the variance is 1.07² — use this in the formula for variance.
variance = $\frac{\sum x^2}{n} - \bar{x}^2 \Rightarrow 1.07^2 = \frac{\sum x^2}{23} - 3.42^2$
So $\sum x^2 = 23 \times (1.07^2 + 3.42^2) = 295.3499$

Do the same for the 37 eruptions that Ellen has timed. The s.d. is 0.97, so the variance is 0.97²
— use this in the formula for variance.
variance = $\frac{\sum y^2}{n} - \bar{y}^2 \Rightarrow 0.97^2 = \frac{\sum y^2}{37} - 3.92^2$
So $\sum y^2 = 37 \times (0.97^2 + 3.92^2) = 603.3701$

Now you can work out the total sum of squares (for all 60 eruptions):
$\sum x^2 + \sum y^2 = 295.3499 + 603.3701 = 898.72$
So the variance for all 60 eruptions is:
variance = $\frac{898.72}{60} - \left(\frac{223.7}{60}\right)^2 = 1.0781... = 1.08$ min² (3 s.f.)
When finding the variance of the 60 durations you use the mean from part a) written as a fraction (or the full decimal) so your answer is as accurate as possible.

c) This means the standard deviation of the durations is $\sqrt{1.0781...} = 1.0383... = 1.04$ min (3 s.f.)

Exercise 2.11 — Coding

Q1 Since $y = \frac{x - 20\,000}{15}$, $\bar{y} = \frac{\bar{x} - 20\,000}{15}$.
This means $\bar{x} = 15 \times 12.4 + 20\,000 = 20\,186$.
s.d. of x = 15 × s.d. of y = 15 × 1.34 = 20.1

Q2 a) All the values are of the form '0.6_', and so if you subtract 0.6 from all the values, and then multiply what's left by 100, you'll end up with coded data values between 1 and 10.
So code the data values using $y = 100(x - 0.6)$, where x is an original data value and y is the corresponding coded value.
This gives y-values of: 1, 7, 3, 3, 6, 5, 4, 8, 4, 2

b) $\bar{y} = \frac{1+7+3+3+6+5+4+8+4+2}{10} = \frac{43}{10} = 4.3$
Find the sum of squares of the coded values, $\sum y^2$.
This is $\sum y^2 = 229$.
So variance = $\frac{\sum y^2}{n} - \bar{y}^2 = \frac{229}{10} - 4.3^2 = 4.41$
This gives a standard deviation of $\sqrt{4.41} = 2.1$
Since $y = 100(x - 0.6)$, $\bar{y} = 100(\bar{x} - 0.6)$
This means: $\bar{x} = \frac{\bar{y}}{100} + 0.6 = \frac{4.3}{100} + 0.6 = 0.643$ cm
Since $y = 100(x - 0.6)$, s.d. of y = 100 × s.d. of x
So s.d. of x = s.d. of y ÷ 100 = 2.1 ÷ 100 = 0.021 cm

Q3 a) All the values are between 4460 and 4550, so subtract 4450 from all the values, and then divide what's left by 10.
You'll end up with coded data values between 1 and 10.
So code the data values using $y = \frac{x - 4450}{10}$, where x is an original data value and y is the corresponding coded value.
This gives y-values of: 10, 6, 3, 8, 3, 2, 9, 4, 10, 5, 1, 7

b) $\bar{y} = \frac{10+6+3+8+3+2+9+4+10+5+1+7}{12}$
$= \frac{68}{12} = 5.66...$

Find the sum of squares of the coded values, $\sum y^2$.
This is $\sum y^2 = 494$.

So variance $= \frac{\sum y^2}{n} - \bar{y}^2 = \frac{494}{12} - (5.66...)^2 = 9.055...$

This gives standard deviation of $\sqrt{9.055...} = 3.009...$

Since $y = \frac{x - 4450}{10}$, $\bar{y} = \frac{\bar{x} - 4450}{10}$

This means: $\bar{x} = 10\bar{y} + 4450 = 10(5.66...) + 4450$
$= 56.66... + 4450 = 4506.66...$
$= 4510$ km (to nearest 10 km)

Since $y = \frac{x - 4450}{10}$, s.d. of y = s.d. of $x \div 10$

So s.d. of $x = 10 \times$ s.d. of $y = 10 \times 3.009...$
$= 30.09... = 30$ km (to nearest 10 km)

Q4 Make a new table showing the class mid-points (x) and their corresponding coded values (y), as well as fy, y^2 and fy^2.

Weight (nearest g)	100-104	105-109	110-114	115-119
Frequency, f	2	6	3	1
Class mid-point, x	102	107	112	117
Coded value, y	0	5	10	15
fy	0	30	30	15
y^2	0	25	100	225
fy^2	0	150	300	225

Then $\bar{y} = \frac{\sum fy}{\sum f} = \frac{75}{12} = 6.25$

variance of $y = \frac{\sum fy^2}{\sum f} - \bar{y}^2 = \frac{675}{12} - 6.25^2 = 17.1875$

This means standard deviation of $y = \sqrt{17.1875} = 4.15$ (3 s.f.)

Now you can convert these back to values for x.
Since $y = x - 102$: $\bar{x} = \bar{y} + 102 = 6.25 + 102 = 108.25$ g
s.d. of x = s.d. of $y = 4.15$ g (3 s.f.)

Q5 **a)** Estimate of the coded mean: $\bar{y} = \frac{262.5}{20} = 13.125$

Estimate of the coded variance:
$\frac{4023.4375}{20} - \left(\frac{262.5}{20}\right)^2 = 28.90625 = 28.9$ (3 s.f.)

[2 marks available — 1 mark for finding the mean, 1 mark for finding the variance]

b) Estimate of original mean: $\bar{x} = 4 \times 13.125 + 2500 = 2552.5$

Estimate of original variance: $(4 \times \sqrt{28.90625})^2 = 462.5$

[3 marks available — 1 mark for finding the original mean, 1 mark for using standard deviation to find the variance, 1 mark for finding the original variance]

You could also calculate the original variance as 4^2 × the coded variance.

Q6 Using the coding $y = x + 2$. Then $\sum y = 7$ and $\sum y^2 = 80$.

So $\bar{y} = \frac{\sum y}{n} = \frac{7}{20} = 0.35$

And the variance of y is: $\frac{\sum y^2}{n} - \bar{y}^2 = \frac{80}{20} - 0.35^2 = 3.8775$

So standard deviation for $y = \sqrt{3.8775} = 1.97$ (3 s.f.)

So $\bar{x} = \bar{y} - 2 = 0.35 - 2 = -1.65$, and
standard deviation of x = standard deviation of $y = 1.97$ (3 s.f.)

Q7 Look at the standard deviations first.

standard deviation of $y = \frac{\text{standard deviation of } x}{\text{b}}$,

so $4.3 = \frac{21.5}{\text{b}} \Rightarrow \text{b} = 5$

So $\bar{y} = \frac{\bar{x} - \text{a}}{5} \Rightarrow 7 = \frac{195 - \text{a}}{5} \Rightarrow \text{a} = 160$

So the equation used by the student was $y = \frac{x - 160}{5}$.

Q8 Add the mid-point of each interval to the table:

y	$0 < y \le 5$	$5 < y \le 10$	$10 < y \le 15$	$15 < y \le 20$	$20 < y \le 25$
Freq, f	22	19	23	p	16
Mid-point, y	2.5	7.5	12.5	17.5	22.5

a) $\bar{y} = 10^6\bar{x} - 100 = 10^6 \times (0.00011195) - 100 = 11.95$

Using the table:
$\bar{y} = [(2.5 \times 22) + (7.5 \times 19) + (12.5 \times 23) + 17.5p$
$+ (22.5 \times 16)] \div [22 + 19 + 23 + p + 16]$

So $\bar{y} = (845 + 17.5p) \div (80 + p) = 11.95$
$\Rightarrow 845 + 17.5p = 956 + 11.95p$
$\Rightarrow 5.55p = 111 \Rightarrow p = 20$

[4 marks available — 1 mark for finding $\bar{y}$, 1 mark for using the table to find an expression for $\bar{y}$, 1 mark for setting up the equation, 1 mark for the correct answer]

b) Add extra rows to the table:

y	$0 < y \le 5$	$5 < y \le 10$	$10 < y \le 15$	$15 < y \le 20$	$20 < y \le 25$
Freq, f	22	19	23	p	16
Mid-point, y	2.5	7.5	12.5	17.5	22.5
y^2	6.25	56.25	156.25	306.25	506.25
fy^2	137.5	1068.75	3593.75	6125	8100

$\sum fy^2 = 137.5 + 1068.75 + 3593.75 + 6125 + 8100 = 19025$
and $\sum f = 22 + 19 + 23 + 20 + 16 = 100$.

So variance of $y = \frac{\sum fy^2}{\sum f} - \bar{y}^2 = \frac{19025}{100} - 11.95^2 = 47.4475$

Standard deviation of $y = \sqrt{47.4475} = 6.8882...$

Standard deviation of $x = (6.888\,214...) \div 10^6$
$= 6.89 \times 10^{-6}$ mm (3 s.f.)

[4 marks available — 1 mark for finding $\sum fy^2$, 1 mark for finding the variance of y, 1 mark for decoding the standard deviation, 1 mark for the final answer in the correct form]

Exercise 2.12 — Comparing Distributions

Q1 The median is higher for Shop B. This shows that the prices in Shop B are generally higher. The median in Shop A is approximately £37 while the median in Shop B is approximately £63, so the difference between the average prices is around £26.

Although the ranges in the two shops are quite similar, the interquartile range (IQR) for Shop B is higher than that for Shop A. This shows that the prices of shoes in Shop B are more varied than the prices in Shop A.

Q2 **a)** For the men: mean $= \frac{\sum x}{n} = \frac{73}{10} = 7.3$ hours

There are 10 values, so the median is halfway between the 5th and 6th values in the ordered list.
So the median is 7 hours.

Don't forget to sort the list before trying to find the median — it's an easy mistake to make.

For the women: mean $= \frac{\sum x}{n} = \frac{85}{10} = 8.5$ hours

Again, there are 10 values, so the median is halfway between the 5th and 6th values. So the median is 8.5 hours.

The mean and median are both higher for the women, so they get between 1 and 1.5 hours more sleep per night, on average, than the men.

b) For the men: s.d. $= \sqrt{\frac{\sum x^2}{n} - \bar{x}^2} = \sqrt{\frac{553}{10} - 7.3^2}$
$= 1.42$ hours (3 s.f.)

For the women: s.d. $= \sqrt{\frac{\sum x^2}{n} - \bar{x}^2} = \sqrt{\frac{749}{10} - 8.5^2}$
$= 1.63$ hours (3 s.f.)

The standard deviation is slightly higher for the women, so the number of hours of sleep for the women varies slightly more from the mean than it does for the men.

Q3 E.g. Class A has a higher median (36 m compared to 27 m) — on average, students in Class A threw the javelin further than students in Class B.
Class B has a lower IQR (15 m compared to 22 m) and a lower range (26 m compared to 36 m) — the distances that students in Class B threw the javelin were more consistent than the distances thrown by students in Class A.
[2 marks available — 1 mark for a valid comparison of location, 1 mark for a valid comparison of dispersion]

Q4 Location: The 50th percentile is the median, so the median for x and y are almost equal — there isn't much difference in the location or "centre" of the two data sets.
Dispersion: The 20th to 80th interpercentile range is 13.6 for data set x, and 14.6 for data set y. This means that the middle 60% of data is more spread out in data set y than data set x.
[3 marks available — 1 mark for comparison of location between data sets, 1 mark for working out an interpercentile range, 1 mark for comparing an interpercentile range between data sets]
You could also have compared a different interpercentile range.

Q5 **a)** Calculate the mean for each sample.

A: $\bar{x} = \frac{\sum fx}{\sum f} = \frac{3598}{141} = 25.517... = 25.5$ cm (3 s.f.)

B: $\bar{x} = \frac{\sum fx}{\sum f} = \frac{4344}{120} = 36.2$ cm

The mean is higher for the river B sample, so the trout are longer on average than trout from the river A sample.

b) Calculate the standard deviation for each sample.

A: s.d. $= \sqrt{\frac{\sum fx^2}{\sum f} - \bar{x}^2} = \sqrt{\frac{96\,376}{141} - (25.5...)^2}$

$= 5.688... = 5.69$ cm (3 s.f.)

B: s.d. $= \sqrt{\frac{\sum fx^2}{\sum f} - \bar{x}^2} = \sqrt{\frac{184\,366}{120} - (36.2)^2}$

$= 15.031... = 15.0$ cm (3 s.f.)

The standard deviation is higher for river B, so the lengths of trout in the river B sample are more varied than the lengths of the trout in the river A sample.

Q6 Read the quartiles off the graphs:

Island A: $Q_1 \approx 8$ °C, $Q_2 \approx 15$ °C, $Q_3 \approx 19$ °C $\Rightarrow$ IQR ≈ 11 °C

Island B: $Q_1 \approx 9.5$ °C, $Q_2 \approx 12$ °C, $Q_3 \approx 15.5$°C $\Rightarrow$ IQR ≈ 6 °C

Island A has a higher median temperature, suggesting that the temperatures on island A are generally hotter than island B.

The data for island A has a larger interquartile range than that of island B — the data for island B is grouped more closely about the median, while the data for island A is more spread out. This suggests that the temperatures on island A tend to vary more than those on island B.
[3 marks available — 1 mark for comparison of location between data sets, 1 mark for working out an interpercentile range, 1 mark for comparing an interpercentile range between data sets]

Exercise 2.13 — Scatter Diagrams and Correlation

Q1 **a)**

b) Strong positive correlation

Q2 **a)**

b) No correlation

Q3 **a)**

b) No — if the student were right, the scatter diagram would show negative correlation. However, the data is scattered randomly, so there is zero correlation between the variables.

Q4 **a)**

b) The data shows overall positive correlation, but there are two clusters of data. One shows some positive correlation, while the other doesn't look correlated at all.

c) The circumference of 3.5 cm or the length of 8.9 cm.

Q5 **a)**

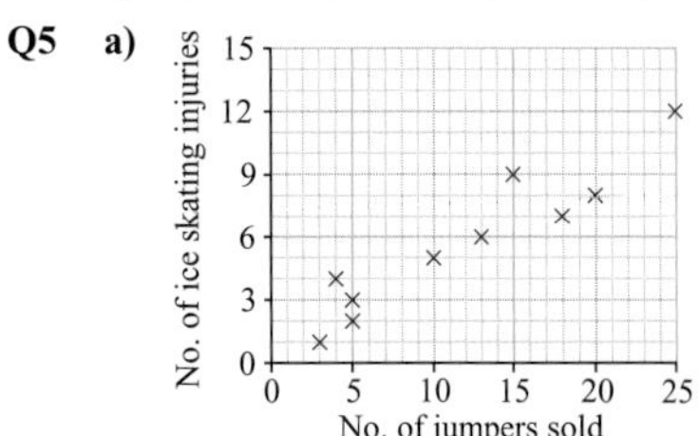

b) The data shows a fairly strong positive correlation.

c) The two things are correlated but the number of woolly jumpers sold is unlikely to increase the number of ice skating-related injuries, or vice versa. A third factor may be involved — e.g. a decrease in outside temperature might be the cause of both trends.

Q6 **a)** (Strong) positive correlation — as the number of cars increases, the number of cafes also increases. *[1 mark]*

b) E.g. While they are correlated, it's unlikely that the amount of traffic is directly related to the number of cafes in a city centre. There is likely to be a third variable that affects both, e.g. a city with a larger population is likely to have more traffic and more demand for cafes in the city centre.
[2 marks available — 1 mark for a suitable explanation of why the statement is incorrect, 1 mark for an example of a third variable]

Q7 a)

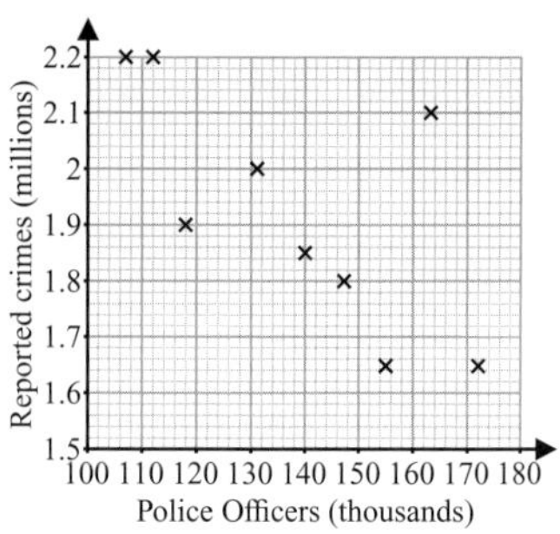

[2 marks available — 2 marks for all points plotted correctly, otherwise 1 mark for at least four points plotted correctly]

b) (Strong) negative correlation — as the number of police officers increases, the number of reported crimes decreases. *[1 mark]*

c) The 2009 data (163, 2.1) could be an outlier as it doesn't fit the general trend of the other data points.
[1 mark for the correct point or year with suitable justification]

Q8 a) (Weak) negative correlation *[1 mark]*

b) E.g. While they are correlated, it's unlikely that the cost of a car is directly related to the number of accidents that car is involved in. There is likely to be a third variable that affects both, e.g. there are fewer expensive cars on the roads, so there is less chance of them being involved in accidents.
[1 mark for a sensible explanation]

c) The outlier is a particularly cheap car, so it is possible that there are fewer of these sold (e.g. it might not have features required by customers). If there were fewer of them on the road, they would be involved in fewer accidents.
[1 mark for a sensible explanation]

Exercise 2.14 — Explanatory and Response Variables

Q1 a) **Explanatory variable**: the time spent practising the piano each week
Response variable: the number of mistakes made in a test at the end of the week.
It is the amount of practice that would determine the performance in the test, not the other way around.

b) **Explanatory variable**: the age of a second-hand car
Response variable: the value of a second-hand car.
It is the age of the car that would affect its value, not the other way around.

c) **Explanatory variable**: the population of a town
Response variable: the number of phone calls made in a town in a week.
It is the population that would affect the number of calls, not the other way around.

d) **Explanatory variable**: the amount of sunlight falling on a plant in an experiment
Response variable: the growth rate of a plant in an experiment
It is the amount of sunlight that would affect the growth rate, not the other way around. (Or you could say that the amount of sunlight can be directly controlled, as this is an experiment.)

Q2 For this question, all answers should be quantitative data.

a) (i) E.g. temperature

(ii) E.g. amount of drug administered/time since drug taken

b) (i) E.g. disposable income/value of house/value of car

(ii) E.g. height of tree/number of leaves or branches/width of trunk

Q3 a) Explanatory: Advertising budget
Response: Volume of sales

b) Explanatory: Production efficiency
Response: Cost

c) Explanatory: Height
Response: IQ (or vice versa)

Q4 a)

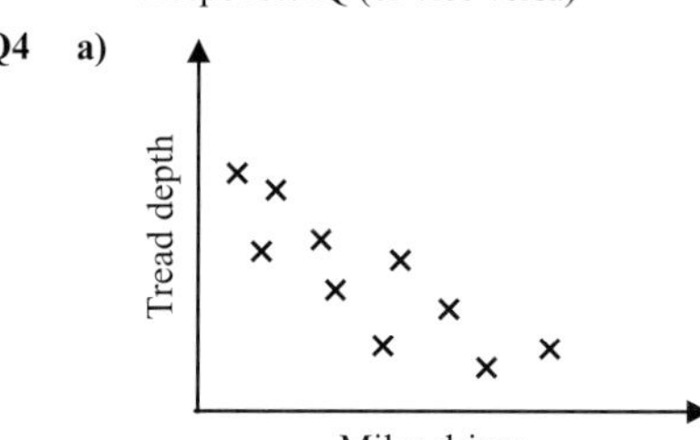

[3 marks available — 1 mark for putting the labels on the correct axes, 1 mark for showing a negative correlation, 1 mark for plotting exactly 10 points]

b) Miles driven is the explanatory (independent) variable as this can be controlled by the driver of the car. The tread depth cannot be directly controlled, and will depend on the number of miles driven, so this is the response (dependent) variable. *[1 mark]*

Exercise 2.15 — Regression Lines

Q1 a) y is the response variable (since this is the regression line of y on x).

b) (i) $1.67 + 0.107 \times 5 = 2.205$

(ii) $1.67 + 0.107 \times 20 = 3.81$

Q2 a) £30 000 *[1 mark]*

b) Substitute $V = 17\,200$ and $a = 8$ into the regression equation:
$17\,200 = 30\,000 - k \times 8 \Rightarrow 12\,800 = 8k \Rightarrow k = 1600$.
k is the amount (in pounds) that the value of the car model decreases by per year.
[3 marks available — 1 mark for substituting into the regression line equation, 1 mark for correct value of k, 1 mark for a sensible explanation]

c) (i) The age of the car is within the range used to generate the model, so it is likely to be a reliable estimate.
[1 mark for a sensible comment with justification]

(ii) This is extrapolation — the age of the car is outside of the range used to generate the model, so this may not be a reliable estimate.
[1 mark for a sensible comment with justification]

Q3 a) $58.8 - 2.47 \times 7 = 41.51$ — so the volunteer would be predicted to have approximately 42 spots.
This is interpolation (since 7 is between 2 and 22, which are the values of x between which data was collected).
This estimate should be reliable.

b) $58.8 - 2.47 \times 0 = 58.8$ — so the volunteer would be predicted to have approximately 59 spots.
This is extrapolation (since 0 is less than 2, which was the smallest value of d for which data was collected).
This estimate may not be reliable.

c) Using the formula for $d = 30$ is extrapolation, since 30 is greater than 22, the largest value of d for which data was collected. The model isn't valid for $d = 30$, since you can't have a negative number of spots. But this doesn't mean that the regression equation is wrong.

Q4 a) (i) 1990s is decade 3, so $d = 3$.
Then $l = 67.6 - 2.7 \times 3 = 59.5$ cm *[1 mark]*

(ii) 2010s is decade 5, so $d = 5$.
Then $l = 67.6 - 2.7 \times 5 = 54.1$ cm *[1 mark]*

b) Set $l = 18$ in the regression equation and solve for d:
$18 = 67.6 - 2.7d \Rightarrow 2.7d = 49.6 \Rightarrow d = 18.3703...$
The average length of the fish in the pond is expected to be less than 18 cm when $d = 18.37...$, which means the first decade where the average length will be lower will be at $d = 19$ i.e. the 2150s.
Assumptions: e.g. the average length of the fish in the pond will continue to decrease according to the model.
This prediction is unreliable as it is extrapolation, as $d = 19$ is outside the range of values for d that were used to create the model. There is no evidence that the decrease in length predicted by the model will continue beyond the known data.
[4 marks available — 1 mark for setting up an equation or inequality to solve, 1 mark for the correct decade, 1 mark for a sensible assumption, 1 mark for a valid explanation mentioning extrapolation]

Q5 a) Positive correlation — B is a positive constant, so when x increases by 1, y will increase by B. *[1 mark]*

b) Substitute both coordinates into the regression line equation and solve the equations simultaneously:
$9.5 = A + 4.5B$ (1)
$17.48 = A + 10.2B$ (2)
(2) – (1): $7.98 = 5.7B \Rightarrow B = 1.4$
When $B = 1.4$, $A = 9.5 - (4.5 \times 1.4) = 3.2$.
[3 marks available — 1 mark for generating two equations to solve simultaneously, 1 mark for the correct value of A, 1 mark for the correct value of B]

c) The regression line equation doesn't give any information about how close the data points lie to the line, so the strength of correlation cannot be interpreted.
[1 mark for a sensible comment]

Chapter 2 Review Exercise

Q1 a) Plot the mid-point of the classes on the x-axis and the frequencies on the y-axis.

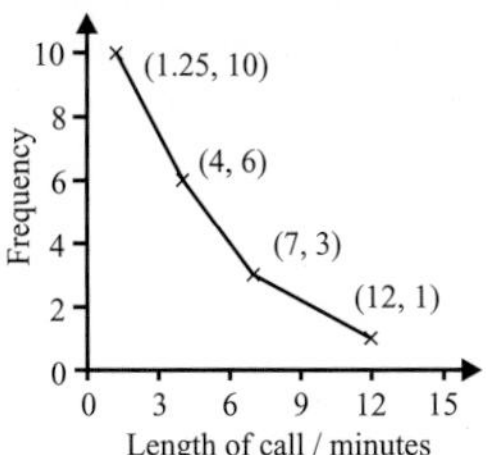

b) First add rows to the table to show class boundaries, the class widths and the frequency densities.

Length of calls	0 - 2	3 - 5	6 - 8	9 - 15
Lower class boundary	0	2.5	5.5	8.5
Upper class boundary	2.5	5.5	8.5	15.5
Class width	2.5	3	3	7
Frequency	10	6	3	1
Frequency density	4	2	1	$\frac{1}{7}$

Then you can draw the histogram:

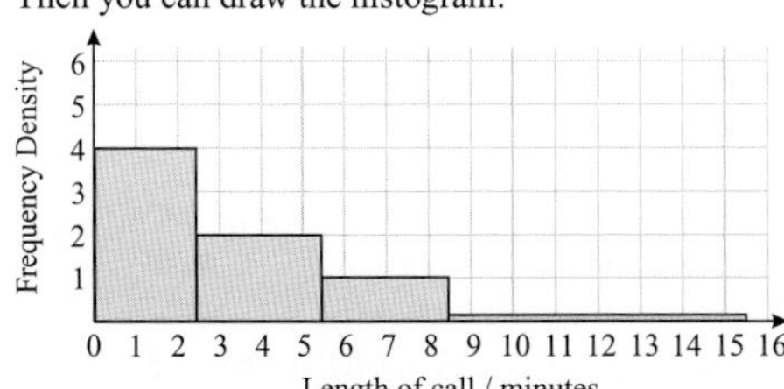

Q2 a) There are 5 people in the 6-7 class, so each large square on the y-axis represents a frequency density of $5 \div 5 = 1$. So, the frequency of the 2-4.5 class interval is $8 \times 2.5 = 20$, and the frequency of the 4.5-6 class is $6 \times 1.5 = 9$. So there are $20 + 9 = 29$ adults with a TLC between 2 and 6 litres.
[2 marks available — 1 mark for finding the scale for frequency density, 1 mark for the final answer]

b) "Less than 5 litres" will be everyone in the 2-4.5 class and approximately $\frac{1}{3}$ of the 4.5-6 class. From part a), the frequency for the 2-4.5 class is 20 and the frequency for the 4.5-6 class is 9. So $20 + \frac{1}{3} \times 9 = 20 + 3 = 23$ adults had a TLC less than 5 litres. *[1 mark]*

c) "Between 4 and 8 litres" will be $\frac{1}{5}$ of the 2-4.5 class, everyone in the 4.5-6 and 6-7 classes and $\frac{1}{2}$ of the 7-9 class.
The frequency of the 7-9 class is $4 \times 2 = 8$, so the number of adults with TLCs in this range is:
$(\frac{1}{5} \times 20) + (1.5 \times 6) + (1 \times 5) + (\frac{1}{2} \times 8) = 22$
So $\frac{22}{30} = 73.33...\%$ of the adults are within this range.
This is quite close to 70%, so these 30 adults are typical of the population.
[3 marks available — 1 mark for calculating the number of adults within 4 and 8 litres, 1 mark for finding this as a percentage of all the adults, 1 mark for the final answer and reasoning]

Q3 a) Add a row showing the values of fx and a column showing the totals $\sum f$ and $\sum fx$ to the table:

No. of live concerts (x)	0	1	2	3	4	5	6	Total
Frequency (f)	2	5	16	15	10	9	8	65
fx	0	5	32	45	40	45	48	215

So the mean is $215 \div 65 = 3.30769... = 3.3$ (2 s.f.)

b) $\frac{n}{2} = \frac{65}{2} = 32.5$, so the median is the 33rd value.
This is in the '3' column, so the median is 3.
The '2' column has the highest frequency, so the mode is 2.

Q4 Add a row showing the values of fx and a column showing the totals $\sum f$ and $\sum fx$ to the table:

x	0	1	2	3	4	Total
f	5	4	4	2	1	16
fx	0	4	8	6	4	22

So the mean is $22 \div 16 = 1.375$
There are 16 values. $16 \div 2 = 8$, so the median is midway between the 8th and 9th values. Both these values are in the column $x = 1$, so the median is 1.
$x = 0$ has the highest frequency, so the mode = 0.

Q5

Speed (mph)	Frequency, f	Mid-point, x	fx
30 - 34	12	32	384
35 - 39	37	37	1369
40 - 44	9	42	378
45 - 50	2	47.5	95

$\sum f = 60$, $\sum fx = 2226$
So estimate of mean $= 2226 \div 60 = 37.1$ mph
$\sum f \div 2 = 60 \div 2 = 30$, so the median is in the class 35 - 39 class. Now you need to sketch that class:

b_1
34.5 a_1 m 39.5
12 a_2 30 49
b_2

Now solve $\frac{a_1}{b_1} = \frac{a_2}{b_2}$. This gives:
$\frac{m - 34.5}{39.5 - 34.5} = \frac{30 - 12}{49 - 12} \Rightarrow \frac{m - 34.5}{5} = \frac{18}{37}$
$\Rightarrow m = 5 \times \frac{18}{37} + 34.5 = 36.932...$
$\Rightarrow$ estimate of median is 36.9 mph (3 s.f.)
The modal class is 35 - 39 mph.

Q6 a) Let the median be x. Then the mode is also x, and the value of the outlier is $2x$. The mode occurs 3 times, and there is one value greater than and one value less than the mode, so the middle three values of the five must all be x. Let the lowest value be y.
So we have the five values: $y \quad x \quad x \quad x \quad 2x$
Using the mean: $\frac{y + 5x}{5} = 6.4$
So $y = 32 - 5x$. That means the lowest value (y) is the difference between 32 and 5 lots of the mode (x).

b) $\frac{y + 2x}{2} = 7$, so $y + 2x = 14$. Solve the equations $y = 32 - 5x$ (1) and $y + 2x = 14$ (2) simultaneously:
Substituting (1) into (2):
$(32 - 5x) + 2x = 14 \Rightarrow 32 - 3x = 14 \Rightarrow 3x = 18 \Rightarrow x = 6$
Substituting $x = 6$ back into (1) gives $y = 32 - (5 \times 6) = 2$
So the five numbers are 2, 6, 6, 6, 12

Q7 a) Highest value = 42, Lowest value = 6
So range = 42 – 6 = 36

b) The data set A in order is:
7, 8, 9, 11, 14, 16, 16, 18, 21, 23, 26, 28, 31, 37, 41
$n = 15 \Rightarrow \frac{n}{4} = 3.75$, so the lower quartile (Q_1) is in position 4 in the ordered list. So $Q_1 = 11$.
$\frac{3n}{4} = 11.25$, so the upper quartile (Q_3) is in position 12 in the ordered list. So $Q_3 = 28$.
So the interquartile range of A = 28 – 11 = 17.

c) The data set B in order is:
6, 12, 15, 15, 15, 19, 24, 24, 25, 30, 33, 36, 38, 40, 42
$n = 15$
$\frac{20}{100} \times n = \frac{20}{100} \times 15 = 3$, meaning the 20th percentile (P_{20}) is halfway between the values in position 3 and position 4 in the ordered list. So $P_{20} = 15$.
$\frac{80}{100} \times n = \frac{80}{100} \times 15 = 12$, meaning the 80th percentile (P_{80}) is halfway between the value in position 12 and 13 in the ordered list. So $P_{80} = \frac{36 + 38}{2} = 37$.
So the 20% to 80% interpercentile range of B is 37 – 15 = 22.

Q8 a) Add a cumulative frequency row to the table:

r	$0 \le r < 2$	$2 \le r < 4$	$4 \le r < 6$	$6 \le r < 8$	$8 \le r < 10$
Freq	2	6	7	4	1
Cumul. freq.	2	8	15	19	20

Then plot the cumulative frequency diagram.

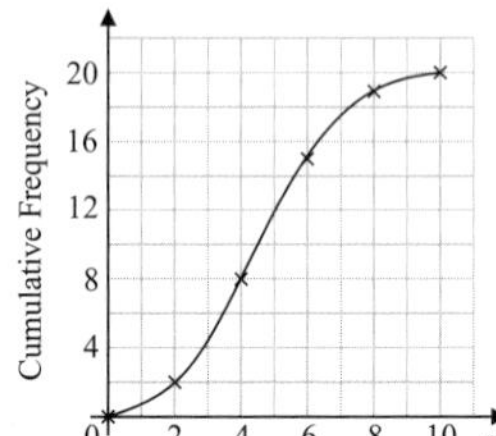

b) (i) Go up from $r = 3$ on the horizontal axis and read off the frequency. The estimated number of r-values less than 3 is 5.

(ii) Go up from $r = 5$ on the horizontal axis and read off the frequency. This gives you the number of r-values less than 5, which is 11.5. Subtract from the total frequency to get the estimated number of r-values more than 5:
20 – 11.5 = 8.5, giving an estimate of 8 or 9 values.

(iii) Go up from the curve from $r = 3.5$ on the horizontal axis and read off the frequency. This gives you the number of r-values less than 3.5, which is 6.5. Repeat from $r = 7$. This gives you the number of r-values less than 7, which is 17. Subtract to get the estimated number of r-values between $r = 3.5$ and $r = 7$:
17 – 6.5 = 10.5, giving an estimate of 10 or 11 values.

c) (i) $\frac{n}{4} = 5$, so go across from 5 on the vertical axis and read off the r-value. So Q_1 is 3.
$\frac{3n}{4} = 15$, so go across from 15 on the vertical axis and read off the r-value. So Q_3 is 6.
So the interquartile range is 6 – 3 = 3.

(ii) $\frac{10}{100} \times n = \frac{10}{100} \times 20 = 2$, so go across from 2 on the vertical axis and read off the r-value. So P_{10} is 2.
$\frac{90}{100} \times n = \frac{90}{100} \times 20 = 18$, so go across from 18 on the vertical axis and read off the r-value. P_{90} is 7.5, so the 10% to 90% interpercentile range is 7.5 – 2 = 5.5.

Q9 a) The middle 80% is the interpercentile range from P_{10} to P_{90}.
P_{10} position = 160 ÷ 10 = 16
Reading from the graph, this is about 63 seconds.
P_{90} position = $\frac{90}{100} \times 160 = 144$
Reading from the graph, this is about 88 seconds.
So the coach should set the qualifying time for the Advanced competition at 63 seconds and for the Intermediate competition at 88 seconds.
[4 marks available — 1 mark for finding the percentiles needed, 1 mark for reading P_{10} from the graph, 1 mark for reading P_{90} from the graph, 1 mark for the final answers]

b) First find the IQR:
Q_1 position = 160 ÷ 4 = 40, which is about 69 seconds.
Q_3 position = (160 ÷ 4) × 3 = 120, which is about 79 seconds.
So the IQR is 79 – 69 = 10 seconds.
So the upper fence is 79 + 1.5 × 10 = 94 seconds.
The cumulative frequency at 94 seconds is approximately 153, so 160 – 153 = 7 of the amateur athletes took longer than 94 seconds. $\frac{7}{160} \times 100 = 4.375\%$, so about 4% of athletes will not get entered for any of the three competitions.
[4 marks available — 1 mark for reading Q_1 and Q_3 from the graph, 1 mark for the upper fence, 1 mark for a method to find the percentage, 1 mark for the final answer]

Q10 a) (i) Worker A's list in order is 2, 3, 4, 4, 5, 5, 5, 7, 10, 12
$\frac{n}{2} = 5$, so the median lies halfway between the 5th and 6th data values. Median = 5 minutes.

(ii) $\frac{n}{4} = 2.5$, so the lower quartile is the 3rd value.
$Q_1 = 4$ minutes.
$\frac{3n}{4} = 7.5$, so the upper quartile is the 8th value.
$Q_3 = 7$ minutes.

(iii) IQR = $Q_3 - Q_1 = 7 - 4 = 3$
Lower fence = $Q_1 - (1.5 \times \text{IQR}) = 4 - (1.5 \times 3) = -0.5$
Upper fence = $Q_3 + (1.5 \times \text{IQR}) = 7 + (1.5 \times 3) = 11.5$
The lower fence is negative so there are no lower outliers. The value 12 is outside the upper fence, so 12 is an outlier.

b) Worker B's list in order is: 4, 4, 6, 7, 8, 8, 9, 9, 10, 11
$\frac{n}{2} = 5$, so the median lies halfway between the 5th and 6th data values. Median = 8 minutes.
$\frac{n}{4} = 2.5$, so the lower quartile is the 3rd value.
$Q_1 = 6$ minutes.
$\frac{3n}{4} = 7.5$, so the upper quartile is the 8th value.
$Q_3 = 9$ minutes.
IQR = $Q_3 - Q_1 = 9 - 6 = 3$
Lower fence = $Q_1 - (1.5 \times \text{IQR}) = 6 - (1.5 \times 3) = 1.5$
Upper fence = $Q_3 + (1.5 \times \text{IQR}) = 9 + (1.5 \times 3) = 13.5$

None of worker B's values are less than the lower fence or more than the upper fence, so there are no outliers for Worker B. Now you can draw box plots for both workers:

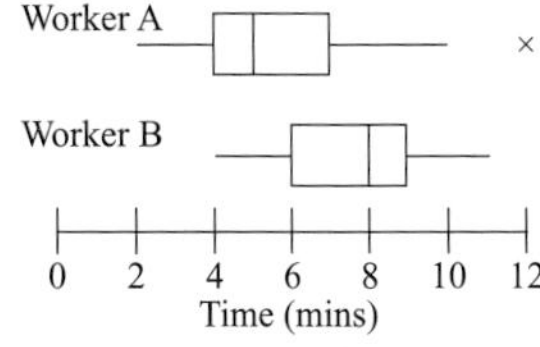

c) Possible answers include:

- The times for Worker B are 3 minutes longer than those for Worker A, on average.
- The IQR for both workers is the same — generally they both work with the same consistency.
- The range for Worker A is larger than that for Worker B. Worker A had a few items he/she could iron very quickly and a few which took a long time.

d) E.g. Worker A would be better to employ, as the median time is less than for Worker B, and the upper quartile is less than the median of Worker B, suggesting that Worker A would generally iron items quicker than Worker B.

Q11 a) 91 seconds *[1 mark]*

b) 109.5 seconds *[1 mark]*

c) From the box plot, $Q_1 = 141$ and $Q_3 = 162$.
So IQR = 162 – 141 = 21 seconds
[2 marks available — 1 mark for finding Q_1 and Q_3 on the box plot, 1 mark for correct IQR]

d) The 90th percentile is the $(20 \div 10) \times 9 = 18^{th}$ value.
A quarter of the total number of people take between 162 and 172 seconds, so there are 5 times in this interval.
So the third time in this interval is the 90th percentile.
$\frac{3}{5}$ into the 162-172 interval is:
$162 + \frac{3}{5} \times (172 - 162) = 162 + \frac{3}{5} \times 10 = 168$ seconds
[3 marks available — 1 mark for finding the 90th percentile, 1 mark for an attempt at estimating, 1 mark for the final answer]

Q12 Total = 11 + 12 + 14 + 17 + 21 + 23 + 27 = 125
Mean = 125 ÷ 7 = 17.85... = 17.9 (3 s.f.)
Variance $= \frac{\sum x^2}{n} - \bar{x}^2 = \frac{2449}{7} - (17.85...)^2 = 30.979...$
So standard deviation $= \sqrt{30.979...} = 5.565... = 5.57$ (3 s.f.)

Q13

Score	Frequency, f	Mid-point, x	fx
100 - 106	6	103	618
107 - 113	11	110	1210
114 - 120	22	117	2574
121 - 127	9	124	1116
128 - 134	2	131	262

$\sum f = 50, \sum fx = 5780, \sum fx^2 = 670\,618$
So estimate of mean = 5780 ÷ 50 = 115.6
Variance $= \frac{\sum fx^2}{\sum f} - \bar{x}^2 = \frac{670\,618}{50} - (115.6)^2 = 49$

Q14 a) The data is not available for this day. *[1 mark]*

b) Mean $= \frac{\sum s}{n} = 104.1 \div 14 = 7.435... = 7.44$ hours (3 s.f.)
Standard deviation $= \sqrt{\frac{\sum s^2}{n} - \left(\frac{\sum s}{n}\right)^2}$
$= 2.959... = 2.96$ hours (3 s.f.)
[3 marks available — 1 mark for correct mean, 1 mark for correct expression for standard deviation, 1 mark for correct standard deviation]

c) Their value for the standard deviation will be lower than the real value because 11.2 is closer to the mean than 12.2.
[2 marks available — 1 mark for saying their value is lower, 1 mark for correct reason]

d) $\bar{s} + 3 \times \text{s.d.} = 7.44 + 3(2.96) = 16.32$
$\bar{s} - 3 \times \text{s.d.} = 7.44 - 3(2.96) = -1.44$
None of the observations are above 16.32 and they cannot be negative, so there are no outliers.
[2 marks available — 1 mark for calculating mean ± three standard deviations, 1 mark for correct explanation]

Q15 a) Let $y = x - 20$, then $\bar{y} = \frac{\sum(x-20)}{n} = \frac{125}{100} = 1.25$
$\bar{x} = \bar{y} + 20 = 1.25 + 20 = 21.25$
s.d. of $y = \sqrt{\frac{\sum y^2}{n} - \bar{y}^2} = \sqrt{\frac{221}{100} - 1.25^2} = 0.8046...$
s.d. of x = s.d. of y = 0.805 (3 s.f.)

b) Lower fence = 21.25 – 2(s.d.) = 21.25 – 2 × 0.805 = 19.64
19.6 is lower than this value, so is an outlier.

Q16

Time	Frequency, f	Mid-point, x	y	fy
30 - 33	3	31.5	–4	–12
34 - 37	6	35.5	0	0
38 - 41	7	39.5	4	28
42 - 45	4	43.5	8	32

$\sum f = 20, \sum fy = 48, \sum fy^2 = 416$
Estimate of mean $(\bar{y}) = 48 \div 20 = 2.4$
So estimate of mean $(\bar{x}) = 2.4 + 35.5 = 37.9$ minutes
Estimated s.d. of $y = \sqrt{\frac{\sum fy^2}{\sum f} - \bar{y}^2} = \sqrt{\frac{416}{20} - (2.4)^2}$
$= \sqrt{15.04} = 3.878...$ minutes
So estimated s.d. of x = 3.88 minutes (3 s.f.)

Q17 a) Add more rows to the table:

y	$-5 \leq y < -3$	$-3 \leq y < 0$	$0 \leq y < 2$	$2 \leq y < 5$	$5 \leq y < 7$	$7 \leq y < 9$
Freq, f	1	7	23	90	55	8
Mid-point	–4	–1.5	1	3.5	6	8
fy	–4	–10.5	23	315	330	64
fy^2	16	15.75	23	1102.5	1980	512

$\sum f = 184, \sum fy = 717.5, \bar{y} = \frac{717.5}{184} = 3.89945...$
So $\bar{x} = 4\bar{y} + 1000 = (4 \times 3.89945...) + 1000$
$= 1015.597... = 1016$ hPa (to the nearest integer)
[3 marks available — 1 mark for a correct method, 1 mark for finding $\bar{y}$, 1 mark for decoding to find $\bar{x}$]

b) From the table in part a) above:
$\sum f = 184, \sum fy^2 = 3649.25$
Variance of $y = \frac{3649.25}{184} - (3.89945...)^2$
$= 4.6271...$
Standard deviation of $y = \sqrt{4.6271...}$
$= 2.15107...$
Decode to get the standard deviation for the original data.
Standard deviation of x = 4 × standard deviation of y
= 4 × 2.15107...
= 8.6042... = 8.60 hPa (3 s.f.)
[3 marks available — 1 mark for finding $\sum fy^2$, 1 mark for finding the coded standard deviation, 1 mark for the final answer]

c) Outliers for the coded values:
$\bar{y} \pm 3 \times$ s.d. of $y = 3.89945... \pm (3 \times 2.15107...)$
So the lower fence is –2.55 (3 s.f.) and the upper fence is 10.4 (3 s.f.). As there is a value in the range $-5 \leq y < -3$, there must be at least one outlier in the data. There may also be outliers in the range $-3 \leq y < 0$, but it's not possible to say for certain without more information.
[3 marks available — 1 mark for method for finding fences, 1 mark for finding the values –2.55 and 10.4, 1 mark for showing that there are outliers in the data]

Q18 $x = \frac{m - 3000}{1000} \Rightarrow m = 1000x + 3000$

$\bar{x} = \frac{\sum x}{n} = 52.4 \div 40 = 1.31$,
so $\bar{m} = 1.31 \times 1000 + 3000 = 4310$ kg

s.d. of $x = \sqrt{\frac{S_{xx}}{n}} = \sqrt{0.245} = 0.494...$,
so s.d. of $m = 0.494... \times 1000 = 494.97... = 495$ kg (3 s.f.)
[4 marks available — 1 mark for $\bar{x}$, 1 mark for $\bar{m}$, 1 mark for s.d. of x, 1 mark for s.d. of m]

Q19 a) Work out the mid-points for each class:
$(0 + 10.5) \div 2 = 5.25$, $(10.5 + 25.5) \div 2 = 18$,
$(25.5 + 40.5) \div 2 = 33$, $(40.5 + 60.5) \div 2 = 50.5$,
$(60.5 + 80.5) \div 2 = 70.5$,
$(80.5 + 120.5) \div 2 = 100.5$

$$\text{Mean} = \frac{\sum fx}{\sum f} = \frac{4501.5}{120} = 37.5125 \text{ miles} = 37.5 \text{ miles (3 s.f.)}$$

$$\text{Standard deviation} = \sqrt{\frac{\sum fx^2}{\sum f} - \bar{x}^2} = \sqrt{\frac{237612.375}{120} - 37.5125^2}$$
$$= 23.935... = 23.9 \text{ miles (3 s.f.)}$$

[3 marks available — 1 mark for correct mean, 1 mark for correct expression for standard deviation, 1 mark for correct standard deviation]

b) Add a cumulative frequency column to the table:

Distance (miles)	Freq.	Cumulative freq.
0 - 10	14	14
11 - 25	29	43
26 - 40	31	74
41 - 60	27	101
61 - 80	13	114
81 - 120	6	120

$\frac{n}{4} = 120 \div 4 = 30$, meaning the lower quartile (Q_1) must lie in the class '11 - 25'. Now you need to sketch that class.

b_1
10.5 a_1 Q_1 25.5
14 a_2 30 43
b_2

Finally, solve $\frac{a_1}{b_1} = \frac{a_2}{b_2}$. This gives:

$$\frac{Q_1 - 10.5}{25.5 - 10.5} = \frac{30 - 14}{43 - 14} \Rightarrow \frac{Q_1 - 10.5}{15} = \frac{16}{29}$$
$$\Rightarrow Q_1 = 15 \times \frac{16}{29} + 10.5 = 18.775... \text{ miles}$$

$\frac{3n}{4} = 3 \times 120 \div 4 = 90$, meaning the upper quartile (Q_3) must lie in the class '41 - 60'. Now sketch that class.

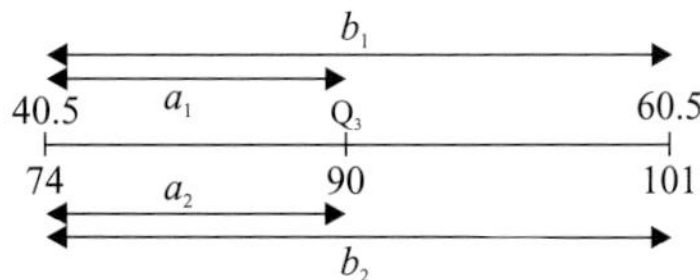

Finally, solve $\frac{a_1}{b_1} = \frac{a_2}{b_2}$. This gives:

$$\frac{Q_3 - 40.5}{60.5 - 40.5} = \frac{90 - 74}{101 - 74} \Rightarrow \frac{Q_3 - 40.5}{20} = \frac{16}{27}$$
$$\Rightarrow Q_3 = 20 \times \frac{16}{27} + 40.5 = 52.351... \text{ miles}$$

So the interquartile range is:
$52.351... - 18.775... = 33.575... = 33.6$ miles (3 s.f.)
[4 marks available — 1 mark for finding positions of Q_1 and Q_3, 1 mark for correct Q_1 value, 1 mark for correct Q_3 value, 1 mark for correct interquartile range]

c) The mean for 2019 is greater, so people travelled further on average than in 2018. The standard deviation is smaller for 2019, so the distance travelled varied less in 2019 than in 2018.
[2 marks available — 1 mark for correctly comparing means, 1 mark for correctly comparing standard deviations]

Q20 a)

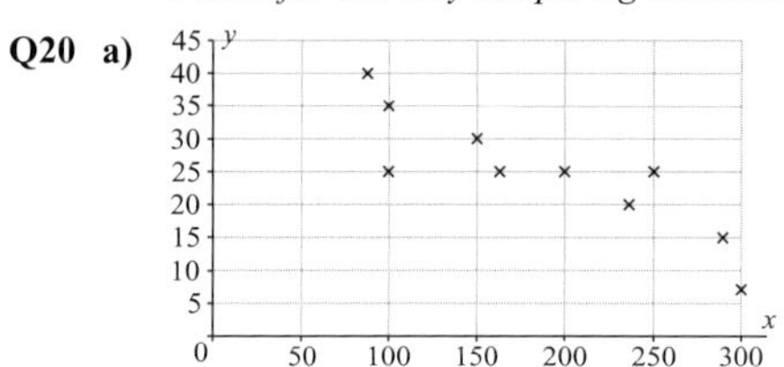

b) The data appears to show strong negative correlation.

Q21 a) (Strong) negative correlation *[1 mark]*

b) (6, 72) and (21, 93) are possible outliers *[1 mark]*

c) E.g. The player happened to play better or worse than usual that week/the score was recorded incorrectly/the player was affected by external factors such as the weather.
[1 mark for a sensible comment]

Q22 a) Explanatory: number of sunny days
Response: number of volleyball-related injuries

b) Explanatory: number of rainy days
Response: number of board game-related injuries

c) Explanatory: a person's disposable income
Response: amount they spend on luxuries

d) Explanatory: number of cups of tea drunk
Response: number of trips to the loo in a day

Q23 a) $m = 3.94r - 94 = 3.94(60) - 94 = 142.4$ g

b) This estimate might not be very reliable because it uses an r-value from outside the range of the original data. It is extrapolation.

Q24 a) There are 8 runners in the 2 - 3 hours class, so each interval on the vertical axis represents $8 \div 2 = 4$ runners.
So there are:
$0.5 \times 32 = 16$ runners in the 3 - 3.5 hours class.
$0.5 \times 36 = 18$ runners in the 3.5 - 4 hours class.
$2 \times 13 = 26$ runners in the 4 - 6 hours class.
$2 \times 6 = 12$ runners in the 6 - 8 hours class.
Use this data to form the following table:

Time (hours)	Frequency, f	Mid-point, x	fx
2 - 3	8	2.5	20
3 - 3.5	16	3.25	52
3.5 - 4	18	3.75	67.5
4 - 6	26	5	130
6 - 8	12	7	84

$\sum f = 80$ and $\sum fx = 353.5$, so the estimate for the mean is

$$\frac{\sum fx}{\sum f} = \frac{353.5}{80} = 4.418... \text{ hours} = 4.42 \text{ hours (3 s.f.)}$$
or 4 hours 25 minutes (to nearest minute)

[6 marks available — 1 mark for working out the value of the vertical axis intervals, 1 mark for two correct frequencies, a further 1 mark for all correct frequencies, 1 mark for mid-point values, 1 mark for sum of fx, 1 mark for correct answer]

b) 'Less than 3 hours 20 minutes' includes the 2 - 3 class and two-thirds of the 3 - 3.5 class, so the number of runners who qualify is: $8 + \frac{2}{3} \times 16 = 18.6... \approx 19$ runners (accept 18)
[2 marks available — 1 mark for finding two-thirds of the 3 - 3.5 hours class, 1 mark for correct answer]

Q25 Find the mid-points of each class:

Height (h cm)	$140 \le h < 150$	$150 \le h < 160$	$160 \le h < 170$	$170 \le h < 180$
Mid-point	145	155	165	175
Freq.	24	36	p	18

Total height = $(145 \times 24) + (155 \times 36) + 165p + (175 \times 18)$
$= 12\,210 + 165p$
Total frequency = $24 + 36 + p + 18 = 78 + p$

The mean is 159 cm, so $\frac{12210 + 165p}{78 + p} = 159$

$\Rightarrow 12\,210 + 165p = 12\,402 + 159p \Rightarrow 6p = 192 \Rightarrow p = 32$

Q26 The middle 70% of the data means 15% of the data is on either side, so you need to find the 15th and 85th percentiles.
There are 184 data values, so P_{15} position = $184 \times \frac{15}{100} = 27.6$, so it is in the $1000 \le v < 2000$ class. Now sketch the class:

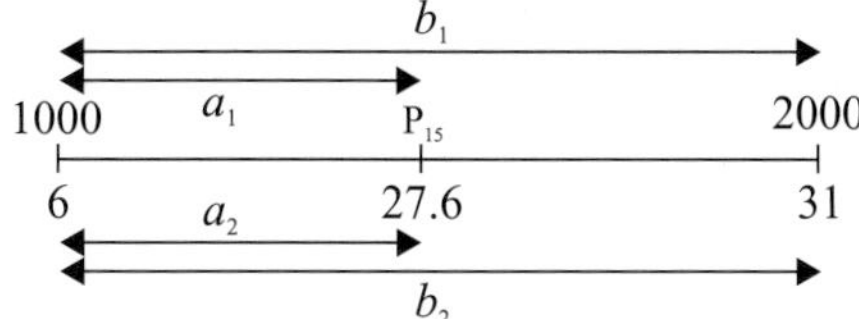

Now, solve $\frac{a_1}{b_1} = \frac{a_2}{b_2}$. This gives

$\frac{P_{15} - 1000}{2000 - 1000} = \frac{27.6 - 6}{31 - 6} \Rightarrow \frac{P_{15} - 1000}{1000} = \frac{21.6}{25}$

$\Rightarrow P_{15} = 1000 \times \frac{21.6}{25} + 1000 = 1864$

P_{85} position = $184 \times \frac{85}{100} = 156.4$, so it is in the $3000 \le v < 4000$ class. Now sketch the class:

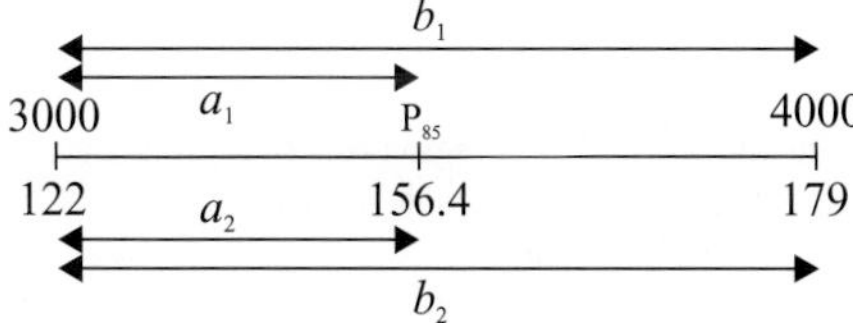

Now, solve $\frac{a_1}{b_1} = \frac{a_2}{b_2}$. This gives

$\frac{P_{85} - 3000}{4000 - 3000} = \frac{156.4 - 122}{179 - 122} \Rightarrow \frac{P_{85} - 3000}{1000} = \frac{34.4}{57}$

$\Rightarrow P_{85} = 1000 \times \frac{34.4}{57} + 3000 = 3604$ (to the nearest integer)

So, $a = 1864$ and $b = 3604$
[5 marks available — 1 mark for identifying the percentiles needed, 1 mark for a correct method to find the percentiles, 1 mark for correct P_{15}, 1 mark for correct P_{85}, 1 mark for stating the values of a and b]

Q27 Median = $Q_2 = 154$, so $Q_3 - 154 = 308 - 2Q_1 \Rightarrow Q_3 + 2Q_1 = 462$
Also, IQR = $Q_3 - Q_1 = 33$
Solve these equations simultaneously by subtracting:
$3Q_1 = 429 \Rightarrow Q_1 = 143$, so $Q_3 = Q_1 + 33 = 176$
Lower fence: $143 - (1.5 \times 33) = 93.5$, so 88 is an outlier.
Upper fence: $176 + (1.5 \times 33) = 225.5$, so 220 is not an outlier.
You also might have spotted from $Q_3 - Q_2 = 2(Q_2 - Q_1)$ that the median (Q_2) is $\frac{2}{3}$ of the way from Q_1 to Q_3.
This means $Q_1 = 154 - \frac{1}{3}(33) = 143$ and $Q_3 = 154 + \frac{2}{3}(33) = 176$.

Q28 **a)** There is a positive correlation between age and cortisol level. *[1 mark for correct answer]*

b) E.g. On average, as a patient gets one year older, their blood cortisol level increases by 0.16 μg/dl.
[1 mark for correct interpretation]

c) E.g. The data was collected from adults, so $a = 10$ is outside the range of the data — the researcher is extrapolating. The relationship between a and c may not continue outside the range of data, so the researcher's claim may not be valid.
[1 mark for correct reasoning]

Chapter 3: Probability

Prior Knowledge Check

Q1 The number of times you would expect the dice to land on 4 if it was unbiased is $\frac{1}{6} \times 60 = 10$ times, which is the number of times recorded. However, you don't have the information about which numbers the dice landed on the other times it was rolled, so you can't say whether the dice is biased or not.

Q2 Total number of pupils in the class = $8 + 4 + 6 + 2 = 20$.
Total number of pupils who play football = $4 + 6 = 10$.
So, probability that a randomly chosen pupil plays football = $\frac{10}{20} = \frac{1}{2}$.

Q3 **a)**

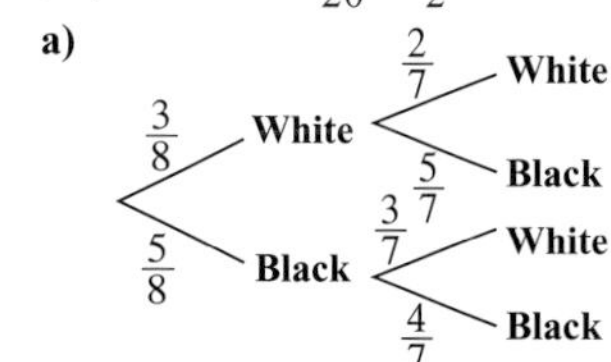

b) P(White, White) = $\frac{3}{8} \times \frac{2}{7} = \frac{6}{56} = \frac{3}{28}$

Exercise 3.1-3.2 — The Basics of Probability and Sample Spaces

Q1 **a)** There are $21 + 10 + 19 + 15 = 65$ seeds in total.
There are 10 poppy seeds, so P(poppy seed) = $\frac{10}{65} = \frac{2}{13}$.

b) $21 + 19 = 40$ of the seeds are marigold or cornflower.
So P(marigold or cornflower) = $\frac{40}{65} = \frac{8}{13}$.

c) $21 + 10 + 19 = 50$ seeds aren't daisy seeds,
so P(not daisy) = $\frac{50}{65} = \frac{10}{13}$.
You could also find P(daisy) = $\frac{15}{65}$ and then subtract it from 1 to find P(not daisy).

Q2 **a)** There is 1 outcome corresponding to the 7 of diamonds, and 52 outcomes in total. So P(7 of diamonds) = $\frac{1}{52}$

b) There is 1 outcome corresponding to the queen of spades, and 52 outcomes in total. So P(queen of spades) = $\frac{1}{52}$

c) There are 4 outcomes corresponding to a '9', and 52 outcomes in total. So P(9 of any suit) = $\frac{4}{52} = \frac{1}{13}$

d) There are 26 outcomes corresponding to a heart or a diamond, and 52 outcomes in total.
So P(heart or diamond) = $\frac{26}{52} = \frac{1}{2}$

Q3 **a)** 6 of the 36 outcomes are prime numbers.
So P(product is a prime number) = $\frac{6}{36} = \frac{1}{6}$

b) 14 of the 36 outcomes are less than 7.
So P(product is less than 7) = $\frac{14}{36} = \frac{7}{18}$

c) 6 of the 36 outcomes are multiples of 10.
So P(product is a multiple of 10) = $\frac{6}{36} = \frac{1}{6}$

Q4 **a)** In the sample space diagram, the numbers at the top of the columns show all the possible outcomes of the dice roll. There are 7 outcomes, and each outcome represents one side, so the dice has 7 sides.

b) The total scores are found by adding the dice and card scores. In the third row the total score is always 5 more than the dice score, so the number on the third card must be 5.

c) There are $5 \times 7 = 35$ possible outcomes.
Seven of the outcomes are less than 7.
So P(total less than 7) = $\frac{7}{35} = \frac{1}{5}$.

Q5 **a)** E.g.

	1	2	3	4	5	6	7	8	9	10
T	•	•	•	•	•	•	•	•	•	•
H	•	•	•	•	•	•	•	•	•	•

b) There are 5 ways of getting an even number and 'tails', and 20 outcomes altogether.
So P(even number and tails) = $\frac{5}{20} = \frac{1}{4}$

Q6 **a)** E.g.

–	1	2	3	4	5	6
1	0	1	2	3	4	5
2	1	0	1	2	3	4
3	2	1	0	1	2	3
4	3	2	1	0	1	2
5	4	3	2	1	0	1
6	5	4	3	2	1	0

b) 6 of the 36 outcomes are zero.
So P(score is zero) = $\frac{6}{36} = \frac{1}{6}$

c) None of the outcomes are greater than 5.
So P(score is greater than 5) = 0

d) The most likely score is the one corresponding to the most outcomes — so it's 1. 10 of the 36 outcomes give a score of 1, so: P(1) = $\frac{10}{36} = \frac{5}{18}$

Q7 **a)** The possible numbers are 0123, 1234, 2345, ... , 6789, so there are 7 four-digit numbers with consecutive digits. There are 10 000 numbers (0000 to 9999),
So the probability is $\frac{7}{10\,000}$.

b) Provided that the number ends in 0 the other three digits can be anything, so there are 10^3 four-digit numbers which end in a 0. The probability is therefore $\frac{1000}{10\,000} = \frac{1}{10}$.
You could have also worked out that the end digit has a 1 in 10 chance of being a 0, so there's a 1 in 10 chance that the four-digit number ends in a 0.

Q8 Start by drawing a sample space diagram to show all the possible outcomes for the two spins combined. Then circle the ones that correspond to the event 'number on spinner 2 is greater than number on spinner 1'.

E.g.

Spinner 2 \ Spinner 1	2	3	5	7	11
10	⦿	⦿	⦿	⦿	•
8	⦿	⦿	⦿	⦿	•
6	⦿	⦿	⦿	•	•
4	⦿	⦿	•	•	•
2	•	•	•	•	•

There are 13 outcomes that correspond to the event 'number on spinner 2 is greater than number on spinner 1', and 25 outcomes altogether. So
P(spinner 2 > spinner 1) = $\frac{13}{25}$

Q9 **a)**

+ (Dice \ Spinner)	0	1	2	3	4
1	1	2	3	4	5
2	2	3	4	5	6
3	3	4	5	6	7
4	4	5	6	7	8
5	5	6	7	8	9
6	6	7	8	9	10

[2 marks available — 1 mark for showing a sample space with 30 outcomes, 1 mark for all correct entries]

b) There are a total of 30 possible outcomes and 10 of the outcomes are at least 7.
So the probability of getting a score of at least 7 is $\frac{10}{30} = \frac{1}{3}$.
[1 mark for the correct answer]

c) If the dice is more likely to land on 1, the probability of getting a final score that includes a 1 from the dice increases. As the highest score that a player can get with a 1 from the dice is 5, the chances of a final score of 7 or more will decrease. Therefore, the probability of getting a score of 7 or more will be less than the probability calculated in b).
[1 mark for a correct reason]

Q10 **a)** According to the ratio, $\frac{13}{27}$ of the fish in the tank are female, so the probability of selecting a female fish is $\frac{13}{27}$.
[1 mark for the correct answer]

b) 143 ÷ 13 = 11, so there are 14 × 11 = 154 male fish in the tank and 297 fish in total.
As 13 fish have already been sold, there are a total of 284 fish left that can be selected, of which, 143 – 6 = 137 are female. So the probability of selecting a female is $\frac{137}{284}$ = 0.482... = 0.48 to 2 d.p.
[2 marks available — 1 mark for finding the total number of fish available for selection, 1 mark for the correct answer]

Q11 **a)** There are 10 odd numbers less than 20, so the probability of selecting a card with an odd number less than 20 on it is $\frac{10}{2k+1}$.

b) There are 50 odd numbers less than 100, and 10 square numbers less than or equal to 100, but 5 of the square numbers are odd (1, 9, 25, 49, 81) so have already been counted. So the probability of selecting a card with a square number less than or equal to 100, or with an odd number less than 100 is $\frac{55}{2k+1}$.

c) There are a total of $2k + 1$ numbers, of which k are even. So the probability of selecting a card with an even number on it is $\frac{k}{2k+1}$.

Q12 **a)** The probability of hitting region A is equal to the area of A divided by the area of the whole target.
Area of A = $\pi \times 5^2 = 25\pi$
Area of whole target = $\pi \times 50^2 = 2500\pi$
So P(hits A) = $\frac{25\pi}{2500\pi} = \frac{1}{100} = 0.01$.
[2 marks available — 1 mark for dividing area of A by area of whole target, 1 mark for the correct simplified answer]

b) **(i)** Area of B = $\pi \times 25^2$ – Area of A = $625\pi - 25\pi = 600\pi$,
so P(hits B) is $\frac{600\pi}{2500\pi} = 0.24$. *[1 mark]*

(ii) Area of C = Area of whole target – Area of A and B
= $2500\pi - 625\pi = 1875\pi$
So P(hits C) = $\frac{1875\pi}{2500\pi} = 0.75$. *[1 mark]*
Alternatively, the probability can be calculated by 1 – 0.24 – 0.01 = 0.75.

c) Jon's coach is likely to be much more experienced at archery, so it is unlikely that their arrow will hit a region at random.
[1 mark for a correct reason]

Exercise 3.3-3.4 — Using Venn Diagrams and Two-Way Tables

Q1 **a)** Total number of ladybirds = 20 + 9 + 1 + 15 + 3 + 2 = 50
Number of red ladybirds = 20 + 15 = 35
Number of orange ladybirds = 1 + 2 = 3
So P(red or orange) = $\frac{35+3}{50} = \frac{38}{50} = \frac{19}{25}$

b) Number of ladybirds that are yellow or have fewer than 10 spots = 20 + 9 + 1 + 3 = 33
So P(yellow or < 10 spots) = $\frac{33}{50}$

Q2 **a)** Label the diagram by starting in the middle with the probability for A and B. Then subtract this probability from P(A) and P(B). And remember to find P(neither A nor B) by subtracting the other probabilities from 1. So:

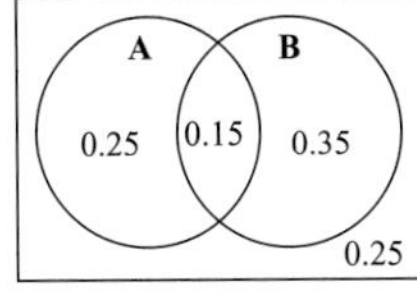

b) Look at the part of A that doesn't overlap with B: P(A and not B) = 0.25

c) Look at the part of B that doesn't overlap with A: P(B and not A) = 0.35

d) Add together all the probabilities contained within A or B or both: P(A or B) = 0.25 + 0.15 + 0.35 = 0.75

e) Look at the area outside both A and B: P(neither A nor B) = 0.25

Q3 **a)** Use the totals to fill in the gaps:
No coffee/BC Tops = 0.51 – 0.16 – 0.11 = 0.24
'No coffee' total = 0.24 + 0.12 + 0.14 = 0.50
'Nenco' total = 1 – 0.18 – 0.50 = 0.32
Nenco/No tea = 0.32 – 0.16 – 0.07 = 0.09
'Cumbria' total = 1 – 0.51 – 0.27 = 0.22
Yescafé/No tea = 0.27 – 0.09 – 0.14 = 0.04
Yescafé/Cumbria = 0.22 – 0.07 – 0.12 = 0.03

	BC Tops	**Cumbria**	**No tea**	**Total**
Nenco	0.16	0.07	**0.09**	**0.32**
Yescafé	0.11	**0.03**	**0.04**	0.18
No coffee	0.24	0.12	0.14	0.50
Total	0.51	**0.22**	0.27	1

b) **(i)** P(Cumbria and Yescafé) = 0.03

(ii) P(Coffee) = 1 – P(No coffee) = 1 – 0.50 = 0.50
You could also find this by adding up the totals for the two brands of coffee:
P(Coffee) = P(Nenco) + P(Yescafé) = 0.32 + 0.18 = 0.50

(iii) P(tea but no coffee) = P(BC Tops and no coffee) + P(Cumbria and no coffee) = 0.24 + 0.12 = 0.36
Another way to find this is P(No coffee) – P(No coffee and no tea) = 0.50 – 0.14 = 0.36

Q4 **a)** **(i)** The total number of pairs produced is 140 + 290 + 320 + 320 + 210 + 450 + 380 = 2110, of which 140 + 210 = 350 are Sporty.
So P(Sporty) = $\frac{350}{2110} = \frac{35}{211}$.

(ii) 320 pairs are Casual and brown, 210 pairs are Sporty and black, so P(Casual and brown, or Sporty and black) is $\frac{530}{2110} = \frac{53}{211}$.
[2 marks available — 1 mark for each correct probability]

b) The total number of Smart pairs produced is 320 + 450 = 770, of which 450 are black.
So P(black, given Smart) = $\frac{450}{770} = \frac{45}{77}$ *[1 mark]*

Q5 **a)** P(A and B and C) = $\frac{3}{32}$ *[1 mark]*

b) The only region of the Venn diagram not included in the event P(A or B' or C) is the region with probability $\frac{3}{16}$, so the probability is $1 - \frac{3}{16} = \frac{13}{16}$. *[1 mark]*

c) The region corresponding to the event P(A and B' and C') is the region with probability $\frac{1}{4}$, so the probability is $\frac{1}{4}$. *[1 mark]*

d) The only region excluded from the event P(A' or B' or C) is the region with probability $\frac{1}{64}$, so the probability is $1 - \frac{1}{64} = \frac{63}{64}$. *[1 mark]*

Q6 **a)** Let M be 'studies maths' and P be 'studies physics'. The total number of students is 144, so that goes in the bottom right-hand corner. You can also fill in the totals for the P row and the M column — these are the total number of students studying each subject. You also know the number that study both:

	M	not M	Total
P	19		38
not P			
Total	46		144

Now you can work out all the missing values:

	M	not M	Total
P	19	38 – 19 = **19**	38
not P	46 – 19 = **27**	98 – 19 = **79**	144 – 38 = **106**
Total	46	144 – 46 = **98**	144

b) M or P has 19 + 27 + 19 = 65 outcomes.
So P(M or P) = $\frac{65}{144}$

c) So you're only interested in the 46 students who study maths. 19 students study maths and physics, so:
P(maths student also studies physics) = $\frac{19}{46}$.

Q7 **a)** P(L and M) = 0.1

b) P(L and N) = 0

c) P(N and not L) = 0.25
Since N doesn't overlap with L, N and not L is just N.

d) P(neither L nor M nor N) = 1 – (0.25 + 0.1 + 0.15 + 0.25) = 0.25

e) P(L or M) = 0.25 + 0.1 + 0.15 = 0.5

f) P(not M) = 0.25 + 0.25 + 0.25 = 0.75
Don't forget to include P(neither L nor M nor N). You could also find P(not M) by doing 1 – P(M) = 1 – (0.1 + 0.15).

Q8 **a)** Number of outcomes not in S or F or G = 200 – (17 + 18 + 49 + 28 + 11 + 34 + 6) = 37
So P(not in S or F or G) = $\frac{37}{200}$

b) You're only interested in those people who have been to France — 49 + 28 + 34 + 11 = 122 people.
The number of people who have been to France **and** Germany = 28 + 34 = 62. So P(G, given F) = $\frac{62}{122} = \frac{31}{61}$

c) Number of outcomes in S and not F = 17 + 18 = 35.
So P(S and not F) = $\frac{35}{200} = \frac{7}{40}$

Q9 **a)** **(i)** L' *[1 mark]*

(ii) L and U' *[1 mark]*

(iii) L' and U *[1 mark]*

b) Total number of people surveyed: 24 + 135 + 36 + 176 = 371.
The Venn diagram looks like this:

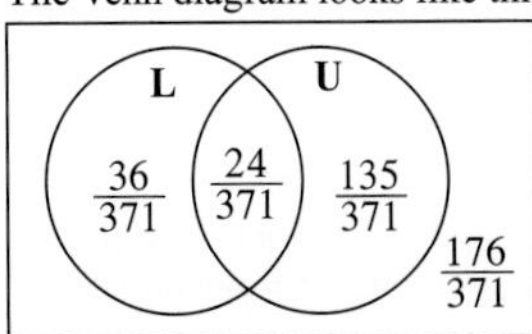

[2 marks available — 1 mark for a Venn diagram with at least one correct probability, 1 mark for a fully correct diagram]

Q10 a) Start by drawing a Venn diagram to represent the information. If H = 'goes to home league matches', A = 'goes to away league matches' and C = 'goes to cup matches', then:

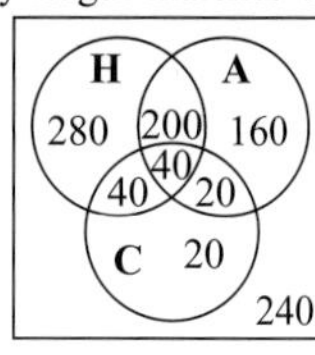

The people who go to exactly 2 types of match are those in (H and A and not C), (H and C and not A), and (A and C and not H). That's 200 + 40 + 20 = 260 people.
So P(2 types of match) = $\frac{260}{1000} = \frac{13}{50}$

b) P(at least 1 type of match) = 1 – P(no matches)
$= 1 - \frac{240}{1000} = \frac{760}{1000} = \frac{19}{25}$

Q11 a) Start by sketching what you know:

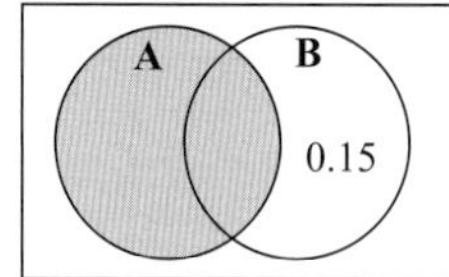

P(A' and B) = 0.15 and the shaded area is P(A) = 0.6, so the area outside the circles is
P(A' and B') = 1 – 0.15 – 0.6 = 0.25.

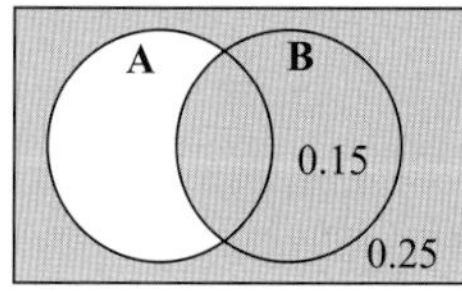

The shaded area in the diagram above is P(A' or B) = 0.48, so the area of the overlap between the two circles is P(A and B) = 0.48 – 0.15 – 0.25 = 0.08 and the unshaded part of the circle for A is P(A and B') = 1 – 0.48 = 0.52.
So the Venn diagram looks like this:

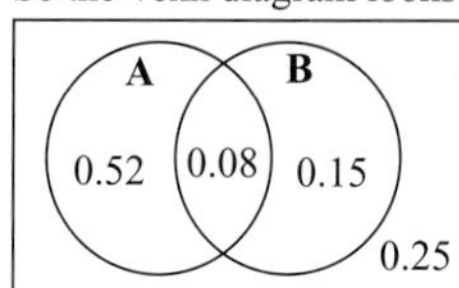

[3 marks available — 1 mark for a Venn diagram with one correct probability, 1 mark for a second correct probability, 1 mark for a fully correct Venn diagram]
You could also use the addition laws covered in the next topic to work out the probabilities in this Venn diagram.

b) (i) P(B) = 0.08 + 0.15 = 0.23 *[1 mark]*

(ii) P((A' or B')') = 1 – P(A' or B')
= 1 – (0.52 + 0.15 + 0.25) = 0.08 *[1 mark]*
Or you could do P((A' or B')') = P(A and B) = 0.08.

Q12 a) The sum of the probabilities must be equal to 1, so
$\frac{n+3}{60} + \frac{3n-1}{120} + \frac{n^2-1}{240} + \frac{1}{4} = 1$
Multiplying through by 240 gives:
$4n + 12 + 6n - 2 + n^2 - 1 + 60 = 240$
$\Rightarrow n^2 + 10n - 171 = 0 \Rightarrow (n-9)(n+19) = 0$
$\Rightarrow n = 9$ or $n = -19$
n cannot equal –19, otherwise some probabilities in the Venn diagram would be negative which is not possible, so $n = 9$.
[3 marks available — 1 mark for deriving an appropriate quadratic equation in n to solve, 1 mark for using an appropriate method to solve, 1 mark for correct value of n]

b) Using the value of n found in a) gives:

(i) P(A) = $\frac{n+3}{60} + \frac{3n-1}{120} = \frac{12}{60} + \frac{26}{120} = \frac{5}{12}$ *[1 mark]*

(ii) P(A and B) = $\frac{3n-1}{120} = \frac{13}{60}$ *[1 mark]*

(iii) P(A' or B) = $1 - \frac{n+3}{60} = 1 - \frac{12}{60} = \frac{4}{5}$ *[1 mark]*

Exercise 3.5 — The Addition Law

Q1 a) P(A') = 1 – P(A) = 1 – 0.3 = 0.7

b) P(A or B) = P(A) + P(B) – P(A and B)
= 0.3 + 0.5 – 0.15 = 0.65

c) P(A' and B') = 1 – P(A or B) = 1 – 0.65 = 0.35
Remember, A' and B' is the complement of A or B.

Q2 a) P(B') = 1 – P(B) = 1 – 0.44 = 0.56

b) P(A or B) = P(A) + P(B) – P(A and B)
= (1 – 0.36) + 0.44 – 0.27 = 0.81

c) P(A and B') = P(A) – P(A and B) = 0.64 – 0.27 = 0.37

d) P(A or B') = P(A) + P(B') – P(A and B')
= 0.64 + 0.56 – 0.37 = 0.83

Q3 Let B = 'car is blue' and E = 'car is an estate'.

a) P(B') = 1 – P(B) = 1 – 0.25 = 0.75

b) P(B or E) = P(B) + P(E) – P(B and E)
= 0.25 + 0.15 – 0.08 = 0.32

c) P(B' and E') = 1 – P(B or E) = 1 – 0.32 = 0.68

Q4 a) P(Y') = 1 – P(Y) = 1 – 0.56 = 0.44

b) P(X and Y) = P(X) + P(Y) – P(X or Y)
= 0.43 + 0.56 – 0.77 = 0.22

c) P(X' and Y') = 1 – P(X or Y) = 1 – 0.77 = 0.23

d) P(X' or Y') = 1 – P(X and Y) = 1 – 0.22 = 0.78

Q5 a) P(C' and D) = P(C') + P(D) – P(C' or D)
= (1 – 0.53) + 0.44 – 0.65 = 0.26

b) P(C' and D') = P(C') – P(C' and D) = 0.47 – 0.26 = 0.21
Just as C = C and D + C and D',
C' = C' and D + C' and D'.

c) P(C' or D') = P(C') + P(D') – P(C' and D')
= 0.47 + 0.56 – 0.21 = 0.82

d) P(C and D) = P(C) + P(D) – P(C or D)
= P(C) + P(D) – [1 – P(C' and D')]
= 0.53 + 0.44 – (1 – 0.21) = 0.18

Q6 Let M = 'has read To Kill a Mockingbird' and A = 'has read Animal Farm'.
Then P(M) = 0.62, P(A') = 0.66, and P(M or A) = 0.79.

a) P(M and A) = P(M) + P(A) – P(M or A)
= 0.62 + (1 – 0.66) – 0.79 = 0.17

b) P(M' and A) = P(A) – P(M and A)
= 0.34 – 0.17 = 0.17

c) P(M' and A') = 1 – P(M or A) = 1 – 0.79 = 0.21

Q7 a) Substituting the given values into the addition law gives 0.56 = 0.24 + P(B) – 0.12, so P(B) = 0.44.
P(B') = 1 – P(B) = 1 – 0.44 = 0.56
[2 marks available — 1 mark for use of addition law, 1 mark for the correct answer]

b) The Venn diagram looks like this:

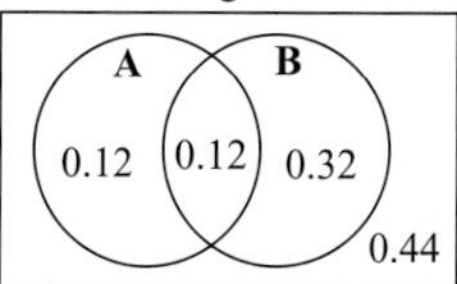

[1 mark for a correct diagram]

Q8 a) 53 + 72 = 125, which is one more than the total number of computer programmers working for the company. So there must be an overlap of at least one person who knows both languages. *[1 mark for a correct reason]*

b) Let A = 'programmer knows Adder' and B = 'programmer knows Baliscript'.
$P(A) = \frac{53}{124}$, $P(B) = \frac{72}{124}$ and $P(A \text{ and } B) = \frac{24}{124}$.
So using the addition law:
$P(A \text{ or } B) = \frac{53}{124} + \frac{72}{124} - \frac{24}{124} = \frac{101}{124}$.
[2 marks available — 1 mark for attempt at using the addition rule, 1 mark for the correct answer]

c) $P(A' \text{ and } B) = P(A) - P(A \text{ and } B) = \frac{48}{124}$
$P(A \text{ and } B') = P(A) - P(A \text{ and } B) = \frac{29}{124}$
So the probability that the programmer knows exactly one of A or B is $\frac{29+48}{124} = \frac{77}{124}$.
[2 marks available — 1 mark for a correct method, 1 mark for the correct answer]

d) The probability that the programmer knows neither A or B is $1 - P(A \text{ or } B) = 1 - \frac{101}{124} = \frac{23}{124}$. *[1 mark]*

Q9 a) Since P(A) + P(B) > 1 then it is possible, at one extreme, that P(A or B) = 1. Therefore the maximum value for $q = 1$.
At the other extreme, it is possible for event A to be a 'sub-event' of B, in which case P(A or B) = P(B) = 0.78.
Therefore the minimum value for $p = 0.78$.
As an example of a 'sub-event', if A is the event that an animal is a cat, and B is the event that an animal is a mammal, since all cats are mammals, event A is completely 'contained' within the event B. In other words, event A must happen whenever event B happens (but not vice-versa).

b) (i) When P(A or B) = 1 then, by using the addition rule, P(A and B) = 0.49 + 0.78 – 1 = 0.27.

(ii) P(A or B) = 1

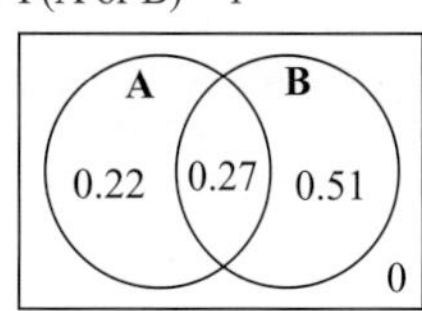

Exercise 3.6 — Mutually Exclusive Events

Q1 a) P(X and Y) = 0

b) P(X or Y) = P(X) + P(Y) = 0.48 + 0.37 = 0.85

c) P(X' and Y') = 1 – P(X or Y) = 1 – 0.85 = 0.15

Q2 a) P(L or M) = P(L) + P(M) = 0.28 + 0.42 = 0.7

b) P(L or N) = P(L) + P(N) = 0.28 + 0.33 = 0.61

c) P(M or N) = P(M) + P(N) – P(M and N)
= 0.42 + 0.33 – 0.16 = 0.59

d) P(L and M and N) = 0

e) Draw 3 circles to represent events L, M and N, making sure that mutually exclusive events don't overlap. As usual, start the labelling with the middle of the overlapping circles and work outwards.

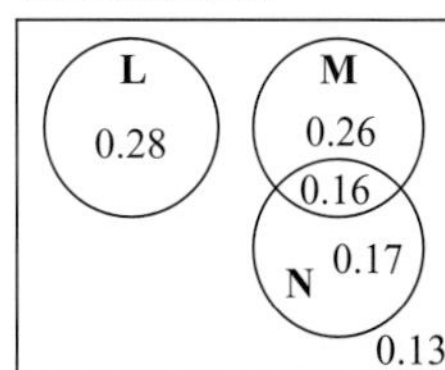

Q3 a) Let B = 'goes bowling', C = 'goes to the cinema', and D = 'goes out for dinner'. All 3 events are mutually exclusive, so: P(B or C) = P(B) + P(C) = 0.17 + 0.43 = 0.6

b) P(doesn't do B, C or D) = P(B' and C' and D')
Since either none of B, C and D happen, or at least one of B, C and D happen, "B' and C' and D'" and "B or C or D" are complementary events. So:
P(B' and C' and D') = 1 – P(B or C or D)
= 1 – [P(B) + P(C) + P(D)] = 1 – (0.17 + 0.43 + 0.22)
= 1 – 0.82 = 0.18

Q4 a) P(A and B) = P(A) + P(B) – P(A or B)
= 0.28 + 0.66 – 0.86 = 0.08
P(A and B) ≠ 0, so A and B aren't mutually exclusive.

b) P(A and C) = P(A) + P(C) – P(A or C)
= 0.28 + 0.49 – 0.77 = 0
P(A and C) = 0, so A and C are mutually exclusive.

c) P(B and C) = P(B) + P(C) – P(B or C)
= 0.66 + 0.49 – 0.92 = 0.23
P(B and C) ≠ 0, so B and C aren't mutually exclusive.

Q5 a) You need to show that P(C and D) = 0.
P(C) = 1 – 0.6 = 0.4
P(C and D) = P(C) – P(C and D') = 0.4 – 0.4 = 0,
so C and D are mutually exclusive.

b) P(C or D) = P(C) + P(D) = 0.4 + 0.25 = 0.65

Q6 As P(A' and B') = 0.61 then
P(A or B) = 1 – P(A' and B') = 1 – 0.61 = 0.39
Using the addition law: P(A) + P(B) = 0.32 + 0.07
= 0.39 = P(A or B), so the events A and B are mutually exclusive.
[2 marks available — 1 mark for correct calculation of appropriate probabilities, 1 mark for correctly showing that A and B are mutually exclusive]

Q7 Out of the total of 50 biscuits, 30 are plain, and 20 are chocolate-coated. Half of the biscuits are in wrappers, so 25 biscuits are in wrappers. Since there are more biscuits in wrappers than there are chocolate-coated ones, there must be some biscuits (at least 5) which are plain and in wrappers. So events P and W can happen at the same time (i.e. P(P and W) ≠ 0), which means they're not mutually exclusive.

Q8 a) As can be seen in the Venn diagram, the regions corresponding to (A and B) and (A and B') do not overlap so the events must be mutually exclusive.

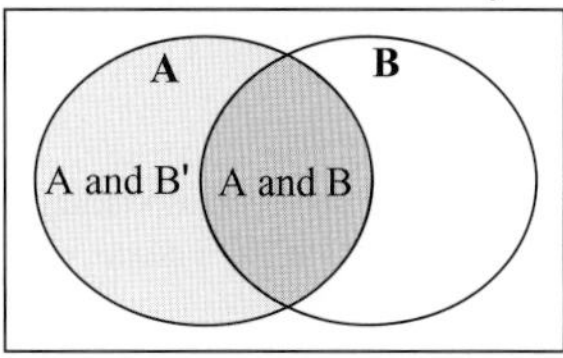

[1 mark for the correct reason supported by a Venn diagram]

b) P(A) = P(A and B) + P(A and B') *[1 mark]*

c) The events (A and B) and (A' and B) are mutually exclusive, so P(B) = P(A and B) + P(A' and B). *[1 mark]*

Q9 a) Using the addition law of probability for events A and B:
P(A or B) = P(A) + P(B) – P(A and B)
Substituting P(B) = P(A and B) gives
P(A or B) = P(A) + P(A and B) – P(A and B)
Hence, P(A) = P(A or B).
[2 marks available — 1 mark for use of addition law, 1 mark for substituting P(B) with P(A and B) to get correct expression for P(A)]

b) P(B) = P(A and B) so on a Venn diagram, the region representing event B must be completely contained in the region representing event A.
Since A and C are mutually exclusive, the region of the Venn diagram representing C is completely separate from the region representing A. Since B is completely inside A, the region representing B must also be completely separate from C. Therefore, B and C are mutually exclusive.

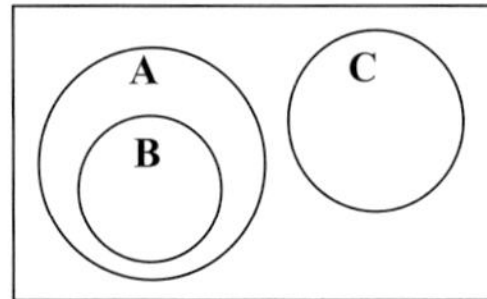

[2 marks available — 1 mark for drawing a correct Venn diagram, 1 mark for a correct explanation]

Q10 a) (i) The Venn Diagram looks like this:

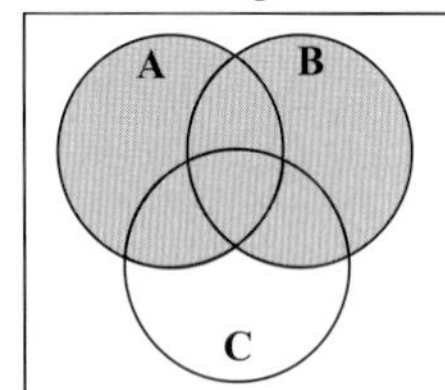

[1 mark]

(ii) The Venn Diagram looks like this:

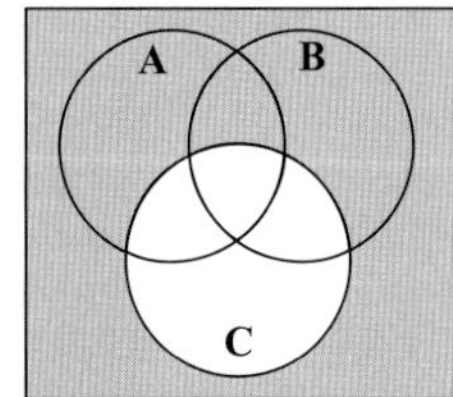

[1 mark]

b) The Venn Diagram looks like this:

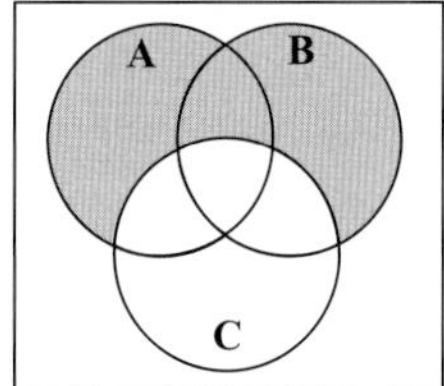

[1 mark]

c) Using a Venn diagram, the regions corresponding to the events (A' and C) and ((A or B) and C') do not overlap (they are mutually exclusive).

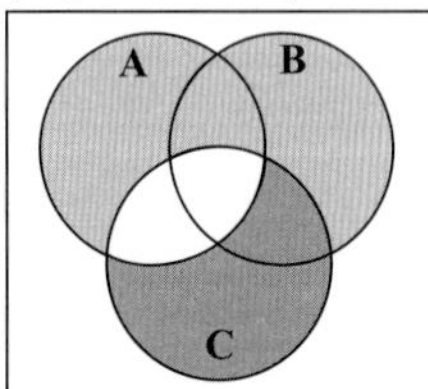

And since P(A' and C) + P((A or B) and C') = 0.36 + 0.64 = 1, P(A and C) must be equal to 0 (as will P(A' and B' and C')) and hence, A and C are mutually exclusive.
[3 marks available — 1 mark for a correct Venn diagram or other working, 1 mark for realising that (A' and C) and ((A or B) and C') are mutually exclusive, 1 mark for a correct explanation]

Exercise 3.7 — Independent Events

Q1 P(X and Y) = P(X)P(Y) = 0.62 × 0.32 = 0.1984

Q2 P(A)P(B) = P(A and B), so:
P(A) = P(A and B) ÷ P(B) = 0.45 ÷ (1 – 0.25) = 0.6

Q3 a) P(X and Y) = P(X)P(Y) = 0.84 × 0.68 = 0.5712

b) P(Y' and Z') = P(Y')P(Z') = (1 – 0.68)(1 – 0.48)
= 0.32 × 0.52 = 0.1664

c) P(X and Z') = P(X)P(Z') = 0.84 × (1 – 0.48)
= 0.84 × 0.52 = 0.4368

d) P(Y' and Z) = P(Y')P(Z) = (1 – 0.68) × 0.48
= 0.32 × 0.48 = 0.1536

Q4 a) P(M and N) = P(M)P(N) = 0.4 × 0.7 = 0.28

b) P(M or N) = P(M) + P(N) – P(M and N)
= 0.4 + 0.7 – 0.28 = 0.82

c) P(M and N') = P(M)P(N') = 0.4 × 0.3 = 0.12

Q5 a) Let A = '1st card is hearts' and B = '2nd card is hearts'. Since the first card is replaced before the second is picked, A and B are independent events.
So P(A and B) = P(A) × P(B).
There are 13 hearts out of the 52 cards,
so P(A) and P(B) both equal $\frac{13}{52} = \frac{1}{4}$.
So P(A and B) = $\frac{1}{4} \times \frac{1}{4} = \frac{1}{16}$.

b) Let A = '1st card is ace of hearts' and B = '2nd card is ace of hearts'. The first card is replaced before the second is picked, so A and B are independent events.
So, P(A and B) = P(A) × P(B). There is 1 'ace of hearts' out of the 52 cards, so P(A) and P(B) both equal $\frac{1}{52}$.
So P(A and B) = $\frac{1}{52} \times \frac{1}{52} = \frac{1}{2704}$.

Q6 a) P(A and B) = P(A) – P(A and B') = 0.58 – 0.36 = 0.22.
Since A and B are independent, P(A)P(B) = P(A and B)
So 0.58 × P(B) = 0.22 ⇒ P(B) = 0.379... = 0.38 to 2 d.p.

b) P(A or B) = P(A) + P(B) – P(A and B)
= 0.58 + 0.379... – 0.22 = 0.739... = 0.74 to 2 d.p.

c) P(A' and B') = 1 – P(A or B)
= 1 – 0.739... = 0.260... = 0.26 to 2 d.p.

Q7 The events '1st sock is black' and '2nd sock is pink' are independent, since Rupa replaces the 1st sock she picks, and mixes up the socks before she picks again.
So P(1st is black and 2nd is pink) = P(1st is black) × P(2nd is pink)
$\frac{1}{25} = \frac{2}{5}$ × P(2nd is pink)
P(2nd is pink) = $\frac{1}{25} \div \frac{2}{5} = \frac{1}{25} \times \frac{5}{2} = \frac{5}{50} = \frac{1}{10}$
So the probability of picking a pink sock is $\frac{1}{10}$.

Q8 The probability of rolling any number on a fair *n*-sided dice is $\frac{1}{n}$, and each roll of the dice is independent.
So P(2 then 5) = $\frac{1}{n} \times \frac{1}{n} = \frac{1}{64} \Rightarrow n^2 = 64 \Rightarrow n = 8$

Q9 <u>A and B</u>: P(A) × P(B) = $\frac{3}{11} \times \frac{1}{3} = \frac{3}{33} = \frac{1}{11}$
P(A) × P(B) = $\frac{1}{11}$ = P(A and B), so A and B are independent.
<u>A and C</u>: P(A) × P(C) = $\frac{3}{11} \times \frac{15}{28} = \frac{45}{308}$
P(A) × P(C) = $\frac{45}{308} \neq \frac{2}{15}$ = P(A and C),
so A and C are not independent.
<u>B and C</u>: P(B) × P(C) = $\frac{1}{3} \times \frac{15}{28} = \frac{15}{84} = \frac{5}{28}$
P(B) × P(C) = $\frac{5}{28}$ = P(B and C), so B and C are independent.

Q10 Let J = 'Jess buys a book', K = 'Keisha buys a book' and L = 'Lucy buys a book'.

a) The probability that all 3 buy a book is P(J and K and L). Since the 3 events are independent, you can multiply their probabilities together to get:
P(J) × P(K) × P(L) = 0.66 × 0.5 × 0.3 = 0.099

b) The probability that at least 2 of them buy a book will be the probability that one of the following happens: J and K and L, or J and K and L', or J and K' and L, or J' and K and L. Since these events are mutually exclusive, you can add their probabilities together to give:

$0.099 + (0.66 \times 0.5 \times 0.7) + (0.66 \times 0.5 \times 0.3) + (0.34 \times 0.5 \times 0.3)$

$= 0.099 + 0.231 + 0.099 + 0.051 = 0.48$

Q11 P(walks to work) × P(drives to work) $= 0.75 \times 0.25 = 0.1875 \neq 0.3125$

So P(walks to work) × P(drives to work) does not equal P('walks to work' and 'drives to work'), so the events are not independent.

Q12 a) The total number of customers during the month was 130.

(i) $\text{P(M)} = \frac{7 + 10 + 3}{130} = \frac{2}{13}$ *[1 mark]*

(ii) $\text{P(Y)} = \frac{29 + 10 + 26}{130} = \frac{1}{2}$ *[1 mark]*

b) M and Y are independent if P(M and Y) = P(M)P(Y).

$\text{P(M)P(Y)} = \frac{2}{13} \times \frac{1}{2} = \frac{1}{13}$

$\text{P(M and Y)} = \frac{10}{130} = \frac{1}{13}$

P(M and Y) = P(M)P(Y) so the events M and Y are independent.

[2 marks available — 1 mark for finding either P(M)P(Y) or P(M and Y), 1 mark for correct reasoning to show the events are independent]

c) $\text{P(L)} = \frac{6 + 26 + 21}{130} = \frac{53}{130}$, $\text{P(Z)} = \frac{4 + 3 + 21}{130} = \frac{28}{130}$

$\text{P(L)P(Z)} = \frac{53}{130} \times \frac{28}{130} = 0.0878...$

$\text{P(L and Z)} = \frac{21}{130} = 0.161...$

P(L and Z) ≠ P(L)P(Z),
so the events L and Z are not independent.

[3 marks available — 1 mark for correctly calculating P(L) and P(Z), 1 mark for finding either P(L)P(Z) or P(L and Z), 1 mark for correct reasoning to show the events are not independent]

Exercise 3.8 — Tree Diagrams

Q1 a) The events are not independent because the probability that Jake wins his 2nd match depends on whether or not he won his 1st match.

b) (i) P(Win then Win) $= 0.6 \times 0.75 = 0.45$

(ii) P(Wins at least 1) = P(Win then Win) + P(Win then Lose) + P(Lose then Win)

$= 0.45 + (0.6 \times 0.25) + (0.4 \times 0.35)$

$= 0.74$

Or you could find 1 – P(Lose then Lose).

Q2 a)

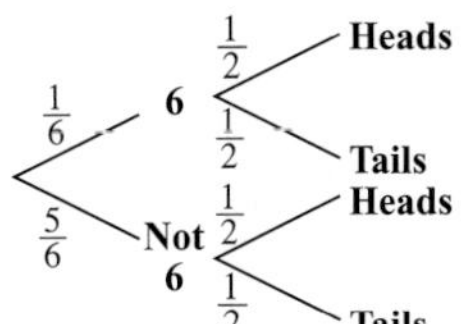

b) P(wins) = P(6 and Tails) $= \frac{1}{6} \times \frac{1}{2} = \frac{1}{12}$

Q3 a) Let D = 'passed driving test' and U = 'intend to go to university'.

0.3 D: 0.75 U, 0.25 U'
0.7 D': 0.75 U, 0.25 U'

Because the events are independent, you could also draw this tree diagram with the 'U' branches first, then the 'D' branches.

b) P(D' and U') $= 0.7 \times 0.25 = 0.175$

Q4 a) The tree diagram looks like this:

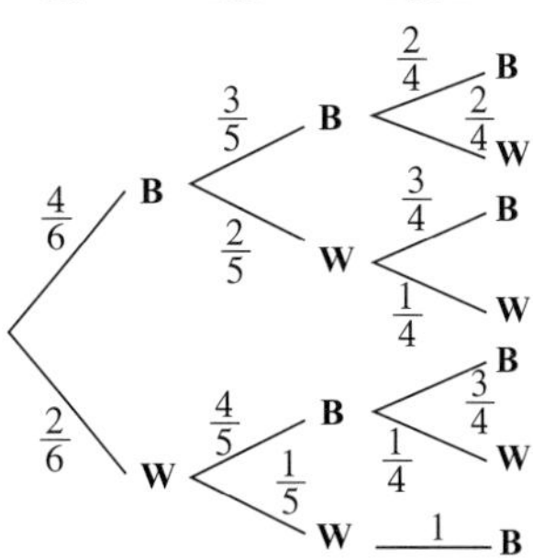

[3 marks available — 1 mark for each correct set of branches (Egg 1, Egg 2, Egg 3)]

You might have shown simplified fractions for some of the branches.

b) P(all 3 eggs brown) = P(BBB) $= \frac{4}{6} \times \frac{3}{5} \times \frac{2}{4} = \frac{1}{5}$ *[1 mark]*

c) The only branch that will not give at least one egg of each colour is BBB.

So P(at least one of each colour) = 1 – P(all 3 eggs brown) $= 1 - \frac{1}{5} = \frac{4}{5}$

[2 marks available — 1 mark for identifying the correct branch(es), 1 mark for the correct answer]

You could also work out the probabilities along each branch that gives at least one egg of each colour and add them up.

d) There are three possible ways of getting exactly one white egg: BBW, BWB and WBB.

$\text{P(BBW)}\ \frac{4}{6} \times \frac{3}{5} \times \frac{2}{4} = \frac{1}{5}$,

$\text{P(BWB)} = \frac{4}{6} \times \frac{2}{5} \times \frac{3}{4} = \frac{1}{5}$,

$\text{P(WBB)} = \frac{2}{6} \times \frac{4}{5} \times \frac{3}{4} = \frac{1}{5}$

So the probability is $\frac{1}{5} + \frac{1}{5} + \frac{1}{5} = \frac{3}{5}$.

[2 marks available — 1 mark for identifying the required combinations, 1 mark for the correct answer]

Q5 Let R = 'orders roast dinner' and let A = 'orders apple pie for pudding'. Then you can draw the following tree diagram:

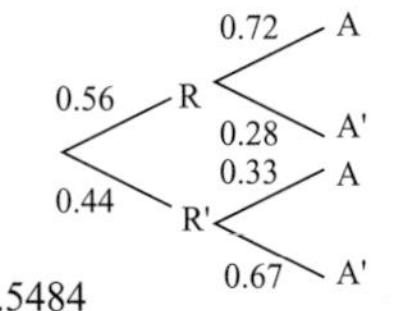

So P(A) = P(R and A) + P(R' and A)

$= (0.56 \times 0.72) + (0.44 \times 0.33) = 0.5484$

Q6 a) Let R_i = 'ball i is red', Y_i = 'ball i is yellow' and G_i = 'ball i is green', for i = 1 and 2. Since the first ball isn't replaced, the second pick depends on the first pick and you get the following tree diagram:

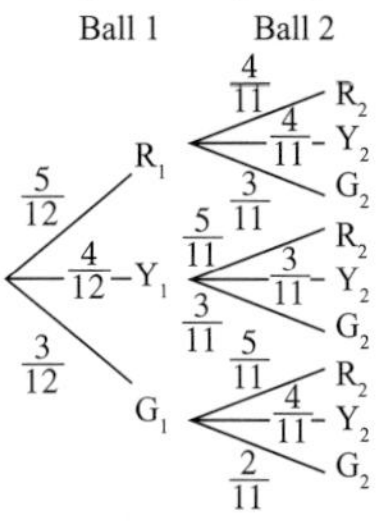

[2 marks available — 1 mark for each correct set of branches (Ball 1, Ball 2)]

b) P(wins) $= \text{P}(R_1 \text{ and } R_2) + \text{P}(Y_1 \text{ and } Y_2) + \text{P}(G_1 \text{ and } G_2)$

$= \left(\frac{5}{12} \times \frac{4}{11}\right) + \left(\frac{4}{12} \times \frac{3}{11}\right) + \left(\frac{3}{12} \times \frac{2}{11}\right)$

$= \frac{20}{132} + \frac{12}{132} + \frac{6}{132} = \frac{38}{132} = \frac{19}{66}$

[2 marks available — 1 mark for multiplying together the correct probabilities, 1 mark for the correct answer]

c) When a ball of one colour is selected then replaced, the proportion of balls of that colour left for the second pick is higher than if it isn't replaced. So the probability of picking the colour again is higher, which means a player is more likely to win.
[1 mark for the correct answer with justification]
You could also answer this question by working out the probability of winning when the ball is replaced and comparing it to the probability of winning without replacing the ball.

Q7 a) Let J_p = 'Juan writes positive review', J_n = 'Juan writes non-positive review', C_p = 'Callum writes positive review', and C_n = 'Callum writes non-positive review'.

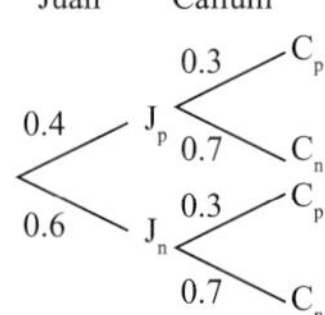

P(exactly one positive review)
$= P(J_p \text{ and } C_n) + P(J_n \text{ and } C_p) = 0.4 \times 0.7 + 0.6 \times 0.3$
$= 0.28 + 0.18 = 0.46$

b) Callum Movie 1 | Callum Movie 2

0.3 C_p — 0.3 C_p, 0.7 C_n
0.7 C_n — 0.3 C_p, 0.7 C_n

P(exactly one positive review)
$= P(C_p \text{ and } C_n) + P(C_n \text{ and } C_p) = 0.3 \times 0.7 + 0.7 \times 0.3$
$= 0.21 + 0.21 = 0.42$

c) Juan Movie 1 | Juan Movie 2 | Juan Movie 3

0.4 J_p — 0.4 J_p (0.4 J_p, 0.6 J_n), 0.6 J_n (0.4 J_p, 0.6 J_n)
0.6 J_n — 0.4 J_p (0.4 J_p, 0.6 J_n), 0.6 J_n (0.4 J_p, 0.6 J_n)

P(exactly one positive review)
$= P(J_p \text{ and } J_n \text{ and } J_n) + P(J_n \text{ and } J_p \text{ and } J_n) + P(J_n \text{ and } J_n \text{ and } J_p)$
$= 0.4 \times 0.6 \times 0.6 + 0.6 \times 0.4 \times 0.6 + 0.6 \times 0.6 \times 0.4$
$= 0.144 + 0.144 + 0.144 = 0.432$

d)

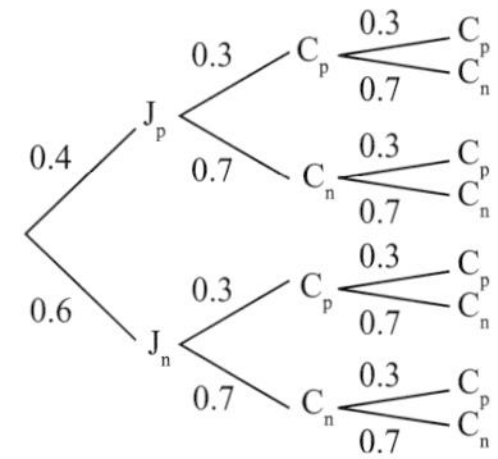

P(exactly one positive review)
$= P(J_p \text{ and } C_n \text{ and } C_n) + P(J_n \text{ and } C_p \text{ and } C_n)$
$+ P(J_n \text{ and } C_n \text{ and } C_p)$
$= 0.4 \times 0.7 \times 0.7 + 0.6 \times 0.3 \times 0.7 + 0.6 \times 0.7 \times 0.3$
$= 0.196 + 0.126 + 0.126 = 0.448$

e)

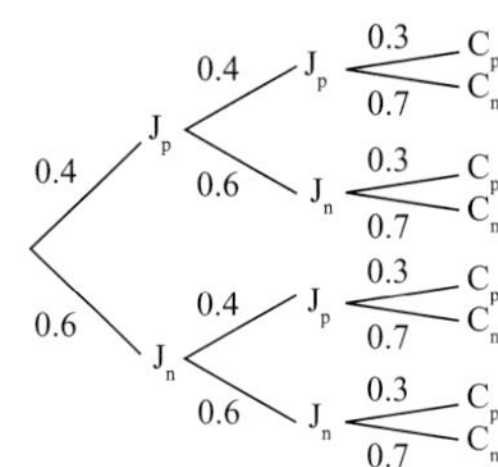

P(exactly one positive review) $= P(J_p \text{ and } J_n \text{ and } C_n)$
$+ P(J_n \text{ and } J_p \text{ and } C_n) + P(J_n \text{ and } J_n \text{ and } C_p)$
$= 0.4 \times 0.6 \times 0.7 + 0.6 \times 0.4 \times 0.7 + 0.6 \times 0.6 \times 0.3$
$= 0.168 + 0.168 + 0.108 = 0.444$

Q8 First find a:
P(knocks over hurdle 1 and hurdle 2) $= 0.2 \times a = 0.08$
$\Rightarrow a = 0.08 \div 0.2 = 0.4$
Each set of branches adds up to 1, so $b = 1 - 0.4 = 0.6$
Now find d:
P(knocks over neither hurdle 1 nor hurdle 2) $= 0.8 \times d = 0.72$
$\Rightarrow d = 0.72 \div 0.8 = 0.9 \Rightarrow c = 1 - 0.9 = 0.1$
So the completed diagram is:

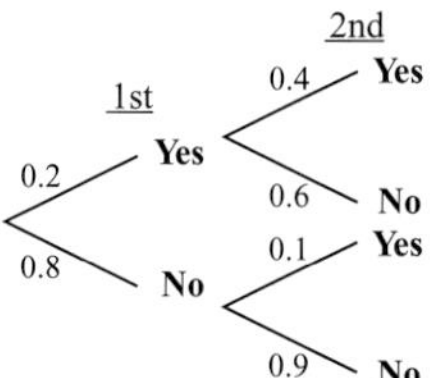

Q9 a) The tree diagram looks like this:

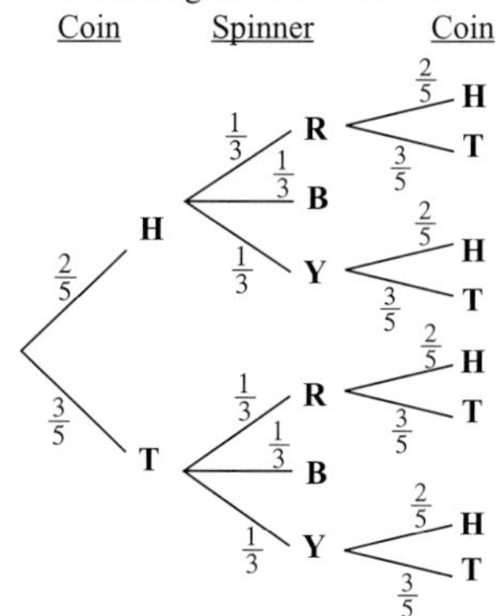

[3 marks available — 1 mark for each correct set of branches (Coin, Spinner, Coin)]

b) There are two possibilities to consider: HRT and TRH.
So the probability of heads, tails and red in any order is:
$$P(HRT) + P(TRH) = \frac{2}{5} \times \frac{1}{3} \times \frac{3}{5} + \frac{3}{5} \times \frac{1}{3} \times \frac{2}{5} = \frac{2}{25} + \frac{2}{25} = \frac{4}{25}$$
[2 marks available — 1 mark for identifying the required possibilities, 1 mark for the correct answer]

c) The two possibilities are HRH and HYH. So the probability of flipping two heads is:
$$P(HRH) + P(HYH) = \frac{2}{5} \times \frac{1}{3} \times \frac{2}{5} + \frac{2}{5} \times \frac{1}{3} \times \frac{2}{5} = \frac{4}{75} + \frac{4}{75} = \frac{8}{75}$$
[2 marks available — 1 mark for identifying the required possibilities, 1 mark for the correct answer]

Chapter 3 Review Exercise

Q1 **a)**

		Dice					
		1	2	3	4	5	6
Coin	H	2	4	6	8	10	12
	T	5	6	7	8	9	10

b) There are 6 × 2 = 12 outcomes in total, and 2 ways of scoring 8. So P(8) = $\frac{2}{12} = \frac{1}{6}$.

c) 9 of the outcomes score more than 5. So P(more than 5) = $\frac{9}{12} = \frac{3}{4}$.

d) There are 6 outcomes where a tail is thrown, and the scores for 3 of them are even. So P(even score when tail thrown) = $\frac{3}{6} = \frac{1}{2}$.

Q2 **a)** Draw a sample space diagram:

+	1	2	3	4	5	6	7	8	9
1	2	3	4	5	6	7	8	9	10
2	3	4	5	6	7	8	9	10	11
3	4	5	6	7	8	9	10	11	12
4	5	6	7	8	9	10	11	12	13
5	6	7	8	9	10	11	12	13	14
6	7	8	9	10	11	12	13	14	15
7	8	9	10	11	12	13	14	15	16
8	9	10	11	12	13	14	15	16	17
9	10	11	12	13	14	15	16	17	18

If the first card is replaced after it is picked, the total number of possible outcomes is 9 × 9 = 81. *[1 mark]*
10 outcomes have a score of 15 or more *[1 mark]*.
So P(score of 15 or more) = $\frac{10}{81}$ *[1 mark]*.

b) If the first card isn't replaced, you can't get the same score on both cards, so the sample space diagram looks like this:

+	1	2	3	4	5	6	7	8	9
1	—	3	4	5	6	7	8	9	10
2	3	—	5	6	7	8	9	10	11
3	4	5	—	7	8	9	10	11	12
4	5	6	7	—	9	10	11	12	13
5	6	7	8	9	—	11	12	13	14
6	7	8	9	10	11	—	13	14	15
7	8	9	10	11	12	13	—	15	16
8	9	10	11	12	13	14	15	—	17
9	10	11	12	13	14	15	16	17	—

There are now 9 × 8 = 72 outcomes in total.
8 outcomes have a score of 15 or more.
[1 mark for both total number of outcomes and number with score ≥15 correct]
So P(score of 15 or more) = $\frac{8}{72} = \frac{1}{9}$ *[1 mark]*.

You don't need to draw the sample space diagram a second time — you can just use your first diagram and spot which scores aren't possible when the first card isn't replaced.

Q3 The probability, in terms of x, of selecting a 10p coin from the bag is $\frac{x}{150}$, so $\frac{1}{6} < \frac{x}{150} < \frac{1}{5} \Rightarrow 25 < x < 30$.
Since x must be an integer, x can be equal to 26, 27, 28 or 29.
[3 marks available — 1 mark for deriving an appropriate inequality in x to solve, 1 mark for the correct solution to the inequality, 1 mark for all correct values of x]

Q4 **a)** The frequencies for each class interval from the table are:
(100 – 70) × 0.5 = 15, (125 – 100) × 2.32 = 58,
(150 – 125) × 3.84 = 96, (180 – 150) × 2.2 = 66, and
(225 – 180) × 0.4 = 18. So the total frequency is 253.
There are 58 apples in the class interval $100 \leq M < 125$, so the probability is $\frac{58}{253}$.
[2 marks available — 1 mark for a correct method to find the frequencies, 1 mark for the correct answer]

b) Add the frequencies of apples in the 3rd, 4th and 5th classes to get the number of apples with a mass at least 125g.
So the probability is $\frac{96 + 66 + 18}{253} = \frac{180}{253}$ *[1 mark]*

c) 165 is the mid-point of the class interval $150 \leq M < 180$.
Since the frequency of this class interval is 66, the frequency of the interval $150 \leq M < 165$ can be estimated to be 33.
So the probability of an apple having a mass 165 g or less can be estimated as $\frac{15 + 58 + 96 + 33}{253} = \frac{202}{253}$.
It has been assumed that the masses of the apples in the class $150 \leq M < 180$ are evenly distributed throughout the class.
[4 marks available — 1 mark for recognising that 165 is the mid-point of the class interval, 1 mark for halving the frequency of the class interval, 1 mark for the correct answer, 1 mark for the correct assumption stated]

Q5 **a)** 50% of 35% is equal to 17.5%, so 17.5% of the total number of coins are copper coins in box A. *[1 mark]*

b) 50% of 35% = 17.5% of the total number of coins are silver and in box A.
60% of 40% = 24% of the total number of coins are silver and in box B.
20% of (100% – 35% – 40%) = 20% of 25% = 5% of the total number of coins are silver and in box C.
Therefore, the probability of choosing a silver coin is 17.5% + 24% + 5% = 46.5% (or 0.465).
[2 marks available — 1 mark for some correct working, 1 mark for the correct answer]

Q6 **a)** 2% of students eat both chips and sausages, so
50% – 2% = 48% eat sausages but not chips, and
20% – 2% = 18% eat chips but not sausages.
100% – 48% – 18% – 2% = 32% eat neither chips nor sausages. Let S be 'eats sausages' and C be 'eats chips':

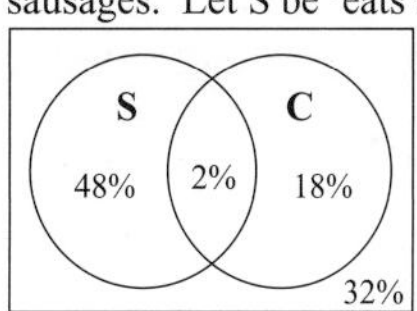

b) 18%

c) 48% + 18% = 66%

d) P(sausages but not chips) = $\frac{48}{100} = 0.48$

e) P(neither sausages nor chips) = $\frac{32}{100} = 0.32$

f) 20% of students eat chips, and 2% eat sausages and chips.
So P(student who eats chips also eats sausages)
$= \frac{2}{20} = \frac{1}{10} = 0.1$

Q7 Draw a Venn diagram with three circles — A for activity holidays, B for beach holidays and S for skiing holidays.
10 people enjoy all three.
25 – 10 = 15 enjoy A and B but not S.
22 – 10 = 12 enjoy A and S but not B.
21 – 10 = 11 enjoy B and S but not A.
41 – 10 – 15 – 12 = 4 enjoy A only.
59 – 10 – 15 – 11 = 23 enjoy B only.
58 – 10 – 12 – 11 = 25 enjoy S only.
Putting this in the Venn diagram gives:

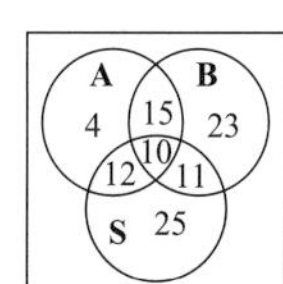

P(likes beach but not skiing holidays)
$= \frac{15 + 23}{100} = \frac{38}{100} = \frac{19}{50}$ (or 0.38)

Q8 Draw a Venn diagram — let C represent the members who are singing in the concert, and T represent those who have been a member for ≥10 years.
18 of the ≥10 years members will be in the concert.
20 – 18 = 2 of the ≥10 years members will not be in the concert.
60 – 18 = 42 of those singing in the concert have not been members for ≥10 years.
75 – 18 – 2 – 42 = 13 members are neither singing in the concert, nor have been a member for ≥10 years.

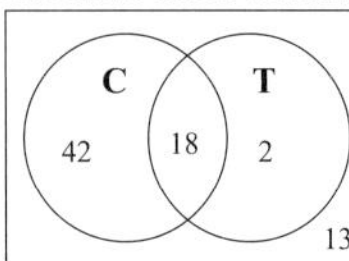

P(<10 years and not in concert) = $\frac{13}{75}$

[3 marks available — 1 mark if all the numbers inside the C and T circles are correct, 1 mark for finding that the number outside the circles is 13, 1 mark for correct probability]

Q9 a) P(drinks coffee) = $\frac{5+3+2+2}{30} = \frac{12}{30} = \frac{2}{5}$

b) P(drinks tea with only milk) = $\frac{7}{30}$

c) P('tea' or 'only sugar')
= P(tea) + P(only sugar) – P('tea' and 'only sugar')
$= \frac{7+4+6+1}{30} + \frac{4+3}{30} - \frac{4}{30}$
$= \frac{18}{30} + \frac{7}{30} - \frac{4}{30} = \frac{21}{30} = \frac{7}{10}$

Q10 From the information in the Venn diagram, derive the simultaneous equations:
$3x + y + 10y + x = 1 \Rightarrow 4x + 11y = 1$ (1)
and $3x + y = 0.46 \Rightarrow 33x + 11y = 5.06$ (2)
(2) – (1): $33x + 11y = 5.06$
$-(4x + 11y = 1)$
$\Rightarrow 29x = 4.06$
$\Rightarrow x = 0.14$,
so $y = 0.46 - 3(0.14) = 0.04$.

[4 marks available — 1 mark for both correct equations derived, 1 mark for use of an appropriate method of solution, 1 mark for correct value of x, 1 mark for correct value of y]

Q11 a) P(clothes or music)
= P(clothes) + P(music) – P(clothes and music)
= 0.7 + 0.4 – 0.2 = 0.9

The question asks for the probability he buys clothes or music or both — when you use the addition rule, as above, the 'or both' option is automatically included.

b) P(neither clothes nor music) = 1 – P(clothes or music)
= 1 – 0.9 = 0.1

You might find it useful to draw a Venn diagram to help with this question.

Q12 a) You can't roll both a 1 and a 3, so the events are mutually exclusive. So P(1 or 3) = P(1) + P(3) = 0.3 + 0.2 = 0.5

b) P(neither 1 nor 3) = 1 – P(1 or 3) = 1 – 0.5 = 0.5

c) (i) Each roll of the dice is independent, so:
P(two 1s) = 0.3 × 0.3 = 0.09

(ii) P(1 then 3) = 0.3 × 0.2 = 0.06

(iii) P(3 then neither 1 nor 3) = 0.2 × 0.5 = 0.1

Q13 a) P(R and S) = P(R) × P(S) = 0.9 × 0.8 = 0.72

b) P(R or S) = P(R) + P(S) – P(R and S)
= 0.9 + 0.8 – 0.72 = 0.98

c) P(R' and S') = P(R') × P(S') = (1 – P(R))(1 – P(S))
= (1 – 0.9)(1 – 0.8) = 0.1 × 0.2 = 0.02

d) P(R' or S') = P(R') + P(S') – P(R' and S')
= 0.1 + 0.2 – 0.02 = 0.28

P(R'), P(S') and P(R' and S') were found in c).

Q14 a) P(A chooses box 4) = $\frac{1}{10}$

b) Contestant A can choose any box, and does so with probability 1. Whichever box contestant A chooses, there are 9 possibilities for B to choose differently from A, so contestant B choosing a different box from A has a probability of $\frac{9}{10}$. As the contestants' choices are independent, the probability that A and B choose different boxes is given by $1 \times \frac{9}{10} = \frac{9}{10}$.

c) Assuming A and B have already selected different boxes, C has 8 possibilities to choose differently from both A and B, so the probability is $\frac{8}{10}$. Similarly, D chooses a box differently from the other three contestants with probability $\frac{7}{10}$. As the choices are independent, the probability that all contestants choose different boxes is $1 \times \frac{9}{10} \times \frac{8}{10} \times \frac{7}{10} = 0.504$.

d) The probability that at least two contestants choose the same box is equal to 1 – 0.504 = 0.496.

Q15 Let M = 'student studies Maths' and A = 'student studies Art'.
P(M) = $\frac{24}{60} = \frac{2}{5}$ and P(A) = $\frac{20}{60} = \frac{1}{3}$
so P(M and A) = $\frac{8}{60} = \frac{2}{15}$

[1 mark for finding P(M), P(A) and P(M and A)]

P(M) × P(A) = $\frac{2}{5} \times \frac{1}{3} = \frac{2}{15}$ *[1 mark]*

So P(M and A) = P(M) × P(A), which means 'student studies Maths' and 'student studies Art' are independent events *[1 mark]*.

Q16 a) Draw a sample space diagram:

+	1	2	3	4	5	6
1	2	3	4	5	6	7
2	3	4	5	6	7	8
3	4	5	6	7	8	9
4	5	6	7	8	9	10
5	6	7	8	9	10	11
6	7	8	9	10	11	12

There are 6 × 6 = 36 outcomes in total.
The scores that are prime are 2, 3, 5, 7 and 11, and these occur 15 times. So P(score is prime) = $\frac{15}{36} = \frac{5}{12}$

b) 4 and 9 are the scores that are square numbers, and these occur 7 times. So P(score is square) = $\frac{7}{36}$

c) It isn't possible for her score to be both a prime number and a square number, so the events P and S are mutually exclusive.

d) Since the events are mutually exclusive,
P(P or S) = P(P) + P(S) = $\frac{5}{12} + \frac{7}{36} = \frac{15+7}{36} = \frac{22}{36} = \frac{11}{18}$

e) The score from the second experiment is unaffected by the score from the first experiment, so the events S_1 and S_2 are independent.

f) P(S_1 and S_2) = P(S_1)P(S_2) = $\frac{7}{36} \times \frac{7}{36} = \frac{49}{1296}$

Q17 a) For A and B to be statistically independent,
P(A and B) = P(A)P(B)

b) P(A) = $\frac{1}{4} + \frac{1}{6} + \frac{1}{12} = \frac{1}{2}$
P(B) = $\frac{1}{4} + \frac{1}{6} + \frac{1}{12} = \frac{1}{2}$
P(C) = $\frac{1}{12} + \frac{1}{12} = \frac{1}{6}$

(i) P(A)P(B) = $\frac{1}{2} \times \frac{1}{2} = \frac{1}{4}$
$= \frac{1}{6} + \frac{1}{12}$ = P(A and B)
So A and B are independent events.

(ii) P(A)P(C) = $\frac{1}{2} \times \frac{1}{6} = \frac{1}{12}$ = P(A and C)
So A and C are independent events.

(iii) P(B)P(C) = $\frac{1}{2} \times \frac{1}{6} = \frac{1}{12}$ = P(B and C)
So B and C are independent events.

Q18 a) The addition law applies to all events A and B, whereas the law that P(A and B) = P(A)P(B) only applies to independent events. So P(A and B) in the addition law cannot be substituted by P(A)P(B) generally.
[1 mark for a correct explanation]

b) Using the information in the Venn diagram,
P(A) = 0.25, P(B) = 0.5, P(C) = 0.4, P(A and B) = 0.125,
P(B and C) = 0.2 and P(A and C) = 0.05.
For two events A and B to be independent,
P(A and B) = P(A)P(B).
So P(A and B) = 0.125 = 0.25 × 0.5 = P(A)P(B),
so A and B are independent.
P(B and C) = 0.2 = 0.5 × 0.4 = P(B)P(C),
so B and C are independent.
P(A and C) = 0.05 ≠ 0.25 × 0.4 = P(A)P(C),
so A and C are not independent.
[3 marks available — 1 mark for attempting to use the probabilities in the Venn diagram, 1 mark for correctly showing independence of two events, 1 mark for correctly showing A and C are not independent]

Q19 For A and B to be independent, P(A and B) = P(A)P(B).

$P(A) = P(A \text{ and } B) + P(A \text{ and } B') = k + \frac{1}{4}$

$P(B) = P(A \text{ and } B) + P(A' \text{ and } B) = k + \frac{1}{6}$

Therefore $\left(k + \frac{1}{4}\right)\left(k + \frac{1}{6}\right) = k \Rightarrow k^2 - \frac{7}{12}k + \frac{1}{24} = 0$

$\Rightarrow 24k^2 - 14k + 1 = 0 \Rightarrow (12k - 1)(2k - 1) = 0$

$\Rightarrow k = \frac{1}{12}$ or $k = \frac{1}{2}$

[4 marks available — 1 mark for use of formula for independence of events, 1 mark for derivation of an appropriate quadratic in k to solve, 1 mark for using an appropriate method to solve, 1 mark for both correct values of k]

Q20 a) The total value will only be > 60p if the 20p and the 50p are selected.
So P(B) = P(20p, 50p) + P(50p, 20p) *[1 mark]*

$= \frac{1}{5} \times \frac{1}{4} + \frac{1}{5} \times \frac{1}{4} = \frac{1}{20} + \frac{1}{20} = \frac{1}{10}$ *[1 mark]*

b) A and B are mutually exclusive — you cannot get a total value that is more than 60p if a 10p is selected, so the events cannot both happen with the same selection of coins.
[2 marks available — 1 mark for B, 1 mark for suitable explanation]

c) If C happens then the second coin must be either a 5p or a 10p. If it's a 5p, then the first coin must be a 10p for A to happen. So P(A and C) = P(10p, 5p) + P(10p, 10p) + P(not 10p, 10p) *[1 mark]*

$= \frac{2}{5} \times \frac{1}{4} + \frac{2}{5} \times \frac{1}{4} + \frac{3}{5} \times \frac{2}{4}$ *[1 mark]*

$= \frac{2}{20} + \frac{2}{20} + \frac{6}{20} = \frac{10}{20} = \frac{1}{2}$ *[1 mark]*

Q21 a) The probabilities on each set of branches add up to 1:

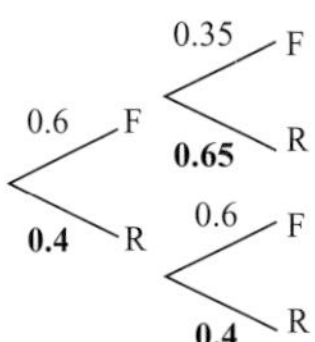

b) P(football on at least one Saturday)
= P(football on both Saturdays)
+ P(football on 1st Sat, rugby on 2nd Sat)
+ P(rugby on 1st Sat, football on 2nd Sat)
= 0.6 × 0.35 + 0.6 × 0.65 + 0.4 × 0.6
= 0.21 + 0.39 + 0.24 = 0.84
You could just add P(football on 1st Saturday) = 0.6 to P(rugby on 1st Sat, football on 2nd Sat) to get the answer. You could also find P(rugby on both Saturdays) and then subtract from 1 to get the answer.

c) P(same sport on both Saturdays)
= P(football on both Saturdays) + P(rugby on both Saturdays)
= 0.6 × 0.35 + 0.4 × 0.4 = 0.21 + 0.16 = 0.37

Q22 a) Can 1 — Can 2 — Can 3

- $\frac{8}{12}$ C
  - $\frac{7}{11}$ C
    - $\frac{6}{10}$ C
    - $\frac{4}{10}$ L
  - $\frac{4}{11}$ L
    - $\frac{7}{10}$ C
    - $\frac{3}{10}$ L
- $\frac{4}{12}$ L
  - $\frac{8}{11}$ C
    - $\frac{7}{10}$ C
    - $\frac{3}{10}$ L
  - $\frac{3}{11}$ L
    - $\frac{8}{10}$ C
    - $\frac{2}{10}$ L

[3 marks available — 1 mark for each correct set of branches (Can 1, Can 2 and Can 3)]

b) P(first can cola and third can lemonade)
= P(CCL) + P(CLL) *[1 mark]*

$= \frac{8}{12} \times \frac{7}{11} \times \frac{4}{10} + \frac{8}{12} \times \frac{4}{11} \times \frac{3}{10}$ *[1 mark]*

$= \frac{224}{1320} + \frac{96}{1320} = \frac{320}{1320} = \frac{8}{33}$ *[1 mark]*

c) P(exactly 2 cans the same)
= P(CCL) + P(CLC) + P(CLL) + P(LCC) + P(LCL) + P(LLC)

$= \frac{8}{12} \times \frac{7}{11} \times \frac{4}{10} + \frac{8}{12} \times \frac{4}{11} \times \frac{7}{10} + \frac{8}{12} \times \frac{4}{11} \times \frac{3}{10} + \frac{4}{12} \times \frac{8}{11} \times \frac{7}{10} + \frac{4}{12} \times \frac{8}{11} \times \frac{3}{10} + \frac{4}{12} \times \frac{3}{11} \times \frac{8}{10}$

$= \frac{224}{1320} + \frac{224}{1320} + \frac{96}{1320} + \frac{224}{1320} + \frac{96}{1320} + \frac{96}{1320}$

$= \frac{960}{1320} = \frac{8}{11}$

You could have done 1 – P(exactly 3 cans the same) to get the answer.
[4 marks available — 1 mark for finding the combinations that give the required result, 1 mark for correct probability for 2 C's and 1 L (or 3 C's if using alternative method), 1 mark for correct probability for 2 L's and 1 C (or 3 L's if using alternative method), 1 mark for correct answer]

Q23 a) Initially there would have been $k + 5$ doughnuts in total.
The tree diagram looks like this:

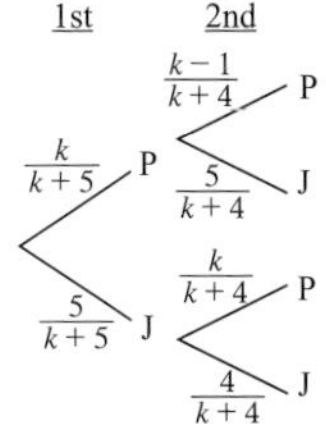

[2 marks available — 1 mark for each correct set of branches (1st doughnut, 2nd doughnut)]

b) To get one of each type there are two possibilities to consider, PJ and JP, both of which have a probability of $\frac{5k}{(k+4)(k+5)}$.

Therefore P(one of each) $= 2 \times \frac{5k}{(k+4)(k+5)} = \frac{11}{24}$

$\Rightarrow \frac{10k}{k^2 + 9k + 20} = \frac{11}{24} \Rightarrow 240k = 11k^2 + 99k + 220$

$\Rightarrow 11k^2 - 141k + 220 = 0 \Rightarrow (11k - 20)(k - 11) = 0$

$\Rightarrow k = 11$ or $k = \frac{20}{11}$.

Since k must be a positive integer, $k = 11$, so there were initially 11 plain doughnuts.
[4 marks available — 1 mark for identifying the relevant possibilities, 1 mark for derivation of an appropriate quadratic equation in k, 1 mark for use of an appropriate method to solve, 1 mark for correct value of k chosen and invalid solution discarded]

Q24 a) The tree diagram looks like this:

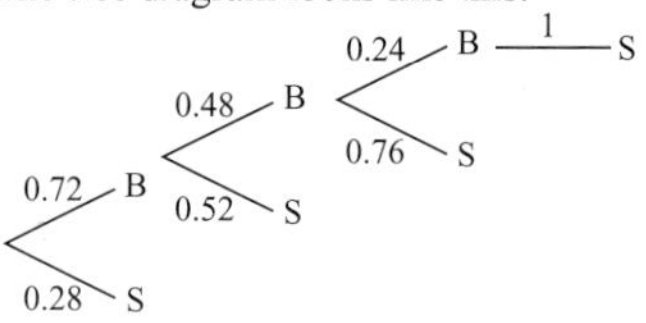

[2 marks available — 1 mark for two correct sets of branches, 1 mark for a fully correct diagram]

b) 3 times *[1 mark]*

c) P(sinks after 1 bounce) = $0.72 \times 0.52 = 0.3744$
$= 0.37$ (to 2 d.p.) *[1 mark]*

d) P(3 bounces) = $0.72 \times 0.48 \times 0.24 = 0.0829...$
$= 0.08$ (to 2 d.p.) *[1 mark]*

Q25 a) P(Medium and Sprinkles) = 0.2, so the expression is probability × total number of ice creams sold, which is $\frac{x}{5}$. *[1 mark]*

b) The value in the cell (Medium and Plain) is $18 - 5 - 6 = 7$. Therefore, the column corresponding to Medium and the bottom row of the table give the equations $7 + \frac{x}{5} + 9 = y$ and $25 + y + 23 = x$.
These can be simplified to the simultaneous equations $5y - x = 80$ and $x - y = 48$. Solving gives $x = 80$ and $y = 32$.
[4 marks available — 1 mark for each correct equation derived, 1 mark for use of an appropriate method of solution, 1 mark for the correct value of x and correct value of y]

c) The entry corresponding to (Large and Sauce) is $0.05 \times 80 = 4$.
The entry corresponding to (Medium and Sprinkles) is $0.2 \times 80 = 16$.
The rest of the entries can be found with straightforward addition and subtraction.

	Small	Medium	Large	Total
Plain	5	7	6	18
Sprinkles	5	16	13	34
Sauce	15	9	4	28
Total	25	32	23	80

[1 mark for all correct entries]

d) (i) P(Large) = $\frac{23}{80}$ *[1 mark]*

(ii) P(Small and Plain) = $\frac{5}{80} = \frac{1}{16}$ *[1 mark]*

(iii) P(Medium or Sprinkles) = $\frac{7 + 16 + 9 + 5 + 13}{80} = \frac{5}{8}$
[1 mark]

Q26 a) The game stops when a 1 is rolled for the first time, so one of the numbers 2, 3, 4, 5 or 6 must be rolled on the first $(n - 1)$ rolls. Since the dice is fair and the rolls are independent then the probability of rolling a 1 on the nth roll is given by the expression $\left(\frac{5}{6}\right)^{n-1} \times \left(\frac{1}{6}\right)$.
[2 marks available — 2 marks for the correct expression, otherwise 1 mark for showing understanding of the independence of the rolls]

b) Substitute $n = 4$ into the expression derived in a) to give $\left(\frac{5}{6}\right)^3\left(\frac{1}{6}\right) = \frac{125}{1296} = 0.096$ to 2 significant figures. *[1 mark]*

c) The two events are mutually exclusive, so the probability is the sum of the individual probabilities.
$\left(\frac{5}{6}\right)^1\left(\frac{1}{6}\right) + \left(\frac{5}{6}\right)^7\left(\frac{1}{6}\right) = 0.185... = 0.19$ (to 2 s.f)
[2 marks available — 1 mark for a correct method, 1 mark for the correct answer]

d) Let A be the event that the number of rolls is at least four, then A' is the event that the number of rolls is at most 3.
Therefore P(A) = 1 – P(A')
$= 1 - \left(\frac{1}{6} + \left(\frac{5}{6} \times \frac{1}{6}\right) + \left(\left(\frac{5}{6}\right)^2 \times \frac{1}{6}\right)\right) = \frac{125}{216}$
$= 0.578... = 0.58$ (to 2 s.f)
[3 marks available — 1 mark for using the formula for probability of a complement, 1 mark for a correct method to find the complement, 1 mark for the correct answer]

Q27 a) Let W be the event that she chooses to walk.
Let C be the event that she chooses to cycle.
The possibilities are:
WWWW WWWC WWCW WCWW CWWW
[1 mark for all correct possibilities]

b) You only need to draw the relevant branches:

0.34 W — 0.34 W — 0.34 W — 0.34 W
0.34 W — 0.34 W — 0.34 W — 0.66 C
0.34 W — 0.34 W — 0.66 C — 0.34 W
0.34 W — 0.66 C — 0.34 W — 0.34 W
0.66 C — 0.34 W — 0.34 W — 0.34 W

The probabilities of the branches are:
0.34^4 for the branch WWWW and $0.34^3 \times 0.66$ for each of the branches WWWC, WWCW, WCWW, CWWW.
Therefore, the probability that Sue walks at least three times in a given week is given by
$0.34^4 + (4 \times 0.34^3 \times 0.66) = 0.117... = 0.12$ (to 2 d.p.)
[3 marks available — 1 mark for a correct tree diagram, 1 mark for using result from a) to identify the relevant branches, 1 mark for the correct answer]

Chapter 4: Statistical Distributions

Prior Knowledge Check

Q1 a) There is only one 6 of clubs, so P(6 of clubs) = $\frac{1}{52}$.

b) 13 out of 52 cards are spades, so P(spade) = $\frac{13}{52} = \frac{1}{4}$.

c) 4 out of 52 cards are aces, so P(ace) = $\frac{4}{52} = \frac{1}{13}$.

d) 5 of the cards are even-numbered diamonds, so P(even-numbered diamond) = $\frac{5}{52}$.

Q2 a) $6! = 6 \times 5 \times 4 \times 3 \times 2 \times 1 = 720$

b) $\frac{20!}{18!} = \frac{18! \times 19 \times 20}{18!} = 19 \times 20 = 380$

c) ${}^7C_6 = \frac{7!}{6!1!} = \frac{7 \times 6!}{6!} = 7$

Exercise 4.1-4.2 — Probability Distributions and Functions

Q1 a) (i) The discrete random variable X is 'number of tails'.
(ii) x could be 0, 1, 2, 3 or 4.

b) (i) The discrete random variable X is 'sum of the two dice scores'.
(ii) x could be 2, 3, 4, 5, 6, 7 or 8.

Q2 a)

a	1	2	3	4	5	6
$P(A = a)$	$\frac{1}{6}$	$\frac{1}{6}$	$\frac{1}{6}$	$\frac{1}{6}$	$\frac{1}{6}$	$\frac{1}{6}$

b) The probability of the score being even is $\frac{3}{6} = \frac{1}{2}$ and the probability of 'otherwise' (the score being odd) is the same. The probability distribution is:

b	0	1
$P(B = b)$	$\frac{1}{2}$	$\frac{1}{2}$

c) C can take 6 values, $c = 5, 10, 15, 20, 25, 30$ (each score × 5) and each one will have probability $\frac{1}{6}$. The probability distribution is:

c	5	10	15	20	25	30
$P(C = c)$	$\frac{1}{6}$	$\frac{1}{6}$	$\frac{1}{6}$	$\frac{1}{6}$	$\frac{1}{6}$	$\frac{1}{6}$

Q3 a) Substitute $x = 1, 2, 3, 4$ into $\frac{x}{10}$ to find the probabilities:

x	1	2	3	4
$P(X = x)$	0.1	0.2	0.3	0.4

b) Substitute $x = 0, 3, 4, 5$ into $0.55 - 0.1x$ to find the probabilities:

x	0	3	4	5
$P(X = x)$	0.55	0.25	0.15	0.05

c) $P(X = x) = 0.2$ for each value of x:

x	10	20	30	40	50
$P(X = x)$	0.2	0.2	0.2	0.2	0.2

d) Substitute $x = 1, 3, 4, 5, 7$ into $0.01x^2$ to find the probabilities:

x	1	3	4	5	7
$P(X = x)$	0.01	0.09	0.16	0.25	0.49

Q4 $X = 0$ if tails is thrown and $X = 1$ if heads is thrown,

so $P(X = x) = \begin{cases} \frac{1}{3} & x = 0 \\ \frac{2}{3} & x = 1 \end{cases}$

Q5 a) (i) $\sum_{\text{all } x} P(X = x) = 0.2 + 0.4 + 0.1 + a = 1$

So, $a = 1 - 0.2 - 0.4 - 0.1 = 0.3$

(ii) $P(X \geq 2) = P(X = 2) + P(X = 3) + P(X = 4)$
$= 0.4 + 0.1 + 0.3 = 0.8$

b) (i) $\sum_{\text{all } x} P(X = x) = 6k = 1$. So, $k = \frac{1}{6}$.

(ii) $P(X \geq 5) = P(X = 9) + P(X = 16) + P(X = 25) + P(X = 36)$
$= 4k = \frac{4}{6} = \frac{2}{3}$

(iii) $P(X \geq 10) = P(X = 16) + P(X = 25) + P(X = 36)$
$= 3k = \frac{3}{6} = \frac{1}{2}$

(iv) $P(3 \leq X \leq 15) = P(X = 4) + P(X = 9) = 2k = \frac{2}{6} = \frac{1}{3}$

(v) $P(X \text{ is divisible by } 3) = P(X = 9 \text{ or } 36)$
$= P(X = 9) + P(X = 36) = 2k = \frac{2}{6} = \frac{1}{3}$

Q6 a) (i) $\sum_{\text{all } x} P(X = x) = k + 4k + 9k = 14k = 1$, so $k = \frac{1}{14}$.

(ii)

x	1	2	3
$P(X = x)$	$\frac{1}{14}$	$\frac{2}{7}$	$\frac{9}{14}$

b) (i) $\sum_{\text{all } x} P(X = x) = k + \frac{k}{2} + \frac{k}{3} = \frac{11k}{6} = 1$, so $k = \frac{6}{11}$.

(ii)

x	1	2	3
$P(X = x)$	$\frac{6}{11}$	$\frac{3}{11}$	$\frac{2}{11}$

c) (i) $\sum_{\text{all } x} P(X = x) = k + 2k + 3k + 4k + 3k + 2k + k = 1$

$16k = 1$, so $k = \frac{1}{16}$.

(ii)

x	1	2	3	4	5	6	7
$P(X = x)$	$\frac{1}{16}$	$\frac{1}{8}$	$\frac{3}{16}$	$\frac{1}{4}$	$\frac{3}{16}$	$\frac{1}{8}$	$\frac{1}{16}$

Q7 Draw a sample space diagram to show all the possible outcomes:

Score on dice 1 (columns), Score on dice 2 (rows)

×	1	2	3	4
1	1	2	3	4
2	2	4	6	8
3	3	6	9	12
4	4	8	12	16

The possible values that X can take are 1, 2, 3, 4, 6, 8, 9, 12, 16. To find the probability of X taking each value, count the number of outcomes that give the value and divide by the total number, 16. So the probability distribution looks like this:

x	1	2	3	4	6	8	9	12	16
$P(X = x)$	$\frac{1}{16}$	$\frac{1}{8}$	$\frac{1}{8}$	$\frac{3}{16}$	$\frac{1}{8}$	$\frac{1}{8}$	$\frac{1}{16}$	$\frac{1}{8}$	$\frac{1}{16}$

$P(3 < X \leq 10) = P(X = 4) + P(X = 6) + P(X = 8) + P(X = 9)$
$= \frac{3}{16} + \frac{1}{8} + \frac{1}{8} + \frac{1}{16} = \frac{1}{2}$

Q8

x	12	13	14	15
$P(X = x)$	$\frac{1}{4}$	$\frac{1}{4}$	$\frac{1}{4}$	$\frac{1}{4}$

$P(X \leq 14) = P(X = 14) + P(X = 13) + P(X = 12)$
$= \frac{1}{4} + \frac{1}{4} + \frac{1}{4} = \frac{3}{4}$

Q9 Let $P(X = 5) = k$. Then $P(X = 2) = 3k$.
$P(X = 0) + P(X = 2) + P(X = 5) + P(X = 10) = 1$,
so $\frac{1}{10} + 3k + k + \frac{1}{10} = 1 \Rightarrow 4k = \frac{8}{10} \Rightarrow k = \frac{1}{5}$

x	0	2	5	10
$P(X = x)$	$\frac{1}{10}$	$\frac{3}{5}$	$\frac{1}{5}$	$\frac{1}{10}$

$P(X > 0) = 1 - P(X = 0) = 1 - \frac{1}{10} = \frac{9}{10}$

You could also add the probabilities of 2, 5 and 10.

Q10 $P(Y = y) = \frac{1}{150}$, $y = 1, 2, ..., 150$
$P(60 < Y \leq 75) = P(Y = 61) + P(Y = 62) + ... + P(Y = 75)$
$= \frac{1}{150} + \frac{1}{150} + ... + \frac{1}{150} = \frac{15}{150} = \frac{1}{10}$

Q11 a) The numbers on the faces are 2, 3, 5 and 7.
If the '2' face is down, $3 + 5 + 7 = 15$.
If the '3' face is down, $2 + 5 + 7 = 14$.
If the '5' face is down, $2 + 3 + 7 = 12$.
If the '7' face is down, $2 + 3 + 5 = 10$.

x	10	12	14	15
$P(X = x)$	$\frac{1}{4}$	$\frac{1}{4}$	$\frac{1}{4}$	$\frac{1}{4}$

[2 marks available — 2 marks for a fully correct table, otherwise 1 mark for one x-value with the correct probability]

b) Each value of X has an equal probability of occurring, and the values are all discrete. *[1 mark]*

c) $P(\text{even}) = P(X = 10) + P(X = 12) + P(X = 14)$
$= \frac{1}{4} + \frac{1}{4} + \frac{1}{4} = \frac{3}{4}$ *[1 mark]*

d) All of the numbers on the dice are now odd. The sum of three odd numbers is always odd, so it is impossible to get an even number, so the probability is 0.
[2 marks available — 1 mark for correct probability of 0, 1 mark for correct explanation]

Q12 Let $P(X = 2) = k$. Then $P(X = 1) = 2k$ and $P(X = 0) = 4k$.
The total probability must be 1, so $k + 2k + 4k = 7k = 1$
$\Rightarrow k = \frac{1}{7}$

x	0	1	2
$P(X = x)$	$\frac{4}{7}$	$\frac{2}{7}$	$\frac{1}{7}$

$P(X \geq 1) = P(X = 1) + P(X = 2) = \frac{2}{7} + \frac{1}{7} = \frac{3}{7}$

Q13 $p(1) = k(1^3 - 6(1^2) + 11(1)) = k(1 - 6 + 11) = 6k$

$p(2) = k(2^3 - 6(2^2) + 11(2)) = k(8 - 24 + 22) = 6k$

$p(3) = k(3^3 - 6(3^2) + 11(3)) = k(27 - 54 + 33) = 6k$

So p(x) is the same for all x, meaning that X has a discrete uniform distribution. The probabilities add up to 1, so:

$6k + 6k + 6k = 18k = 1 \Rightarrow k = \frac{1}{18}$

[3 marks available — 1 mark for finding at least one correct probability in terms of k, 1 mark for correct justification of discrete uniform distribution, 1 mark for correct value of k]

Q14 a) The total probability must be 1, so

$\frac{1}{10k} + \frac{1}{20k} + \frac{k}{30} + \frac{k}{40} + \frac{k}{50} = 1$

$\Rightarrow \frac{(2+1)}{20k} + \frac{(20k + 15k + 12k)}{600} = 1$

$\Rightarrow \frac{90}{600k} + \frac{47k^2}{600k} = 1 \Rightarrow \frac{(90 + 47k^2)}{600k} = 1$

$\Rightarrow 90 + 47k^2 = 600k \Rightarrow 47k^2 - 600k + 90 = 0$

[2 marks available — 1 mark for setting the sum of the probabilities equal to 1, 1 mark for rearranging to quadratic equation]

b) Use the quadratic formula with $a = 47$, $b = -600$, $c = 90$:

$k = \frac{-(-600) \pm \sqrt{(-600)^2 - 4 \times 47 \times 90}}{2 \times 47}$

$\Rightarrow k = 12.614...$ or $k = 0.151...$

Since $k > 1$, $k = 12.6$ (3 s.f.)

[2 marks available — 1 mark for correctly substituting into the quadratic formula, 1 mark for showing the correct result]

c) $P(X \leq 20) = \frac{1}{10k} + \frac{1}{20k} = \frac{3}{20k}$

$k = 12.6$ so $P(X \leq 20) = \frac{3}{20 \times 12.6} = \frac{1}{84} = 0.0119$ (3 s.f.)

[2 marks available — 1 mark for adding correct probabilities, 1 mark for final answer]

Q15 $P(2a \leq X \leq b) = \frac{a}{2b} + \frac{3a}{2b} = \frac{2}{3} \Rightarrow \frac{4a}{2b} = \frac{2}{3} \Rightarrow 6a = 2b$

$\Rightarrow b = 3a$

The probabilities add to 1 and $P(2a \leq X \leq b) = \frac{2}{3}$, so:

$\frac{1}{2b} + \frac{2}{3} + \frac{1}{2a} = 1 \Rightarrow \frac{a+b}{2ab} = \frac{1}{3} \Rightarrow 3(a + b) = 2ab$

Substitute $b = 3a$ into $3(a + b) = 2ab$:

$3(a + 3a) = 2a(3a) \Rightarrow 12a = 6a^2 \Rightarrow a^2 - 2a = 0$

$\Rightarrow a(a - 2) = 0 \Rightarrow a = 0$ or $a = 2$

Since a and b are non-zero, $a = 2$ and $b = 3(2) = 6$.

[5 marks available — 1 mark for equation from $P(2a \leq X \leq b)$, 1 mark for equation from the sum of probabilities, 1 mark for method of solving, 1 mark for correct value of a, 1 mark for correct value of b]

Exercise 4.3 — The Cumulative Distribution Function

Q1 a) Add up the probabilities to work out the values of F(x):

$F(1) = P(X \leq 1) = P(X = 1) = 0.1$

$F(2) = P(X \leq 2) = P(X = 2) + P(X = 1) = 0.2 + 0.1 = 0.3$

$F(3) = P(X \leq 3) = P(X = 3) + P(X = 2) + P(X = 1)$
$= 0.3 + 0.2 + 0.1 = 0.6$

$F(4) = P(X \leq 4) = P(X = 4) + P(X = 3) + P(X = 2) + P(X = 1)$
$= 0.2 + 0.3 + 0.2 + 0.1 = 0.8$

$F(5) = P(X \leq 5)$
$= P(X = 5) + P(X = 4) + P(X = 3) + P(X = 2) + P(X = 1)$
$= 0.2 + 0.2 + 0.3 + 0.2 + 0.1 = 1$

Using all this information, the cumulative distribution function is:

x	1	2	3	4	5
F(x)	0.1	0.3	0.6	0.8	1

b) Add up the probabilities to work out the values of F(x):

$F(-2) = P(X \leq -2) = P(X = -2) = \frac{1}{5}$

$F(-1) = P(X \leq -1) = P(X = -1) + P(X = -2) = \frac{1}{5} + \frac{1}{5} = \frac{2}{5}$

$F(0) = P(X \leq 0) = P(X = 0) + P(X = -1) + P(X = -2)$
$= \frac{1}{5} + \frac{1}{5} + \frac{1}{5} = \frac{3}{5}$

$F(1) = P(X \leq 1)$
$= P(X = 1) + P(X = 0) + P(X = -1) + P(X = -2)$
$= \frac{1}{5} + \frac{1}{5} + \frac{1}{5} + \frac{1}{5} = \frac{4}{5}$

$F(2) = P(X \leq 2)$
$= P(X = 2) + P(X = 1) + P(X = 0)$
$+ P(X = -1) + P(X = -2)$
$= \frac{1}{5} + \frac{1}{5} + \frac{1}{5} + \frac{1}{5} + \frac{1}{5} = 1$

Using all this information, the cumulative distribution function is:

x	–2	–1	0	1	2
F(x)	$\frac{1}{5}$	$\frac{2}{5}$	$\frac{3}{5}$	$\frac{4}{5}$	1

c) Add up the probabilities to work out the values of F(x):

$F(1) = P(X \leq 1) = P(X = 1) = 0.3$

$F(2) = P(X \leq 2) = P(X = 2) + P(X = 1) = 0.2 + 0.3 = 0.5$

$F(3) = P(X \leq 3) = P(X = 3) + P(X = 2) + P(X = 1)$
$= 0.3 + 0.2 + 0.3 = 0.8$

$F(4) = P(X \leq 4) = P(X = 4) + P(X = 3) + P(X = 2) + P(X = 1)$
$= 0.2 + 0.3 + 0.2 + 0.3 = 1$

Using all this information, the cumulative distribution function is:

x	1	2	3	4
F(x)	0.3	0.5	0.8	1

d) Add up the probabilities to work out the values of F(x):

$F(2) = P(X \leq 2) = P(X = 2) = \frac{1}{2}$

$F(4) = P(X \leq 4) = P(X = 4) + P(X = 2) = \frac{1}{4} + \frac{1}{2} = \frac{3}{4}$

$F(8) = P(X \leq 8) = P(X = 8) + P(X = 4) + P(X = 2)$
$= \frac{1}{8} + \frac{1}{4} + \frac{1}{2} = \frac{7}{8}$

$F(16) = P(X \leq 16)$
$= P(X = 16) + P(X = 8) + P(X = 4) + P(X = 2)$
$= \frac{1}{16} + \frac{1}{8} + \frac{1}{4} + \frac{1}{2} = \frac{15}{16}$

$F(32) = P(X \leq 32)$
$= P(X = 32) + P(X = 16) + P(X = 8)$
$+ P(X = 4) + P(X = 2)$
$= \frac{1}{32} + \frac{1}{16} + \frac{1}{8} + \frac{1}{4} + \frac{1}{2} = \frac{31}{32}$

$F(64) = P(X \leq 64)$
$= P(X = 64) + P(X = 32) + P(X = 16)$
$+ P(X = 8) + P(X = 4) + P(X = 2)$
$= \frac{1}{32} + \frac{1}{32} + \frac{1}{16} + \frac{1}{8} + \frac{1}{4} + \frac{1}{2} = 1$

Using all this information, the cumulative distribution function is:

x	2	4	8	16	32	64
F(x)	$\frac{1}{2}$	$\frac{3}{4}$	$\frac{7}{8}$	$\frac{15}{16}$	$\frac{31}{32}$	1

Q2 a) You need to draw up a table showing the cumulative distribution function, so work out the values of F(x):

$F(1) = P(X = 1) = 0.3$

$F(2) = P(X = 2) + P(X = 1) = 0.1 + 0.3 = 0.4$

$F(3) = P(X = 3) + P(X = 2) + P(X = 1)$
$= 0.45 + 0.1 + 0.3 = 0.85$

$F(4) = P(X = 4) + P(X = 3) + P(X = 2) + P(X = 1)$
$= 0.15 + 0.45 + 0.1 + 0.3 = 1$

So the cumulative distribution function looks like this:

x	1	2	3	4
F(x)	0.3	0.4	0.85	1

(i) $P(X \leq 3) = F(3) = 0.85$

(ii) $P(1 < X \leq 3) = P(X \leq 3) - P(X \leq 1) = 0.85 - 0.3 = 0.55$

b) Again, start by working out the values of F(x):

$F(-2) = P(X = -2) = \frac{1}{10}$

$F(-1) = P(X = -1) + P(X = -2) = \frac{2}{5} + \frac{1}{10} = \frac{1}{2}$

$F(0) = P(X = 0) + P(X = -1) + P(X = -2) = \frac{1}{10} + \frac{2}{5} + \frac{1}{10} = \frac{3}{5}$

$F(1) = P(X = 1) + P(X = 0) + P(X = -1) + P(X = -2)$
$= \frac{1}{5} + \frac{1}{10} + \frac{2}{5} + \frac{1}{10} = \frac{4}{5}$

$F(2) = P(X = 2) + P(X = 1) + P(X = 0) + P(X = -1) + P(X = -2)$
$= \frac{1}{5} + \frac{1}{5} + \frac{1}{10} + \frac{2}{5} + \frac{1}{10} = 1$

So the cumulative distribution function looks like this:

x	–2	–1	0	1	2
F(x)	$\frac{1}{10}$	$\frac{1}{2}$	$\frac{3}{5}$	$\frac{4}{5}$	1

(i) $P(X \le 0) = F(0) = \frac{3}{5}$

(ii) $P(X > 0) = 1 - F(0) = 1 - \frac{3}{5} = \frac{2}{5}$

Here you use the fact that all the probabilities add up to 1 — i.e. $P(X \le 0) + P(X > 0) = 1$.

Q3 a) Use the probability function to work out the values of F(x).

$F(1) = P(X = 1) = \frac{1}{8}$

$F(2) = P(X = 2) + P(X = 1) = \frac{1}{8} + \frac{1}{8} = \frac{2}{8} = \frac{1}{4}$

$F(3) = P(X = 3) + P(X = 2) + P(X = 1) = \frac{1}{8} + \frac{1}{8} + \frac{1}{8} = \frac{3}{8}$

Because you are adding on a constant term of $\frac{1}{8}$ each time, the rest are easy to work out:

$F(4) = \frac{4}{8} = \frac{1}{2}$, $F(5) = \frac{5}{8}$, $F(6) = \frac{6}{8} = \frac{3}{4}$,

$F(7) = \frac{7}{8}$, $F(8) = \frac{8}{8} = 1$

So the cumulative distribution function looks like this:

x	1	2	3	4	5	6	7	8
F(x)	$\frac{1}{8}$	$\frac{1}{4}$	$\frac{3}{8}$	$\frac{1}{2}$	$\frac{5}{8}$	$\frac{3}{4}$	$\frac{7}{8}$	1

[2 marks available — 2 marks for a fully correct table, otherwise 1 mark for at least two correct values of F(x)]

b) (i) $P(X \le 3) = F(3) = \frac{3}{8}$ *[1 mark]*

(ii) $P(3 < X \le 7) = P(X \le 7) - P(X \le 3) = \frac{7}{8} - \frac{3}{8} = \frac{4}{8} = \frac{1}{2}$

[2 marks available — 1 mark for using correct values, 1 mark for correct answer]

Q4 a) $P(X = 5) = P(X \le 5) - P(X \le 4) = 1 - 0.9 = 0.1$
$P(X = 4) = P(X \le 4) - P(X \le 3) = 0.9 - 0.6 = 0.3$
$P(X = 3) = P(X \le 3) - P(X \le 2) = 0.6 - 0.3 = 0.3$
$P(X = 2) = P(X \le 2) - P(X \le 1) = 0.3 - 0.2 = 0.1$
$P(X = 1) = P(X \le 1) = 0.2$

So the probability distribution is:

x	1	2	3	4	5
p(x)	0.2	0.1	0.3	0.3	0.1

Always check that the probabilities add up to 1 — if they don't, you know for sure that you've gone wrong.

b) $P(X = 1) = P(X \le 1) - P(X \le 0) = 1 - 0.7 = 0.3$
$P(X = 0) = P(X \le 0) - P(X \le -1) = 0.7 - 0.2 = 0.5$
$P(X = -1) = P(X \le -1) - P(X \le -2) = 0.2 - 0.1 = 0.1$
$P(X = -2) = P(X \le -2) = 0.1$

So the probability distribution is:

x	–2	–1	0	1
p(x)	0.1	0.1	0.5	0.3

c) $P(X = 64) = P(X \le 64) - P(X \le 32) = 1 - \frac{3}{4} = \frac{1}{4}$

$P(X = 32) = P(X \le 32) - P(X \le 16) = \frac{3}{4} - \frac{1}{2} = \frac{1}{4}$

$P(X = 16) = P(X \le 16) - P(X \le 8) = \frac{1}{2} - \frac{1}{4} = \frac{1}{4}$

$P(X = 8) = P(X \le 8) - P(X \le 4) = \frac{1}{4} - \frac{1}{8} = \frac{1}{8}$

$P(X = 4) = P(X \le 4) - P(X \le 2) = \frac{1}{8} - \frac{1}{32} = \frac{3}{32}$

$P(X = 2) = P(X \le 2) = \frac{1}{32}$

So the probability distribution is:

x	2	4	8	16	32	64
p(x)	$\frac{1}{32}$	$\frac{3}{32}$	$\frac{1}{8}$	$\frac{1}{4}$	$\frac{1}{4}$	$\frac{1}{4}$

Q5 a) The total probability must be 1, so

$\frac{k}{30} + \frac{(3k-2)}{60} + \frac{k}{20} + \frac{(2k-1)}{30} + \frac{k}{15} = 1$

$\Rightarrow \frac{2k + 3k - 2 + 3k + 4k - 2 + 4k}{60} = 1$

$\Rightarrow \frac{16k - 4}{60} = 1 \Rightarrow 16k = 64 \Rightarrow k = 4$

[2 marks available — 1 mark for using sum of probabilities = 1, 1 mark for correct answer]

b) First draw up the probability distribution:

x	1	4	9	16	25
$P(X = x)$	$\frac{2}{15}$	$\frac{1}{6}$	$\frac{1}{5}$	$\frac{7}{30}$	$\frac{4}{15}$

Use the probability distribution to work out the values of F(x).

$F(1) = P(X = 1) = \frac{2}{15}$

$F(4) = P(X = 4) + P(X = 1) = \frac{1}{6} + \frac{2}{15} = \frac{3}{10}$

$F(9) = P(X = 9) + P(X = 4) + P(X = 1) = \frac{1}{5} + \frac{1}{6} + \frac{2}{15} = \frac{1}{2}$

$F(16) = P(X = 16) + P(X = 9) + P(X = 4) + P(X = 1)$
$= \frac{7}{30} + \frac{1}{5} + \frac{1}{6} + \frac{2}{15} = \frac{11}{15}$

$F(25) = P(X = 25) + P(X = 16) + P(X = 9) + P(X = 4) + P(X = 1)$
$= \frac{4}{15} + \frac{7}{30} + \frac{1}{5} + \frac{1}{6} + \frac{2}{15} = 1$

So the cumulative distribution function looks like this:

x	1	4	9	16	25
F(x)	$\frac{2}{15}$	$\frac{3}{10}$	$\frac{1}{2}$	$\frac{11}{15}$	1

[2 marks available — 2 marks for a fully correct table, otherwise 1 mark for at least two correct values of F(x)]

c) $P(X \ge 16) = 1 - F(9) = 1 - \frac{1}{2} = \frac{1}{2}$ *[1 mark]*

d) $P(4 < X \le 16) = F(16) - F(4) = \frac{11}{15} - \frac{3}{10} = \frac{13}{30}$

[2 marks available — 1 mark for using correct values, 1 mark for correct answer]

Q6 $P(X = 4) = P(X \le 4) - P(X \le 3) = 1 - 0.8 = 0.2$
$P(X = 3) = P(X \le 3) - P(X \le 2) = 0.8 - a$
$P(X = 2) = P(X \le 2) - P(X \le 1) = a - 0.3$
$P(X = 1) = P(X \le 1) = 0.3$

Now $P(X = 2) = P(X = 3)$ so $0.8 - a = a - 0.3$, so $2a = 1.1$, so $a = 0.55$.
So $P(X = 2) = P(X = 3) = 0.25$

So the probability distribution is:

x	1	2	3	4
p(x)	0.3	0.25	0.25	0.2

Q7 a) $F(3) = P(X \le 3) = \sum_{\text{all } x} P(X = x) = 1$

So $\frac{(3+k)^2}{25} = 1 \Rightarrow (3+k)^2 = 25$

$\Rightarrow 3 + k = 5 \Rightarrow k = 2$

To find the probability distribution, you need to find the probability of each outcome:

$P(X = 3) = P(X \le 3) - P(X \le 2) = F(3) - F(2)$

$= \frac{(3+2)^2}{25} - \frac{(2+2)^2}{25} = \frac{25}{25} - \frac{16}{25} = \frac{9}{25}$

$P(X = 2) = P(X \le 2) - P(X \le 1) = F(2) - F(1)$

$= \frac{(2+2)^2}{25} - \frac{(1+2)^2}{25} = \frac{16}{25} - \frac{9}{25} = \frac{7}{25}$

$P(X = 1) = P(X \le 1) = F(1) = \frac{(1+2)^2}{25} = \frac{9}{25}$

So the table looks like:

x	1	2	3
$P(X = x)$	$\frac{9}{25}$	$\frac{7}{25}$	$\frac{9}{25}$

b) $F(3) = P(X \le 3) = \sum_{\text{all } x} P(X = x) = 1$

So $\frac{(3+k)^3}{64} = 1 \Rightarrow (3+k)^3 = 64 \Rightarrow 3 + k = 4 \Rightarrow k = 1$

To find the probability distribution you need to find the probability of each outcome:

$P(X = 3) = P(X \le 3) - P(X \le 2) = F(3) - F(2)$

$= \frac{(3+1)^3}{64} - \frac{(2+1)^3}{64} = \frac{64}{64} - \frac{27}{64} = \frac{37}{64}$

$P(X = 2) = P(X \le 2) - P(X \le 1) = F(2) - F(1)$

$= \frac{(2+1)^3}{64} - \frac{(1+1)^3}{64} = \frac{27}{64} - \frac{8}{64} = \frac{19}{64}$

$P(X = 1) = P(X \le 1) = F(1) = \frac{(1+1)^3}{64} = \frac{8}{64} = \frac{1}{8}$

So the table looks like:

x	1	2	3
$P(X = x)$	$\frac{1}{8}$	$\frac{19}{64}$	$\frac{37}{64}$

c) $F(3) = P(X \le 3) = \sum_{\text{all } x} P(X = x) = 1$, so $2^{(3-k)} = 1$.

For 2 to the power of something to be equal to 1, the power must be 0, so $3 - k = 0 \Rightarrow k = 3$.
To find the probability distribution, you need to find the probability of each outcome:

$P(X = 3) = P(X \le 3) - P(X \le 2) = F(3) - F(2)$

$= 2^{(3-3)} - 2^{(2-3)} = 2^0 - 2^{-1} = 1 - \frac{1}{2} = \frac{1}{2}$

$P(X = 2) = P(X \le 2) - P(X \le 1) = F(2) - F(1)$

$= 2^{(2-3)} - 2^{(1-3)} = 2^{-1} - 2^{-2} = \frac{1}{2} - \frac{1}{4} = \frac{1}{4}$

$P(X = 1) = P(X \le 1) = F(1) = 2^{(1-3)} = 2^{-2} = \frac{1}{4}$

So the table looks like:

x	1	2	3
$P(X = x)$	$\frac{1}{4}$	$\frac{1}{4}$	$\frac{1}{2}$

Q8 a) $F(x_3) = 1$ so $\frac{(x_3 - 1)^2}{64} = 1$

$\Rightarrow (x_3 - 1)^2 = 64 \Rightarrow x_3 - 1 = \pm 8 \Rightarrow x_3 = -7$ or $x_3 = 9$

You know that x_3 is positive so $x_3 = 9$.

$P(X = x_3) = 1 - F(7) = 1 - \frac{(7-1)^2}{64} = 1 - \frac{36}{64} = \frac{28}{64} = \frac{7}{16}$

[2 marks available — 1 mark for correct x_3, 1 mark for correct $P(X = x_3)$]

b) $\frac{(x_2 - 1)^2}{64} = \frac{1}{4} \Rightarrow (x_2 - 1)^2 = 16 \Rightarrow x_2 - 1 = \pm 4$

$\Rightarrow x_2 = -3$ or $x_2 = 5$

You know that x_2 is positive so $x_2 = 5$.

$P(X = 7) = F(7) - F(5) = \frac{36}{64} - \frac{1}{4} = \frac{20}{64} = \frac{5}{16}$

[2 marks available — 1 mark for correct x_2, 1 mark for correct $P(X = 7)$]

c) $F(x_2) = \frac{1}{4}$, so $P(X = x_2) + P(X = x_1) = \frac{1}{4}$

$\Rightarrow 3P(X = x_1) + P(X = x_1) = \frac{1}{4}$

$\Rightarrow 4P(X = x_1) = \frac{1}{4} \Rightarrow P(X = x_1) = \frac{1}{16}$

$P(X = x_1) = F(x_1) = \frac{(x_1 - 1)^2}{64} = \frac{1}{16}$

$\Rightarrow (x_1 - 1)^2 = 4 \Rightarrow x_1 - 1 = \pm 2 \Rightarrow x_1 = -1$ or $x_1 = 3$

You know that x_1 is positive so $x_1 = 3$.

[2 marks available — 1 mark for correct value for $F(x_1)$, 1 mark for correct x_1]

Q9 a) $F(x)$ means the probability that the larger score on the dice is no larger than x. This means both dice must score no more than x, where $x = 1, 2, 3, 4, 5$ or 6. The probability that one dice will score no more than x is $\frac{x}{6}$, so the probability that both will score no more than x is $\frac{x}{6} \times \frac{x}{6} = \frac{x^2}{36}$.

Two dice rolls are completely independent, so the probabilities can just be multiplied together.

So $F(x) = \frac{x^2}{36}$, $x = 1, 2, 3, 4, 5, 6$.

b) To find the probability distribution you need to find the probability of each outcome:

$P(X = 6) = P(X \le 6) - P(X \le 5) = \frac{6^2}{36} - \frac{5^2}{36}$

$= \frac{36}{36} - \frac{25}{36} = \frac{11}{36}$

$P(X = 5) = P(X \le 5) - P(X \le 4) = \frac{5^2}{36} - \frac{4^2}{36}$

$= \frac{25}{36} - \frac{16}{36} = \frac{9}{36} = \frac{1}{4}$

$P(X = 4) = P(X \le 4) - P(X \le 3) = \frac{4^2}{36} - \frac{3^2}{36}$

$= \frac{16}{36} - \frac{9}{36} = \frac{7}{36}$

$P(X = 3) = P(X \le 3) - P(X \le 2) = \frac{3^2}{36} - \frac{2^2}{36}$

$= \frac{9}{36} - \frac{4}{36} = \frac{5}{36}$

$P(X = 2) = P(X \le 2) - P(X \le 1) = \frac{2^2}{36} - \frac{1^2}{36}$

$= \frac{4}{36} - \frac{1}{36} = \frac{3}{36} = \frac{1}{12}$

$P(X = 1) = P(X \le 1) = \frac{1^2}{36} = \frac{1}{36}$

So the table looks like:

x	1	2	3	4	5	6
$P(X = x)$	$\frac{1}{36}$	$\frac{1}{12}$	$\frac{5}{36}$	$\frac{7}{36}$	$\frac{1}{4}$	$\frac{11}{36}$

Exercise 4.4 — Binomial Coefficients

Q1 a) All 6 letters are different, so there are $6! = 720$ different arrangements.

b) All 8 letters are different, so there are $8! = 40\,320$ different arrangements.

c) If all 4 letters were different, there would be $4! = 24$ different arrangements. But since two of the letters are the same, you need to divide this by $2! = 2$.
So there are $4! \div 2! = 12$ different arrangements.

d) If all 5 letters were different, there would be $5! = 120$ different arrangements. But since two of the letters are the same, you need to divide this by $2! = 2$.
So there are $5! \div 2! = 60$ different arrangements.

e) If all 9 letters were different, there would be $9! = 362\,880$ different arrangements. But since two of the letters are the same, you need to divide this by $2! = 2$.
So there are $9! \div 2! = 181\,440$ different arrangements.

f) If all 8 letters were different, there would be $8! = 40\,320$ different arrangements. But since four of the letters are the same, you need to divide this by $4! = 24$.
So there are $8! \div 4! = 1680$ different arrangements.

g) If all 7 letters were different, there would be $7! = 5040$ different arrangements. But there are two Ts and two Rs, so you need to divide this by 2! twice. So there are $7! \div 2! \div 2! = 1260$ different arrangements.

h) If all 10 letters were different, there would be $10! = 3\,628\,800$ different arrangements. But there are five Ss and two Es, so you need to divide this by 5! and 2!. So there are $10! \div 5! \div 2! = 15\,120$ different arrangements.

i) If all 8 letters were different, there would be $8! = 40\,320$ different arrangements. But there are two Ss, two Ts and two Rs, so you need to divide this by 2! three times. So there are $8! \div 2! \div 2! \div 2! = 5040$ different arrangements.

Q2 $\binom{20}{11} = \frac{20!}{11!9!} = 167\,960$ different ways

Q3 a) $\binom{10}{3} = \binom{10}{7} = \frac{10!}{3!7!} = 120$ ways

b) $\binom{10}{5} = \frac{10!}{5!5!} = 252$ ways

c) $\binom{10}{1} = \binom{10}{9} = \frac{10!}{1!9!} = 10$ ways

d) $\binom{10}{8} = \binom{10}{2} = \frac{10!}{8!2!} = 45$ ways

Q4 a) $\binom{20}{10} = \frac{20!}{10!10!} = 184\,756$ ways

b) $\binom{20}{14} = \binom{20}{6} = \frac{20!}{14!6!} = 38\,760$ ways

c) $\binom{20}{2} = \binom{20}{18} = \frac{20!}{2!18!} = 190$ ways

d) $\binom{20}{5} = \binom{20}{15} = \frac{20!}{5!15!} = 15\,504$ ways

Q5 a) $\binom{11}{4} = \binom{11}{7} = \frac{11!}{4!7!} = 330$ ways

b) $\binom{11}{6} = \binom{11}{5} = \frac{11!}{6!5!} = 462$ ways

c) $\binom{11}{8} = \binom{11}{3} = \frac{11!}{8!3!} = 165$ ways

d) $\binom{11}{11} = \binom{11}{0} = \frac{11!}{11!0!} = 1$ way

e) $\binom{11}{5} = \binom{11}{6} = \frac{11!}{5!6!} = 462$ ways

f) $\binom{11}{9} = \binom{11}{2} = \frac{11!}{9!2!} = 55$ ways

Q6 a) If all 15 bottles were different, there would be 15! different arrangements. But there are 7 bottles of one type and 4 bottles of another type, so you need to divide this by 7! and 4!. So there are $15! \div 7! \div 4! = 10\,810\,800$ different arrangements.
[1 mark]

b) There are 4 bottles of one type, 3 bottles of a second type, and 4 bottles of a third type, so you need to divide 15! by 4!, 3! and 4!. So there are now $15! \div 4! \div 3! \div 4! = 378\,378\,000$ different arrangements.
[1 mark]

Q7 A contestant will win without having to answer all eight questions if they answer six out of the first seven questions correctly.
$\binom{7}{6} = \frac{7!}{6!(7-6)!} = 7$, so there are 7 ways in which a contestant can win without answering all 8 questions.
You don't need to include the possibility of getting the first 7 correct, as if they get the first 6 correct, the game will end, regardless of what would have happened on the 7th question.

Q8 a) There are six choices of colour for the first peg, six choices for the second peg, and so on.
$6 \times 6 \times 6 \times 6 = 6^4 = 1296$

b) As the order is irrelevant, you just need to work out how many ways 4 colours can be chosen from 6 options.
$\binom{6}{4} = \frac{6!}{4!2!} = 15$ ways

Q9 $\binom{12}{x} = \frac{12!}{x!(12-x)!} = 792 \Rightarrow x!(12-x)! = \frac{12!}{792}$
$\Rightarrow x!(12-x)! = 604\,800$
Deduce x by trial and error:
$x = 1$: $1!\,11! = 39\,916\,800$
$x = 2$: $2!\,10! = 7\,257\,600$
$x = 3$: $3!\,9! = 2\,177\,280$
$x = 4$: $4!\,8! = 967\,680$
$x = 5$: $5!\,7! = 604\,800$, so $x = 5$.
[3 marks available — 1 mark for using the binomial coefficient, 1 mark for method to find x, 1 mark for the correct answer]

Q10 $\binom{n}{3} = 2\binom{n-1}{2} \Rightarrow \frac{n!}{3!(n-3)!} = \frac{2(n-1)!}{2!(n-1-2)!}$
$\Rightarrow \frac{n!}{6(n-3)!} = \frac{(n-1)!}{(n-3)!} \Rightarrow n! = 6(n-1)!$
$\Rightarrow \frac{n!}{(n-1)!} = 6 \Rightarrow \frac{n(n-1)!}{(n-1)!} = 6 \Rightarrow n = 6$
[4 marks available — 1 mark for setting up an equation with binomial coefficients, 1 mark for simplifying by evaluating factorials, 1 mark for a correct method to solve the simplified equation, 1 mark for correct answer]

Exercise 4.5 — The Binomial Distribution

Q1 a) Not a binomial distribution
— the number of trials is not fixed.

b) Here, X will follow a binomial distribution.
$X \sim B(2000, 0.005)$.

c) Here, Y will follow a binomial distribution. $Y \sim B(10, 0.5)$.

Q2 E.g. Kaitlin is assuming that there is a constant probability of it being sunny on a given day, which isn't valid.

Q3 The number of trials is fixed (i.e. the 15 acts), each trial can either succeed or fail, X is the total number of successes, and the probability of success is the same each time if the trials are independent. So to model this situation with a binomial distribution, you would need to assume that all the trials are independent.

Q4 The number of trials is fixed, each trial can either succeed or fail, and X is the total number of successes. To make the probability of success the same each time, the cards would need to be replaced, and to make each pick independent you could shuffle the pack after replacing the picked cards.
If this is done, then $X \sim B(10, \frac{3}{13})$.

Q5 The number of trials is fixed (650), each trial can either succeed or fail, X is the total number of successes, and the probability of each button falling off is the same if the trials are independent. So to model this situation with a binomial distribution, you would need to assume that all the trials are independent (i.e. the probability of each separate button falling off should not depend on whether any other button has fallen off).
If this assumption is satisfied, then $X \sim B(650, 0.001)$.

Q6 a) E.g. All trials are independent if the probability of one customer answering their call has no impact on the probability of other customers answering their call. *[1 mark]*

b) Any two from:
E.g. The number of trials is fixed — it is the number of customers called (150).
Each trial involves success or failure — call answered or not answered.
The probability of success is the same each time — the probability the call being answered is 45%.
The variable is the number of successes — the number of calls answered.
[2 marks available — 1 mark for each of two correct points]

c) $X \sim B(150, 0.45)$ *[1 mark]*

Q7 a) Any two from:
E.g. There is a fixed number of trials (the 8 songs selected).
Each trial is either a success (a song is not longer than 3 minutes) or failure (a song is longer than 3 minutes).
All trials are independent (the length of one song does not influence the length of another).
The probability of success is the same for each trial (each song is assumed to have a 20% chance of not being longer than 3 minutes).
The variable X is the total successes (the number of songs that aren't longer than 3 minutes).
[2 marks available — 1 mark for each correct reason]

b) The probability of a song being longer than 3 minutes is 0.8, so the probability of a song not being longer than 3 minutes is $1 - 0.8 = 0.2$. So $X \sim B(8, 0.2)$. *[1 mark]*

Exercise 4.6 — Using the Binomial Probability Function

Q1 a) Use the binomial probability function with $n = 10$ and $p = 0.14$.

(i) $P(X = 2) = \binom{10}{2} \times 0.14^2 \times (1 - 0.14)^{10-2}$
$= \frac{10!}{2!8!} \times 0.14^2 \times 0.86^8 = 0.264$ (3 s.f.)

(ii) $P(X = 4) = \binom{10}{4} \times 0.14^4 \times (1 - 0.14)^{10-4}$
$= \frac{10!}{4!6!} \times 0.14^4 \times 0.86^6 = 0.0326$ (3 s.f.)

(iii) $P(X = 5) = \binom{10}{5} \times 0.14^5 \times (1 - 0.14)^{10-5}$
$= \frac{10!}{5!5!} \times 0.14^5 \times 0.86^5 = 0.00638$ (3 s.f.)

b) Use the binomial probability function with $n = 8$ and $p = 0.27$.

(i) $P(X = 3) = \binom{8}{3} \times 0.27^3 \times (1 - 0.27)^{8-3}$
$= \frac{8!}{3!5!} \times 0.27^3 \times 0.73^5 = 0.229$ (3 s.f.)

(ii) $P(X = 5) = \binom{8}{5} \times 0.27^5 \times (1 - 0.27)^{8-5}$
$= \frac{8!}{5!3!} \times 0.27^5 \times 0.73^3 = 0.0313$ (3 s.f.)

(iii) $P(X = 7) = \binom{8}{7} \times 0.27^7 \times (1 - 0.27)^{8-7}$
$= \frac{8!}{7!1!} \times 0.27^7 \times 0.73^1 = 0.000611$ (3 s.f.)

c) Use the binomial probability function with $n = 22$ and $p = 0.55$.

(i) $P(X = 10) = \binom{22}{10} \times 0.55^{10} \times (1 - 0.55)^{22-10}$
$= \frac{22!}{10!12!} \times 0.55^{10} \times 0.45^{12} = 0.113$ (3 s.f.)

(ii) $P(X = 15) = \binom{22}{15} \times 0.55^{15} \times (1 - 0.55)^{22-15}$
$= \frac{22!}{15!7!} \times 0.55^{15} \times 0.45^7 = 0.0812$ (3 s.f.)

(iii) $P(X = 20) = \binom{22}{20} \times 0.55^{20} \times (1 - 0.55)^{22-20}$
$= \frac{22!}{20!2!} \times 0.55^{20} \times 0.45^2 = 0.000300$ (3 s.f.)

Q2 a) Use the binomial probability function with $n = 12$ and $p = 0.7$.

(i) $P(X \geq 11) = P(X = 11) + P(X = 12)$
$= \frac{12!}{11!1!} \times 0.7^{11} \times 0.3^1 + \frac{12!}{12!0!} \times 0.7^{12} \times 0.3^0$
$= 0.07118... + 0.01384... = 0.0850$ (3 s.f.)

(ii) $P(8 \leq X \leq 10) = P(X = 8) + P(X = 9) + P(X = 10)$
$= \frac{12!}{8!4!} \times 0.7^8 \times 0.3^4 + \frac{12!}{9!3!} \times 0.7^9 \times 0.3^3$
$+ \frac{12!}{10!2!} \times 0.7^{10} \times 0.3^2$
$= 0.23113... + 0.23970... + 0.16779...$
$= 0.639$ (3 s.f.)

(iii) $P(X > 9) = P(X = 10) + P(X = 11) + P(X = 12)$
$= 0.16779... + 0.07118... + 0.01384$
$= 0.253$ (3 s.f.)

Part (iii) has been worked out using the results found in (i) and (ii).

b) Use the binomial probability function with $n = 20$ and $p = 0.16$.

(i) $P(X < 2) = P(X = 0) + P(X = 1)$
$= \frac{20!}{0!20!} \times 0.16^0 \times 0.84^{20} + \frac{20!}{1!19!} \times 0.16^1 \times 0.84^{19}$
$= 0.03059... + 0.11653... = 0.147$ (3 s.f.)

(ii) $P(X \leq 3) = P(X = 0) + P(X = 1) + P(X = 2) + P(X = 3)$
$= 0.03059... + 0.11653...$
$+ \frac{20!}{2!18!} \times 0.16^2 \times 0.84^{18}$
$+ \frac{20!}{3!17!} \times 0.16^3 \times 0.84^{17}$
$= 0.03059... + 0.11653...$
$+ 0.21087... + 0.24099...$
$= 0.599$ (3 s.f.)

(iii) $P(1 < X \leq 4) = P(X = 2) + P(X = 3) + P(X = 4)$
$= 0.21087... + 0.24099...$
$+ \frac{20!}{4!16!} \times 0.16^4 \times 0.84^{16}$
$= 0.21087... + 0.24099...$
$+ 0.19509... = 0.647$ (3 s.f.)

c) Use the binomial probability function with $n = 30$ and $p = 0.88$.

(i) $P(X > 28) = P(X = 29) + P(X = 30)$
$= \frac{30!}{29!1!} \times 0.88^{29} \times 0.12^1$
$+ \frac{30!}{30!0!} \times 0.88^{30} \times 0.12^0$
$= 0.088369... + 0.021601... = 0.110$ (3 s.f.)

(ii) $P(25 < X < 28) = P(X = 26) + P(X = 27)$
$= \frac{30!}{26!4!} \times 0.88^{26} \times 0.12^4$
$+ \frac{30!}{27!3!} \times 0.88^{27} \times 0.12^3$
$= 0.204693... + 0.222383...$
$= 0.427$ (3 s.f.)

(iii) $P(X \geq 27) = P(X = 27) + P(X = 28)$
$+ P(X = 29) + P(X = 30)$
$= 0.222383... + \frac{30!}{28!2!} \times 0.88^{28} \times 0.12^2$
$+ 0.088369... + 0.021601...$
$= 0.222383... + 0.174729...$
$+ 0.088369... + 0.021601...$
$= 0.507$ (3 s.f.)

d) Use the binomial probability function with $n = 14$ and $p = 0.62$.

(i) $P(X = 6) = \binom{14}{6} \times 0.62^6 \times (1 - 0.62)^{14-6}$
$= \frac{14!}{6!8!} \times 0.62^6 \times (1 - 0.62)^8 = 0.0742$ (3 s.f.)

(ii) $P(X \geq 12) = P(X = 12) + P(X = 13) + P(X = 14)$
$= \frac{14!}{12!2!} \times 0.62^{12} \times 0.38^2$
$+ \frac{14!}{13!1!} \times 0.62^{13} \times 0.38^1$
$+ \frac{14!}{14!0!} \times 0.62^{14} \times 0.38^0$
$= 0.042394... + 0.010641... + 0.0012401...$
$= 0.05427... = 0.0543$ (3 s.f.)

(iii) $P(X \leq 11) = 1 - P(X \geq 12) = 1 - 0.05427...$
$= 0.946$ (3 s.f.)

The key here is to spot that this is the "opposite" to part (ii), so you can use that to find the answer.

Q3 a) Use the binomial probability function with $n = 5$ and $p = \frac{1}{2}$.

(i) $P(X \leq 4) = 1 - P(X > 4) = 1 - P(X = 5)$
$= 1 - \frac{5!}{5!0!} \times \left(\frac{1}{2}\right)^5 \times \left(\frac{1}{2}\right)^0$
$= 1 - 0.03125 = 0.969$ (3 s.f.)

(ii) $P(X > 1) = 1 - P(X \leq 1) = 1 - P(X = 0) - P(X = 1)$
$= 1 - \frac{5!}{0!5!} \times \left(\frac{1}{2}\right)^0 \times \left(\frac{1}{2}\right)^5 - \frac{5!}{1!4!} \times \left(\frac{1}{2}\right)^1 \times \left(\frac{1}{2}\right)^4$
$= 1 - 0.03125 - 0.15625 = 0.813$ (3 s.f.)

(iii) $P(1 \leq X \leq 4) = 1 - P(X = 0) - P(X = 5)$
$= 1 - \frac{5!}{0!5!} \times \left(\frac{1}{2}\right)^0 \times \left(\frac{1}{2}\right)^5$
$- \frac{5!}{5!0!} \times \left(\frac{1}{2}\right)^5 \times \left(\frac{1}{2}\right)^0$
$= 1 - 0.03125 - 0.03125 = 0.938$ (3 s.f.)

b) Use the binomial probability function with $n = 8$ and $p = \frac{2}{3}$.

(i) $P(X < 7) = 1 - P(X \geq 7) = 1 - P(X = 7) - P(X = 8)$
$= 1 - \frac{8!}{7!1!} \times \left(\frac{2}{3}\right)^7 \times \left(\frac{1}{3}\right)^1 - \frac{8!}{8!0!} \times \left(\frac{2}{3}\right)^8 \times \left(\frac{1}{3}\right)^0$
$= 1 - 0.156073... - 0.039018 = 0.805$ (3 s.f.)

(ii) $P(X \geq 2) = 1 - P(X < 2) = 1 - P(X = 0) - P(X = 1)$
$= 1 - \frac{8!}{0!8!} \times \left(\frac{2}{3}\right)^0 \times \left(\frac{1}{3}\right)^8 - \frac{8!}{1!7!} \times \left(\frac{2}{3}\right)^1 \times \left(\frac{1}{3}\right)^7$
$= 1 - 0.00015241... - 0.00243865...$
$= 0.997$ (3 s.f.)

(iii) $P(0 \leq X \leq 8) = 1$

This must be 1, as X can only take values from 0 to 8.

c) Use the binomial probability function with $n = 6$ and $p = \frac{4}{5}$.

(i) $P(X > 0) = 1 - P(X = 0) = 1 - \frac{6!}{0!6!} \times \left(\frac{4}{5}\right)^0 \times \left(\frac{1}{5}\right)^6$
$= 1 - 0.000064 = 1.00$ (3 s.f.)

(ii) $P(X \geq 3) = 1 - P(X < 3)$
$= 1 - P(X = 0) - P(X = 1) - P(X = 2)$
$= 1 - \frac{6!}{0!6!} \times \left(\frac{4}{5}\right)^0 \times \left(\frac{1}{5}\right)^6$
$- \frac{6!}{1!5!} \times \left(\frac{4}{5}\right)^1 \times \left(\frac{1}{5}\right)^5 - \frac{6!}{2!4!} \times \left(\frac{4}{5}\right)^2 \times \left(\frac{1}{5}\right)^4$
$= 1 - 0.000064 - 0.001536 - 0.01536$
$= 0.983$ (3 s.f.)

(iii) $P(1 \leq X < 6) = P(X > 0) - P(X = 6)$
$= 0.999936 - \frac{6!}{6!0!} \times \left(\frac{4}{5}\right)^6 \times \left(\frac{1}{5}\right)^0$
$= 0.999936 - 0.262144$
$= 0.738$ (3 s.f.)

Remember to use the non-rounded value for P(X > 0).

Q4 a) Let X = number of heads, $n = 9$ and p = P(heads) = $\frac{2}{5}$, so $X \sim B(9, \frac{2}{5})$.

$P(X = 2) = \binom{9}{2} \times \left(\frac{2}{5}\right)^2 \times \left(\frac{3}{5}\right)^7 = 0.161$ (3 s.f.)

b) $P(X = 5) = \binom{9}{5} \times \left(\frac{2}{5}\right)^5 \times \left(\frac{3}{5}\right)^4 = 0.167$ (3 s.f.)

c) Getting 9 tails means getting 0 heads.

$P(X = 0) = \binom{9}{0} \times \left(\frac{2}{5}\right)^0 \times \left(\frac{3}{5}\right)^9 = 0.0101$ (3 s.f.)

You could also use the binomial probability function for the number of tails to find P(9 tails), using P(tails) = $\left(\frac{3}{5}\right)$.

Q5 a) $X \sim B(8, 0.1)$ *[1 mark]*

b) $P(X = 4) = \binom{8}{4} \times 0.1^4 \times 0.9^4 = 0.00459$ (3 s.f.) *[1 mark]*

c) $P(X = 0) = \binom{8}{0} \times 0.1^0 \times 0.9^8 = 0.9^8 = 0.430$ (3 s.f.) *[1 mark]*

Q6 a) X is the number of sixes rolled, $n = 5$ and p = P(roll a six) = $\frac{1}{6}$, so $X \sim B(5, \frac{1}{6})$.

$P(X = 2) = \binom{5}{2} \times \left(\frac{1}{6}\right)^2 \times \left(\frac{5}{6}\right)^3 = 0.161$ (3 s.f.)

b) X is the number of fives rolled, $n = 5$ and p = P(roll a five) = $\frac{1}{6}$, so $X \sim B(5, \frac{1}{6})$.

$P(X \geq 1) = 1 - P(X = 0) = 1 - \binom{5}{0} \times \left(\frac{1}{6}\right)^0 \times \left(\frac{5}{6}\right)^5$
$= 1 - 0.40187... = 0.598$ (3 s.f.)

c) X is the number of threes rolled, $n = 5$ and p = P(roll a three) = $\frac{1}{6}$, so $X \sim B(5, \frac{1}{6})$.

$P(X > 3) = P(X = 4) + P(X = 5)$
$= \binom{5}{4} \times \left(\frac{1}{6}\right)^4 \times \left(\frac{5}{6}\right)^1 + \binom{5}{5} \times \left(\frac{1}{6}\right)^5 \times \left(\frac{5}{6}\right)^0$
$= 0.003215... + 0.0001286... = 0.00334$ (3 s.f.)

d) X is the number of scores more than two rolled, $n = 5$ and p = P(roll more than a two) = $\frac{2}{3}$, so $X \sim B(5, \frac{2}{3})$.

$P(X = 3) = \binom{5}{3} \times \left(\frac{2}{3}\right)^3 \times \left(\frac{1}{3}\right)^2 = 0.329$ (3 s.f.)

e) X is the number of scores that are multiples of 3 (i.e. three or six), $n = 5$ and p = P(roll three or six) = $\frac{1}{3}$, so $X \sim B(5, \frac{1}{3})$.

$P(X = 0) = \binom{5}{0} \times \left(\frac{1}{3}\right)^0 \times \left(\frac{2}{3}\right)^5 - 0.132$ (3 s.f.)

f) X is the number of square number scores (i.e. one or four), $n = 5$ and p = P(roll one or four) = $\frac{1}{3}$, so $X \sim B(5, \frac{1}{3})$.

$P(X \leq 4) = 1 - P(X = 5) = 1 - \binom{5}{5} \times \left(\frac{1}{3}\right)^5 \times \left(\frac{2}{3}\right)^0$
$= 1 - 0.004115... = 0.996$ (3 s.f.)

Q7 a) There are 12 answers, which are either 'correct' or 'incorrect'. The student guesses at random so the questions are answered independently of each other and the probability of a correct answer is $\frac{1}{3}$. So $X \sim B(12, \frac{1}{3})$.

b) $P(X < 3) = P(X = 0) + P(X = 1) + P(X = 2)$
$= \frac{12!}{0!12!} \times \left(\frac{1}{3}\right)^0 \times \left(\frac{2}{3}\right)^{12} + \frac{12!}{1!11!} \times \left(\frac{1}{3}\right)^1 \times \left(\frac{2}{3}\right)^{11}$
$+ \frac{12!}{2!10!} \times \left(\frac{1}{3}\right)^2 \times \left(\frac{2}{3}\right)^{10}$
$= 0.00770... + 0.04624... + 0.12717...$
$= 0.181$ (3 s.f.)

Q8 Let X represent the number of ripe avocados Seb picks. Then $X \sim B(3, 0.225)$.

$P(X = 3) = \frac{3!}{3!0!} \times 0.225^3 \times 0.775^0 = 0.0114$ (3 s.f.)

You're only able to use the binomial distribution because Seb replaces each avocado after he picks it — otherwise the probability of picking a ripe avocado would change each time.

Q9 Let X represent the number of defective items. Then $X \sim B(15, 0.05)$, and you need to find $P(1 \leq X \leq 3)$.

$P(1 \leq X \leq 3) = P(X = 1) + P(X = 2) + P(X = 3)$
$= \frac{15!}{1!14!} \times 0.05^1 \times 0.95^{14} + \frac{15!}{2!13!} \times 0.05^2 \times 0.95^{13} + \frac{15!}{3!12!} \times 0.05^3 \times 0.95^{12}$
$= 0.36575... + 0.13475... + 0.03072...$
$= 0.531$ (3 s.f.)

Q10 a) Let the random variable X represent the number of 'treble-20's the player gets in a set of 3 darts. Then $X \sim B(3, 0.75)$.

$P(X \geq 2) = P(X = 2) + P(X = 3)$

$P(X = 2) = \binom{3}{2} \times 0.75^2 \times (1 - 0.75) = 0.421875$

$P(X = 3) = \binom{3}{3} \times 0.75^3 \times (1 - 0.75)^0 = 0.421875$

So $P(X \geq 2) = 0.421875 + 0.421875$
$= 0.84375 = 0.844$ (3 s.f.)

b) Now let X represent the number of 'treble-20's the player scores with 30 darts. Then $X \sim B(30, 0.75)$.
You need to find $P(X \geq 26)$.

$P(X \geq 26) = P(X = 26) + P(X = 27) + P(X = 28) + P(X = 29) + P(X = 30)$
$= 0.06042... + 0.02685... + 0.00863... + 0.00178... + 0.00017...$
$= 0.0979$ (to 3 s.f.)

Q11 a) Let the random variable X represent the number of people in the sample who intend to switch their energy supplier. Then $X \sim B(50, 0.35)$. *[1 mark]*

b) $P(X = 20) + P(X = 30)$
$= \binom{50}{20} \times 0.35^{20} \times 0.65^{30} + \binom{50}{30} \times 0.35^{30} \times 0.65^{20}$
$= 0.087508... + 0.00017930... = 0.0877$ (3 s.f.)
[2 marks available — 1 mark for a correct method, 1 mark for correct answer]

c) Fewer than 3 people not intending to switch their energy supplier is the same as 48 or more people intending to switch their energy supplier. So it is given by

$P(X \geq 48) = P(X = 48) + P(X = 49) + P(X = 50)$
$= \binom{50}{48} \times 0.35^{48} \times 0.65^2 + \binom{50}{49} \times 0.35^{49} \times 0.65^1 + 0.35^{50}$
$= 6.7488... \times 10^{-20} + 1.4832... \times 10^{-21} + 1.5973... \times 10^{-23}$
$= 6.899 \times 10^{-20}$
[3 marks available — 1 mark for a correct method, 1 mark for at least one correct probability, 1 mark for correct answer in standard form]

Q12 a) $P(X \geq 14) = P(X = 14) + P(X = 15)$
$= \binom{15}{14} \times p^{14} \times (1 - p)^1 + \binom{15}{15} \times p^{15} \times (1 - p)^0$
$= 15p^{14}(1 - p) + p^{15} = p^{14}(15 - 14p)$

[3 marks available — 1 mark for the correct method, 2 marks for the correct simplified answer, otherwise 1 mark for correct answer not in its simplest form]

b) $P(X = 4) = P(X = 11)$
$\Rightarrow \binom{15}{4} \times p^4 \times (1 - p)^{11} = \binom{15}{11} \times p^{11} \times (1 - p)^4$
$\Rightarrow p^4(1 - p)^{11} = p^{11}(1 - p)^4 \Rightarrow (1 - p)^7 = p^7$
$\Rightarrow 1 - p = p \Rightarrow 2p = 1 \Rightarrow p = 0.5$
[3 marks available — 1 mark for setting up the equation, 1 mark for simplifying, 1 mark for showing the correct result]

Exercise 4.7 — Using Binomial Tables to Find Probabilities

Q1 a) $P(X \leq 2) = 0.5256$

b) $P(X \leq 7) = 0.9996$

c) $P(X \leq 9) = 1.0000$

d) $P(X < 10) = P(X \leq 9) = 1.0000$

e) $P(X < 5) = P(X \leq 4) = 0.9219$

f) $P(X < 4) = P(X \leq 3) = 0.7759$

g) $P(X < 6) = P(X \leq 5) = 0.9803$

h) $P(X < 2) = P(X \leq 1) = 0.2440$

Q2 a) $P(X > 3) = 1 - P(X \leq 3) = 1 - 0.0905 = 0.9095$

b) $P(X > 6) = 1 - P(X \leq 6) = 1 - 0.6098 = 0.3902$

c) $P(X > 10) = 1 - P(X \leq 10) = 1 - 0.9907 = 0.0093$

d) $P(X \geq 5) = 1 - P(X < 5) = 1 - P(X \leq 4) = 1 - 0.2173 = 0.7827$

e) $P(X \geq 3) = 1 - P(X < 3) = 1 - P(X \leq 2) = 1 - 0.0271 = 0.9729$

f) $P(X \geq 13) = 1 - P(X < 13) = 1 - P(X \leq 12)$
$= 1 - 0.9997 = 0.0003$

g) $P(X > 11) = 1 - P(X \leq 11) = 1 - 0.9981 = 0.0019$

h) $P(X \geq 1) = 1 - P(X < 1) = 1 - P(X \leq 0) = 1 - 0.0005 = 0.9995$

Q3 a) $P(X = 7) = P(X \leq 7) - P(X \leq 6) = 0.6010 - 0.4166 = 0.1844$

b) $P(X = 12) = P(X \leq 12) - P(X \leq 11)$
$= 0.9940 - 0.9804 = 0.0136$

c) $P(2 < X \leq 4) = P(X \leq 4) - P(X \leq 2)$
$= 0.1182 - 0.0121 = 0.1061$

d) $P(10 < X \leq 15) = P(X \leq 15) - P(X \leq 10)$
$= 1.0000 - 0.9468 = 0.0532$

e) $P(7 \leq X \leq 10) = P(X \leq 10) - P(X \leq 6)$
$= 0.9468 - 0.4166 = 0.5302$

f) $P(3 \leq X < 11) = P(X \leq 10) - P(X \leq 2)$
$= 0.9468 - 0.0121 = 0.9347$

Q4 Define a new random variable $Y \sim B(25, 0.2)$.

a) $P(X \geq 17) = P(Y \leq 8) = 0.9532$

b) $P(X \geq 20) = P(Y \leq 5) = 0.6167$

c) $P(X > 14) = P(Y < 11) = P(Y \leq 10) = 0.9944$

d) $P(X = 21) = P(Y = 4) = P(Y \leq 4) - P(Y \leq 3)$
$= 0.4207 - 0.2340 = 0.1867$

e) $P(3 \leq X < 14) = P(11 < Y \leq 22) = P(Y \leq 22) - P(Y \leq 11)$
$= 1.0000 - 0.9985 = 0.0015$

f) $P(12 \leq X < 18) = P(7 < Y \leq 13) = P(Y \leq 13) - P(Y \leq 7)$
$= 0.9999 - 0.8909 = 0.1090$

Q5 Let X represent the number of children with green eyes. Then $X \sim B(30, 0.18)$. Since $p = 0.18$ isn't a value in the binomial tables, use the c.d.f. on your calculator.
$P(X < 10) = P(X \leq 9) = 0.96768... = 0.9677$ (to 4 s.f.)

Q6 Let X represent the number of faulty items. Then $X \sim B(25, 0.05)$, so use the table for $n = 25$.
$P(X < 6) = P(X \leq 5) = 0.9988$

Q7 Let X represent the number of times the coin lands on heads. Then $X \sim B(15, 0.85)$. 0.85 isn't in the binomial tables, so let $Y = 15 - X$, where $Y \sim B(15, 0.15)$.
You can then use the tables for Y:
$P(11 \leq X < 14) = P(10 < X \leq 13) = P(1 < Y \leq 4)$
$= P(Y \leq 4) - P(Y \leq 1) = 0.9383 - 0.3186 = 0.6197$

Q8 a) The probability of a car having a mileage of more than 50 000 miles is $1 - 0.9 = 0.1$, so $X \sim B(40, 0.1)$. *[1 mark]*

b) $P(X \leq 6) = 0.9005$ *[1 mark]*

c) $P(X = 3) = P(X \leq 3) - P(X \leq 2)$
$= 0.4231 - 0.2228 = 0.2003$
[2 marks available — 1 mark for a correct method, 1 mark for the correct answer]

Q9 X represents the number of newspapers undelivered in a week, $n = 7$ and $p = 0.05$, so $X \sim B(7, 0.05)$. Use the table for $n = 7$:
$P(X > 1) = 1 - P(X \leq 1) = 1 - 0.9556 = 0.0444$

Q10 a) Let X represent the number of spam emails Abbie receives. Then $X \sim B(25, 0.65)$. *[1 mark]*

b) 0.65 isn't in the binomial tables, so let $Y = 25 - X$, where $Y \sim B(25, 0.35)$. You can then use the tables for Y:
$P(X = 10) = P(Y = 15) = P(Y \leq 15) - P(Y \leq 14)$
$= 0.9971 - 0.9907 = 0.0064$
[2 marks available — 1 mark for the correct method, 1 mark for the correct answer]

c) Let Z represent the total number of days that Abbie receives exactly 10 spam emails. This assumes e.g. that Abbie receives 25 emails every day for the five days.
From part b), the probability that she receives exactly 10 spam emails is 0.0064, so $Z \sim B(5, 0.0064)$.
$P(Z \geq 2) = 1 - P(Z \leq 1) = 1 - 0.999595... = 0.000404$ (3 s.f.)
[4 marks available — 1 mark for using answer from part b) to find the new binomial distribution, 1 mark for identifying an assumption that has been made in using the binomial distribution, 1 mark for correct method for finding $P(Z \geq 2)$, 1 mark for correct answer]

d) E.g. It is unrealistic that someone would receive exactly the same number of emails every day.
[1 mark for a suitable explanation of why the assumption made may not be sensible]

Exercise 4.8 — Using Binomial Tables 'Backwards'

Q1 a) Use the table for $n = 8$ and the column for $p = 0.35$. Reading down the column tells you that $P(X \leq 2) = 0.4278$, so $a = 2$.

b) $P(X < b) = 0.9747$, so $P(X \leq b - 1) = 0.9747$.
From the table, $P(X \leq 5) = 0.9747$.
So $b - 1 = 5$, which means that $b = 6$.

c) $P(X > c) = 0.8309$, so $P(X \leq c) = 1 - P(X > c)$
$= 1 - 0.8309 = 0.1691$.
From the table, $P(X \leq 1) = 0.1691$, which means that $c = 1$.

d) $P(X \geq d) = 0.1061$, so $P(X < d) = 1 - P(X \geq d)$
$= 1 - 0.1061 = 0.8939$.
This means that $P(X \leq d - 1) = 0.8939$.
From the table, $P(X \leq 4) = 0.8939$, which means that $d - 1 = 4$, so $d = 5$.

Q2 a) Use the table for $n = 12$ and the column for $p = 0.4$.
$P(X < e) = 0.2253$, so $P(X \leq e - 1) = 0.2253$.
From the table, $P(X \leq 3) = 0.2253$.
So $e - 1 = 3$, which means that $e = 4$.

b) From the table, $P(X \leq 6) = 0.8418$, so $f = 6$.

c) $P(X \geq g) = 0.0003$, so $P(X < g) = 1 - P(X \geq g)$
$= 1 - 0.0003 = 0.9997$.
This means that $P(X \leq g - 1) = 0.9997$.
From the table, $P(X \leq 10) = 0.9997$, which means that $g - 1 = 10$, so $g = 11$.

d) $P(X > h) = 0.0573$, so $P(X \leq h) = 1 - P(X > h)$
$= 1 - 0.0573 = 0.9427$.
From the table, $P(X \leq 7) = 0.9427$, which means that $h = 7$.

Q3 a) Use the table for $n = 30$ and the column for $p = 0.15$.
$P(X < i) = 0.9903$, so $P(X \leq i - 1) = 0.9903$.
From the table, $P(X \leq 9) = 0.9903$. So $i - 1 = 9 \Rightarrow i = 10$.

b) $P(X \geq j) = 0.2894$, so $P(X < j) = 1 - P(X \geq j)$
$= 1 - 0.2894 = 0.7106$.
This means that $P(X \leq j - 1) = 0.7106$.
From the table, $P(X \leq 5) = 0.7106$, so $j - 1 = 5 \Rightarrow j = 6$.

c) $P(X > k) = 0.9520$, so $P(X \leq k) = 1 - P(X > k)$
$= 1 - 0.9520 = 0.0480$.
From the table, $P(X \leq 1) = 0.0480$, so $k = 1$.

d) $P(X \geq l) = 0.1526$, so $P(X < l) = 1 - P(X \geq l)$
$= 1 - 0.1526 = 0.8474$.
This means that $P(X \leq l - 1) = 0.8474$.
From the table, $P(X \leq 6) = 0.8474$, so $l - 1 = 6 \Rightarrow l = 7$.

Q4 a) Use the table for $n = 40$ and the column for $p = 0.45$.
$P(X < a) = 0.9233$, so $P(X \leq a - 1) = 0.9233$.
From the table, $P(X \leq 22) = 0.9233$.
So $a - 1 = 22 \Rightarrow a = 23$. *[1 mark]*

b) $P(X > b) = 0.3156$, so $P(X \leq b) = 1 - P(X > b)$
$= 1 - 0.3156 = 0.6844$.
From the table, $P(X \leq 19) = 0.6844$, so $b = 19$.
[2 marks available — 1 mark for correct method, 1 mark for correct answer]

c) You need to find the maximum value c, such that $P(X \leq c) < 0.6$. From the table $P(X \leq 18) = 0.5651$ and $P(X \leq 19) = 0.6844$, so the maximum value is $c = 18$.
[2 marks available — 1 mark for correct method, 1 mark for correct answer]

Q5 a) Use the table for $n = 25$ and the column for $p = 0.25$.
From the table, $P(X \leq 3) = 0.0962$, so $a = 3$. *[1 mark]*

b) $P(X \geq b) = 0.4389$, so $P(X < b) = 1 - P(X \geq b)$
$= 1 - 0.4389 = 0.5611$.
This means that $P(X \leq b - 1) = 0.5611$.
From the table, $P(X \leq 6) = 0.5611$, so $b - 1 = 6$, so $b = 7$.
[2 marks available — 1 mark for correct method, 1 mark for correct answer]

c) You need to find the minimum value c, such that $P(X > c) < 0.1$, or $P(X \leq c) > 0.9$. From the table, $P(X \leq 8) = 0.8506$, but $P(X \leq 9) = 0.9287$, so the minimum value is $c = 9$.
[2 marks available — 1 mark for correct method, 1 mark for correct answer]

Q6 a) $X \sim B(40, p)$ *[1 mark]*

b) $P(X = 3) = 0.0816$, so $P(X \leq 3) - P(X \leq 2) = 0.0816$
Using the table for $n = 40$, calculate the difference between the rows for $x = 2$ and $x = 3$:
$p = 0.15$: $P(X \leq 3) - P(X \leq 2) = 0.1302 - 0.0486 = 0.0816$
So $p = 0.15$
[3 marks available — 1 mark for use of $P(X \leq 3) - P(X \leq 2)$, 1 mark for correct method, 1 mark for the correct answer]

Q7 $P(7 < X \leq 10) = 0.3840$, so $P(X \leq 10) - P(X \leq 7) = 0.3840$.
Using the table for $n = 30$, calculate the difference between the rows for $x = 7$ and $x = 10$.
$p = 0.35$: $P(X \leq 10) - P(X \leq 7) = 0.5078 - 0.1238 = 0.3840$
So $a = 0.35$
[3 marks available — 1 mark for use of $P(X \leq 10) - P(X \leq 7)$, 1 mark for correct method, 1 mark for the correct answer]

Q8 Let X be the number of cans they hit. Then $X \sim B(10, k)$.
$P(X \geq 8) = 0.9298 \Rightarrow P(X \leq 7) = 1 - 0.9298 = 0.0702$
This entry is not in the statistical tables across the row of $x = 7$ for $n = 10$, which indicates that $k > 0.5$.
So convert 'successes' to 'failures' to use the tables.
Let Y be the number of cans they don't hit.
Then $Y \sim B(10, 1 - k)$ and $P(X \geq 8) = P(Y \leq 2) = 0.9298$.
Looking along the row for $x = 2$, $1 - k = 0.1 \Rightarrow k = 0.9$.
[4 marks available — 1 mark for finding $P(X \leq 7)$, 1 mark for deducing $k > 0.5$, 1 mark for alternative distribution, 1 mark for the correct answer]

Q9 **a)** Let X be the score of someone who guesses the answer to each question. Then $X \sim B(30, 0.25)$.
Use the table for $n = 30$ and the column for $p = 0.25$.
You need to find the minimum value m for which $P(X \geq m) \leq 0.1$. This is the minimum value m for which $P(X < m) \geq 0.9$, or $P(X \leq m - 1) \geq 0.9$.

$P(X \leq 10) = 0.8943$, but $P(X \leq 11) = 0.9493$. This means that $m - 1 = 11$, so the pass mark should be at least 12.

b) This time you need to find the minimum value m for which $P(X \geq m) < 0.01$. This is the minimum value m for which $P(X < m) > 0.99$, or $P(X \leq m - 1) > 0.99$.

$P(X \leq 12) = 0.9784$, but $P(X \leq 13) = 0.9918$. This means that $m - 1 = 13$, so the pass mark should be at least 14.

Q10 Here, $X \sim B(20, 0.5)$. You need $P(X \geq x) < 0.05$.
This means $P(X < x) > 0.95$, or $P(X \leq x - 1) > 0.95$.

Use the table for $n = 20$, and the column for $p = 0.5$.
$P(X \leq 13) = 0.9423$, but $P(X \leq 14) = 0.9793$.
This means that $x - 1 = 14$, so x should be at least 15.

Q11 **a)** Let X be the number of successful spins.
Then $X \sim B(5, 0.25)$. Use the table for $n = 5$ and column for $p = 0.25$.
$P(X \geq b) = 0.1035$, so $P(X < b) = 1 - P(X \geq b)$
$= 1 - 0.1035 = 0.8965$
This means that $P(X \leq b - 1) = 0.8965$.
From the table, $P(X \leq 2) = 0.8965$, which means that $b - 1 = 2$, so $b = 3$ — they need 3 successful spins.

b) Use the table for $n = 10$ and column for $p = 0.25$.
You need to find the minimum value g for which $P(X \geq g) \leq 0.1035$. This is the minimum value g for which $P(X < g) \geq 0.8965$, or $P(X \leq g - 1) \geq 0.8965$.
$P(X \leq 3) = 0.7759$, but $P(X \leq 4) = 0.9219$.
This means that $g - 1 = 4$, so $g = 5$.

Q12 $p > 0.5$ means the answer cannot be found directly from the tables, so convert 'successes' to 'failures'. Let $Y \sim B(6, 1 - p)$.
There are 6 trials and a is non-zero, so it can be deduced from $P(a < X \leq a + 3)$ that $a \geq 1$ and $a + 3 \leq 6$, so $1 \leq a \leq 3$.

$P(a < X \leq a + 3) = P(X = a + 1) + P(X = a + 2) + P(X = a + 3)$
As there are 6 trials in total, this is the same as
$P(Y = 6 - (a + 1)) + P(Y = 6 - (a + 2)) + P(Y = 6 - (a + 3))$
$= P(Y = 5 - a) + P(Y = 4 - a) + P(Y = 3 - a)$
$= P(3 - a \leq Y \leq 5 - a)$
$= P(Y \leq 5 - a) - P(Y \leq 2 - a)$
$a \neq 3$ as when $a = 3$, $2 - a = -1$.
So either $a = 1$ and $P(Y \leq 4) - P(Y \leq 1) = 0.4673$
or $a = 2$ and $P(Y \leq 3) - P(Y \leq 0) = 0.4673$
Looking across columns in the table:
If $1 - p = 0.05$: $P(Y \leq 4) - P(Y \leq 1) = 0.0328$
$P(Y \leq 3) - P(Y \leq 0) = 0.2648$
If $1 - p = 0.1$: $P(Y \leq 4) - P(Y \leq 1) = 0.1142$
$P(Y \leq 3) - P(Y \leq 0) = 0.4673$
So $1 - p = 0.1$ and so $p = 0.9$ and $a = 2$.

Exercise 4.9 — Modelling Real Problems with B(n, p)

For the questions in this exercise, working for using the binomial tables has been shown where possible. You could also have used a calculator to answer these questions.

Q1 **a)** Each person who passes can be considered a separate trial, where 'success' means they take a leaflet, and 'failure' means they don't. Since there is a fixed number of independent trials (50), a constant probability of success (0.25), and X is the total number of successes, $X \sim B(50, 0.25)$.
[1 mark]

b) $P(X > 4) = 1 - P(X \leq 4) = 1 - 0.0021 = 0.9979$
[2 marks available — 1 mark for correct method, 1 mark for correct answer]

c) $P(X = 10) = P(X \leq 10) - P(X \leq 9)$
$= 0.2622 - 0.1637 = 0.0985$
[2 marks available — 1 mark for correct method, 1 mark for correct answer]

Q2 **a)** E.g. If the cards were not returned to the pack, the probability of picking a heart would change and the trials would not be independent. Shuffling also ensures that the trials are independent.

b) Let X represent the number of people picking a heart.
Then $X \sim B(50, 0.25)$.
$P(X = 15) = P(X \leq 15) - P(X \leq 14)$
$= 0.8369 - 0.7481 = 0.0888$

c) $P(X > 20) = 1 - P(X \leq 20) = 1 - 0.9937 = 0.0063$

Q3 **a)** Let X be the number of positive responses to the drug.
Then $X \sim B(20, 0.88)$. *[1 mark]*

b) **(i)** $P(X \leq 17) = 0.437$ (3 s.f.) *[1 mark]*

(ii) $P(X = 17) = 0.224$ (3 s.f.) *[1 mark]*
You could use the cumulative distribution function for (i) and the binomial probability function for (ii).

c) $P(X > r) < 0.35 \Rightarrow 1 - P(X \leq r) < 0.35 \Rightarrow P(X \leq r) > 0.65$
Find the probabilities that lie either side of 0.65:
$P(X \leq 17) = 0.4368...$ and $P(X \leq 18) = 0.7109...$
The minimum value of r that gives $P(X \leq r) > 0.65$ and thus $P(X > r) < 0.35$ is 18.
[3 marks available — 1 mark for correct method, 1 mark for interpreting probabilities, 1 mark for correct answer]

Q4 **a)** Let X represent the number of plants in a tray with yellow flowers. Then $X \sim B(15, 0.35)$.
Using binomial tables for $n = 15$ and $p = 0.35$:
$P(X = 5) = P(X \leq 5) - P(X \leq 4) = 0.5643 - 0.3519 = 0.2124$

b) P(more yellow flowers than white flowers)
$= P(X \geq 8) = 1 - P(X < 8) = 1 - P(X \leq 7)$
$= 1 - 0.8868 = 0.1132$

Q5 **a)** The probability of Simon being able to solve each crossword needs to remain the same, and all the outcomes need to be independent (i.e. Simon solving or not solving a puzzle one day should not affect whether he will be able to solve it on another day).

b) $P(X = 4) = \frac{18!}{4!14!} \times p^4 \times (1 - p)^{14}$

$P(X = 5) = \frac{18!}{5!13!} \times p^5 \times (1 - p)^{13}$

Putting these equal to each other gives:

$$\frac{18!}{4!14!} \times p^4 \times (1 - p)^{14} = \frac{18!}{5!13!} \times p^5 \times (1 - p)^{13}$$

Dividing by things that appear on both sides gives:

$$\frac{1 - p}{14} = \frac{p}{5} \Rightarrow 5 = 19p \Rightarrow p = \frac{5}{19} = 0.263 \text{ (3 s.f.)}$$

You can divide both sides by p^4, $(1 - p)^{13}$ and 18! immediately. Write 14! as 14 × 13! and 5! as 5 × 4! to simplify further.

Q6 **a)** **(i)** The player will not win a prize if they roll a 3, 4, 5 or 6 on three consecutive occasions:

P(no prize) = $\left(\frac{4}{6}\right)^3 = \frac{8}{27}$

P(prize) = 1 – P(no prize), so P(prize) = $1 - \frac{8}{27} = \frac{19}{27}$

[2 marks available — 1 mark for a correct method, 1 mark for the correct answer]

(ii) $X \sim B(10, \frac{19}{27})$. There are a fixed number of games (10) and each game is either a success (wins a prize) or a failure (fails to win a prize). Each game is independent from the others, the probability of success is always the same ($\frac{19}{27}$), and the discrete random variable X is the number of prizes won.

[1 mark for a suitable model with correct justification]

b) Let $X \sim B(10, \frac{19}{27})$, then

$P(X \geq 5) = 1 - P(X \leq 4) = 1 - 0.0446... = 0.955$ (3 s.f.)

[2 marks available — 1 mark for correct method, 1 mark for correct answer]

The probability $\frac{19}{27}$ does not appear in the binomial tables so you have to use a calculator to find $P(X \leq 4)$.

c) Find the largest value of x such that $P(X \leq x) < 0.1$.

$P(X \leq 3) = 0.0098$, $P(X \leq 4) = 0.0447$, $P(X \leq 5) = 0.1440$

So the largest possible value of x is 4.

[2 marks available — 1 mark for correct method, 1 mark for correct answer]

Q7 The probability distribution is $X \sim B(40, 0.15)$.

a) $P(X = 3) = P(X \leq 3) - P(X \leq 2)$
$= 0.1302 - 0.0486 = 0.0816$ *[1 mark]*

b) $P(X < 6) = P(X \leq 5) = 0.4325$ *[1 mark]*

c) $P(5 \leq X \leq 10) = P(X \leq 10) - P(X \leq 4)$
$= 0.9701 - 0.2633 = 0.7068$

[2 marks available — 1 mark for correct method, 1 mark for correct answer]

d) You're looking for $P(X \geq t) < 0.01 \Rightarrow P(X \leq t - 1) > 0.99$

$P(X \leq 11) = 0.9880$

$P(X \leq 12) = 0.9957 \Rightarrow t - 1 = 12 \Rightarrow t = 13$

So the minimum value of t that would cause production to stop is 13.

[3 marks available — 1 mark for correct method, 1 mark for finding a correct probability, 1 mark for the correct answer]

Q8 **a)** $X \sim B(12, 0.36)$

$P(X = 0) = (1 - 0.36)^{12} = 0.00472$ (3 s.f.) *[1 mark]*

b) More than half of the orders means 7 or more.

$P(X \geq 7) = 1 - P(X \leq 6) = 1 - 0.902978... = 0.0970$ (3 s.f.)

[2 marks available — 1 mark for correct method, 1 mark for correct answer]

The probability 0.36 does not appear in the binomial tables so you have to use a calculator to find $P(X \leq 6)$.

c) **(i)** $P(X < 3) = P(X \leq 2) = 0.135$ (3 s.f.) *[1 mark]*

(ii) Let Y be the number of ten-minute periods for which fewer than 3 orders are cancelled. The probability of fewer than 3 orders being cancelled is the answer to part c)(i), so $Y \sim B(6, 0.135...)$.

$P(Y = 4) = \binom{6}{4} \times (0.135...)^4 \times (1 - 0.135...)^2$

$= 0.00375$ (3 s.f.)

[3 marks available — 1 mark for using answer from part c) (i) to find the new binomial distribution, 1 mark for correct method for finding P(Y = 4), 1 mark for correct answer]

Chapter 4 Review Exercise

For the questions in this exercise, working for using the binomial tables has been shown where possible. You could also have used a calculator to answer these questions.

Q1 **a)** $\sum_{\text{all } y} P(Y = y) = 0.5 + k + k + 3k = 0.5 + 5k = 1$, so $k = 0.1$

[1 mark]

b) $P(Y < 2) = P(Y = 0) + P(Y = 1) = 0.5 + 0.1 = 0.6$ *[1 mark]*

Q2 Draw a sample space diagram to show the possible scores:

Score on dice 2 \ Score on dice 1	1	2	3	4	5	6
1	2	3	4	5	6	7
2	3	4	5	6	7	8
3	4	5	6	7	8	9
4	5	6	7	8	9	10
5	6	7	8	9	10	11
6	7	8	9	10	11	12

From the diagram you can see there are 36 possible outcomes. Scores of 3, 6, 9 and 12 give 3 points. There are 2 + 5 + 4 + 1 = 12 ways of scoring 3 points, so the probability of scoring 3 points is $\frac{12}{36} = \frac{1}{3}$.

Scores of 5 and 10 give 5 points. There are 4 + 3 = 7 ways of scoring 5 points, so the probability of scoring 5 points is $\frac{7}{36}$.

Scores of 7 only give 7 points. There are 6 ways of scoring 7 points, so the probability of scoring 7 points is $\frac{6}{36} = \frac{1}{6}$

All other scores give 2 points, so the probability of scoring 2 points is $1 - \frac{1}{3} - \frac{7}{36} - \frac{1}{6} = \frac{11}{36}$.

Now you can draw a probability distribution table:

x	2	3	5	7
$P(X = x)$	$\frac{11}{36}$	$\frac{1}{3}$	$\frac{7}{36}$	$\frac{1}{6}$

$P(X \leq 5) = P(X = 2) + P(X = 3) + P(X = 5)$
$= \frac{11}{36} + \frac{1}{3} + \frac{7}{36} = \frac{5}{6}$

You could also have subtracted P(X = 7) from 1.

Q3 **a)** One out of six sides has a 1, so P(roll a 1) = $1 \div 6 = \frac{1}{6}$

Two out of six sides has a 2, so P(roll a 2) = $2 \div 6 = \frac{1}{3}$

Three out of six sides has a 3, so P(roll a 3) = $3 \div 6 = \frac{1}{2}$

y	1	2	3
$P(Y = y)$	$\frac{1}{6}$	$\frac{1}{3}$	$\frac{1}{2}$

[2 marks available — 2 marks for a fully correct table, otherwise 1 mark for one y-value with the correct probability]

b) $P(Y < 3) = 1 - P(Y = 3) = 1 - \frac{1}{2} = \frac{1}{2}$ *[1 mark]*

You could also add together P(Y = 1) and P(Y = 2).

c) P(even product) = P(1 then 2) + P(2 then 1) + P(2 then 2) + P(2 then 3) + P(3 then 2)

$= \left(\frac{1}{6} \times \frac{1}{3}\right) + \left(\frac{1}{3} \times \frac{1}{6}\right) + \left(\frac{1}{3} \times \frac{1}{3}\right) + \left(\frac{1}{3} \times \frac{1}{2}\right) + \left(\frac{1}{2} \times \frac{1}{3}\right)$

$= \frac{1}{18} + \frac{1}{18} + \frac{1}{9} + \frac{1}{6} + \frac{1}{6} = \frac{5}{9}$

[2 marks available — 1 mark for appropriate method, 1 mark for correct answer]

Q4 **a)** Substitute $x = 2, 4, 6, 8$ into kx^2:

x	2	4	6	8
$P(X = x)$	$4k$	$16k$	$36k$	$64k$

$\sum_{\text{all } x} P(X = x) = 120k = 1$. So, $k = \frac{1}{120}$.

[2 marks available — 1 mark for correctly writing each probability in terms of k, 1 mark for correct value of k]

b) 2 is the only prime number on the spinner.

$P(2) = 4k = \frac{4}{120} = \frac{1}{30}$

$P(\text{tails and prime}) = \frac{1}{2} \times \frac{1}{30} = \frac{1}{60}$

[2 marks available — 1 mark for correct probability of prime number, 1 mark for correct answer]

Q5 **a)** $\sum_{\text{all } x} P(X = x) = k + 2k + 3k + (4^2)k + (5^2)k = 1$

$\Rightarrow 47k = 1 \Rightarrow k = \frac{1}{47}$

[2 marks available — 1 mark for correctly writing each probability in terms of k, 1 mark for correct value of k]

b) $P(X = 2) = 2k = \frac{2}{47}$ *[1 mark]*

c) $P(X \leq 3.5) = P(X \leq 3) = \frac{1}{47} + \frac{2}{47} + \frac{3}{47} = \frac{6}{47}$ *[1 mark]*

d) $P(2.1 \leq X \leq 4.2) = P(3 \leq X \leq 4) = \frac{3}{47} + \frac{4^2}{47} = \frac{19}{47}$

[2 marks available — 1 mark for correct method, 1 mark for correct answer]

Q6 **a)** $\frac{k}{4} + \frac{k^2}{16} + \frac{k^2}{32} + \frac{k}{16} = 1 \Rightarrow \frac{10k + 3k^2}{32} = 1$

$\Rightarrow 3k^2 + 10k = 32 \Rightarrow 3k^2 + 10k - 32 = 0$

[2 marks available — 1 mark for setting the sum of probabilities equal to 1, 1 mark for rearranging to the correct quadratic equation]

b) $3k^2 + 10k - 32 = 0 \Rightarrow (3k + 16)(k - 2) = 0$

$\Rightarrow k = -\frac{16}{3}$ or $k = 2$

k cannot be a negative number because $P(X = 2)$ and $P(X = 36)$ can't be negative, so $k = 2$.

[2 marks available — 1 mark for solving quadratic equation, 1 mark for explaining why k = 2 is only valid solution]

c) As M is discrete, this is the same as $P(8 \leq M \leq 24)$.

$P(8 \leq M \leq 24) = P(M = 8) + P(M = 24)$

$= \frac{2^2}{16} + \frac{2^2}{32} = \frac{12}{32} = \frac{3}{8}$

[2 marks available — 1 mark for correct method, 1 mark for correct answer]

Q7 Add up the probabilities to work out the values of $F(w)$:

$F(0.2) = P(W \leq 0.2) = P(W = 0.2) = 0.2$

$F(0.3) = P(W \leq 0.3) = P(W = 0.2) + P(W = 0.3) = 0.2 + 0.2 = 0.4$

$F(0.4) = P(W \leq 0.4) = P(W = 0.2) + P(W = 0.3) + P(W = 0.4)$
$= 0.2 + 0.2 + 0.3 = 0.7$

$F(0.5) = P(W \leq 0.5)$
$= P(W = 0.2) + P(W = 0.3) + P(W = 0.4) + P(W = 0.5)$
$= 0.2 + 0.2 + 0.3 + 0.3 = 1$

w	0.2	0.3	0.4	0.5
$F(w)$	0.2	0.4	0.7	1

Q8 **a)** Substitute $x = 1, 2, 3, 4, 5$ into $\frac{(x+2)}{25}$ to find the values of $P(X = x)$:

x	1	2	3	4	5
$P(X = x)$	$\frac{3}{25}$	$\frac{4}{25}$	$\frac{5}{25}$	$\frac{6}{25}$	$\frac{7}{25}$

Add up the probabilities to work out the values of $F(x)$:

$F(1) = P(X \leq 1) = P(X = 1) = \frac{3}{25}$

$F(2) = P(X \leq 2) = P(X = 1) + P(X = 2) = \frac{3}{25} + \frac{4}{25} = \frac{7}{25}$

$F(3) = P(X \leq 3) = P(X = 1) + P(X = 2) + P(X = 3)$
$= \frac{3}{25} + \frac{4}{25} + \frac{5}{25} = \frac{12}{25}$

$F(4) = P(X \leq 4) = P(X = 1) + P(X = 2) + P(X = 3) + P(X = 4)$
$= \frac{3}{25} + \frac{4}{25} + \frac{5}{25} + \frac{6}{25} = \frac{18}{25}$

$F(5) = P(X \leq 5)$
$= P(X = 1) + P(X = 2) + P(X = 3) + P(X = 4) + P(X = 5)$
$= \frac{3}{25} + \frac{4}{25} + \frac{5}{25} + \frac{6}{25} + \frac{7}{25} = 1$

x	1	2	3	4	5
$F(x)$	$\frac{3}{25}$	$\frac{7}{25}$	$\frac{12}{25}$	$\frac{18}{25}$	1

(i) $P(X \leq 3) = \frac{12}{25}$

(ii) $P(1 < X \leq 3) = P(X \leq 3) - P(X \leq 1) = \frac{12}{25} - \frac{3}{25} = \frac{9}{25}$

b) $P(X = x) = \frac{1}{6}$ for each value of x:

x	1	2	3	4	5	6
$P(X = x)$	$\frac{1}{6}$	$\frac{1}{6}$	$\frac{1}{6}$	$\frac{1}{6}$	$\frac{1}{6}$	$\frac{1}{6}$

$F(1) = P(X \leq 1) = P(X = 1) = \frac{1}{6}$

$F(2) = P(X \leq 2) = P(X = 1) + P(X = 2) = \frac{1}{6} + \frac{1}{6} = \frac{1}{3}$

$F(3) = P(X \leq 3) = P(X = 1) + P(X = 2) + P(X = 3)$
$= \frac{1}{6} + \frac{1}{6} + \frac{1}{6} = \frac{1}{2}$

$F(4) = P(X \leq 4) = P(X = 1) + P(X = 2) + P(X = 3) + P(X = 4)$
$= \frac{1}{6} + \frac{1}{6} + \frac{1}{6} + \frac{1}{6} = \frac{2}{3}$

$F(5) = P(X \leq 5)$
$= P(X = 1) + P(X = 2) + P(X = 3) + P(X = 4) + P(X = 5)$
$= \frac{1}{6} + \frac{1}{6} + \frac{1}{6} + \frac{1}{6} + \frac{1}{6} = \frac{5}{6}$

$F(6) = P(X \leq 6)$
$= P(X = 1) + P(X = 2) + P(X = 3) + P(X = 4) + P(X = 5) + P(X = 6)$
$= \frac{1}{6} + \frac{1}{6} + \frac{1}{6} + \frac{1}{6} + \frac{1}{6} + \frac{1}{6} = 1$

x	1	2	3	4	5	6
$F(x)$	$\frac{1}{6}$	$\frac{1}{3}$	$\frac{1}{2}$	$\frac{2}{3}$	$\frac{5}{6}$	1

(i) $P(X \leq 3) = \frac{1}{2}$

(ii) $P(3 < X < 6) = P(X \leq 5) - P(X \leq 3) = \frac{5}{6} - \frac{1}{2} = \frac{1}{3}$

Q9 **a)** $P(Y \leq 0.3) = F(0.3) = \frac{0.3}{2} = 0.15$ *[1 mark]*

b) $P(Y = 0.4) = F(0.4) - F(0.3)$
$= 2 \times 0.4 - \frac{0.3}{2} = 0.8 - 0.15 = 0.65$

[2 marks available — 1 mark for correct method, 1 mark for correct answer]

c) $P(0.2 \leq Y \leq 0.4) = F(0.4) - F(0.1)$
$= 2 \times 0.4 - \frac{0.1}{2} = 0.8 - 0.05 = 0.75$

[2 marks available — 1 mark for correct method, 1 mark for correct answer]

Q10 a) As q is the largest value on the spinner, $F(q) = 1$.
As p is second largest value, $F(q) = F(p) + P(q)$.
So $0.5 + \frac{q}{20} = 1 \Rightarrow q = 10$
[2 marks available — 1 mark for using F(q) = 1, 1 mark for correct answer]

b) $1 + 2 + 3 + p + 10 = 16 + p$
Triangular numbers are 1, 3, 6, 10, 15, 21, 28, 36, ...
$3 < p < 10$, so the sum of the numbers must be 21 and $p = 5$.
[2 marks available — 1 mark for correct method, 1 mark for correct answer]

Q11 a) There are 21 balls in total, which can be arranged in 21! different ways. But since 15 are identical, you need to divide this by 15!
So there are $21! \div 15! = 39\,070\,080$ different ways.

b) There are 16 counters in total, which can be arranged in 16! different ways. But since there are 4 of each colour, you need to divide this by 4! four times. So there are $16! \div 4! \div 4! \div 4! \div 4! = 63\,063\,000$ different ways.

c) There are 12 counters in total, which can be arranged in 12! different ways. But since 7 are identical and another 5 are identical, you need to divide this by 7! and 5!.
So there are $12! \div 7! \div 5! = 792$ different ways.

d) There are 7 coin tosses in total, which can be arranged in 7! different ways. But you know there are 3 heads and 4 tails, so you need to divide this by 3! and 4!.
So there are $7! \div 3! \div 4! = 35$ different ways.

Q12 a) This is $\binom{10}{6} = \frac{10!}{6!(10-6)!} = 210$
[2 marks available — 2 marks for correct answer, otherwise 1 mark for substituting in correct numbers to calculate binomial coefficient]

b) There are $\binom{10}{4}$ ways of choosing four different flavoured doughnuts.
$\binom{10}{6} = \binom{10}{4}$, so the number of ways doesn't change.
[1 mark for correct explanation]

Q13 a) Binomial — there are a fixed number of independent trials (30) with two possible results ('prime' / 'not prime'), a constant probability of success ($p = 0.5$), and the random variable is the total number of successes.

b) Not binomial — the probability of being dealt an ace changes with each card dealt, since the total number of cards decreases as each card is dealt.

c) Not binomial — the number of trials is not fixed.

Q14 a) X is the number of heads, $n = 10$, $p = 0.5$, so $X \sim B(10, 0.5)$
$P(X = 8) = \frac{10!}{8!2!} \times 0.5^8 \times 0.5^2 = 0.04394... = 0.0439$ (3 s.f.)

b) $X \sim B(10, 0.5)$ as in part a)
$P(X \geq 8) = P(X = 8) + P(X = 9) + P(X = 10)$
$= 0.04394... + \frac{10!}{9!1!} \times 0.5^9 \times 0.5^1 + \frac{10!}{10!0!} \times 0.5^{10} \times 0.5^0$
$= 0.04394... + 0.00976... + 0.00097...$
$= 0.0547$ (3 s.f.)

Q15 a) $P(X = 4) = \frac{14!}{4!10!} \times 0.27^4 \times 0.73^{10} = 0.229$ (3 s.f.)

b) $P(X < 2) = P(X = 0) + P(X = 1)$
$= \frac{14!}{0!14!} \times 0.27^0 \times 0.73^{14} + \frac{14!}{1!13!} \times 0.27^1 \times 0.73^{13}$
$= 0.0122... + 0.0631... = 0.0754$ (3 s.f.)

c) $P(5 < X \leq 8) = P(X = 6) + P(X = 7) + P(X = 8)$
$= \frac{14!}{6!8!} \times 0.27^6 \times 0.73^8 + \frac{14!}{7!7!} \times 0.27^7 \times 0.73^7 + \frac{14!}{8!6!} \times 0.27^8 \times 0.73^6$
$= 0.0938... + 0.0396... + 0.0128...$
$= 0.146$ (3 s.f.)

d) $P(X \geq 11) = P(X = 11) + P(X = 12) + P(X = 13) + P(X = 14)$
$= \frac{14!}{11!3!} \times 0.27^{11} \times 0.73^3 + \frac{14!}{12!2!} \times 0.27^{12} \times 0.73^2 + \frac{14!}{13!1!} \times 0.27^{13} \times 0.73^1 + \frac{14!}{14!0!} \times 0.27^{14} \times 0.73^0$
$= 0.0000787... + 0.0000072... + 0.00000041... + 0.000000010...$
$= 0.0000864$ (3 s.f.)
You could also use the binomial probability and cumulative distribution functions on your calculator.

Q16 a) If one canopy has an imperfection, this has no effect on whether or not other canopies have imperfections, so trials are independent. *[1 mark]*
The other conditions for modelling with a binomial distribution are implied by the question, so are not assumptions.

b) Let X represent the number of canopies that have an imperfection. Then $X \sim B(30, 0.01)$. *[1 mark]*

c) $P(X = 2) = \binom{30}{2} \times (0.01)^2 \times (1 - 0.01)^{28} = 0.0328$ (3 s.f.)
[1 mark]

Q17 a) $X \sim B(40, 0.45)$ *[1 mark]*

b) $P(X = 12) = \frac{40!}{12!28!} \times 0.45^{12} \times (1 - 0.45)^{40-12}$
$= 0.0207$ (3 s.f.) *[1 mark]*

c) $P(X < 2) = P(X = 0) + P(X = 1)$
$= \frac{40!}{0!40!} \times 0.45^0 \times 0.55^{40} + \frac{40!}{1!39!} \times 0.45^1 \times 0.55^{39}$
$= 1.39 \times 10^{-9}$ (3 s.f.)
[2 marks available — 1 mark for correct method, 1 mark for correct answer]

Q18 a) Each day can be considered a separate trial, where 'success' means Darshan is late to college and 'failure' means he is not late. Since there is a fixed number of trials (5 days), a constant probability of success (0.2), and X is the total number of successes, $X \sim B(5, 0.2)$.
[1 mark for suitable model with correct justification]

b) (i) $P(X = 1) = \frac{5!}{1!4!} \times 0.2^1 \times 0.8^4 = 0.4096$ *[1 mark]*

(ii) Using the binomial table for $n = 5$ and the column for $p = 0.2$:
$P(X > 2) = 1 - P(X \leq 2) = 1 - 0.9421 = 0.0579$
You could also use the binomial probability function to find P(X = 0), P(X = 1) and P(X = 2), then subtract them from 1 to get the answer.
[2 marks available — 1 mark for using 1 – P(X ≤ 2) or another correct method, 1 mark for correct answer]

Q19 For $X \sim B(25, 0.15)$, use the table for $n = 25$ and column for $p = 0.15$. For $Y \sim B(15, 0.65)$, define a new random variable $Z = 15 - Y$, so $Z \sim B(15, 0.35)$.
Use the table for $n = 15$ and column for $p = 0.35$.
You could also use the binomial c.d.f. function on your calculator for Y.

a) $P(X \leq 3) = 0.4711$

b) $P(X \leq 7) = 0.9745$

c) $P(X \leq 15) = 1.0000$

d) $P(2 < X < 8) = P(X \leq 7) - P(X \leq 2)$
$= 0.9745 - 0.2537 = 0.7208$

e) $P(Y \leq 3) = P(Z \geq 12) = 1 - P(Z \leq 11) = 1 - 0.9995 = 0.0005$

f) $P(Y \leq 7) = P(Z \geq 8) = 1 - P(Z \leq 7) = 1 - 0.8868 = 0.1132$

g) $n = 15$, so $P(Y \leq 15) = 1$

h) $P(Y \geq 9) = P(Z \leq 6) = 0.7548$

i) $P(8 \leq Y < 13) = P(2 < Z \leq 7) = P(Z \leq 7) - P(Z \leq 2)$
$= 0.8868 - 0.0617 = 0.8251$

Q20 a) Use the table for $n = 20$ and column for $p = 0.4$.
$P(X \leq 15) = 0.9997$

b) Use the table for $n = 40$ and column for $p = 0.15$.
$P(X < 4) = P(X \leq 3) = 0.1302$

c) Use the table for $n = 25$ and column for $p = 0.45$.
$P(X > 7) = 1 - P(X \leq 7) = 1 - 0.0639 = 0.9361$

d) Define a new random variable $Y = 50 - X$, so $Y \sim B(50, 0.2)$.
Use the table for $n = 50$ and column for $p = 0.2$.
$P(X \geq 40) = P(Y \leq 10) = 0.5836$

e) Define a new random variable $Y = 30 - X$, so $Y \sim B(30, 0.3)$.
Use the table for $n = 30$ and column for $p = 0.3$.
$P(X = 20) = P(Y = 10) = P(Y \leq 10) - P(Y \leq 9)$
$= 0.7304 - 0.5888 = 0.1416$

f) Define a new random variable $Y = 10 - X$, so $Y \sim B(10, 0.25)$.
Use the table for $n = 10$ and column for $p = 0.25$.
$P(X = 7) = P(Y = 3) = P(Y \leq 3) - P(Y \leq 2)$
$= 0.7759 - 0.5256 = 0.2503$

Q21 a) Use the table for $n = 30$ and column for $p = 0.35$.
$P(X \leq a) = 0.8737$.
From the table $P(X \leq 13) = 0.8737$, so $a = 13$.
[1 mark]

b) $P(X \geq b) = 0.8762$, so $P(X \leq b - 1) = 1 - P(X \geq b)$
$= 1 - 0.8762 = 0.1238$. From the table
$P(X \leq 7) = 0.1238$. So $b - 1 = 7$, which means that $b = 8$.
[2 marks available — 1 mark for correct method, 1 mark for correct answer]

c) You need to find the maximum value c, such that
$P(X \leq c) < 0.05$. From the table $P(X \leq 5) = 0.0233$ and
$P(X \leq 6) = 0.0586$, so the maximum value is $c = 5$.
[2 marks available — 1 mark for correct method, 1 mark for correct answer]

Q22 a) Let X represent the number of days on which there is at least one call. Then $X \sim B(30, 0.05)$.
There's a fixed number of trials (30 days), and each trial involves "success" (the person gets at least one call) or "failure" (the person gets no calls).
The variable X is the total number of successes.
The probability of success is the same on each day (5%).
Each trial is independent (the number of calls on one day does not affect the number of calls on another day).
[1 mark for suitable model with correct justification]

b) Use the table for $n = 30$ and column for $p = 0.05$.
$P(X < 5) = P(X \leq 4) = 0.9844$ *[1 mark]*

Q23 a) There's a fixed number of independent trials (40) with 'success' meaning a person uses the voucher and 'failure' meaning they don't, a constant probability of success (0.15) and X is the total number of successes. $X \sim B(40, 0.15)$.
[1 mark for suitable model with correct justification]

b) Use the table for $n = 40$ and column for $p = 0.15$.
$P(X \geq 10) = 1 - P(X \leq 9) = 1 - 0.9328 = 0.0672$
[2 marks available — 1 mark for correct method, 1 mark for correct answer]

c) $P(X = 6) = P(X \leq 6) - P(X \leq 5) = 0.6067 - 0.4325 = 0.1742$
[2 marks available — 1 mark for correct method, 1 mark for correct answer]
You could also find $P(X = 6)$ using the binomial probability function.

Q24 a) There are 12 chocolates in the selection box and the probability of Forrest liking each chocolate is 0.7.
Let X be the number of chocolates that Forrest likes, so $X \sim B(12, 0.7)$. Define a new random variable where $Y = 12 - X$. So $Y \sim B(12, 0.3)$.
$P(X = 10) = P(Y = 2) = P(Y \leq 2) - P(Y \leq 1)$
$= 0.2528 - 0.0850 = 0.1678$

b) If the box contains more chocolates Forrest likes than chocolates he dislikes, there must be at least 7 chocolates he likes. So you need to find $P(X \geq 7)$ using the new random variable Y as defined in part a):
$P(X \geq 7) = P(Y \leq 5) = 0.8822$

Q25 a) $X \sim B(10, 0.4)$ *[1 mark]*

b) Fewer than half of the drinks is fewer than 5.
$P(X < 5) = P(X \leq 4) = 0.6331$ *[1 mark]*

c) 75% of 10 is 7.5, so find $P(X \geq 8)$:
$P(X \geq 8) = 1 - P(X \leq 7) = 1 - 0.9877 = 0.0123$
[2 marks available — 1 mark for correct method, 1 mark for correct answer]

d) Either 4 or 5 drinks containing caffeine is the same as
$P(3 < X \leq 5) = P(X \leq 5) - P(X \leq 3)$
$= 0.8338 - 0.3823 = 0.4515 \approx 45\%$
[2 marks available — 1 mark for correct method, 1 mark for correct answer]

Q26 This is choosing 2 members from n possible members.
$\binom{n}{2} = \frac{n!}{2!(n-2)!} = 120 \Rightarrow \frac{n(n-1)}{2} = 120$
$\Rightarrow n^2 - n - 240 = 0 \Rightarrow (n - 16)(n + 15) = 0$
$\Rightarrow n = 16$ or $n = -15$. n must be positive, so $n = 16$.
To simplify the equation, use the fact that $n! \div (n-2)! = n(n-1)$, i.e. $(n \times (n-1) \times (n-2) \times (n-3) \times \ldots) \div ((n-2) \times (n-3) \times \ldots) = n \times (n-1)$

Q27 a) The probability of Messy being able to dribble past the player needs to remain the same each time, and all the outcomes need to be independent.

b) To solve part b), use the binomial probability function to find $P(X = 3)$ and $P(X = 4)$ in terms of p.
$P(X = 3) = \frac{11!}{3!8!} \times p^3 \times (1-p)^8 = 165 \times p^3 \times (1-p)^8$
$P(X = 4) = \frac{11!}{4!7!} \times p^4 \times (1-p)^7 = 330 \times p^4 \times (1-p)^7$
Then set these expressions equal to each other and solve to find p.
$P(X = 3) = P(X = 4)$,
so $165 \times p^3 \times (1-p)^8 = 330 \times p^4 \times (1-p)^7$
Dividing both sides by 165, p^3 and $(1-p)^7$ gives:
$1 - p = 2p \Rightarrow p = \frac{1}{3}$

Q28 a) Let X be the 'number of successfully completed shots per day', then $X \sim B(24, 0.12)$.
(i) $P(X = 3) = 0.239$ (3 s.f.)
(ii) $P(X \geq 2) = 1 - P(X \leq 1) = 1 - 0.1987... = 0.801$ (3 s.f.)
[3 marks available — 1 mark for using the correct binomial distribution, 1 mark for each correct answer]
You could use the binomial probability function for (i) and the cumulative distribution function for (ii).

b) Let Y be the random variable 'the number of days when there are at least 2 successful attempts at the shot', so using $P(X \geq 2)$ from part a)(ii), $Y \sim B(7, 0.8013...)$.
$P(Y \geq 4) = 1 - P(Y \leq 3) = 1 - 0.0326 = 0.967$ (3 s.f.)
[3 marks available — 1 mark for using answer from part a) (ii) to find the new binomial distribution, 1 mark for correct method for finding $P(Y \geq 4)$, 1 mark for correct answer]

c) E.g. It is unlikely that the probability of success is fixed. The snooker player should get better at completing the shot with more practice, so the probability of them being successful should increase over time.
[2 marks available — 1 mark for identifying an assumption that has been made in using the binomial distribution, 1 mark for a suitable explanation of why it may not be a sensible assumption]

Q29 a) Let X represent the number of cracked eggs in a box, so $X \sim B(12, 0.08)$.

$P(X > 2) = 1 - P(X \leq 2) = 1 - P(X = 0) - P(X = 1) - P(X = 2)$

$= 1 - \frac{12!}{0!12!} \times 0.08^0 \times 0.92^{12} - \frac{12!}{1!11!} \times 0.08^1 \times 0.92^{11} - \frac{12!}{2!10!} \times 0.08^2 \times 0.92^{10}$

$= 1 - 0.367... - 0.383... - 0.183...$

$= 0.0651... = 0.0652$ (3 s.f.)

You could also have found $P(X \leq 2)$ using your calculator and subtracted it from 1 to get $P(X > 2)$.

[2 marks available — 1 mark for correct method for finding P(X > 2), 1 mark for correct answer]

b) Let Y represent the number of defective boxes in a crate. The probability of a box being defective is the answer to part a), so $Y \sim B(8, 0.0651...)$

$P(Y > 1) = 1 - P(Y \leq 1) = 1 - P(Y = 0) - P(Y = 1)$

$= 1 - \frac{8!}{0!8!} \times (0.0651...)^0 \times (0.9348...)^8 - \frac{8!}{1!7!} \times (0.0651...)^1 \times (0.9348...)^7$

$= 1 - 0.583... - 0.325... = 0.0915$ (3 s.f.)

[3 marks available — 1 mark for using answer from part a) to find the new binomial distribution, 1 mark for correct method for finding P(Y > 1), 1 mark for correct answer]

c) E.g. It is unlikely that the eggs are cracked independently of each other. If one egg is cracked due to the box being dropped, for example, then other eggs within that box are more likely to be cracked.

[2 marks available — 1 mark for identifying an assumption that has been made in using the binomial distribution, 1 mark for a suitable explanation of why it may not be a sensible assumption]

Chapter 5: Statistical Hypothesis Testing

Prior Knowledge Check

Q1 a) From the tables, $P(X \leq 12) = 0.8209$

b) $P(X < 5) = P(X \leq 4) = 0.0160$

c) $P(X > 8) = 1 - P(X \leq 8) = 1 - 0.2998 = 0.7002$

Q2 a) $X \sim B(50, 0.3)$

b) $P(X < 15) = P(X \leq 14) = 0.4468$

Exercise 5.1 — Null and Alternative Hypotheses

Q1 a) The probability that a seed germinates.

b) 0.9

c) Call the probability p. Then the null hypothesis is $H_0: p = 0.9$.

d) The alternative hypothesis is that the probability has increased, i.e. $H_1: p > 0.9$.

e) The test is one-tailed.

Q2 a) The probability that a mouse is caught each week.

b) 0.7

c) Call the probability p. Then the null hypothesis is $H_0: p = 0.7$.

d) The alternative hypothesis is that the probability of catching a mouse has decreased, i.e. $H_1: p < 0.7$.

e) The test is one-tailed.

Q3 a) The team is interested in the population parameter p, the probability that a randomly selected teenager has the antibody present.

b) The null hypothesis is that the probability is the same, $H_0: p = 0.35$. The alternative hypothesis is that the probability is different, $H_1: p \neq 0.35$.

c) The test is two-tailed.

Q4 The council want to know if more than 16% of residents are now aware of the grants. Let p be the probability that a randomly selected resident knows about the grants. Then $H_0: p = 0.16$ and $H_1: p > 0.16$.

Q5 The owner wants to know if the proportion of customers buying a jar of chilli chutney has changed. Let p be the proportion of customers who buy a jar of chilli chutney. Then $H_0: p = 0.03$ and $H_1: p \neq 0.03$.

Q6 Boyd wants to know if the proportion of gym members that watch Australian soaps is higher than the claim of 40%. Let p be the probability that a randomly selected gym member watches Australian soaps. Then $H_0: p = 0.4$ and $H_1: p > 0.4$.

Q7 Elena wants to know if the probability of the new brand of battery lasting more than 18 months is higher than 0.64. Let p be the probability that a battery from the new brand lasts for more than 18 months. Then $H_0: p = 0.64$, $H_1: p > 0.64$. This is a one-tailed test.

Q8 a) Let p be the proportion of students who do not reach the expected standard. Then $H_0: p = 0.2$ and $H_1: p \neq 0.2$.

b) The test is two-tailed.

Q9 a) That there has been a change/increase/decrease in the probability of collecting over 2000 litres in a day since the feed was changed.

b) Let p be the probability of collecting over 2000 litres of milk a day. Then $H_0: p = 0.95$ and $H_1: p \neq 0.95$ / $p < 0.95$ / $p > 0.95$.

c) The test is two-tailed if testing whether the probability has changed. The test is one-tailed if testing whether the probability has decreased or increased.

Exercise 5.2 — Significance Levels and Test Statistics

Q1 a) Let p be the proportion of customers buying homemade ice cream. Then $H_0: p = 0.15$ and $H_1: p \neq 0.15$. It's a two-tailed test.

b) X = the number of customers in the sample who buy the shopkeeper's homemade ice cream.

c) 9 is not in the critical region, so there is insufficient evidence to reject H_0 in favour of H_1.

d) The actual significance level is $0.0460 + 0.0301 = 0.0761$ or 7.61%.

Q2 a) Let p be the proportion of light bulbs that last less than 800 hours. Then $H_0: p = 0.4$ and $H_1: p > 0.4$

b) X = the number of light bulbs in the sample lasting less than 800 hours.

c) $X = 30 - 13 = 17$ is in the critical region, so there is sufficient evidence at the 5% level to reject H_0 in favour of H_1.

Q3 a) E.g. X is the number of luxury boxes of the 50 that get gift wrapped. Let p be the proportion of luxury boxes that get gift wrapped. Then $H_0: p = 24 \div 60 = 0.4$ and $H_1: p \neq 0.4$

b) 14 is not in the critical region, so there is insufficient evidence at the 10% level to reject H_0 in favour of H_1.

Q4 a) Let p be the proportion of bags with a mass exceeding 205 g. Then $H_0: p = 0.95$ and $H_1: p < 0.95$.

b) She is only interested in whether the proportion of bags with a mass exceeding 205 g is lower than claimed, not higher.

c) The p-value is less than the significance level ($0.0026 < 0.05$), so she has enough evidence at the 5% level to reject H_0.

Exercise 5.3 — Hypothesis Tests for a Binomial Distribution

Q1 a) Let p be the probability of the spinner landing on 7. Then $H_0: p = 0.1$ and $H_1: p > 0.1$. Let X be the number of times the spinner lands on 7 in 50 spins. Then under H_0, $X \sim B(50, 0.1)$.

b) Let p be the probability of Eli being stopped at the traffic lights. Then $H_0: p = 0.25$ and $H_1: p < 0.25$. Let X be the number of times Eli is stopped in 2 weeks. Then under H_0, $X \sim B(14, 0.25)$.

c) Let p be the probability that a driver gets lost on any journey. Then $H_0: p = 0.025$ and $H_1: p \neq 0.025$. Let X be the number of journeys where the driver gets lost in the sample of 100. Then under H_0, $X \sim B(100, 0.025)$.

d) Let p be the probability that a randomly selected student has seen the film. Then $H_0: p = 0.5$ and $H_1: p > 0.5$. Let X be the number of students in the sample who have seen the film. Then under H_0, $X \sim B(30, 0.5)$.

Q2 a) If Charlotte cannot read minds, she would just be guessing a number between 1 and 5, and so the probability of getting it right would be 0.2. Let p be the probability of Charlotte guessing correctly. Then $H_0: p = 0.2$ and $H_1: p > 0.2$.

b) Let X be the number of times Charlotte guesses correctly in the sample. Then under H_0, $X \sim B(10, 0.2)$.

c) From the tables:
$P(X \geq 4) = 1 - P(X \leq 3) = 1 - 0.8791 = 0.1209 > 0.05$.

So there is not significant evidence at the 5% level to reject H_0 in favour of Charlotte's claim.

Q3 Let p = the proportion of students who think chicken dinosaurs are good value. Then $H_0: p = 0.45$ and $H_1: p < 0.45$. The significance level $\alpha = 0.1$. Let X be the number of students in the sample who think chicken dinosaurs are good value. Then under H_0, $X \sim B(50, 0.45)$. Now from the tables:
$P(X \leq 16) = 0.0427 < 0.1$.
So there is significant evidence at the 10% level to reject H_0 in favour of Ellen's claim that fewer students think chicken dinosaurs are good value.
[5 marks available — 1 mark for defining p and stating the hypotheses, 1 mark for defining X and stating the correct distribution and parameters for X, 1 mark for calculation of P(X ≤ 16) = 0.0427, 1 mark for comparison of p-value to significance level, 1 mark for a suitable written conclusion in context]
In fact, there is even significant evidence at the 5% level to reject H_0 because $P(X \leq 16) = 0.0427 < 0.05$.

Q4 a) Let p = the proportion of customers using at least one voucher. Then $H_0: p = 0.25$ and $H_1: p \neq 0.25$.
[1 mark for defining p and stating hypotheses]

b) Let X be the number of customers in the sample who used at least one voucher. Then under H_0, $X \sim B(30, 0.25)$.
The significance level $\alpha = 0.05$ but since it's a two-tailed test, you'll need $\frac{\alpha}{2} = 0.025$.
From the tables:
$P(X \geq 13) = 1 - P(X \leq 12) = 1 - 0.9784 = 0.0216 < 0.025$
So there is significant evidence at the 5% level to reject H_0 in favour of the alternative hypothesis that the proportion of customers using at least one voucher has changed.
[4 marks available — 1 mark for defining X and stating the correct distribution and parameters for X, 1 mark for calculation of P(X ≥ 13) = 0.0216, 1 mark for comparison of p-value to significance level, 1 mark for a suitable written conclusion in context]

Q5 Let p = the probability of drawing a Heart from Alice's pack of cards. In a standard pack, the probability of drawing a Heart would be 0.25. So $H_0: p = 0.25$ and $H_1: p \neq 0.25$.
The significance level $\alpha = 0.05$ but since it's a two-tailed test, you'll need $\frac{\alpha}{2} = 0.025$. Let X be the number of Hearts drawn from the pack. Then under H_0, $X \sim B(15, 0.25)$.
So from the tables:
$P(X \geq 8) = 1 - P(X \leq 7) = 1 - 0.9827 = 0.0173 < 0.025$.
So there is significant evidence at the 5% level to reject H_0 in favour of the alternative hypothesis that the pack is not a standard pack.
[5 marks available — 1 mark for defining p and stating the hypotheses, 1 mark for defining X and stating the correct distribution and parameters for X, 1 mark for calculation of P(X ≥ 8) = 0.0173, 1 mark for comparison of p-value to significance level, 1 mark for a suitable written conclusion in context]
To work out which tail of a two-tailed test you want, find the expected value of X. For binomial distributions, the expected value is np, e.g. in this question, it's 15 × 0.25 = 3.75. The observed value 8 > 3.75, so you're interested in the upper tail.

Q6 Let p = the proportion of John's pupils who gain distinctions. Then $H_0: p = 0.25$ and $H_1: p \neq 0.25$. The significance level $\alpha = 0.01$ but since it's a two-tailed test, you'll need $\frac{\alpha}{2} = 0.005$.
Let X be the number of John's exam candidates who get distinctions. Then under H_0, $X \sim B(12, 0.25)$. So from the tables:
$P(X \geq 6) = 1 - P(X \leq 5) = 1 - 0.9456 = 0.0544 > 0.005$.
So there is not significant evidence at the 1% level to reject H_0 in favour of the alternative hypothesis that the number of distinctions has changed.
[5 marks available — 1 mark for defining p and stating the hypotheses, 1 mark for defining X and stating the correct distribution and parameters for X, 1 mark for calculation of P(X ≥ 6) = 0.0544, 1 mark for comparison of p-value to significance level, 1 mark for a suitable written conclusion in context]

Q7 Let p = the proportion of the birds that are rare. Then $H_0: p = 0.15$ and $H_1: p \neq 0.15$. The significance level is $\alpha = 0.1$ but the test is two-tailed so you'll need $\frac{\alpha}{2} = 0.05$.
Let X be the number of rare birds in the sample.
Then under H_0, $X \sim B(40, 0.15)$.
Now from the tables, $P(X \leq 2) = 0.0486 < 0.05$.
So there is significant evidence at the 10% level to reject H_0 in favour of the alternative hypothesis that the number of rare birds is different with the new birdseed.
[5 marks available — 1 mark for defining p and stating the hypotheses, 1 mark for defining X and stating the correct distribution and parameters for X, 1 mark for calculation of P(X ≤ 2) = 0.0486, 1 mark for comparison of p-value to significance level, 1 mark for a suitable written conclusion in context]

Q8 Let p = the proportion of customers who buy Pigeon Spotter Magazine. Then H_0: $p = 0.1$ and H_1: $p \neq 0.1$.
The significance level is $\alpha = 0.05$ but the test is two-tailed so you'll need $\frac{\alpha}{2} = 0.025$. Let X = the number of customers who buy the magazine in the sample. Then under H_0, $X \sim B(50, 0.1)$.
Now from the tables: $P(X \geq 8) = 1 - P(X \leq 7) = 1 - 0.8779$
$= 0.1221 > 0.025$.

So there is not significant evidence at the 5% level to reject H_0 in favour of the alternative hypothesis that the number of customers buying the magazine is different in the new shop.
[5 marks available — 1 mark for defining p and stating the hypotheses, 1 mark for defining X and stating the correct distribution and parameters for X, 1 mark for calculation of P(X ≥ 8) = 0.1221, 1 mark for comparison of p-value to significance level, 1 mark for a suitable written conclusion in context]

Q9 Let p = the proportion of cookies sold that are white chocolate chip flavour. Then H_0: $p = 0.32$ and H_1: $p \neq 0.32$.
The significance level $\alpha = 0.1$ but since it's a two-tailed test, you'll need $\frac{\alpha}{2} = 0.05$. Let X be the number of customers in the sample who buy a white chocolate chip cookie. Then under H_0, $X \sim B(50, 0.32)$. Using your calculator's binomial cdf: $P(X \leq 11) = 0.0832$ (4 d.p.) > 0.05.
There is no significant evidence at the 10% level to reject H_0 and to support the alternative hypothesis that the proportion of cookies sold that are white chocolate chip has changed.
[5 marks available — 1 mark for defining p and stating the hypotheses, 1 mark for defining X and stating the correct distribution and parameters for X, 1 mark for calculation of P(X ≤ 11) = 0.0832, 1 mark for comparison of p-value to significance level, 1 mark for a suitable written conclusion in context]

Q10 Let p = the proportion of clients who pass the driving test first time. Then H_0: $p = 0.7$ and H_1: $p < 0.7$. The significance level $\alpha = 0.01$. Let X be the number of people in the sample who passed their driving test on their first attempt.
Then under H_0, $X \sim B(8, 0.7)$.
You'll need to use the tables to find $P(X \leq 4)$, but the probability is greater than 0.7, so you need to do the usual trick for this, or find this probability using a calculator.

Let Y = the number of people in the sample who didn't pass first time, then $Y \sim B(8, 0.3)$ under H_0. From the tables:
$P(X \leq 4) = P(Y \geq 4) = 1 - P(Y \leq 3) = 1 - 0.8059 = 0.1941 > 0.01$

There is not significant evidence at the 1% level to reject H_0 in favour of H_1, so Hati's claim is not upheld at the 1% level.
[5 marks available — 1 mark for defining p and stating the hypotheses, 1 mark for defining X and stating the correct distribution and parameters for X, 1 mark for calculation of P(X ≤ 4) = 0.1941, 1 mark for comparison of p-value to significance level, 1 mark for a suitable written conclusion in context]

Q11 Let p = the proportion of games that the footballer scores a goal in for her new team. Then H_0: $p = 0.55$ and H_1: $p \neq 0.55$.
The significance level $\alpha = 0.05$ but since it's a two-tailed test, you'll need $\frac{\alpha}{2} = 0.025$. Let X be the number of games the footballer scores in out of the 30 games played for her new team.
Then under H_0, $X \sim B(30, 0.55)$.
This probability is higher than 0.5 so you need to introduce another random variable, Y (or use a calculator).
Let Y be the number of games the footballer doesn't score in out of the 30 games played for her new team.
Then under H_0, $Y \sim B(30, 0.45)$, where $Y = 30 - X$.
From the tables: $P(X \geq 22) = P(Y \leq 8) = 0.0312 > 0.025$
So there is no significant evidence at the 5% level to reject H_0 in favour of the alternative hypothesis that the proportion of games she scores in has changed.
[5 marks available — 1 mark for defining p and stating the hypotheses, 1 mark for defining X and stating the correct distribution and parameters for X, 1 mark for calculation of P(X ≥ 22) = 0.0312, 1 mark for comparison of p-value to significance level, 1 mark for a suitable written conclusion in context]

Q12 Let p = the proportion of days on which Yawen gets a detention.
Then H_0: $p = 0.17$ and H_1: $p < 0.17$.
The significance level $\alpha = 0.05$. Let X be the number of days she gets detention out of the N days in the new school year.
Then under H_0, $X \sim B(N, 0.17)$.
If after N days, she has had no detentions ($X = 0$), and this is significant evidence at the 5% level to reject H_0, then $P(X = 0) < 0.05$
Using your calculator's binomial cdf or pdf (or otherwise):
$N = 16 \Rightarrow P(X = 0) = 0.0507$
$N = 17 \Rightarrow P(X = 0) = 0.0421$
Therefore the lowest number of days needed to provide sufficient evidence to reject H_0 at the 5% level is 17 days.
[5 marks available — 1 mark for defining p and stating the hypotheses, 1 mark for defining X and stating the correct distribution and parameters for X in terms of N, 1 mark for using the conditions for rejecting H_0 to form an inequality, 1 mark for calculating at least one binomial probability correctly, 1 mark for the correct answer with justification]

Exercise 5.4 — Critical Regions for Binomial Hypothesis Tests

Q1 **a)** Let p = the proportion of pupils reaching the top reading level. So H_0: $p = 0.25$ and H_1: $p > 0.25$. Let X be the number of pupils in the sample that are reaching the top reading level. Then under H_0, $X \sim B(20, 0.25)$.
You're looking for the smallest value x such that $P(X \geq x) \leq 0.05$. Using the tables,
$P(X \geq 9) = 1 - P(X \leq 8) = 1 - 0.9591 = 0.0409$
$P(X \geq 8) = 1 - P(X \leq 7) = 1 - 0.8982 = 0.1018$
So the critical region is $X \geq 9$.

b) The actual significance level is 0.0409 or 4.09%.

Q2 Let p = the proportion of pupils giving up Miss Cackle's potion-making class after year 9. So H_0: $p = 0.2$ and H_1: $p < 0.2$.
Let X be the number of pupils in the class of 30 that give up potion-making after year 9. Then under H_0, $X \sim B(30, 0.2)$.
You're interested in the low values since you're looking for a decrease. $P(X \leq 2) = 0.0442$ and $P(X \leq 3) = 0.1227$
This means the critical region is $X \leq 2$.
The actual significance level is 0.0442 or 4.42%.

Q3 a) Let p = the proportion of people who have booked their summer holiday by February 1st. Then $H_0: p = 0.35$ and $H_1: p < 0.35$. Let X be the number of people in the sample who have booked their holiday. Then under H_0, $X \sim B(15, 0.35)$. Using the tables,
$P(X \leq 1) = 0.0142$ and $P(X \leq 2) = 0.0617$.
This means the critical region is $X \leq 1$.
[4 marks available — 1 mark for defining p and stating the hypotheses, 1 mark for defining X and stating the correct distribution and parameters for X, 1 mark for clear evidence of a correct method to find the critical region, 1 mark for stating the correct critical region]

b) The actual significance level is 0.0142 or 1.42%. *[1 mark]*

c) 3 does not lie in the critical region so the result is not significant at the 5% level. *[1 mark]*

Q4 a) Let p = the proportion of sports centre members who play squash. So $H_0: p = 0.15$ and $H_1: p > 0.15$. Let X be the number of members in the sample who play squash at the sports centre. Then under H_0, $X \sim B(40, 0.15)$.
You're interested in the high values since you're looking for an increase.
From the tables:
$P(X \geq 10) = 1 - P(X \leq 9) = 1 - 0.9328 = 0.0672$
$P(X \geq 11) = 1 - P(X \leq 10) = 1 - 0.9701 = 0.0299$
So the critical region is $X \geq 11$.
[4 marks available — 1 mark for defining p and stating the hypotheses, 1 mark for defining X and stating the correct distribution and parameters for X, 1 mark for clear evidence of a correct method to find the critical region, 1 mark for stating the correct critical region]

b) The actual significance level is 0.0299 or 2.99%. *[1 mark]*

c) 12 is in the critical region so the result is significant at the 5% level. *[1 mark]*

Q5 a) Let p = the proportion of days on which she gets a headache. So $H_0: p = 0.3$ and $H_1: p \neq 0.3$. Let X be the number of days out of the 40 on which she gets a headache. Then under H_0, $X \sim B(40, 0.3)$. Since this is a two-tailed test, you need to find two critical regions, one at each tail.
Lower tail: $P(X \leq 6) = 0.0238$ and $P(X \leq 7) = 0.0553$
So the critical region for this tail is $X \leq 6$.
Upper tail: $P(X \geq 17) = 1 - P(X \leq 16) = 1 - 0.9367 = 0.0633$
$P(X \geq 18) = 1 - P(X \leq 17) = 1 - 0.9680 = 0.0320$
So the critical region for this tail is $X \geq 18$.
This means the critical region is $X \leq 6$ or $X \geq 18$.
[5 marks available — 1 mark for defining p and stating the hypotheses, 1 mark for defining X and stating the correct distribution and parameters for X, 1 mark for clear evidence of a correct method to find the critical region, 1 mark for the correct lower limit, 1 mark for the correct upper limit]

b) $X = 9$ is not in the critical region, so Isla has insufficient evidence to reject the null hypothesis at the 10% level.
[1 mark for explaining that the null hypothesis should not be rejected]

c) E.g. A binomial model may not be suitable as the probabilities of getting headaches on subsequent days might not be independent / the probability might not be constant and may vary based on other factors / etc.
[1 mark for a suitable criticism]

Q6 Let p = proportion of southern local councils who provide weekly collections. So $H_0: p = 0.4$ and $H_1: p \neq 0.4$. Let X be the number of southern councils in the sample that offer a weekly collection. Then under H_0, $X \sim B(25, 0.4)$. Since this is a two-tailed test, you need to find two critical regions, one at each tail.
Lower tail: $P(X \leq 4) = 0.0095$ and $P(X \leq 5) = 0.0294$
The closest probability to 0.025 is 0.0294 so the critical region for this tail is $X \leq 5$.
Upper tail: $P(X \geq 15) = 1 - P(X \leq 14) = 1 - 0.9656 = 0.0344$
$P(X \geq 16) = 1 - P(X \leq 15) = 1 - 0.9868 = 0.0132$
The closest probability to 0.025 is 0.0344 so the critical region for this tail is $X \geq 15$. So the critical region is $X \leq 5$ or $X \geq 15$.
The actual significance level is
$0.0344 + 0.0294 = 0.0638$, or 6.38%.

Q7 Let p = proportion of customers spending over £25.
So $H_0: p = 0.3$ and $H_1: p \neq 0.3$. Let X be the number of customers in the sample who spend more than £25. Then under H_0, $X \sim B(50, 0.3)$. Since this is a two-tailed test, you need to find two critical regions, one at each tail.
Lower tail: $P(X \leq 9) = 0.0402$ and $P(X \leq 10) = 0.0789$
The probability must be less than 0.05, so the critical region for this tail is $X \leq 9$.
Upper tail: $P(X \geq 21) = 1 - P(X \leq 20) = 1 - 0.9522 = 0.0478$
$P(X \geq 20) = 1 - P(X \leq 19) = 1 - 0.9152 = 0.0848$
The probability must be less than 0.05, so the critical region for this tail is $X \geq 21$. So the critical region is $X \leq 9$ or $X \geq 21$.
The actual significance level is
$0.0402 + 0.0478 = 0.088$, or 8.8%.

Q8 Let p = the proportion of people reporting an improvement in symptoms. Then $H_0: p = 0.15$ and $H_1: p > 0.15$.
Let X be the number of people in the test who report an improvement in symptoms. Then $X \sim B(50, 0.15)$ under H_0.
You're interested in the high values. From the tables:
$P(X \geq 15) = 1 - P(X \leq 14) = 1 - 0.9947 = 0.0053$
$P(X \geq 14) = 1 - P(X \leq 13) = 1 - 0.9868 = 0.0132$
The probability must be less than 0.01
so the critical region is $X \geq 15$.
The actual significance level is 0.0053 or 0.53%.

Q9 Let p = the proportion of five-year-old boys who believe they have magical powers. Then $H_0: p = 0.05$ and $H_1: p \neq 0.05$.
Let X be the number of five-year-old boys in the sample who believe they have magical powers. Then under H_0, $X \sim B(50, 0.05)$. The test is two-tailed so you need to consider the upper and lower ends of the binomial distribution.
From the tables: $P(X \leq 0) = 0.0769$
This is as close to 0.05 as you can possibly get, so the critical region for the lower tail is $X = 0$.
$P(X \geq 6) = 1 - P(X \leq 5) = 1 - 0.9622 = 0.0378$
$P(X \geq 5) = 1 - P(X \leq 4) = 1 - 0.8964 = 0.1036$
So the closest probability to 0.05 is 0.0378 and so the critical region for the higher tail is $X \geq 6$.
So the critical region is $X = 0$ or $X \geq 6$.
The actual significance level is
$0.0769 + 0.0378 = 0.1147$ or 11.47%.

Q10 a) Let p = the proportion of trains run by the new operator that arrive late. Then $H_0: p = 0.25$ and $H_1: p < 0.25$.
Let X = the number of trains in the sample that arrive late.
Then under H_0, $X \sim B(20, 0.25)$.
You're interested in the low values since you're looking for a decrease in the proportion of trains arriving late.
From the tables: $P(X \leq 2) = 0.0913$
$P(X \leq 3) = 0.2252$
The probability must be less than 0.1, so the critical region is $X \leq 2$.
[4 marks available — 1 mark for defining p and stating the hypotheses, 1 mark for defining X and stating the correct distribution and parameters for X, 1 mark for clear evidence of a correct method to find the critical region, 1 mark for stating the correct critical region]

b) 2 is within the critical region, so there is sufficient evidence at the 10% level to reject H_0 and to support the claim that the service has improved. *[1 mark]*

Q11 a) Let p = the proportion of customers the salesman can persuade to get a loyalty card. Then $H_0: p = 0.6$ and $H_1: p > 0.6$. Let X be the number of customers he persuades in the sample. Then $X \sim B(12, 0.6)$ under H_0.
This probability is higher than 0.5 so you need to introduce another random variable, Y (or use a calculator).
Let Y be the number of customers he doesn't persuade, then $Y \sim B(12, 0.4)$ under H_0.
Then you're looking for a value x such that $P(X \geq x) \leq 0.05$, i.e. $P(Y \leq y) \leq 0.05$, where $y = 12 - x$.
$P(Y \leq 1) = 0.0196$ and $P(Y \leq 2) = 0.0834$
So the critical region is $Y \leq 1$, i.e. $X \geq 11$.

b) The actual significance level is 0.0196 or 1.96%.

c) 10 doesn't lie in the critical region so this result is not significant at the 5% level.

Q12 Let p = the proportion of customers who buy children's books. Then $H_0: p = 0.65$ and $H_1: p \neq 0.65$. Let X be the number of customers in the sample who buy children's books.
Then under H_0, $X \sim B(15, 0.65)$.
This probability is higher than 0.5 so you need to introduce another random variable, Y (or use a calculator).
Let Y be the number of customers in the sample who don't buy children's books. Then under H_0, $Y \sim B(15, 0.35)$.

The test is two-tailed so you need to consider the upper and lower ends of the binomial distribution.
To get the upper tail of the distribution for X, you need to look at the lower tail of the distribution for Y, and vice versa.
From the tables — upper tail for X:
$P(X \geq 14) = P(Y \leq 1) = 0.0142$
$P(X \geq 13) = P(Y \leq 2) = 0.0617$
The probability must be as close to 0.025 as possible, so the critical region for the upper tail is $X \geq 14$.
Lower tail:
$P(X \leq 6) = P(Y \geq 9) = 1 - P(Y \leq 8) = 1 - 0.9578 = 0.0422$
$P(X \leq 5) = P(Y \geq 10) = 1 - P(Y \leq 9) = 1 - 0.9876 = 0.0124$

So the closest probability to 0.025 is 0.0124 and so the critical region for the lower tail is $X \leq 5$.
So the critical region is $X \leq 5$ or $X \geq 14$.

The actual significance level is
$0.0142 + 0.0124 = 0.0266$ or 2.66%.

Q13 a) Let p = the proportion of parrots that prefer Polly-No-Meal to the next best-selling brand. Then $H_0: p = 0.8$ and $H_1: p < 0.8$.
Let X be the number of parrots out of the sample of 10 parrots who prefer Polly-No-Meal to the next best-selling brand. Then under H_0, $X \sim B(10, 0.8)$.
This probability is higher than 0.5 so you need to introduce another random variable, Y (or use a calculator).
Let Y be the number of parrots that do not prefer Polly-No-Meal to the next best-selling brand, then $Y \sim B(10, 0.2)$ under H_0.
Then you're looking for a value x such that $P(X \leq x) \leq 0.05$, i.e. $P(Y \geq y) \leq 0.05$, where $y = 10 - x$. From the tables:
$P(X \leq 6) = P(Y \geq 4) = 1 - P(Y \leq 3) = 1 - 0.8791 = 0.1209$
$P(X \leq 5) = P(Y \geq 5) = 1 - P(Y \leq 4) = 1 - 0.9672 = 0.0328$
So the critical region is $X \leq 5$.
So 6 of the 10 parrots in Ava's test preferred Polly-No-Meal.

b) She now has a sample of size 20, of which 12 preferred Polly-No-Meal, and 8 did not.
Let Z be the number of parrots out of both samples that do not prefer Polly-No-Meal to the next best-selling brand.
Then under H_0, $Z \sim B(20, 0.2)$.
From the tables:
$P(Z \geq 8) = 1 - P(Z \leq 7) = 1 - 0.9679 = 0.0321$
$0.0321 < 0.05$, so this is significant — Ava now has enough evidence at the 5% level to reject H_0 and conclude that the company's claim is exaggerated.

Chapter 5 Review Exercise

Q1 H_1 should simply be that $p > 0.15$, not that it is 0.25 — he should test for a rejection of the null hypothesis, not an acceptance of another specific probability. The test is one-tailed, since he is exploring specifically whether the probability has changed in favour of getting through without stopping.

Q2 a) Let p = the proportion of packets containing fewer than 12 sweets. Then $H_0: p = 0.09$ and $H_1: p < 0.09$

b) This is a one-tailed test.

Q3 Let p be the probability that an item is faulty.
Then $H_0: p = 0.05$, $H_1: p \neq 0.05$. Let X be the number of faulty items in the sample. Then under H_0, $X \sim B(50, 0.05)$.

Q4 a) X is the number of songs out of 50 that he does not like on Tunes FM.
Watch out — the hypotheses specify the probability of ***not*** *liking a song.*

b) He will reject H_0, because $50 - 36 = 14$ is within the critical region.

Q5 a) The population parameter is p, the probability that Tina answers a question correctly.
Then $H_0: p = 0.84$, $H_1: p > 0.84$.

b) The test statistic, X, is the number of questions in the sample that Tina answers correctly.
Then under H_0, $X \sim B(10, 0.84)$.

c) You need to find $P(X \geq 9)$ — use the binomial probability function or your calculator's cdf:
$P(X \geq 9) = P(X = 9) + P(X = 10) = 0.3331... + 0.1749...$
$= 0.5080$ (4 d.p.) > 0.05.

So there is not significant evidence at the 5% level to reject H_0 in favour of Tina's claim that she is better at quizzes.

Q6 a) $H_0: p = 0.2$ and $H_1: p < 0.2$. Significance level $\alpha = 0.05$.
Under H_0, $X \sim B(20, 0.2)$. $P(X \leq 2) = 0.2061 > 0.05$
There is insufficient evidence at the 5% level of significance to reject H_0.

b) $H_0: p = 0.4$ and $H_1: p > 0.4$. Significance level $\alpha = 0.01$.
Under H_0, $X \sim B(20, 0.4)$.
$P(X \geq 15) = 1 - P(X \leq 14) = 1 - 0.9984 = 0.0016 < 0.01$
There is sufficient evidence at the 1% level of significance to reject H_0.

Q7 Let p be the probability of getting heads when the coin is flipped.
Then $H_0: p = 0.5$ and $H_1: p > 0.5$. The test is one-tailed as she claims the coin is biased towards heads.
Let X = the number of times the coin lands on heads when flipped 20 times. Significance level $\alpha = 0.05$.
Then under H_0, $X \sim B(20, 0.5)$.
From the tables: $P(X \geq 13) = 1 - P(X \leq 12)$
$= 1 - 0.8684 = 0.1316$
If you use the calculator function, you might get probabilities to more decimal places, but they will round to the values shown.
$0.1316 > 0.05$, so there is no significant evidence to reject H_0 in favour of the alternative hypothesis that the coin is biased towards heads.
[5 marks available — 1 mark for defining p and stating the hypotheses, 1 mark for defining X and stating the correct distribution and parameters for X, 1 mark for calculation of P(X ≥ 13) = 0.1316, 1 mark for comparison of p-value to significance level, 1 mark for a suitable written conclusion in context]

Q8 a) Let p = the proportion of rolls that score a five.
Then $H_0: p = 0.2$ and $H_1: p > 0.2$.
[1 mark for defining p and stating the hypotheses]

b) Let X be the number of fives scored in 20 rolls. Then under H_0, $X \sim B(20, 0.2)$
The test is one-tailed as she suspects the dice is biased towards rolling a 5. She rolled 9 fives so find $P(X \geq 9)$.
From the tables $P(X \geq 9) = 0.0100$, so the range of significance levels which would cause her to reject the null hypothesis is $\geq 1\%$.
[3 marks available — 1 mark for defining X and stating the correct distribution and parameters for X, 1 mark for calculation of P(X ≥ 9) = 0.0100, 1 mark for the correct range]

Q9 Let p = the proportion of pages that contain an error.
Then $H_0: p = 0.05$ and $H_1: p \neq 0.05$.
The significance level $\alpha = 0.05$ but since it's a two-tailed test, you'll need $\frac{\alpha}{2} = 0.025$.
Let X be the number of pages in the sample of 50 that contain errors. Then under H_0, $X \sim B(50, 0.05)$.
The expected number of pages with errors is $50 \times 0.05 = 2.5$, so you're interested in the lower tail.
So from the tables, $P(X \leq 2) = 0.5405 > 0.025$.
So there is not significant evidence at the 5% level to reject H_0 in favour of the alternative hypothesis that the error rate is significantly different.
[5 marks available — 1 mark for defining p and stating the hypotheses, 1 mark for defining X and stating the correct distribution and parameters for X, 1 mark for finding P(X ≤ 2) = 0.5405, 1 mark for comparing the p-value to the significance level, 1 mark for suitable written conclusion in context]

Q10 Let p be the proportion of students who gain an A grade.
Then $H_0: p = 0.25$, $H_1: p \neq 0.25$. The significance level $\alpha = 0.05$ but since it's a two-tailed test, you'll need $\frac{\alpha}{2} = 0.025$.
Let X = the number of the teacher's students who gained an A grade with the new exam board. Then under H_0, $X \sim B(40, 0.25)$. The expected number of A grades is $40 \times 0.25 = 10$, so you're interested in the lower tail.
From the tables, $P(X \leq 9) = 0.4395$
$0.4395 > 0.025$ so there is no significant evidence at the 5% level to reject H_0 in favour of the alternative hypothesis that the proportion of students gaining A grades has changed under the new exam board.
[5 marks available — 1 mark for defining p and stating the hypotheses, 1 mark for defining X and stating the correct distribution and parameters for X, 1 mark for finding P(X ≤ 9) = 0.4395, 1 mark for comparing the p-value to the significance level, 1 mark for suitable written conclusion in context]

Q11 a) Let p = the proportion of this variety of orchid seeds that germinate using the new fertiliser. Then $H_0: p = 0.15$ and $H_1: p > 0.15$. Significance level $\alpha = 0.05$.
Let X be the number of orchid seeds that germinate from the 20 seeds planted. Then under H_0, $X \sim B(20, 0.15)$.
This assumes e.g. that the probability of a seed germinating remains constant, and that the germination of one seed is independent of any other seed in the batch.
From the tables: $P(X \geq 7) = 1 - P(X \leq 6)$
$= 1 - 0.9781 = 0.0219$

$0.0219 < 0.05$ so there is significant evidence at the 5% level to reject H_0 in favour of the alternative hypothesis that the proportion of seeds germinating using the new fertiliser is higher.
[6 marks available — 1 mark for defining p and stating the hypotheses, 1 mark for defining X and stating the correct distribution and parameters for X, 1 mark for a sensible assumption in context, 1 mark for finding P(X ≥ 7) = 0.0219, 1 mark for comparing the p-value to the significance level, 1 mark for suitable written conclusion in context]

b) E.g. It may not be true that the chance of one seed germinating is independent of the others, as neighbouring seeds will be competing for the same resources such as light, nutrients, etc. *[1 mark for a suitable explanation]*

Q12 $H_0: p = 0.3$ and $H_1: p < 0.3$. Then $X \sim B(10, 0.3)$ under H_0.
You're interested in the low values since you're looking for a decrease. From the tables:
$P(X = 0) = 0.0282$ and $P(X \leq 1) = 0.1493$
The probability must be less than 0.05 so the critical region is $X = 0$.

Q13 a) Let p = the proportion of positive reviews on the website since the changes were made.
Then $H_0: p = 0.45$ and $H_1: p > 0.45$.
Let X be the number of positive reviews in the sample.
Then $X \sim B(20, 0.45)$ under H_0.
You're interested in the high values since you're looking for an increase. From the tables:
$P(X \geq 14) = 1 - P(X \leq 13) = 1 - 0.9786 = 0.0214$
$P(X \geq 15) = 1 - P(X \leq 14) = 1 - 0.9936 = 0.0064$
The probability must be less than 0.01 so the critical region is $X \geq 15$.

b) Actual significance level is 0.0064 or 0.64%

c) Acceptance region: $X < 15$ (or $X \leq 14$)

Q14 a) The test is one-tailed — his alternative hypothesis is examining whether the proportion is specifically less than that given.

b) $X \sim B(50, 0.1)$ under H_0. You're interested in the low values since you're looking for fewer than 10% of eggs to contain a toy.
From the tables: $P(X \leq 1) = 0.0338$ and $P(X \leq 2) = 0.1117$.
The probability must be less than 0.05, so the possible values of X are 0 or 1.

Q15 a) Let p = the proportion of days he goes for a jog.
Then $H_0: p = 0.4$ and $H_1: p < 0.4$.
Let X be the number of days he goes for a jog in the first week of the new year. Then under H_0, $X \sim B(7, 0.4)$.
You're interested in the low values since you're looking for a decrease. From the tables:
$P(X = 0) = 0.0280$ and $P(X \leq 1) = 0.1586$
The probability must be less than 0.1 so the critical region is $X = 0$.
[4 marks available — 1 mark for defining p and stating the hypotheses, 1 mark for defining X and stating the correct distribution and parameters for X, 1 mark for clear evidence of a correct method to find the critical region, 1 mark for stating the correct critical region]

b) $X = 1$ is outside the critical region, so there is insufficient evidence to reject the null hypothesis, or to support Cherlan's suspicion that he is less motivated.
[1 mark for a correct comment]

c) E.g. the sample is too small to be conclusive / a binomial model may not be appropriate (e.g. if the probability that he goes for a jog isn't constant or if it's dependent on whether or not he went for a jog the day before) / etc.
[1 mark for a suitable comment]

Q16 a) Let p = the proportion of students who are happy with the bus service. Then $H_0: p = 0.85$ and $H_1: p \neq 0.85$.
Let X be the number of students in the sample from the second school who are happy with their bus company.
Then under H_0, $X \sim B(100, 0.85)$.
This probability is higher than 0.5 so you need to introduce another random variable, Y (or use a calculator). Let Y be the number of students in the sample from the second school who are not happy with their bus company.
Then under H_0, $Y \sim B(100, 0.15)$, where $Y = 100 - X$.
The test is two-tailed so you need to consider the upper and lower ends of the binomial distribution.

Using your calculator's binomial cdf — upper tail:
$P(Y \leq 8) = P(X \geq 92) = 0.0275$ (4 d.p.)
$P(Y \leq 9) = P(X \geq 91) = 0.0551$ (4 d.p.)
0.0551 is closer to 0.05, so the critical region for the upper tail is $X \geq 91$.
Lower tail:
$P(Y \geq 21) = P(X \leq 79) = 1 - P(Y \leq 20)$
$= 1 - 0.9337 = 0.0663$ (4 d.p.)
$P(Y \geq 22) = P(X \leq 78) = 1 - P(Y \leq 21)$
$= 1 - 0.9607 = 0.0393$ (4 d.p.)
The closest probability to 0.05 is 0.0393 so the critical region for the lower tail is $X \leq 78$.
So the critical region is $X \leq 78$ or $X \geq 91$.
[5 marks available — 1 mark for defining p and stating the hypotheses, 1 mark for defining X and stating the correct distribution and parameters for X, 1 mark for clear evidence of a correct method to find the critical region, 1 mark for the correct lower limit, 1 mark for the correct upper limit]

b) The actual significance level is $0.0551 + 0.0393 = 0.0944$ or 9.44%. *[1 mark]*

c) 75 lies inside the critical region, so the result is significant at the 10% level. *[1 mark]*

Q17 a) Let p be the proportion of households who use the cleaning product. Then $H_0: p = 0.7$, $H_1: p \neq 0.7$ *[1 mark]*

b) Let X = the number of households surveyed who use the cleaning product. Then under H_0, $X \sim B(50, 0.7)$.
To use the tables, since $p > 0.5$, introduce another random variable Y = the number of households surveyed who do not use the product (or use a calculator).
Then under H_0, $Y \sim B(50, 0.3)$, where $Y = 50 - X$.
The test is two-tailed so you need to consider the upper and lower ends of the binomial distribution.
From the tables — upper tail:
$P(Y \leq 9) = P(X \geq 41) = 0.0402$
$P(Y \leq 8) = P(X \geq 42) = 0.0183$
The probability needs to be less than 0.025, so the critical region for the upper tail is $X \geq 42$.
Lower tail:
$P(Y \geq 22) = P(X \leq 28) = 1 - P(Y \leq 21) = 1 - 0.9749 = 0.0251$
$P(Y \geq 23) = P(X \leq 27) = 1 - P(Y \leq 22) = 1 - 0.9877 = 0.0123$
The probability needs to be less than 0.025, so the critical region for the lower tail is $X \leq 27$.
So the critical region is $X \leq 27$ or $X \geq 42$.

The actual significance level is $0.0183 + 0.0123 = 0.0306$ or 3.06%
[5 marks available — 1 mark for stating the correct distribution and parameters for X or Y, 1 mark for finding probabilities using the correct distribution, 1 mark for the correct upper limit, 1 mark for the correct lower limit, 1 mark for correct value of the actual significance level]

c) 26 is inside the critical region, so there is significant evidence at the 5% level, to reject H_0 in favour of H_1. There is evidence to doubt the claim that 70% of households use the product.
[2 marks available — 1 mark for comparing 26 to the critical region, 1 mark for a suitable comment in context]

Q18 a) Let p = the proportion of children who choose the building blocks. Then $H_0: p = 0.4$ and $H_1: p \neq 0.4$.
Let X be the number of children who choose the building blocks out of the 40 children. Then under H_0, $X \sim B(40, 0.4)$.
The test is two-tailed so you need to consider the upper and lower ends of the binomial distribution.
From the tables — upper tail:
$P(X \geq 21) = 1 - 0.9256 = 0.0744$
$P(X \geq 22) = 1 - 0.9608 = 0.0392$
The probability needs to be less than 0.05, so the critical region for the upper tail is $X \geq 22$.
Lower tail:
$P(X \leq 11) = 0.0709$
$P(X \leq 10) = 0.0352$
The probability needs to be less than 0.05, so the critical region for the lower tail is $X \leq 10$.
So the critical region is $X \leq 10$ or $X \geq 22$.
[5 marks available — 1 mark for defining p and stating the hypotheses, 1 mark for defining X and stating the correct distribution and parameters for X, 1 mark for clear evidence of a correct method to find the critical region, 1 mark for the correct upper limit, 1 mark for the correct lower limit]

b) 20 is not in the critical region, so there is insufficient evidence to reject H_0 at the 10% level. There is not significant evidence that the proportion of children choosing the building blocks was different in the younger age group.
[2 marks available — 1 mark for comparing 20 to the critical region, 1 mark for a suitable comment in context]

c) E.g. making the toys of similar appeal to those in the original experiment / not leading children to one toy or another through gesture or suggestion / making sure each child chose independently from the others.
[1 mark for a sensible answer]

Q19 a) According to the Venn diagram, 599 out of 1198 diners ordered exactly two courses. So the proportion of diners who ordered exactly two courses was 0.5.
Let p = the proportion of diners who order exactly two courses. Then $H_0: p = 0.5$ and $H_1: p > 0.5$.
Let X be the number of diners who order exactly two courses out of the 40 diners. Then under H_0, $X \sim B(40, 0.5)$.
From the tables:
$P(X \geq 26) = 1 - P(X \leq 25) = 1 - 0.9597 = 0.0403$.
$0.0403 < 0.05$ so there is significant evidence at the 5% level to reject H_0 in favour of the alternative hypothesis that the proportion of diners ordering exactly two courses is higher and the incentive is working.
[5 marks available — 1 mark for defining p and stating the hypotheses, 1 mark for defining X and stating the correct distribution and parameters for X, 1 mark for finding P(X ≥ 26) = 0.0403, 1 mark for comparing the p-value to the significance level, 1 mark for suitable written conclusion in context]

b) You're interested in the high values since you're looking for an increase. From the tables:
$P(X \geq 24) = 1 - P(X \leq 23) = 1 - 0.8659 = 0.1341$
$P(X \geq 25) = 1 - P(X \leq 24) = 1 - 0.9231 = 0.0769$
The probability must be less than 0.1, so the critical region is $X \geq 25$.
[2 marks available — 1 mark for clear evidence of a correct method to find the critical region, 1 mark for stating the correct critical region]

Q20 a) Under H_0, $X \sim B(20, 0.5)$.
The test is two-tailed as he wants to test whether the pack is biased toward either red or black. The expected number of red cards is $20 \times 0.5 = 10$, so you're interested in the upper tail. From the tables $P(X \geq 12) = 0.2517$.
The test is two-tailed so the minimum significance level needed to reject the null hypothesis is $0.2517 \times 2 = 0.5034$ or 50.34%.

b) E.g. That there is not enough evidence to conclude that his pack of cards doesn't contain equal numbers of red and black cards and that he needs to perform more trials to investigate further.

Q21 a) Let p = the proportion of students who approve of the canteen. Then $H_0: p = 0.68$ and $H_1: p \neq 0.68$.
The significance level $\alpha = 0.01$ but since it's a two-tailed test, you'll need $\frac{\alpha}{2} = 0.005$. Let X = the number of students from the 42 surveyed who approve of the canteen.
Then under H_0, $X \sim B(42, 0.68)$.
The expected value for $X = 42 \times 0.68 = 28.56$.
$34 > 28.56$ so you're interested in the upper tail.
You can't look up these values of n and p in the tables, so use your calculator's binomial cdf:
$P(X \geq 34) = 1 - P(X \leq 33) = 1 - 0.9533...$
$= 0.0467$ (4 d.p.) > 0.005,
so there is no significant evidence at the 1% level to reject H_0 in favour of the alternative hypothesis that the approval rating for the canteen has changed.
[5 marks available — 1 mark for defining p and stating the hypotheses, 1 mark for defining X and stating the correct distribution and parameters for X, 1 mark for finding P(X ≥ 34) = 0.0467, 1 mark for comparing the p-value to the significance level, 1 mark for suitable written conclusion in context]

b) E.g. students' opinions may not be independent as groups of friends are likely to have similar opinions.
E.g. people who dislike the canteen are less likely to eat there and so won't be fairly represented in the sample.
[1 mark for a suitable comment]

Chapter 6: Quantities and Units in Mechanics

Prior Knowledge Check

Q1 a) 3200 m = 3200 ÷ 1000 = 3.2 km
b) 825 mm = 825 ÷ 10 = 82.5 cm
c) 0.07 km = 0.07 × 1000 = 70 m

Q2 Convert to kilograms: 2500 g = 2500 ÷ 1000 = 2.5 kg
0.5 tonnes = 0.5 × 1000 = 500 kg
So the total is 2.5 + 45 + 500 = 547.5 kg

Exercise 6.1 — S.I. units

Q1 a) velocity = 7 ms^{-1} or 7 m/s
b) displacement = 0.2 m
c) time = 5 seconds
d) acceleration = 2.6 ms^{-2} or 2.6 m/s^2
e) speed = 9 ms^{-1} or 9 m/s
f) area = 1020 m^2

Q2 a) metres × metres × metres = m^3
b) kilograms ÷ m^3 = kg m^{-3} or kg/m^3
c) kilograms × ms^{-1} = kg m s^{-1} or kg m/s
d) metres ÷ seconds^2 ÷ seconds = $\text{ms}^{-2} \div \text{s} = \text{ms}^{-3}$
e) newtons × metres = $\text{kg m s}^{-2} \times \text{m} = \text{kg m}^2\text{s}^{-2}$ or $\text{kg m}^2/\text{s}^2$
f) newtons ÷ $\text{m}^2 = \text{kg m s}^{-2} \div \text{m}^2 = \text{kg m}^{-1}\text{s}^{-2}$ or $\text{kg/(m s}^2)$

Exercise 6.2 — Modelling in Mechanics

Q1 W
Assumptions:
The apple is modelled as a particle.
The apple is initially at rest.
Air resistance can be ignored.
There are no other external forces acting.
The effect of gravity (g) is constant.

Q2
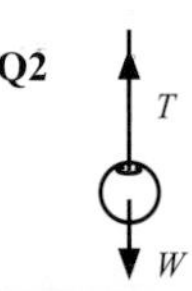

Assumptions:
The conker is modelled as a particle.
The shoelace is a light, inextensible string.
There are no other external forces acting.

Q3
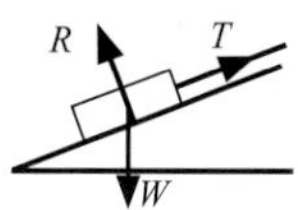

Assumptions:
The sledge is modelled as a particle.
The surface of the slope is smooth (it's icy).
The rope is a light, inextensible string.
The rope is parallel to the slope.
No other external forces are acting.

Q4 a)
Assumptions:
The box is modelled as a particle.
The floor is smooth (it's polished).
There are no other external forces acting.

b)
Assumptions:
The crate is modelled as a particle.
The rope is light and inextensible.
The floor is rough.
There are no other external forces acting.

Q5
Assumptions:
The package is modelled as a particle.
The stick is light and rigid.
The ground is rough.
There are no other external forces acting.

Q6 a)
Assumptions:
The car is modelled as a particle.
The angle of the slope is constant.
The surface is rough.
There are no other external forces acting.

b)
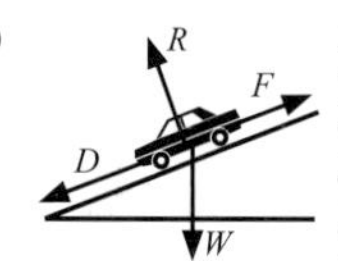

Assumptions:
The car is modelled as a particle.
The angle of the slope is constant.
The surface is rough.
There are no other external forces acting.

Q7
Assumptions: The man and the lorry are both modelled as particles. The rope is light and inextensible, and remains taut.
The road is rough.
No resistance forces slow the strongman's motion.
There are no other external forces acting.

Q8
Assumptions:
The toboggan is modelled as a particle.
The slope is smooth.
No other external forces are acting.

Q9
Assumptions:
The pendulum is modelled as a particle.
The string is light and inextensible.
The rod is thin, straight and rigid.
The rod is horizontal.

Q10
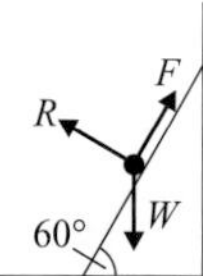

[2 marks available — 1 mark for an appropriate diagram, 1 mark for all forces correctly labelled]

Q11 a) A body in contact with a rough surface will experience a frictional force which will act to oppose motion, whereas a body in contact with a smooth surface will not experience a frictional force.

b) A wire is light and inextensible whereas a rod isn't always.

c) A peg is a fixed support from which a body can hang or rest on, whereas a pulley is a smooth, fixed support that a string can pass over.

Q12

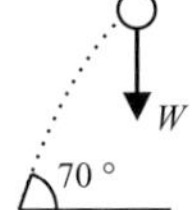

Once the ball is in motion, there are no other forces acting on it other than its own weight.

Q13

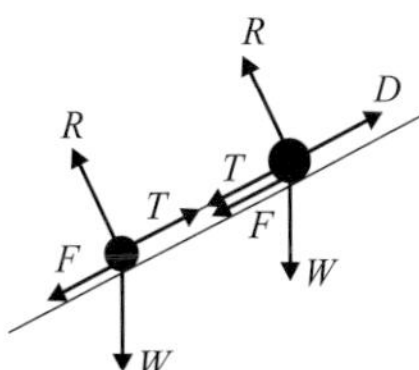

Assumptions:
The car and trailer are modelled as particles.
Air resistance can be ignored.
The rope is light and inextensible.
The road is rough.
No other external forces are acting.

Technically, you can't assume the reaction forces are the same, so they should be labelled as R_1 and R_2 (as should the F and W forces), but this is not required for full marks.
[5 marks available — 1 mark for an appropriate diagram, 1 mark for at least five correctly labelled forces, 1 mark for all correctly labelled forces, 1 mark for each correct assumption made up to a maximum of 2 marks]

Chapter 6 Review Exercise

Q1 $P = \frac{W}{t}$, so $\text{Nms}^{-1} = \text{Ws}^{-1}$
Work done is in Nm.
Energy = force × distance = Nm
[2 marks available — 1 mark for deriving the units for work done or energy, 1 mark for deriving the units for both]

Q2 v is in ms^{-1} (given)
u is in ms^{-1} (given)
at is in $\text{ms}^{-2} \times \text{s} = \text{ms}^{-1}$ *[1 mark]*

Q3 s is in m (given)
ut is in $\text{ms}^{-1} \times \text{s} = \text{m}$
$\frac{1}{2}at^2$ is in $\text{ms}^{-2} \times \text{s}^2 = \text{m}$ *[1 mark]*

Q4 The SI units for density are kg/m^3.
Dividing g/cm^3 by 1000 gives kg/cm^3, then multiplying by 1 000 000 gives kg/m^3. This is equivalent to multiplying by 1000.

Q5 E is in Nm. $E = \lambda x^2 \Rightarrow \text{Nm} = \lambda\text{m}^2$
Rearranging gives λ in $\frac{\text{Nm}}{\text{m}^2} = \frac{\text{N}}{\text{m}}$
$\text{N} = \text{kgms}^{-2}$, so λ is in $\frac{\text{kgms}^{-2}}{\text{m}} = \text{kgs}^{-2}$
[2 marks available — 1 mark for substituting the correct SI units into the formula, 1 mark for the correct answer]

Q6 For the first 6 km:
6 km = 6000 m, 30 000 cm/min = 300 m/min = 5 m/s
6000 m ÷ 5 m/s = 1200 s
Then she cycles for:
0.0125 days = 0.3 hours = 18 minutes = 1080 seconds
So she cycled for 1080 + 1200 = 2280 seconds
[3 marks available — 1 mark for calculating the time taken for the first 6 km, 2 marks for the correct answer in the correct units, otherwise 1 mark for the correct answer not in the correct units]

Q7 **a)** ma is in kgms^{-2}
$\frac{mv}{t^2}$ is in $\frac{\text{kgms}^{-1}}{\text{s}^2} = \text{kgms}^{-3}$
$\frac{v^2}{a} \times \frac{m}{t^2}$ is in $\frac{\text{m}^2\text{s}^{-2}\text{kg}}{\text{ms}^{-2} \times \text{s}^2} = \text{kgms}^{-2}$
$\frac{ma}{t}$ is in $\frac{\text{kgms}^{-2}}{\text{s}} = \text{kgms}^{-3}$
ma is equivalent to $\frac{v^2}{a} \times \frac{m}{t^2}$ and $\frac{mv}{t^2}$ is equivalent to $\frac{ma}{t}$

b) $v \times s$ is in $\text{ms}^{-1} \times \text{m} = \text{m}^2\text{s}^{-1}$
$\frac{Fvt}{ms}$ is in $\frac{\text{kgms}^{-2}\text{ms}^{-1}\text{s}}{\text{kgm}} = \text{ms}^{-2}$
$vs \div t$ is in $\text{ms}^{-1} \times \text{m} \div \text{s} = \text{m}^2\text{s}^{-2}$
So, only $\frac{Fvt}{ms}$ has equivalent units to acceleration.

Q8 W is weight, F is friction, R is reaction/normal reaction, N is reaction/normal reaction, T is thrust, tension or compression.

Q9 **a)** Offering a frictional force which opposes motion.
b) Offering no (or negligible) frictional force.
c) A flat surface.
d) An object.

Q10 (1) model, (2) simple, (3) inaccurate, (4) harder, (5) light, (6) static, (7) equilibrium, (8) rigid, (9) inextensible

Q11 **a)** The surface is horizontal at the point of contact between it and the particle. *[1 mark]*

b)

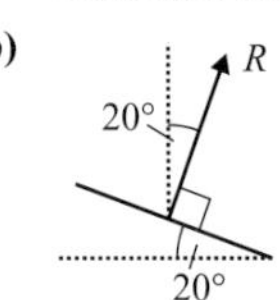

The surface is at an angle of 20° to the horizontal at the point of contact between it and the particle. *[1 mark]*
The reaction force is always at 90° to the surface.

Q12

Assumptions:
The object is modelled as a particle.
No other external forces are acting.

Technically, you can't assume the reaction forces are the same, so they could be labelled as R_1 and R_2.

Q13 y is in m, so $0.5x^2$ and 3 are also in m.
$0.5x^2$ is in (the units of 0.5) × s^2.
So, the units of 0.5 must be in ms^{-2}.
[2 marks available — 1 mark for correct units for 3, 1 mark for correct units for 0.5]

Chapter 7: Kinematics

Prior Knowledge Check

Q1 **a)** The fastest speed is the steepest gradient, so $\frac{18-8}{5-4} = \frac{10}{1} = 10 \text{ ms}^{-1}$

b) The particle is at rest when gradient = 0, so the total rest time is (4 – 2) + (6 – 5) = 3 seconds

Q2 **a)** $\int 4x^3 + 6x^{-2} - 7 \, dx = x^4 - 6x^{-1} - 7x + C$

b) $\frac{dy}{dx} = 10x - x^{-\frac{1}{2}}$

Q3 $\frac{dy}{dx} = 3x^2 - 8x + 4$
$3x^2 - 8x + 4 = 0 \Rightarrow (3x-2)(x-2) = 0 \Rightarrow x = \frac{2}{3}, x = 2$
when $x = \frac{2}{3}$, $y = \left(\frac{2}{3}\right)^3 - 4\left(\frac{2}{3}\right)^2 + 4\left(\frac{2}{3}\right) - 1 = \frac{5}{27}$
when $x = 2$, $y = 2^3 - 4(2)^2 + 4(2) - 1 = -1$
The stationary points are $\left(\frac{2}{3}, \frac{5}{27}\right)$ and $(2, -1)$.
$\frac{d^2y}{dx^2} = 6x - 8$, so for $\left(\frac{2}{3}, \frac{5}{27}\right)$, $6\left(\frac{2}{3}\right) - 8 = -4$,
so $\frac{d^2y}{dx^2} < 0$ and $\left(\frac{2}{3}, \frac{5}{27}\right)$ is a maximum.
For $(2, -1)$, $6(2) - 8 = 4$, so $\frac{d^2y}{dx^2} > 0$ and $(2, -1)$ is a minimum.

Exercise 7.1-7.2 — Displacement-Time Graphs

Q1 The velocity is given by the gradient of the graph.

First stage: $v = \text{gradient} = \frac{(40-0)\text{ km}}{(0.5-0)\text{ h}} = 80\text{ kmh}^{-1}$

Second stage: $v = \frac{(60-40)\text{ km}}{(1-0.5)\text{ h}} = 40\text{ kmh}^{-1}$

Third stage: $v = \frac{(60-60)\text{ km}}{(1.5-1)\text{ h}} = 0\text{ kmh}^{-1}$

Fourth stage: $v = \frac{(0-60)\text{ km}}{(2-1.5)\text{ h}} = -120\text{ kmh}^{-1}$

Q2 **a)** You need to calculate the time taken to travel between B and C. The coach travels 60 km at 40 kmh^{-1}, so the time taken is: 60 km ÷ 40 kmh^{-1} = 1.5 hours.

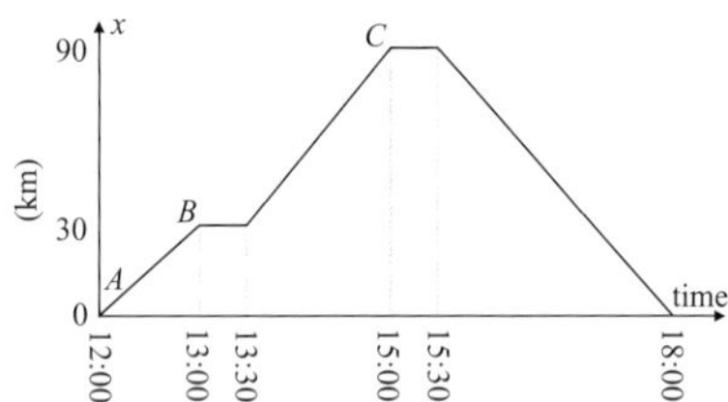

b) $v = -\frac{90\text{ km}}{2.5\text{ h}} = -36\text{ kmh}^{-1}$

c) Total distance travelled = 30 km + 60 km + 90 km = 180 km

$\text{speed} = \frac{\text{distance}}{\text{time}} = \frac{180\text{ km}}{6\text{ h}} = 30\text{ kmh}^{-1}$

Q3 **a)** First stage: $v = \text{gradient} = \frac{(60-0)\text{ m}}{(25-0)\text{ s}} = 2.4\text{ ms}^{-1}$

Second stage: $v = \frac{-60-60}{70-25} = -2.67\text{ ms}^{-1}$ (3 s.f.)

Third stage: $v = \frac{-60-(-60)}{110-70} = 0\text{ ms}^{-1}$

Fourth stage: $v = \frac{30-(-60)}{130-110} = 4.5\text{ ms}^{-1}$

Fifth stage: $v = \frac{0-30}{150-130} = -1.5\text{ ms}^{-1}$

b) **(i)** Total distance = 60 + 120 + 90 + 30 = 300 m

(ii) She begins and ends at $s = 0$, so her total displacement is 0, i.e. 60 – 120 + 90 – 30 = 0

c) $\text{Speed} = \frac{\text{distance}}{\text{time}} = \frac{300}{150} = 2\text{ ms}^{-1}$

Q4 **a)** The horizontal lines show where the horse stopped, which are both at 60 m. The total time was (50 – 30) + (100 – 90) = 30 seconds.
[2 marks available — 1 mark for the distance, 1 mark for the time]

b) The graph is steepest between 50 and 60 seconds (or 100 and 110 seconds). The speed is 60 ÷ 10 = 6 ms^{-1}.
[2 marks available — 1 mark for correctly identifying one or both areas of the graph, 1 mark for finding the correct speed]

c) 80 + 60 + 60 + 60 = 260 m *[1 mark]*

d) 260 ÷ 110 = 2.4 ms^{-1} (1 d.p.) *[1 mark]*

e) –140 ÷ 110 = –1.3 ms^{-1} (1 d.p.) *[1 mark]*

Q5 The man travels 5 mph × 1 h = 5 miles from 13:00 to 14:00, then 3 mph × 1 h = 3 miles from 14:00 to 15:00.

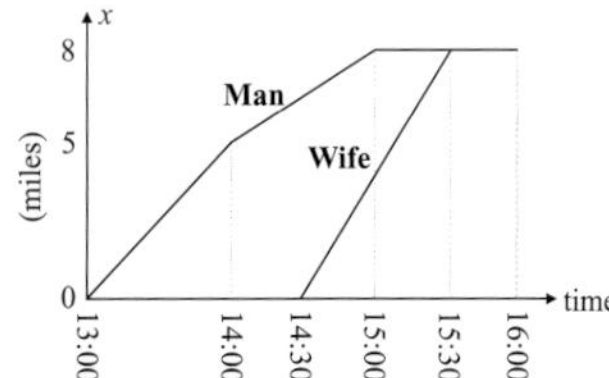

Q6 **a)**

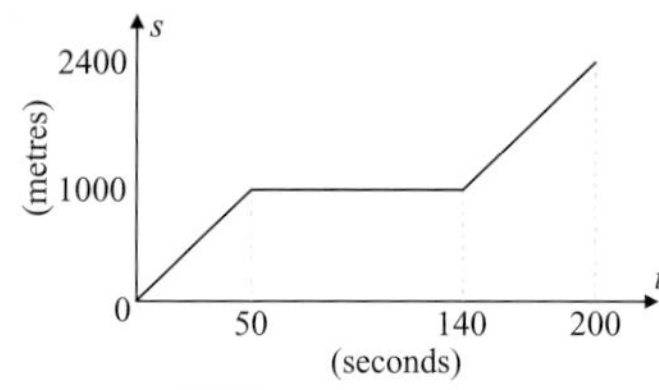

b) $\text{Speed} = \frac{1000\text{ m}}{50\text{ s}} = 20\text{ ms}^{-1}$

c) The train travelled 2400 – 1000 = 1400 m between $t = 140$ and $t = 200$ (i.e. in 60 seconds).
So $U = \frac{1400\text{ m}}{60\text{ s}} = 23.3\text{ ms}^{-1}$ (3 s.f.)

d) $\text{Average speed} = \frac{2400\text{ m}}{200\text{ s}} = 12\text{ ms}^{-1}$

Q7 B and C.
B: the displacement from home would increase over time.
C: the distance travelled would increase over time (the graph is correct if it had been 'distance from starting point').
The bee maintains a constant distance from the hive when it is circling — the bee is moving in this scenario even though the graph shows a horizontal line.

Q8 **a)**

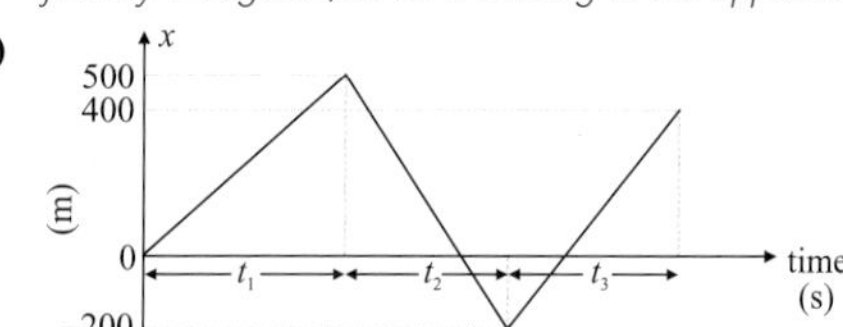

b) Reading from the distance-time graph, the distance travelled is 120 m.

Q9 **a)** 500 m – 700 m + 600 m = 400 m
The 700 m is subtracted because his velocity for that part of the journey is negative, so he is walking in the opposite direction.

b)

c) The gradient of each part of the graph is equal to the velocity during that stage. You already know the velocities, and the distances, for each stage, so you can use them to find the times.

$u = \frac{500}{t_1} \Rightarrow t_1 = \frac{500}{u}$

$-2u = \frac{-700}{t_2} \Rightarrow t_2 = \frac{350}{u}$

$1.5u = \frac{600}{t_3} \Rightarrow t_3 = \frac{400}{u}$

$\text{Total time} = t_1 + t_2 + t_3 = \frac{500}{u} + \frac{350}{u} + \frac{400}{u}$
$= \frac{1250}{u}$ seconds

d) $\text{Average speed} = \frac{\text{total distance}}{\text{total time}}$
$= (500 + 700 + 600) \div \frac{1250}{u} = \frac{36u}{25}\text{ ms}^{-1}$

Q10 **a)**

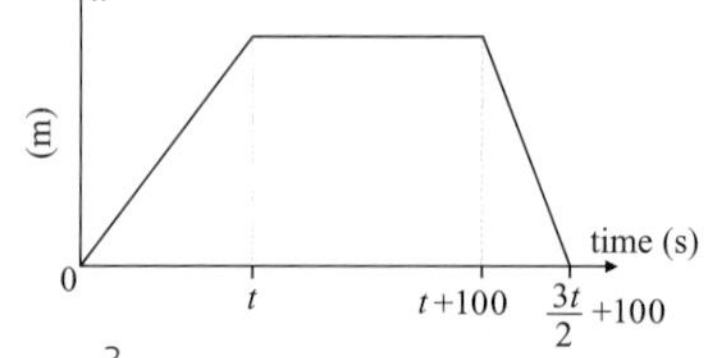

The $\frac{3}{2}t + 100$ comes from the fact that the car returns home at twice the speed that it travelled away from home, so must take half as long (i.e. $\frac{t}{2}$ seconds).
So the total time is: $t + 100 + \frac{t}{2} = \frac{3}{2}t + 100$

b) Total distance = speed × time
So distance covered in first part of journey = ut m
Car travels same distance in return journey,
so total distance travelled = $2ut$ m.

c) Average speed
$$= \frac{\text{total distance}}{\text{total time}} = \frac{2ut}{\frac{3}{2}t + 100} = \frac{4ut}{3t + 200}\ \text{ms}^{-1}$$

Exercise 7.3 — Velocity-Time Graphs

Q1 The bus accelerates uniformly from rest to a velocity of 20 kmh^{-1} in 2 min. It then travels at this speed for 18 min, before decelerating uniformly to 10 kmh^{-1} in 5 min. Finally, it decelerates uniformly to rest in 10 min.

Q2 **a)** Acceleration is given by the gradient of the graph.
$$a = \text{gradient} = \frac{(15-0)\ \text{ms}^{-1}}{(5-0)\ \text{s}} = 3\ \text{ms}^{-2}$$

b) $a = \frac{((-15)-0)\ \text{ms}^{-1}}{(60-40)\ \text{s}} = -0.75\ \text{ms}^{-2}$

c) $a = \frac{(0-(-15))\ \text{ms}^{-1}}{(70-60)\ \text{s}} = 1.5\ \text{ms}^{-2}$

Q3 **a)**

b) Total distance = area under the graph
$$\text{Area} = \frac{1}{2} \times [(210-30) + 270] \times V = \frac{1}{2} \times 450 \times V = 225V$$
So 6.3 km = 6300 m = $225V \Rightarrow V = 6300 \div 225 = 28$ ms^{-1}

c) Deceleration is the part of the graph with a negative gradient.
$$\text{Area} = \frac{1}{2} \times (270-210) \times 28 = 840\ \text{m}$$

Q4 **a)**

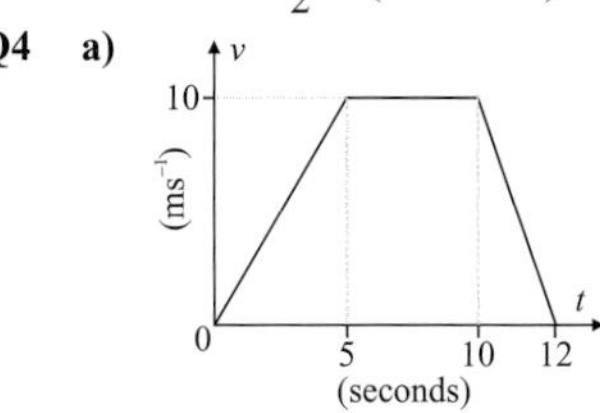

[2 marks available — 1 mark for correct shape, 1 mark for correct labels]

b) Total distance = area under graph
$$\text{Area} = \frac{1}{2}[(10-5) + 12] \times 10 = 85\ \text{m}$$
[2 marks available — 1 mark for a correct method to calculate the area, 1 mark for the correct answer]

c) $10 \div 5 = 2$ ms^{-2} *[1 mark]*

d) The cat travels 85 m in 12 seconds, so has an average velocity of $85 \div 12 = 7.1$ ms^{-1} (1 d.p.) *[1 mark]*

Q5 **a)**

b) Split the area up into a rectangle and a triangle:
$$\text{Area} = 10T + \frac{(50-10) \times T}{2} = 30T$$

c) The gradient gives the acceleration, so considering the time the particle is accelerating:
$$4 = \frac{(50-10)}{t_1} \Rightarrow t_1 = 10$$
Now considering the time it is decelerating:
$$-10 = \frac{(10-50)}{t_2} \Rightarrow t_2 = 4$$
x is the area under the graph while the particle is accelerating:
$$x = 10t_1 + \frac{(50-10) \times t_1}{2} = (10 \times 10) + \frac{40 \times 10}{2} = 300\ \text{m}$$
y is the area under the graph while the particle is decelerating:
$$y = 10t_2 + \frac{(50-10) \times t_2}{2} = (10 \times 4) + \frac{40 \times 4}{2} = 120\ \text{m}$$
T is just the sum of t_1 and t_2: $T = 10 + 4 = 14$ s

Q6 **a)** The gradient gives the acceleration, so:
$$a = 0.375 = \frac{15}{t} \Rightarrow t = 40\ \text{s}$$
So it takes the train 40 s to reach the signal box.

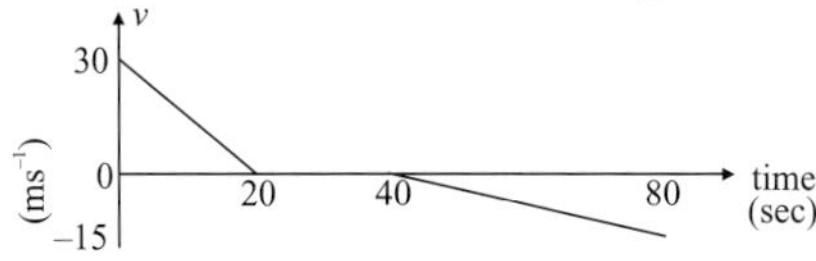

b) Gradient $= -\frac{30}{20} = -1.5$
So the train decelerates at a rate of 1.5 ms^{-2}

c) The distance is given by the area under the graph from $t = 0$ s to $t = 20$ s: distance $= \frac{30 \times 20}{2} = 300$ m
You could also have found the area under the graph from t = 40 s to t = 80 s — the distance is the same.

Q7 **a)** Taking upwards as positive:

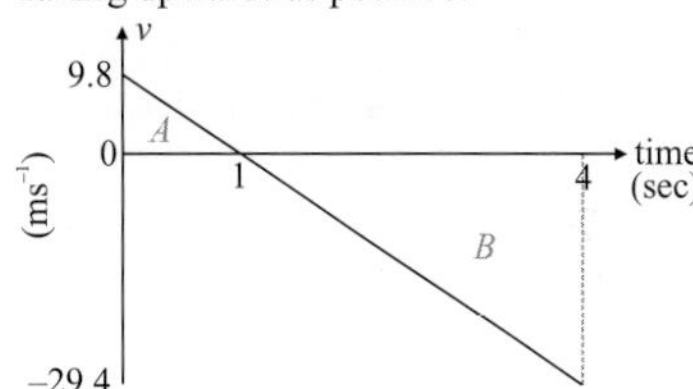

If you took downwards as positive, your graph should be the same as this, but flipped vertically, i.e. sloping upwards from –9.8 ms⁻¹ to 29.4 ms⁻¹.

b) **(i)** As the stone travels upwards, it will slow down until it reaches its highest point, where it will have velocity $v = 0$ ms^{-1}. The distance the stone travels from the cliff edge to its highest point is equal to its displacement during this time. This is given by the area marked A on the graph.
$$\text{Area } A = \frac{1 \times 9.8}{2} = 4.9$$
So distance from cliff to highest point is 4.9 m.

(ii) As the stone falls from its highest point to the sea, its speed will increase from 0 ms^{-1} to 29.4 ms^{-1}. The distance the stone travels from its highest point to the sea is equal to the magnitude of its displacement during this time. This is given by the area marked B on the graph.
$$\text{Area } B = \frac{3 \times -29.4}{2} = -44.1\ \text{m}$$
So the stone travels 44.1 m downwards from its highest point to the sea.

(iii) The height of the cliff is equal to the magnitude of the stone's final displacement from its starting point. Find this by adding the areas of A and B:
$4.9 + (-44.1) = -39.2$ m
So the height of the cliff is 39.2 m.
You can also think of the height of the cliff as being the difference between your answers to (i) and (ii): $44.1 - 4.9 = 39.2$ m.

Q8 **a)** 12 ms^{-1} *[1 mark]*
This is just the highest point on the graph.

b) The steepest line with positive gradient is Justin's line segment between 0 and 2 seconds. This represents an acceleration of $6 \div 2 = 3$ ms^{-2}.
[2 marks available — 1 mark for identifying the correct section/time period, 1 mark for the correct answer]

c) Mo ran $(12 \times 6) \div 2 = 36$ m in the first 6 seconds. At 12 ms^{-1}, it took $64 \div 12 = 5.333...$ seconds to run the remaining 64 m. Time taken $= 6 + 5.333... = 11.333...$ s.
Justin ran $(2 \times 6) \div 2 = 6$ m in the first 2 seconds and $(10 + 6) \times 3 \div 2 = 24$ m in the next 3 seconds.
At 10 ms^{-1}, it took $70 \div 10 = 7$ seconds to run the remaining 70 m. Time taken $= 2 + 3 + 7 = 12$ seconds.
So Mo ran 100 m in the quicker time.
[4 marks available — 1 mark for Mo's distance in the first 6 seconds, 1 mark for Mo's total time, 1 mark for Justin's distance in the first 5 seconds, 1 mark for Justin's total time with a correct conclusion]

d) No. Justin was ahead of Mo for at least the first two seconds, as his velocity was higher during this entire period.
[1 mark for correct answer with reasoning]

e) E.g. the model assumes that the acceleration of both sprinters changed from one constant value to another in an instant.
[1 mark for any sensible answer]

Exercise 7.4 — Constant Acceleration Equations

Q1 **a)** $u = 0, v = 12, a = a, t = 5$
$v = u + at$
$12 = 0 + 5a \Rightarrow a = 12 \div 5 = 2.4$ ms^{-2}

b) $s = s, u = 0, v = 12, t = 5$
$s = \left(\frac{u+v}{2}\right)t$
$s = \left(\frac{0+12}{2}\right) \times 5 = 30$ m

Q2 **a)** $18 \times 1000 \div 60^2 = 5$ ms^{-1}

b) $s = 50, u = 5, v = 0, t = t$
$s = \left(\frac{u+v}{2}\right)t$
$50 = \left(\frac{5+0}{2}\right)t \Rightarrow t = 50 \div 2.5 = 20$ s

c) $s = 50, u = 5, v = 0, a = a$
$v^2 = u^2 + 2as$
$0 = 5^2 + 2a \times 50$
$2a = -5^2 \div 50 \Rightarrow a = -0.25$
So the cyclist decelerates at a rate of 0.25 ms^{-2}

Q3 **a)** $s = 60, u = 5, v = 25, a = a$
$v^2 = u^2 + 2as$
$25^2 = 5^2 + (2a \times 60)$
$625 = 25 + 120a \Rightarrow a = 600 \div 120 = 5$ ms^{-2}

b) Acceleration is constant. The skier is modelled as a particle travelling in a straight line.

Q4 **a)** From the first post to the second post:
$s = 18, u = u, a = a, t = 2$
$s = ut + \frac{1}{2}at^2$
$18 = 2u + \frac{1}{2}a \times 2^2$
$18 = 2u + 2a \Rightarrow 9 = u + a \Rightarrow u = 9 - a$ ①
From the first post to the third post:
$s = 36, u = u, a = a, t = 3$
$s = ut + \frac{1}{2}at^2$
$36 = 3u + \frac{1}{2}a \times 3^2$
$36 = 3u + 4.5a \Rightarrow 12 = u + 1.5a$ ②
Substituting ① into ②: $12 = (9 - a) + 1.5a$
$3 = 0.5a \Rightarrow a = 6$ ms^{-2}

b) Use expression for u from part a): $u = 9 - a = 9 - 6 = 3$ ms^{-1}

Q5 **a)** $s = 30, u = 0, v = 6, a = a$
$v^2 = u^2 + 2as$
$6^2 = 0^2 + 2 \times a \times 30$
$36 = 60a \Rightarrow a = 36 \div 60 = 0.6$ ms^{-2}

b) $s = 30, u = 0, v = 6, a = 0.6, t = t$
$s = \left(\frac{u+v}{2}\right)t$
$30 = \left(\frac{0+6}{2}\right)t \Rightarrow 30 = 3t \Rightarrow t = 10$ seconds
You could have also used $v = u + at$ here.

Q6 **a)** $u = 0, v = 40, t = 2, a = a$
$v = u + at$
$40 = 2a \Rightarrow a = 20$ cms^{-2}
[2 marks available — 1 mark for using a suvat equation to find a, 1 mark for the correct answer]

b) $s = \left(\frac{u+v}{2}\right)t$
$s = \left(\frac{0+40}{2}\right)2 = 40$ cm
[2 marks available — 1 mark for using a suvat equation to find s, 1 mark for the correct answer]

Q7 **a)** $u = 1.2, v = 0.7, a = -0.4, t = t$
$v = u + at$
$0.7 = 1.2 + (-0.4)t \Rightarrow t = -0.5 \div -0.4 = 1.25$ seconds

b) $s = s, u = 1.2, v = 0, a = -0.4$
$v^2 = u^2 + 2as$
$0^2 = 1.2^2 + 2 \times -0.4 \times s \Rightarrow s = -1.2^2 \div -0.8 = 1.8$ m
So the block will stop before falling off the table if the table is longer than 1.8 m.

Q8 **a)** $u = 6, v = 0, t = 3, a = a$
$v = u + at$
$0 = 6 + 3a \Rightarrow a = -2$ ms^{-2}
We must assume that the acceleration is uniform.
[3 marks available — 1 mark for correctly using a suvat equation to find a, 1 mark for the correct answer, 1 mark for a correct assumption]

b) $v^2 = u^2 + 2as$
$0 = 6^2 + (2 \times -2 \times s) \Rightarrow s = 9$ m
[2 marks available — 1 mark for using a suvat equation to find s, 1 mark for the correct answer]

Q9 **a)** $s = 800, u = 10, a = a, t = 40$
$s = ut + \frac{1}{2}at^2$
$800 = 10 \times 40 + (\frac{1}{2} \times a \times 40^2) = 400 + 800a$
$\Rightarrow a = 0.5$ ms^{-2}
[2 marks available — 1 mark for using a suvat equation to find a, 1 mark for the correct answer]

b) $v = u + at$
$v = 10 + (0.5 \times 40) = 30 \text{ ms}^{-1}$
60 miles per hour $= 60 \times 1609 = 96\,540 \text{ mh}^{-1}$
$96\,540 \text{ mh}^{-1} = 96\,540 \div (60 \times 60) = 26.816... \text{ ms}^{-1}$
So accelerating at a constant rate would involve breaking the speed limit.
[4 marks available — 1 mark for using a suvat equation to find v, 1 mark for the correct value of v, 1 mark for converting 30 ms^{-1} to miles per hour or 60 miles per hour to ms^{-1}, 1 mark for the correct conclusion with reasoning]

Q10 a) $s = 300,\ u = 0,\ a = 6,\ t = t$
$s = ut + \frac{1}{2}at^2$
$300 = 0 \times t + (\frac{1}{2} \times 6 \times t^2) \Rightarrow 3t^2 = 300 \Rightarrow t^2 = 100$
$t = 10$ seconds (time can't be negative, so reject $t = -10$).
[2 marks available — 1 mark for using a suvat equation to find t, 1 mark for the correct answer]

b) For stage 1: $v = u + at = 0 + 6 \times 10 = 60 \text{ ms}^{-1}$
For stage 2:
$u_2 = 60,\ v_2 = 0,\ s_2 = 150,\ t_2 = t_2$
$s = \left(\frac{u+v}{2}\right)t \Rightarrow 150 = \left(\frac{60+0}{2}\right)t_2 \Rightarrow t_2 = 5$ seconds
[3 marks available — 1 mark for finding the final velocity for stage 1, 1 mark for using a suvat equation to find t, 1 mark for the correct answer]

Q11 a) For the first 5 seconds: $s_1 = s_1,\ u_1 = 6,\ a_1 = 1,\ t_1 = 5$
$s = ut + \frac{1}{2}at^2$
$s_1 = 6 \times 5 + (\frac{1}{2} \times 1 \times 5^2) = 42.5 \text{ m}$
[2 marks available — 1 mark for using a suvat equation to find s, 1 mark for the correct answer]

b) $v = u + at$
$v_1 = 6 + (1 \times 5) = 11 \text{ ms}^{-1}$
[2 marks available — 1 mark for using a suvat equation to find v, 1 mark for the correct answer]

c) For the second interval: $s_2 = s_2,\ v_2 = 14,\ u_2 = 11,\ a_2 = 2$
$v^2 = u^2 + 2as$
$14^2 = 11^2 + (2 \times 2 \times s_2) \Rightarrow s_2 = 18.75 \text{ m}$
[2 marks available — 1 mark for using a suvat equation to find s, 1 mark for the correct answer]

d) $v = u + at$
$14 = 11 + (2 \times t_2) \Rightarrow t_2 = 1.5$ seconds
[2 marks available — 1 mark for using a suvat equation to find t, 1 mark for the correct answer]

e) Total time $= 5 + 1.5 + \frac{60}{14} = 10.785...$ seconds.
Total displacement $= 42.5 + 18.75 + 60 = 121.25$ m.
Average velocity = displacement ÷ time
$= 121.25 \div 10.785... = 11.2 \text{ ms}^{-1}$ (1 d.p.)
[3 marks available — 1 mark for the total time, 1 mark for the total displacement, 1 mark for the average velocity]

Q12 If $s < 150$, she won't hit the obstacle.
$v^2 = u^2 + 2as$ rearranges to give $\frac{v^2 - u^2}{2a} = s$.
$v = 0$ and $u = 30$, so $\frac{v^2 - u^2}{2a} < 150 \Rightarrow \frac{-900}{2a} < 150$
Since a must be negative, $-900 > 300a \Rightarrow a < -3 \text{ ms}^{-2}$
[4 marks available — 1 mark for making s the subject, 1 mark for expressing a correct inequality, 1 mark for substituting into the inequality, 1 mark for the correct answer]

Q13
U ms^{-1} → 20 ms^{-1} → tunnel 20 ms^{-1} → U ms^{-1} →
$t = 0$ $t = 15$ $t = 40$ $t = 70$

a) While the bus is in the tunnel, $s = s,\ u = 20,\ a = 0,\ t = 25$
$s = ut + \frac{1}{2}at^2$
$s = (20 \times 25) + 0 = 500 \text{ m}$

b) Before the tunnel: $s = s_1,\ u = U,\ v = 20,\ t = 15$
$s_1 = \left(\frac{u+v}{2}\right)t \Rightarrow s_1 = \left(\frac{U+20}{2}\right) \times 15$
After tunnel: $s = s_2,\ u = 20,\ v = U,\ t = 30$
$s_2 = \left(\frac{u+v}{2}\right)t = \left(\frac{20+U}{2}\right) \times 30$
Total distance travelled $= s_1 + 500 + s_2$:
$1580 = 15\left(\frac{U+20}{2}\right) + 500 + 30\left(\frac{20+U}{2}\right)$
$1080 = 45\left(\frac{U+20}{2}\right) \Rightarrow 48 = U + 20 \Rightarrow U = 28 \text{ ms}^{-1}$

Exercise 7.5 — Gravity

Q1 $s = s,\ u = 0,\ a = 9.8,\ t = 3$
$s = ut + \frac{1}{2}at^2$
$s = 0 + \frac{1}{2} \times 9.8 \times 3^2 = 44.1 \text{ m}$

Q2 $u = 14,\ v = 0,\ a = -9.8,\ t = t$
$v = u + at$
$0 = 14 - 9.8t \Rightarrow t = 14 \div 9.8 = 1.43$ seconds (3 s.f.)

Q3 a) $s = 5,\ u = 0,\ a = 9.8,\ t = t$
$s = ut + \frac{1}{2}at^2$
$5 = 0 + \frac{1}{2} \times 9.8 \times t^2$
$t^2 = 1.02... \Rightarrow t = 1.01$ s (3 s.f.)

b) $s = 5,\ u = 0,\ v = v,\ a = 9.8$
$v^2 = u^2 + 2as$
$v^2 = 0 + 2 \times 9.8 \times 5 \Rightarrow v^2 = 98 \Rightarrow v = 9.90 \text{ ms}^{-1}$ (3 s.f.)

Q4 a) $s = s,\ u = 0,\ a = 9.8,\ t = 4$
$s = ut + \frac{1}{2}at^2$
$s = 0 + \frac{1}{2} \times 9.8 \times 4^2 = 78.4 \text{ m}$
[2 marks available — 1 mark for using a suvat equation to find s, 1 mark for the correct answer]

b) $v = u + at$
$v = 0 + 9.8 \times 4 = 39.2 \text{ ms}^{-1}$
[2 marks available — 1 mark for using a suvat equation to find v, 1 mark for the correct answer]

Q5 a) Taking upwards as positive:
$s = s,\ u = 30,\ v = 0,\ a = -9.8$
$v^2 = u^2 + 2as$
$0 = 30^2 + (2 \times -9.8 \times s)$
$s = 900 \div 19.6 = 45.918... = 45.9$ m (3 s.f.)

b) $s = 0,\ u = 30,\ a = -9.8,\ t = t$
$s = ut + \frac{1}{2}at^2$
$0 = 30t + \frac{1}{2} \times -9.8t^2$
$0 = 30t - 4.9t^2$
$0 = t(30 - 4.9t) \Rightarrow t = 0$ or $(30 - 4.9t) = 0$
$30 = 4.9t \Rightarrow t = 30 \div 4.9 = 6.1224... = 6.12$ s (3 s.f.)

c) $u = 30,\ v = v,\ a = -9.8,\ t = 2$
$v = u + at$
$v = 30 + (-9.8 \times 2) = 10.4 \text{ ms}^{-1}$
v is positive, so the object is moving upwards.

Q6 a) Taking upwards as positive: $u = u,\ v = -20,\ a = -9.8,\ t = 3$
$v = u + at$
$-20 = u - 9.8 \times 3 \Rightarrow u = 9.4 \text{ ms}^{-1}$

b) $s = -d,\ v = -20,\ a = -9.8,\ t = 3$
$s = vt - \frac{1}{2}at^2$
$-d = (-20 \times 3) + (4.9 \times 9) \Rightarrow d = 15.9 \text{ m}$

Q7 a) Taking upwards as positive: $s = s, u = 8, v = 0, a = -9.8$
$v^2 = u^2 + 2as$
$0 = 8^2 + (2 \times -9.8s)$
$s = 64 \div 19.6 = 3.265...$
Thrown from 5 m above ground,
so max height = 3.265... + 5 = 8.27 m (3 s.f.)

b) $s = 8 - 5 = 3, u = 8, a = -9.8, t = t$
$s = ut + \frac{1}{2}at^2$
$3 = 8t + \frac{1}{2} \times -9.8t^2 \Rightarrow 4.9t^2 - 8t + 3 = 0$
Solve using the quadratic formula:
$t = \frac{8 \pm \sqrt{8^2 - (4 \times 4.9 \times 3)}}{9.8}$
$t = 0.583...$ or $t = 1.049...$
So required time is given by:
1.049... – 0.583... = 0.465 s (3 s.f.)

Q8 a) Take upwards as positive.
p is the time that the object is at its highest point.
So $u = 24.5, v = 0, a = -9.8, t = p$
$v = u + at$
$0 = 24.5 - 9.8p \Rightarrow p = 24.5 \div 9.8 = 2.5$ s

b) q is the time that the object lands. From the graph, this is 29.4 m below the point of projection.
$s = -29.4, u = 24.5, a = -9.8, t = q$
$s = ut + \frac{1}{2}at^2 \Rightarrow -29.4 = 24.5q - \frac{1}{2}(9.8)q^2$
Dividing each term by 4.9, and rearranging:
$q^2 - 5q - 6 = 0 \Rightarrow (q - 6)(q + 1) = 0 \Rightarrow q = 6$ or $q = -1$
q is a time, and must be positive, so $q = 6$ s

c) r is the object's max height.
$s = s, u = 24.5, v = 0, a = -9.8$
$v^2 = u^2 + 2as$
$0 = 24.5^2 + (2 \times -9.8s) \Rightarrow s = 24.5^2 \div 19.6 = 30.625$
The object was projected from 29.4 m above the ground, so:
$r = 30.625 + 29.4 = 60.025$ m

Q9 a) Object B would travel more quickly, since they both have the same starting velocity but the acceleration due to gravity is higher on the Earth.
[1 mark for the correct answer with a correct explanation]

b) Take downwards as positive: $s = 10, u = 0, v = v, a = 1.62$
$v^2 = u^2 + 2as$
$v^2 = 0^2 + (2 \times 1.62 \times 10)$
$v^2 = 32.4 \Rightarrow v = 5.7$ ms^{-1} (1 d.p.)
[2 marks available — 1 mark for using a suvat equation to find v, 1 mark for the correct answer]

c) Take upwards as positive: $s = 10, u = u, v = 0, a = -9.8$
$v^2 = u^2 + 2as$
$0 = u^2 + (2 \times -9.8 \times 10)$
$u^2 = 196 \Rightarrow u = 14$ ms^{-1}
[2 marks available — 1 mark for using a suvat equation to find u, 1 mark for the correct answer]

d) E.g. the differences in the air resistance, caused by differences in the atmospheres.
[1 mark for any sensible answer]

Q10 a) Take upwards as positive: $s = -1.7, u = 9, a = -9.8, t = t$
$s = ut + \frac{1}{2}at^2$
$-1.7 = 9t + \frac{1}{2} \times (-9.8)t^2 \Rightarrow 4.9t^2 - 9t - 1.7 = 0$
Solve using the quadratic formula:
$t = \frac{9 \pm \sqrt{(-9)^2 - (4 \times 4.9 \times -1.7)}}{9.8}$
$t = -0.172...$ or $t = 2.009...$
t must be positive, so $t = 2.01$ seconds (2 d.p)
You may have used $v^2 = u^2 + 2as$ to find v then used this in $v = u + at$, which avoids dealing with a quadratic.
[4 marks available — 1 mark for substituting all values in correctly, 1 mark for a correct method to find the values of t, 1 mark for rejecting the incorrect value of t, 1 mark for the correct answer]

b) Taking upwards as positive: $v = 0, u = 9, a = -9.8, s = s$
$v^2 = u^2 + 2as$
$0^2 = 9^2 + (2 \times -9.8 \times s)$
$19.6s = 81 \Rightarrow s = 4.132...$ m = 4.13 m (2 d.p.)
[2 marks available — 1 mark for using a suvat equation to find s, 1 mark for the correct answer]

c) Taking upwards as positive:
$v = 0, u = u, a = -9.8, s = 4.132... + 2 = 6.132...$
$v^2 = u^2 + 2as$
$0^2 = u^2 + (2 \times -9.8 \times 6.132...)$
$u^2 = 120.2 \Rightarrow u = 10.963...$ ms^{-1} or $-10.963...$ ms^{-1}
u must be positive, so $u = 11.0$ ms^{-1} (3 s.f.)
[2 marks available — 1 mark for using a suvat equation to find u, 1 mark for the correct answer]

Q11 Taking downwards as positive:
The closer to the ground it is projected from, the less initial velocity will be needed to hit the ground in 0.2 s.
The minimum displacement is 70 cm + 1.2 m = 1.9 m.
$s = 1.9, u = u, a = 9.8, t = 0.2$
$s = ut + \frac{1}{2}at^2$
$1.9 = 0.2u + \frac{1}{2} \times 9.8 \times 0.2^2$
$0.2u = 1.704 \Rightarrow u = 8.52$
So the minimum speed is 8.52 ms^{-1}.
[3 marks available — 1 mark for choosing least displacement, 1 mark for using a suvat equation to find u, 1 mark for the correct answer]

Q12 a) Take downwards as positive:
$s = s, u = 0, a = 9.8, t = 2$
$s = ut + \frac{1}{2}at^2$
$s = 0 + (\frac{1}{2} \times 9.8 \times 2^2) = 19.6$
So the height was 19.6 m.

b) $v = u + at$
$v = 0 + 9.8 \times 2 = 19.6$
So the speed was 19.6 ms^{-1}.

c) $v = v, u = -29.4, a = 9.8, s = 19.6$
$v^2 = u^2 + 2as$
$v^2 = (-29.4)^2 + (2 \times 9.8 \times 19.6)$
$v^2 = 1248.52 \Rightarrow v = \pm 35.334...$
So the ball hits the ground with a speed of 35.3 ms^{-1} (3 s.f.)

d) $v = u + at$
$35.334... = -29.4 + 9.8t$
$9.8t = 64.734... \Rightarrow t = 6.60$ seconds (3 s.f.)

e) E.g. there is no air resistance.

Q13 Consider the motion from the tree to where it reaches 2 ms^{-1}:
$u = 0, v = 2, a = 9.8, t = t$
$v = u + at$
$2 = 0 + 9.8t \Rightarrow t = 0.204...$ seconds.
So the total time of the fall was 0.304... seconds.
Now consider the whole journey:
$u = 0, a = 9.8, t = 0.304...$ seconds
$s = ut + \frac{1}{2}at^2$
$s = 0 + \frac{1}{2} \times 9.8 \times 0.304...^2 = 0.453...$ m.
The acorn fell from 0.45 m (2 d.p.) above the ground.
You could also work out s for each stage of the drop separately and then add them together.

Q14 a) Taking upwards as positive:
$s = s, u = 12, v = 0, a = -9.8$
$v^2 = u^2 + 2as$
$0 = 12^2 - 2 \times 9.8s$
$s = 144 \div 19.6 = 7.3469... = 7.35$ m (3 s.f.)

b) $u = 12, v = 0, a = -9.8, t = t$
$v = u + at$
$0 = 12 - 9.8t \Rightarrow t = 12 \div 9.8 = 1.2244... = 1.22$ s (3 s.f.)

c) Distance between 5th and 8th floors = 7.3469...
So distance between each floor = 7.3469... ÷ 3
Distance between ground and 5th floor = 5(7.3469... ÷ 3) = 12.244...
So $s = -12.244...$, $u = 12$, $v = v$, $a = -9.8$
$v^2 = u^2 + 2as = 12^2 + (2 \times -9.8 \times -12.244...)$
$v^2 = 384 \Rightarrow v = 19.595... = 19.6\ \text{ms}^{-1}$ (3 s.f.)

Q15 a) Take upwards as positive:
$s = 77.5$, $u = 40$, $a = -9.8$, $t = t$
$s = ut + \frac{1}{2}at^2$
$77.5 = 40t - 4.9t^2 \Rightarrow 4.9t^2 - 40t + 77.5 = 0$
Solve using the quadratic formula:
$$t = \frac{40 \pm \sqrt{(-40)^2 - (4 \times 4.9 \times 77.5)}}{9.8}$$
$t = 3.163...$ or $t = 5$ seconds.
[4 marks available — 1 mark for substituting all values in correctly, 1 mark for a correct method to find the values of t, 1 mark for each correct value of t]
You may have used another suvat equation to find the velocities where s = 77.5, and then used your answers to find t without dealing with a quadratic.

b) From part a) and using symmetry of the velocity-time graph, the time when the particle reaches its greatest height is
$t = \frac{3.163... + 5}{2} = 4.081...$ seconds.
Again, using symmetry, the other time is
4.081... + (4.081... – 3.5) = 4.663... seconds.
[2 marks available — 1 mark for using the symmetry of the graph, 1 mark for the correct answer]

Q16 a) Take upwards as positive.
When the projectile is moving between the two targets:
$s = 120$, $u = u$, $a = -9.8$, $t = 3$
$s = ut + \frac{1}{2}at^2$
$120 = 3u + \frac{1}{2}(-9.8 \times 3^2)$
$3u = 164.1$
$u = 54.7\ \text{ms}^{-1}$ — this is the speed of the projectile as it passes the first target. When the projectile is moving between the point of projection and the first target:
$s = 150$, $u = u$, $v = 54.7$, $a = -9.8$
$v^2 = u^2 + 2as$
$54.7^2 = u^2 + (2 \times -9.8 \times 150)$
$u^2 = 5932.09 \Rightarrow u = 77.020...$
So the projectile is projected at 77.0 ms⁻¹ (3 s.f.)

b) $s = s$, $u = 77.020...$, $v = 0$, $a = -9.8$
$v^2 = u^2 + 2as$
$0 = 77.020...^2 + (2 \times -9.8s)$
$s = 77.020...^2 \div 19.6 = 302.657...$
The projectile is projected from 50 m below ground, so the max height above ground is:
302.657... – 50 = 252.657... = 253 m (3 s.f.)

c) $u = 77.020...$, $v = 54.7$, $a = -9.8$, $t = t$
$v = u + at$
$54.7 = 77.020... - 9.8t$
$t = (77.020... - 54.7) \div 9.8 = 2.2775... = 2.28$ s (3 s.f.)

Exercise 7.6 — More Complicated Problems

Q1 a) Displacement is the area under the graph.
Using area of a trapezium: $s = \left(\frac{u+v}{2}\right)t$

b) Substitute $t = \frac{v-u}{a}$ into $s = \left(\frac{u+v}{2}\right)t$:
$s = \left(\frac{u+v}{2}\right)\left(\frac{v-u}{a}\right)$
$\Rightarrow 2as = (u + v)(v - u)$
$\Rightarrow 2as = uv - u^2 + v^2 - vu$
$\Rightarrow v^2 = u^2 + 2as$

Q2 a) For the acceleration period, $a = \frac{5}{8}\ \text{ms}^{-2}$
For the deceleration period, $a = -2.5\ \text{ms}^{-2}$.
So the graph would be steeper during the deceleration period.
[2 marks available — 1 mark for acceleration, 1 mark for the correct answer with reason]

b) $u = 5$, $v = 0$, $a = -2.5$, $t = t$
$v = u + at$
$0 = 5 - 2.5t \Rightarrow t = 2$ seconds
[2 marks available — 1 mark for the correct use of a suvat equation to find t, 1 mark for the correct answer]

c) During acceleration, $s = \left(\frac{u+v}{2}\right)t = 5 \times 8 \div 2 = 20$ m.
During the period of constant velocity, $s = 5 \times 20 = 100$ m.
During deceleration, $v^2 = u^2 + 2as$.
$0 = 5^2 + (2 \times -2.5s) \Rightarrow s = 5$ m. The total distance is 125 m.
[2 marks available — 1 mark for a correct method, 1 mark for the correct answer]
You could also sketch a velocity-time graph for the situation and find the area underneath it using the formula for the area of a trapezium.

Q3 a) $s = 28$, $u = 2$, $v = 6$, $t = t$
$s = \left(\frac{u+v}{2}\right)t$
$28 = \left(\frac{2+6}{2}\right)t = 4t \Rightarrow t = 7$ s

b)

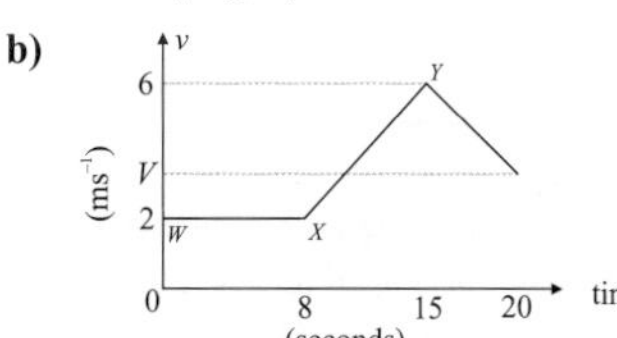

c) Area under the graph gives the distance travelled.

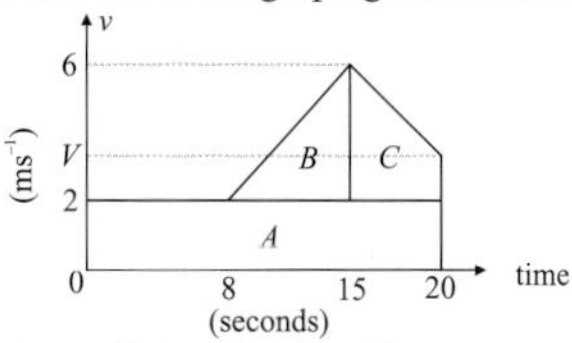

Area of $A = 20 \times 2 = 40$
Area of $B = \left(\frac{7 \times 4}{2}\right) = 14$
Area of $C = \left(\frac{4 + (V-2)}{2}\right) \times 5 = 5 + 2.5V$
Total area = $40 + 14 + 5 + 2.5V = 59 + 2.5V$
Total distance travelled is 67 m, so:
$59 + 2.5V = 67 \Rightarrow 2.5V = 8 \Rightarrow V = 3.2\ \text{ms}^{-1}$

Q4 a)

b) The motorbike overtakes the van T seconds after setting off. At this point, the two vehicles will have covered the same distance since $t = 0$, so the areas under the graphs up to this point will be the same. Van area = $14 \times T$
Motorbike area = $\left(\frac{T + (T-20)}{2}\right) \times 18 = 18T - 180$
Making the two areas equal to each other:
$14T = 18T - 180 \Rightarrow 4T = 180 \Rightarrow T = 45$ seconds

Q5 a) Write down the *suvat* variables for X and Y, considering the movement of each car separately. In each case, take the direction that the car moves as being positive.

$u_X = 15$, $a_X = 1$, $t_X = t$
$u_Y = 20$, $a_Y = 2$, $t_Y = t$

Using $s = ut + \frac{1}{2}at^2$:

$s_X = 15t + \frac{1}{2}t^2$
$s_Y = 20t + t^2$

They collide when $s_X + s_Y = 30$:

$15t + \frac{1}{2}t^2 + 20t + t^2 = 30$

$35t + \frac{3}{2}t^2 = 30$

Multiplying throughout by 2 and rearranging:
$3t^2 + 70t - 60 = 0$
Solve using the quadratic formula:

$t = \frac{-70 \pm \sqrt{70^2 - (4 \times 3 \times (-60))}}{6}$

$t = 0.8277...$ or $t = -24.161...$ so $t = 0.828$ s (3 s.f.)

b) Use $v = u + at$ on the two cars separately. Again, take the direction of motion as being positive for each car.
X: $v_X = 15 + 0.8277... = 15.8$ ms^{-1} (3 s.f.)
Y: $v_Y = 20 + 2(0.8277...) = 21.7$ ms^{-1} (3 s.f.)

c) $s = ut + \frac{1}{2}at^2$
$s_X = (15 \times 0.8277...) + \frac{1}{2}(0.8277...)^2$
$s_X = 12.759... = 12.8$ m (3 s.f.)

Q6 a)

b) The cyclists are cycling alongside each other after 11 seconds, so they have the same displacement, i.e. the areas under the graphs are equal.
Area under Ava's graph:

$7U + \frac{1}{2} \times (11 - 7) \times (V + U) = 9U + 2V$

Area under Budi's graph:

$\frac{1}{2} \times (5 + 11) \times V = 8V$

So $8V = 9U + 2V \Rightarrow 6V = 9U \Rightarrow V = \frac{3}{2}U$

c) Area under Budi's graph $= 8V = 36$ m
So $V = 4.5$ ms^{-1} and $U = \frac{2}{3} \times V = 3$ ms^{-1}.

Q7 a)

b) From P to Q: $u = 15$, $v = U$, $a = 3$, $t = 4$
$v = u + at$
$U = 15 + (3 \times 4) = 27$ ms^{-1}

c) The area under the graph from P to Q is:
$\frac{1}{2} \times (15 + 27) \times 4 = 84$
So the distance from P to Q is 84 m.
The area under the graph from Q to R is $27 \times 6 = 162$
So the distance from Q to R is 162 m.
The total distance travelled is 405 m, so the distance the particle travels in coming to rest is: $405 - 162 - 84 = 159$ m
So from R to rest: $s = 159$, $u = U = 27$, $v = 0$, $t = T$

$s = \left(\frac{u+v}{2}\right)t \Rightarrow 159 = \left(\frac{27}{2}\right)T \Rightarrow T = 11.777...$
$= 11.8$ s (3 s.f.)

So the particle comes to rest $10 + 11.8 = 21.8$ s (3 s.f.) after passing P.

d) Gradient of graph $= \frac{0 - U}{T} = \frac{-27}{11.777...} = -2.292...$
So it decelerates at a rate of 2.29 ms^{-2} (3 s.f.)

Q8 a) (i) Convert velocity of golf cart A to ms^{-1}:
27 kmh^{-1} × 1000 ÷ (60 × 60) = 7.5 ms^{-1}

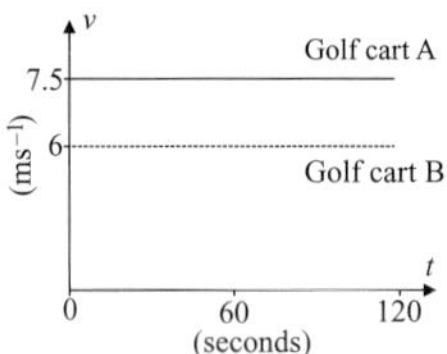

[2 marks available — 1 mark for evaluating each velocity in the same unit, 1 mark for the correct graph with labels]

(ii) Golf cart A: distance = 7.5 ms^{-1} × 120 s = 900 m
Golf cart B: distance = 6 ms^{-1} × 120 s = 720 m

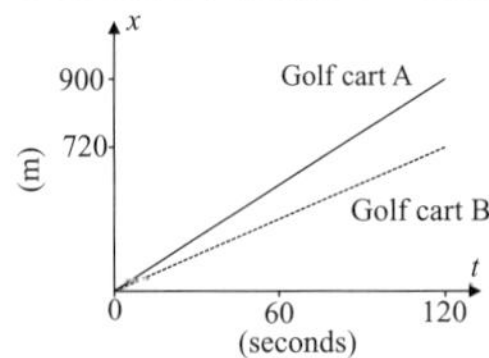

[2 marks available — 1 mark for evaluating each displacement in the same unit, 1 mark for the correct graph with labels]

b) Golf cart A travels 900 m and golf cart B travels 720 m in the first two minutes. Golf cart A then travels 50 m more before coming to a stop.
So after the first two minutes, golf cart B must travel a further 950 – 720 = 230 m to reach golf cart A.
$s = 230$, $u = 6$, $a = -0.06$, $t = t$

$s = ut + \frac{1}{2}at^2$

$230 = 6t + \frac{1}{2} \times -0.06\,t^2 \Rightarrow 0.03t^2 - 6t + 230 = 0$
Solve using the quadratic formula:

$t = \frac{-(-6) \pm \sqrt{(-6)^2 - (4 \times 0.03 \times 230)}}{2 \times 0.03}$

$t \approx 51.7$ or $t \approx 148.3$
Reject $t = 148.3$, since golf cart B would stop the first time it reaches the same distance as golf cart A, so $t = 51.7$ seconds.
So golf cart B travelled for $51.7 + 120 = 171.7$ seconds in total.
[4 marks available — 1 mark for using a suvat equation to find t, 1 mark for a correct method to solve the quadratic, 1 mark for each correct value of t]

Q9 a)

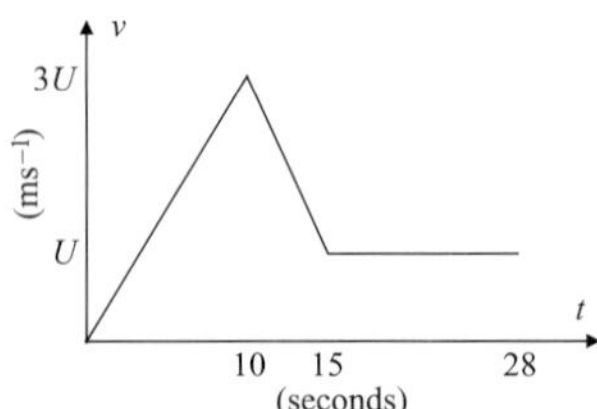

b) $u = 3U$, $v = U$, $a = a$, $t = 5$
$v = u + at$
$U = 3U + 5a \Rightarrow a = -\frac{2}{5}U$

c) Area under the graph:

$304 = \frac{1}{2} \times 10 \times 3U + \frac{1}{2} \times 5 \times (3U - U) + 13U$
$= 15U + 5U + 13U = 33U$

$U = 304 \div 33 = 9.21$ ms^{-1} (3 s.f.)

Q10 a) Using $s = ut + \frac{1}{2}at^2$ and taking up as positive:
Ball A: $s = s_A$, $u = 0$, $a = -9.8$, $t = t$
$s_A = 0t + \frac{1}{2} \times -9.8 \times t^2 = -4.9t^2$
Ball B: $s = s_B$, $u = 6$, $a = -9.8$, $t = t$
$s_B = 6t + \frac{1}{2} \times -9.8 \times t^2 = 6t - 4.9t^2$
After t seconds, Ball A is $(8 + s_A)$ above the ground, where s_A is negative, and Ball B is $(4 + s_B)$ above the ground, where s_B is positive. Since they must be in the same place at the same time in order to collide, they collide when:
$8 - 4.9t^2 = 4 + 6t - 4.9t^2 \Rightarrow 4 = 6t \Rightarrow t = \frac{2}{3}$ seconds

b) Height above ground $= 4 + s_B = 4 + 6\left(\frac{2}{3}\right) - 4.9\left(\frac{2}{3}\right)^2$
$= 5.822... = 5.82$ m (3 s.f.)
You could have done $8 - 4.9(2/3)^2 = 5.82$ m instead.

Q11 a) Write down the *suvat* variables for the two balls:
$u_1 = 5$, $a_1 = -0.5$, $t_1 = t$
$u_2 = 4$, $a_2 = 0$, $t_2 = t - 3$
Using $s = ut + \frac{1}{2}at^2$:
First ball: $s_1 = 5t + \frac{1}{2}(-0.5)t^2 = 5t - 0.25t^2$
Second ball: $s_2 = 4(t - 3) + 0 = 4t - 12$
They are level when $s_1 = s_2$: $5t - 0.25t^2 = 4t - 12$
Multiplying throughout by 4 and rearranging:
$t^2 - 4t - 48 = 0$
Solve using the quadratic formula or by completing the square:
$(t - 2)^2 - 52 = 0 \Rightarrow t - 2 = \pm\sqrt{52} \Rightarrow t = 2 \pm \sqrt{52}$
$\Rightarrow t = 9.2111...$ or $t = -5.2111...$
So the second ball passes the first ball 9.21 s (3 s.f.) after the first ball is rolled.

b) Using $s_2 = 4t - 12$ from part a):
$s_2 = (4 \times 9.2111...) - 12 = 24.844... = 24.8$ m (3 s.f.)

c) Find the time that the first ball comes to rest using $v = u + at$ with $v = 0$: $0 = 5 - 0.5t \Rightarrow t = 10$ s
Now find the distance the first ball travels in this time using $s = ut + \frac{1}{2}at^2$:
$s_1 = (5 \times 10) + \frac{1}{2}(-0.5 \times 10^2) = 25$ m
Find the distance the second ball travels in 15 s using $s = ut + \frac{1}{2}at^2$:
$s_2 = 4(15 - 3) + 0 = 48$ m
So the second ball is 48 m – 25 m = 23 m ahead.

Q12 a) Using $s = ut + \frac{1}{2}at^2$:
Car X: $s = s_X$, $u = 16$, $a = 0$, $t = t$
$s_X = 16t$
Car Y: $s = s_Y$, $u = 28$, $a = -3$, $t = t$
$s_Y = 28t - \frac{3}{2}t^2$
$16t = 28t - \frac{3}{2}t^2 \Rightarrow \frac{3}{2}t^2 - 12t = 0 \Rightarrow \frac{3}{2}t(t - 8) = 0$
The cars are level again at $t = 8$ seconds.

b) $s = s_X = 16 \times 8 = 128$ m

Q13 a)

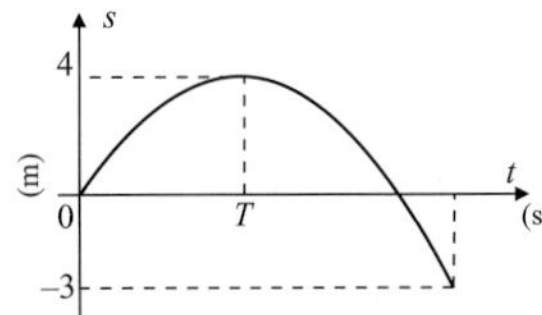

b) Consider the motion between $t = 0$ and $t = T$, taking up as positive:
$s = 4$, $v = 0$, $a = -9.8$, $t = T$
$s = vt - \frac{1}{2}at^2$
$4 = 0T - \frac{1}{2} \times -9.8 \times T^2 \Rightarrow T^2 = 4 \div 4.9$
$\Rightarrow T = \frac{2\sqrt{10}}{7} = 0.9035... = 0.904$ seconds (3 s.f.)

c) Consider the motion from $t = T$ until it hits the ground, taking down as positive:
$s = 7$, $u = 0$, $v = v$, $a = 9.8$
$v^2 = u^2 + 2as$
$v^2 = 0^2 + 2 \times 9.8 \times 7 = 137.2$
$v = \sqrt{137.2} = 11.71... = 11.7$ ms^{-1} (3 s.f.)

Q14 a)

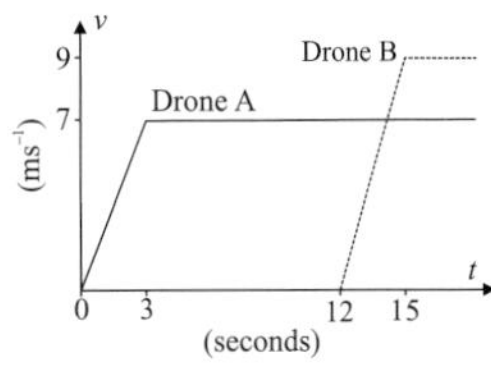

[3 marks available — 1 mark for each correctly drawn line for Drones A and B, 1 mark for correct labels]

b) Let the time when they are level be T. Find the area under each graph (each area is a trapezium, with a side on the line $t = T$).
Drone A: $\frac{1}{2} \times (T + T - 3) \times 7 = 7T - 10.5$
Drone B: $\frac{1}{2} \times (T - 12 + T - 15) \times 9 = 9T - 121.5$
At time T, Drone B has travelled 50 m less than Drone A, so
$7T - 10.5 = 9T - 121.5 + 50$
$\Rightarrow 7T - 10.5 = 9T - 71.5$
$\Rightarrow 2T = 61 \Rightarrow T = 30.5$ seconds
[4 marks available – 1 mark for the distance for Drone A in terms of T, 1 mark for the distance for Drone B in terms of T, 1 mark for an equation linking the two correctly, 1 mark for the correct answer]

Q15 a) Take upwards as the positive direction.
Find the time that ball B is at its highest point:
$u_B = 5$, $v_B = 0$, $a_B = -9.8$, $t_B = t$
$v = u + at$
$0 = 5 - 9.8t \Rightarrow t = 5 \div 9.8 = 0.5102...$
Now find the displacement of ball A at this time (remembering that A is released 1 s before B):
$u_A = 0$, $a_A = -9.8$, $t_A = 1 + 0.5102... = 1.5102...$
$s = ut + \frac{1}{2}at^2$
$s = 0 + \frac{1}{2}(-9.8 \times 1.5102...^2) = -11.1755...$
So ball A has travelled 11.2 m (3 s.f.)

b) Using $s = ut + \frac{1}{2}at^2$:
Ball A: $u_A = 0$, $a_A = -9.8$, $t_A = t$
$s = 0 + \frac{1}{2}(-9.8t^2) = -4.9t^2$
Ball B: $u_B = 5$, $a_B = -9.8$, $t_B = t - 1$
$s = 5(t - 1) + \frac{1}{2} \times -9.8(t - 1)^2$
$s = 5t - 5 - 4.9(t^2 - 2t + 1)$
$s = 14.8t - 9.9 - 4.9t^2$
So A has moved $4.9t^2$ m down from a height of 40 m, and B has moved $(14.8t - 9.9 - 4.9t^2)$ m up from a height of 10 m. A and B are at the same level when:
$40 - 4.9t^2 = 10 + 14.8t - 9.9 - 4.9t^2$
$\Rightarrow 39.9 = 14.8t \Rightarrow t = 39.9 \div 14.8 = 2.6959...$
So they become level 2.70 seconds (3 s.f.) after A is dropped.

c) Using $s = -4.9t^2$ (from part b)) for ball A:
$s = -4.9 \times (2.6959...)^2 = -35.6138...$
$40 - 35.6138... = 4.3861...$
So they are 4.39 m (3 s.f.) above the ground.

Exercise 7.7 — Displacement with Non-Uniform Acceleration

Q1 **a)** $s = 2(3)^3 - 4(3)^2 + 3 = 54 - 36 + 3 = 21$ m

b) $v = \frac{ds}{dt} = 6t^2 - 8t$

c) $v = 6(3)^2 - 8(3) = 54 - 24 = 30$ ms^{-1}

Q2 **a)** $s = \frac{1}{3}(4)^4 - 2(4)^3 + 3(4)^2 = \frac{256}{3} - 128 + 48 = \frac{16}{3}$ m

b) $a = \frac{dv}{dt} = \frac{d^2s}{dt^2}$, so first differentiate to find v:

$v = \frac{4}{3}t^3 - 6t^2 + 6t$

Then differentiate again to find a: $a = 4t^2 - 12t + 6$

When $t = 3$, $a = 4(3)^2 - 12(3) + 6 = 36 - 36 + 6 = 6$ ms^{-2}

Q3 **a)** When $t = 0$, $s = 0^4 + 0^3 + 2(0)^2 = 0$, and

$v = \frac{ds}{dt} = 4t^3 + 3t^2 + 4t = 4(0)^3 + 3(0)^2 + 4(0) = 0$

[4 marks available — 1 mark for verifying the initial displacement, 1 mark for differentiating with respect to t, 1 mark for a correct expression for v, 1 mark for verifying the initial velocity]

b) $a = \frac{dv}{dt} = 12t^2 + 6t + 4$

When $t = 5$, $a = 12(5)^2 + 6(5) + 4 = 334$ ms^{-2}

[3 marks available — 1 mark for differentiating velocity with respect to time, 1 mark for the correct expression for acceleration in terms of t, 1 mark for the correct answer]

Q4 **a)** $v = \frac{ds}{dt} = t^4 - 8t^3 + 21t^2 - 20t + 5$

At $t = 0$, $v = 0^4 - 8(0)^3 + 21(0)^2 - 20(0) + 5 = 5$ ms^{-1}

b) $a = \frac{dv}{dt} = 4t^3 - 24t^2 + 42t - 20$

At $t = 2$, $a = 4(2)^3 - 24(2)^2 + 42(2) - 20$
$= 32 - 96 + 84 - 20 = 0$ ms^{-2}

Q5 **a)** $f(t) = t^2(t - 3)(t - 4) = t^4 - 7t^3 + 12t^2$

$f(0) = (0)^4 - 7(0)^3 + 12(0)^2 = 0$, so the s-intercept is (0, 0)

$t^2(t - 3)(t - 4) = 0$, so $t = 0$, 3 and 4

So the graph meets the horizontal axis at 0, 3 and 4:

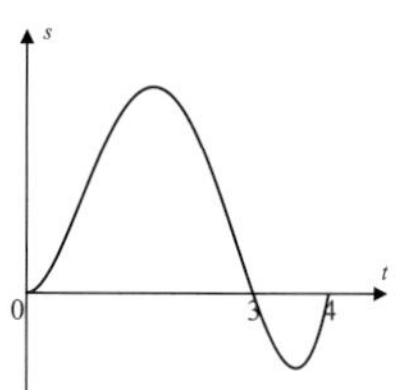

[4 marks available — 1 mark for the general shape, 1 mark for each correct x-intercept]

b) When $t = 2$, $s = 2^2(2 - 3)(2 - 4) = 8$ m *[1 mark]*

c) $s = t^2(t - 3)(t - 4) = t^4 - 7t^3 + 12t^2$, so

$v = \frac{ds}{dt} = 4t^3 - 21t^2 + 24t$ and $a = \frac{dv}{dt} = 12t^2 - 42t + 24$

When $t = 3.5$, $a = 12(3.5)^2 - 42(3.5) + 24 = 24$ ms^{-2}

[4 marks available — 1 mark for differentiating with respect to t, 1 mark for the correct expression for v, 1 mark for the correct expression for a, 1 mark for the correct answer]

Q6 **a)** You're given the 3 points where the cubic graph crosses the x-axis, so you know the roots of the function.

$s(t) = k(t - 3)(t - 5)(t - 10)$

$s(1) = k \times -2 \times -4 \times -9 = -72k$

$-72k = 14.4 \Rightarrow k = -0.2$

So $s(t) = -0.2(t - 3)(t - 5)(t - 10)$

[4 marks available — 1 mark for the factorised expression, 1 mark for including k in the factorised expression, 1 mark for substituting t = 1 and s = 14.4, 1 mark for the correct answer]

b) $s(4) = -0.2 \times 1 \times -1 \times -6 = -1.2$ m *[1 mark]*

c) $s = -0.2(t - 3)(t - 5)(t - 10)$
$= -0.2(t^2 - 8t + 15)(t - 10)$
$= -0.2(t^3 - 18t^2 + 95t - 150)$
$= -0.2t^3 + 3.6t^2 - 19t + 30$

$v = \frac{ds}{dt} = -0.6t^2 + 7.2t - 19$

$v(4) = -0.6(4)^2 + 7.2(4) - 19 = 0.2$ ms^{-1}

[4 marks available — 1 mark for getting s in a form that can be differentiated, 1 mark for differentiating with respect to t, 1 mark for a correct expression for v, 1 mark for the correct value of v when t = 4]

d) $a(t) = \frac{dv}{dt} = -1.2t + 7.2$

Equate velocity and acceleration functions:

$-1.2t + 7.2 = -0.6t^2 + 7.2t - 19$

Rearranging gives $0.6t^2 - 8.4t + 26.2 = 0$

Solve using the quadratic formula:

$t = \frac{-(-8.4) \pm \sqrt{(-8.4)^2 - (4 \times 0.6 \times 26.2)}}{1.2}$

$t \approx 4.7$ or $t \approx 9.3$

So there are two times where the numerical values are equal.

[4 marks available — 1 mark for the correct expression for a, 1 mark for equating this to v, 1 mark for correct use of quadratic formula, 1 mark for establishing there is a solution for t ≥ 0]

You could also have just shown that the discriminant is positive and that the coefficients of t^2 and t have opposite signs to prove there's at least one real, positive solution as required.

Q7 **a)** $s = 0.2(t - 5)^3 - 3(t - 5)^2$ (for $t \geq 5$) *[1 mark]*

b) Particle A: $s = 0.2(10)^3 - 3(10)^2 = -100$ m.

Particle B: $s = 0.2(5)^3 - 3(5)^2 = -50$ m.

So the distance between them is 50 m.

[2 marks available — 1 mark for the at least one correct displacement of A or B, 1 mark for the correct answer]

c) Particle A: $v = \frac{ds}{dt} = 0.6t^2 - 6t$

When $t = 10$, $v = 0.6(10)^2 - 6(10) = 0$.

Substitute $t = 5$ into the expression for v to find B's velocity:

When $t = 5$, $v = 0.6(5)^2 - 6(5) = -15$ ms^{-1}

So the difference in the speeds is 15 ms^{-1}.

[4 marks available – 1 mark for differentiating s with respect to t, 1 mark for the correct expression for v, 1 mark for at least one correct velocity of A or B, 1 mark for the correct answer]

You could have differentiated $s = 0.2(t - 5)^3 - 3(t - 5)^2$ and substituted in $t = 10$, but this is a bit trickier.

Exercise 7.8 — Velocity and Acceleration Equations

Q1 **a)** $s = \int v\,dt = \int (1 + 6t + 6t^2 - 4t^3)\,dt$
$= t + 6\left(\frac{t^2}{2}\right) + 6\left(\frac{t^3}{3}\right) - 4\left(\frac{t^4}{4}\right) + C$
$= t + 3t^2 + 2t^3 - t^4 + C$

When $t = 0$, $s = 0$: $0 = 0 + 3(0)^2 + 2(0)^3 - 0^4 + C \Rightarrow C = 0$

So $s = t + 3t^2 + 2t^3 - t^4$

b) At $t = 2$: $s = 2 + 3(2)^2 + 2(2)^3 - 2^4$
$= 2 + 12 + 16 - 16 = 14$ cm

$v = 1 + 6(2) + 6(2)^2 - 4(2)^3$
$= 1 + 12 + 24 - 32 = 5$ cm s^{-1}

Q2 **a)** $s = \int v\,dt = \int (12t^3 - 18t^2 + 2t)\,dt$
$= 12\left(\frac{t^4}{4}\right) - 18\left(\frac{t^3}{3}\right) + 2\left(\frac{t^2}{2}\right) + C$
$= 3t^4 - 6t^3 + t^2 + C$

When $t = 0$, $s = 2$: $2 = 3(0)^4 - 6(0)^3 + (0)^2 + C \Rightarrow 2 = C$

So $s = 3t^4 - 6t^3 + t^2 + 2$

b) When $t = 2$, $s = 3(2)^4 - 6(2)^3 + (2)^2 + 2$
$= 48 - 48 + 4 + 2 = 6$ m

When $t = 2$, $v = 12(2)^3 - 18(2)^2 + 2(2) = 96 - 72 + 4 = 28$ ms^{-1}

Q3 $v = \int a\,dt = \int (3t^3 - 9t^2 + 4t + 6)\,dt$
$= 3\left(\frac{t^4}{4}\right) - 9\left(\frac{t^3}{3}\right) + 4\left(\frac{t^2}{2}\right) + 6t + C_1$
$= \frac{3}{4}t^4 - 3t^3 + 2t^2 + 6t + C_1$

When $t = 2$, $v = 6$: $6 = \frac{3}{4}(2)^4 - 3(2)^3 + 2(2)^2 + 6(2) + C_1$
$= 12 - 24 + 8 + 12 + C_1$
$= 8 + C_1 \Rightarrow C_1 = -2$

So $v = \frac{3}{4}t^4 - 3t^3 + 2t^2 + 6t - 2$

Then, $s = \int v\,dt = \int (\frac{3}{4}t^4 - 3t^3 + 2t^2 + 6t - 2)\,dt$
$= \frac{3}{4}\left(\frac{t^5}{5}\right) - 3\left(\frac{t^4}{4}\right) + 2\left(\frac{t^3}{3}\right) + 6\left(\frac{t^2}{2}\right) - 2t + C_2$
$= \frac{3}{20}t^5 - \frac{3}{4}t^4 + \frac{2}{3}t^3 + 3t^2 - 2t + C_2$

When $t = 0$, $s = 0$:

$0 = \frac{3}{20}(0)^5 - \frac{3}{4}(0)^4 + \frac{2}{3}(0)^3 + 3(0)^2 - 2(0) + C_2 \Rightarrow C_2 = 0$

So $s = \frac{3}{20}t^5 - \frac{3}{4}t^4 + \frac{2}{3}t^3 + 3t^2 - 2t$

Q4 $v = \int a\,dt = \int (-6t^2 + 6t - 6)\,dt = -6\left(\frac{t^3}{3}\right) + 6\left(\frac{t^2}{2}\right) - 6t + C$
$= -2t^3 + 3t^2 - 6t + C$

When $t = 0$, $v = 0$: $0 = -2(0)^3 + 3(0)^2 - 6(0) + C \Rightarrow C = 0$

So $v = -2t^3 + 3t^2 - 6t$

When $t = 1$, $v = -2(1)^3 + 3(1)^2 - 6(1) = -2 + 3 - 6 = -5\text{ ms}^{-1}$

Since the velocity is negative, the shuttlecock is moving downwards.

Q5 **a)** When $t = 2$, $v = 3(2)^2 - 4(2) = 4\text{ ms}^{-1}$ *[1 mark]*

b) $a = \frac{dv}{dt} = 6t - 4$ *[1 mark]*

c) $s = \int v\,dt = t^3 - 2t^2 + C$

When $t = 2$, $s = 0$: $0 = 2^3 - 2(2)^2 + C \Rightarrow C = 0$

So $s = t^3 - 2t^2$

[2 marks available — 1 mark for integrating v with respect to time, 1 mark for the correct answer]

Q6 **a)** $v = 2^3 + 4(2)^2 = 24\text{ ms}^{-1}$ *[1 mark]*

b) $s = \int v\,dt = \frac{t^4}{4} + \frac{4t^3}{3} + C$

When $t = 0$, $s = 4 \Rightarrow C = 4$

So $s = \frac{t^4}{4} + \frac{4t^3}{3} + 4$

[2 marks available — 1 mark for integrating v with respect to time, 1 mark for the correct answer]

c) When $t = 3$, $s = \frac{3^4}{4} + \frac{4 \times 3^3}{3} + 4 = 60.25$ m *[1 mark]*

Q7 $v = \int a\,dt = \int t + 4\,dt = \frac{t^2}{2} + 4t + C$

When $t = 5$, $v = 6$: $6 = \frac{5^2}{2} + 4(5) + C$
$= 12.5 + 20 + C \Rightarrow C = -26.5$

When $a = 6$, $t = 2$: $v = \frac{2^2}{2} + 4 \times 2 - 26.5 = -16.5\text{ ms}^{-1}$

Q8 **a)** $x = \int v\,dt = t + \frac{1}{3}t^3 + C$

$x(2)$ is $2 \times x(4) \Rightarrow 2 + \frac{8}{3} + C = 2(4 + \frac{64}{3} + C)$
$\Rightarrow \frac{14}{3} + C = \frac{152}{3} + 2C \Rightarrow C = -46$

So $x = t + \frac{1}{3}t^3 - 46$

[4 marks available — 1 mark for integrating with respect to t, 1 mark for correct integral, 1 mark for equating x(2) and 2 × x(4), 1 mark for the full expression for x]

b) $a = \frac{dv}{dt} = 2t$. So when $t = 8$, $a = 16\text{ ms}^{-2}$.

[2 marks available — 1 mark for differentiating with respect to t, 1 mark for the correct answer]

Q9 $v = \int a\,dt = \int (-3t^2 + 6t - 4)\,dt$
$= -3\left(\frac{t^3}{3}\right) + 6\left(\frac{t^2}{2}\right) - 4t + C_1$
$= -t^3 + 3t^2 - 4t + C_1$

When $t = 1$, $v = 0$: $0 = -(1)^3 + 3(1)^2 - 4(1) + C_1$
$= -1 + 3 - 4 + C_1 \Rightarrow C_1 = 2$

So $v = -t^3 + 3t^2 - 4t + 2$

$s = \int v\,dt = \int (-t^3 + 3t^2 - 4t + 2)\,dt$
$= -\left(\frac{t^4}{4}\right) + 3\left(\frac{t^3}{3}\right) - 4\left(\frac{t^2}{2}\right) + 2t + C_2$
$= -\frac{1}{4}t^4 + t^3 - 2t^2 + 2t + C_2$

When $t = 0$, $s = 2$: $2 = -\frac{1}{4}(0)^4 + (0)^3 - 2(0)^2 + 2(0) + C_2$
$\Rightarrow 2 = C_2$

So $s = -\frac{1}{4}t^4 + t^3 - 2t^2 + 2t + 2$

Q10 **a)** Since a is a quadratic, v is a cubic.

Roots of v are at $t = 2$, 4 and 6, so $v(t) = k(t - 2)(t - 4)(t - 6)$

$v(0) = 24$, so $24 = k \times -2 \times -4 \times -6 = -48k \Rightarrow k = -0.5$

So $v = -0.5(t - 2)(t - 4)(t - 6)$

[3 marks available — 1 mark for deducing that v is a cubic, 1 mark for the correct linear factors, 1 mark for finding k]

b) Expanding the brackets in the expression above for v gives:

$v = -0.5t^3 + 6t^2 - 22t + 24$

$s = \int v\,dt = -\frac{t^4}{8} + 2t^3 - 11t^2 + 24t + C$

It is given that $C = 10$, so when $t = 5$,

$v = -\frac{5^4}{8} + 2(5)^3 - 11(5)^2 + 24(5) + 10$
$= 26.875 = 26.9$ m (3 s.f.)

[4 marks available — 1 mark for the correct expansion, 1 mark for attempting to integrate, 1 mark for the correct expression for v, 1 mark for the correct answer]

Exercise 7.9 — Maximum and Minimum Points

Q1 **a)** $s = 2t^4 - 8t^3 + 8t^2$

At $t = 2$, $s = 2(2)^4 - 8(2)^3 + 8(2)^2 = 32 - 64 + 32 = 0$

So the yo-yo is released from $s = 0$ when $t = 0$, and at time $t = 2$, the yo-yo returns to $s = 0$.

b) $\frac{ds}{dt} = 8t^3 - 24t^2 + 16t$

At maximum displacement, $\frac{ds}{dt} = 0$

$\Rightarrow 8t^3 - 24t^2 + 16t = 0 \Rightarrow t^3 - 3t^2 + 2t = 0$
$\Rightarrow t(t^2 - 3t + 2) = 0 \Rightarrow t(t - 1)(t - 2) = 0$

So $t = 0$, $t = 1$ or $t = 2$

Check for negative $\frac{d^2s}{dt^2} = 24t^2 - 48t + 16$:

At $t = 0$, $\frac{d^2s}{dt^2} = 24(0)^2 - 48(0) + 16$
$= 16 > 0$ (local minimum)

At $t = 1$, $\frac{d^2s}{dt^2} = 24(1)^2 - 48(1) + 16$
$= -8 < 0$ (local maximum)

At $t = 2$, $\frac{d^2s}{dt^2} = 24(2)^2 - 48(2) + 16$
$= 16 > 0$ (local minimum)

So the maximum displacement is at time $t = 1$:

$s = 2(1)^4 - 8(1)^3 + 8(1)^2 = 2$

So the maximum displacement (length of the string) is 2 feet.

Q2 **a)** $v = t^3 - 6t^2 + 9t \Rightarrow \frac{dv}{dt} = 3t^2 - 12t + 9$

At maximum velocity, $\frac{dv}{dt} = 0$:

$\Rightarrow 3t^2 - 12t + 9 = 0 \Rightarrow t^2 - 4t + 3 = 0 \Rightarrow (t - 1)(t - 3) = 0$

So $t = 1$ or $t = 3$

Check for negative $\frac{d^2v}{dt^2} = 6t - 12$:

When $t = 1$, $\frac{d^2v}{dt^2} = 6(1) - 12 = 6 - 12 = -6 < 0$ (local maximum)

When $t = 3$, $\frac{d^2v}{dt^2} = 6(3) - 12 = 18 - 12 = 6 > 0$ (local minimum)

So the cat reaches its maximum velocity at time $t = 1$ s.

b) $s = \int v\,dt = \int (t^3 - 6t^2 + 9t)\,dt = \left(\frac{t^4}{4}\right) - 6\left(\frac{t^3}{3}\right) + 9\left(\frac{t^2}{2}\right) + C$
$= \frac{1}{4}t^4 - 2t^3 + \frac{9}{2}t^2 + C$

At $t = 0$, $s = 5$: $5 = \frac{1}{4}(0)^4 - 2(0)^3 + \frac{9}{2}(0)^2 + C \Rightarrow C = 5$

Now find s at time $t = 2$:

$s = \frac{1}{4}t^4 - 2t^3 + \frac{9}{2}t^2 + 5 = \frac{1}{4}(2)^4 - 2(2)^3 + \frac{9}{2}(2)^2 + 5$
$= 4 - 16 + 18 + 5 = 11$ m

Q3 a) $s = 2 + 3t - 2t^2 \Rightarrow v = \frac{ds}{dt} = 3 - 4t$

$\frac{ds}{dt} = 0 \Rightarrow 3 - 4t = 0 \Rightarrow t = \frac{3}{4}$

$\frac{d^2s}{dt^2} = -4 < 0$ so $t = \frac{3}{4}$ must be a maximum.

The function is a quadratic so the maximum must be the overall maximum.

At $t = \frac{3}{4}$, $s = 2 + 3\left(\frac{3}{4}\right) - 2\left(\frac{3}{4}\right)^2$
$= 2 + \frac{9}{4} - \frac{9}{8} = 3\frac{1}{8} = 3.125$ m

So the maximum displacement is 3.125 m.

b) $s = t^2 + t^3 - 1.25t^4 \Rightarrow \frac{ds}{dt} = 2t + 3t^2 - 5t^3$

$\frac{ds}{dt} = 0 \Rightarrow 2t + 3t^2 - 5t^3 = 0$
$\Rightarrow -t(5t^2 - 3t - 2) = 0 \Rightarrow -t(5t + 2)(t - 1) = 0$

So $t = 0$, $t = -0.4$ or $t = 1$

We can ignore $t = -0.4$ as we are only interested in $t \geq 0$. Check for negative $\frac{d^2s}{dt^2} = 2 + 6t - 15t^2$:

At $t = 0$, $\frac{d^2s}{dt^2} = 2 + 6(0) - 15(0)^2 = 2 > 0$ (local minimum)

At $t = 1$, $\frac{d^2s}{dt^2} = 2 + 6(1) - 15(1)^2 = -7 < 0$ (local maximum)

The graph of $s = t^2 + t^3 - 1.25t^4$ looks like this:

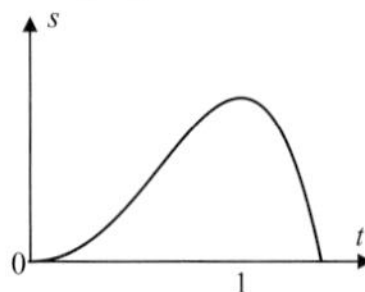

So the maximum displacement happens at $t = 1$:
$s = 1 + 1 - 1.25(1) = 0.75$ m

c) $s = -3t^4 + 8t^3 - 6t^2 + 16 \Rightarrow \frac{ds}{dt} = -12t^3 + 24t^2 - 12t$

$\frac{ds}{dt} = 0 \Rightarrow -12t^3 + 24t^2 - 12t = 0 \Rightarrow t^3 - 2t^2 + t = 0$
$\Rightarrow t(t^2 - 2t + 1) = 0 \Rightarrow t(t - 1)^2 = 0$

So $t = 0$ or $t = 1$

Check for negative $\frac{d^2s}{dt^2} = -36t^2 + 48t - 12$

At $t = 0$, $\frac{d^2s}{dt^2} = -36(0)^2 + 48(0) - 12$
$= -12 < 0$ (local maximum)

At $t = 1$, $\frac{d^2s}{dt^2} = -36(1)^2 + 48(1) - 12$
$= -36 + 48 - 12 = 0$

So there could be a maximum, minimum or point of inflection at $t = 1$. There are two possible local maximums, so check the value of s at both:

At $t = 0$, $s = -3(0)4 + 8(0)3 - 6(0)2 + 16 = 16$ m

At $t = 1$, $s = -3(1)4 + 8(1)3 - 6(1)2 + 16$
$= -3 + 8 - 6 + 16 = 15$ m

The graph of $s = -3t^4 + 8t^3 - 6t^2 + 16$ looks like this:

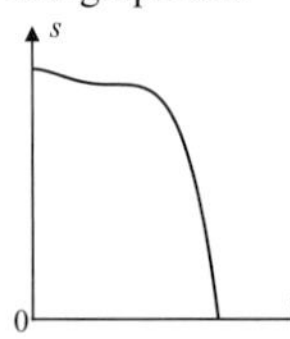

So the maximum displacement happens at $t = 0$, where $s = 16$ m.

Q4 a) $s = 15t + 6t^2 - t^3 \Rightarrow v = \frac{ds}{dt} = 15 + 12t - 3t^2$

$\frac{dv}{dt} = 12 - 6t$

$\frac{dv}{dt} = 0 \Rightarrow 12 - 6t = 0 \Rightarrow t = 2$

$\frac{d^2v}{dt^2} = -6 < 0$ so $t = 2$ must give a maximum.

The function for v is a quadratic so the maximum must be the overall maximum.

At $t = 2$, $v = 15 + 12(2) - 3(2)^2 = 15 + 24 - 12 = 27$

So the maximum velocity is 27 ms^{-1}.

b) $s = \frac{-t^5}{20} + \frac{t^4}{4} - \frac{t^3}{3} + 11t \Rightarrow v = \frac{ds}{dt} = -\frac{1}{4}t^4 + t^3 - t^2 + 11$

$\frac{dv}{dt} = -t^3 + 3t^2 - 2t$

$\frac{dv}{dt} = 0 \Rightarrow -t^3 + 3t^2 - 2t = 0 \Rightarrow -t(t^2 - 3t + 2) = 0$
$\Rightarrow -t(t - 1)(t - 2) = 0$

So $t = 0$, $t = 1$ or $t = 2$

Check for negative $\frac{d^2v}{dt^2} = -3t^2 + 6t - 2$

At $t = 0$, $\frac{d^2v}{dt^2} = -3(0)^2 + 6(0) - 2 = -2 < 0$ (local maximum)

At $t = 1$, $\frac{d^2v}{dt^2} = -3(1)^2 + 6(1) - 2 = 1 > 0$ (local minimum)

At $t = 2$, $\frac{d^2v}{dt^2} = -3(2)^2 + 6(2) - 2 = -2 < 0$ (local maximum)

The graph of $v = -\frac{1}{4}t^4 + t^3 - t^2 + 11$ looks like this:

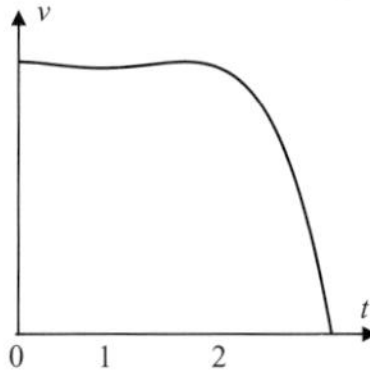

There are two local maximums, so check the value of s at both.

At $t = 0$, $v = -\frac{1}{4}(0)^4 + 0^3 - 0^2 + 11 = 11$ ms^{-1}

At $t = 2$, $v = -\frac{1}{4}(2)^4 + 2^3 - 2^2 + 11$
$= -4 + 8 - 4 + 11 = 11$ ms^{-1}

So the maximum velocity is 11 ms^{-1} and it reaches this velocity twice: once at t = 0 and again at t = 2.

Q5 $a = \frac{dv}{dt} = -t^3 + 6t^2 + 4$

$\frac{da}{dt} = -3t^2 + 12t = 0 \Rightarrow 3t(-t + 4) = 0 \Rightarrow t = 0$ or $t = 4$

Check for negative $\frac{d^2a}{dt^2} = -6t + 12$

At $t = 0$, $\frac{d^2a}{dt^2} = 12 > 0$ (local minimum)

At $t = 4$, $\frac{d^2a}{dt^2} = -12 < 0$ (local maximum)

The graph of $a = -t^3 + 6t^2 + 4$ looks like:

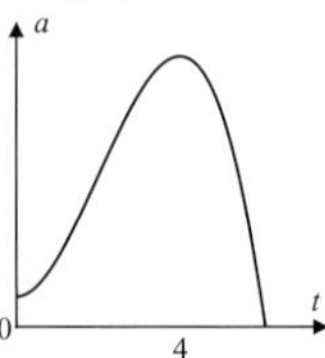

So the maximum acceleration occurs at $t = 4$.

At $t = 4$, $a = -(4)^3 + 6(4)^2 + 4 = -64 + 96 + 4 = 36$ ms^{-2}

Q6 a) When $t = 0$, $s = 3(0)^2 + 2(0) + 5 = 5$ m *[1 mark]*

b) $v = \frac{ds}{dt} = 6t + 2$ *[1 mark]*

c) $t \geq 0$ so $s = 3t^2 + 2t + 5$ is increasing for all values of t. So the minimum displacement must occur when $t = 0$ $\Rightarrow s = 5$ m.

[2 marks available — 1 mark for justifying that t = 0 gives the minimum, 1 mark for the correct answer]

Q7 a) Stationary points for s indicate a change of direction:

$\frac{ds}{dt} = 3t^2 - 28t + 56 = 0$

Solve using the quadratic formula:

$t = \frac{28 \pm \sqrt{(-28)^2 - (4 \times 3 \times 56)}}{6}$

$t \approx 2.9$ or $t \approx 6.4$

The displacement function is a cubic with a positive coefficient of t^3, so $t = 2.9$ represents a local maximum and $t = 6.4$ is a local minimum.

[4 marks available — 1 mark for differentiating, 1 mark for the whole derivative correct, 1 mark for finding the correct values of t, 1 mark for identifying the local maximum and minimum correctly with explanation]

You could have found the second derivative to determine the local minimum and maximum here too.

b) Stationary points for v are indicated by $\frac{dv}{dt} = 0$.

$\frac{dv}{dt} = 6t - 28 = 0 \Rightarrow t = \frac{14}{3}$

When $t = \frac{14}{3}$, $v = 3\left(\frac{14}{3}\right)^2 - 28\left(\frac{14}{3}\right) + 56 = -9.333...$

$= -9.3$ (1 d.p.)

$v = -9.3$ ms^{-1} is a minimum, since v is a quadratic with a positive coefficient of t^2.

[4 marks available — 1 mark for differentiating, 1 mark for the correct expression for the derivative, 1 mark for correct t value, 1 mark for correct answer with explanation]

Q8 a) Stationary points for s are indicated by $\frac{ds}{dt} = 0$.

$\frac{ds}{dt} = -3t^2 + 12t - 11 = 0$

Solve using the quadratic formula:

$t = \frac{-12 \pm \sqrt{12^2 - (4 \times -3 \times -11)}}{-6}$

$t = 1.422... = 1.4$ (1 d.p.) or $t = 2.577... = 2.6$ (1 d.p.)

The displacement function is a negative cubic, so $t = 1.4$ represents a minimum displacement and $t = 2.6$ gives a maximum displacement:

$s = -(2.577...)^3 + 6(2.577...)^2 - 11(2.577...) + 6$

$= 0.3849... = 0.385$ m (3 s.f.)

At the extremes of the range: $t = 1$, $s = 0$ and $t = 3$, $s = 0$.

So the maximum displacement is 0.385 m.

[5 marks available — 1 mark for differentiating, 1 mark for the whole derivative correct, 1 mark for finding the correct values of t, 1 mark for the correct choice of t with justification, 1 mark for the correct answer]

b) Stationary points for v are indicated by $\frac{dv}{dt} = 0$.

$\frac{dv}{dt} = -6t + 12 = 0 \Rightarrow t = 2$.

When $t = 2$, $v = -3(2)^2 + 12(2) - 11$

$= -12 + 24 - 11 = 1$ ms^{-1}

This gives a maximum, since v is a quadratic with a negative coefficient of t^2.

[4 marks available — 1 mark for differentiating, 1 mark for the correct derivative, 1 mark for correct t value, 1 mark for the correct answer with justification]

Q9 a) $v = \frac{ds}{dt} = 2t - 8$

When $t = 10$, $v = 2(10) - 8 = 12$ ms^{-1}

[2 marks available — 1 mark for the correct expression for v, 1 mark for the correct answer]

b) As the graph is a u-shaped quadratic, the minimum displacement is indicated by a stationary point, i.e. where $\frac{ds}{dt} = 0$. $\frac{ds}{dt} = 2t - 8 = 0 \Rightarrow t = 4$

When $t = 4$, $s = 4^2 - 8(4) + 12 = -4$ m.

[2 marks available — 1 mark for finding t, 1 mark for the correct answer]

c) The car is to the left of the marked point when the graph of s against t is below the horizontal axis. $s = t^2 - 8t + 12$ factorises to give $s = (t - 6)(t - 2)$, and is a u-shaped quadratic, so the car is to the left from 2 to 6 seconds, for a total of 4 seconds.

[2 marks available — 1 mark for correctly factorising the quadratic, 1 mark for the correct range given]

Q10 $s = \frac{1}{6}t^4 - 2t^3 + 5t^2 + 2t \Rightarrow v = \frac{ds}{dt} = \frac{2}{3}t^3 - 6t^2 + 10t + 2$

$\frac{dv}{dt} = 2t^2 - 12t + 10$

$\frac{dv}{dt} = 0 \Rightarrow 2t^2 - 12t + 10 = 0 \Rightarrow t^2 - 6t + 5 = 0$

$\Rightarrow (t - 1)(t - 5) = 0 \Rightarrow t = 1$ or $t = 5$

At $t = 1$, $v = \frac{2}{3}(1)^3 - 6(1)^2 + 10(1) + 2$

$= \frac{2}{3} - 6 + 10 + 2 = 6.67$ ms^{-1} (3 s.f.)

At $t = 5$, $v = \frac{2}{3}(5)^3 - 6(5)^2 + 10(5) + 2$

$= \frac{250}{3} - 150 + 50 + 2 = -14.7$ ms^{-1} (3 s.f.)

Its greatest speed is 14.7 ms^{-1} in the negative direction.

Q11 a) $v = \int a \, dt = \int (2t - 6t^2) \, dt = t^2 - 2t^3 + C$

When $t = 0$, $v = 1$: $1 = (0)^2 - 2(0)^3 + C \Rightarrow C = 1$ ms^{-1}

So $v = t^2 - 2t^3 + 1$

Maximum velocity will occur when $a = 0$:

$a = 2t(1 - 3t) = 0 \Rightarrow t = 0$ and $t = \frac{1}{3}$

Check for negative $\frac{d^2v}{dt^2} = \frac{da}{dt} = 2 - 12t$

At $t = 0$, $\frac{d^2v}{dt^2} = 2 > 0$ (local minimum)

At $t = \frac{1}{3}$, $\frac{d^2v}{dt^2} = -2 < 0$ (local maximum)

The graph of $v = t^2 - 2t^3 + 1$ looks like this:

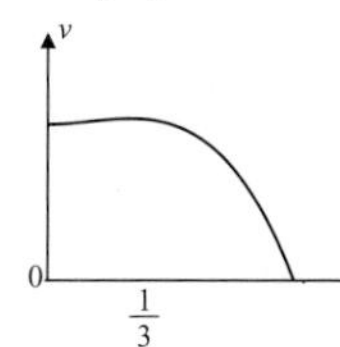

So the maximum velocity happens at $t = \frac{1}{3}$ and

$v = \left(\frac{1}{3}\right)^2 - 2\left(\frac{1}{3}\right)^3 + 1 = 1.037... = 1.04$ ms^{-1} (3 s.f.)

b) $s = \int v \, dt = \int (t^2 - 2t^3 + 1) \, dt = \frac{1}{3}t^3 - \frac{1}{2}t^4 + t + D$

You want displacement from the starting position, so you can say $s = 0$ at $t = 0$, i.e. $D = 0$.

So $s = \frac{1}{3}t^3 - \frac{1}{2}t^4 + t$.

Maximum displacement occurs when $v = \frac{ds}{dt} = 0$:

$t^2 - 2t^3 + 1 = 0 \Rightarrow 2t^3 - t^2 - 1 = 0$

Using the Factor Theorem:

$2(1)^3 - (1)^2 - 1 = 0$, so $(t - 1)$ is a factor.

So using e.g. algebraic division: $(t - 1)(2t^2 + t + 1) = 0$

The discriminant of the quadratic factor is < 0, so it has no real roots, so the only real solution is $t = 1$.

Check that $\frac{d^2s}{dt^2} = a = 2t - 6t^2$ is negative at $t = 1$:

At $t = 1$, $a = 2 - 6 = -4 < 0$ (local maximum)

So maximum displacement happens at $t = 1$ and

$s = \frac{1}{3}(1)^3 - \frac{1}{2}(1)^4 + (1) = \frac{5}{6}$ m $= 0.833$ m (3 s.f.)

Q12 $v = \int a\,dt = \int (6t - 4)\,dt = 3t^2 - 4t + C$

The conditions both involve s, so you can't use them to find the value of C yet. But you can still integrate — just remember that C is a constant.

$s = \int v\,dt = \int (3t^2 - 4t + C)\,dt = t^3 - 2t^2 + Ct + D$, where C and D are constants.

Now use your conditions to find C and D:

At $t = 0$, $s = 0$: $(0)^3 - 2(0)^2 + C(0) + D = 0 \Rightarrow D = 0$
At $t = 1$, $s = 0$: $(1)^3 - 2(1)^2 + C(1) = 0 \Rightarrow -1 + C = 0 \Rightarrow C = 1$
So $s = t^3 - 2t^2 + t$ and $v = 3t^2 - 4t + 1$

A local maximum will occur when $v = 0$:

$v = 3t^2 - 4t + 1 = 0 \Rightarrow (3t - 1)(t - 1) = 0 \Rightarrow t = \frac{1}{3}$ or $t = 1$

Check for negative $\frac{d^2s}{dt^2} = a = 6t - 4$:

At $t = \frac{1}{3}$, $a = 6 \times \frac{1}{3} - 4 = -2 < 0$ (local maximum)
At $t = 1$, $a = 6 \times 1 - 4 = 2 > 0$ (local minimum)

So the maximum displacement for $0 \le t \le 1$ happens at $t = \frac{1}{3}$, and $s = \left(\frac{1}{3}\right)^3 - 2\left(\frac{1}{3}\right)^2 + \left(\frac{1}{3}\right) = \frac{4}{27} = 0.148$ m (3 s.f.)

Chapter 7 Review Exercise

Q1 B: in order for the average velocity to be negative, the object must have had negative velocity at some point in the journey.
C: since velocity is overall displacement divided by time, a negative displacement will give a negative velocity.

Q2 A: $v = \text{gradient} = \frac{80 - 0}{1 - 0} = 80$ kmh^{-1}

B: $v = \frac{120 - 80}{2.5 - 1} = 26.7$ kmh^{-1} (3 s.f.)

C: $v = \frac{120 - 120}{3 - 2.5} = 0$ kmh^{-1}

D: $v = \frac{200 - 120}{4 - 3} = 80$ kmh^{-1}

Q3 a) Find the distance between Appleton and Broughby using distance = speed × time:
Distance = 160 km/h × 0.25 h = 40 km

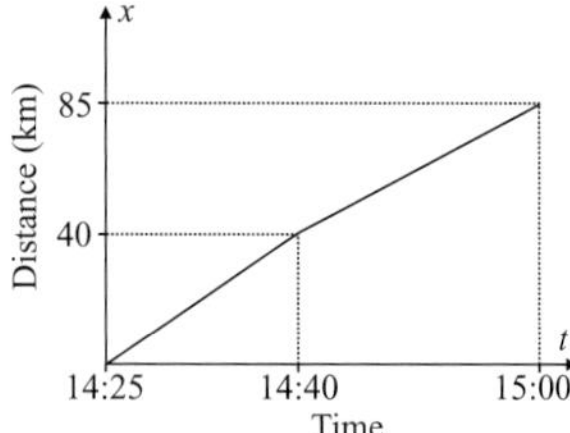

[2 marks available — 1 mark for correct shape of graph, 1 mark for correct labels]

The time axis could give time elapsed rather than times on a clock.

b) No — the movement is linear and in the same direction.
[1 mark for correct answer with explanation]

Q4 Maximum velocity = 0.5 ms^{-2} × 5 s = 2.5 ms^{-1}
Time taken to decelerate = 2.5 ms^{-1} ÷ 0.25 ms^{-2} = 10 s

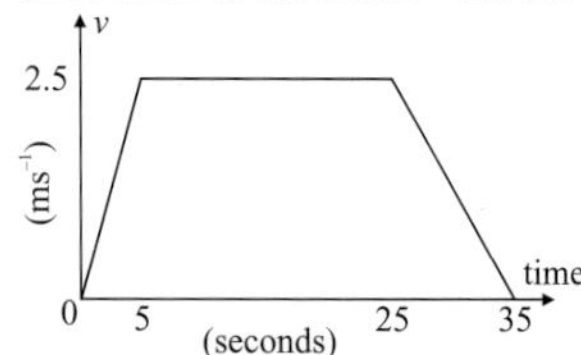

Distance travelled = area under graph
$= \frac{1}{2} \times (35 + 20) \times 2.5 = 68.75$ m

Q5 a) $a = \text{gradient} = \frac{5 - 0}{3 - 0} = 1.67$ ms^{-2} (3 s.f.)

b) $a = \frac{0 - 5}{6 - 5} = -5$ ms^{-2}, so deceleration = 5 ms^{-2}

c) Distance travelled = area under graph
$= (5 \times 2) + (\frac{1}{2} \times 5 \times 1) = 12.5$ m

Q6 a) 3 seconds (between 15 and 18 seconds) *[1 mark]*

b) Find the area under the graph.
Split the area into a trapezium, triangle and rectangle:

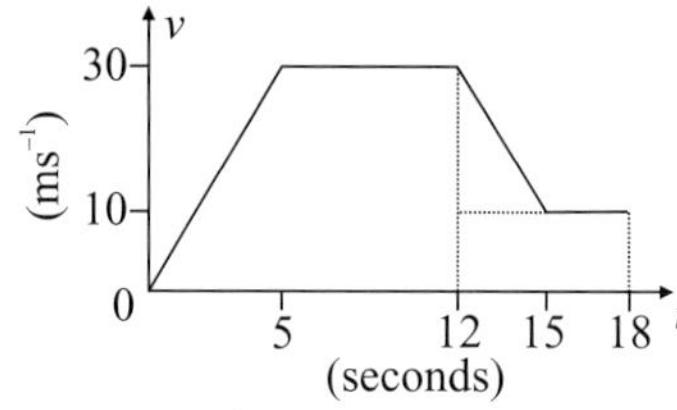

Trapezium: $\frac{1}{2} \times (12 + 7) \times 30 = 285$ m

Triangle: $\frac{1}{2} \times (3 \times 20) = 30$ m

Rectangle: $6 \times 10 = 60$ m
So total area = 285 + 30 + 60 = 375 m
[3 marks available — 1 mark for one area calculated correctly, 1 mark for a second area calculated correctly, 1 mark for the correct answer]

c) The car reaches 12 ms^{-1} between 0 and 5 seconds. As the acceleration is constant up to 30 ms^{-1} at 5 seconds, the car reaches 12 ms^{-1} at $\frac{12}{30} \times 5 = 2$ seconds.
[2 marks available — 1 mark for a correct method, 1 mark for correct answer]

You could also work out the acceleration as 30 ms^{-1} ÷ 5 s = 6 ms^{-2} and realise that it would take 2 seconds to reach 12 ms^{-1}.

Q7 a) The diver reaches his greatest height when his velocity is 0 ms^{-1} for the first time after diving, i.e. at $t = 0.4$ seconds. *[1 mark]*

b) Acceleration is the gradient of the line, so at $t = 5$, the gradient is $\frac{-2 - 0}{5 - 2.3} = -0.741$ ms^{-2} (3 s.f.)
[2 marks available — 1 mark for attempting to find the gradient at t = 5, 1 mark for correct answer]

The negative acceleration means he's accelerating towards the surface at that point — the graph has been plotted using downwards as the positive direction.

c) Distance covered = area under the graph. The diver reaches his highest point at $t = 0.4$ s and enters the water at $t = 1.8$ s when he starts to decelerate. So the distance covered from the highest point to hitting the water is:
$\frac{1}{2} \times (1.8 - 0.4) \times 14 = 9.8$ m
Then find the height the diver reaches above the diving board in the initial jump:
$\frac{1}{2} \times 0.4 \times 4 = 0.8$ m
So the height of the board is 9.8 – 0.8 = 9 m.
[4 marks available — 1 mark for identifying that the diver enters the water at t = 1.8 s, 1 mark for finding the distance covered from the greatest height, 1 mark for finding the distance between the greatest height and the board, 1 mark for correct final answer]

Q8 a) $s = s$, $u = 6$, $a = 0.2$, $t = 20$
$s = ut + \frac{1}{2}at^2$
$s = 6 \times 20 + \frac{1}{2} \times 0.2 \times 20^2 = 120 + 40 = 160$ m

b) $u = 6$, $v = v$, $a = 0.2$, $t = 20$
$v = u + at$
$v = 6 + 0.2 \times 20 = 6 + 4 = 10$ ms^{-1}

Q9 E.g. the child will keep moving forward until the deceleration causes them to reverse direction.
$u = 3, v = 0, a = -0.85, t = t$
$v = u + at$
$0 = 3 - 0.85t \Rightarrow t = 3.529...$ s
The return takes the same time because a is constant, so the total time is $3.529... \times 2 = 7.06$ seconds (3 s.f.)
There are a few different ways to solve this.
[3 marks available — 1 mark for using either the symmetry of the motion or the fact that displacement = 0, 1 mark for a correct and consistent method, 1 mark for correct final answer]

Q10 $s = s, u = 11, v = 0, a = -3.8$
$v^2 = u^2 + 2as$
$0 = 11^2 + 2 \times -3.8 \times s \Rightarrow s = \frac{11^2}{2 \times 3.8} = 15.9$ m (3 s.f.)
$15.9 < 25$, so yes, the horse will stop before the edge.
There are other ways of doing this — e.g. you could have worked out the deceleration necessary to stop within 25 m and checked that this is less than the given deceleration.

Q11 Consider the motion in two parts:
Stage 1: $s = s_1, u = 0, v = v, a = 1.5$
$v^2 = u^2 + 2as$
$v^2 = 0 + 2 \times 1.5 \times s_1 \Rightarrow v = \sqrt{3s_1}$
In Stage 2, the initial velocity u is the same as the final velocity $v = \sqrt{3s_1}$ from Stage 1, and $s = 32 - s_1$, so:
Stage 2: $s = 32 - s_1, u = \sqrt{3s_1}, v = 0, a = -1$
$v^2 = u^2 + 2as$
$0 = 3s_1 + 2 \times -1 \times (32 - s_1)$
$\Rightarrow 5s_1 = 64 \Rightarrow s_1 = 12.8$ m
Then looking again at Stage 1: $s = 12.8, u = 0, a = 1.5, t = t$
$s = ut + \frac{1}{2}at^2$
$12.8 = 0t + \frac{1}{2} \times 1.5 \times t^2 \Rightarrow t = 4.131...$ s
And for Stage 2: $s = 19.2, v = 0, a = -1, t = t$
$s = vt - \frac{1}{2}at^2$
$19.2 = 0t - \frac{1}{2} \times -1 \times t^2 \Rightarrow t = 6.196...$ s
So the total time is $4.131... + 6.196... = 10.3$ s (3 s.f.)
Again, there are different methods you could have used to solve this.
[6 marks available — 1 mark each for a correctly applied suvat equation for each stage, 1 mark for using a value from the first stage in the second to eliminate one of the unknowns, 1 mark for correctly using the total distance travelled to form an equation in t, 1 mark for correct calculation of the time taken for at least one stage of the motion, 1 mark for the correct final answer]

Q12 a) Take upwards as the positive direction.
$s = s, u = 35, v = 0, a = -9.8$
$v^2 = u^2 + 2as$
$0 = 35^2 + 2 \times -9.8 \times s \Rightarrow s = \frac{35^2}{2 \times 9.8} = 62.5$ m

b) Take upwards as the positive direction.
$s = 0, u = 35, a = -9.8, t = t$
You want to find the two times t where $s = 0$:
$s = ut + \frac{1}{2}at^2$
$0 = 35t - 4.9t^2 \Rightarrow 0 = t(35 - 4.9t)$
$\Rightarrow t = 0$ or $t = \frac{35}{4.9} = 7.14$ (3 s.f.)
So the particle is in the air for 7.14 seconds.
You could also have found the time to reach the maximum height and doubled it, or found the time when v = –u, because the motion is symmetrical.

Q13 a) Take downwards as the positive direction.
$s = 30, u = u, v = 25, a = 9.8$
$v^2 = u^2 + 2as$
$25^2 = u^2 + 2 \times 9.8 \times 30$
$u^2 = 25^2 - 2 \times 9.8 \times 30 \Rightarrow u = \sqrt{37} = 6.08$ ms^{-1} (3 s.f.)

b) $s = 20, u = \sqrt{37}, a = 9.8, t = t$
$s = ut + \frac{1}{2}at^2$
$20 = \sqrt{37}t + 4.9t^2 \Rightarrow 4.9t^2 + \sqrt{37}t - 20 = 0$
$t = \frac{-\sqrt{37} + \sqrt{37 - 4 \times 4.9 \times -20}}{9.8} = 1.49$ s (3 s.f.)
You only need to take the positive root since time t > 0.

c) Any suitable reason — e.g. the carriage is likely to be affected by air resistance (or friction), the carriage is too large to be modelled as a particle.

Q14 a) Taking upwards as positive:
$u = 20, v = 0, a = -9.8, t = t$
$v = u + at$
$0 = 20 - 9.8t \Rightarrow t = 2.0408... = 2.04$ s (3 s.f.)
[3 marks available — 1 mark for using the correct suvat equation, 1 mark for correct working, 1 mark for correct final answer]

b) Taking upwards as positive:
$s = s, u = 20, a = -9.8, t = 5.24$
$s = ut + \frac{1}{2}at^2$
$s = 20 \times 5.24 + \frac{1}{2} \times -9.8 \times 5.24^2 = -29.74...$
So the height of the cliff is 29.7 m (3 s.f.)
[3 marks available — 1 mark for using the correct suvat equation, 1 mark for correct working, 1 mark for correct final answer]

Q15 a) Anish: $u = 0, v = v, a = 1.5, t = 3$
$v = u + at$
$v = 0 + 1.5 \times 3 = 4.5$ ms^{-1}

Bethany accelerating:
$u = 0, v = v, a = 1.8, t = 5$
$v = u + at$
$v = 0 + 1.8 \times 5 = 9$ ms^{-1}

Bethany decelerating:
$u = 9, v = v, a = -2, t = 3$
$v = u + at$
$v = 9 + (-2 \times 3) = 9 - 6 = 3$ ms^{-1}

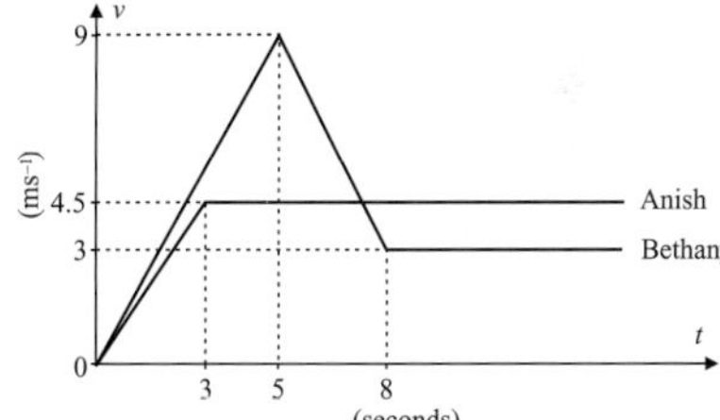

[3 marks available — 1 mark for each correctly plotted line shape, 1 mark for correct labels]

b) Find the time it takes each runner to reach 60 m using the areas under the graph at each stage:
For Anish:
Distance covered while accelerating:
$\frac{1}{2} \times 3 \times 4.5 = 6.75$ m.
He then runs $60 - 6.75 = 53.25$ m at a constant speed of 4.5 ms^{-1}, which takes $53.25 \div 4.5 = 11.83...$ s
So his total time is $11.83... + 3 = 14.83...$ seconds.

For Bethany:
Distance covered while accelerating:
$\frac{1}{2} \times 5 \times 9 = 22.5$ m
Distance covered while decelerating:
$\frac{1}{2} \times 3 \times (9 + 3) = 18$ m
She then runs $60 - 22.5 - 18 = 19.5$ m at a constant speed of 3 ms^{-1}, which takes $19.5 \div 3 = 6.5$ seconds.
Her total time is $5 + 3 + 6.5 = 14.5$ seconds.
So Bethany wins the race.
[6 marks available — 1 mark for using areas under the graph to find times, 1 mark for each correct method for each person, 1 mark for each correct time for each person, 1 mark for stating with reasoning that Bethany wins the race]

Q16 a)

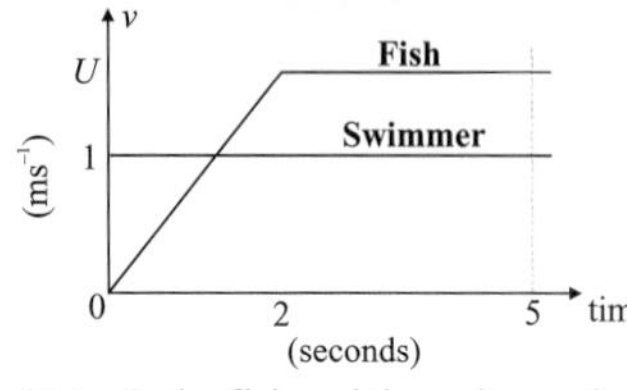

b) At $t = 5$, the fish and the swimmer have travelled the same distance, so the areas under each graph are equal.
So $1 \times 5 = \frac{1}{2} \times 2 \times U + 3U \Rightarrow 5 = 4U \Rightarrow U = 1.25$ ms^{-1}
You have enough information to use other suvat equations here — they should all give the same answer.

Q17 a) '7 + T' may be to the left or the right of 13.

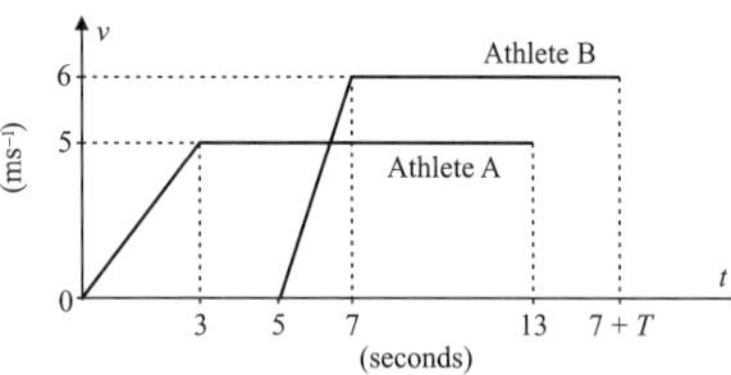

[5 marks available — 1 mark for the shape of both graphs correct, 1 mark for two correctly labelled points on athlete A, 1 mark for all correctly labelled points on athlete A, 1 mark for two correctly labelled points on athlete B, 1 mark for all correctly labelled points on athlete B]

b) They are both running at 5 ms^{-1} when the graphs intersect. For athlete B's acceleration stage, $v = u + at$ gives $5 = 0 + 3t$ $\Rightarrow t = 1.66...$ seconds. Athlete B doesn't start until 5 seconds so both athletes travel at the same velocity after $5 + 1.66... = 6.67$ seconds (3 s.f).
[3 marks available — 1 mark for 5 ms^{-1}, 1 mark for deriving equation for athlete 2, 1 mark for the correct answer]

c) Find the area under each graph (both are trapeziums).
Athlete 1: $\frac{1}{2} \times (10 + 13) \times 5 = 57.5$,
Athlete 2: $\frac{1}{2} \times ((7 + T - 5) + (7 + T - 7)) \times 6$
$= 6T + 6 = 57.5 \Rightarrow T = 8.583...$
So athlete 2's total time is $(8.583... + 7) - 5 = 10.583...$ s
Athlete 1 takes 13 seconds, so Athlete 2 is quicker by 2.42 seconds (3 s.f.).
[4 marks available — 1 mark for distance run, 1 mark for using formula to find t, 1 mark for athlete 2's total time, 1 mark for the correct answer]

Q18 a) Velocity $= \frac{ds}{dt}$, so differentiate s:
$v = \frac{ds}{dt} = t^3 - 3t^2 - 2t$
When $t = 5$, $v = (5)^3 - 3(5)^2 - 2(5) = 40$ ms^{-1}

b) Acceleration $= \frac{dv}{dt} = \frac{d^2s}{dt^2}$, so differentiate v:
$a = \frac{dv}{dt} = 3t^2 - 6t - 2$
When $t = 2$, $a = 3(2)^2 - 6(2) - 2 = -2$ ms^{-2}

Q19 a) $v = \int a\, dt = \int (12 - 3t^2)\, dt = 12t - t^3 + C$
When $t = 0$, $v = 4$: $4 = 12(0) - (0)^3 + C \Rightarrow C = 4$
So $v = 12t - t^3 + 4$

b) When $t = 3$: $v = 12(3) - (3)^3 + 4 = 36 - 27 + 4 = 13$ ms^{-1}
$a = 12 - 3(3)^2 = 12 - 27 = -15$ ms^{-2}

Q20 $a = \frac{dv}{dt}$, so $v = \int a\, dt = \int (4t^2 - 9t + 32)\, dt$
$= \frac{4}{3}t^3 - \frac{9}{2}t^2 + 32t + C$
The particle starts from rest, so $v = 0$ at $t = 0 \Rightarrow C = 0$
So $v = \frac{4}{3}t^3 - \frac{9}{2}t^2 + 32t$
$v = \frac{ds}{dt}$, so integrate again to find s:
$s = \int v\, dt = \int \left(\frac{4}{3}t^3 - \frac{9}{2}t^2 + 32t\right) dt = \frac{1}{3}t^4 - \frac{3}{2}t^3 + 16t^2 + D$
Initial displacement is 0, so $D = 0$.
Then at $t = 2$, $s = \frac{1}{3}(2)^4 - \frac{3}{2}(2)^3 + 16(2)^2$
$= 57.33...$ m $= 57.3$ m (3 s.f.)
[6 marks available — 1 mark for attempting to integrate the acceleration, 1 mark for correct expression for v, 1 mark for finding constant of integration C, 1 mark for integrating to find an expression for s, 1 mark for finding the constant of integration D, 1 mark for correctly evaluating at t = 2]

Q21 Particle X: displacement-time graph (2), velocity-time graph (6)
Particle Y: displacement-time graph (1), velocity-time graph (4)
Particle Z: displacement-time graph (3), velocity-time graph (5)

Q22 a) At $t = 0$, $s = 8(0)^2 - \frac{1}{2}(0)^4 = 0$
At $t = 4$, $s = 8(4)^2 - \frac{1}{2}(4)^4 = 8 \times 16 - \frac{1}{2} \times 256 = 0$
The object is released from $s = 0$ at $t = 0$, so at $t = 4$, it returns to its initial position.

b) At the point of greatest displacement the velocity of the particle is zero.
$\frac{ds}{dt} = 16t - 2t^3 = 0 \Rightarrow 2t(8 - t^2) = 0$
$\Rightarrow t = 0$ or $t = \sqrt{8}$ $(t > 0)$
When $t = 0$, $s = 0$.
When $t = \sqrt{8}$, $s = 8(\sqrt{8})^2 - \frac{1}{2}(\sqrt{8})^4 = 64 - 32 = 32$ m
So the maximum displacement is 32 m.

Q23 a) When $t = 5$, $v = 21 - 7(5) = -14$ ms^{-1} *[1 mark]*

b) For $0 \le t \le 3$:
$s = \int v\, dt = \frac{3t^2}{2} - \frac{t^3}{3} + C_1$
When $t = 0$, $s = 0 \Rightarrow C_1 = 0$
When $t = 3$, $s = \frac{3(3)^2}{2} - \frac{(3)^3}{3} = 4.5$
For $t \ge 3$:
$s = \int v\, dt = 21t - 3.5t^2 + C_2$
We know from the first equation that $s = 4.5$ when $t = 3$, so
$4.5 = 21(3) - 3.5(3)^2 + C_2 \Rightarrow C_2 = -27$
When $t = 5$, $s = 21(5) - 3.5(5)^2 - 27$
$= 105 - 87.5 - 27 = -9.5$ m
[6 marks available — 1 mark for a correct expression for s for the first 3 seconds, 1 mark for finding C_1, 1 mark for equating expressions for s at t = 3, 1 mark for a correct expression for s for when t is greater than or equal to 3 seconds, 1 mark for finding C_2, 1 mark for the correct answer]

Q24 a) $s = 1.5^4 = 5.0625$ m *[1 mark]*

b) $s = t^3$ and $s = t^4$ are increasing functions for $t \ge 0$ and $s = -t^3 + 24$ is a decreasing function for $t \ge 0$.
Together, the functions are continuous, so the maximum value of s occurs when $t = 2$, giving $s = 2^4 = 16$ m.
[3 marks available — 1 mark for correctly identifying increasing/decreasing functions, 1 mark for a reference to the continuity of the functions, 1 mark for the correct answer]

c) $v = \frac{ds}{dt} = -3t^2$
When $t = 2.5$, $v = -3(2.5)^2 = -18.75$ ms^{-1}
[3 marks available — 1 mark for differentiating, 1 mark for the correct derivative, 1 mark for the correct answer]

Q25 a) a is an increasing function, so the maximum value will occur when $t = 3$, giving $a = 0.25 \times 3^2 = 2.25$ ms^{-2}.
[2 marks available — 1 mark for the justification, 1 mark for the correct answer]

b) $v = \int a\,dt = \frac{t^3}{12} + C$

When $t = 0$, $v = 0 \Rightarrow C = 0$

So $v = \frac{t^3}{12}$

[3 marks available — 1 mark for attempting to integrate, 1 mark for finding C, 1 mark for the correct answer]

c) $s = \int v\,dt = \frac{t^4}{48} + D$

When $t = 0$, $s = 0 \Rightarrow D = 0$

So $s = \frac{t^4}{48}$

[3 marks available — 1 mark for attempting to integrate, 1 mark for finding D, 1 mark for the correct answer]

d) When $t = 2$, $s = \frac{1}{3}$. When $t = 3$, $s = \frac{27}{16}$.

So the change in displacement was $\frac{27}{16} - \frac{1}{3} = 1.35$ (3 s.f.).

[3 marks available — 1 mark for each value of s, 1 mark for the correct answer]

e) Less — e.g. velocity is an increasing function, so the rate of increase of displacement is also increasing.

[1 mark for the correct answer with justification]

Q26 a) $420 - 360 = 60$ seconds

b) Distance walked by person A: $450 + 450 = 900$ m

Distance walked by person B: $450 + 650 = 1100$ m

So person B's distance was greater by 200 m.

c) Person A's displacement was greater by 450 m.

d) Person B achieved the greatest speed — this is indicated by the steepest part of the graph, between 420 and 600 seconds.

Speed $= 650 \div 180 = 3.6$ ms^{-1}

The gradient is negative here, but the question asks for a speed rather than velocity.

e) The line from (420, 0) to (600, 450) has a gradient of $\frac{450}{180} = 2.5$ and has equation $y = 2.5x + c$.

Substituting in (420, 0) gives $0 = 1050 + c$, so the line has equation $y = 2.5x - 1050$.

The line from (420, 650) to (600, 0) has a gradient of $\frac{-650}{180} = \frac{-65}{18}$ and has equation $y = \frac{-65}{18}x + c$.

Substituting in (600, 0) gives $0 = \frac{-6500}{3} + c$,

so the line has equation $y = \frac{-65}{18}x + \frac{6500}{3}$.

The people are at the same distance at the intersection of these two lines, so where $\frac{-65}{18}x + \frac{6500}{3} = 2.5x - 1050$,

which gives $\frac{9650}{3} = \frac{55x}{9}$ and $x = 526$ seconds.

Q27 a) Take upwards as the positive direction.

From passing the first target to passing the second:

$s = 30$, $u = u$, $a = -9.8$, $t = 2$

$s = ut + \frac{1}{2}at^2$

$30 = 2u - 4.9 \times 4 \Rightarrow u = 49.6 \div 2 = 24.8$

The projectile is travelling at 24.8 ms^{-1} at the first target.

So for the motion from the point of projection until the first target is reached:

$s = 30$, $u = u$, $v = 24.8$, $a = -9.8$

$v^2 = u^2 + 2as$

$24.8^2 = u^2 + 2 \times -9.8 \times 30$

$u = \sqrt{24.8^2 + 2 \times 9.8 \times 30} = 34.68... = 34.7$ ms^{-1} (3 s.f.)

b) From the first target to maximum height:

$s = s$, $u = 24.8$, $v = 0$, $a = -9.8$

$v^2 = u^2 + 2as$

$0^2 = 24.8^2 + 2 \times -9.8 \times s \Rightarrow s = \frac{24.8^2}{2 \times 9.8} = 31.4$ (3 s.f.)

The maximum height is 31.4 m above the first target, so $31.4 + 20 = 51.4$ m above the ground.

c) 30 m above the ground is 40 m above the point of projection, so from the point of projection, taking upwards as positive:

$s = 40$, $u = 34.68...$, $a = -9.8$, $t = t$

$s = ut + \frac{1}{2}at^2$

$40 = 34.68...t + \frac{1}{2} \times -9.8 \times t^2$

$\Rightarrow 4.9t^2 - 34.68...t + 40 = 0$

$t = \frac{-(-34.68...) \pm \sqrt{(-34.68...)^2 - 4 \times 4.9 \times 40}}{9.8}$

$\Rightarrow t = 1.450...$ and $t = 5.628...$

The projectile is more than 40 m from the point of projection between these two times, i.e. it is 30 m above the ground for $5.628... - 1.450... = 4.18$ s (3 s.f.)

Q28 a) Take upwards as the positive direction.

Particle A: $s = s_A$, $u = 0$, $a = -9.8$, $t = t$

Particle B: $s = s_B$, $u = 3$, $a = -9.8$, $t = t - 2$

When B is at its highest point, $v = 0$.

For particle B, $v = u + at$

$0 = 3 - 9.8(t - 2) \Rightarrow t = \frac{15}{49} + 2 = \frac{113}{49}$

When $t = \frac{113}{49}$, using $s = ut + \frac{1}{2}at^2$ on particle A,

$s_A = 0t - 4.9\left(\frac{113}{49}\right)^2 = -26.1$ m (3 s.f.)

i.e. a distance of 26.1 m.

b) Using $s = ut + \frac{1}{2}at^2$,

$s_A = 0t - 4.9t^2 = -4.9t^2$

$s_B = 3(t-2) - 4.9(t-2)^2$

$= 3t - 6 - 4.9(t^2 - 4t + 4)$

$= 3t - 6 - 4.9t^2 + 19.6t - 19.6$

$= -25.6 + 22.6t - 4.9t^2$

So after t seconds, A is $35 - 4.9t^2$ from the ground and B is $5 - 25.6 + 22.6t - 4.9t^2$ from the ground:

$35 - 4.9t^2 = -20.6 + 22.6t - 4.9t^2$

$55.6 = 22.6t \Rightarrow t = 2.46$ s (3 s.f.)

c) $35 - 4.9\left(\frac{55.6}{22.6}\right)^2 = 5.34$ m (3 s.f.)

Use the unrounded value of t from part b) — the rounding could give you the wrong answer.

Q29 $s = -\frac{1}{40}t^4 - \frac{1}{15}t^3 + 2t^2 \Rightarrow v = \frac{ds}{dt} = -\frac{1}{10}t^3 - \frac{1}{5}t^2 + 4t$

$\frac{dv}{dt} = -\frac{3}{10}t^2 - \frac{2}{5}t + 4 = 0 \Rightarrow -3t^2 - 4t + 40 = 0$

$\Rightarrow 0 = 3t^2 + 4t - 40$

$t = \frac{-4 \pm \sqrt{4^2 - 4 \times 3 \times -40}}{6}$, so $t = 3.045...$ s

(The other value of t is negative.)

Substitute this into the equation for velocity:

$v = -\frac{1}{10}(3.045...)^3 - \frac{1}{5}(3.045...)^2 + 4(3.045...)$

$= 7.5022...$ ms^{-1} $= 7.50$ ms^{-1} (3 s.f.)

Chapter 8: Forces and Newton's Laws

Prior Knowledge Check

Q1 a) Magnitude $= \sqrt{12^2 + 9^2} = \sqrt{225} = 15$

Direction $\theta = \tan^{-1}\left(\frac{9}{12}\right) = 36.9°$ (1 d.p.)

b) Magnitude $= \sqrt{3^2 + 5^2} = \sqrt{34} = 5.8$ (1 d.p.)

Direction $\theta = \tan^{-1}\left(\frac{-5}{3}\right) = -59.0° = 301.0°$ (1 d.p.)

c) Magnitude $= \sqrt{2^2 + 2^2} = \sqrt{8} = 2.8$ (1 d.p.)

$\tan^{-1}\left(\frac{2}{-2}\right) = -45°$, so direction $\theta = 180° - 45° = 135°$

d) Magnitude $= \sqrt{4^2 + 8^2} = \sqrt{80} = 8.9$ (1 d.p.)

$\tan^{-1}\left(\frac{-8}{-4}\right) = 63.43...°$, so direction $\theta = 180° + 63.43...°$ $= 243.4°$ (1 d.p.)

Q2 **a)** **(i)** There is no friction between the crate and the slope.
(ii) The string has negligible mass.

b) There are three forces acting on the crate:
The weight of the crate, W
The normal reaction of the plane on the crate, N
The tension in the string pulling on the crate, T

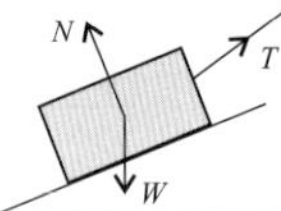

Q3 $s = s,\ u = 0\ \text{ms}^{-1},\ v = v,\ a = 5\ \text{ms}^{-2},\ t = 6\ \text{s}$

a) $v = u + at = 0 + (5 \times 6) = 30\ \text{ms}^{-1}$

b) $s = ut + \frac{1}{2}at^2 = (0 \times 6) + \left(\frac{1}{2} \times 5 \times 6^2\right) = 90\ \text{m}$

Exercise 8.1 — Treating Forces as Vectors

Q1 **a)** Magnitude = 7 N, Direction $\theta = 0°$

b) Magnitude = $\sqrt{2^2 + 2^2} = \sqrt{8} = 2.83$ N (3 s.f.)
Direction $\theta = \tan^{-1}\left(\frac{2}{2}\right) = \tan^{-1}(1) = 45°$

c) Magnitude = $\sqrt{3^2 + 4^2} = \sqrt{25} = 5$ N
Direction $\theta = \tan^{-1}\left(\frac{4}{3}\right) = 53.1°$ (1 d.p.)

d) Magnitude = $\sqrt{(-3)^2 + 4^2} = \sqrt{25} = 5$ N
Angle above the negative horizontal $\alpha = \tan^{-1}\left(\frac{4}{3}\right) = 53.1...°$
So direction $\theta = 180° - \alpha = 126.9°$ (1 d.p.)

e) Magnitude = $\sqrt{12^2 + (-5)^2} = \sqrt{169} = 13$ kN
Angle below the positive horizontal $\alpha = \tan^{-1}\left(\frac{5}{12}\right) = 22.6...°$
So direction $\theta = 360° - \alpha = 337.4°$ (1 d.p.)

f) Magnitude = $\sqrt{(-1)^2 + (-4)^2} = \sqrt{17} = 4.12$ N (3 s.f.)
Angle below the negative horizontal $\alpha = \tan^{-1}\left(\frac{4}{1}\right) = 75.9...°$
So direction $\theta = 180° + \alpha = 256.0°$ (1 d.p.)

Q2 **a)** Magnitude = $\sqrt{3^2 + 1^2} = \sqrt{10} = 3.16$ N (3 s.f.)
Direction $\theta = \tan^{-1}\left(\frac{1}{3}\right) = 18.4°$ (1 d.p.)

b) Magnitude = $\sqrt{(-4)^2 + (-2)^2} = \sqrt{20} = 4.47$ N (3 s.f.)
Angle below the negative horizontal $\alpha = \tan^{-1}\left(\frac{2}{4}\right) = 26.5...°$
So direction $\theta = 180° + \alpha = 206.6°$ (1 d.p.)

c) Magnitude = $\sqrt{12^2 + (-3)^2} = \sqrt{153} = 12.4$ N (3 s.f.)
Angle below the positive horizontal $\alpha = \tan^{-1}\left(\frac{3}{12}\right) = 14.0...°$
So direction $\theta = 360° - \alpha = 346.0°$ (1 d.p.)

d) Magnitude = $\sqrt{(-0.5)^2 + 0.5^2} = 0.707$ kN (3 s.f.)
Angle above the negative horizontal $\alpha = \tan^{-1}\left(\frac{0.5}{0.5}\right) = 45°$
So direction $\theta = 180° - \alpha = 135°$

e) Magnitude = 11 N, Direction $\theta = 270°$

f) Magnitude = $\sqrt{15^2 + 25^2} = \sqrt{850} = 29.2$ kN (3 s.f.)
Direction $\theta = \tan^{-1}\left(\frac{25}{15}\right) = 59.0°$ (1 d.p.)

g) Magnitude = $\sqrt{(-5)^2 + (-7)^2} = \sqrt{74} = 8.60$ N (3 s.f.)
Angle below the negative horizontal $\alpha = \tan^{-1}\left(\frac{7}{5}\right) = 54.46...°$
So direction $\theta = 180° + \alpha = 234.5°$ (1 d.p.)

h) Magnitude = $\sqrt{(-8)^2 + 9^2} = \sqrt{145} = 12.0$ N (3 s.f.)
Angle above the negative horizontal $\alpha = \tan^{-1}\left(\frac{9}{8}\right) = 48.36...°$
So direction $\theta = 180° - \alpha = 131.6°$ (1 d.p.)

Q3

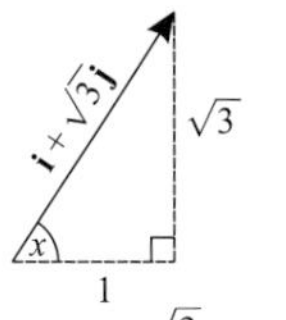

$\tan x = \frac{\sqrt{3}}{1} \Rightarrow x = \tan^{-1}(\sqrt{3}) = 60°$

Q4 Magnitude = $\sqrt{15^2 + (-8)^2} = \sqrt{289} = 17$ kN
Angle below the positive horizontal $\alpha = \tan^{-1}\left(\frac{8}{15}\right) = 28.07...°$
So direction $\theta = 360° - \alpha = 331.9°$ (1 d.p.)

Q5 Magnitude = $\sqrt{(56a)^2 + (-42a)^2} = \sqrt{4900a^2} = 70a$
$70a = 35 \Rightarrow a = 0.5$

Q6 E.g. use the cosine rule with the triangle formed by **a** and **b**.

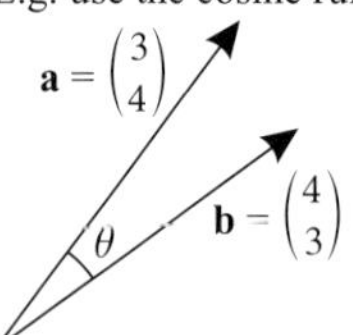

$|\mathbf{a}| = |\mathbf{b}| = \sqrt{3^2 + 4^2} = 5,\ |\mathbf{b} - \mathbf{a}| = \sqrt{1^2 + (-1)^2} = \sqrt{2}$

$\cos\theta = \frac{5^2 + 5^2 - \sqrt{2}^2}{2 \times 5 \times 5} = \frac{48}{50} \Rightarrow \theta = \cos^{-1}(0.96) = 16.3°$ (1 d.p.)

Q7

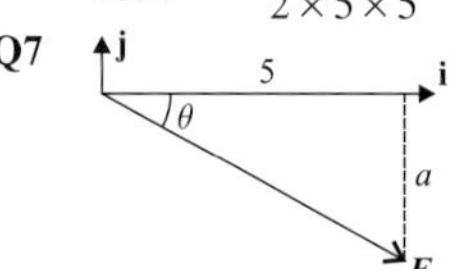

So $F = (5\mathbf{i} - a\mathbf{j})$ N.

$|F| = \sqrt{5^2 + (-a)^2} = 6\text{ N} \Rightarrow 5^2 + a^2 = 36 \Rightarrow 25 + a^2 = 36$
$\Rightarrow a^2 = 11 \Rightarrow a = \sqrt{11}$

(Ignore the negative root as $a > 0$)

Q8 $\boldsymbol{F}_2$ is a multiple of $\boldsymbol{F}_1$ so, for some real value of a, $\boldsymbol{F}_2 = \begin{pmatrix} 3a \\ 2a \end{pmatrix}$ N
$\Rightarrow \sqrt{(3a)^2 + (2a)^2} = 8 \Rightarrow a = \pm\frac{8}{\sqrt{13}} = \pm 2.218...$
$\boldsymbol{F}_1$ and $\boldsymbol{F}_2$ act in the same direction,
so a must be positive $\Rightarrow \boldsymbol{F}_2 = \begin{pmatrix} 6.66 \\ 4.44 \end{pmatrix}$ N (3 s.f.)

[4 marks available — 1 mark for identifying $\boldsymbol{F}_1$ as a multiple of $\boldsymbol{F}_2$, 1 mark for equating the magnitude to 8, 1 mark for finding the multiple, 1 mark for the correct answer]

Q9 $(-1)^2 + a^2 = 3^2 + 5^2 = 34 \Rightarrow a = \pm\sqrt{33} = \pm 5.74$ (3 s.f.)

[3 marks available — 1 mark for each side of the equation for equal magnitudes, 1 mark for the correct answer]

Q10 **a)** $|\boldsymbol{F}| = \sqrt{2^2 + 1^2} = \sqrt{5}$
$\boldsymbol{F}_1$ acts directly downwards, so it has no horizontal component.
If $\boldsymbol{F}_1 = (0, a)$, $\sqrt{0^2 + a^2} = 5 + \sqrt{5}$
$\Rightarrow a = -5 - \sqrt{5} = -7.236...$
So $\boldsymbol{F}_1 = \begin{pmatrix} 0 \\ -7.24 \end{pmatrix}$ N (2 d.p.)

[2 marks available — 1 mark for the magnitude of $\boldsymbol{F}_1$, 1 mark for the correct answer]

b) $\frac{1}{\sqrt{5}}\begin{pmatrix} 2 \\ -1 \end{pmatrix}\text{ N} = \begin{pmatrix} 2 \\ -1 \end{pmatrix} \div \sqrt{5} = \begin{pmatrix} 0.89 \\ -0.45 \end{pmatrix}$ N (2 d.p.)

[2 marks available — 2 marks for the correct answer, otherwise 1 mark for attempting to multiply by $\frac{1}{\sqrt{5}}$]

Q11 **a)** Taking up and right as positive directions:
$\boldsymbol{F} = \begin{pmatrix} 3 \\ -2 \end{pmatrix}$ and $\boldsymbol{G} = \begin{pmatrix} -1 \\ 4 \end{pmatrix}$

$|\boldsymbol{F}| = \sqrt{3^2 + 2^2} = \sqrt{13} = 3.61$ N (3 s.f.) and
$|\boldsymbol{G}| = \sqrt{1^2 + 4^2} = \sqrt{17} = 4.12$ N (3 s.f.)

[3 marks available — 1 mark for a correct method, 1 mark for each correct answer]

b) E.g. use the cosine rule with the triangle formed by **F** and **G**.

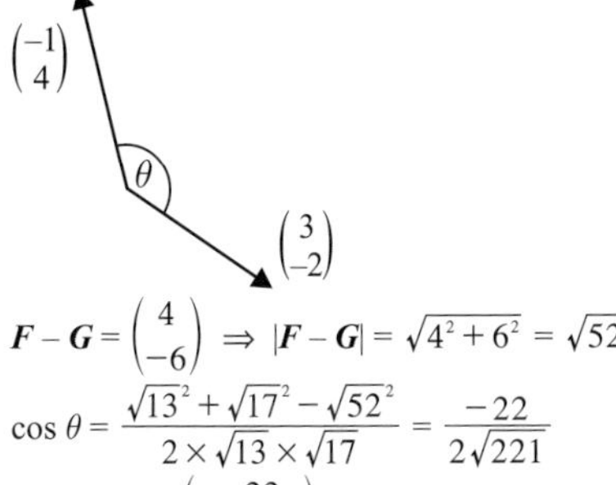

$$\boldsymbol{F} - \boldsymbol{G} = \begin{pmatrix}4\\-6\end{pmatrix} \Rightarrow |\boldsymbol{F} - \boldsymbol{G}| = \sqrt{4^2 + 6^2} = \sqrt{52}$$

$$\cos\theta = \frac{\sqrt{13}^2 + \sqrt{17}^2 - \sqrt{52}^2}{2 \times \sqrt{13} \times \sqrt{17}} = \frac{-22}{2\sqrt{221}}$$

$$\Rightarrow \theta = \cos^{-1}\left(\frac{-22}{2\sqrt{221}}\right) = 137.7° \text{ (1 d.p.)}$$

[2 marks available — 1 mark for a correct method, 1 mark for the correct answer]

c) If $\boldsymbol{G} = \begin{pmatrix}a\\4\end{pmatrix}$ then $|\boldsymbol{G}| = \sqrt{a^2 + 4^2}$

$|\boldsymbol{F}| = \sqrt{13}$ and $2|\boldsymbol{F}| = 2\sqrt{13}$

$a^2 + 4^2 = (2\sqrt{13})^2 = 52 \Rightarrow a = \pm 6$ and $\boldsymbol{G} = \begin{pmatrix}\pm 6\\4\end{pmatrix}$

*[3 marks available — 1 mark for squaring components of **G**, 1 mark for equating that to $(2\sqrt{13})^2$, 1 mark for the correct answer]*

Exercise 8.2 — Resultant Forces and Equilibrium

Q1 Since the object is in equilibrium, there is no resultant force.
Resolving vertically (↑): $T - 8 = 0 \Rightarrow T = 8$ N

Q2 To find the resultant, add the components:
$(8\mathbf{i} + 5\mathbf{j}) + (3\mathbf{i} - 2\mathbf{j}) = (8 + 3)\mathbf{i} + (5 - 2)\mathbf{j} = (11\mathbf{i} + 3\mathbf{j})$ N

Q3 **a)** Add the components:
$(-7\mathbf{i} - 9\mathbf{j}) + (3\mathbf{i} - 2\mathbf{j}) = (-7 + 3)\mathbf{i} + (-9 - 2)\mathbf{j} = (-4\mathbf{i} - 11\mathbf{j})$ N

b) The particle is now in equilibrium, so the total resultant force must be 0. So the third force $F = (4\mathbf{i} + 11\mathbf{j})$ N

Q4 Resultant force $= (200 - 30)\mathbf{i} + ((-100) + (-50))\mathbf{j} = (170\mathbf{i} - 150\mathbf{j})$ N

Q5 Since the object is in equilibrium, the resultant force has **i** and **j** components of zero. Resolving in the **i** direction:
$3 + x - 5 = 0 \Rightarrow x = 2$

Q6

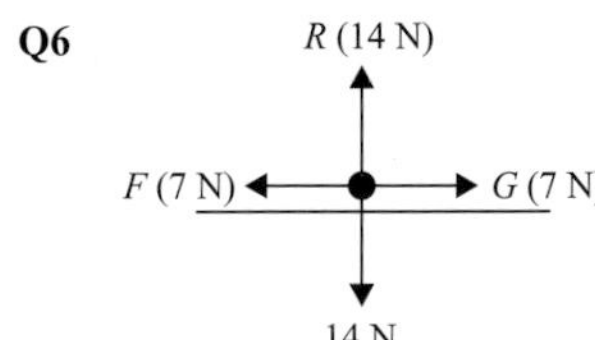

[2 marks available — 1 mark for each pair of forces correctly positioned and labelled]

Q7 Since the object is in equilibrium, the resultant force has **i** and **j** components of zero.

Resolving in each direction: $\begin{pmatrix}3 - 2 + b\\a + 1 + 7\end{pmatrix} = \begin{pmatrix}0\\0\end{pmatrix}$

So $a + 1 + 7 = 0 \Rightarrow a = -8$
$3 - 2 + b = 0 \Rightarrow b = -1$

Q8 **a)**

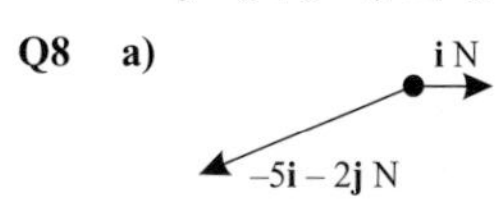

b) $(-5\mathbf{i} - 2\mathbf{j}) + (\mathbf{i}) = -4\mathbf{i} - 2\mathbf{j}$ N

c) $(-4\mathbf{i} - 2\mathbf{j}) + (4\mathbf{i} + \mathbf{j}) + F = 0 \Rightarrow -\mathbf{j} + F = 0 \Rightarrow F = \mathbf{j}$ N

Q9 Taking upwards on the y-axis and right on the x-axis to be positive:

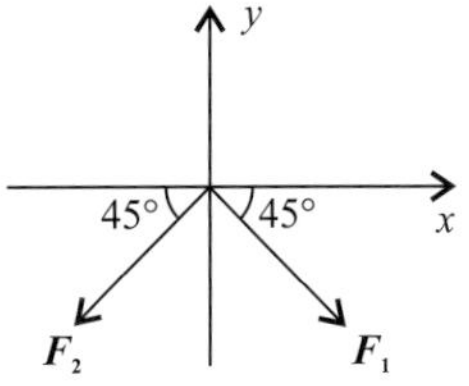

So $\boldsymbol{F}_1$ will have a positive **i** component and a negative **j** component and $\boldsymbol{F}_2$ will have negative **i** and **j** components.

As $\boldsymbol{F}_1$ has double the magnitude of $\boldsymbol{F}_2$, let $\boldsymbol{F}_1 = \begin{pmatrix}2a\\-2a\end{pmatrix}$ and $\boldsymbol{F}_2 = \begin{pmatrix}-a\\-a\end{pmatrix}$, where a is positive.

$$\begin{pmatrix}2a\\-2a\end{pmatrix} + \begin{pmatrix}-a\\-a\end{pmatrix} + \begin{pmatrix}-3\\c\end{pmatrix} = \begin{pmatrix}0\\0\end{pmatrix}$$

So $2a + (-a) + (-3) = 0 \Rightarrow a = 3$
$-2a + (-a) + c = 0 \Rightarrow c = 9$

$\boldsymbol{F}_1 = \begin{pmatrix}6\\-6\end{pmatrix}$ and $\boldsymbol{F}_2 = \begin{pmatrix}-3\\-3\end{pmatrix}$

[6 marks available — 1 mark for each correct algebraic expression for the first two forces, 1 mark for the correct equation relating the three forces, 1 mark for each of c, F_1 and F_2]

Q10 The second force has a horizontal component which is double its vertical component, so let the second force be $\begin{pmatrix}2b\\b\end{pmatrix}$.

$$\begin{pmatrix}2b\\b\end{pmatrix} + \begin{pmatrix}4\\a\end{pmatrix} = \begin{pmatrix}6\\-2\end{pmatrix}$$

So $2b + 4 = 6 \Rightarrow 2b = 2 \Rightarrow b = 1$
$b + a = -2 \Rightarrow a = -2 - b \Rightarrow a = -3$

E.g. use the cosine rule with the triangle formed by **F** and **G**.

$\boldsymbol{F} = \begin{pmatrix}2\\1\end{pmatrix}$

θ

$\boldsymbol{G} = \begin{pmatrix}4\\-3\end{pmatrix}$

$|\boldsymbol{F}| = \sqrt{2^2 + 1^2} = \sqrt{5}$, $|\boldsymbol{G}| = \sqrt{4^2 + 3^2} = 5$,

$$\boldsymbol{G} - \boldsymbol{F} = \begin{pmatrix}2\\-4\end{pmatrix} \Rightarrow |\boldsymbol{G} - \boldsymbol{F}| = \sqrt{2^2 + 4^2} = \sqrt{20}$$

$$\cos\theta = \frac{\sqrt{5}^2 + 5^2 - \sqrt{20}^2}{2 \times \sqrt{5} \times 5} = \frac{10}{10\sqrt{5}}$$

$$\theta = \cos^{-1}\left(\frac{1}{\sqrt{5}}\right) = 63.4° \text{ (1 d.p.)}$$

[6 marks available — 1 mark for a correct algebraic expression for the second force, 1 mark for the correct equation relating the forces, 1 mark for b, 1 mark for a, 1 mark for a correct method to find the angle between the vectors, 1 mark for the correct answer]

Exercise 8.3-8.4 — Newton's Laws of Motion

Q1 $F_{net} = ma$
$F_{net} = 15 \times 4 = 60$ N

Q2 **a)** $F_{net} = ma$
$10 = 5a \Rightarrow a = 2$ ms^{-2}

b) Use a constant acceleration equation.
$u = 0, v = v, a = 2, t = 8$
$v = u + at$
$v = 0 + (2 \times 8) = 16$ ms^{-1}

Q3 $F_{net} = ma$
$8 = 5a \Rightarrow a = 1.6$ ms^{-2}, horizontally in the direction of the resultant force.
[2 marks available — 1 mark for the correct size, 1 mark for the correct direction]

Q4 $F_{net} = ma$

$3 = 2a \Rightarrow a = 1.5 \text{ ms}^{-2}$

$v = u + at$

$v = -5 + 1.5 \times 2 \Rightarrow v = -2 \text{ ms}^{-1}$

[2 marks available — 1 mark for finding a, 1 mark for finding v]

Q5

T

a

$18g$

Resolving vertically (↑):

$F_{net} = ma$

$T - 18g = 18 \times 0.4$

$\Rightarrow T = 7.2 + 176.4 = 183.6 \text{ N}$

Q6 **a)** $F_{net} = ma$

$18 = 5m \Rightarrow m = 18 \div 5 = 3.6 \text{ kg}$

b) $u = 0, v = v, a = 5, t = 4$

$v = u + at$

$v = 0 + (5 \times 4) = 20 \text{ ms}^{-1}$

c) $R - mg = 0 \Rightarrow R = 3.6 \times 9.8 = 35.28 \text{ N}$

Q7 **a)** $u = 0, v = 2.5, a = a, t = 4$

$v = u + at$

$2.5 = 0 + 4a \Rightarrow a = 0.625 \text{ ms}^{-2}$

b)

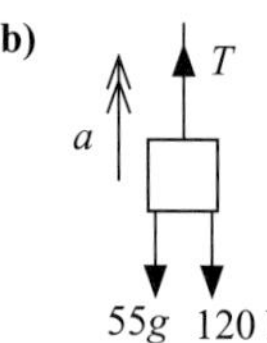

Resolving vertically (↑):

$F_{net} = ma$

$T - 120 - 55g = 55 \times 0.625$

$T = 34.375 + 120 + 539 = 693 \text{ N (3 s.f.)}$

Q8 $v = u + at$

$3 = 5 + 10a \Rightarrow a = -0.2 \text{ ms}^{-2}$

$F_{net} = ma$

$F = 2 \times -0.2 \Rightarrow F = 0.4 \text{ N}$ parallel to motion, but in the opposite direction.

[2 marks available — 1 mark for finding a, 1 mark for finding F]

Q9

1.5 N

a

$0.3g$

Resolving vertically (↓):

$0.3g - 1.5 = 0.3a \Rightarrow a = 1.44 \div 0.3 = 4.8 \text{ ms}^{-2}$

$u = 0, a = 4.8, s = s, t = 12$

$s = ut + \frac{1}{2}at^2$

$s = 0 + \left(\frac{1}{2} \times 4.8 \times 12^2\right) = 345.6 \text{ m}$

Remember that if something is dropped, its initial velocity is zero.

Q10 $v = u + at$

$8 = 0 + 4a \Rightarrow a = 2 \text{ ms}^{-2}$

$F_{net} = ma$

$5 = 2m \Rightarrow m = 2.5 \text{ kg}$

$W = mg$, so $W = 2.5g \text{ N} = 24.5 \text{ N}$

The vertical forces are in equilibrium so $W = R = 24.5 \text{ N}$

[4 marks available — 1 mark for a, 1 mark for correctly linking force with acceleration, 1 mark for m, 1 mark for finding R]

Q11 **a)** $\mathbf{F}_{net} = m\mathbf{a}$

$8\mathbf{i} - 2\mathbf{j} = 10\mathbf{a} \Rightarrow \mathbf{a} = (0.8\mathbf{i} - 0.2\mathbf{j}) \text{ ms}^{-2}$

b) $|a| = \sqrt{0.8^2 + (-0.2)^2} = 0.8246... = 0.825 \text{ ms}^{-2} \text{ (3 s.f.)}$

c) $u = 0, v = v, a = 0.8246..., t = 6$

$v = u + at$

$v = 0 + (0.8246... \times 6) = 4.947... = 4.95 \text{ ms}^{-1} \text{ (3 s.f.)}$

Q12 $u = (0\mathbf{i} + 0\mathbf{j}), v = (32\mathbf{i} + 24\mathbf{j}), a = a, t = 2$

$v = u + at$

$(32\mathbf{i} + 24\mathbf{j}) = (0\mathbf{i} + 0\mathbf{j}) + 2a \Rightarrow a = (16\mathbf{i} + 12\mathbf{j}) \text{ ms}^{-2}$

$F_{net} = ma$

$(8\mathbf{i} + 6\mathbf{j}) = m(16\mathbf{i} + 12\mathbf{j})$

$\mathbf{i}$: $8 = 16m \Rightarrow m = 8 \div 16 = 0.5 \text{ kg}$

Check with $\mathbf{j}$: $6 = 12m \Rightarrow m = 6 \div 12 = 0.5 \text{ kg}$

Q13 **a)** $u = (0\mathbf{i} + 0\mathbf{j}), v = (30\mathbf{i} + 20\mathbf{j}), a = a, t = 10$

$v = u + at$

$(30\mathbf{i} + 20\mathbf{j}) = (0\mathbf{i} + 0\mathbf{j}) + 10a \Rightarrow a = (3\mathbf{i} + 2\mathbf{j}) \text{ ms}^{-2}$

$F_{net} = ma = 2(3\mathbf{i} + 2\mathbf{j}) = (6\mathbf{i} + 4\mathbf{j}) \text{ N}$

b) $(10\mathbf{i} - 3\mathbf{j}) + x = 6\mathbf{i} + 4\mathbf{j}$

$x = (6 - 10)\mathbf{i} + (4 + 3)\mathbf{j} = (-4\mathbf{i} + 7\mathbf{j}) \text{ N}$

$|x| = \sqrt{(-4)^2 + 7^2} = 8.062... = 8.06 \text{ N (3 s.f.)}$

Q14 **a)** $u = 0, v = (6\mathbf{i} - 9\mathbf{j}), a = a, t = 3$

$v = u + at$

$(6\mathbf{i} - 9\mathbf{j}) = 0 + 3a \Rightarrow a = (2\mathbf{i} - 3\mathbf{j}) \text{ ms}^{-2}$

$F_{net} = ma \Rightarrow (10\mathbf{i} - 15\mathbf{j}) = x(2\mathbf{i} - 3\mathbf{j}) \Rightarrow x = 5$

b) The other force $= (10\mathbf{i} - 15\mathbf{j}) - (\mathbf{i} + 7\mathbf{j}) = (9\mathbf{i} - 22\mathbf{j})$

Magnitude $= \sqrt{9^2 + (-22)^2} = \sqrt{565} = 23.8 \text{ N (3 s.f.)}$

Q15 **a)** $\begin{pmatrix}4\\6\end{pmatrix} = 2 \times \begin{pmatrix}2\\3\end{pmatrix}$, so the forces are parallel and act in the same direction. As the cars start from the same point, the motion will be along the same path.

[1 mark for the correct explanation]

b) Collision occurs when displacement is equal.

Using $F_{net} = ma$:

Car 1: $\begin{pmatrix}2\\3\end{pmatrix} = 2a_1 \Rightarrow a_1 = \begin{pmatrix}1\\1.5\end{pmatrix}$

Car 2: $\begin{pmatrix}4\\6\end{pmatrix} = 2a_2 \Rightarrow a_2 = \begin{pmatrix}2\\3\end{pmatrix}$

$u = 0$, and s is the same for each car, so using $s = ut + \frac{1}{2}at^2$ with the $\mathbf{i}$ components of the acceleration vectors:

$\frac{1}{2}(1)t^2 = \frac{1}{2}(2)(t - 2)^2 \Rightarrow 0 = t^2 - 8t + 8$

$\Rightarrow t = 4 + 2\sqrt{2} = 6.828...$, or $t = 4 - 2\sqrt{2} = 1.171...$

(You would get the same values using the $\mathbf{j}$ *components.)*

It can't be 1.171... seconds, as car 2 hasn't started to move at this point. So the collision happens 6.828... = 6.8 seconds (1 d.p.) after car 1 set off.

[7 marks available — 1 mark for each acceleration, 1 mark for an expression for s in terms of t for each car, 1 mark for a valid equation in t, 1 mark for both values of t, 1 mark for accepting the correct value of t]

Exercise 8.5 — Connected Particles

Q1 **a)**

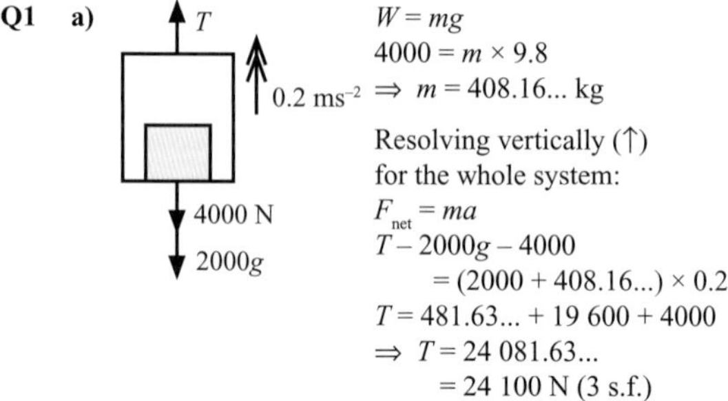

$W = mg$

$4000 = m \times 9.8$

$\Rightarrow m = 408.16... \text{ kg}$

Resolving vertically (↑) for the whole system:

$F_{net} = ma$

$T - 2000g - 4000$
$= (2000 + 408.16...) \times 0.2$

$T = 481.63... + 19\,600 + 4000$

$\Rightarrow T = 24\,081.63...$
$= 24\,100 \text{ N (3 s.f.)}$

b)

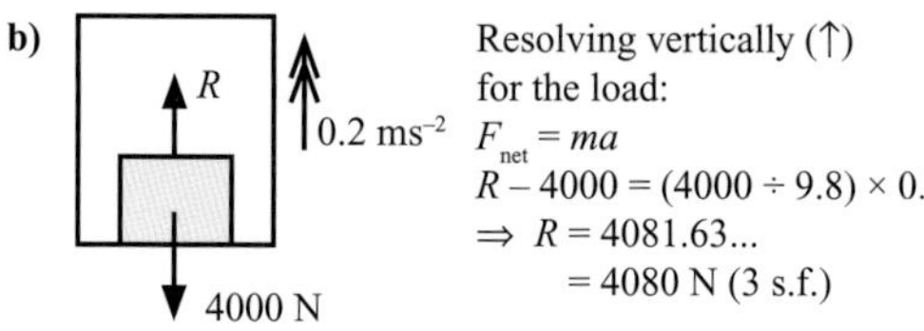

Resolving vertically (↑) for the load:

$F_{net} = ma$

$R - 4000 = (4000 \div 9.8) \times 0.2$

$\Rightarrow R = 4081.63...$
$= 4080 \text{ N (3 s.f.)}$

Q2 a)

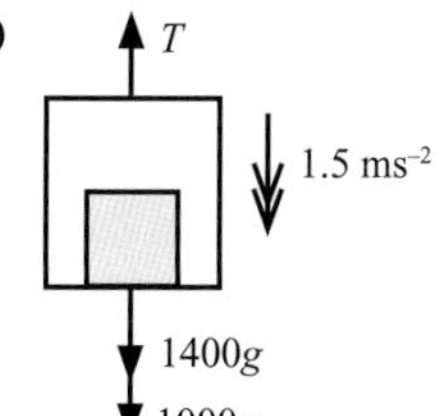

1400g

1000g

Resolving vertically (↓) for whole system:
$2400g - T = 2400 \times 1.5$
$\Rightarrow T = 19\,920$ N

b)

R
1.5 ms⁻²
1400g

Resolving vertically (↓) for the load:
$1400g - R = 1400 \times 1.5$
$\Rightarrow R = 11\,620$ N

c) The lift is now falling freely under gravity, so $a = g$:
$u = 0, v = v, a = 9.8, s = 30$
$v^2 = u^2 + 2as$
$v^2 = 2 \times 9.8 \times 30 = 588 \Rightarrow v = 24.2$ ms⁻¹ (3 s.f.)

Q3 a) Taking upwards to be the positive direction:
$F_{net} = ma$
$11\,124 - 1080g = 1080 \times a \Rightarrow 540 = 1080 \times a$
$\Rightarrow a = 0.5$ ms⁻²
[2 marks available — 1 mark for using F = ma, 1 mark for the correct answer]

b) $F_{net} = ma$
$R - 80g = 80 \times 0.5 \Rightarrow R = 824$ N
[2 marks available — 1 mark for using F = ma, 1 mark for the correct answer]

Q4 a) Resolving horizontally for the whole system, taking the direction of acceleration as positive:
$F_{net} = ma$
$P = 3500 \times 0.3 = 1050$ N
The tractor and trailer are decelerating, so the acceleration (and the force P) are in the opposite direction to the motion of the system.

b) Resolving horizontally for the trailer:
$F_{net} = ma$
$T = 1500 \times 0.3 = 450$ N

c) E.g. The tractor and trailer are modelled as particles, there are no external forces (e.g. air resistance) acting, the coupling is horizontal, the braking force generated by the tractor is constant, the tractor and trailer are moving in a straight line on horizontal ground.

Q5 a)

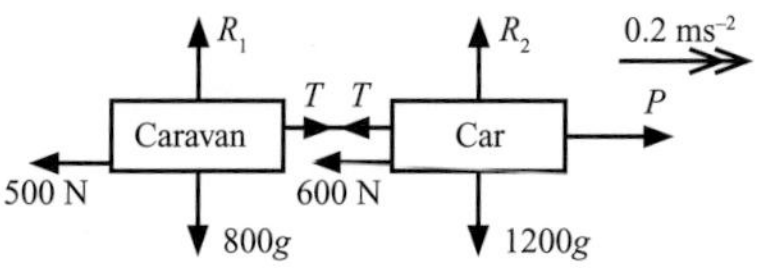

Resolving horizontally (→) for the whole system:
$F_{net} = ma$
$P - 500 - 600 = 2000 \times 0.2 \Rightarrow P = 1500$ N

b) Resolving horizontally (→) for the caravan:
$T - 500 = 800 \times 0.2 \Rightarrow T = 660$ N

c) $F_{net} = ma$
$-500 = 800a \Rightarrow a = -0.625$ ms⁻²
$u = 20, v = 0, a = -0.625, t = t$
$v = u + at$
$0 = 20 - 0.625t \Rightarrow t = 32$ s

Q6 a)

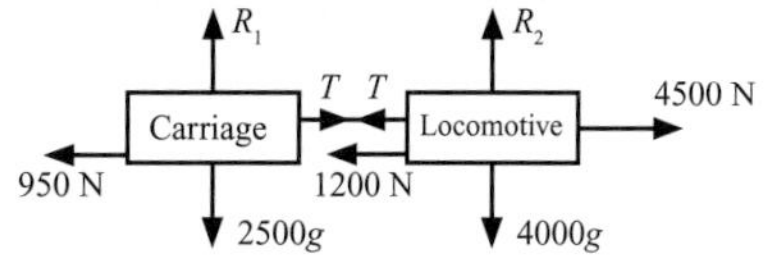

Resolving horizontally (→) for the whole system:
$F_{net} = ma$
$4500 - 1200 - 950 = (4000 + 2500)a = 6500a$
$\Rightarrow 2350 = 6500a \Rightarrow a = 0.361... = 0.36$ ms⁻² (2 d.p.)

b) Resolving horizontally (→) for the carriage:
$-950 = 2500a \Rightarrow a = -0.38$ ms⁻²
$s = s, u = 30, a = -0.38, t = 5$
$s = ut + \frac{1}{2}at^2 = 30 \times 5 + \frac{1}{2} \times -0.38 \times 5^2 = 145.25$ m

Q7 a)

R₁
R₂
T T
1900 N
Trailer
Car
200 N
400 N
400g
900g

Resolving horizontally (→) for the whole system:
$F_{net} = ma$
$1900 - 600 = 1300a \Rightarrow a = 1$ ms⁻²
[2 marks available — 1 mark for using F = ma, 1 mark for the correct answer]

b) Resolving horizontally (→) for the trailer:
$F_{net} = ma$
$T - 200 = 400 \times 1 \Rightarrow T = 600$ N
[2 marks available — 1 mark for using F = ma, 1 mark for the correct answer]

c) Resolving horizontally (→) for the whole system:
$F_{net} = ma$
$1900 - 700 = 1800a \Rightarrow a = 0.666...$ ms⁻²
Let $u = x$ and $v = x + 10$. Then using $v = u + at$:
Before the load: $x + 10 = x + 1 \times t \Rightarrow t = 10$
After the load: $x + 10 = x + 0.666... \times t \Rightarrow t = 15$.
$15 - 10 = 5$, so it takes 5 seconds longer.
[4 marks available — 1 mark for using F = ma, 1 mark for a, 1 mark for one value of t, 1 mark for the correct difference]

Q8 a)

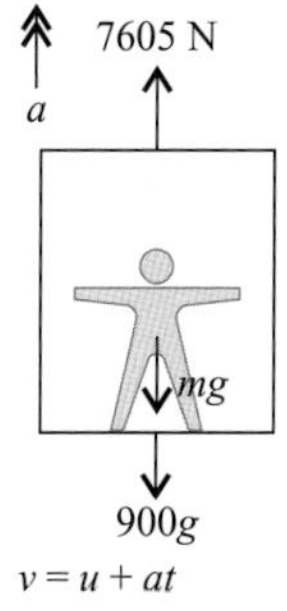

$v = u + at$
$0 = 20 + 10a \Rightarrow a = -2$ ms⁻²
Resolving vertically (↑) for the whole system:
$F_{net} = ma$
$7605 - (900 + m)g = (900 + m) \times -2 \Rightarrow m = 75$ kg
[3 marks available — 1 mark for finding a, 1 mark for using F = ma, 1 mark for the correct answer]

b) Resolving vertically (↑) for the person:
$F_{net} = ma$
$R - 75g = 75 \times -2 \Rightarrow R = 585$ N
[2 marks available — 1 mark for using F = ma, 1 mark for the correct answer]

c) Distance needed for the lift to gain a velocity of 20 ms^{-1}, accelerating from rest at the bottom of the shaft:
$v^2 = u^2 + 2as \Rightarrow 400 = 0 + 2 \times 1.2 \times s \Rightarrow s = 166.6...$ m.
The lift then continues to move upwards, decelerating to come to rest.
$v^2 = u^2 + 2as \Rightarrow 0 = 400 - 4s \Rightarrow s = 100$ m
So the minimum height of the shaft is:
$166.6... + 100 = 267$ m (3 s.f.)
[3 marks available — 1 mark for each separate distance and 1 mark for the minimum height]

Exercise 8.6 — Pegs and Pulleys

Q1 a)

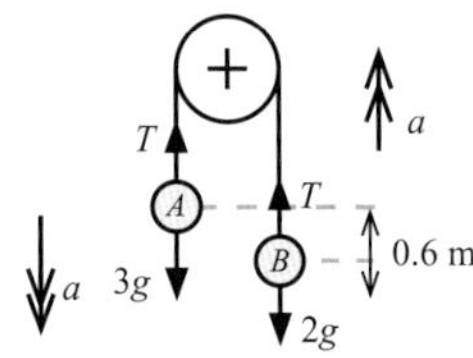

b) Resolving vertically (↓) for A:
$F_{net} = ma$
$3g - T = 3a$ ①
Resolving vertically (↑) for B:
$F_{net} = ma$
$T - 2g = 2a$ ②
① + ②: $g = 5a \Rightarrow a = 9.8 \div 5 = 1.96$ ms^{-2}
The particles will become level when they have each moved 0.3 m.
$u = 0, a = 1.96, s = 0.3, t = t$
$s = ut + \frac{1}{2}at^2$
$0.3 = \frac{1}{2} \times 1.96 \times t^2$
$t^2 = 0.306... \Rightarrow t = 0.5532... = 0.553$ s (3 s.f.)

Q2 a) Resolving vertically (↑) for A:
$F_{net} = ma$
$T - 2g = 2a$ ①
Resolving vertically (↓) for B:
$F_{net} = ma$
$6g - T = 6a$ ②
① + ②: $4g = 8a \Rightarrow a = 4.9$ ms^{-2}
[3 marks available — 1 mark for each correct equation, 1 mark for a]

b) $T - 2g = 2 \times 4.9 \Rightarrow T = 29.4$ N *[1 mark]*

Q3 a) $u = 0, a = a, s = 5, t = 2$
$s = ut + \frac{1}{2}at^2$
$5 = \frac{1}{2} \times a \times 2^2 \Rightarrow a = 5 \div 2 = 2.5$ ms^{-2}
Resolving vertically (↓) for A:
$F_{net} = ma$
$35g - T = 35 \times 2.5 \Rightarrow T = 343 - 87.5 = 255.5$ N

b) Resolving vertically (↑) for B:
$F_{net} = ma$
$T - Mg = 2.5M$
$255.5 = 12.3M \Rightarrow M = 20.8$ kg (3 s.f.)

Q4 a) Resolving horizontally (→) for A:
$F_{net} = ma$
$T = 5a$ ①
Resolving vertically (↓) for B: $7g - T = 7a$ ②
Substituting ① into ②: $7g - 5a = 7a$
$7g = 12a \Rightarrow a = 7g \div 12 = 5.716... = 5.72$ ms^{-2} (3 s.f.)

b) Using ①:
$T = 5a = 5 \times 5.716... = 28.583... = 28.6$ N (3 s.f.)

c) The string is light and inextensible, the pulley is fixed and smooth, the horizontal surface is smooth, no other external forces are acting, A doesn't hit the pulley, B doesn't hit the floor, the string doesn't break, the pulley doesn't break, the string between A and the pulley is horizontal, the string is initially taut, the acceleration due to gravity is constant at 9.8 ms^{-2}.

Q5

Resolving horizontally (→) for the 2 kg mass:
$F_{net} = ma$
$16 = 2a \Rightarrow a = 8$ ms^{-2}
Resolving vertically (↓) for the M kg mass:
$F_{net} = ma$
$Mg - 16 = 8M \Rightarrow (g - 8)M = 16$
$\Rightarrow M = \frac{16}{g - 8} = 8.89$ kg (2 d.p.)

Q6 a)

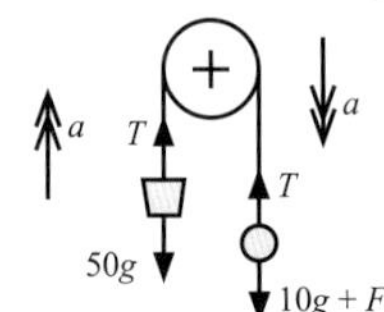

b) First find the acceleration.
$u = 0, s = 12, a = a, t = 20$
$s = ut + \frac{1}{2}at^2$
$12 = \frac{1}{2} \times a \times 20^2 \Rightarrow a = 0.06$ ms^{-2}
Now resolving vertically (↑) for the bucket:
$F_{net} = ma$
$T - 50g = 50 \times 0.06 \Rightarrow T = 493$ N

c) Resolving vertically (↓) for the counterweight:
$F_{net} = ma$
$10g + F - T = 10 \times 0.06$
$\Rightarrow F = 0.6 - 98 + 493 = 395.6$ N

d)

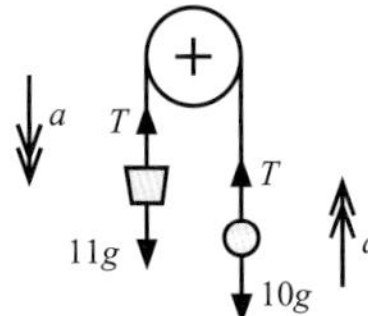

Resolving vertically (↓) for the bucket:
$11g - T = 11a$ ①
Resolving vertically (↑) for the counterweight:
$T - 10g = 10a$ ②
① + ②:
$g = 21a \Rightarrow a = 0.466...$ ms^{-2}
$u = 0, v = v, s = 12$
$v^2 = u^2 + 2as$
$v^2 = 2 \times 0.466... \times 12 = 11.2 \Rightarrow v = 3.35$ ms^{-1} (3 s.f.)

Q7 a) Resolving vertically (↓) for P:
$2.5g - T = 2.5a$ ①
Resolving vertically (↑) for Q:
$T - 1.5g = 1.5a$ ②
① + ②: $g = 4a \Rightarrow a = \frac{g}{4} = 2.45 \text{ ms}^{-2}$

b) For Q: $s = s, u = 0, a = 2.45, t = 0.8$
$s = ut + \frac{1}{2}at^2 \Rightarrow s = 0 + \frac{1}{2} \times 2.45 \times 0.8^2 = 0.784 \text{ m}$
So total height above the ground is 2 + 0.784 m = 2.784 m.

c) For P: $s = 2, u = 0, v = v, a = 2.45$
$v^2 = u^2 + 2as$
$v^2 = 0 + 2 \times 2.45 \times 2 \Rightarrow v = \sqrt{9.8} = 3.13 \text{ ms}^{-1}$ (3 s.f.)

Q8 a) A has a greater mass than B, so A will accelerate downwards and B will accelerate upwards.
Resolving vertically (↓) for A:
$15g - T = 15a$ ①
Resolving vertically (↑) for B:
$T - 12g = 12a$ ②
① + ②: $3g = 27a \Rightarrow a = 1.088... = 1.09 \text{ ms}^{-2}$ (3 s.f.)

b) The force exerted on the pulley by the string is $2T$.
Using ②:
$T = 12a + 12g = (12 \times 1.088...) + (12 \times 9.8)$
$T = 130.66... \Rightarrow 2T = 261.33... = 261 \text{ N}$ (3 s.f.)

c) First find the speed of the particles when A hits the ground:
$u = 0, v = v, a = 1.088..., s = 6$
$v^2 = u^2 + 2as$
$v^2 = 2 \times 1.088... \times 6 = 13.066... \Rightarrow v = 3.614...$
Now considering the motion of B as it moves freely under gravity, taking upwards as positive:
$u = 3.614..., v = 0, a = -9.8, t = t$
$v = u + at$
$0 = 3.614... - 9.8t \Rightarrow t = 0.368... = 0.369 \text{ s}$ (3 s.f.)

Q9 a)

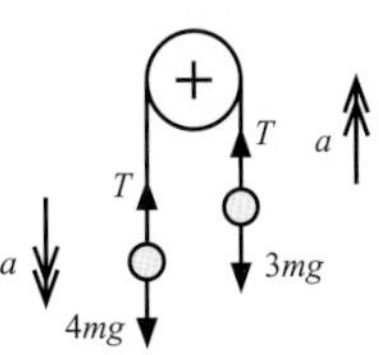

Resolving vertically (↓) for the $4m$ kg mass:
$F_{net} = ma$
$4mg - T = 4ma$ ①
Resolving vertically (↑) for the $3m$ kg mass:
$F_{net} = ma$
$T - 3mg = 3ma$ ②
① + ②: $mg = 7ma \Rightarrow a = 1.4 \text{ ms}^{-2}$,
which is independent of m.
[4 marks available — 1 mark for using F = ma, 1 mark for forming two simultaneous equations, 1 mark for attempting to solve simultaneously, 1 mark for finding a and concluding that it is independent of m]

b) Using equation ② from part a):
$T = 3m \times (g + 1.4) \Rightarrow T = 33.6m$,
so the tension is proportional to m. *[1 mark]*
You could also have just rearranged either of equation 1 or 2 from part a) to show $T = 4m(g - a)$ or $T = 3m(g + a)$ respectively and left it at that.

Q10 Split the motion into two parts. The first part is from the particles being released to P striking the pulley.
Resolving vertically (↓) for Q:
$F_{net} = ma$
$10g - T = 10a$ ①
Resolving horizontally (→) for P:
$F_{net} = ma$
$T = 8a$ ②
Substituting ② into ①:
$10g - 8a = 10a \Rightarrow 10g = 18a \Rightarrow a = 5.444...$
Use this to find the time between the point that the particles are released and the point that P hits the pulley:
$u = 0, a = 5.444..., s = 4, t = t$
$s = ut + \frac{1}{2}at^2$
$4 = \frac{1}{2} \times 5.444... \times t^2 \Rightarrow t^2 = 1.469... \Rightarrow t = 1.212...$
Also find the speed of the particles at this point:
$v = u + at$
$v = 0 + (5.444... \times 1.212...) = 6.599...$
Now consider the second part of the motion — Q falling freely under gravity:
$u = 6.599..., a = 9.8, s = 9 - 4 = 5, t = t$
$s = ut + \frac{1}{2}at^2$
$5 = (6.599...)t + 4.9t^2 \Rightarrow 4.9t^2 + (6.599...)t - 5 = 0$
Using the quadratic formula:
$t = \frac{-6.599... \pm \sqrt{(6.599...)^2 - (4 \times 4.9 \times -5)}}{9.8}$
So $t = 0.540...$ or $t = -1.887...$
t must be positive, so take $t = 0.540...$
So the total time taken is:
$1.212... + 0.540... = 1.752... = 1.75 \text{ s}$ (3 s.f.)

Q11 a)

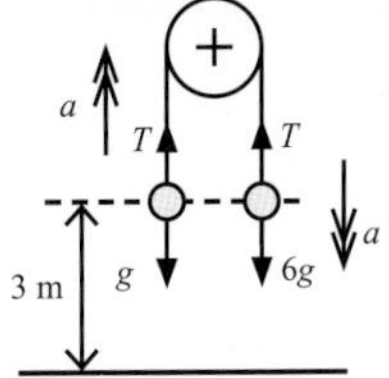

Resolving vertically (↓) for the 6 kg mass:
$F_{net} = ma$
$6g - T = 6a$ ①
Resolving vertically (↑) for the 1 kg mass:
$F_{net} = ma$
$T - g = a$ ②
① + ②: $5g = 7a \Rightarrow a = 7 \text{ ms}^{-2}$
[4 marks available — 1 mark for using F = ma, 1 mark for forming two simultaneous equations, 1 mark for attempting to solve simultaneously, 1 mark for finding a]

b) $T - g = a \Rightarrow T - g = 7 \Rightarrow T = 16.8 \text{ N}$ *[1 mark]*

c) As particle B hits the ground:
$s = -3 \text{ m}, u = 0 \text{ ms}^{-1}, v = v, a = -7 \text{ ms}^{-2}, t = t$
$s = ut + \frac{1}{2}at^2 \Rightarrow -3 = -3.5t^2$
$\Rightarrow t = 0.92... = 0.9$ seconds (1 d.p.) *[1 mark]*

d) $v = u + at \Rightarrow v = 7 \times 0.92... \Rightarrow v = 6.48... \text{ ms}^{-1}$.
From then, the lighter particle continues to move up under the influence of gravity:
$v^2 = u^2 + 2as \Rightarrow 0 = (6.48...)^2 + 2(-g)s \Rightarrow 0 = 42 - 2gs$
$\Rightarrow s = 2.14...$ m. So the maximum height is
$3 + 2.14... = 5.14... = 5.1 \text{ m}$ (1 d.p.).
[3 marks available — 1 mark for finding v, 1 mark for s, 1 mark for total height reached]

Exercise 8.7 — Harder Problems involving Pegs and Pulleys

Q1 **a)** Resolving horizontally (←) for A:
$T - F = 6a \Rightarrow 6a = 12 - 10 = 2$
$a = 2 \div 6 = 0.333 \text{ ms}^{-2}$ (3 s.f.)

b) Resolving vertically (↓) for B:
$Mg - T = Ma \Rightarrow Mg - Ma = 12$
$M(9.8 - 0.333...) = 12$
$M = 12 \div 9.466... = 1.27$ kg (3 s.f.)

Q2 For B: $s = 1.5, u = 0, a = a, t = 3$
$s = ut + \frac{1}{2}at^2$
$1.5 = 0 + \frac{1}{2} \times a \times 9 \Rightarrow a = \frac{1}{3} \text{ ms}^{-2}$
Resolving horizontally (→) for A:
$F_{net} = ma$
$T - 15 = 3a = 3 \times \frac{1}{3} = 1 \Rightarrow T = 16$ N
Resolving vertically (↓) for B:
$F_{net} = ma$
$Mg - T = Ma$
$Mg - 16 = \frac{1}{3}M \Rightarrow M(g - \frac{1}{3}) = 16 \Rightarrow M = 1.69$ kg (3 s.f.)

Q3 **a)**

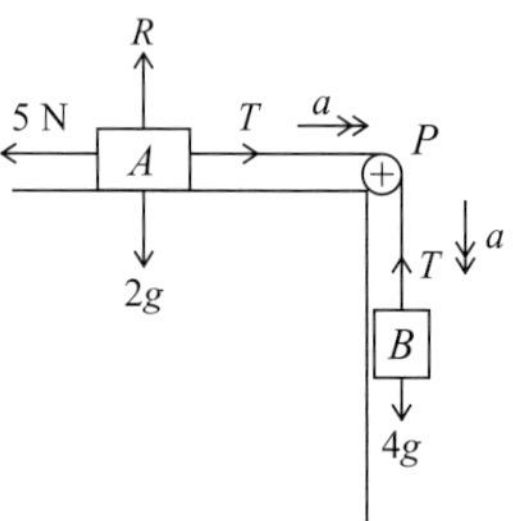

Resolving horizontally (→) for A:
$F_{net} = ma$
$T - 5 = 2a$ ①
Resolving vertically (↓) for B:
$F_{net} = ma$
$4g - T = 4a$ ②
① + ②: $4g - 5 = 6a \Rightarrow a = 5.7 \text{ ms}^{-2}$
[4 marks available — 1 mark for using F = ma, 1 mark for forming two simultaneous equations, 1 mark for attempting to solve simultaneously, 1 mark for finding a]

b) $T - 5 = 2 \times 5.7 \Rightarrow T = 16.4$ N *[1 mark]*

c) There is no movement, so $a = 0$.
Resolving horizontally (→) for A:
$F_{net} = ma \Rightarrow T - F = 0 \Rightarrow T = F$
Resolving vertically (↓) for B:
$F_{net} = ma \Rightarrow 4g - T = 0 \Rightarrow T = 4g = 39.2$ N
So $F = T = 39.2$ N
[2 marks available — 1 mark for T = 39.2 N, 1 mark for F = 39.2 N]

Q4 For the slab: $u = 0, v = 2, a = a, t = 6$
$v = u + at$
$2 = 0 + 6a \Rightarrow a = \frac{1}{3} \text{ ms}^{-2}$
Resolving vertically (↑) for the slab:
$F_{net} = ma$
$T - 300g = 300 \times \frac{1}{3} \Rightarrow T = 100 + 300g = 3040$ N
Resolving horizontally (→) for the buggy:
$F_{net} = ma$
$12000 - 3040 - F = 4500 \times \frac{1}{3}$
$\Rightarrow F = 12000 - 3040 - 1500 = 7460$ N

Q5 **a)** $u = 0,\ v = 3,\ a = a,\ t = 5$
$v = u + at$
$3 = 0 + 5a \Rightarrow a = 0.6 \text{ ms}^{-2}$
Resolving vertically (↑) for the crate:
$T - 250g = 250a \Rightarrow T = 250 \times 0.6 + 250 \times 9.8$
$= 150 + 2450 = 2600$ N
Resolving horizontally (←) for the truck:
$D - T - F = 4000a$
$\Rightarrow D = 4000 \times 0.6 + 2600 + 500 = 2400 + 3100 = 5500$ N

b) Resolving horizontally again (←) for the truck:
$5500 - 500 = 4000a \Rightarrow a = 5000 \div 4000 = 1.25 \text{ ms}^{-2}$

c) Take upwards (↑) as the positive direction.
Find the height that the crate reaches before the rope snaps (i.e. its displacement during the first 5 seconds):
$s = s,\ u = 0,\ v = 3,\ a = 0.6,\ t = 5$
$s = \frac{1}{2}(u + v)t = 0.5 \times 3 \times 5 = 7.5$ m
You could've used a different suvat equation to find s.
After the rope snaps: $s = -7.5,\ u = 3,\ a = -9.8,\ t = t$
$s = ut + \frac{1}{2}at^2 \Rightarrow -7.5 = 3t - 4.9t^2 \Rightarrow 4.9t^2 - 3t - 7.5 = 0$
Using the quadratic formula:
$$t = \frac{3 \pm \sqrt{(-3)^2 - (4 \times 4.9 \times (-7.5))}}{9.8} = \frac{3 \pm \sqrt{9 + 147}}{9.8}$$
$t = -0.9683...$ ($t < 0$ so ignore) or $t = 1.5806...$
So the crate hits the ground 1.58 seconds (to 3 s.f.) after the rope snaps.

d) Some possible answers include:
– The pulley is assumed to be smooth, which is likely to be inaccurate. The model could be improved by accounting for the friction in the pulley.
– The driving force and the resistance force are given as constant, but it would be more accurate to assume that they vary with time and include that in the model.
– The falling crate would experience air resistance as it fell, so if the model were updated to include that, it would be more realistic.

Q6 **a)** B only needs to overcome the friction acting on A to move it — B is not lifting A, only sliding it. For equilibrium with maximum friction, $T = Mg$ and $T = 3$, so $M = 0.3$ kg (1 d.p.).
So where $M > \frac{3}{g}$ kg (≈ 0.31 kg), movement occurs.
[4 marks available — 1 mark for explanation, 1 mark for each correct equation from F_{net} = ma, 1 mark for the correct inequality]

b) Resolving horizontally (→) for A:
$F_{net} = ma$
$T - 3 = 3 \times 2 \Rightarrow T = 9$ N
Resolving vertically (↓) for B:
$F_{net} = ma$
$Mg - T = 2M \Rightarrow 9.8M - 2M = 9 \Rightarrow M = 1.15$ kg (3 s.f.)
[4 marks available — 1 mark for using F = ma, 1 mark for forming two correct equations, 1 mark for finding T, 1 mark for finding M]

Q7 **a)** For $t = 1$, $s = ut + \frac{1}{2}at^2 \Rightarrow 3 = \frac{1}{2}a \Rightarrow a = 6 \text{ ms}^{-2}$
And for $t = 3$, $s = ut + \frac{1}{2}at^2 \Rightarrow 3 = \frac{9}{2}a \Rightarrow a = 0.666... \text{ ms}^{-2}$
So $0.666... \text{ ms}^{-2} < a < 6 \text{ ms}^{-2}$
[2 marks available — 1 mark for each correct bound on the value of a]

b) Resolving horizontally (→) for A:
$F_{net} = ma$
$T - 300 = 60a$ ①
Resolving vertically (↓) for B:
$F_{net} = ma$
$Mg - T = Ma$ ②
① + ②: $Mg - 300 = Ma + 60a \Rightarrow a = \frac{Mg - 300}{M + 60}$
$0.666... < a < 6 \Rightarrow 0.666... < \frac{Mg - 300}{M + 60} < 6$
$\Rightarrow 0.666...M + 40 < Mg - 300$ and $Mg - 300 < 6M + 360$
$\Rightarrow 9.133...M > 340$ and $3.8M < 660$
$\Rightarrow 37.2 \text{ kg} < M < 173.7 \text{ kg}$ (1 d.p.)
[7 marks available — 1 mark for using F = ma, 1 mark for forming two simultaneous equations, 1 mark for attempting to solve simultaneously, 1 mark for an expression for a in terms of M, 1 mark for any correct inequality, 1 mark for each correct bound on the value of M]

Chapter 8 Review Exercise

Q1 a) Magnitude = $\sqrt{5^2 + 12^2} = 13$ kN
Direction $\theta = \tan^{-1}\left(\frac{12}{5}\right) = 67.38...° = 67.4°$ (3 s.f.)

b) Magnitude = $\sqrt{2^2 + (-5)^2} = \sqrt{29} = 5.39$ N (3 s.f.)
Angle below the positive horizontal $\alpha = \tan^{-1}\left(\frac{5}{2}\right) = 68.1..°$
So direction $\theta = 360° - \alpha = 292°$ (3 s.f.)

c) Magnitude = $\sqrt{(-3)^2 + 8^2} = \sqrt{73} = 8.54$ kN (3 s.f.)
Angle above the negative horizontal $\alpha = \tan^{-1}\left(\frac{8}{3}\right) = 69.4...°$
So direction $\theta = 180° - \alpha = 111°$ (3 s.f.)

d) Magnitude = $\sqrt{(-4)^2 + (-11)^2} = \sqrt{137} = 11.7$ N (3 s.f.)
Angle below the negative horizontal $\alpha = \tan^{-1}\left(\frac{11}{4}\right) = 70.0...°$
So direction $\theta = 180° + \alpha = 250°$ (3 s.f.)

Q2

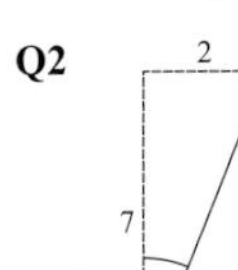

$\theta = \tan^{-1}\left(\frac{2}{7}\right) = 15.9°$ (3 s.f.)

Q3 a) Resultant force = $\begin{pmatrix} 11 \\ -6 \end{pmatrix} + \begin{pmatrix} -8 \\ 4 \end{pmatrix} = \begin{pmatrix} 3 \\ -2 \end{pmatrix}$ N

b) The object is in equilibrium, so the resultant force is 0,
i.e. $\begin{pmatrix} 3 \\ -2 \end{pmatrix} + F = \begin{pmatrix} 0 \\ 0 \end{pmatrix} \Rightarrow F = \begin{pmatrix} -3 \\ 2 \end{pmatrix}$ N
So $|F| = \sqrt{(-3)^2 + 2^2} = \sqrt{13} = 3.6$ N (1 d.p.)
Angle above the negative horizontal $\alpha = \tan^{-1}\left(\frac{2}{3}\right) = 33.69...°$
So direction $\theta = 180° - \alpha = 146.3°$ (1 d.p.)

Q4 a) $\begin{pmatrix} 4 \\ -3 \end{pmatrix}$ N *[1 mark]*

b) $(3\mathbf{i} + 4\mathbf{j})$ N *[1 mark]*

Q5 a) $R = F_1 + F_2 + F_3 = (2\mathbf{i} + a\mathbf{j}) + (3a\mathbf{i} - 2b\mathbf{j}) + (b\mathbf{i} + 2\mathbf{j})$
$= [(2 + 3a + b)\mathbf{i} + (a - 2b + 2)\mathbf{j}]$ N
[2 marks available — 1 mark for attempting to add the forces, 1 mark for correct answer]

b) $\tan 45° = \frac{a}{2} \Rightarrow a = 2 \times \tan 45° \Rightarrow a = 2$ *[1 mark]*

c) $R = (2 + 6 + b)\mathbf{i} + (2 - 2b + 2)\mathbf{j} = (8 + b)\mathbf{i} + (4 - 2b)\mathbf{j}$
$3\sqrt{10} = |\mathbf{R}| = \sqrt{(8 + b)^2 + (4 - 2b)^2}$
$= \sqrt{(64 + 16b + b^2) + (16 - 16b + 4b^2)}$
$= \sqrt{80 + 5b^2}$
So $90 = 5b^2 + 80 \Rightarrow 5b^2 = 10 \Rightarrow b^2 = 2 \Rightarrow b = \pm\sqrt{2}$
[3 marks available — 1 mark for finding the magnitude of R in terms of b, 1 mark for forming a quadratic, 1 mark for both correct values]

Q6 a) Let $\mathbf{F} = \begin{pmatrix} a \\ a \end{pmatrix}$ N, so $a^2 + a^2 = 5^2 \Rightarrow 2a^2 = 25 \Rightarrow a = \frac{\sqrt{25}}{\sqrt{2}}$
$= \frac{5}{\sqrt{2}} = \frac{5\sqrt{2}}{2}$, so $\mathbf{F} = \begin{pmatrix} \frac{5\sqrt{2}}{2} \\ \frac{5\sqrt{2}}{2} \end{pmatrix}$ N.
[2 marks available — 1 mark for two equal components, 1 mark for the correct answer]

b) $\begin{pmatrix} -\frac{5\sqrt{2}}{2} \\ \frac{5\sqrt{2}}{2} \end{pmatrix}$ N and $\begin{pmatrix} \frac{5\sqrt{2}}{2} \\ -\frac{5\sqrt{2}}{2} \end{pmatrix}$ N
[2 marks available — 1 mark for each correct answer]

Q7 a) $\begin{pmatrix} -4 \\ 6 \end{pmatrix} + \begin{pmatrix} 1 \\ -7 \end{pmatrix} = \begin{pmatrix} -3 \\ -1 \end{pmatrix}$ N *[1 mark]*

b) $\sqrt{(-3)^2 + (-1)^2} = \sqrt{10} = 3.16... = 3.2$ N (2 s.f.)
[2 marks available — 1 mark for a correct method, 1 mark for the correct answer]

c) $\alpha = \tan^{-1}\left(\frac{1}{3}\right) = 18.43...°$
$\begin{pmatrix} -3 \\ -1 \end{pmatrix}$ lies in the bottom left quadrant,
so $\theta = 180° + 18.43...° = 198°$ (3 s.f.)
[2 marks available — 1 mark for a correct method, 1 mark for the correct answer]

d) $\begin{pmatrix} 3 \\ 4 \end{pmatrix} - \begin{pmatrix} -3 \\ -1 \end{pmatrix} = \begin{pmatrix} 6 \\ 5 \end{pmatrix}$ N *[1 mark]*

Q8 $|\mathbf{F}| = \sqrt{4^2 + a^2} = \sqrt{a^2 + 16}$, $|\mathbf{G}| = \sqrt{2^2 + a^2} = \sqrt{a^2 + 4}$
$\mathbf{G} - \mathbf{F} = \begin{pmatrix} 6 \\ 0 \end{pmatrix} \Rightarrow |\mathbf{G} - \mathbf{F}| = 6$
Using the cosine rule:
$\cos\theta = \frac{a^2 + 16 + a^2 + 4 - 36}{2\sqrt{a^2 + 16}\sqrt{a^2 + 4}} = \frac{2a^2 - 16}{2\sqrt{(a^2 + 16)(a^2 + 4)}}$
$= \frac{a^2 - 8}{\sqrt{(a^2 + 16)(a^2 + 4)}}$ as required.
[3 marks available — 1 mark for finding the magnitudes in terms of a, 1 mark for attempting to use the cosine rule, 1 mark for rearranging to obtain the required result]

Q9 Resolving horizontally (→):
$F_{net} = ma$
$2 = 1.5a \Rightarrow a = \frac{4}{3}$ ms^{-2}
$u = 0, v = v, a = \frac{4}{3}, t = 3$
$v = u + at$
$v = 0 + \frac{4}{3} \times 3 \Rightarrow v = 4$ ms^{-1}

Q10 $u = 0, v = 3, a = a, t = 6$
$v = u + at$
$3 = 0 + 6a \Rightarrow a = \frac{1}{2}$ ms^{-2}
Resolving horizontally (→):
$F_{net} = ma = 7 \times \frac{1}{2} = 3.5$ N

Q11 300 g = 0.3 kg
$F_{net} = ma = 0.3 \times 5 = 1.5$ N

Q12 $s = 5, u = 0, a = a, t = 1.2$
$s = ut + \frac{1}{2}at^2 \Rightarrow 5 = \frac{1}{2}a(1.2)^2 \Rightarrow a = 6.94...$ ms^{-2}
$F_{net} = ma \Rightarrow 8g - R = 8 \times 6.94... \Rightarrow R = 22.84... = 22.8$ N (1 d.p.)
[3 marks available — 1 mark for finding a, 1 mark for correctly linking force with acceleration, 1 mark for finding R]

Q13 $F_{net} = ma$
$3 - 1.2 = 4a \Rightarrow 1.8 = 4a \Rightarrow a = 0.45$ ms^{-2}
$s = s, u = 10, a = 0.45, t = 4$
So $s = ut + \frac{1}{2}at^2 \Rightarrow s = 10 \times 4 + \frac{1}{2} \times 0.45 \times 4^2 \Rightarrow s = 43.6$ m
[3 marks available — 1 mark for using F = ma, 1 mark for finding a, 1 mark for finding s]

Q14 a) Taking upwards as positive:
$s = 2.7, u = 0, a = a, t = 3$
$s = ut + \frac{1}{2}at^2$
$2.7 = 0 + \frac{1}{2} \times a \times 3^2 \Rightarrow a = 0.6 \text{ ms}^{-2}$

b) Resolving vertically (↑):
$F_{net} = ma$
$T - 3g = 3 \times 0.6 \Rightarrow T = 1.8 + 3 \times 9.8 = 31.2 \text{ N}$

Q15

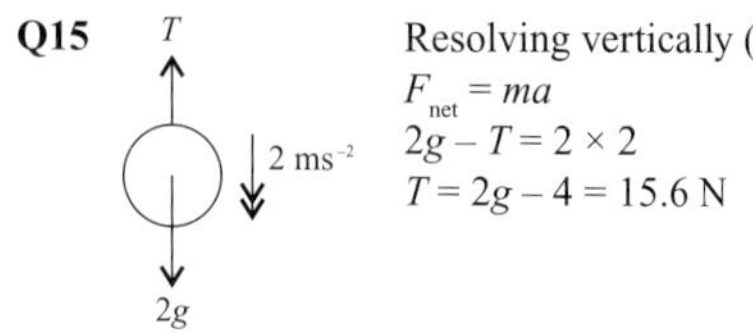

Resolving vertically (↓):
$F_{net} = ma$
$2g - T = 2 \times 2$
$T = 2g - 4 = 15.6 \text{ N}$

Q16 $F = ma \Rightarrow 15\mathbf{i} + 9\mathbf{j} = 6a \Rightarrow a = 2.5\mathbf{i} + 1.5\mathbf{j} \text{ ms}^{-2}$
$v = v, u = 0, a = 2.5\mathbf{i} + 1.5\mathbf{j}, t = 4$
$v = u + at \Rightarrow v = 4(2.5\mathbf{i} + 1.5\mathbf{j}) \Rightarrow v = 10\mathbf{i} + 6\mathbf{j} \text{ ms}^{-1}$
[2 marks available — 1 mark for finding a, 1 mark for v]

Q17 a) $F_{net} = ma$
$(4\mathbf{i} - 2\mathbf{j}) = 4a \Rightarrow a = (\mathbf{i} - \frac{1}{2}\mathbf{j}) \text{ ms}^{-2}$

b) $F_{net} = ma$
$(4\mathbf{i} - 2\mathbf{j}) + (-\mathbf{i} + 2\mathbf{j}) = 3\mathbf{i}$
$3\mathbf{i} = 4a \Rightarrow a = 0.75\mathbf{i} \text{ ms}^{-2}$
$|\mathbf{a}| = \sqrt{0.75^2 + 0^2} = 0.75 \text{ ms}^{-2}$

Q18 a) Resultant force $= (24\mathbf{i} + 18\mathbf{j}) + (6\mathbf{i} + 22\mathbf{j}) = 30\mathbf{i} + 40\mathbf{j}$
Magnitude $= \sqrt{30^2 + 40^2} = 50 \text{ N}$
$F_{net} = ma$
$50 = 8a \Rightarrow a = 6.25 \text{ ms}^{-2}$
Direction of acceleration is the same as the direction of the resultant force, i.e. $\theta = \tan^{-1}\left(\frac{40}{30}\right) = 53.13...° = 53.1°$ (3 s.f.)
You could also have found the vector form of the acceleration and used that to find its magnitude.

b) $s = s, u = 0, a = 6.25, t = 3$
$s = ut + \frac{1}{2}at^2$
$s = 0 + \frac{1}{2} \times 6.25 \times 3^2 = 28.125 \text{ m}$

Q19 a) $\alpha = \tan^{-1} \frac{5}{12} = 22.619...°$, and it's in the upper right quadrant, so $\theta = 22.6°$ (1 d.p.)
[2 marks available — 1 mark for a correct method, 1 mark for the correct answer]

b) $F_{net} = ma \Rightarrow -1.2\mathbf{i} - 0.5\mathbf{j} = 5a \Rightarrow a = (-0.24\mathbf{i} - 0.1\mathbf{j}) \text{ ms}^{-2}$
$|a| = \sqrt{(-0.24)^2 + (-0.1)^2} \Rightarrow |a| = 0.26 \text{ ms}^{-2}$
The direction of acceleration is parallel to and opposite to the direction of initial movement, so:
$v^2 = u^2 + 2as \Rightarrow 0 = (12^2 + 5^2) + 2 \times -0.26s$
$\Rightarrow s = 325 \text{ m}$
*[3 marks available — 1 mark for finding –0.24**i** – 0.1**j**, 1 mark for finding 0.26 ms⁻², 1 mark for finding s]*

Q20 a)

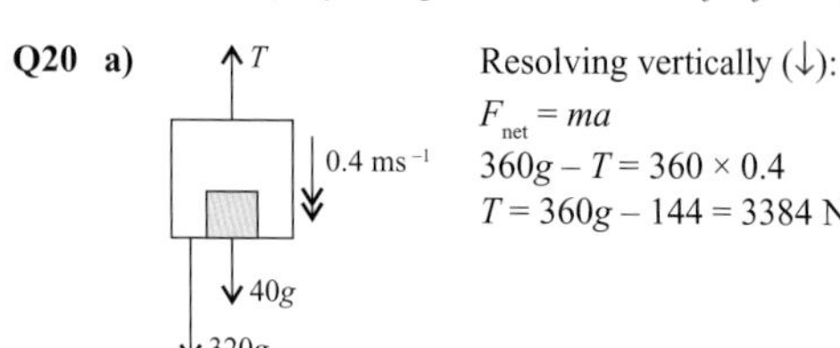

Resolving vertically (↓):
$F_{net} = ma$
$360g - T = 360 \times 0.4$
$T = 360g - 144 = 3384 \text{ N}$

b)

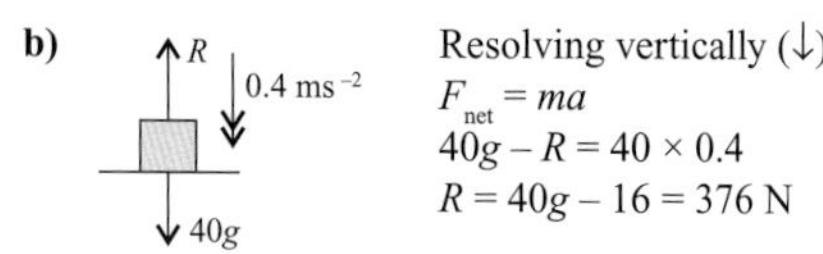

Resolving vertically (↓):
$F_{net} = ma$
$40g - R = 40 \times 0.4$
$R = 40g - 16 = 376 \text{ N}$

Q21 a)

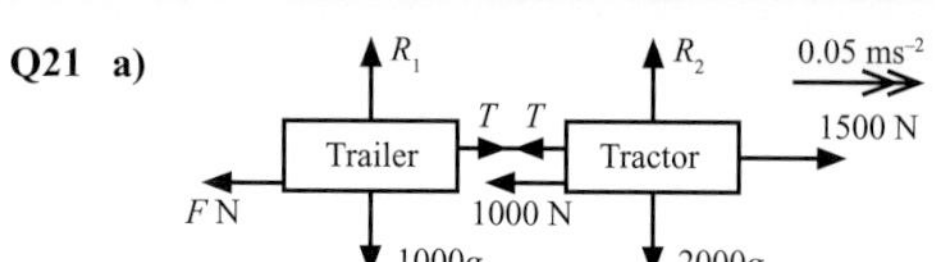

Resolving horizontally (→) for the whole system:
$F_{net} = ma$
$1500 - 1000 - F = 3000 \times 0.05$
$500 - F = 150 \Rightarrow F = 350 \text{ N}$

b) E.g. Resolving horizontally (→) for the trailer:
$F_{net} = ma$
$T - 350 = 1000 \times 0.05$
$T = 350 + 50 = 400 \text{ N}$
You could have resolved forces for the tractor instead and got the same value for T.

Q22 a)

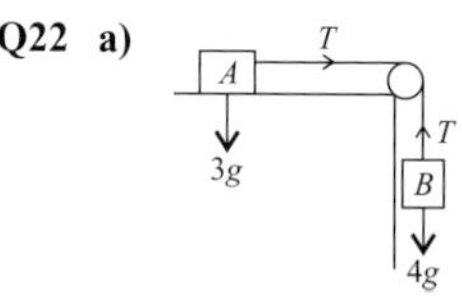

Resolving horizontally (→) for A:
$T = 3a$ ①
Resolving vertically (↓) for B:
$4g - T = 4a$ ②
① + ②: $4g = 7a \Rightarrow a = \frac{4g}{7} = 5.6 \text{ ms}^{-2}$

b) $T = 3a = 3 \times 5.6 = 16.8 \text{ N}$

c) E.g. No other external forces are acting, A doesn't hit the pulley, B doesn't hit the ground, the string doesn't break, the pulley doesn't break, the string between A and the pulley is horizontal, the string is initially taut, the acceleration due to gravity is constant at 9.8 ms⁻².

Q23

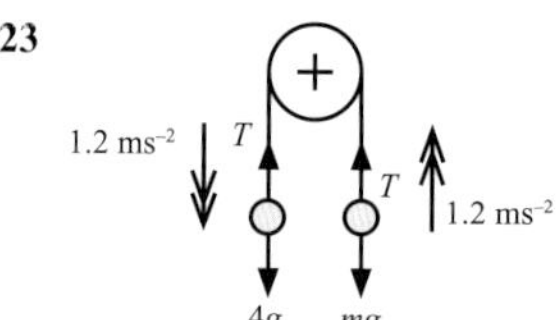

Resolving vertically (↓) for the 4 kg particle:
$F_{net} = ma$
$4g - T = 4 \times 1.2 \Rightarrow T = 4g - 4.8 = 34.4 \text{ N}$
Resolving vertically (↑) for the m kg particle:
$F_{net} = ma$
$T - mg = 1.2m$
$34.4 - mg = 1.2m \Rightarrow 34.4 = m(g + 1.2)$
$\Rightarrow m = \frac{34.4}{g + 1.2} = 3.13 \text{ kg}$ (3 s.f.)

Q24 Resolving horizontally (→) for A:
Particle A is on a frictionless surface, so $T = F_{net}$
$F_{net} = ma \Rightarrow T = 2 \times 5.9 \Rightarrow T = 11.8 \text{ N}$
Resolving vertically (↓) for B:
F_{net} = weight of $B - T$
$F_{net} = ma \Rightarrow mg - 11.8 = m \times 5.9 \Rightarrow (g - 5.9)m = 11.8$
$\Rightarrow m = 11.8 \div (g - 5.9) \Rightarrow m = 3.03 \text{ kg}$ (3 s.f.)
[4 marks available — 1 mark for a correct equation for T, 1 mark for T, 1 mark for a correct equation for m, 1 mark for m]

Q25 a) Resolving vertically (↑) for A:

$F_{net} = ma$

$T - mg = ma$ ①

Resolving vertically (↓) for B:

$F_{net} = ma$

$(m + 5)g - T = (m + 5)a$ ②

① + ②: $(m + 5)g - mg = (m + 5)a + ma$

$5g = (2m + 5)a \Rightarrow a = \frac{5 \times 9.8}{2m+5} = \frac{49}{2m+5}$

[4 marks available — 1 mark for using F = ma, 1 mark for finding equations of motion for A and B, 1 mark for solving simultaneously to find a, 1 mark for simplifying into the correct form]

b) From ①:

$T - mg = ma \Rightarrow 36.75 - mg = \frac{49}{2m+5}m$

Rearranging gives: $36.75(2m + 5) - mg(2m + 5) = 49m$

$\Rightarrow 19.6m^2 + 24.5m - 183.75 = 0$

Using the quadratic formula, $m = 2.5$ or -3.75. Ignore the negative solution as mass $m > 0$, so $m = 2.5$ kg.

[4 marks available — 1 mark for substituting T and a into an appropriate equation of motion, 1 mark for rearranging into a solvable form, 1 mark for using the quadratic formula, 1 mark for the correct value of m]

c) When B hits the ground A will be 1 m higher than its initial height, so it will be 2 m from the ground. A will then continue to move vertically. Find the velocity when B hits the ground:

$s = 1, u = 0, v = v, a = \frac{49}{2 \times 2.5 + 5} = 4.9$

$v^2 = u^2 + 2as$

$v^2 = 0 + 2 \times 1 \times 4.9 = 9.8 \Rightarrow v = 3.13...\ \text{ms}^{-1}$

So for the vertical movement of A after B hits the ground:

$s = s, u = 3.13..., v = 0, a = -9.8$

$v^2 = u^2 + 2as$

$0 = 3.13...^2 + 2 \times -9.8 \times s \Rightarrow s = 0.5$ m

The greatest height above the floor is 2 m + 0.5 m = 2.5 m

[4 marks available — 1 mark for using an appropriate suvat equation, 1 mark for finding the speed of A when B hits the ground, 1 mark for finding the vertical movement of A after B hits the ground, 1 mark for final answer]

Q26 Resolving vertically (↓) for B:

$F_{net} = ma$

$8g - T = 8 \times 0.5 \Rightarrow T = 8g - 4 \Rightarrow T = 74.4$ N

Resolving horizontally (→) for A:

$F_{net} = ma$

$T - F = 10 \times 0.5 \Rightarrow 74.4 - F = 5 \Rightarrow F = 69.4$ N

Q27 a)

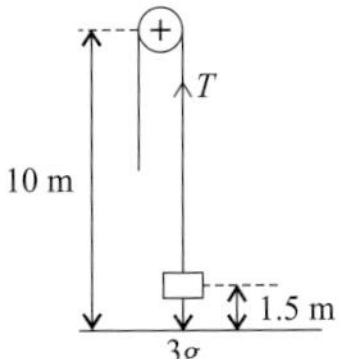

$s = 9.5 - 1.5 = 8$ m, $u = 0, a = a, t = 4$

$s = ut + \frac{1}{2}at^2 \Rightarrow 8 = \frac{1}{2} \times 16a \Rightarrow a = 1$

$F_{net} = ma$

$T - 3g = 3a \Rightarrow T = 3g + 3 \Rightarrow T = 32.4$ N

[3 marks available — 1 mark for finding a, 1 mark for using F = ma, 1 mark for finding T]

b) $F_{net} = ma$

$382.4 - 35g = 35a \Rightarrow a = 1.12...\ \text{ms}^{-2}$

$s = 10 - 1.5 - 0.5 = 8$ m

$s = ut + \frac{1}{2}at^2$

$8 = \frac{1}{2} \times 1.12... \times t^2 \Rightarrow t = 3.77... = 3.8$ seconds (1 d.p.)

[3 marks available — 1 mark for using F = ma, 1 mark for finding a, 1 mark for finding t]

Q28 a)

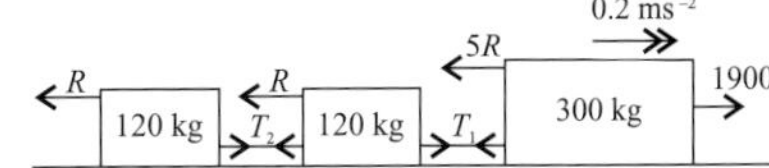

Considering only the horizontal forces acting at the start of the solution, resolve horizontally (→) for the whole system:

$F_{net} = ma$

$1900 - 5R - R - R = 540 \times 0.2$

$\Rightarrow 7R = 1900 - 108 \Rightarrow R = 256$ N

[3 marks available — 1 mark for using F = ma, 1 mark for resolving forces, 1 mark for the correct value of R]

b) Resolving horizontally (→) for the end sled:

$F_{net} = ma$

$T_2 - 256 = 120 \times 0.2 \Rightarrow T_2 = 280$ N

[2 marks available — 1 mark for using F = ma, 1 mark for the correct tension]

c) Resolving horizontally (→) for the snowmobile:

$F_{net} = ma$

$1900 - (5 \times 256) - T_1 = 300 \times 0.2$

$T_1 = 1900 - 1280 - 60 = 560$ N

You could have resolved for the first sled instead.

[2 marks available — 1 mark for using F = ma, 1 mark for the correct tension]

d) There is a resistance of 256 N for each sled. The maximum driving force is 2500 N and the snowmobile has a resistance of 1280 N, so the maximum possible number of sleds is:

$(2500 - 1280) \div 256 = 4.76...$ so the snowmobile can pull 4 sleds. Resolving horizontally (→) when there are 4 sleds:

$F_{net} = ma$

$2500 - (5 + 4) \times 256 = (300 + 4 \times 120)a$

$2500 - (9 \times 256) = 780a$

$\Rightarrow 196 = 780a \Rightarrow a = 0.251\ \text{ms}^{-2}$ (3 s.f.)

[5 marks available — 1 mark for identifying that the total resistive force must be less than the driving force, 1 mark for calculating the maximum whole number of sleds, 1 mark for using F = ma, 1 mark for resolving for the new system, 1 mark for the correct acceleration]

Q29 $|\mathbf{F}_1| = \sqrt{1^2 + 8^2} = \sqrt{65}$, so for $\mathbf{F}_2$, $\sqrt{4^2 + k^2} = \sqrt{65}$

$\Rightarrow 16 + k^2 = 65 \Rightarrow k = \pm\sqrt{49} = \pm 7$

When $k = 7$, $\mathbf{F}_2 - \mathbf{F}_1 = -5\mathbf{i} - \mathbf{j}$ N $\Rightarrow |\mathbf{F}_2 - \mathbf{F}_1| = \sqrt{5^2 + 1^2} = \sqrt{26}$

Using the cosine rule:

$\cos\theta = \frac{\sqrt{65}^2 + \sqrt{65}^2 - \sqrt{26}^2}{2\sqrt{65}\sqrt{65}} = \frac{104}{130}$

$\Rightarrow \theta = \cos^{-1}\left(\frac{4}{5}\right) = 36.9°$ (1 d.p.)

When $k = -7$, $\mathbf{F}_2 - \mathbf{F}_1 = -5\mathbf{i} - 15\mathbf{j}$ N

$\Rightarrow |\mathbf{F}_2 - \mathbf{F}_1| = \sqrt{5^2 + 15^2} = \sqrt{250}$

Using the cosine rule:

$\cos\theta = \frac{\sqrt{65}^2 + \sqrt{65}^2 - \sqrt{250}^2}{2\sqrt{65}\sqrt{65}} = \frac{-120}{130}$

$\Rightarrow \theta = \cos^{-1}\left(-\frac{12}{13}\right) = 157.4°$ (1 d.p.)

[5 marks available — 1 mark for a correct method to calculate the magnitude, 1 mark for both values of k, 1 mark for a correct method to find the angle between vectors, 1 mark for each correct answer]

Q30 a) Resultant force = $-3\mathbf{i} + 4\mathbf{i} + 2\mathbf{j} - \mathbf{j} = (\mathbf{i} + \mathbf{j})$ N
Magnitude = $\sqrt{1^2 + 1^2} = \sqrt{2} = 1.4$ N (1 d.p.)
Direction = $\tan^{-1}\frac{1}{1} = 45°$
[3 marks available — 1 mark for finding the resultant force, 1 mark for the correct magnitude, 1 mark for the correct direction]

b) Let the resultant force be $a\mathbf{i} + b\mathbf{j} = 7$, with a and b both positive. Resolve the resultant force into **i** and **j** components:

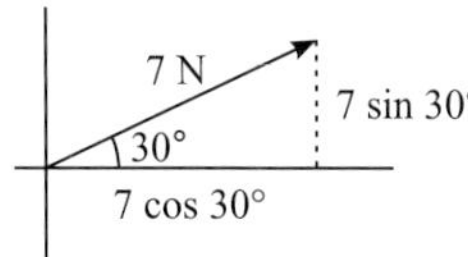

$a = 7\cos 30° \Rightarrow a = 6.062...$
$b = 7\sin 30° \Rightarrow b = 3.5$
Let the third force be $(c\mathbf{i} + d\mathbf{j})$ N, then adding to the resultant force found in part a) gives:
$1 + c = 6.062... \Rightarrow c = 5.062...$
and $1 + d = 3.5 \Rightarrow d = 2.5$,
so the third force = $(5.1\mathbf{i} + 2.5\mathbf{j})$ N (1 d.p.)
[7 marks available — 1 mark for each component of the resultant force, 1 mark for a, 1 mark for b, 1 mark for using a and b to attempt to find c and d, 1 mark for finding c or d, 1 mark for finding the third force]
Alternatively you could write the magnitude and direction of the 7 N force in terms of a and b, then solve simultaneously.

Q31 a) The resultant force only acts in a horizontal direction — i.e. there's no vertical component to the resultant force, so $b - a + 2 = 0 \Rightarrow a = b + 2$
[2 marks available — 1 mark for any valid equation in a and b, 1 mark for the correct answer]

b) $a + 2b - 11 = 0$ (1)
$b - a + 2 = 0$ (2)
(1) + (2): $3b = 9 \Rightarrow b = 3$
(2): $3 - a + 2 = 0 \Rightarrow a = 5$
[2 marks available — 1 mark for a, 1 mark for b]

c) (i) 45° means the horizontal and vertical components are equal, so $a + 2b - 11 = b - a + 2 \Rightarrow b = 13 - 2a$
[2 marks available — 1 mark for any valid equation in a and b, 1 mark for the correct answer]

(ii) The vertical component of the resultant force must be positive, so $b - a + 2 > 0$. Then $b = 13 - 2a$
$\Rightarrow (13 - 2a) - a + 2 > 0 \Rightarrow a < 5$
$b = 13 - 2a \Rightarrow a = \frac{1}{2}(13 - b)$
$\Rightarrow b - \frac{1}{2}(13 - b) + 2 > 0 \Rightarrow b > 3$
[3 marks available — 1 mark for a correct inequality in either a or b, 1 mark for a < 5, 1 mark for b > 3]
You could also have used the horizontal component of the resultant force to find both inequalities.

Q32 a) $m = 8 \div 1000 = 0.008$ kg
$a = \begin{pmatrix}20\\50\end{pmatrix} \div 100 = \begin{pmatrix}0.2\\0.5\end{pmatrix}$ ms^{-2}
As the acceleration is a vector, you need to multiply both components by m:
$F_{net} = ma \Rightarrow F = 0.008 \times \begin{pmatrix}0.2\\0.5\end{pmatrix} \Rightarrow F = \begin{pmatrix}0.0016\\0.004\end{pmatrix}$ N
[2 marks available — 1 mark for the correct units, 1 mark for the correct answer]

b) For Marble B:
$F_{net} = ma \Rightarrow \begin{pmatrix}0.004\\0.01\end{pmatrix} = 0.008a_B \Rightarrow a_B = \begin{pmatrix}0.5\\1.25\end{pmatrix}$ ms^{-2}
Using $s = ut + \frac{1}{2}at^2$:
$|a_A| = \sqrt{0.2^2 + 0.5^2} = \frac{\sqrt{29}}{10}$, $u_A = 0$, $t_A = t$
$\Rightarrow s_A = \frac{\sqrt{29}}{20}t^2$
$|a_B| = \sqrt{0.5^2 + 1.25^2} = \frac{\sqrt{29}}{4}$, $u_B = 0$, $t_B = t - 4$
$\Rightarrow s_B = \frac{\sqrt{29}}{8}(t-4)^2$
For one marble to have travelled twice as far as the other, either $2s_A = s_B$ or $s_A = 2s_B$.
For $2s_A = s_B$, $\frac{\sqrt{29}}{10}t^2 = \frac{\sqrt{29}}{8}(t-4)^2$
$\Rightarrow \frac{4\sqrt{29}}{40}t^2 = \frac{5\sqrt{29}}{40}(t-4)^2 \Rightarrow 4t^2 = 5(t-4)^2$
$\Rightarrow 4t^2 = 5t^2 - 40t + 80 \Rightarrow 0 = t^2 - 40t + 80$
$\Rightarrow t = 20 \pm 8\sqrt{5}$ seconds
$\Rightarrow t = 2.1$ seconds or 37.9 seconds (1 d.p.)
For $s_A = 2s_B$, $\frac{\sqrt{29}}{20}t^2 = \frac{\sqrt{29}}{4}(t-4)^2$
$\Rightarrow \frac{\sqrt{29}}{20}t^2 = \frac{5\sqrt{29}}{20}(t-4)^2 \Rightarrow t^2 = 5(t-4)^2$
$\Rightarrow t^2 = 5t^2 - 40t + 80 \Rightarrow 0 = 4t^2 - 40t + 80$
$\Rightarrow 0 = t^2 - 10t + 20 \Rightarrow t = 5 \pm \sqrt{5}$ seconds
$\Rightarrow t = 7.2$ seconds or 2.8 seconds (1 d.p.)
Reject values less than 4 as Marble B doesn't start moving until 4 seconds, so one of the marbles travelling twice as far as the other occurs after 7.2 seconds and 37.9 seconds (1 d.p.).
[7 marks available — 1 mark for a_B, 1 mark for an expression for s_A in terms of t, 1 mark for an expression for s_B in terms of t, 1 mark for each quadratic in terms of t, 1 mark for any two solutions for t, 1 mark for both correct answers with justification for rejecting the other solutions]

Q33 a) Resistive force of engine = $0.05 \times 1200g = 60g$ N
Resistive force of carriage = $0.05 \times 800g = 40g$ N

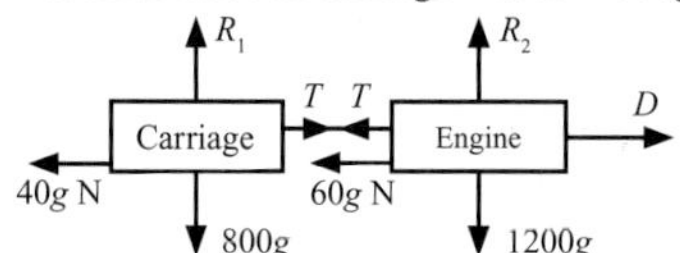

$v = 10$ ms^{-1}, $u = 0$ ms^{-1}, $a = a$, $t = 10$ s:
$v = u + at \Rightarrow 10 = 10a \Rightarrow a = 1$ ms^{-2}
Let D be the driving force of the engine, so:
$F_{net} = ma \Rightarrow D - 60g - 40g = 2000 \times 1 \Rightarrow D = 2980$ N
For $v = 15$ ms^{-1}, $u = 0$ ms^{-1}, $a = a$, $t = 10$ s:
$v = u + at \Rightarrow 15 = 10a \Rightarrow a = 1.5$ ms^{-2}
Let m be the mass of the load in the carriage, so:
$F_{net} = ma$
$\Rightarrow 2980 - 0.05(1200g + 200g + mg) = (1400 + m) \times 1.5$
$\Rightarrow 2980 - 0.49(1400 + m) = 2100 + 1.5m$
$\Rightarrow 2980 - 686 - 0.49m = 2100 + 1.5m \Rightarrow 194 = 1.99m$
$\Rightarrow m = 97.487... = 97.5$ kg (3 s.f.)
[6 marks available — 1 mark for calculating the acceleration for the first scenario, 1 mark for using F = ma for the first scenario, 1 mark for the correct value of D, 1 mark for calculating the acceleration for the second scenario, 1 mark for using F = ma for the second scenario, 1 mark for the correct answer]

b) Resolving horizontally (→) for the engine:
When $a = 1$: $F_{net} = ma \Rightarrow D - T_1 - 60g = 1200 \times 1$
$\Rightarrow T_1 = 2980 - 588 - 1200 = 1192$ N
When $a = 1.5$: $F_{net} = ma \Rightarrow D - T_2 - 60g = 1200 \times 1.5$
$\Rightarrow T_2 = 2980 - 588 - 1800 = 592$ N
So the difference is $1192 - 592 = 600$ N.
[4 marks available — 1 mark for a correct equation for the resultant force in each scenario, 1 mark for at least one tension force correctly calculated, 1 mark for the correct answer]
You could also resolve forces on the carriage — you'd get the same answer either way.

Q34 Find the time in two sections — the time taken for A to hit the pulley, and the time taken for B to hit the ground under gravity after the string breaks.

Find the acceleration of the particles:
Resolving horizontally (→) for A:
$F_{net} = ma$
$T = 0.5a$ ①
Resolving vertically (↓) for B:
$F_{net} = ma$
$0.75g - T = 0.75a$ ②
① + ②: $0.75g = 1.25a \Rightarrow a = 0.6g = 5.88 \text{ ms}^{-2}$
Then using *suvat*: $s = 2$, $u = 0$, $a = 5.88$, $t = t$
$s = ut + \frac{1}{2}at^2$
$2 = 0 + \frac{1}{2} \times 5.88 \times t^2$
$t^2 = 0.680... \Rightarrow t = 0.8247...$ seconds

For B at the instant A hits the pulley:
$s = 2$, $u = 0$, $v = v$, $a = 5.88$
$v^2 = u^2 + 2as$
$v^2 = 0 + 2 \times 5.88 \times 2 \Rightarrow v = \frac{14\sqrt{3}}{5} = 4.849.... \text{ ms}^{-1}$
Then find the time taken for B to fall the remaining 1 m to the ground under gravity:
$s = 1$, $u = \frac{14\sqrt{3}}{5}$, $a = 9.8$, $t = t$
$s = ut + \frac{1}{2}at^2$
$1 = \frac{14\sqrt{3}}{5}t + \frac{1}{2} \times 9.8 \times t^2 \Rightarrow 4.9t^2 + \frac{14\sqrt{3}}{5}t - 1 = 0$
Using the quadratic formula:

$$t = \frac{-\frac{14\sqrt{3}}{5} \pm \sqrt{\left(\frac{14\sqrt{3}}{5}\right)^2 - 4 \times 4.9 \times -1}}{9.8} = 0.1751... \text{ s}$$

(Ignore the negative solution since time $t > 0$)
So the total time between the particles being released and B hitting the ground is:
$0.8247... + 0.1751... = 0.999... = 1.00$ s (3 s.f.)

Practice Paper

Q1 a) (i) Daily mean air temperature
(ii) Daily mean pressure
[1 mark for both correct]

b) There is a weak negative correlation between daily mean air temperature and daily mean pressure. (OR As daily mean air temperature increases, daily mean pressure decreases.)
[1 mark]

c) For every 1 °C increase in daily mean air temperature there is a decrease of 0.45 hPa in the daily mean pressure.
[1 mark for correct interpretation in context]

d) (i) $P = -0.45T + 1029$
$= (-0.45 \times 10) + 1029$
$= -4.5 + 1029$
$= 1024.5$ hPa
[1 mark for correct answer]

(ii) 10 °C is not within the range of data used to find the equation of the regression line. Therefore the prediction will be unreliable as it is an extrapolation.
[1 mark for correctly reasoning that extrapolation can lead to unreliable predictions]

Q2 a) E.g. some days have 'tr' (i.e. "trace of rain") as the entry in the column for daily total rainfall. Philippa will need to decide how to deal with these entries if she selects one — for instance, by discarding and randomly choosing other days.
[1 mark for correctly identifying a difficulty]

b) (i) $\sum y = 4 + 0 + 224 + 6 + 152 + 20 = 406$
[1 mark for correct answer]

(ii) $\sum y^2 = 4^2 + 0^2 + 224^2 + 6^2 + 152^2 + 20^2$
$= 16 + 0 + 50\,176 + 36 + 23\,104 + 400$
$= 73\,732$
[1 mark for correct answer]

c) $\bar{y} = \frac{406}{6} = 67.666... = 67.7$ (3 s.f.)

s.d. $= \sqrt{\frac{73\,732}{6} - \left(\frac{406}{6}\right)^2} = 87.805...$
$= 87.8$ (3 s.f.)
[2 marks available — 1 mark for correct mean to an appropriate degree of accuracy, 1 mark for correct standard deviation to an appropriate degree of accuracy]

d) Rearranging the coding gives $x = \frac{y+2}{10} = 0.1y + 0.2$
standard deviation of x values
$= 0.1 \times$ standard deviation of y values
$= 0.1 \times 87.805...$
$= 8.7805...$
$= 8.78$ mm (3 s.f.)
[1 mark for correct answer to appropriate degree of accuracy]

Q3 a) S and M are independent, so
P(S and M) = P(S) × P(M)
$\Rightarrow 0.06 = 0.4(y + 0.06)$
$\Rightarrow 0.06 = 0.4y + 0.024$
$\Rightarrow y = 0.09$
All probabilities in the diagram must sum to 1
$\Rightarrow 0.3 + 0.09 + 0.06 + 0.27 + 0.07 + x = 1$
$\Rightarrow x = 0.21$
[3 marks available — 1 mark for correct use of formula for independent events, 1 mark for correct value of x, 1 mark for correct value of y]

b) P(Mandarin or Spanish but not both) = 0.09 + 0.07 + 0.27
= 0.43
[1 mark for correct answer — allow for errors carried forward from part a)]

c) Systematic sampling
[1 mark for correct answer]

Q4 a) The median is the $\frac{80}{2} = 40^{\text{th}}$ value.
$\Rightarrow$ median is in the class interval $10 \le x < 15$.
[2 marks available — 1 mark for position of median, 1 mark for identifying correct class interval]

b) Sketch the class interval $10 \le x < 15$:

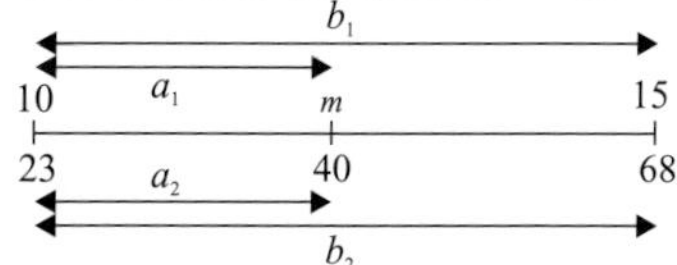

Solve $\frac{a_1}{b_1} = \frac{a_2}{b_2}$ — this gives: $\frac{m-10}{15-10} = \frac{40-23}{68-23}$
$\Rightarrow \frac{m-10}{5} = \frac{17}{45} \Rightarrow m = 5 \times \frac{17}{45} + 10 = 11.888...$
$\Rightarrow m = 11.9$ N (to 3 s.f.)
[3 marks available — 1 mark for setting up equation to solve, 1 mark for correct rearrangement, 1 mark for correct answer to an appropriate degree of accuracy]

c) IQR = $Q_3 - Q_1 = 14.2 - 9.4 = 4.8$
$Q_3 + (1.5 \times \text{IQR}) = 14.2 + 1.5 \times 4.8 = 21.4$
Since 28.8 > 21.4, 28.8 is an outlier.
[1 mark for correct demonstration using given formula]

Q5 a) Let X be the number of infected plants. Then $X \sim B(30, 0.3)$
$P(X \ge 12) = 1 - P(X \le 11) = 1 - 0.8407 = 0.1593$
[2 marks available — 1 mark for 1 – P(X ≤ 11), 1 mark for correct answer]

b) Let p = the proportion of plants infected by the fungus. So $H_0: p = 0.3$ and $H_1: p > 0.3$. Let X be the number of plants in the sample that are infected.
Then under H_0, $X \sim B(25, 0.3)$. Significance level is 0.05, so you want to find x such that $P(X \geq x) \leq 0.05$.
$P(X \leq 10) = 0.9022 \Rightarrow P(X \geq 11) = 0.0978 > 0.05$
$P(X \leq 11) = 0.9558 \Rightarrow P(X \geq 12) = 0.0442 < 0.05$
So the critical region is $X \geq 12$.
[3 marks available — 1 mark for correct hypotheses, 1 mark for clear evidence of a correct method to find the critical region, 1 mark for stating the correct critical region]

c) $X = 10$ is not in the critical region, so the biologist should not reject the null hypothesis. So there is not significant evidence at the 5% level to suggest that the probability that a given potato plant is infected has been underestimated.
[2 marks available — 1 mark for explaining that the null hypothesis should not be rejected, 1 mark for correct conclusion in context]

d) A binomial distribution may not be appropriate as the probability that plants are infected may be affected by the surrounding plants. So you cannot assume the trials are independent.
[1 mark for correct reasoning]

Q6 a) Resultant force = $\boldsymbol{F}_1 + \boldsymbol{F}_2$

$$= \begin{pmatrix} 2.5 \\ -2 \end{pmatrix} + \begin{pmatrix} 9.5 \\ 5.5 \end{pmatrix} = \begin{pmatrix} 12 \\ 3.5 \end{pmatrix} \text{N}$$

$\Rightarrow$ magnitude = $\sqrt{12^2 + 3.5^2} = 12.5$ N
[3 marks available — 1 mark for finding resultant force, 1 mark for correct use of magnitude formula, 1 mark for correct answer with correct units]

b) Using $F_{net} = ma$:
$12.5 = 2m \Rightarrow m = 6.25$ kg
[2 marks available — 1 mark for correct use of Newton's 2nd law, 1 mark for correct answer with correct units]

Q7 a) $a = \frac{dv}{dt}$
$\Rightarrow a = -0.9 + 0.2t$
When $t = 0$, $a = -0.9 + 0.2(0) = -0.9$
So the initial acceleration is -0.9 ms^{-2}
and the magnitude of initial acceleration is 0.9 ms^{-2}
[2 marks available — 1 mark for correct differentiation, 1 mark for correct magnitude with correct units]

b) Q is at rest when $v = 0$
$\Rightarrow 1.4 - 0.9t + 0.1t^2 = 0$
$\Rightarrow 14 - 9t + t^2 = 0$
$\Rightarrow (t - 2)(t - 7) = 0$
$\Rightarrow t = 2$ seconds and $t = 7$ seconds are the times when Q is instantaneously at rest
[2 marks available — 1 mark for deriving an appropriate quadratic equation to solve in any form, 1 mark for both correct solutions to the quadratic]

c) The displacement function of Q is $s = \int v \, dt$
$\Rightarrow s = \frac{7}{5}t - \frac{9}{20}t^2 + \frac{1}{30}t^3$
Note that the constant of integration will be equal to 0 since Q is at the origin when t = 0.

A sketch of the velocity-time graph for Q shows that it has both positive and negative displacement in the first 7 seconds of its motion (since the area between the curve and the t-axis lies above and then below the t-axis).

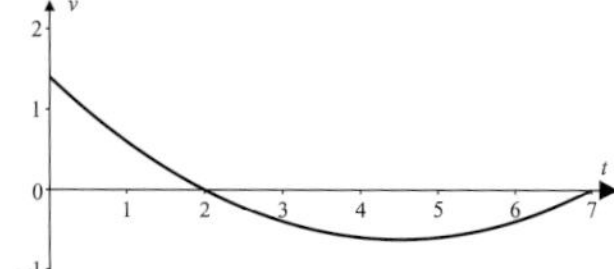

So to find the distance travelled by Q, calculate

$$s = \int_0^2 v \, dt - \int_2^7 v \, dt$$

$$\int_0^2 v \, dt = \left[\frac{7}{5}t - \frac{9}{20}t^2 + \frac{1}{30}t^3\right]_0^2$$
$$= \left(\frac{7}{5}(2) - \frac{9}{20}(2)^2 + \frac{1}{30}(2)^3\right) - \left(\frac{7}{5}(0) - \frac{9}{20}(0)^2 + \frac{1}{30}(0)^3\right)$$
$$= \left(\frac{14}{5} - \frac{36}{20} + \frac{8}{30}\right) - 0$$
$$= \frac{19}{15}$$

$$\int_2^7 v \, dt = \left[\frac{7}{5}t - \frac{9}{20}t^2 + \frac{1}{30}t^3\right]_2^7$$
$$= \left(\frac{7}{5}(7) - \frac{9}{20}(7)^2 + \frac{1}{30}(7)^3\right) - \frac{19}{15}$$
$$= \left(\frac{49}{5} - \frac{441}{20} + \frac{343}{30}\right) - \frac{19}{15}$$
$$= -\frac{25}{12}$$

$$s = \frac{19}{15} - \left(-\frac{25}{12}\right) = \frac{67}{20} = 3.35 \text{ m}$$

[4 marks available — 1 mark for correct displacement function, 1 mark for determining that Q has both positive and negative displacement, 1 mark for clear attempt at finding positive and negative displacements, 1 mark for correct answer with correct units]

Q8 a) For S, you have $u = 25$ ms^{-1}, $a = -9.8$ ms^{-2}
Using the formula:
$s = ut + \frac{1}{2}at^2$
$= 25t - 4.9t^2$
For T, you have $u = 32$ ms^{-1}, $a = -9.8$ms^{-2}
Using the same formula:
$s = 32t' - 4.9t'^2$, where $t' = t - 1$

Then $32t' - 4.9t'^2 = 32(t - 1) - 4.9(t - 1)^2$
When the stones collide, they have the same displacement from the point of projection.
$\Rightarrow 25t - 4.9t^2 = 32(t - 1) - 4.9(t - 1)^2$
$= -4.9t^2 + 41.8t - 36.9$
$\Rightarrow 25t = 41.8t - 36.9 \Rightarrow 16.8t = 36.9 \Rightarrow t = 2.196...$
$\Rightarrow s = 25(2.196...) - 4.9(2.196...)^2 = 31.27...$
So S and T collide 31.3 m (3 s.f.) above the point of projection.

For the motion of S when $t = 2.196...$, taking up as positive:
$v = v$, $u = 25$, $a = -9.8$, $t = 2.196...$
$v = u + at$
$v = 25 - 9.8 \times 2.196... = 3.475...$
$\Rightarrow$ speed of S is 3.475 ms^{-1} directed upwards.
T started off later and with a higher velocity, so has a higher velocity than S at point of impact, so T is also travelling upwards. So S and T are travelling in the same direction at the time of collision.
[7 marks available — 1 mark for correct derivation of equation for trajectory of S, 1 mark for correct derivation of equation for trajectory of T, 1 mark for correctly equating both equations, 1 mark for correct solution to resulting equation to find t, 1 mark for correct height with correct units, 1 mark for clear attempt at determining the velocities of either S or T, 1 mark for correct directions of S and T relative to one another]

b) E.g. Air resistance and other resistance forces can be ignored and so g = 9.8 ms^{-2} can be used as the magnitude of the acceleration.
[1 mark for any valid explanation]

Q9 **a)** Resolving vertically (↑) for the whole system:
$F_{net} = ma$
$T - 650g = 650 \times 0.05 \Rightarrow T = 6402.5$ N
[2 marks available — 1 mark for derivation of equation for T, 1 mark for correct value for T with correct units]

b) **(i)** Resolving vertically (↑) for the load:
$F_{net} = ma$
$R - 600g = 600 \times 0.05$
$R = 600 \times 9.8 + 600 \times 0.05 = 5910$ N
You could have resolved forces on the cage using the value of T calculated in part a).

(ii) Newton's 3rd law says that the normal reaction force exerted by the floor of the cage on the load will be the same size as R.
[3 marks available — 1 mark for derivation of equation for R, 1 mark for correct value for R with correct units, 1 mark for correct reason with appropriate reference to Newton's 3rd law]

c) Area under graph = distance travelled
During the initial acceleration: $v = v$, $u = 0$, $a = 0.05$, $t = 6$
$v = u + at$
$v = 0 + 0.05 \times 6 = 0.3 \text{ ms}^{-1}$
$\Rightarrow$ velocity of the cage after 6 seconds is 0.3 ms^{-1}

Area $= (0.5 \times 6 \times 0.3) + (3k \times 0.3) + (0.5 \times k \times 0.3) = 9.3$
$\Rightarrow 0.9 + 0.9k + 0.15k = 9.3$
$\Rightarrow 8.4 = 1.05k \Rightarrow k = 8$

During the final deceleration: $v = 0$, $u = 0.3$, $a = a$, $t = 8$
$v = u + at$
$0 = 0.3 + 8a \Rightarrow a = -0.0375 \text{ ms}^{-2}$
$\Rightarrow$ deceleration is 0.0375 ms^{-2}
[4 marks available — 1 mark for clearly demonstrating that area under graph = distance travelled, 1 mark for finding the speed of the cage after 6 seconds, 1 mark for finding the value of k, 1 mark for correct value of deceleration with correct units (award final mark even if minus sign given with answer)]

A

Acceleration
The rate of change of an object's velocity with respect to time.

Addition law
A formula linking the probability of two events both happening and the probability that at least one of them happens.

Alternative hypothesis
The statement that you will accept instead if you decide to reject the null hypothesis in a hypothesis test. It gives a range of values for the parameter and is usually written H_1.

Assumption
A simplification of a real-life situation used in a model.

B

Base units
The basic S.I. units of measurement, which can be used to derive all other S.I. units.

Beam
A long, thin, straight body.

Bearing
A direction, given as an angle measured clockwise from north.

Biased sample
A sample that does not fairly represent the population it is taken from.

Binomial distribution B(n, p)
A discrete probability distribution modelling the number of successes x in n independent trials when the probability of success in each trial is p.

Bivariate data
Data that comes as an ordered pair of variables (x, y).

Box plot
A diagram showing the median, quartiles and greatest/least values of a data set, as well as any outliers.

C

Census
A survey in which information is collected from every single member of the population.

Coding
Coding means transforming all the readings in a data set to make the numbers easier to work with.

Complement (of an event A)
The group of all outcomes corresponding to event A not happening.

Component
The effect of a vector in a given direction.

Compression
The force in a compressed rod. Another word for thrust.

Constant
A fixed numerical value in an expression.

Correlation
A relationship between two variables showing that they change together to some extent. (A correlation does not necessarily mean a causal relationship.)

Critical region
The set of all values of the test statistic that would cause you to reject the null hypothesis.

Critical value
The value of the test statistic at the edge of the critical region.

Cumulative distribution function
A function, F(x), that gives the probability that a random variable, X, will be less than or equal to a particular value, x.

Cumulative frequency
The total frequency for all the classes in a data set up to and including a given class.

Cumulative frequency diagram
A graph plotting cumulative frequency of a data set.

D

Deceleration
An acceleration where the object's speed is decreasing.

Dependent variable
Another name for the response variable.

Derived units
Units of measurement that can be made by combining S.I. base units.

Discrete random variable
A random variable with 'gaps' between its possible values.

Dispersion
Measures of dispersion describe how spread out data values are.

Displacement
A vector measurement of an object's distance from a particular point.

E

Equilibrium
A state where there is no resultant force acting on a body, hence the body is at rest (or moving with constant velocity).

Event
An event is a 'group' of one or more possible outcomes.

Explanatory variable
In an experiment, the variable you can control, or the one that you think is affecting the other.

Extrapolation
Predicting a value of y corresponding to a value of x outside the range for which you have data.

F

Fence
If a data value lies outside a fence, then it is an outlier.

Finite population
A population for which it is possible and practical to count the members.

Force
An influence that can change the motion of a body (i.e. cause an acceleration).

Frequency density
The frequency of a class divided by its class width.

Friction
A frictional force is a resistive force due to roughness between a body and surface. It always acts against motion, or likely motion.

G

g
Acceleration due to gravity.
g is usually assumed to be 9.8 ms^{-2}.

H

Histogram
A diagram showing the frequencies with which a continuous variable falls in particular classes — the frequency of a class is proportional to the area of a bar.

Hypothesis
A statement that you want to test.

Hypothesis test
A method of testing a hypothesis using observed sample data.

I

i unit vector
The standard horizontal unit vector (i.e. along the x-axis).

Independent events
If the probability of an event B happening doesn't depend on whether or not an event A happens, events A and B are independent.

Independent variable
Another name for the explanatory variable.

Inextensible
Describes a body that can't be stretched. (Usually a string or wire.)

Infinite population
A population for which it is impossible or impractical to count the members.

Interpercentile range
The difference between the values of two given percentiles.

Interpolation
Predicting a value of y corresponding to a value of x within the range for which you have data.

Interquartile range
A measure of dispersion. It's the difference between the upper quartile and the lower quartile.

J

j unit vector
The standard vertical unit vector (i.e. along the y-axis).

K

Kinematics
The study of the motion of objects.

L

Light
Describes a body that is modelled as having no mass.

Linear interpolation
Method of estimating a measure (e.g. the median, quartiles or percentiles) of a grouped data set by assuming the readings within each class are evenly spread.

Linear regression
A method for finding the equation of a line of best fit on a scatter diagram.

Location
Measures of location show where the 'centre' of the data lies.

Lower quartile
The value that 25% of data values in a data set are less than or equal to.

M

Magnitude
The size of a quantity.
The magnitude of a vector is the distance between its start point and end point.

Mean
A measure of location — it's the sum of a set of data values, divided by the number of data values.

Median
A measure of location — it's the value in the middle of the data set when all the data values are in order of size.

Mode
A measure of location — it's the most frequently occurring data value.

Mode of a discrete random variable
The value that the random variable is most likely to take — i.e. the one with the highest probability.

Model
A mathematical description of a real-life situation, in which certain assumptions are made about the situation.

Modulus of a vector
Another name for the vector's magnitude.

Mutually exclusive
Events are mutually exclusive (or just 'exclusive') if they have no outcomes in common, and so can't happen at the same time.

N

Normal reaction
The reaction force from a surface acting on an object. Acts at 90° to the surface.

Null hypothesis
A statement that gives a specific value to the parameter in a hypothesis test. Usually written H_0.

Glossary

One-tailed test
A hypothesis test is 'one-tailed' if the alternative hypothesis is specific about whether the parameter is greater or less than the value specified by the null hypothesis. E.g. it says $p < a$ or $p > a$ for a parameter p and constant a.

Opportunity sampling
A method of selecting a sample from a population in which a sample is selected at a time and place which is convenient for the sampler. Also known as convenience sampling.

Outcome
One of the possible results of a trial or experiment.

Outlier
A freak piece of data lying a long way from the majority of the values in a data set.

P

Parameter (statistics)
A quantity that describes a characteristic of a population.

Particle
A body whose mass is considered to act at a single point, so its dimensions don't matter.

Peg
A fixed support that a body can hang from or rest on.

Percentiles
The percentiles (P_1-P_{99}) divide an ordered data set into 100 parts.

Plane
A flat surface.

Population
The whole group of every single thing (person, animal, item etc.) that you want to investigate in a statistical test.

Position vector
The position of a point relative to a fixed origin, O, given in vector form.

Probability distribution for a discrete random variable
A table showing all the possible values that a random variable can take, plus the probability that it takes each value.

Probability function
A function that generates the probabilities of a discrete random variable taking each of its possible values.

Pulley
A wheel, usually modelled as fixed and smooth, over which a string passes.

Q

Qualitative variable
A variable that takes non-numerical values.

Quantitative variable
A variable that takes numerical values.

Quartiles
The three quartiles Q_1, Q_2 and Q_3 divide an ordered data set into four parts.

Quota sampling
A method of selecting a sample from a population by dividing it into categories and sampling a set number of individuals from each category, but not selecting them at random.

R

Random variable
A variable taking different values with different probabilities.

Range
A measure of dispersion. It's the difference between the highest value and the lowest value.

Resistance
A force acting in the opposite direction to the movement of an object.

Resolving
Splitting a vector up into components.

Response variable
In an experiment, the variable you think is being affected.

Rest
Describes a body that is not moving. Often used to describe the initial state of a body.

Resultant (force or vector)
The single force/vector that has the same effect as two or more forces/vectors added together.

Rigid
Describes a body that does not bend.

Rod
A long, thin, straight, rigid body.

Rough
Describes a surface for which a frictional force will oppose the motion of a body in contact with the surface.

S

Sample
A selection of members from a population. Information from the sample is used to deduce information about the population as a whole.

Sample space
The set of all possible outcomes of a trial.

Scalar
A quantity that has a magnitude but not a direction.

Scatter diagram
Graph showing the two variables in a bivariate data set plotted against each other.

Set
A collection of objects or numbers (called elements).

S.I. Units
System of measurements based on fixed scientific constants.

Significance level (α)
Determines how unlikely the observed value of the test statistic needs to be (under H_0) before rejecting the null hypothesis in a hypothesis test.

Significant result
The observed value of a test statistic is significant if, under H_0, it has a probability lower than the significance level.

Simple random sampling
A method of selecting a sample from a population in which every member is equally likely to be chosen and each selection is independent of every other selection.

Smooth
Describes a surface for which there is no friction between the surface and a body in contact with it.

Speed
The magnitude of an object's velocity.

Standard deviation
A measure of dispersion calculated by taking the square root of the variance.

Static
Describes a body that is not moving. Often used to describe a body in equilibrium.

Statistic
A quantity that is calculated using only known observations from a sample.

Stratified sampling
A method of selecting a random sample from a population in which the population is divided into categories and the proportions of each category in the population are matched in the sample.

String
A thin body, usually modelled as being light and inextensible.

Survey
A way of collecting information about a population by questioning people or examining items.

Systematic sampling
A method of selecting a sample from a population in which every nth member is chosen from a full list of the population.

T

Taut
Describes a string or wire that is experiencing a tension force and is tight and straight.

Tension
The force in a taut wire or string.

Test statistic
A statistic calculated from sample data that is used to decide whether or not to reject the null hypothesis in a hypothesis test.

Thin
Describes a body that is modelled as having no thickness, only length.

Thrust
The force in a compressed rod.

Tree diagram
Tree diagrams show probabilities for sequences of two or more events.

Trial
A process (e.g. an experiment) with different possible outcomes.

Two-tailed test
A hypothesis test is 'two-tailed' if the alternative hypothesis specifies only that the parameter doesn't equal the value specified by the null hypothesis. E.g. it says $p \neq a$ for a parameter p and constant a.

Two-way table
A way of representing a probability problem involving combinations of two events in a table, where each cell of the table represents a different combined event.

U

Unit vector
A vector of magnitude one unit.

Upper quartile
The value that 75% of data values in a data set are less than or equal to.

Variance
A measure of dispersion from the mean.

Vector
A quantity that has both a magnitude and a direction.

Velocity
The rate of change of an object's displacement with respect to time.

Venn diagram
A Venn diagram shows how a collection of objects is split up into different groups, where everything in a group has something in common. In probability, the objects are outcomes, and the groups are events.

Weight
The force due to a body's mass and the effect of gravity: $W = mg$.

Wire
A thin, inextensible, rigid, light body.

Index

The binomial cumulative distribution function

The values below show $P(X \le x)$, where $X \sim B(n, p)$.

	p =	0.05	0.10	0.15	0.20	0.25	0.30	0.35	0.40	0.45	0.50
n = 5	x = 0	0.7738	0.5905	0.4437	0.3277	0.2373	0.1681	0.1160	0.0778	0.0503	0.0313
	1	0.9774	0.9185	0.8352	0.7373	0.6328	0.5282	0.4284	0.3370	0.2562	0.1875
	2	0.9988	0.9914	0.9734	0.9421	0.8965	0.8369	0.7648	0.6826	0.5931	0.5000
	3	1.0000	0.9995	0.9978	0.9933	0.9844	0.9692	0.9460	0.9130	0.8688	0.8125
	4	1.0000	1.0000	0.9999	0.9997	0.9990	0.9976	0.9947	0.9898	0.9815	0.9688
n = 6	x = 0	0.7351	0.5314	0.3771	0.2621	0.1780	0.1176	0.0754	0.0467	0.0277	0.0156
	1	0.9672	0.8857	0.7765	0.6554	0.5339	0.4202	0.3191	0.2333	0.1636	0.1094
	2	0.9978	0.9842	0.9527	0.9011	0.8306	0.7443	0.6471	0.5443	0.4415	0.3438
	3	0.9999	0.9987	0.9941	0.9830	0.9624	0.9295	0.8826	0.8208	0.7447	0.6563
	4	1.0000	0.9999	0.9996	0.9984	0.9954	0.9891	0.9777	0.9590	0.9308	0.8906
	5	1.0000	1.0000	1.0000	0.9999	0.9998	0.9993	0.9982	0.9959	0.9917	0.9844
n = 7	x = 0	0.6983	0.4783	0.3206	0.2097	0.1335	0.0824	0.0490	0.0280	0.0152	0.0078
	1	0.9556	0.8503	0.7166	0.5767	0.4449	0.3294	0.2338	0.1586	0.1024	0.0625
	2	0.9962	0.9743	0.9262	0.8520	0.7564	0.6471	0.5323	0.4199	0.3164	0.2266
	3	0.9998	0.9973	0.9879	0.9667	0.9294	0.8740	0.8002	0.7102	0.6083	0.5000
	4	1.0000	0.9998	0.9988	0.9953	0.9871	0.9712	0.9444	0.9037	0.8471	0.7734
	5	1.0000	1.0000	0.9999	0.9996	0.9987	0.9962	0.9910	0.9812	0.9643	0.9375
	6	1.0000	1.0000	1.0000	1.0000	0.9999	0.9998	0.9994	0.9984	0.9963	0.9922
n = 8	x = 0	0.6634	0.4305	0.2725	0.1678	0.1001	0.0576	0.0319	0.0168	0.0084	0.0039
	1	0.9428	0.8131	0.6572	0.5033	0.3671	0.2553	0.1691	0.1064	0.0632	0.0352
	2	0.9942	0.9619	0.8948	0.7969	0.6785	0.5518	0.4278	0.3154	0.2201	0.1445
	3	0.9996	0.9950	0.9786	0.9437	0.8862	0.8059	0.7064	0.5941	0.4770	0.3633
	4	1.0000	0.9996	0.9971	0.9896	0.9727	0.9420	0.8939	0.8263	0.7396	0.6367
	5	1.0000	1.0000	0.9998	0.9988	0.9958	0.9887	0.9747	0.9502	0.9115	0.8555
	6	1.0000	1.0000	1.0000	0.9999	0.9996	0.9987	0.9964	0.9915	0.9819	0.9648
	7	1.0000	1.0000	1.0000	1.0000	1.0000	0.9999	0.9998	0.9993	0.9983	0.9961
n = 9	x = 0	0.6302	0.3874	0.2316	0.1342	0.0751	0.0404	0.0207	0.0101	0.0046	0.0020
	1	0.9288	0.7748	0.5995	0.4362	0.3003	0.1960	0.1211	0.0705	0.0385	0.0195
	2	0.9916	0.9470	0.8591	0.7382	0.6007	0.4628	0.3373	0.2318	0.1495	0.0898
	3	0.9994	0.9917	0.9661	0.9144	0.8343	0.7297	0.6089	0.4826	0.3614	0.2539
	4	1.0000	0.9991	0.9944	0.9804	0.9511	0.9012	0.8283	0.7334	0.6214	0.5000
	5	1.0000	0.9999	0.9994	0.9969	0.9900	0.9747	0.9464	0.9006	0.8342	0.7461
	6	1.0000	1.0000	1.0000	0.9997	0.9987	0.9957	0.9888	0.9750	0.9502	0.9102
	7	1.0000	1.0000	1.0000	1.0000	0.9999	0.9996	0.9986	0.9962	0.9909	0.9805
	8	1.0000	1.0000	1.0000	1.0000	1.0000	1.0000	0.9999	0.9997	0.9992	0.9980
n = 10	x = 0	0.5987	0.3487	0.1969	0.1074	0.0563	0.0282	0.0135	0.0060	0.0025	0.0010
	1	0.9139	0.7361	0.5443	0.3758	0.2440	0.1493	0.0860	0.0464	0.0233	0.0107
	2	0.9885	0.9298	0.8202	0.6778	0.5256	0.3828	0.2616	0.1673	0.0996	0.0547
	3	0.9990	0.9872	0.9500	0.8791	0.7759	0.6496	0.5138	0.3823	0.2660	0.1719
	4	0.9999	0.9984	0.9901	0.9672	0.9219	0.8497	0.7515	0.6331	0.5044	0.3770
	5	1.0000	0.9999	0.9986	0.9936	0.9803	0.9527	0.9051	0.8338	0.7384	0.6230
	6	1.0000	1.0000	0.9999	0.9991	0.9965	0.9894	0.9740	0.9452	0.8980	0.8281
	7	1.0000	1.0000	1.0000	0.9999	0.9996	0.9984	0.9952	0.9877	0.9726	0.9453
	8	1.0000	1.0000	1.0000	1.0000	1.0000	0.9999	0.9995	0.9983	0.9955	0.9893
	9	1.0000	1.0000	1.0000	1.0000	1.0000	1.0000	1.0000	0.9999	0.9997	0.9990

The binomial cumulative distribution function (continued)

	$p =$	0.05	0.10	0.15	0.20	0.25	0.30	0.35	0.40	0.45	0.50
$n = 12$	$x = 0$	0.5404	0.2824	0.1422	0.0687	0.0317	0.0138	0.0057	0.0022	0.0008	0.0002
	1	0.8816	0.6590	0.4435	0.2749	0.1584	0.0850	0.0424	0.0196	0.0083	0.0032
	2	0.9804	0.8891	0.7358	0.5583	0.3907	0.2528	0.1513	0.0834	0.0421	0.0193
	3	0.9978	0.9744	0.9078	0.7946	0.6488	0.4925	0.3467	0.2253	0.1345	0.0730
	4	0.9998	0.9957	0.9761	0.9274	0.8424	0.7237	0.5833	0.4382	0.3044	0.1938
	5	1.0000	0.9995	0.9954	0.9806	0.9456	0.8822	0.7873	0.6652	0.5269	0.3872
	6	1.0000	0.9999	0.9993	0.9961	0.9857	0.9614	0.9154	0.8418	0.7393	0.6128
	7	1.0000	1.0000	0.9999	0.9994	0.9972	0.9905	0.9745	0.9427	0.8883	0.8062
	8	1.0000	1.0000	1.0000	0.9999	0.9996	0.9983	0.9944	0.9847	0.9644	0.9270
	9	1.0000	1.0000	1.0000	1.0000	1.0000	0.9998	0.9992	0.9972	0.9921	0.9807
	10	1.0000	1.0000	1.0000	1.0000	1.0000	1.0000	0.9999	0.9997	0.9989	0.9968
	11	1.0000	1.0000	1.0000	1.0000	1.0000	1.0000	1.0000	1.0000	0.9999	0.9998
$n = 15$	$x = 0$	0.4633	0.2059	0.0874	0.0352	0.0134	0.0047	0.0016	0.0005	0.0001	0.0000
	1	0.8290	0.5490	0.3186	0.1671	0.0802	0.0353	0.0142	0.0052	0.0017	0.0005
	2	0.9638	0.8159	0.6042	0.3980	0.2361	0.1268	0.0617	0.0271	0.0107	0.0037
	3	0.9945	0.9444	0.8227	0.6482	0.4613	0.2969	0.1727	0.0905	0.0424	0.0176
	4	0.9994	0.9873	0.9383	0.8358	0.6865	0.5155	0.3519	0.2173	0.1204	0.0592
	5	0.9999	0.9978	0.9832	0.9389	0.8516	0.7216	0.5643	0.4032	0.2608	0.1509
	6	1.0000	0.9997	0.9964	0.9819	0.9434	0.8689	0.7548	0.6098	0.4522	0.3036
	7	1.0000	1.0000	0.9994	0.9958	0.9827	0.9500	0.8868	0.7869	0.6535	0.5000
	8	1.0000	1.0000	0.9999	0.9992	0.9958	0.9848	0.9578	0.9050	0.8182	0.6964
	9	1.0000	1.0000	1.0000	0.9999	0.9992	0.9963	0.9876	0.9662	0.9231	0.8491
	10	1.0000	1.0000	1.0000	1.0000	0.9999	0.9993	0.9972	0.9907	0.9745	0.9408
	11	1.0000	1.0000	1.0000	1.0000	1.0000	0.9999	0.9995	0.9981	0.9937	0.9824
	12	1.0000	1.0000	1.0000	1.0000	1.0000	1.0000	0.9999	0.9997	0.9989	0.9963
	13	1.0000	1.0000	1.0000	1.0000	1.0000	1.0000	1.0000	1.0000	0.9999	0.9995
	14	1.0000	1.0000	1.0000	1.0000	1.0000	1.0000	1.0000	1.0000	1.0000	1.0000
$n = 20$	$x = 0$	0.3585	0.1216	0.0388	0.0115	0.0032	0.0008	0.0002	0.0000	0.0000	0.0000
	1	0.7358	0.3917	0.1756	0.0692	0.0243	0.0076	0.0021	0.0005	0.0001	0.0000
	2	0.9245	0.6769	0.4049	0.2061	0.0913	0.0355	0.0121	0.0036	0.0009	0.0002
	3	0.9841	0.8670	0.6477	0.4114	0.2252	0.1071	0.0444	0.0160	0.0049	0.0013
	4	0.9974	0.9568	0.8298	0.6296	0.4148	0.2375	0.1182	0.0510	0.0189	0.0059
	5	0.9997	0.9887	0.9327	0.8042	0.6172	0.4164	0.2454	0.1256	0.0553	0.0207
	6	1.0000	0.9976	0.9781	0.9133	0.7858	0.6080	0.4166	0.2500	0.1299	0.0577
	7	1.0000	0.9996	0.9941	0.9679	0.8982	0.7723	0.6010	0.4159	0.2520	0.1316
	8	1.0000	0.9999	0.9987	0.9900	0.9591	0.8867	0.7624	0.5956	0.4143	0.2517
	9	1.0000	1.0000	0.9998	0.9974	0.9861	0.9520	0.8782	0.7553	0.5914	0.4119
	10	1.0000	1.0000	1.0000	0.9994	0.9961	0.9829	0.9468	0.8725	0.7507	0.5881
	11	1.0000	1.0000	1.0000	0.9999	0.9991	0.9949	0.9804	0.9435	0.8692	0.7483
	12	1.0000	1.0000	1.0000	1.0000	0.9998	0.9987	0.9940	0.9790	0.9420	0.8684
	13	1.0000	1.0000	1.0000	1.0000	1.0000	0.9997	0.9985	0.9935	0.9786	0.9423
	14	1.0000	1.0000	1.0000	1.0000	1.0000	1.0000	0.9997	0.9984	0.9936	0.9793
	15	1.0000	1.0000	1.0000	1.0000	1.0000	1.0000	1.0000	0.9997	0.9985	0.9941
	16	1.0000	1.0000	1.0000	1.0000	1.0000	1.0000	1.0000	1.0000	0.9997	0.9987
	17	1.0000	1.0000	1.0000	1.0000	1.0000	1.0000	1.0000	1.0000	1.0000	0.9998
	18	1.0000	1.0000	1.0000	1.0000	1.0000	1.0000	1.0000	1.0000	1.0000	1.0000

The binomial cumulative distribution function (continued)

$p =$	0.05	0.10	0.15	0.20	0.25	0.30	0.35	0.40	0.45	0.50
$n = 25$ $x = 0$	0.2774	0.0718	0.0172	0.0038	0.0008	0.0001	0.0000	0.0000	0.0000	0.0000
1	0.6424	0.2712	0.0931	0.0274	0.0070	0.0016	0.0003	0.0001	0.0000	0.0000
2	0.8729	0.5371	0.2537	0.0982	0.0321	0.0090	0.0021	0.0004	0.0001	0.0000
3	0.9659	0.7636	0.4711	0.2340	0.0962	0.0332	0.0097	0.0024	0.0005	0.0001
4	0.9928	0.9020	0.6821	0.4207	0.2137	0.0905	0.0320	0.0095	0.0023	0.0005
5	0.9988	0.9666	0.8385	0.6167	0.3783	0.1935	0.0826	0.0294	0.0086	0.0020
6	0.9998	0.9905	0.9305	0.7800	0.5611	0.3407	0.1734	0.0736	0.0258	0.0073
7	1.0000	0.9977	0.9745	0.8909	0.7265	0.5118	0.3061	0.1536	0.0639	0.0216
8	1.0000	0.9995	0.9920	0.9532	0.8506	0.6769	0.4668	0.2735	0.1340	0.0539
9	1.0000	0.9999	0.9979	0.9827	0.9287	0.8106	0.6303	0.4246	0.2424	0.1148
10	1.0000	1.0000	0.9995	0.9944	0.9703	0.9022	0.7712	0.5858	0.3843	0.2122
11	1.0000	1.0000	0.9999	0.9985	0.9893	0.9558	0.8746	0.7323	0.5426	0.3450
12	1.0000	1.0000	1.0000	0.9996	0.9966	0.9825	0.9396	0.8462	0.6937	0.5000
13	1.0000	1.0000	1.0000	0.9999	0.9991	0.9940	0.9745	0.9222	0.8173	0.6550
14	1.0000	1.0000	1.0000	1.0000	0.9998	0.9982	0.9907	0.9656	0.9040	0.7878
15	1.0000	1.0000	1.0000	1.0000	1.0000	0.9995	0.9971	0.9868	0.9560	0.8852
16	1.0000	1.0000	1.0000	1.0000	1.0000	0.9999	0.9992	0.9957	0.9826	0.9461
17	1.0000	1.0000	1.0000	1.0000	1.0000	1.0000	0.9998	0.9988	0.9942	0.9784
18	1.0000	1.0000	1.0000	1.0000	1.0000	1.0000	1.0000	0.9997	0.9984	0.9927
19	1.0000	1.0000	1.0000	1.0000	1.0000	1.0000	1.0000	0.9999	0.9996	0.9980
20	1.0000	1.0000	1.0000	1.0000	1.0000	1.0000	1.0000	1.0000	0.9999	0.9995
21	1.0000	1.0000	1.0000	1.0000	1.0000	1.0000	1.0000	1.0000	1.0000	0.9999
22	1.0000	1.0000	1.0000	1.0000	1.0000	1.0000	1.0000	1.0000	1.0000	1.0000
$n = 30$ $x = 0$	0.2146	0.0424	0.0076	0.0012	0.0002	0.0000	0.0000	0.0000	0.0000	0.0000
1	0.5535	0.1837	0.0480	0.0105	0.0020	0.0003	0.0000	0.0000	0.0000	0.0000
2	0.8122	0.4114	0.1514	0.0442	0.0106	0.0021	0.0003	0.0000	0.0000	0.0000
3	0.9392	0.6474	0.3217	0.1227	0.0374	0.0093	0.0019	0.0003	0.0000	0.0000
4	0.9844	0.8245	0.5245	0.2552	0.0979	0.0302	0.0075	0.0015	0.0002	0.0000
5	0.9967	0.9268	0.7106	0.4275	0.2026	0.0766	0.0233	0.0057	0.0011	0.0002
6	0.9994	0.9742	0.8474	0.6070	0.3481	0.1595	0.0586	0.0172	0.0040	0.0007
7	0.9999	0.9922	0.9302	0.7608	0.5143	0.2814	0.1238	0.0435	0.0121	0.0026
8	1.0000	0.9980	0.9722	0.8713	0.6736	0.4315	0.2247	0.0940	0.0312	0.0081
9	1.0000	0.9995	0.9903	0.9389	0.8034	0.5888	0.3575	0.1763	0.0694	0.0214
10	1.0000	0.9999	0.9971	0.9744	0.8943	0.7304	0.5078	0.2915	0.1350	0.0494
11	1.0000	1.0000	0.9992	0.9905	0.9493	0.8407	0.6548	0.4311	0.2327	0.1002
12	1.0000	1.0000	0.9998	0.9969	0.9784	0.9155	0.7802	0.5785	0.3592	0.1808
13	1.0000	1.0000	1.0000	0.9991	0.9918	0.9599	0.8737	0.7145	0.5025	0.2923
14	1.0000	1.0000	1.0000	0.9998	0.9973	0.9831	0.9348	0.8246	0.6448	0.4278
15	1.0000	1.0000	1.0000	0.9999	0.9992	0.9936	0.9699	0.9029	0.7691	0.5722
16	1.0000	1.0000	1.0000	1.0000	0.9998	0.9979	0.9876	0.9519	0.8644	0.7077
17	1.0000	1.0000	1.0000	1.0000	0.9999	0.9994	0.9955	0.9788	0.9286	0.8192
18	1.0000	1.0000	1.0000	1.0000	1.0000	0.9998	0.9986	0.9917	0.9666	0.8998
19	1.0000	1.0000	1.0000	1.0000	1.0000	1.0000	0.9996	0.9971	0.9862	0.9506
20	1.0000	1.0000	1.0000	1.0000	1.0000	1.0000	0.9999	0.9991	0.9950	0.9786
21	1.0000	1.0000	1.0000	1.0000	1.0000	1.0000	1.0000	0.9998	0.9984	0.9919
22	1.0000	1.0000	1.0000	1.0000	1.0000	1.0000	1.0000	1.0000	0.9996	0.9974
23	1.0000	1.0000	1.0000	1.0000	1.0000	1.0000	1.0000	1.0000	0.9999	0.9993
24	1.0000	1.0000	1.0000	1.0000	1.0000	1.0000	1.0000	1.0000	1.0000	0.9998
25	1.0000	1.0000	1.0000	1.0000	1.0000	1.0000	1.0000	1.0000	1.0000	1.0000

The binomial cumulative distribution function (continued)

	$p =$	0.05	0.10	0.15	0.20	0.25	0.30	0.35	0.40	0.45	0.50
$n = 40$	$x = 0$	0.1285	0.0148	0.0015	0.0001	0.0000	0.0000	0.0000	0.0000	0.0000	0.0000
	1	0.3991	0.0805	0.0121	0.0015	0.0001	0.0000	0.0000	0.0000	0.0000	0.0000
	2	0.6767	0.2228	0.0486	0.0079	0.0010	0.0001	0.0000	0.0000	0.0000	0.0000
	3	0.8619	0.4231	0.1302	0.0285	0.0047	0.0006	0.0001	0.0000	0.0000	0.0000
	4	0.9520	0.6290	0.2633	0.0759	0.0160	0.0026	0.0003	0.0000	0.0000	0.0000
	5	0.9861	0.7937	0.4325	0.1613	0.0433	0.0086	0.0013	0.0001	0.0000	0.0000
	6	0.9966	0.9005	0.6067	0.2859	0.0962	0.0238	0.0044	0.0006	0.0001	0.0000
	7	0.9993	0.9581	0.7559	0.4371	0.1820	0.0553	0.0124	0.0021	0.0002	0.0000
	8	0.9999	0.9845	0.8646	0.5931	0.2998	0.1110	0.0303	0.0061	0.0009	0.0001
	9	1.0000	0.9949	0.9328	0.7318	0.4395	0.1959	0.0644	0.0156	0.0027	0.0003
	10	1.0000	0.9985	0.9701	0.8392	0.5839	0.3087	0.1215	0.0352	0.0074	0.0011
	11	1.0000	0.9996	0.9880	0.9125	0.7151	0.4406	0.2053	0.0709	0.0179	0.0032
	12	1.0000	0.9999	0.9957	0.9568	0.8209	0.5772	0.3143	0.1285	0.0386	0.0083
	13	1.0000	1.0000	0.9986	0.9806	0.8968	0.7032	0.4408	0.2112	0.0751	0.0192
	14	1.0000	1.0000	0.9996	0.9921	0.9456	0.8074	0.5721	0.3174	0.1326	0.0403
	15	1.0000	1.0000	0.9999	0.9971	0.9738	0.8849	0.6946	0.4402	0.2142	0.0769
	16	1.0000	1.0000	1.0000	0.9990	0.9884	0.9367	0.7978	0.5681	0.3185	0.1341
	17	1.0000	1.0000	1.0000	0.9997	0.9953	0.9680	0.8761	0.6885	0.4391	0.2148
	18	1.0000	1.0000	1.0000	0.9999	0.9983	0.9852	0.9301	0.7911	0.5651	0.3179
	19	1.0000	1.0000	1.0000	1.0000	0.9994	0.9937	0.9637	0.8702	0.6844	0.4373
	20	1.0000	1.0000	1.0000	1.0000	0.9998	0.9976	0.9827	0.9256	0.7870	0.5627
	21	1.0000	1.0000	1.0000	1.0000	1.0000	0.9991	0.9925	0.9608	0.8669	0.6821
	22	1.0000	1.0000	1.0000	1.0000	1.0000	0.9997	0.9970	0.9811	0.9233	0.7852
	23	1.0000	1.0000	1.0000	1.0000	1.0000	0.9999	0.9989	0.9917	0.9595	0.8659
	24	1.0000	1.0000	1.0000	1.0000	1.0000	1.0000	0.9996	0.9966	0.9804	0.9231
	25	1.0000	1.0000	1.0000	1.0000	1.0000	1.0000	0.9999	0.9988	0.9914	0.9597
	26	1.0000	1.0000	1.0000	1.0000	1.0000	1.0000	1.0000	0.9996	0.9966	0.9808
	27	1.0000	1.0000	1.0000	1.0000	1.0000	1.0000	1.0000	0.9999	0.9988	0.9917
	28	1.0000	1.0000	1.0000	1.0000	1.0000	1.0000	1.0000	1.0000	0.9996	0.9968
	29	1.0000	1.0000	1.0000	1.0000	1.0000	1.0000	1.0000	1.0000	0.9999	0.9989
	30	1.0000	1.0000	1.0000	1.0000	1.0000	1.0000	1.0000	1.0000	1.0000	0.9997
	31	1.0000	1.0000	1.0000	1.0000	1.0000	1.0000	1.0000	1.0000	1.0000	0.9999
	32	1.0000	1.0000	1.0000	1.0000	1.0000	1.0000	1.0000	1.0000	1.0000	1.0000

	$p =$	0.05	0.10	0.15	0.20	0.25	0.30	0.35	0.40	0.45	0.50
$n = 50$	$x = 0$	0.0769	0.0052	0.0003	0.0000	0.0000	0.0000	0.0000	0.0000	0.0000	0.0000
	1	0.2794	0.0338	0.0029	0.0002	0.0000	0.0000	0.0000	0.0000	0.0000	0.0000
	2	0.5405	0.1117	0.0142	0.0013	0.0001	0.0000	0.0000	0.0000	0.0000	0.0000
	3	0.7604	0.2503	0.0460	0.0057	0.0005	0.0000	0.0000	0.0000	0.0000	0.0000
	4	0.8964	0.4312	0.1121	0.0185	0.0021	0.0002	0.0000	0.0000	0.0000	0.0000
	5	0.9622	0.6161	0.2194	0.0480	0.0070	0.0007	0.0001	0.0000	0.0000	0.0000
	6	0.9882	0.7702	0.3613	0.1034	0.0194	0.0025	0.0002	0.0000	0.0000	0.0000
	7	0.9968	0.8779	0.5188	0.1904	0.0453	0.0073	0.0008	0.0001	0.0000	0.0000
	8	0.9992	0.9421	0.6681	0.3073	0.0916	0.0183	0.0025	0.0002	0.0000	0.0000
	9	0.9998	0.9755	0.7911	0.4437	0.1637	0.0402	0.0067	0.0008	0.0001	0.0000
	10	1.0000	0.9906	0.8801	0.5836	0.2622	0.0789	0.0160	0.0022	0.0002	0.0000

$n = 50$ table continues on next page

The binomial cumulative distribution function (continued)

$p =$	0.05	0.10	0.15	0.20	0.25	0.30	0.35	0.40	0.45	0.50
$n = 50$ $x = 11$	1.0000	0.9968	0.9372	0.7107	0.3816	0.1390	0.0342	0.0057	0.0006	0.0000
12	1.0000	0.9990	0.9699	0.8139	0.5110	0.2229	0.0661	0.0133	0.0018	0.0002
13	1.0000	0.9997	0.9868	0.8894	0.6370	0.3279	0.1163	0.0280	0.0045	0.0005
14	1.0000	0.9999	0.9947	0.9393	0.7481	0.4468	0.1878	0.0540	0.0104	0.0013
15	1.0000	1.0000	0.9981	0.9692	0.8369	0.5692	0.2801	0.0955	0.0220	0.0033
16	1.0000	1.0000	0.9993	0.9856	0.9017	0.6839	0.3889	0.1561	0.0427	0.0077
17	1.0000	1.0000	0.9998	0.9937	0.9449	0.7822	0.5060	0.2369	0.0765	0.0164
18	1.0000	1.0000	0.9999	0.9975	0.9713	0.8594	0.6216	0.3356	0.1273	0.0325
19	1.0000	1.0000	1.0000	0.9991	0.9861	0.9152	0.7264	0.4465	0.1974	0.0595
20	1.0000	1.0000	1.0000	0.9997	0.9937	0.9522	0.8139	0.5610	0.2862	0.1013
21	1.0000	1.0000	1.0000	0.9999	0.9974	0.9749	0.8813	0.6701	0.3900	0.1611
22	1.0000	1.0000	1.0000	1.0000	0.9990	0.9877	0.9290	0.7660	0.5019	0.2399
23	1.0000	1.0000	1.0000	1.0000	0.9996	0.9944	0.9604	0.8438	0.6134	0.3359
24	1.0000	1.0000	1.0000	1.0000	0.9999	0.9976	0.9793	0.9022	0.7160	0.4439
25	1.0000	1.0000	1.0000	1.0000	1.0000	0.9991	0.9900	0.9427	0.8034	0.5561
26	1.0000	1.0000	1.0000	1.0000	1.0000	0.9997	0.9955	0.9686	0.8721	0.6641
27	1.0000	1.0000	1.0000	1.0000	1.0000	0.9999	0.9981	0.9840	0.9220	0.7601
28	1.0000	1.0000	1.0000	1.0000	1.0000	1.0000	0.9993	0.9924	0.9556	0.8389
29	1.0000	1.0000	1.0000	1.0000	1.0000	1.0000	0.9997	0.9966	0.9765	0.8987
30	1.0000	1.0000	1.0000	1.0000	1.0000	1.0000	0.9999	0.9986	0.9884	0.9405
31	1.0000	1.0000	1.0000	1.0000	1.0000	1.0000	1.0000	0.9995	0.9947	0.9675
32	1.0000	1.0000	1.0000	1.0000	1.0000	1.0000	1.0000	0.9998	0.9978	0.9836
33	1.0000	1.0000	1.0000	1.0000	1.0000	1.0000	1.0000	0.9999	0.9991	0.9923
34	1.0000	1.0000	1.0000	1.0000	1.0000	1.0000	1.0000	1.0000	0.9997	0.9967
35	1.0000	1.0000	1.0000	1.0000	1.0000	1.0000	1.0000	1.0000	0.9999	0.9987
36	1.0000	1.0000	1.0000	1.0000	1.0000	1.0000	1.0000	1.0000	1.0000	0.9995
37	1.0000	1.0000	1.0000	1.0000	1.0000	1.0000	1.0000	1.0000	1.0000	0.9998
38	1.0000	1.0000	1.0000	1.0000	1.0000	1.0000	1.0000	1.0000	1.0000	1.0000

These are the formulas you'll be given in the exam, but make sure you know exactly when you need them and how to use them.

Standard Deviation

Standard deviation = $\sqrt{\text{variance}}$

Interquartile range = IQR = $Q_3 - Q_1$

For a set of n values $x_1, x_2, \ldots x_i, \ldots x_n$

$$S_{xx} = \sum(x_i - \bar{x})^2 = \sum x_i^2 - \frac{\left(\sum x_i\right)^2}{n}$$

$$\text{Standard deviation} = \sqrt{\frac{S_{xx}}{n}} = \sqrt{\frac{\sum x^2}{n} - \bar{x}^2}$$

Probability

P(A') = 1 – P(A)

Kinematics

For motion in a straight line with constant acceleration:

$$v = u + at \qquad s = ut + \frac{1}{2}at^2$$

$$s = \left(\frac{u+v}{2}\right)t \qquad s = vt - \frac{1}{2}at^2$$

$$v^2 = u^2 + 2as$$

MESMT52